S·M·A·L·L BUSINESS

MANAGEMENT AND ENTREPRENEURSHIP

S·M·A·L·L
B·U·S·I·N·E·S·S

MANAGEMENT AND ENTREPRENEURSHIP

OLIVE D. CHURCH, PH.D.
Professor of Business Education
The University of Wyoming

SRA®
SCIENCE RESEARCH ASSOCIATES, INC.
Chicago, Toronto, Henley-on-Thames, Sydney
A Subsidiary of IBM

Acquisition Editor	**Susan L. Fisher**
Project Editor	**James C. Budd**
Compositor	**Bi-Comp, Inc.**
Illustrator	**House of Graphics**
Text Designer	**Barbara Ravizza**
Cover Designer	**Janet Bollow**
Cover Photo by	**Steve Niedorf**
	© **Steve Niedorf, 1983,**
	Image Bank

Library of Congress Cataloging in Publication Data

Church, Olive D.,
  Small business management and entrepreneurship.

  Includes index.
    1. Small business—United States—Management.
  2. New business enterprises—United States—Management.
  I. Title.
  HD62.7.C48   1984   658'.022   83-16444
  ISBN 0-574-20715-5

Copyright © Science Research Associates, Inc. 1984.
All rights reserved.
Printed in the United States of America.
10 9 8 7 6 5 4 3 2 1

Table of Contents

Preface • 1

UNIT I • THINK "SMALL" BUSINESS • 7

1 • Small Business in the Economy	9
2 • Satisfactions, Risks, Failures, and Challenges	29
3 • Business Classifications	49
4 • Franchises, Existing Businesses, and Family Businesses	75
5 • Deciding What Kind of Business to Open	91

UNIT II • PLANNING THE SMALL BUSINESS • 109

6 • The Comprehensive Business Plan	111
7 • Studying the Market	131
8 • Selecting the Location	151
9 • Facilities and Layout	177
10 • Legal Structures and Staffing	195
11 • Establishing Price and Credit Policies	217

UNIT III • ORGANIZING FOR BUSINESS • 241

12 • Financing the Enterprise	243
13 • Legal, Tax, and Insurance Needs	265
14 • Establishing the Records and Office Systems	289
15 • Microcomputer Systems in the Small Business	315
16 • Purchasing and Promotion	335

UNIT IV • MANAGING AND CONTROLLING THE SMALL BUSINESS • 363

17 • The Systems Approach to Management	365
18 • Market Research, Advertising, and Selling	389
19 • Training, Motivating, and Supervising Employees	409
20 • Managing the Physical Environment; Security and Safety	435
21 • Taking Stock; Managing Adjustments	455

APPENDIXES • 475

A • Self-Assessment Tools and Exercises	475
B • Decision-Making Tools and Activities	485
C • Checklist for Going into Business	491
D • References and Resources	497

INDEX • 509

Preface

Successful owners of small enterprises apply to their organizations the knowledge and skills gleaned from specific disciplines. These include accounting, business law, communications, economics, finance, human relations, management, marketing, office systems, personnel management, and psychology. This book could have been arranged according to these topics.

However, entrepreneurs do not use these disciplines in consecutive order or isolated situations. They plan and organize their businesses toward getting ready for opening day. Then they implement their plans and manage their operations from that day forward.

The organization of this text is based on this logic. Backgrounds from the academic disciplines noted above are presented in context, *at the time most needed*, and are integrated within the overall topics of planning, organizing, and managing and controlling.

Many people who own businesses seldom manage them. They go into business because they want a second income, a tax shelter, or a hobby. They hire managers to run these companies. The latter may study small business management but are not necessarily interested in how to start their own.

People who plan, organize, finance, and operate their own businesses are called *entrepreneurs*. This book was written primarily for entrepreneurs.

Organization of the Text

The five chapters of Unit I are designed to introduce you to small business and its role in the United States' economy and list some of the risks and challenges encountered in business ownership. The topics previewed there will be expanded in subsequent units and chapters. The unit also defines and describes many types of businesses as well as the characteristics of successful entrepreneurs. Although you may have some idea about what kind of business you want to own, it is important that you identify numerous other possibilities. Included are exercises and tools to help you assess yourself and make decisions.

The next three units follow the management sequence: they move from planning, organizing, and implementing to controlling. Unit II outlines the specific information you should gather and the planning decisions you must make before seeking financial assistance.

Unit III opens with the finance chapter and provides additional background on how to organize a business and its interactive elements. With the last chapter you will be organizing to purchase inventory and promote your business for the grand opening. At the close of this unit, you will revise your business plan, based on your preparation of checklists and financial statements.

Unit IV assumes that you have now planned and organized your business. The chapters in this unit address the management topics that will face you as an entrepreneur with an operating business. Although you will be introduced to a decision-making method during the exploratory unit, this technique and others will be applied in the last unit to managing the numerous interactive factors of small business.

The Writing Style

The "You" approach is used in every chapter, a strategy designed to get you involved in thinking, planning and organizing, and making decisions based on your particular situation and inclinations. Factual data about entrepreneurship and small business management theory are presented in third-person writing style. This information comes from interviewing numerous entrepreneurs and also from academic literature and is pertinent to everyone who goes into business. You should try to interpret this information and apply it to your own case.

The Business Plan

The central focus of this textbook is to help you prepare the comprehensive business plan introduced at the beginning of the unit on planning. Don't expect to be able to finalize the plan, however, until you have explored all the subsequent topics and related activities.

Your business plan should be as real as possible. If you are already in business or expect to launch your company while using this book (or soon thereafter), the plan should reflect the actual data you've gathered and the decisions you've made. Checklists for gathering and analyzing data appear throughout the book.

Building a Human Resource Network

You are advised to conduct interviews and to observe businesses in operation. Get in the habit of asking questions as you shop or pay bills, eat out, fill your gas tank, pick up a load of wood or gravel, talk with a door-to-door salesperson or vending machine owner, or participate in leisure-time activities. As you travel across town in the backseat of a taxi, find out if the driver is self-employed. Use the time it takes to reach your destination to interview the driver.

Most entrepreneurs are delighted to talk about their businesses and the challenges they have encountered. Ask these people why they are in business for themselves. Invite their recommendations.

Making appointments with practicing entrepreneurs and business specialists (e.g., accountant, banker, attorney) is recommended throughout the text. If you are serious about operating an enterprise, you can build an important human-resource network of people who can advise and assist you, both now and later.

Back in the classroom or in small discussion groups you will share the results of your findings with colleagues. The latter can also help you modify preconceived ideas about small business ownership. With those whom you establish long-term relationships, you should be able to develop another human-resource network to help you later, when you open your own business.

End-of-chapter activities include discussions and debates. Use these assignments to practice oral communication, persuasion, and negotiation skills. Entrepreneurs need these skills; they use them every day. Although the questions are also designed for reviewing chapter content, they should stimulate your thinking in context with interviewing business owners and sharing your findings with classmates.

The Author's Motivation and Background

I was born into a business family. In adulthood, as sole proprietor or as a partner, I have owned businesses that processed raw materials, sold retail and wholesale merchandise, and provided hospitality and business services. In addition to my university position, I also currently head a consulting firm where my colleagues and I frequently counsel with owners of small business. I have experienced the same frustrations and problems that most entrepreneurs encounter in dealing with suppliers, customers, employees, competition, and cash flow. I also hold degrees in business administration and vocational education and am experienced in educational teaching and administration.

Too few people, it seems, understand what it takes to succeed in business, why profit is essential, and why worker productivity and involvement are so critical. Moreover, many owners of small businesses launch their enterprises with limited knowledge and unrealistic expectations. Together, these frustrations and concerns motivated me to write this book.

Entrepreneurs and You

Entrepreneurs operate wherever business takes place or can be generated. This book incorporates many of the stories and business experiences of entrepreneurs from every business classification and size, whether newcomers or old-timers, whether they run a family-owned business or a franchise operation.

These people's enterprises are located in downtown areas, on business "strips," or along highways. They can be found in shopping malls, high-rise buildings, or beautifully landscaped industrial parks. They are housed in resort locations, along popular and highly traveled byways, tucked in out-of-the-way places, or in an individual's home or garage. They can be found in isolated forests and mining locales, on farms and ranches, or in villages and cities. Whether these enterprises are described in context or in minicases, be assured that the people who run them are all real human beings—with very real problems, failures, or successes.

You probably would not try to overhaul your auto without a thorough knowledge of what makes an engine work—of how it is put together and what it takes to troubleshoot its ills. Yet too many people have apparently come to believe that there is no more to operating a business effectively than having the specific skills associated with a particular trade, product, or service.

If you are planning to start a business, no matter what your current situation is or how you expect your career to unfold, this book will help you put yourself squarely in the center of the action. You will imagine yourself starting several different types of businesses and then taking the necessary steps to open and manage them. You will learn how businesses operate and what it takes to make a profit. As you conduct your own primary research through interviews and observations, you will get a "feeling" for the challenges, risks, and problems involved in running your own enterprise.

> Nothing in the world can take the place of persistence. Talent will not; nothing is more common than unsuccessful men of talent. Genius will not . . . the world is full of educated derelicts. Persistence and determination alone are omnipotent. The slogan, "press on" has solved and always will solve the problems of the human race. (Calvin Coolidge, 30th President of the United States)

I would like to thank the following reviewers, who helped throughout the many drafts this text has undergone:

Joseph Abbruscato, Scottsdale Community College (Arizona); E. Terry Deiderick, Director, Small Business Institute, Youngstown State University (Ohio); Phillip Foster, Metropolitan State College (Colorado); Virginia Phillips, Youngstown State University (Ohio); Joseph Platts, Miami-Dade Community College (Florida); Joseph Ryan, Saddleback College (California); Warren Weber, California State Polytechnic Institute; Roland Whitsell, Volunteer State Community College (Tennessee); and William Wright, Mt. Hood Community College (Oregon).

J. M. GARZA
BARBER SHOP

UNIT 1

THINK "SMALL" BUSINESS

Business enterprises are as varied and colorful as the people who run them—the entrepreneurs. These businesses provide a wide range of products and services, whether through retail or wholesale outlets, construction or extraction industries (such as farming, forestry, and mining), transportation or utilities, manufacturing plants, or service establishments. They may be organized as sole proprietorships, partnerships, or corporations. They may operate from a hole-in-the-wall facility, a beautiful site, or a home.

People with many diverse skills and talents find satisfaction and success as entrepreneurs. Yet there are certain clear differences among those who fail, those who merely survive, and those who achieve phenomenal rewards. In this book we will examine the traits and skills of the successful entrepreneurs and discover how these owners launched and continue to operate their businesses.

Although these business people encounter many challenges and rewards, many risks and pitfalls await the unwary or ill-prepared. However, those who sincerely desire success can undertake appropriate training and studies. Planning, organization, and the willingness to take risks and to stand by your decisions can significantly increase your chances of success.

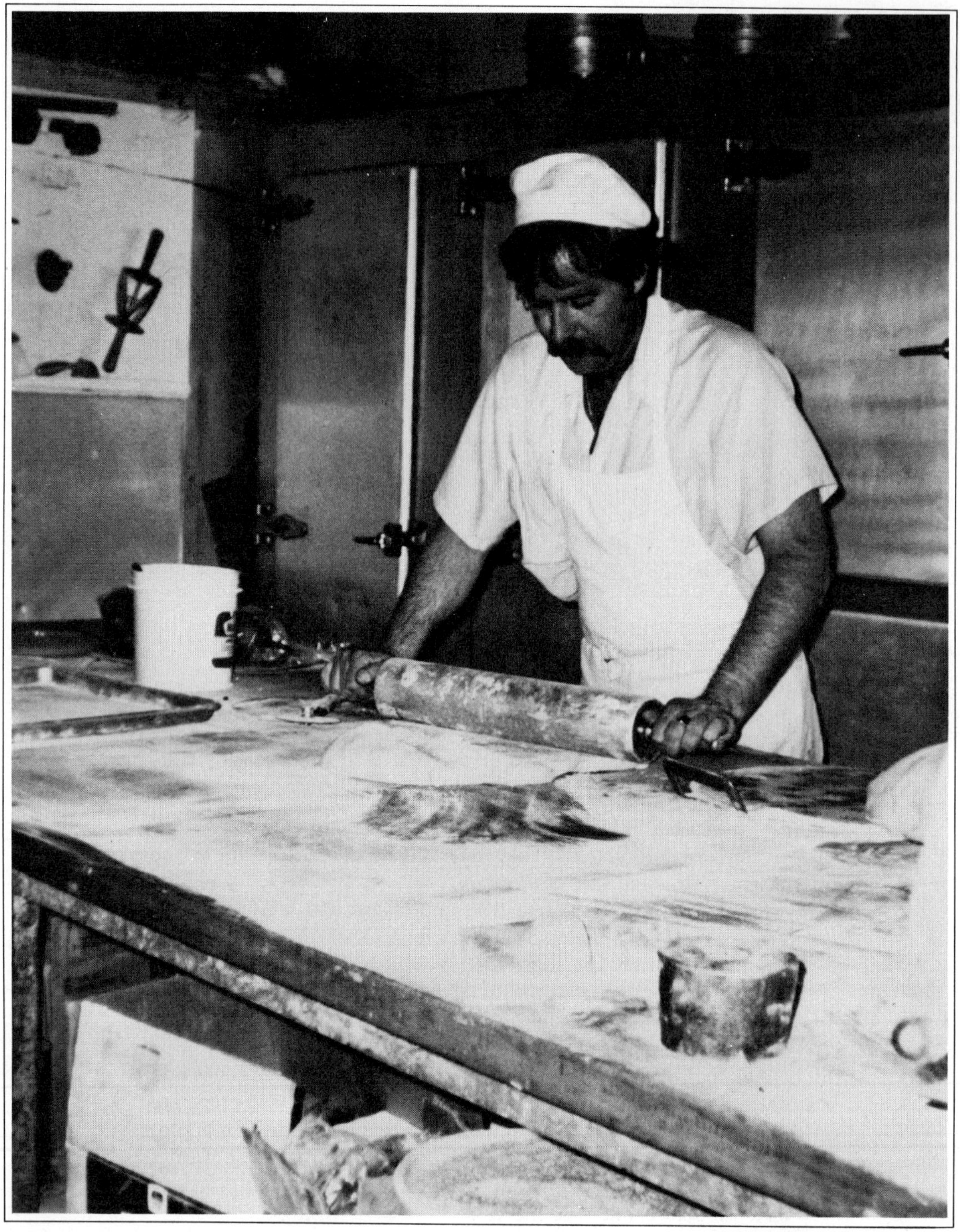

chapter 1

Small Business in the Economy

Objectives

1. Define the profit motive and its significance in the free enterprise system.

2. Describe issues facing owners of small business in the American economy.

3. Discuss the economic climate today and debate the future of small business.

THE AMERICAN ENTREPRENEUR

Historically, small businesses have provided many innovations and new jobs throughout the United States. Small businesses have also supplied many products, services and deliveries to virtually every village, farm, town, and city in the nation. According to recent statistics (see Figure 1.1), approximately 14 million businesses, or 99 percent of the total number of American business, can be categorized as "small."[1]

Perhaps you, like many others before you, have dreamed of starting your own business. People become entrepreneurs for many different reasons, but some reasons are more obvious, while others are simply misconceptions. How often have you heard someone say:

"Wouldn't it be great to get out from under the eye of my supervisor?"

"I've always wanted to see my name over the door of my own firm."

"At the end of a day I'd like to empty that cash drawer into my pockets!"

But running your own business is not as easy as it may seem. There can be problems with the inventory, getting the right goods delivered on time. Employ-

**FIGURE 1.1
Constitution of the American Small-Business Population.** There are approximately 14 million small businesses in the United States, but a large proportion of these are part-time operations.

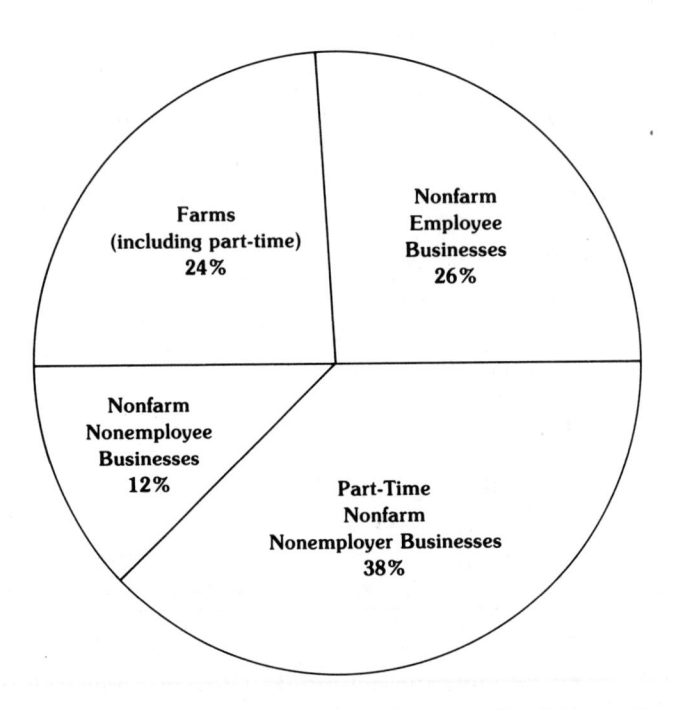

Farms (including part-time) 24%
Nonfarm Employee Businesses 26%
Nonfarm Nonemployee Businesses 12%
Part-Time Nonfarm Nonemployer Businesses 38%

Courtesy of the National Federation of Independent Business (NFIB) Research and Education Foundation

Sources: Estimated from *Statistics of Income*, Internal Revenue Service and *Current Population Survey*, Department of Commerce, Bureau of the Census.

ees are often absent or late just when they are needed most. Then there are the slow days, when you feel sure that no customer or client will ever walk through the door again. Yet the overhead costs and expenses continue to mount, whether or not anyone buys. These costs include rent (or mortgage payments), utilities, advertising, taxes, employee wages, and the money invested in stock, equipment, or machines. And if you need to borrow money to get started, you'll also be paying back the loan each month.

Suppose though that you have a specific skill or talent or that you have gained a great deal of experience working for someone else in a particular trade, service, industry, or store. You are eager to make it on your own. Perhaps instead of a retail store or service establishment you have a unique business plan that you believe you can launch from your home. You plan to start with a very little initial outlay of funds. You might choose to run this new business at night and on weekends, while you keep working full- or part-time elsewhere until your company can pay its own way and provide you with a living wage.

In fact, most large companies have started small—from someone's basement or backyard or in a nondescript rented establishment. Henry Ford began his automotive experiments in his barn with bicycles; Frank L. Carney, Pizza Hut's founder, paid his way through college by making pizzas in a hole-in-the-wall kitchen that had carry-out facilities only.

Naomi Sims was bothered by the lack of hairpieces available to black women. She traveled around collecting hair samples by asking for snips from the heads of people she met! Three years after she launched her wig collection, she grossed over $5 million in sales.[2]

Donald Douglas, with aeronautical engineering degree in hand and only a drafting board, set up business in the back room of a barber shop. Today his multibillion-dollar corporation stands in the forefront of the aerospace industry.

Steve Jobs and Stephen Wozniak, both in their early twenties, started Apple Computer from Jobs' dining room and garage. At age 26, Jobs held over 7 million shares of the corporation—worth nearly $200 million.[3]

Debbie Fields, who began baking chocolate-chip cookies when she was 13, opened a tiny 325-square-foot shop on a side street. Four years later, at the age of 24, she was the owner of a chain of 21 chocolate-chip cookie stores that was grossing over $6 million.

Young people are not the only ones who have demonstrated a willingness to take entrepreneurial risks (see Figure 1.2). Consider Colonel Sanders, who introduced his fried-chicken recipe and gained worldwide attention after the age of 70. He had already failed in several other business ventures but, undaunted, he finally succeeded.

Hobbies often lead to business ventures. Anne and Frank Kitchens developed their separate careers along parallel lines. After training professionally, Frank became an excellent chef working for others as an employee, while Anne learned the business side of food management. They amused themselves and their friends by entertaining with lavish gourmet dinners until at last they decided to start their own business. Instead of tackling the food industry by opening a

FIGURE 1.2
Age Starting Business. People in all age groups become entrepreneurs. Most people start their businesses between the ages of 25 and 40.

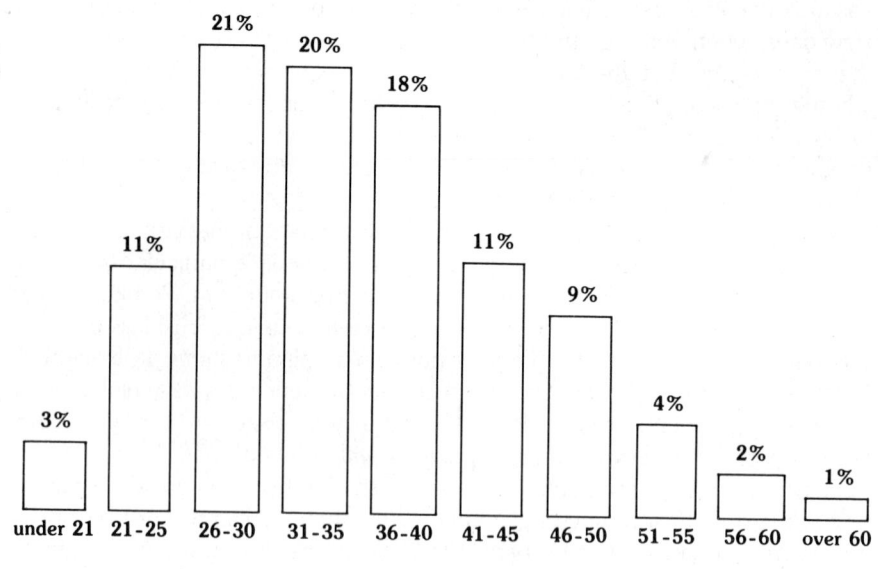

Age	Percentage
under 21	3%
21-25	11%
26-30	21%
31-35	20%
36-40	18%
41-45	11%
46-50	9%
51-55	4%
56-60	2%
over 60	1%

Courtesy of the National Federation of Independent Business (NFIB)

restaurant or retail bakery, they chose to start a wholesale pastry-baking business.

In their business plan they estimated they needed a $10,000 capital investment; as a margin of safety they raised $20,000 (from both savings and by borrowing). It took eight months before they began to show a profit, but by the end of their second year the business had grossed $350,000.

What does it take to achieve such phenomenal success? According to Sandra Brown, president of a firm that grosses several million dollars a year:

> You have to want to win . . . and you need courage and energy. It takes a lot of guts and it's lonely. When problems come home to roost, they come home to you. And don't try to go into business without enough money. Most important, you must be the kind of person who can always regenerate yourself, make yourself happy, and thrive on being alone.[4]

Not everyone embarks on business ventures alone, however. Some people form partnerships in order, among other reasons, to pool both expertise and capital. Nevertheless, you need to invest a great deal of work and energy to get an enterprise off the ground. Frank and Anne Kitchens can attest to that; they each worked 18 hours a day in order to make their pastry business operational. Optimism and perseverance in the face of multiple problems are also a must. While establishing themselves, the Kitchens found it necessary to give 90-day payment terms. This meant that in the first few months they were operating with a negative cash flow, at a time when they needed money badly.

"The first few months were torture!" says Anne. "Things were going wrong every day. We had enough crises to last a lifetime. Things got so busy we began sleeping at the bakery. Sometimes we'd just drop down on the flour sacks."

Beginning with one employee in addition to themselves, the Kitchens eventually hired 12 people. They have sought to maintain the standards that have guided their enterprise: "We believe quality is what people want, and we try to charge a fair and reasonable price to maintain that quality."[5]

The Enterprise—What Is It?

Webster's defines *enterprise* as "an undertaking, especially one which involves activity, courage, energy; an important or daring project. . . . The character or disposition that leads one to attempt the difficult, the untried." One synonym is *venture*. Basically, a business enterprise is any operation in which one engages for the purpose of making money, although some people have other motivations. Most people feel, however, that—given the amount of time and energy one must devote to operating a business—if they couldn't expect to make a reasonable profit or income, it would make more sense for them to work for others.

An *entrepreneur*, according to Webster's, is: "an employer as the person who assumes the risk and the management of a business." Risk is a key factor; the willingness to take risks—along with knowledge and a bit of luck—often spells the difference between those who fail, those who barely survive, and the truly successful.

How Small Is "Small"?

There are many definitions of small business. The 1980 White House Conference on Small Business decided that a small business is one that employs 500 people or less.[6] Qualitatively, we might expect a small business to involve independence, enterprise, and an obvious personal touch—that the owners know the names and perhaps the circumstances of their employees and many of their regular customers. (see Figure 1.3.)

THE AMERICAN ECONOMIC SYSTEM

Economics studies the relationship between human wants and needs and society's efforts to satisfy these wants and needs by utilizing available goods and services. People have two types of needs: biological and psychological. As people become more affluent, they grow more interested in satisfying their psychological wants. In societies where the standard of living is relatively high, these psychological wants become dominant. Status symbols and social status are concepts of an affluent society.

**FIGURE 1.3
Percentage of Gross Product Originated by Small Business.** Small businesses' share of economic activity since the mid-1960s. The share of big business has remained relatively constant. Government's share has increased.

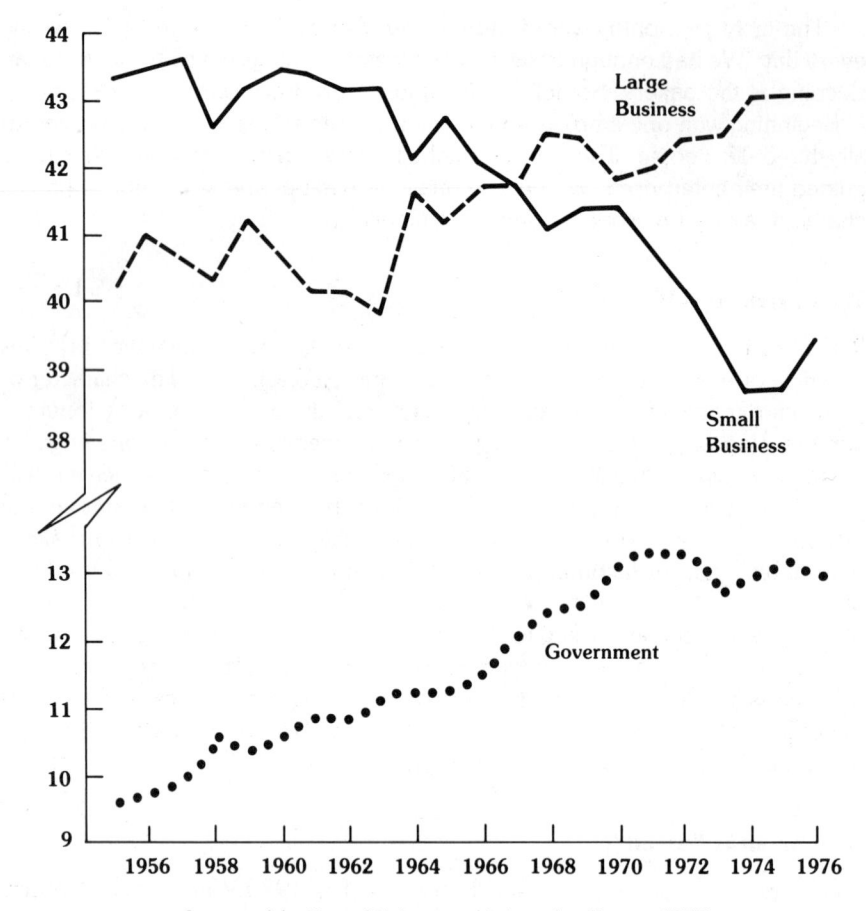

Courtesy of the National Federation of Independent Business (NFIB)

In a free-enterprise system, different television manufacturers, for example, compete for a share of the same market. One company will try to provide features in its set that other companies can't or don't offer, in an attempt to attract more customers. In a controlled economic system, by comparison, consumers have but two options—to buy the single standard model available or to go without. In a free-enterprise system, the competition among various firms means that people have more products from which to choose.

Gross National Product (GNP)

The United States remains unrivaled in the world for its total output of goods and services. The output of California alone, for example, exceeds that of Africa. Pennsylvania almost equals Australia in economic power, and Nebraska's economy is as big as Ireland's. America's 25 Eastern states, with the District of Columbia, virtually equal the output of the number-two nation, the Soviet Union ($1379 billion versus $1393 billion, according to 1980 statistics).[7]

Actually, America's total output now approaches $3 trillion, a figure that boggles the mind. Three trillion dollars equals $4 million spent daily from the birth of Christ to the present day. Or, illustrated another way, $3 trillion would buy more than three-fourths of America's 54 million single-family houses (which cost an average of $79,000 each in the early 1980s).[8]

Since the nineteenth century, the share of U.S. national output of goods and services accounted for by small business has declined. This decline leveled off in the 1950s, with small business responsible for just over half of all private production (see Table 1.1).

New Jobs and Innovations from Small Business

Despite the decline in its contribution to the GNP, small business still plays a key role in the U.S. economy in areas such as employment and innovations. Inventors often choose to market their new product through small business, whose greater flexibility and greater openness to risk makes it the ideal vehicle for such ventures.

TABLE 1.1 Distribution of Employment in Companies with less than 100 and less than 500 Employees, by Industry Division

INDUSTRY DIVISION	PERCENTAGE OF FIRMS WITH LESS THAN 100 EMPLOYEES — Small Business Data Base	PERCENTAGE OF FIRMS WITH LESS THAN 100 EMPLOYEES — Enterprise Statistics	PERCENTAGE OF FIRMS WITH LESS THAN 500 EMPLOYEES — Small Business Data Base	PERCENTAGE OF FIRMS WITH LESS THAN 500 EMPLOYEES — Enterprise Statistics
All industries	33.8%	40.1%	46.8%	52.5%
Agriculture, Forestry, Fisheries	66.8	NA	76.6	NA
Mining	13.8	30.0	19.7	44.8
Construction	70.0	68.9	83.7	82.0
Manufacturing	16.1	16.1	28.3	28.9
Transportation, Communications, Utilities	18.1	NA	24.5	NA
Wholesale trade	68.5	73.0	83.0	88.8
Retail trade	56.8	54.0	65.8	62.4
Finance, Insurance, Real estate	31.8	NA	46.3	NA
Services	32.0	59.1	51.3	75.7

Note: Mining and Services sectors in the two sources are not comparable. NA = "not available."

Sources: Small Business Data Base tabulated by Brookings Institution from Dun and Bradstreet's Market Identifier File; and Department of Commerce, Bureau of the Census, 1977 Enterprise Statistics, General Report on Industrial Organization, Table 3.

Supply and Demand

The interaction of supply and demand helps to determine whether and how well people will be able to satisfy their needs and wants. But this interaction is not a simple one, since it is influenced by many peripheral factors. These include (1) the business factors of production, distribution, and consumption; (2) the human factors of producers, distributors, and consumers; and (3) the environmental factors of natural resources, capital facilities, and population.

The price of any good or service is the amount of money for which it can be purchased, as determined by supply and demand. Thus production and consumption are assumed to equalize price. It is usually said that the demand for a product will be increased by a low price and decreased by a high price and the supply will be increased by a high price and decreased by a low price. When this principle applies, price tends to move toward the equilibrium point at which the quantity of goods offered for sale will equal the quantity demanded.

This explanation makes the relationship between supply and demand sound fairly straightforward. Unfortunately, however, the balance does not always work as predicted. I say "unfortunately," because if entrepreneurs could count on this principle to operate as it's supposed to in the marketplace, they might find it much easier not only to establish prices but also to make more accurate financial forecasts. One example of how far off the relationship can get is the Boston service station that successfully sold its gasoline for 12 cents more per gallon than most other stations in the city, including those within a half-dozen blocks. Asked why they bought their gas there customers grinned, or shrugged their shoulders, or even looked surprised. Their reasons ranged from "I don't know, I've always come here" to "The gas must be better if it costs more."[9]

Competition

The particular structure of business competition is made more complex and flexible by a common medium of exchange, money, which is exchanged for a multiplicity of resources. The medium of exchange focuses attention on the pursuit of revenue, in competition with others, as a common denominator for the trade-off between resources.[10]

The free-enterprise system usually offers people with imagination, energy, and drive the opportunity to achieve profit, recognition, and prestige by doing a better job or providing a better service than others. The essence of the free-enterprise system is competition. It is competition that makes people who are already doing a good job try harder—that makes them try to improve on their own past record as well as on the performance and/or contribution of others.

Competition in a free-enterprise system takes several forms. One company may offer a high-quality product at a relatively high price while another company offers a similar product of lesser quality at a lower price. It is left to the consumers to evaluate their needs and decide how much they can or are willing to pay.

Companies can often stimulate a demand for a particular product or service through advertising. Indeed, how could we learn about new and/or better items without advertising? How long would it take for a product to become known to the majority without advertising?

The entrepreneur who wants to be successful must seek to provide a little extra service, a little better product, or in some other way to improve upon the competition. Although many businesses fail each year, many survive. Those that succeed perform services or offer merchandise for sale in such a way as to satisfy the community in which they operate. When the business no longer satisfies a sufficient number of people, it fails.

You do not have to be the best manager or have the biggest store in order to compete successfully. It's a relative matter. If you see a need for a new store in a growing community and begin operating before anyone else, you can get a head start on the competition. If the location is good, you will soon have business neighbors, but even then they may not be direct competition since they may represent different products and services and actually bring more business to the locale.

Competition and the Profit Motive

Competition in a free-enterprise system means at least two things: for the entrepreneur it means the freedom to enter any business venture desired and compete with those already in existence, while for the consumer it means the freedom to purchase any of the goods and services offered by these various firms. As used here, *profit* (or *net income*) represents the excess of money received from a business transaction over the costs of operating to achieve that sale.

"Whatever the Traffic Will Bear"

One guideline used by some companies to establish prices is "whatever the traffic will bear." And indeed, like some of the customers at the Boston gas station, many consumers believe that "if it costs more, it must be better."

Yet these consumers would only have to shop around to discover the wide range of prices available for just about any product or service. Why then will they pay two to ten times as much for an item as it costs elsewhere? Perhaps they are dazzled by those entrepreneurs who offer their goods and services at the higher prices into believing that the product is really superior. This impression may be reinforced by advertising campaigns. One television commercial for a hair-color product frankly admits that the price is high: the model closes her sales pitch by declaring "It costs more, but I'm worth it!"

Snob appeal? Perhaps, but those people who can afford it—and some who cannot—are often willing to pay for such "prestige" products, regardless of their quality.

Determining Markup

Suppose a manufacturing company produces zacks and sells them directly to consumers. (See Figure 1.4.) The markup on each zack is $32.50. Markup is the difference between direct costs and sale price. Markup must cover all indirect costs in addition to profit. Note that the profit on each zack is only $2.50 out of a markup of $32.50.

"No Customers, No Business"

The number of customers available and willing to buy ultimately determines the success of any business, whether retail, wholesale, agricultural, manufacturing, or distributionary. Wherever products are offered, "the customer is king!"

Sometimes national, even international issues can affect the customer supply. Consider the 1982 Tylenol scare. Tampering with the product led to several deaths in the Chicago area. With the growing consumer fears came an informal boycott of a product that had previously captured nearly 20 percent of the total market for aspirin and related products. Pharmacies cooperated with Johnson and Johnson, the manufacturer of Tylenol, to pull the product out of the market. Thus not only the druggists and other retail establishments, but also the manufacturer and the wholesalers, were affected. Johnson and Johnson lost about $100 million.[11]

National boycotts can occur for a variety of reasons. Some influential groups boycott the products of companies whose commercials support television programs that include excessive violence.[12] Unfavorable national publicity about a company and its products or services can also cause customers to abandon it en masse.

The snowball can begin rolling at any of several levels. The Tylenol scare started in one locale, Chicago. Negative publicity about a major manufacturer operates on a national scale. The health of other business sectors can affect your business. In the early 1980s, for example, consumers stopped buying houses, cars, and household appliances because interest rates on loans and other credit were simply too high. All these are extraneous factors beyond the control of any single entrepreneur.

When customers do not buy, there is no business! Or at any rate, business activity can slow down considerably, and at every level—if, that is, the trend affects more than a single locale or business. Thus a reduction in customers and purchases at the retail level can snowball "uphill" to touch both the manufacturers who produce the products and the distributors who make them available to retailers.

On a smaller, purely local scale, any number of causes can produce an informal boycotting of a company or of its products and services. Thus it is extremely important for an entrepreneur to build goodwill by developing a reputation for dealing honestly and courteously with customers. Without customers, there can be no business; and without business, there can be no profits.

Small Business in the Economy

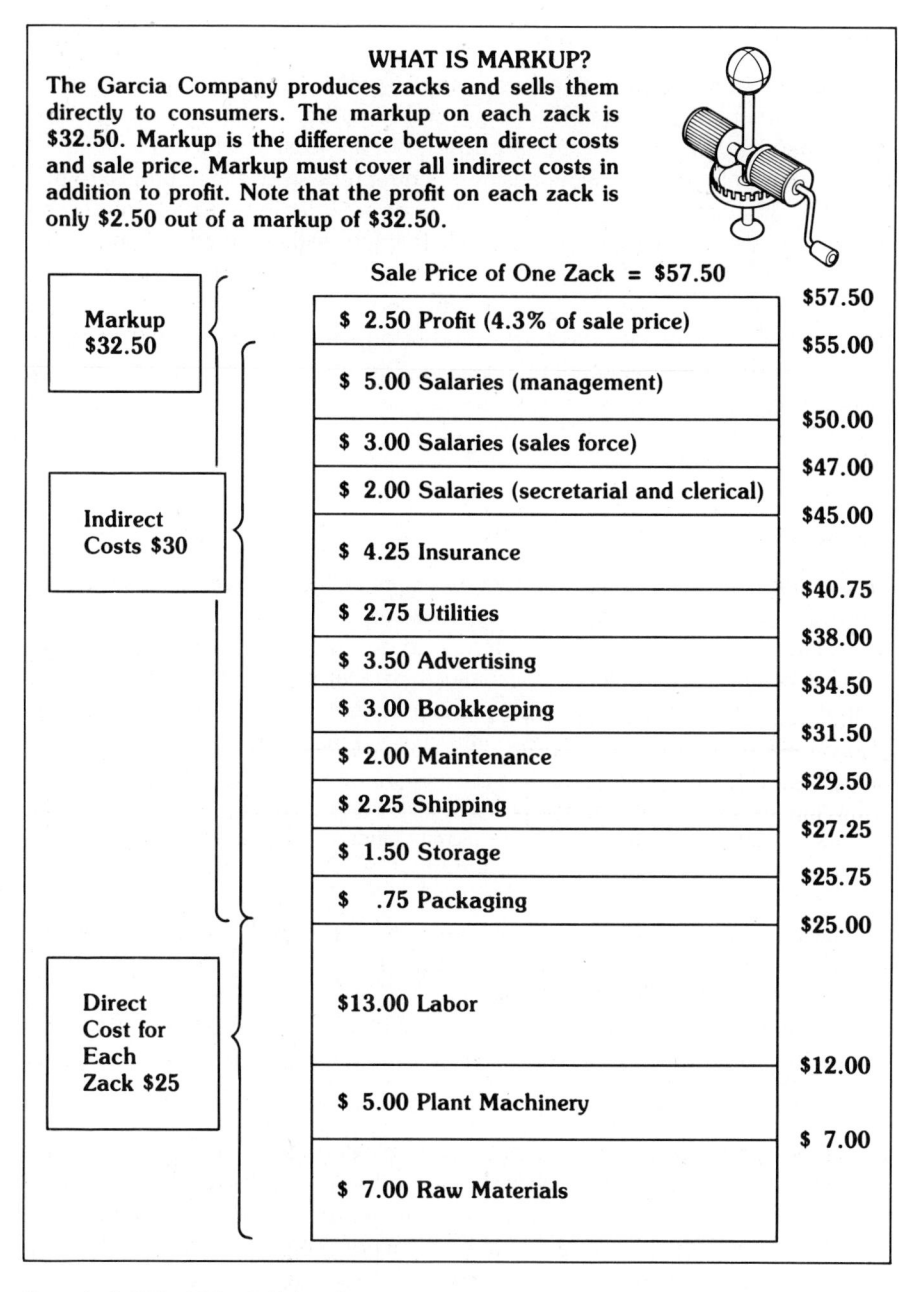

WHAT IS MARKUP?
The Garcia Company produces zacks and sells them directly to consumers. The markup on each zack is $32.50. Markup is the difference between direct costs and sale price. Markup must cover all indirect costs in addition to profit. Note that the profit on each zack is only $2.50 out of a markup of $32.50.

Sale Price of One Zack = $57.50

Category	Item	Cumulative
Markup $32.50	$ 2.50 Profit (4.3% of sale price)	$57.50 / $55.00
	$ 5.00 Salaries (management)	$50.00
	$ 3.00 Salaries (sales force)	$47.00
	$ 2.00 Salaries (secretarial and clerical)	$45.00
Indirect Costs $30	$ 4.25 Insurance	$40.75
	$ 2.75 Utilities	$38.00
	$ 3.50 Advertising	$34.50
	$ 3.00 Bookkeeping	$31.50
	$ 2.00 Maintenance	$29.50
	$ 2.25 Shipping	$27.25
	$ 1.50 Storage	$25.75
	$ .75 Packaging	$25.00
Direct Cost for Each Zack $25	$13.00 Labor	$12.00
	$ 5.00 Plant Machinery	$ 7.00
	$ 7.00 Raw Materials	

Copyright © 1980—Milliken Publishing Co.

FIGURE 1.4 What Is Markup? (*Courtesy of Milliken Publishing Co.*).

What Happens to Profit?

Naturally, business owners expect some financial return for themselves from their investment of money, time, energy, and expertise. However, they often use the money they take in for other purposes, not the least of which is to funnel it directly back into improving the business. Entrepreneurs use their profits: to buy new machinery; to improve, expand, or open new facilities; to hire more employees or raise salaries and give bonuses; to improve their purchasing power by buying in greater bulk and receiving case or truckload discounts; to pay creditors or decrease loan or mortgage indebtedness; to research how to improve products and services, decrease costs, and so on; and to increase the advertising budget. Any of these expenditures can lead in turn to more income. Finally, from profits come the taxes companies pay.

Business Cycles

Free-enterprise economies go through what are called "cyclical fluctuations." A business cycle is a recurring sequence of events and associated activities; each event leads to the next until the entire cycle is completed.

In all business cycles there is usually a parallel relationship among prices, output, income, employment, and profit. Employment and incomes are high and business expands during prosperity cycles, while in recessionary cycles all these factors contract.

During the recession of the early 1980s, businesses failed at an alarming rate: figures for early 1982 reported a 55-percent increase in bankruptcies over the previous 12 months.[13] Indicators included:

> *Sluggish growth in profits.* Many companies have, at best, had modest profits growth, and at worst, losses in recent years. Thus, firms are forced to raise outside cash for new investments and current production.
>
> *High interest rates.* Firms have relied on short-term borrowing because they are unwilling to lock themselves into years of near-record interest rates on long-term bonds.[14]

Yet the recessionary picture is not always bleak. Innovative business owners invariably find ways to cope, no matter how adverse conditions are. Among the steps some successful business owners use to combat downswings in the economy are: extending the due date of debts, renegotiating the terms of repayment, arranging interim loans to tide the company over a rough time, selling off money-losing units, and even merging with other companies. In fact, a recession can prove a plus for owners who are flexible and can take fast action. In downturns, they usually trim production and cut costs, and may also slash capital spending, thus lowering their current cash requirements.

The Future of Small Business

The 1982 *Report of the President on the State of Small Business* draws some pertinent distinctions between large and small companies. Small business it reports, are more sensitive to high interest rates, high inflation, and downturns in the business cycle. Simultaneously, small companies operate at a disadvantage in the debt and equity capital markets. Nevertheless, it is small business that generates opportunities for many new jobs and innovations in products and services.

In the United States, dynamic economic change is a certainty. This trend has meant continued growth in the number of small businesses. The 1982 report indicated that new businesses continue to form at a rate of about 2 to 4 percent annually—even, apparently, during recessions. Additionally, the number of businesses with employees and the number of businesses operated by self-employed persons with no employees are increasing at approximately equal rates.[15] (See Figure 1.5.)

THE CHALLENGES FACING ENTREPRENEURS

From 1974 to 1979 the Survey Research Center of the University of Michigan asked over 2 million new high school graduates what sort of work setting they preferred. The results showed that young Americans strongly prefer an entrepreneurial setting: i.e., employment with a small enterprise rather than in a large bureaucratic organization.[16]

FIGURE 1.5
Trends in the Small-Business Population

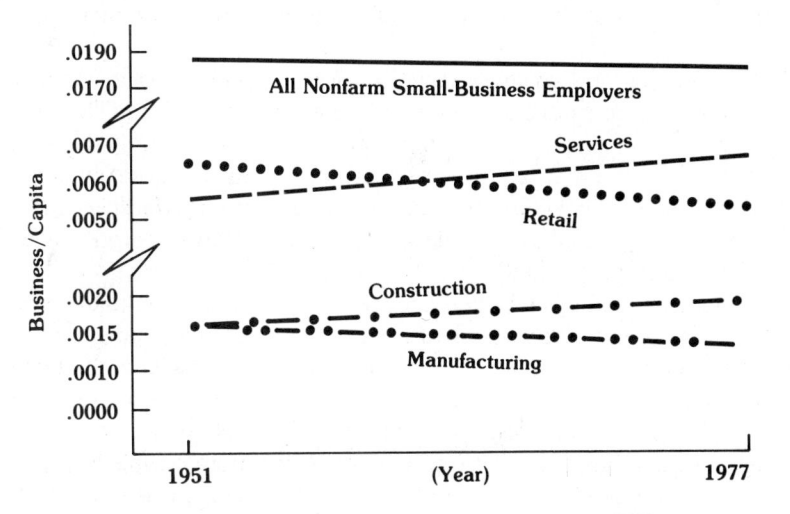

Courtesy of the National Federation of Independent Business (NFIB)

Owning your own business, however, involves not only satisfactions but also numerous challenges. A successful enterprise doesn't "just happen." You need a great deal of information besides some special skills, talents, and possibly experience working as an employee in a related industry.

Many would-be entrepreneurs, unfortunately, do not comprehend the rudiments of economic planning, systematic management, and continual control. They think that their technical expertise is all they need. Indeed, some experts argue that being in the right place at the right time with the right product or service is the key to success. But that success can't happen without an effective plan for marketing and distribution—"getting there first with the best."

Steps in the Planning Process

Part of advance planning and organization is gathering data, conducting informal interviews, and observing related businesses. You can draw on entrepreneurial contacts by visiting with owners of businesses similar to yours. You should definitely contact such other human resources as an attorney, a banker or loan officer, and an accountant. Although you may plan to start small, you will still need knowledge and experience that you obtain by seeking the advice of experts. Other sources of information are trade and professional journals, books, seminars, and courses, and personnel from the chamber of commerce and the Small Business Administration (SBA).

You should conduct a market-feasibility study of the community in which you wish to operate. Is there a need for the product or service you plan to offer? Are there potential customers? For example, a community of 20,000 with three bath-and-body boutiques would hardly be able to keep those stores open, much less support a fourth one. You also need to determine a good location for your enterprise. Can you afford to move into one or more of the identified "best places"?

To answer this and other financial questions, you'll need to identify your current assets. Your skills and experience count, to be sure. Equally significant, though, is whether you can obtain the capital needed to open the business and to operate it for the first few months (perhaps a year or more) until you can realize a profit. You'll need money for, among other things: facilities and equipment, advertising, supplies, materials, and stock (if your enterprise is to be a store or manufacturing plant).

Consider how you will raise the necessary capital and if you have to borrow, plan to make regular loan payments. Know, too, that few loans are made to inexperienced first-time entrepreneurs, particularly those with limited collateral (other assets against which loans can be made), no matter how sanguine you are about the potential profits. Your chances will be better if you have prepared a comprehensive business plan (see Chapter 6 for more on this topic).

Some entrepreneurs report that their greatest challenge was how to raise the needed capital. Others claim that it was the task of adjusting their dreams to the reality—the hard work, the long hours, the tremendous expenditures of energy, and the anxiety of wondering if the decisions they make will eventually bear fruit.

Sufficient funding—although you can't launch a successful business without it—is not necessarily the most essential ingredient for success. The most essential ingredient is financial planning and control. According to Beatrice Fitzpatrick, former director of the American Women's Economic Development Corporation: "There is a scientific approach to running a business. Women in particular have to recognize and make use of the entrepreneurial skills they've always had—managing a household and volunteer projects, for instance—and apply these to their own advantage."[17]

Advice from the Experienced

One banker advises potential entrepreneurs—particularly those who have limited capital and a low credit rating—to seek partners. "Most entrepreneurs," he says, "want to hold on to everything themselves, and don't want to give up a piece of the action. People starting out are reluctant to bring in partners, and that's where most loan proposals die."[18]

Several successful business people add the following advice:

> If you want to start your own business, first decide whether your idea, product or service is realistic; whether there is a need for it; and whether the business will take advantage of your strongest attributes. Then secure venture capital, or start-up money.
>
> You can have all the talent in the world, but if you can't sell yourself, your talent may not be worth much in the business world.
>
> Dedication is the word. If you're washing dishes, you have to be willing to get your hands in the sink!
>
> Expect to have dry spells (lack of customers or pending deals). The wait can be hair-raising, but the results are often worth it.
>
> You have to know what you're doing. Also, take all the courses and read all you can.
>
> Plan! Work out your direction, but be spontaneous enough to respond to the reality of the situation. Creative planning and creative *un*-planning are both essential.[19]

SUMMARY

Small businesses are a complex mixture of many different ownership types, sizes, and locations. Census statistics show that small businesses appear in all industry categories. Many are family owned and operated or individually owned and operated. They are located all across the United States, many in large cities but a significant portion in small towns. Small businesses are as diverse and disparate as the American population.

Many of our forebears started their own enterprises and, at least as a dream, the idea continues to be powerful. With realistic perceptions of what small-business ownership involves, together with thorough planning, you too can become successful in entrepreneurship.

DISCUSSION QUESTIONS

Draw on your own experience and opinions, as well as what you have read above, to consider the following questions.

1. Naomi Sims had gained a worldwide reputation as a model before launching her Naomi Sims Collection of wigs and hairpieces. How much of her success do you suppose was based on her already "having a name" and contacts in the business world? How much on her business acumen? Debate the truth of the byword, "It's not *what* you know, but *who*."
2. What do you think Debbie Fields did "right" that enabled her to expand her first tiny chocolate-chip cookie store into a chain of 21? Describe some other highly successful business ventures you know of. What traits seem to separate the highly successful from the mediocre?
3. How do you account for the entrepreneurial achievements of people who are described as "eighth-grade millionaires"—i.e., supposedly unschooled people? How much do you think luck contributes to entrepreneurial success?
4. Discuss business cycles in relation to the current economic climate—local, regional, and national. What would you say is the outlook for success, given the present economy of the enterprises with which you are most familiar (perhaps one or more you might have considered opening)?
5. Evaluate the advice given by some experienced businesspeople and entrepreneurs. Does this advice apply to your own experience and to that of businesspeople you have known?

MINICASE

Michael and Megan wanted to go into business when Michael got out of the army, but they had no idea what they could do. Finding a plumbing and heating franchise for sale in their hometown, they pooled their resources and made the plunge. The couple reported that initially they did not know how to sell the products, how to service them, nor even how to establish the books for an effective recordkeeping system. The franchise, however, provided the training. Since opening their business five years ago they have had their problems, to be sure, but have yet to regret becoming "their own boss(es)." Now they plan to return to school for training in using microcomputers.

Compare this approach to going into business with that of a person who already has skills, training, and work experience in the particular product or service he or she will be offering. Also consider why this couple are planning to obtain more training.

ACTIVITIES AND EXERCISES

1. Individually or in teams, interview entrepreneurs in one or more small businesses. Ask them, "If you had it to do over again, what would you do differently? Why?" Observe the business informally and note what interests you or puzzles you. Be ready to share the results of your findings, as noted below.
2. Organize into small groups for discussion. If possible, each group should contain at least one person who is familiar with small business operations, as a current owner or manager, as a former entrepreneur, or from associating with family or friends who are owners.

Share your interview findings as well as your personal experiences. Raise questions that you and members of your group would like to answer through this textbook and related experiences.

NOTES

1. Small Business Administration (SBA), *The State of Small Business: A Report of the President* (Washington, D.C.: U.S. Government Printing Office, March 1982), p. 3.
2. Bena Kay and Frances Ruffin, "How to Make a Million Before You're 34," *Redbook,* May 1977, pp. 60–64.
3. Stewart Also, II, "An Apple on Every Desk," *Inc.,* October 1981, pp. 50–51.
4. Kaye and Ruffin, "Million."
5. Alexandra Penney, "Baking Together, A Work of Love," *Working Woman,* October 1977, pp. 37–39.
6. This conference was convened in compliance with the 1980 Small Business Economic Policy Act. It produced the President's first annual report on the state of small business (SBA, "Small Business Administration"). According to a White House senior policy adviser, this report is "the most definitive Presidential statement ever on small business." It summarizes for the first time most of what's known about the relationship between small business and the rest of the world.
7. "An Economic Force That None Can Equal," *U.S. News & World Report,* April 5, 1982, p. 40.
8. Monroe W. Karmin, with Robert J. Morse, "An Economy That Speaks in Trillions," *U.S. News & World Report,* June 14, 1982, pp. 72–73.
9. "Sunday Morning News, with Charles Kuralt," CBS TV, August 8, 1982.

10. Bruce D. Henderson, "The Anatomy of Competition," *Journal of Marketing*, Vol. 47 (Spring 1983), pp. 7–11.
11. "Sixty Minutes," CBS TV, December 19, 1982.
12. Eugene H. Methvin, "TV Violence: The Shocking New Evidence," *Reader's Digest*, January 1983, pp. 49–53.
13. Monroe W. Karmin, "Business Failures—A New Wave to Come?" *U.S. News & World Report,* May 3, 1982, p. 82.
14. Judith B. Gardner, "Companies Going Broke—How Big a Danger?" *U.S. News & World Report,* November 30, 1981, pp. 91–92.
15. *The State of Small Business: A Report of the President,* 1982.
16. Small Business Administration, *Economic Research on Small Business* (Washington, D.C.: U.S. Government Printing Office, 1981), p. ii.
17. Fran Weinstein, "How to Become an Entrepreneur," *Working Woman,* December 1977, pp. 14–15.
18. From an interview with a bank loan officer who asked to remain anonymous (Denver, Colorado, January 1983).
19. Weinstein, "Entrepreneur."

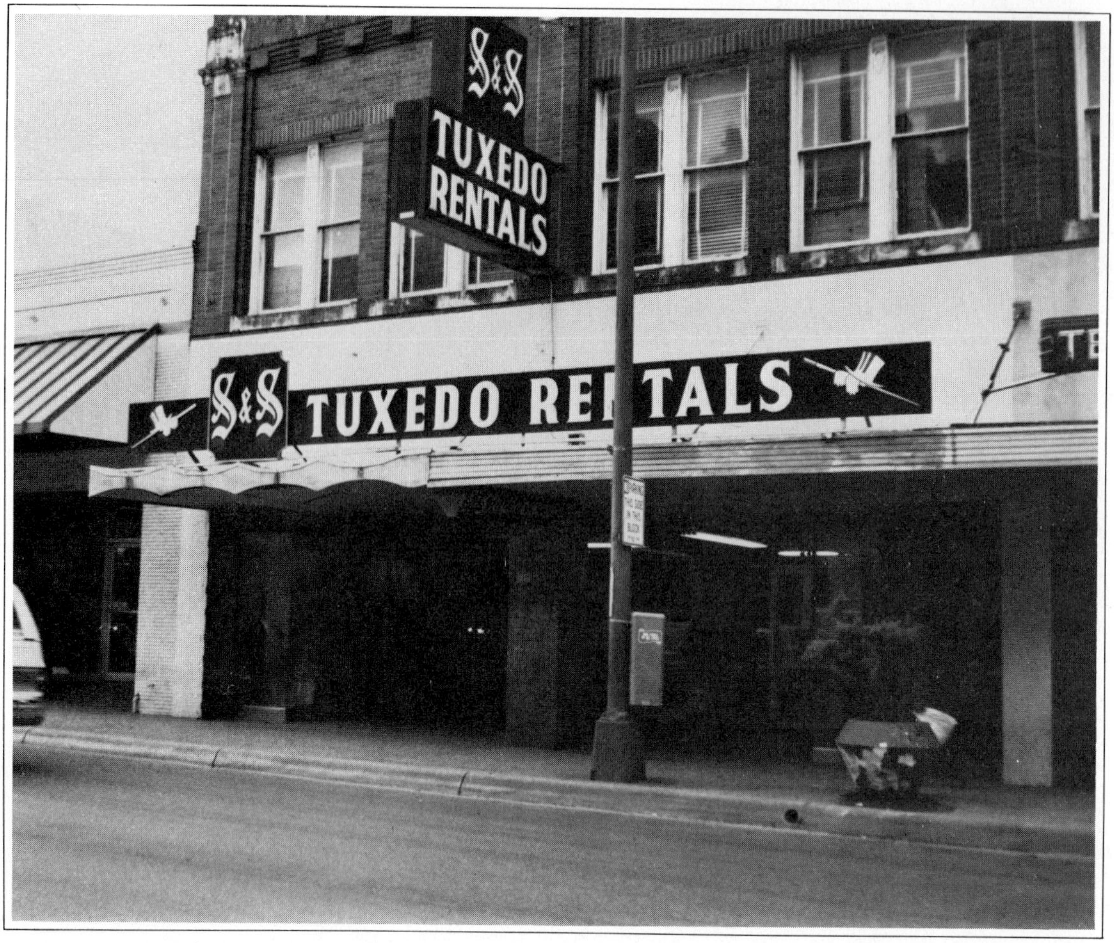
S&S
TUXEDO
RENTALS
S&S

c·h·a·p·t·e·r ·2·

Satisfactions, Risks, Failures, and Challenges

Objectives

1. Identify satisfactions you hope to find from small business ownership.

2. Describe some of the risks faced by business owners you have met and tell how they dealt with their problems.

3. Formulate opinions about what differentiates those entrepreneurs who will probably fail from those who will survive and prosper.

4. Design a plan to ensure the support of family members who will be affected by your decision to go into business and include provisions for continuity and survival of the business.

Although most people expect to make money from their businesses, there are other satisfactions to be derived from business ownership beyond profit alone. These satisfactions are as diverse as are the people who go into business for themselves.

But with these satisfactions come risk and the possibility of failure. The first year of a new business is its most critical. Expenditures often overtake the amount of revenue coming in while the new owner is facing numerous problems simultaneously and for the first time. In a time of economic and business fluctuations, unskilled, misinformed, inexperienced, or otherwise incapable management can result in increased business mortality. To survive in such times, you need not only technical or operational know-how but also considerable managerial skill.

Finally, remember that you won't be able to keep your work life totally separate from your personal, social, or family life. If you are married, you will have to think about how your spouse and children will fit in with your entrepreneurial business plans and work. Even if you are and remain single, you may need the participation—or at least the moral support—of family and friends.

SATISFACTIONS

Top on the list of satisfactions reported by entrepreneurs (in interviews and in literature) are: personal satisfaction, independence, and profits. This rank order may surprise those who are mostly profit-oriented. Yet the opportunity to realize a higher income is not of paramount concern to some people, although of course the business must eventually produce a profit—or it will face bankruptcy. (See Figure 2.1.)

Self-fulfillment and growing self-esteem account for much of the satisfaction to be realized from entrepreneurship. The knowledge that, as Naomi Sims says, "I am mistress of my own destiny"[1] is apparently worth plenty.

Other important satisfactions reported by entrepreneurs include the opportunity to gain power, prestige, and influence; to make investments; to achieve security; to enjoy the adventure; and to apply one's skills and experience to a venture of one's own making.

Opportunity to Exert Influence

We have all experienced the authority of others, from parents and teachers to employers. Owning a small business gives us a unique, satisfying chance to have power and influence ourselves. As master or mistress of our own destiny, we gain some measure of control over our work, time, and decisions.

Investment Options

The fact that satisfactions are represented in monetary terms does not necessarily imply that they are adequately described by a single return factor. In the investment context, it is realistic to recognize short-run return, liquidity, and capital-gains potential, among others, as distinct factors deemed important by the owner-investor.[2]

Small business is one way of making your money work for you outside the standard avenues of bank accounts, money markets, stocks and bonds, and real estate. The entrepreneur, win or lose, has control. People who have saved money from their salaries, an inheritance, or other investments sometimes find that owning a business serves as a tax shelter.

Security

Admittedly you face many risks when you start a business venture. But there is a certain measure of security as well. Whatever you do, short of going bankrupt, you have no employer to fire you for infractions of any rules or because of personality conflicts or because the company has suffered an economic setback.

**FIGURE 2.1
Small-Business Sales and Earnings.** Unlike most wage and salary workers, small business owners cannot count on constant earnings (profits). These levels vary considerably from quarter to quarter and year to year.

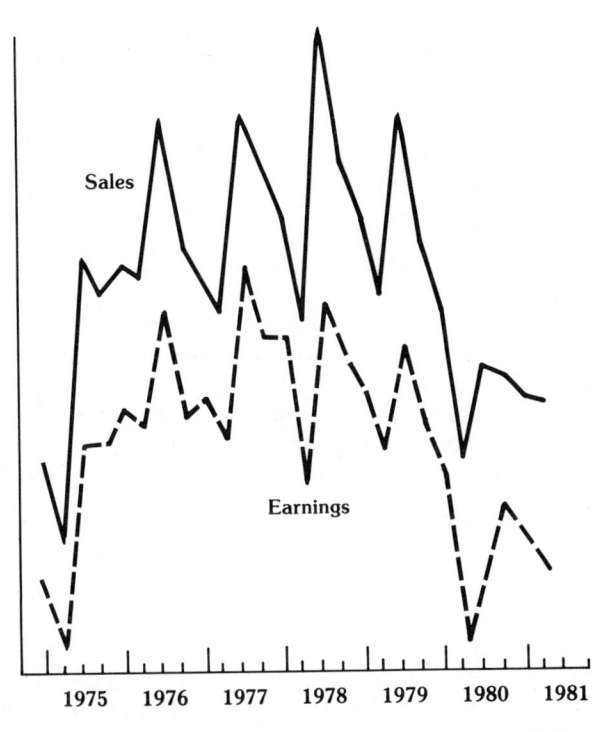

Courtesy of the National Federation of Independent Business (NFIB)

Adventure

Facing and surmounting the various risks associated with entrepreneurship can be an adventure. You never know what will happen next with the economy, the competition, or numerous other uncontrollable factors. Some people also find it an adventure to introduce innovative ideas, products, or services on the market.

RISKS IN ENTREPRENEURSHIP

Decision analysis involving risky prospects with monetary outcomes—and, in particular, investment opportunities with uncertain returns—has long been a subject of interest to decision theorists and practitioners. One approach focuses directly on a decision maker's preferences among risky prospects. The Von Neumann-and-Morgenstern model asserts that prospects and returns can be evaluated via a utility function such that the relative worth of a risky prospect is the expected utility of its possible returns. The expected-utility model has been the prominent approach in describing or predicting actual preference behavior.[3]

The opportunity for getting higher pay-offs comes with taking higher risks. "Nothing ventured, nothing gained" is a cliche that applies to small business. This truism is illustrated in the following example:

> Suppose you decide to invest in snow-removal equipment. You may plan to spend very little money on advertising and to make your service known through word of mouth, by posting notices on laundromat bulletin boards, or by placing small ads in the newspaper classified section. If you choose to buy a small motor-driven, hand-pushed implement for $1000 or less, your earning potential will be limited, no matter how much time you devote to clearing snow from sidewalks and driveways. If the winter is particularly snowy and if news of your service does get around, you could gross several hundred dollars. On the other hand, if the winter proves dry, with few clients and little work available, you will lose less than you would have if you had invested more.
>
> Now suppose, instead, that you purchase a three-quarter-ton pickup with four-wheel drive and attach an automatic snow-removal device to the front, which you can operate from within the cab. This time the monetary outlay could run to $15,000 or more. You can of course pay for the truck and the snow-removal equipment by installments and amortize the cost over several years. This plan implies that you are serious about your business and will remain with it for several seasons. It also significantly increases the potential for earnings, because you can also offer to clear roads as well as driveways, at a much higher price per job. You should also devote more money to the advertising budget, using printed and broadcast media among other outlets. If you are going to invest more money in equipment, if you're serious enough to plan a lengthy time investment, then your advertising plan should be commensurate. (Imagine opening a multimillion-dollar manufacturing plant to produce jet airplanes, with the only marketing gimmick a series of cards mounted at local laundromats!)

If you planned to retain a full-time job elsewhere, then you would need to hire someone to drive the truck in your absence. Your gross earnings might reach thousands of dollars with this expanded plan. Unfortunately, you still face the risks of a dry winter, competition from similar services, and not getting enough customers to make the venture pay.

Any business may face risks such as: cost increases, competition, changing consumer tastes and technology, changes in government regulations, and catastrophe. (See Table 2.1.)

Cost Increases

Retail, distributive trade, and production enterprises have to buy products and raw materials. Every business, however, has expenses: not only the cost of supplies and materials but also of utilities, rent, advertising, and employee

TABLE 2.1 Problems Facing Small Business

MOST IMPORTANT PROBLEM	Construction	Manufacturing	Transportation	Wholesale	Retail	Agriculture	Financial Services	Nonprofessional Services	Professional Services	All firms
Taxes	12%	11%	16%	13%	12%	8%	7%	18%	17%	13%
Inflation	8	8	8	7	12	20	7	28	13	12
Inadequate demand for product	19	40	24	26	26	19	9	12	8	23
Interest rates and financing	33	18	24	30	22	35	40	14	23	25
Minimum wage laws, cost of labor	7	4	2	3	3	3	2	5	8	4
Other government regulations, red tape	6	4	8	4	3	2	20	6	10	6
Competition from large business	2	4	6	9	12	2	7	2	3	6
Quality of labor	3	4	2	1	3	*	*	7	5	3
Shortage of fuels, materials or goods	*	*	*	*	*	*	*	1	*	*
Other; no answer	10	7	10	7	7	11	8	7	13	8
Total	100%	100%	100%	100%	100%	100%	100%	100%	100%	100%
Number of firms	251	259	50	200	646	90	164	232	134	2026
Percent of firms	12%	13%	2%	10%	32%	4%	8%	12%	7%	

* Less than 0.5%.
Courtesy: National Federation of Independent Business (NFIB).

wages. In an inflationary economy, business people also must anticipate that their expenses will escalate each year. In a recessionary climate the reverse is true. But although expenses will decrease, so may sales and, thus, profits.

Competition

You may begin your business by conducting a thorough marketing survey, but you can't always predict what the competition will do tomorrow. Although the initial location you choose for your small independent hamburger stand may be ideal, consider what will happen to the business if a McDonald's moves in down the street. Existing competitors can also do battle in a variety of ways, from introducing new products and lowering their prices to offering new services and sales gimmicks. Once operational, your marketing plan, including advertising, sales, consumer give-away games, etc., needs to be continually updated so you can keep up with and outdo your competitors.

All of these strategies cost money, of course, but the end result is to attract more buying customers than your competitors. You should allow for such business risks and costs in your overall business plan (see Chapters 6, 7, 16, and 18).

Changing Tastes, Technologies, and Economics

Consumers are fickle. Fads come and go. You should plan for changes in consumers' tastes. If you don't, you may be stuck with unsellable goods or have to scramble to devise more appealing products and services. You should also monitor the economic climate and be ready for the dry spells that can occur during recessions when consumers change their spending habits to buy less.

You as an entrepreneur must try to anticipate economic fluctuations and consumers' reactions. You might think you'd need a crystal ball to predict accurately. However, using good marketing research techniques can help you alleviate these problems (see Chapters 7 and 18 for more discussion of these issues).

Modern technology is characterized by rapid and often dramatic growth. It came upon us suddenly and without warning. We were unprepared for it and we must quickly learn to adapt. Both the number of innovations and their rates of development are increasing. "The time scales of technological progress do not match the time scales of our decision-making processes, with disastrous results for our ability to design rational policies."[4]

Here's an example in the extreme: anybody who operates a store or manufacturing plant that only sells or makes high-button shoes won't be staying in business very long. However, many enterprising entrepreneurs today are opening businesses to manufacture and retail products that were unheard of only a few years ago. Many new companies have formed since the early 1970s as a result of innovations in semiconductor and transistor technology. Video-game and microcomputer companies such as Atari, Apple, Radio Shack, and CPT sprang up. Established firms also expanded their lines, until by the early 1980s

FIGURE 2.2 A converted gasoline station. Changes in politics or technology can contribute to poor business. The wise entrepreneur finds some other use for facilities before going bankrupt. This owner converted his gasoline station to a car wash and parking lot.

such companies as IBM, Burroughs, and Texas Instruments were also known for producing low-cost microprocessors.

Technological innovations have made such enterprises possible but this also brings competition to traditional companies whose merchandise and services are becoming obsolete. Unless consumers need or like your product, they will not buy. Although the high-button shoes example makes this principle obvious, other more subtle technological and social changes also often affect business.

The oil embargo of the early 1970s, for instance, caused many independent gasoline stations to either quit or go bankrupt. In some instances, new enterprises under construction never got a chance to open their doors. Gasoline and oil products were simply not available, except to those established franchisees who had already secured their source of supply. Such changes represented by these examples occur because of a complicated combination of political, technological, and international economic conditions occurring in the macro-economy. (See Figure 2.2)

In short, whether a company is small, medium, or large, its owner(s) must be aware of new and emerging trends and be ready to adapt. Research and development expenses, in some cases, are another cost to build into the expanded business plan. An ability to recognize current trends and project new ones can help you attain success. (See Figure 2.3).

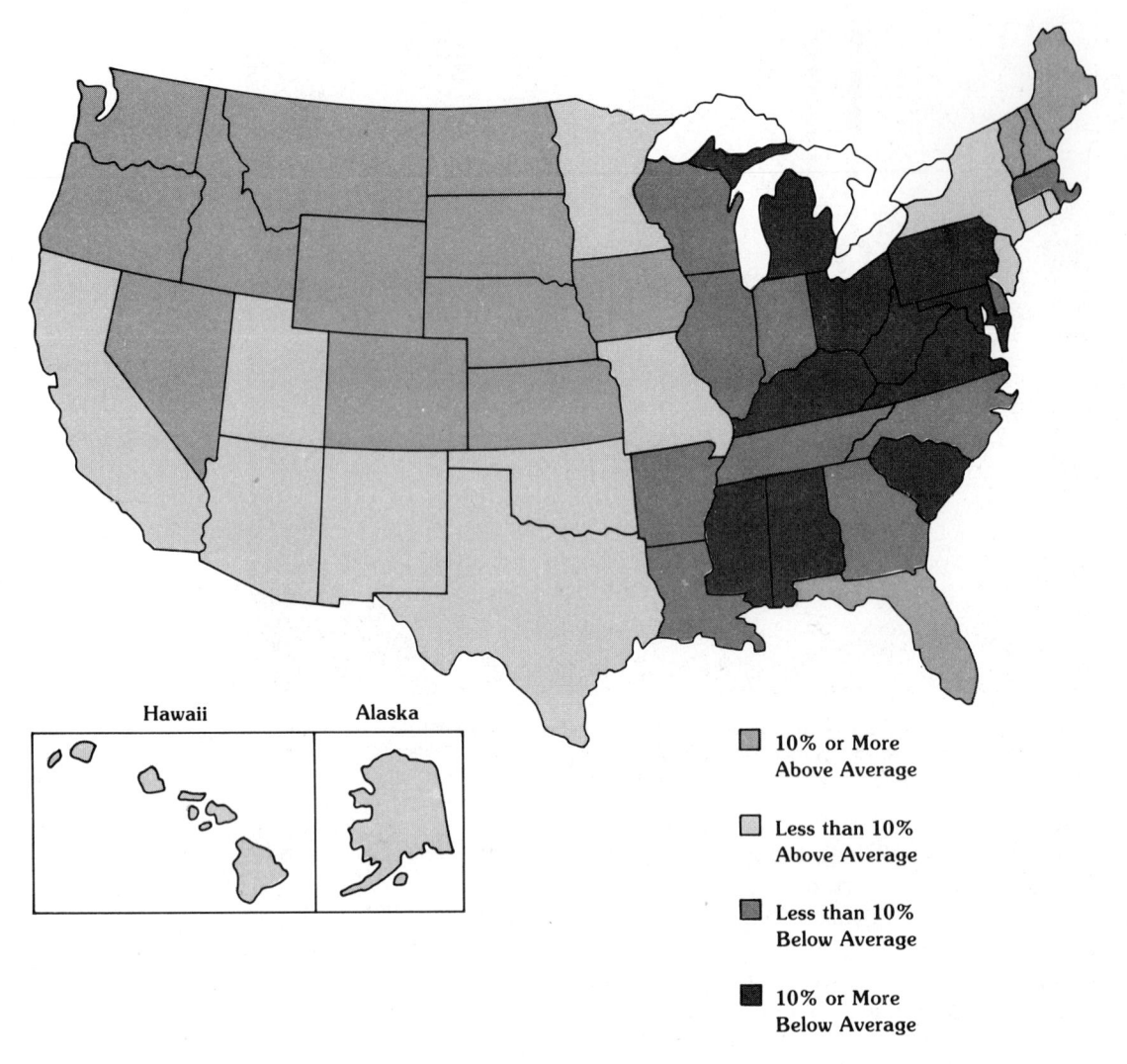

FIGURE 2.3 Small Business by State. The number of small businesses per capita varies from state to state. Some of the reasons for this variance include: differences in per capita income, farm population, and the number of big businesses.

Source: Developed from *County Business Patterns, 1977*, U.S. Department of Commerce, Bureau of the Census.

Courtesy of the National Federation of Independent Business (NFIB)

Changes in Government Regulations

It is extremely difficult to deal with the many different sets of federal, state, and local regulations. Each year many new regulations emerge, and the entrepreneur must keep abreast of these as well as current laws and requirements. The cost of filling out required forms alone can escalate operating expenses.

There is the risk of penalty for failing to comply. Various research studies conducted for the U.S. Small Business Administration have suggested several ways the SBA could help owners of small businesses: (1) by establishing one-stop small-business centers, (2) by consolidating and thus eliminating duplication of services from numerous agencies, and (3) by developing an ombudsman system.[5]

Other recommendations made by a 1981 commission that reported to the SBA include:

1. Exempt business from the minor but burdensome paperwork requirements of many federal agencies and regulatory commissions;
2. Establish two-tiered regulations: one set for large businesses and the other for small businesses;
3. Totally exempt small businesses from some regulations, especially those of the Occupational Safety and Health Administration (OSHA);
4. Establish an Office of Small Business Affairs in each regulatory commission to represent the interests of small business;
5. Require the SBA's Office of Advocacy to review all proposed regulations that affect small business; and
6. Require cost/benefit analyses for all proposed regulations.[6]

Until such time as these and other changes are made, however, entrepreneurs had better seek expert advice to be sure that their small business is in compliance with all relevant requirements. Tax laws also change every year, and it often takes a competent accountant to keep up with the requirements and allowable deductions (see Chapter 13).

Entrepreneurs face many risks, many because of external forces. To be successful, owners must be aware of how their businesses operate within the macroenvironment. Decisions emerging from the political, governmental, and technological actions of others come under this category.

Catastrophe

Unforeseen circumstances invariably crop up: anything from vandalism to fire, flood, hurricane, tornado, and earthquake. Entrepreneurs typically arrange for product liability insurance, Workers' Compensation, and employee bonding (see also Chapter 13).

Small businesses are also vulnerable to theft, both from outside and from within. Security measures to avoid robberies and shoplifting can be costly. White-collar crime and associated internal thefts cost the nation's businesses approximately $45 billion per year. How does the entrepreneur prevent employee pilferage? (See Chapter 20 for more on this topic.)

Perhaps the biggest risk in launching an enterprise is the fear of failing or of losing one's money and time. Fear, of course, is a state of mind rather than a risk per se. Nevertheless, people who are more security-conscious than others—

those who strongly prefer to have a regular weekly or monthly paycheck—may fear whether their business could generate enough income to support them, much less the enterprise itself. Such fears make it hard for such people to reach effective business decisions, particularly those that appear to involve a gamble.

CAUSES OF BUSINESS FAILURES

It may seem that focusing on the many risks and pitfalls facing would-be entrepreneurs is a negative approach to studying small business ownership. But such forewarning can help you as an entrepreneur anticipate potential problems. You can reduce risk by thorough planning. A review of why some people fail can help you prepare a more successful venture (see Figure 2.4).

FIGURE 2.4
Number of business failures in 10,000 firms, from 1978 through 1981

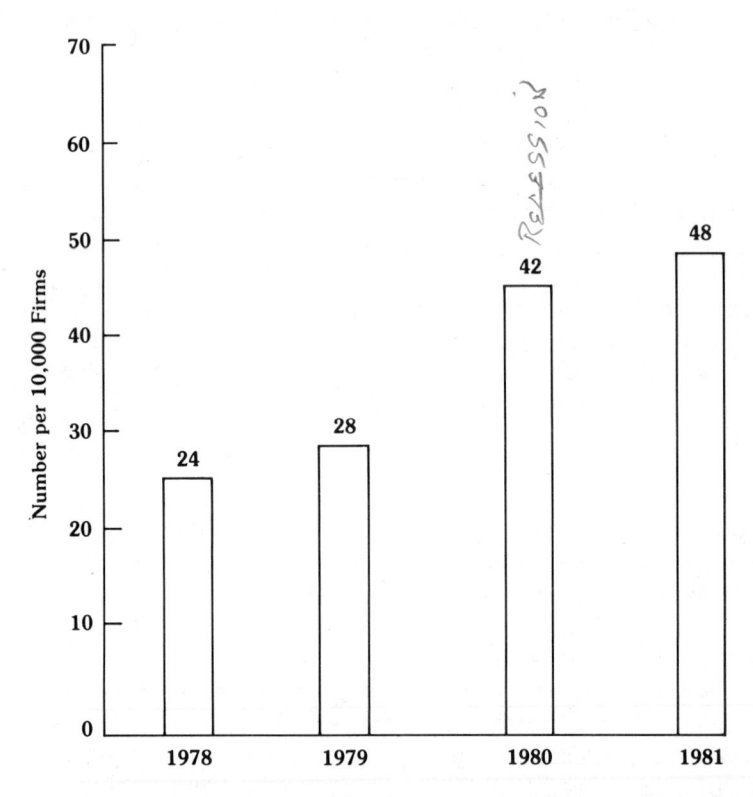

Year	Number per 10,000 Firms
1978	24
1979	28
1980	42
1981	48

Source: Devised from data in "The State of Small Business: A Report of the President, Transmitted to the Congress, March 1982," *The Annual Report on Small Business and Competition of the U.S. Small Business Administration,* U.S. Government Printing Office, Washington, 1982.

Poor Management

Data on small business failures seem to indicate that poor management is primarily the cause; i.e., deficient bookkeeping, inadequate inventory control, lack of market data, incompetent personnel management, etc. For example, in 1977–78, 55 percent of the small-business failures studied in Canada were attributed to poor management.[7]

Dun & Bradstreet reports that nearly 50 percent of new businesses fail within their first five years. If you can maintain operations that long, your statistical chances of success grow exponentially. For instance, only one out of five firms fails after 10 years in operation.[8]

Although this picture may be dismal, things would be even worse if we didn't have the right at least to try. In a free-enterprise system, a person is free to enter business, free to succeed, free to fail, and free also to try again. This, supposedly, is what an economic democracy is all about.

Poor or incompetent management comes in several forms, such as unbalanced experience and inexperience either in management or in the technical, product-related aspects of business. A review of these and of miscellaneous other causes of failure may help you identify your potential strengths and weaknesses.

Unbalanced Experience

Someone with unbalanced experience has a better background in one or two of the important aspects of business than in the others. The aspects of business include marketing; production (or productivity); human relations (with customers, employees, suppliers, and others); accounting and recordkeeping; and supervision of personnel, products, services, and physical details. (See Figure 2.5.) The entrepreneur must continually and systematically keep track of all these areas and be ready to take positive action to improve conditions in any one of them.

Entrepreneurs who have unbalanced experience, however, may focus most of their attention on the production end and neglect the other aspects of their business. Other entrepreneurs may concentrate on customer sales and public relations while ignoring in-house operations.

Management versus Technical Experience

Research has shown that financial management, marketing management, and meeting government regulations are cited frequently by entrepreneurs as problem areas. Studies also indicate that entrepreneurs most often need assistance in planning, financial information systems, and marketing analysis.[9]

The integrated strategic management framework in small businesses comprises a number of elements. They include: the owner-manager's objectives and

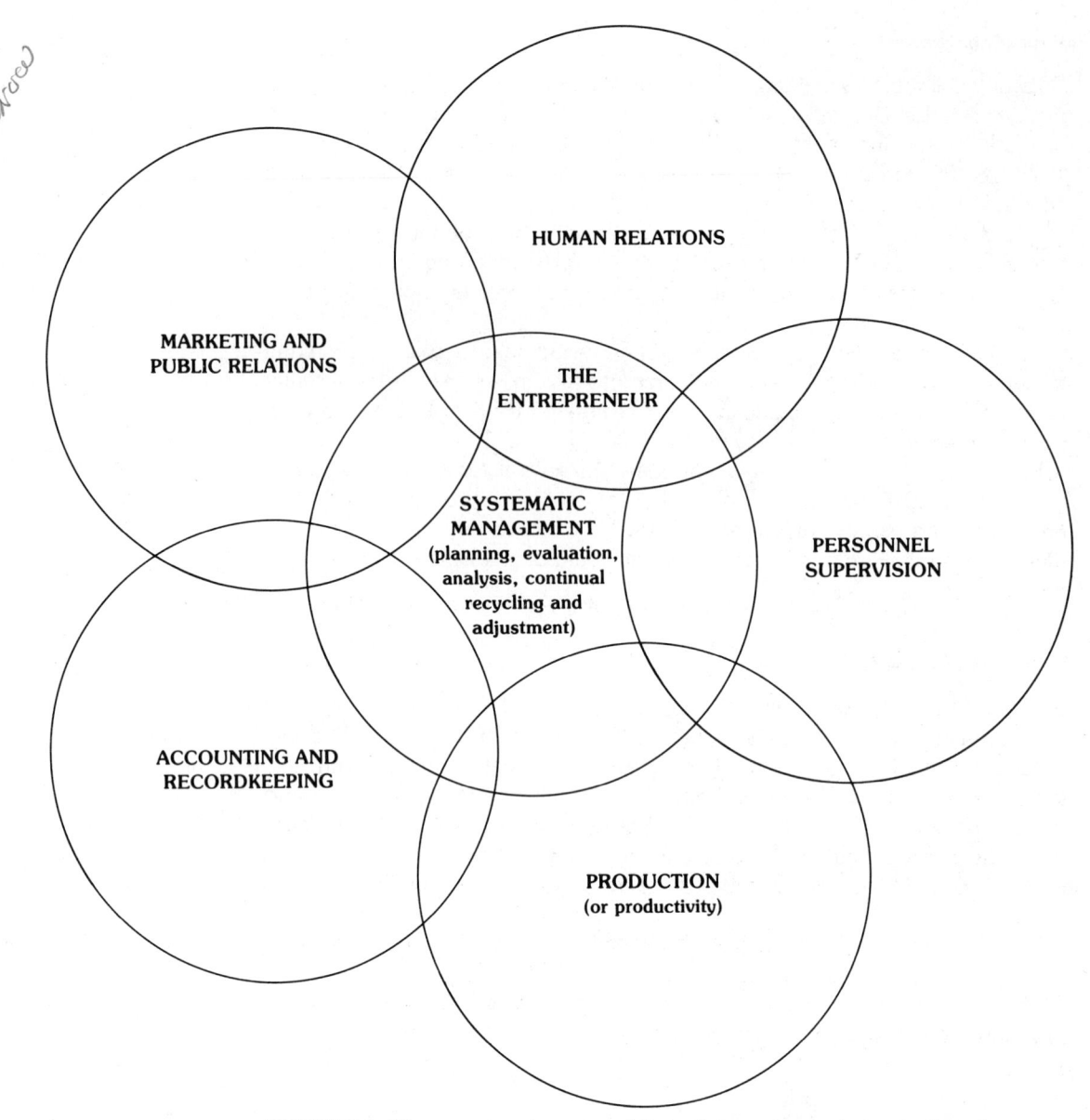

FIGURE 2.5 There are many interactive skills needed to manage a business effectively.

personal characteristics, the strengths and weaknesses of the enterprise, the business environment, and management and market strategies.[10] (See also Chapters 17 through 21.)

Strengths and weaknesses. Among the 16 items selected for analysis in a Canadian study of small businesses, the ability to manage its cash was the most important strength cited by the most profitable companies. The next most important variable was innovativeness, followed by strengths in location, in marketing, productivity of employees, quality control and overall image of the firm. On the other hand, the losing firms tended to emphasize quality but could not produce quality items at competitive costs. They also reported a lower percentage of sales in their immediate markets than the more profitable businesses and they modified their merchandise or introduced new products less frequently. Finally, the losing entrepreneurs reported having poor locations and rated themselves as lacking managerial competence.[11]

It appears that innovativeness, know-how, and creativity are important for success in small business. However, these qualities are not sufficient alone to generate success. Entrepreneurs also need to develop managerial competence as well, particularly in cash management.

Those with inexperience "in the line," on the other hand, may have a financial, marketing, legal, or accounting background but little technical experience with a particular product or service. However, technical competence in knowledge of the product or service is not enough; management skills are also required.

Miscellaneous Causes of Failure

Some owners run into trouble through excessive expenses, poor collections, inadequate sales, inventory troubles, a bad location, and competitive weakness.

Expenses sometimes run higher than anticipated. You may need to plan for inflation, both as you start your business and throughout its operation. But whatever the economic climate, expenses should be kept under control (see Chapter 14).

To get and keep customers you may have to let them buy on credit. But what if they don't pay up? A reasonable percentage must be allowed for bad debts if credit is given (see also Chapters 12 and 14).

If you misjudge the customers' needs, tastes, and purchasing patterns you may not be able to sell your product. Dry seasons, fluctuations in the economy, unanticipated actions from the competition, and inadequate pricing policies may also cut into your business. You and your employees should also develop effective sales techniques and the technical skills for demonstrating equipment (see Chapters 18 and 19).

Sometimes owners stock too many or too few products. Too much of your money can get tied up in the cost of goods, whether acquired for resale, purchased as raw materials, or used as operating supplies. And you may suffer from late or incomplete deliveries, caused by suppliers, distributors, or transportation firms (see also Chapter 16).

Misled by an inaccurate or too limited marketing survey, entrepreneurs sometimes set up shop in a location where consumer traffic or purchasing patterns are not adequate to support the enterprise. Even if the choice were appropriate at first, the community may change. The downtown shopping area may be abandoned in favor of neighborhood malls; a new freeway or interstate highway may bypass the store, restaurant, or motel. Meanwhile, the emergence of additional competitors, nearby or across town, can also affect the value of the selected site (see Chapter 8).

Insufficient operating funds may hinder your ability to compete effectively, whether through the products/services you offer or through initiating a successful marketing program. Could you live through a price war started by competitors who have greater financial resources? Perhaps they can afford to lose money for an extended period, but what about you?

These and many other one-time-only and subtle but nonetheless significant problems can emerge to challenge the ingenuity of the entrepreneur. Is it worth it? Some people find surmounting this continuing row of barriers not only stimulating and exciting but actually half the fun of going into business for themselves. Are you one of these people?

FAMILY CHALLENGES

A business does well if it clears expenses for the first period of its operation, usually several months if not a year or more. It takes time to build a reputation and a clientele. Questions you, as the entrepreneur, will want to ask yourself include:

- "Do I have enough money to take care of my family responsibilities for at least six months while the business is getting on its feet?"
- "Is my family as enthusiastic over my plans as I am?"
- "What additional burdens will my decision to go into business place upon the members of my family—spouse, children, and parents, even perhaps my brothers and sisters? Can they deal with having less money to spend for a while, doing extra household duties, or having to help me run the business?"
- "What will be the hours of the business? What demands will it make upon time—my own, plus that of other family members? Who will be at home to run the household and to take care of the children?"

Marriages have sometimes been dissolved because the husbands were "married to their businesses." The same can happen to marriages in which the wife or both spouses head businesses. Is your business worth this risk? If not, arrange ahead of time to reconcile the demands both of your business and of your spouse and/or family. Otherwise, not only will you and your family be cheated of the pleasures of a good family life but the anxieties and difficulties created may prevent you from doing your best in the business. Many businesses are successful because both marriage partners, even children, contribute to the operations. We've all heard the term, "ma and pa business." You may have been raised in such a situation and consider this mutual sharing natural. But your spouse may feel that home and family should be kept separate from business.

You should give all the affected members of your family (nuclear or extended) a chance to air their opinions on this important question. The only way to make certain that your family will back you and will assist you in facing the new problems that can arise for family and business alike is to obtain consensus.

Continuity and Survival of Businesses

In 1983 the Small Business Administration supported research projects designed to examine the involvement of female family members in the operation and/or management of family-owned businesses. Would women, for example, retain ownership of a business after the death of their husbands, or did they tend to lose the businesses to outsiders? Did they have to pay inheritance taxes on what was all along as much theirs as their husbands'?

The National Family Business Council estimates that there are over 2 million family-owned businesses in America. The majority of these are small businesses. The report said:

> It is popularly assumed that women are discouraged directly and subtly from participation in their families' businesses and that women who participate do so often without compensation or officers' status. Anecdotal accounts suggest that it is not uncommon for a family business to be sold out of the family or to come under the leadership of a distant blood relative or relation by marriage when potential company leadership among wives or daughters has not been considered.[12]

The objectives of these SBA research projects were to:

1. Identify factors that encourage or discourage female participation in the operation, management, and continuity of family businesses.
2. Determine reasons for women's inclusion in or exclusion from the management and/or operation of the businesses. Factors examined included but were not limited to: the personal aspirations, perceptions, and perspectives of both the women and men of the family; and the formal and informal business and technical training of family members.
3. Recommend ways to encourage female members to participate effectively in managing and operating the businesses.[13]

This research on small business has revealed that not every family entrepreneurship has made due provisions for the survival of the business and for the needs of family members when the primary owner/manager dies or becomes incapacitated. Providing insurance coverage for the survivor(s) is one method of protecting their personal income. But where they have the interest and expertise, the surviving family member(s) may also want to continue operating the company.

Opportunities for daughters of men engaged in small-business enterprises may be expanding. Don Jonovic, vice-president of the Center for Family Business in Cleveland, reports a recent 30-percent increase in the number of daughters attending the Center's Succession Seminars. Jonovic also estimates that at least half a million women could become owners/managers of some of this country's 2 million family-owned companies, if they are prepared to assume control.[14]

SUMMARY

Most failures are caused by the impatience of budding entrepreneurs who rush into business without adequate preparation. If you do not have the experience, if you cannot muster the capital, and if you lack the qualifications—technical, managerial, personal, or familial—you should wait until you have acquired these essentials. For once you have failed it is doubly difficult to begin anew, and banks and creditors are more reluctant than before to loan you money. Moreover, your self-esteem may have sunk to an all-time low, sapping your ability to jump the new hurdles.

Nevertheless, there are numerous satisfactions involved in owning one's own business, not the least of which is to have control over the profit and the managerial decisions. For many people such satisfactions are sufficient compensation for the risks and challenges.

The two major causes of business failure seem to be incompetence and a lack of capital. Not only do you need adequate funds with which to launch your venture but you also need maturity and experience in dealing with people and the readiness to tackle each of the interdependent components of entrepreneurship.

Once you use up your capital, it is gone. Your first blush of enthusiasm will have evaporated—unless of course, like Colonel Sanders, you are one of those people who only grow more determined with each "failure" that they will show the world they can do it! Prepare yourself carefully, now. Learn from the experiences of the successful—and not so successful—entrepreneurs discussed above. When you think you have sufficient assets to go into business for yourself, your chances will be better.

DISCUSSION QUESTIONS

1. From among the satisfactions discussed, which one(s) most appeal to you? Why? Discuss your feelings about these satisfactions with your peers, classmates, or family. Add to the list any others that come to mind or that other entrepreneurs have told you about.
2. What is the point of discussing the failures and accomplishments of others? In brief, do you believe it is more enlightening to concentrate on positive aspects only and to avoid the negative? If so, why? If not, why not?

3. From the list of problems that can threaten a firm's success, discuss specific examples within your experience and analyze what factors may have contributed to these failures. Also discuss alternative actions the business owners might have taken to circumvent internal or external problems.
4. Discuss the stories of entrepreneurs you know who have or have not successfully managed all the various aspects of their businesses (see Figure 2.5 in this chapter). How important is it to focus attention on each? How significant is the omission of any one or more segments?
5. Debate whether it's preferable to enter the small-business arena with training and/or experience in a product or service line or in management, accounting, or finance. If appropriate, organize a small panel to debate both sides of the issue before the group, or divide the group into halves and have each champion one approach. Designate a recorder to report pros and cons for each side and tally the results. Use your personal experience and knowledge of successful and mediocre operations as a basis for the discussion. Analyze the points made by each side and summarize.
6. Identify from which direction—technical or managerial—you personally are coming. Discuss compensatory factors and what you can do to increase your knowledge of the areas you have less experience with.

MINICASE

Bryon and Elizabeth entered a marital and a business partnership simultaneously. First they sold Watkins products door to door, one canvassing the left side of the street while the other sold along the right. By the time their only child was five, Dorothy was "filing" the sales slips numerically in the backseat of the car.

Later they opened a service station, then an auto agency, and finally a motel and restaurant. Elizabeth and Dorothy pumped gas, changed tires, handled all the office and accounting work, and purchased, inventoried, and sold auto parts. Also to Elizabeth fell the maintenance work, from electrical to plumbing repairs and the supervision of remodeling.

Grown by then, Dorothy took responsibility for credit and collections (repossessing cars from bad-debt customers despite violent threats to her person and to her family in some cases). Mother and daughter also served as maids, cooks, and waitresses in their motel and restaurant, later assuming supervision when each of the companies had expanded enough to warrant hiring a full rank of employees.

Meanwhile, Bryon assumed the presidency of each company, making all of the policy decisions and serving as salesman and liaison with financial institutions. Upon his death, Elizabeth and Dorothy discovered to their horror that although their names appeared on the firms' letterheads, neither was officially recorded as a company officer. Dorothy left home. Elizabeth had to sell the businesses to raise enough capital to pay inheritance taxes and to meet the many other financial obligations Bryon had assumed without consulting her.

In this situation, what might Bryon or Elizabeth have done differently to enable Elizabeth to keep the businesses intact after Bryon's death? Discuss other issues you find at stake here, remembering that the family's history extends over a period of approximately 40 years, beginning with the couple's marriage during the early years of the Great Depression.

ACTIVITIES AND EXERCISES

1. Interview successful entrepreneurs to determine what risk factors (from among those listed) they have found most prevalent. Add to the list any others they describe.
2. If you know any business owners who have closed their doors, interview them if possible to find out the reasons. Note whether they had failed to derive the satisfactions they had anticipated or whether they decided to close because they couldn't manage the risk factors, financial problems, or other causes. Be ready to share your findings.
3. Interview the owners of one or more family-owned businesses about the allocation of duties, the division of authority (among spouses, children, extended relatives, etc.), and the arrangements—if any—for the business's survival and continuity in case of one individual's death or incapacity.

NOTES

1. Bena Kaye and Frances Ruffin, "How to Make a Million before You're 34," *Redbook,* May 1977, pp. 60–64.
2. Mustafa R. Yilmaz, "Risk-Return Analysis with Particular Attention to Large Losses and Satisfactory Gains," *Decision Sciences,* July 1983, pp. 299–311.
3. D. Hakneman and A. Tversky, "Prospect Theory: An Analysis of Decision under Risk," *Econometrica,* Vol. 47, 1979, pp. 263–91.
4. Louis A. Girifalco, "The Dynamics of Technological Change," *The Wharton Magazine,* Fall 1982, pp. 31–37.
5. Small Business Administration, "Compilation of All Recommendations," *The Environment for Entrepreneurship and Small Business* (Washington, D.C.: U.S. Government Printing Office, 1981), p. 5.

    Webster's defines *ombudsman* as "a public official appointed to investigate citizens' complaints against local or national government agencies that may be infringing on the rights of individuals."
6. SBA, "Compilation," p. 5.
7. Rajeswararao Chaganti and Radharao Chaganti, "A Profile of Profitable and Not-So-Profitable Small Businesses," *Journal of Small Business Management,* July 1983, pp. 43–51.

8. Dun & Bradstreet, *Failure Rates of New Business Ventures* (New York: Dun and Bradstreet, 1977), p. 10.
9. Thomas C. Dandridge and Murpha A. Sewall, "A Priority Analysis of the Problems of Small Business Managers," *American Journal of Small Business,* October 1978, pp. 28–36.
10. LaRue T. Hosmer. *Strategic Management* (Englewood Cliffs, NJ: Prentice-Hall, 1982).
11. Chaganti and Chaganti, "Profile."
12. Small Business Administration, "Women's Involvement in Small Family-Owned Businesses," RFP no. 82–83 (Washington, D.C.: July 22, 1982).
13. Ibid.
14. Andrea Fooner, "Dad & Daughter, Inc.," *Working Woman,* January 1983, pp. 79–82.

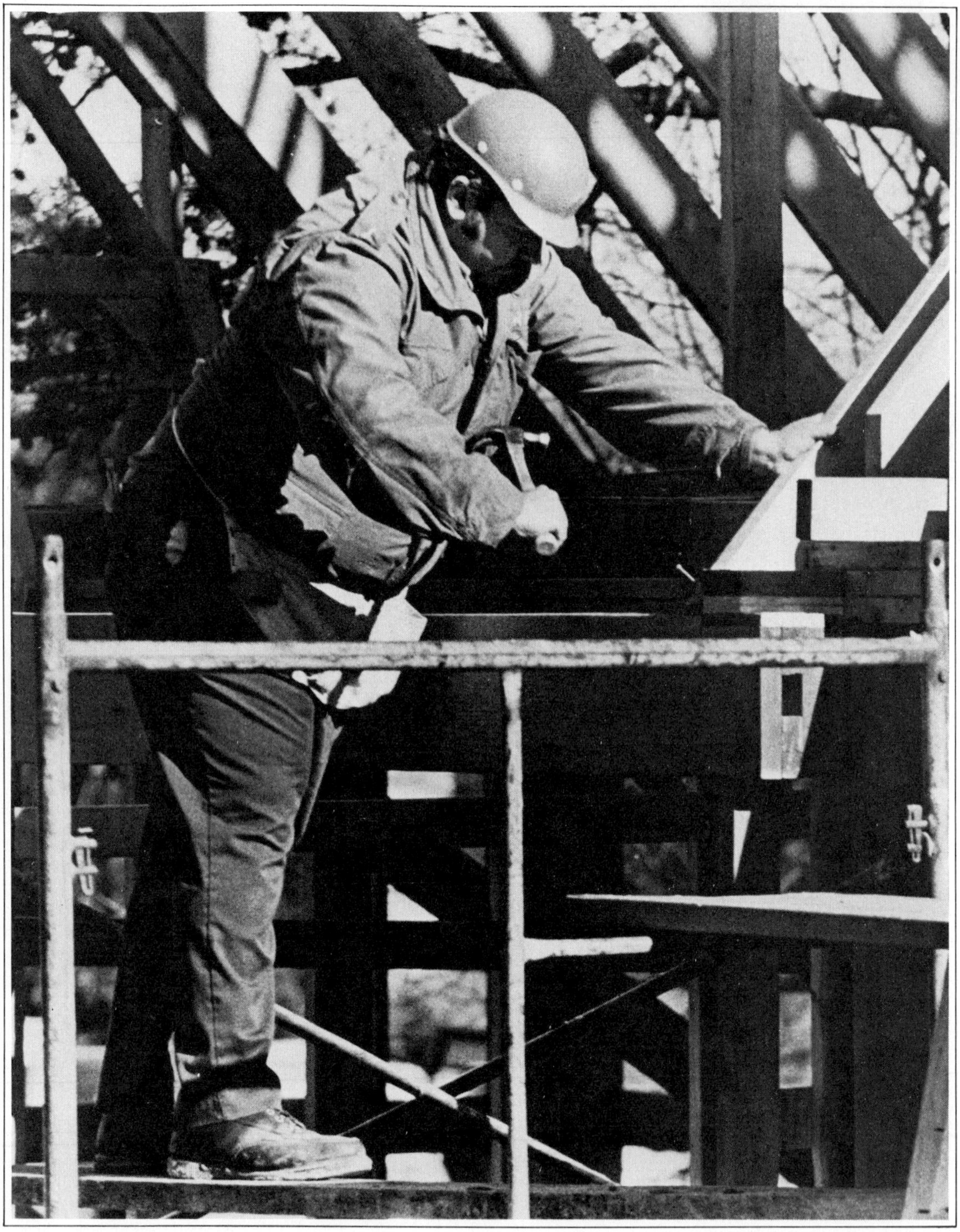

chapter 3

Business Classifications

Objectives

1. List examples of small businesses from each classification.

2. Describe owner qualifications typifying these businesses and give some exceptions to the rule; e.g., how entrepreneurs can compensate for lack of training and experience.

3. Compare home-based and self-employed enterprises of different types on the basis of profit potential and entrepreneurial satisfaction.

4. Decide why people are attracted by classified ads to spend time and money on fruitless or even fraudulent ventures.

BUSINESS CATEGORIES

Dividing enterprises into several categories can help you decide what sort of business you would like to open. Most businesses can be placed in one or more of these broad categories: retail trade; extraction, including agriculture and mining; manufacturing and processing; wholesale trade and distribution; construction; transportation and communications; and service establishments, including professional and financial services. Some states and regions also support a tourism and recreation industry. (See Figure 3.1.)

Sources of information about small enterprises are these: IRS's Statistics of Income series (reporting on 14.7 million businesses), the Census Bureau's Enterprise Statistics (5.6 million businesses), the Small Business Administration's

FIGURE 3.1
Small Business by Industry, 1977. According to NFIB and other fact-gathering agencies, retail trade and service industries account for most of the activity in small business.

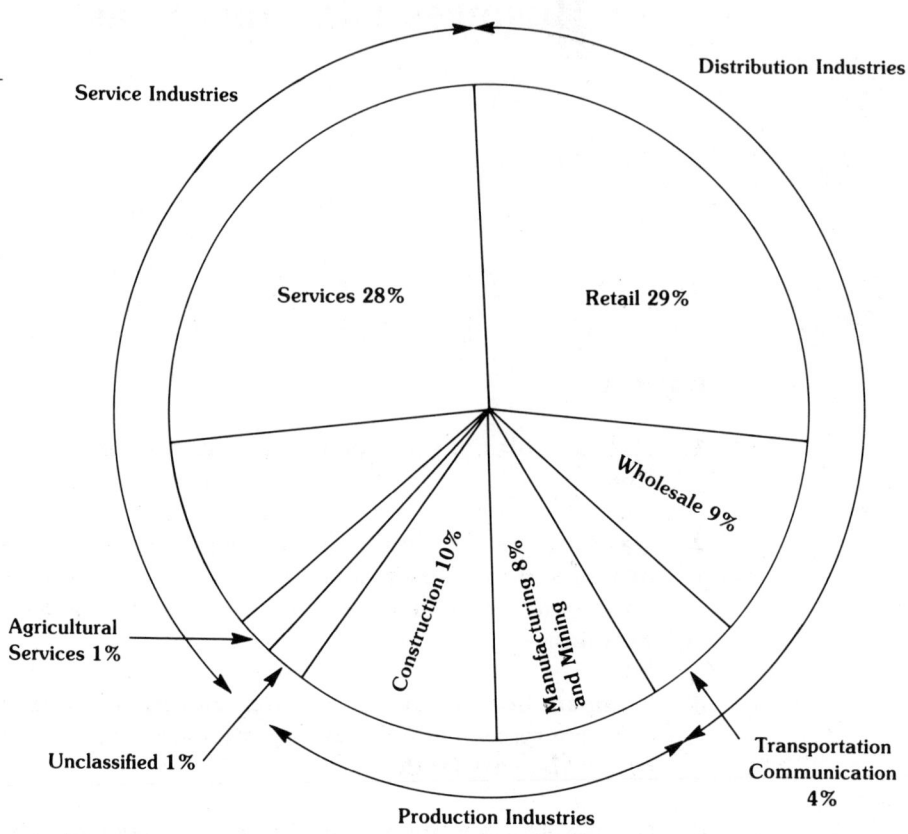

Service Industries — Distribution Industries

Services 28%
Retail 29%
Wholesale 9%
Construction 10%
Manufacturing and Mining 8%
Transportation Communication 4%
Agricultural Services 1%
Unclassified 1%

Production Industries

Source: Developed from *County Business Patterns,* 1977, U.S. Department of Commerce, Bureau of the Census.

Courtesy of the National Federation of Independent Business (NFIB)

Small Business Data Base (3.7 million businesses), Dun & Bradstreet, Standard and Poors, Robert Morris, and U.S. and state statistical abstracts. The latter are important sources at local and regional levels.

The Standard Industrial Code (SIC) classifies enterprises into major classifications, with numerous subcategories for each. Table 3.1 shows the number of employees by classification and Table 3.2 shows company profits after tax as a percentage of net sales.

Retail Trade

At least two criteria define the retail establishment: it sells goods direct to consumers and it deals with products. Although the businesses whose beginnings

TABLE 3.1 Establishments and Enterprises by Industry Classification and Number of Employees

INDUSTRY DIVISION	TOTAL	0–4	5–9	10–19	20–49	50–99
Retail Trade						
Establishments	1,426,979	697,985	290,360	153,207	106,495	41,738
Enterprises	1,164,650	685,487	261,351	120,680	70,165	17,849
Services						
Establishments	955,493	486,640	168,128	93,393	65,812	32,518
Enterprises	805,033	479,411	155,310	78,511	48,537	19,601
Construction						
Establishments	577,360	369,295	94,386	51,000	30,716	10,322
Enterprises	540,749	365,764	90,055	47,115	26,353	7,048
Wholesale Trade						
Establishments	470,873	194,527	101,859	64,748	48,554	20,134
Enterprises	373,834	189,891	92,070	51,499	28,815	28,815
Manufacturing						
Establishments	538,198	121,603	76,612	61,370	60,085	31,313
Enterprises	337,223	119,266	72,033	55,032	48,947	20,535
Finance, Insurance, Real estate						
Establishments	392,377	160,306	52,859	34,682	30,695	18,451
Enterprises	262,332	156,490	47,337	28,448	17,941	6,216
Transportation, Communications, Utilities						
Establishments	189,283	64,420	31,550	22,351	17,401	8,199
Enterprises	129,081	63,126	28,721	18,550	11,732	3,690
Agriculture, Forestry, Fisheries						
Establishments	107,961	66,452	21,066	9,651	5,240	1,721
Enterprises	98,578	65,210	19,505	8,230	3,943	998
Mining						
Establishments	40,044	12,391	5,857	5,033	4,263	2,032
Enterprises	25,396	12,011	5,103	3,929	2,688	872

Source: Small Business Data Base tabulated by Brookings Institution from Dun and Bradstreet's Market Identifier File.

TABLE 3.2 Company Profits after Tax as a Percentage of Net Sales, by Major Industry Groups and Number of Employees, 1978

	NUMBER OF EMPLOYEES	
MAJOR GROUPS	20–99	100–499
Farms: Crops	8.03	2.72
Farms: Livestock	4.75	2.54
Agricultural Services	8.20	12.72
Metal Mining	−.07	—
Anthracite Mining	0.45	2.06
Bituminous Coal	7.78	8.37
Oil, Gas Extraction	11.94	12.31
Nonmetallic Mining	7.38	8.37
General Contractors	3.02	2.57
Heavy Construction	4.23	3.12
Special Trade Construction	3.41	2.53
Food Products	2.70	3.33
Textile Mill Products	2.73	1.30
Apparel and Other Textile Products	2.90	2.68
Lumber, Wood Products	4.73	6.10
Furniture, Fixtures	3.51	3.55
Paper Products	3.64	2.20
Printing, Publishing	37.18	7.23
Chemicals	5.81	9.01
Petroleum Products	4.78	5.01
Rubber Products	4.06	3.68
Leather Products	3.55	2.79
Stone, Clay, Glass Products	4.83	6.12
Primary Metal Products	2.91	3.95
Fabricated Metal Products	3.89	4.23
Machinery except Electrical	4.36	4.75
Electric, Electronic Equipment	4.70	6.19
Transportation Equipment	3.87	5.13
Instruments	5.83	5.39
Miscellaneous Manufacturing	5.62	4.54
Railroad Transportation	11.08	12.30
Local Transportation	3.75	−3.04
Trucking and Warehousing	3.28	2.99
Water Transportation	7.74	2.93
Air Transportation	2.47	6.44
Pipeline Transportation	14.45	21.36
Transportation Services	3.45	8.61
Communication	13.69	14.83
Utilities	6.76	5.88
Wholesale Durable	2.85	2.01
Wholesale Nondurable	1.93	2.00

(continued on next page)

	NUMBER OF EMPLOYEES	
MAJOR GROUPS	20–99	100–499
Building Materials	3.14	2.21
General Merchandise Stores	1.38	2.14
Food Stores	1.65	2.19
Automotive Dealers, Service Stations	1.40	1.26
Apparel Stores	3.08	2.63
Furniture Stores	2.97	2.52
Eating & Drinking Places	5.25	5.27
Miscellaneous Retail	3.10	2.57
Banking	15.30	10.17
Credit Agencies	12.67	10.60
Commodity Brokers	2.19	8.65
Insurance Carriers	7.94	7.12
Insurance Agents	8.21	11.65
Real Estate	14.58	8.13
Holding Investment Offices	9.26	11.17
Hotels, Motels	9.01	4.90
Personal Services	5.27	4.57
Business Services	5.66	3.76
Auto Repair Services	4.27	13.72
Miscellaneous Repairs	8.46	4.50
Motion Pictures	4.29	2.92
Recreation, excluding Motion Pictures	5.09	8.09
Health Services	4.01	−3.90
Educational Services	6.06	5.51
Social Services	5.83	7.75
Museums	19.09	25.55
Nonprofit Organizations	7.80	9.07
Miscellaneous Services	6.17	5.94

Note: A dash indicates that the sample was insufficient for statistical accuracy. Generally, 25 observations were required to provide a minimal degree of acceptability. Data are preliminary and subject to revision.

Source: Small Business Data Base tabulated by Brookings Institution from the Dun and Bradstreet Financial Statistics for 1978.

were traced in Chapter 1 have for the most part grown into sprawling organizations, note that they all deal with products: Ford Motor Company sells vehicles and parts; Pizza Hut, food and beverages; Naomi Sims' Creations, wigs and hairpieces; Apple, microcomputers and related products; McDonnel-Douglas, airplanes and spacecraft; Debbie Fields' stores, chocolate-chip cookies; Colonel Sanders' Kentucky Fried Chicken, chicken; and Anne and Frank Kitchens, pastry products.

Three of these companies—Pizza Hut, Kentucky Fried Chicken, and the chocolate-chip-cookie stores—are large-scale retail establishments that expand through franchises or chains. The other companies manufacture goods to sell to distributors and/or directly to consumers.

Retailing offers many opportunities to the would-be entrepreneur. You can start small, even without employees. Nor do you usually need special training, although related work experience can help you be aware of customer habits and buying needs and equip you with overall managerial expertise. In most cases you will need to find an appropriate location and to purchase both stock and equipment (such as counters and showcases).

Many of the people who sell products through home parties or door to door are often independent entrepreneurial agents for the companies involved.

Some of these enterprises operate as multilevel marketing companies. That is, as a distributor recruits new distributors and their monthly sales reach a specified volume, he or she becomes a supervisor and earns commissions not only from his or her own retail sales but also from the sales made by the distributors.

Companies that offer such opportunities include Amway, Shaklee, and Mary Kaye Cosmetics. Only people with the title of supervisor (and above) are classified as entrepreneurs. They are responsible not only for their own company operations but also for training, aiding, and supplying the distributors responsible to them.

One problem with getting into this type of operation is that neophyte distributors often believe they can accumulate vast riches with little time, effort, or monetary investment. Not so. As with any enterprise, a great deal of all three kinds of investment are required for success. Yet many energetic, devoted, and enterprising people have become successful at just such businesses as these. Interviews with a representative sample of the latter, however, also suggest that expenses for inventory, training, promotions, and continuing operations are consistent with those of any other similar enterprise. In short, nothing is either free or easy but, given hard work, long hours, and a realistic idea of what you're getting into, there are profits to be made through direct marketing.

Mary Bayer, Mary Kaye supervisor, by 1983 had the first and only pink Cadillac in the state of Wyoming (pink Cadillacs are manufactured only for Mary Kaye supervisors who have earned such a mark of distinction). She has distributors in Wyoming and four other states. Having originally started her business part-time while she continued to teach, she has now gone full-time into an operation that demands a great deal of time and energy but offers many exciting and rewarding benefits.

Extraction: Agriculture, Mining, etc.

Extractive operations, such as agriculture, commercial fishing, mining, and forestry, grow, collect, or quarry raw materials from nature.

Suppose you have maple trees growing on your property. To make and sell maple-sugar products either direct to consumers at a roadside stand or to distributors, you must first collect and process the raw material.

Agriculture classification

Other examples of entrepreneurs and enterprises in this classification are: farmers, horticulturists, forestry and logging entrepreneurs; sand and gravel operators; miners of coal, copper, silver, gold, diamonds, uranium, etc.; and petroleum extractors. A related group, although one can't exactly call them "extractors," are ranchers, dairy farmers, and fishers.

Many farms and ranches, whether small, medium, or large in acreage, production, and profits, are family enterprises. So too are various other extraction enterprises. According to John English, director of the Mine Safety and Health Administration's nationwide training program, approximately 200 of the 1700 coal mines in Kentucky alone are "ma-and-pa" operations. In the eight-state Rocky Mountain region, nearly two-thirds of the 6000 nonmetal mining companies are small sand-and-gravel firms.[1]

Many small operators also provide support services for the large extraction industries. Independent well servicers, for example, may take calls from small offices or their homes. What they need to go into business is a truck or van and some equipment. People who have worked in oil fields and in other mining operations often start their own small businesses to fill needs whose existence they discover while on the job.

Forestry and logging enterprises also account for many of the small-business operations in this category. One person alone, or with only a few employees,

One person alone or with a few employees—and a truck, logging equipment and skills—can establish a logging enterprise.

Many sand-and-gravel operations operate as small businesses and are included in the extraction classification.

and equipped with a truck and minimal but appropriate equipment can establish an independent logging venture. Small sawmills also appear throughout forestry locales to accommodate these loggers.

Manufacturing and Processing

Manufacturers process raw materials into finished products. Manufacturing companies are often big businesses, because it frequently takes a great deal of money to procure the needed facilities, equipment, and raw materials and to employ the number of workers necessary to perform the required tasks. We all know the names of major corporations that mass-produce motor vehicles, airplanes, appliances, and electronic and computerized equipment. In fact, however, these companies actually use and assemble many small parts that may be manufactured by much smaller firms. There are approximately 600 of these smaller producers to each larger one, and another 3000 or so retailers also support the needs of each of these major corporations.

There are thus many opportunities for small manufacturing firms. In fact, more than 90 percent of manufacturers employ fewer than 100 people, and 66 percent employ fewer than 20. These enterprises include printing shops, machine shops, meat-packing plants, cabinet shops, and food and beverage producers. Craftspeople who make such things as furniture and jewelry also count in this group, whether they make their goods by hand or by machine.

Suppose you have discovered a way of producing some attractive gadget in your basement. You have developed the expertise and believe the product has a market. Your investment includes your expenditures for the raw materials, the time it takes you to create your masterpiece, and the time and money it takes to advertise and distribute your product.

Corinne McGrady discovered how easily she could bend plastic into a thousand shapes after placing it for a minute over a simple hot wire. With equipment no more elaborate than that, she designed and manufactured magazine racks, tables, picture frames, and finally a see-through cookbook stand. The stand was her prize creation. She felt certain it would be a success because other people frequently attempted to copy the design. After "shouting at them, even picketing these 'thieves'," she ultimately sued one of them in court to protect her invention and won. Fortunately, she had had the foresight to seek legal advice during her start-up period and had copyrighted the design.

With both husband and children working, the family spent several years of weekends and evenings in their basement, painstakingly bending sheets of clear plastic over homemade heating machines. During this period they turned out as many as eight cookbook stands per minute. When the net annual income approached $10,000, the company expanded to new headquarters, invested in more sophisticated manufacturing equipment, and hired a full staff of workers to handle product assembly as well as advertising, purchasing, shipping, and recordkeeping.[2]

Wholesale Trade and Distribution

Wholesalers or distributors neither produce or retail products. Rather, they are middlemen: they process, package, label, store, and/or transport food and other products. Wholesalers buy large quantities of products from extractive or production companies and sell them in smaller lots to other businesses. A wholesaler might, for example, purchase 2000 stoves and sell a dozen or so to each individual retailer, who in turn sells stoves one at a time to consumers. Some distributors pick a special market (hospitals, schools, hotels and motels, or restaurants), while others do not.

Construction

This classification includes contractors and subcontractors who specialize in such areas as carpentry, masonry, plumbing, electricity, floor-covering installation, painting and paperhanging, civil engineering, roofing and siding, and sheet-metal and dry-wall work.

Land developers, who buy land to develop as housing tracts, shopping malls, industrial parks, and so on, are also included in this broad classification. Thus architects and civil engineers (with or without employees) can work as entrepreneurs in subcontracting their skills to larger developers and construction companies.

Construction classification

Construction classification

Well-trained people in these fields have usually completed an apprenticeship, training program, or college degree, which can take five years or more. Most people also gain considerable work experience before launching their own businesses. Some, however, start small, establishing a part-time operation before committing all of their time and resources to an independent enterprise.

For instance, some contractors build a house, then move into it (to save their family from having to pay for other housing) while constructing a second house. Then they put the first house up for sale and the family moves into the second. Once such entrepreneurs develop a backlog of capital, they can hire employees and build more than one house (or other building) simultaneously.

One could also operate a remodeling service along these lines. As word gets around, the entrepreneur can expand operations and go full-time into the venture, using subcontractors for areas in which he or she has less expertise.

Many full-scale medium or large construction companies started small, either as described above or by forming a partnership or corporation to obtain start-up or expansion capital. Because many building contracts are large and time-consuming as well as expensive for the potential client, the construction industry is highly dependent on economic and related factors, including current and projected interest rates.

Small-company entrepreneurs sometimes compensate for recessionary cycles by developing and advertising their related skills. Thus a carpenter may expand on his basic expertise by offering to remodel, to build cabinets, to paint, to put up wallpaper, and so on. Other small-business owners in the construction trades must find other jobs—even work for others—during these slack periods. Large construction companies, on the contrary, are able as usual to bid on municipal projects or on those funded by large corporations, which are less sensitive to economic downturns.

Transportation and Communications

Transportation.   Enterprises in this category include boat charter or rental services; trucking; bus, taxi, and limousine services; aviation; and vehicle repairs.

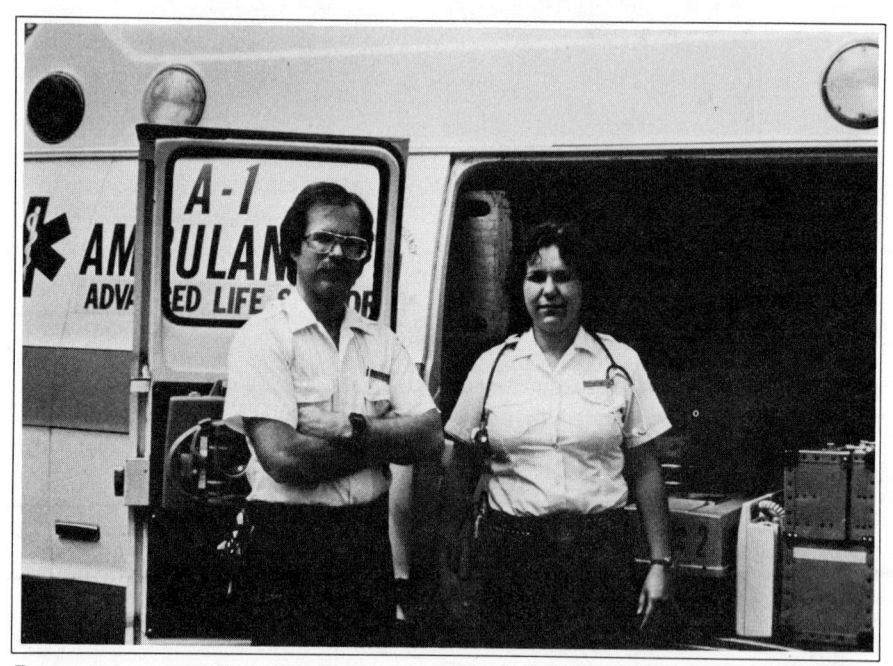

Transportation and medical or professional services are cross-referenced when people operate an ambulance service.

(People who sell autos, trucks, recreation vehicles, cycles, and so on may also count as retailers or wholesalers.)

Many trucking firms are actually small owner-driver operations, in which one semitruck van comprises the entire fleet. The costs can be prohibitive for the budding entrepreneur, however; one needs to finance $100,000 or more for the purchase price of one tractor-truck with van, complete with spare tires, repair tools, and minimal replacement parts and loading equipment.

Aviation also requires a high initial investment for the airplane(s) or helicopter(s). Those who love flying, if they can afford the start-up costs, can, however, turn their hobby to a profit by giving flying lessons, providing a charter service, spraying crops with insecticides, or establishing a rescue and emergency/health transportation service.

Such endeavors as driving a taxicab or a limousine, repairing vehicles, or running a travel agency represent the least expensive ways for an entrepreneur to break into the transportation field. Entering into a partnership or forming a corporate legal structure can help you obtain the capital you need to launch a larger enterprise.

Communications. This category includes such entrepreneurial areas as broadcast or print media, photography, printing, and commercial or industrial communications. Subcontractors or freelance operators may provide services related to package design, commercial or industrial design, paste-up layouts,

Small radio stations are included in the communications classification.

silk-screen printing, phototypesetting, photographs (including aerial photography), book or journal binding, and drafting.

You need special training for most of these skills. Working for someone else in a related company is an excellent way to get a background.

The idea of owning a TV or radio station, a newspaper, or a magazine may seem farfetched because of the amount of capital required for facilities and equipment, not to mention the expertise you'd need.

But the area of print media also includes newsletters, which can be produced at comparatively low cost (perhaps out of one's home, with mail-order subscriptions and distribution). And as for broadcast media, it is a fact that all the television shows, commercials, and movies that you can see on TV or at movie houses represent no more than 20 percent of the total production of the film and videotape industry. The other 80 percent of all audiovisual materials originate in the non-Hollywood world of special-purpose media. All manner of businesses and industries, as well as educational institutions and government agencies, require such special products.[3]

Perhaps the most prevalent private use of audiovisual materials is for instruction. It's estimated that $30 billion is spent annually in the United States to train or retrain approximately 3.7 million employees.[4] Many of these materials simply illustrate how to do some task. If you have expertise in a particular area, plus writing abilities, you might find this field appealing.

Services

This broad category includes everything from personal services to professional, financial, business, hospitality, and recreation services.

Professional services. This area includes doctors, dentists, and other medical specialists who operate as small businesses as well as lawyers, accountants, and consultants of every variety. To be professional one needs many years of formal education and must either meet the requirements imposed for licensing or accrediting or pass the tests administered by a professional board. Both individuals and companies use professional services. This category also includes architects, chiropractors, nurses, pharmacists, psychologists, and teachers who operate their own businesses.[5]

Financial. Establishments providing financial services deal primarily with investments, loans, and money in the form of stocks and bonds, financial papers, and transfers. Examples in this category include: commercial and all-purpose banks, savings-and-loan associations, trust companies, loan companies, insurance agencies, stock brokerages, mutual-funds groups, hospitalization plans and retirement funds. Although these are more likely handled by medium or large companies, entrepreneurs often form partnerships or closely held corporations to establish such firms.

A travel agency is a business or personal service and may often be cross-referenced with the transportation classification.

Public accounting firms and real estate agencies might be counted here, although their operations can also be classed as business or professional services. Realtors perform a personal, business, or financial service, depending on the purpose for which the property is being acquired.

Independent insurance agents sometimes work out of their homes or from one- or two-person offices. So do real estate agents. In both fields one needs experience and licensing in order to operate. You must pass state tests to obtain a sales and broker's license, and at least one broker must be on hand in any real estate office.

Business services. Business services are those provided by one firm to meet the economic and business needs of another firm or of individuals. These enterprises include accounting and legal firms, sign companies, repair shops, advertising agencies, janitorial and security companies, rental operations, temporary-help firms, and employment agencies.

Some businesses have their own repair shops, but others hire independent entrepreneurs to fix their appliances, motor vehicles, computers, photographic equipment, radios, TVs, stereos, and other electronic machines.

Office-support agencies provide typing and clerical services, bookkeeping, data processing, and word-processing services. Entrepreneurs may work alone out of an office, freelance from their homes, hire employees to assist, or use part-time workers who respond on call.

Information processing, according to such futurists as Alvin Toffler and John Naisbitt, is not only the wave of the future but is here now, outstripping industrial development by far. "In the United states," says Naisbitt, "we're creating new companies at the rate of 600,000 annually, compared to no more than 93,000 in 1950, at the height of the industrial period."[6] Of these new companies, many are responding with innovations from the rapidly emerging technology, ranging from electronic office services to video games (see also Chapter 15).

Personal services. There are enterprises to fill the consumer's every conceivable need or want. The possibilities include barber and beauty shops; funeral homes; upholstery shops; jewelry, shoe, leather, or watch repair shops; dry-cleaning establishments and laundries; and television, radio, appliance, and auto repair firms. Most of these operations require some specialized training and experience.

One needs less of a formal background to open a referral agency. Here the entrepreneur works to identify potential customers who need (or can be enticed

Bonnie operates her personal service beauty shop from her home.

to want) things done and to discover workers (often part-time) who can serve these needs; e.g., temporary help to serve clerical, medical, and security needs, among numerous others. The entrepreneur's role is to get these two groups together—for a fee, of course. The business owner does the legwork, such as making telephone calls, keeping financial and other records (legal, insurance, payroll, work-completion logs, etc.) and solves problems that require effective management, articulate communications, and human relations skills. Referral companies also arrange for house-cleaning, yard care, diaper-laundering, catering, and baby-, plant-, or house-sitting.

Many personal services offer "how to" courses and other training or educational opportunities. They teach people how to maintain and repair motor vehicles, household equipment, and the house itself; how to do macrame or needlepoint; how to prepare their own income taxes; how to program their personal computer; how to belly dance; and on and on. Such courses have become ever more popular.

Hospitality and recreation services. Hospitality services involve every type and socioeconomic level of hotel, motel, and restaurant. Recreation services provide entertainment, recreation, and leisure-time and tourism-related activities at, among other places, cinemas, bowling alleys, skating rinks, swim-

Hospitality and recreation is another service classification. Hospitality includes motels, hotels, and all types of restaurants. Recreation includes all leisure-time and recreational type businesses. Tourism enterprises are often associated with either hospitality or recreation.

ming pools, ski, golf, and tennis resorts, lakes, private parks, marinas, camping grounds, and dude ranches. The physical-fitness craze has supported many new businesses, such as jogging lanes and facilities, gymnasiums, recreation clubs, health spas, and weight-control clinics.

FURTHER OPTIONS

Specialty Firms

Large population centers can and do support many specialty firms. Look over the kinds of retail, service and manufacturing firms listed below to find any that are not yet established in your community that might appeal to you and to consumers. You can also try to determine which of the categories reviewed above these firms fit into.[7]

- aerobic dance classes
- art-show promoting
- balloon vending
- bartender trade school
- bartering club
- catalogue distribution
- collection agencies
- computerized dating service
- contest promoting
- co-op laundry
- customized rug making
- flea market
- food and party catering
- franchise analysis
- gold mining
- handwriting analysis
- interior decorating
- kite making
- liquidated goods broker
- making original clothing
- manufacturing sculptured candles
- mobile locksmithing
- newsletter publishing
- personalized shopping
- pet cemetery
- pet grooming
- private mailbox or safe-deposit box center
- quick photocopying
- rental list publishing
- self-improvement seminars or seminar promoting
- selling antiques
- selling backpacking equipment
- selling pipes, plants, T-shirts, used books, vitamins, or waterbeds
- swap-meet promoting
- teachers' agencies
- videocassette rental
- videotaping service
- wilderness or camping guide service

Typical of astute specialty entrepreneurship was the way that the booming box-office business of *E.T.* (a movie portraying an alien creature trapped on earth and befriended by a little boy, which has grossed over $169 million) was soon surpassed by entrepreneurs with related ideas. Over 45 manufacturing firms were quickly licensed to produce such *E.T.* items as dolls, underwear, posters, shoelaces, lunch kits, storybooks, night-lights, brush and comb sets, clocks and watches, bedding, T-shirts, footwear, tablewear, greeting cards, electronic games, and calendars. Likewise, merchandise items featuring characters and scenes from *Star Wars* earned their marketers $1.5 billion.

Working at Home

People who work at home may fit into any of the above categories or a combination thereof. There is a growing trend for people to work at home. With the advent of microprocessors and telecommunications devices, "the electronic cottage," as Alvin Toffler calls the home of the future, could emerge as the center for a variety of business and computer-related activities.[8]

Some people will continue to work for others, operating their home office as a satellite department. Others, however, are already working as freelance business owners, using their house as the base. Although many of these occupations require special training and experience, many others do not: e.g., door-to-door salespeople, mail-order operators, and party-givers (such as independent dealers representing products from Avon, Mary Kaye Cosmetics, Tupperware, Shaklee, Amway, and Cambridge).

Home-based operations don't always have to expand into bigger and fancier facilities. Many self-employed people do and will continue to use their homes as their only headquarters. Examples include construction, trade, and technical people such as carpenters, electricians, plumbers, and repair operators who work out of a garage or truck and take service calls from their homes; independent agents, including real-estate and insurance people; professionals; artists (sculptors, writers, composers, etc.); and consultants, counselors, tutors, music teachers, and freelancers in a variety of fields.

Mail-order enterprises, too, can be operated from the home. Some of these establishments may, however, expand enough to need extra space for warehousing, storage, packing, and shipping and may thus have to move to bigger facilities as the business grows.

People interested in developing a part-time business at home include "moonlighters," retired citizens living on fixed incomes, people with handicaps, and homemaker-parents. Books such as *Profits at Your Doorstep*, by Judith Eichler Weber and Karol White, can provide ideas and guidance in these efforts.

Weber's and White's list of home-based businesses includes those dealing with animals and pets, antiques, baby-sitting, bookkeeping, bookselling, catering, clocks and watches, electrical appliances, furniture and woodworking, glass and jewelry, home improvement and repairs, inventions, painting and picture-framing, photography, plants, stamps and coins, and typing services. (A bibliography of books about home-based enterprises is available from the SBA, "Small Business Bibliography," no. 2.)

Barbara Brabec, author of another SBA bibliography and also of the book *Creative Cash*, describes how handicraft hobbies, if properly marketed, can

Many small businesses are run from the home. This woman is able to run a profitable business without an additional rent charge.

become home-based businesses. She lists crafts such as: basketry, batik, ceramics, decorating, painting and design, dollhouses and miniatures, dyeing and spinning, embroidery and stitchery, furniture and finishing, jewelry and enameling, graphic arts, glass and leather, macrame, needlepoint, printing and silk-screening, quilting and applique, rug-making, sculpture, sewing and weaving, and woodworking and woodcarving. (For the list of references about home crafts sales, ask for SBA "Small Business Bibliography," no. 1.)

APPEALS TO THE UNWARY

The classified advertisement section of many popular tabloids include sections titled "Business Opportunities," "Money Making Opportunities," and so on.

Although some of these ads describe legitimate operations, too frequently they are designed to attract the unwary. Not all of the advertisers are themselves unscrupulous, however; often they, too, have been led to believe that they can find literally thousands of customers via the mails.

U.S. Postmaster General Herschler, speaking of the various types of money-by-mail frauds, has warned: "If it's too good to be true—it probably is!" He cites two types of scam: (1) the fake manufacturing scheme where you are supposed to assemble something and then return it to the company, and (2) the "stuff envelopes" plan—they send you a flier (such as "How to Make Big Bucks!") and you duplicate it (at your own expense) and mail it out to hundreds of others.

Herschler added that it is only when enough people complain that the Post Office takes action. "There are just too many ads in too many magazines to check on all of them," he states. But the government does follow through when several complaints are received about any one advertisement. "Of course in most cases people can ask for a refund; but the fact is, few people will bother.[9]

Those plans that are neither legal nor effective are typically no more than a chain-letter method of seeking money through the mail. The tip-off to a fraudulent scheme is its promise of fabulous profits to be made quickly with only a low investment of time and money, and with no experience or training. Sample pitchlines are:

"Earn up to $968 per week or $50,000 in three months . . ."

"Earnings of $2,000 monthly possible by offering leases and loans to professionals . . ."

"1000 percent profit possible bronzing baby shoes . . ."

"Earn thousands selling how-to books, manuals and directories . . ."

"Start sensational home business. Fantastic profits. No experience or investment necessary; people work for YOU . . ."

"$300 weekly spare time, mailing sales letters . . ."

"Big money possible getting people to do the work for you, invest only $12.50 . . ."

"$1000 weekly possible stuffing and mailing envelopes. Easy guaranteed program . . ."[10]

Although many of these advertisements ask you to do no more than "write for free details," the resulting piece is often a slick sales campaign that describes in easy, step-by-step fashion how you can realize the fabulous income promised. Far too many people, it would appear, still cling to dreams of easy money with little work, of "pie in the sky." Because people are both vulnerable and gullible, these schemes continue to proliferate. It is also sad but true that many of the respondents are among those who can least afford to invest even the smallest amount of money.

> ### RESEARCH ON MAIL APPEALS
>
> As part of the research conducted for this book, I answered over 200 "get-rich-quick" ads. I also wrote personally to nearly 100 of these mail-order entrepreneurs. Most of those who responded admitted they hadn't made any money as yet, although in many instances they had already spent thousands of dollars—yet they "hoped to make a killing soon!" Fewer than 20 percent had been involved in their particular mail-order enterprise for more than six months. Another 18 percent had gone out of business between the time they had placed the classified ad and its publication (my letters came back marked, "Box closed, no forwarding address"). Three dozen people wrote personal letters describing their disillusionment and recommending that I "not get involved." The remainder ignored the request for factual results, sending only more glowing accounts on mimeographed pages describing other surefire money-making schemes.
>
> Some people advertised no business venture at all, but merely asked for contributions ("Please HELP!"). Their reasons for soliciting ranged from personal tragedies—health or welfare problems or victimization by natural disasters or criminals—to a need to get specialized training so that they could find a job and support their families. Three out of the 40 ads to which I responded asked people to invest in their invention and promised vaguely to return the contributions later (in what form was unclear). These pleas are typically published under the "Personal" section, or "HELP!" headings in the classified advertisements.
>
> As an experiment, I contributed $1 to each of 40 advertisers whose notices appeared in five leading tabloids and magazines. Accompanying the contributions was a request for results, together with a self-addressed stamped envelope. Given that ads in national publications can cost from a low of $29 to a high of $85-plus (depending on the number of words and the magazine's rates), I was curious to know if placing this type of open-ended ad was a viable money-making enterprise. Of course, if the plan had indeed proved successful, these innovators would presumably have continued advertising. Over the next six months, not one of the 40 advertised a second time. Fifty percent of the recipients of my dollar responded. All gave bleak reports; their intake ranged from a low of $1 (this writer's) to a high of $7.

SUMMARY

Businesses can be classified, according to their products or services and how they are offered, into these categories: extraction, manufacturing, construction, transportation and communications, retail or wholesale trade, and various services. The range of company types within any given classification is broad. New entrepreneurs, hesitant to invest considerable time, energy, and money, may wish to launch their firms from their home. People should be wary, though, of risking their all on the type of enterprise, sometimes advertised in tabloids, that promises a fantastic return with little or no investment or expertise.

DISCUSSION QUESTIONS

1. Review each business classification. Cite examples of businesses you know of from:
   a. prior or present work experience
   b. family, friends, or neighbors who are entrepreneurs,
   c. interviews and observations.
2. What types of enterprises do you imagine could succeed in the fields of information processing, electronics, and televideo communications? Why, or why not?
3. Discuss the attraction of starting a "new venture," something new to your community or unheard of entirely. Brainstorm to produce new ideas. Debate the pros and cons of trying something new and different.
4. Think up some ventures you could start and operate successfully from your home, either now or in the near future.
5. Debate the attractiveness to would-be entrepreneurs of the money-making schemes advertised in national tabloids. Why do people invest money and time in such nebulous promises? What recommendations would you make "to the unwary"?

MINICASE

Sally began taking vitamins and using cosmetics that she obtained from a supervisor-distributor of a well-known multilevel marketing company. She liked the products so much she asked about becoming a distributor herself. Because of her willingness to work long, hard hours and her ability to make contacts with people, she was soon selling over $3000 worth of products retail.

If she could maintain this level of orders, she would soon qualify to become a supervisor herself. She would oversee other distributors and earn a commission from their orders as well as from her own retail sales. The problem was that if she and her distributors did not sell enough goods to pay for the specified minimum monthly order from the company, she would have to pay the difference out of her own savings.

Several times during the first few years she did in fact operate "in the red." She might have grown discouraged, as many of the distributors who had signed on with her did, and dropped out. But she recognized that this business was like any other, that there would be both good days and bad. Unlike many other people, instead of quitting she increased her efforts.

Today she considers herself a success. Besides seeing her company level off with gross earnings of over $100,000 annually (or about $35,000 in net income), she has also earned as bonuses for herself and her family four new cars and yearly trips to sales conventions.

With this story and your own experiences and ideas in mind, discuss the following issues:

a. the percentage of people who actually do succeed in such ventures as opposed to those who think they will make it big but don't;
b. what factors may have contributed to Sally's success and to other people's failure;
c. whether this and similar operations appeal to you personally, and why or why not;
d. what recommendations you would make to someone interested in becoming a distributor for a multilevel marketing company, where you earn not only from your own retail sales but also by recruiting distributors and earning commissions on their sales.

ACTIVITIES AND EXERCISES

Select a type of business or businesses within a given category and visit two or more such firms. Observe the operations and interview the key personnel, such as the owners or managers. Ask them about the advantages and disadvantages of opening this type of business. If they had it to do over again, would they go into business for themselves? If so, would they choose a different kind of enterprise?

NOTES

1. John English, Director of Mine Training and Safety, Mining Safety and Health Administration, U.S. Department of Labor, Washington, D.C. From an interview conducted at the Denver MSHA offices, regional headquarters for the Rocky Mountain region, June 1982.
2. Mike McGrady, *The Kitchen Sink Papers* (New York: Doubleday, 1975), pp. 5–9.
3. Olive Church and Anne Schatz, "Communications and Media Career Module," *Office Systems and Careers* (Boston: Allyn and Bacon, 1981), pp. 170–72.
4. Roger Sullivan, "Impacts and Trends of Communications Technology in Education and Training," speech given at the conference of American Society of Trainers and Developers, Boston, March 17, 1982.

5. Some definitions of small businesses exclude farming enterprises, professionals (doctors, dentists, lawyers, etc.), and sole proprietorships that operate from the home or employ no workers. The statistics reported reflect this exclusion. However, these categories are included among the classifications examined here in order to broaden the scope of entrepreneurship possibilities.
6. Interview with John Naisbitt in "Restructuring of America," *U.S. News & World Report,* January 3, 1983, pp. 49–50.
7. These business types were noted on site, in the "Yellow Page" advertisements of metropolitan telephone books (Los Angeles, Kansas City, Denver, and Chicago), and in U.S. Department of Labor, Bureau of Labor Statistics, "Small Business Occupations," Bulletin no. 2075-26, 1980–81.
8. Alvin Toffler, "The Electronic Cottage," *The Third Wave* (New York: William Morrow, 1980), pp. 194–207.
9. Interview with Postmaster General Hershler, (independent television station), Denver, December 12, 1982.
10. These ads appear frequently in national tabloids of the kind sold in supermarkets, including *Star, National Enquirer, Popular Mechanics,* various mystery magazines, and so on.

Look for Summer Fun Prizes under Gold Caps!
Coca-Cola
16
Look for Summer Fun Prizes under Gold Caps!
Coca-Cola
16
Coke
Coca-Cola

c·h·a·p·t·e·r ·4·

Franchises, Existing Businesses, and Family Businesses

Objectives

1. Define a franchise and describe the relationship between franchiser and franchisee in various types of agreements.

2. Explain advantages and disadvantages of operating a franchise as compared to owning an independent business.

3. Compare buying an existing business with starting your own.

4. Give advantages and disadvantages of joining and/or assuming ownership of a family business.

There are several ways to go into business besides starting your own independent, new enterprise. You can open a franchise, buy an existing business, or join a family-owned enterprise with a view toward eventually assuming ownership.

FRANCHISES

The International Franchise Association defines a franchise as a continuing relationship between the franchiser and the franchisee in which the franchiser supplies its knowledge, image, success, and manufacturing and marketing techniques to the franchisee for a consideration. A franchise is a legal agreement between a company and an entrepreneur.

The *franchiser* may be a manufacturer, a wholesaler, or a service company. The *franchisee*, or entrepreneur, receives permission to offer the franchiser's goods or services for sale in a particular locale as well as permission to use the company's name and help in starting, advertising, and managing the company. Thus when you buy a franchise you are buying the trade name of an already proven product or service and the *right* to do business.

The failure rate for franchises is somewhat lower than that of independent businesses. In setting up a franchise you avoid the precarious first steps of starting your own business, since the franchise idea already has been conceived, packaged, and refined. Since the guidelines for management have often been created from A to Z, you have the opportunity to benefit from both the mistakes and the successes of others.

The Background of Franchising

Early franchise arrangements involved automobile dealerships and gasoline service stations as well as such soft-drink companies as Coca-Cola and local brewing companies. Auto dealerships and gasoline stations accounted for about 50 percent of retail franchise sales.

Many retail stores are also franchises. Walk through any big shopping mall and you'll find the same familiar names. The past few decades have seen the growth of many other types of franchises as well, including those providing fast foods, entertainment and recreation, and personal and business services.

According to the International Franchise Association, the largest franchise operations (in number of outlets) in the United States are General Motors, Ford, and Midas Muffler (automobiles, products and services); Standard Oil, Exxon, Texaco, and other major oil companies (petroleum products); McDonald's (fast foods); 7-11 (convenience and self-service stores); Coca-Cola (soft drinks); and Holiday Inns (hotels and motels).[1]

Types of Franchises

There are four types of franchises. The first involves manufacturers and wholesalers: e.g., soft-drink companies and breweries. Because it is difficult for the

Early franchises consisted of automobile dealerships, products, and gasoline stations. Fast-food, service, and other retail franchises are now common.

manufacturer to produce the entire finished product, it franchises the recipes and special ingredients (such as the syrup to produce Coca-Cola) to the franchisee. The latter assembles and bottles the products and distributes them to retailers. In this type of arrangement, the franchisee participates in some of the production.

The second type of franchise involves wholesalers and retailers. The wholesaler, as the franchiser, is able to buy in volume from manufacturers and can in turn pass these savings on to the franchised retail outlets that market the products. Examples are such automotive product lines as Western Auto Supply and Goodyear.

The third arrangement has the manufacturer as franchiser supplying the retailer as franchisee with the entire stock, a complete product line. Naturalizer shoe stores and Midas Muffler shops are examples. Consumers enter these establishments knowing the products they can expect to find and the quality and reputation of the products. The franchisee has very little decision-making authority over the products offered.

The fourth franchise relationship is based on brand name. A given product or products may or may not be part of the deal, although fast-food establishments would use a certain recipe or at least a specific menu. In addition to such franchises as McDonald's, Kentucky Fried Chicken, and Baskin-Robbins, there are motels (e.g., Holiday Inns) auto-rental firms (e.g., Hertz and Budget Rent-A-Car), and a variety of service establishments.

Requirements and Benefits

The franchisee agrees to follow specific marketing and operating procedures. A *limited* franchise, however, requires less of the franchisee than does an *extensive* franchise. With the former, you purchase the right to sell a particular brand and agree to place a certain number and volume of orders each year. With the latter you agree to abide by certain standards—but you also benefit from the marketing, management, and financial experience of the franchiser. (See Figure 4.1.)

Samuel Downey, founder and chief executive officer of Downey Automotive, Inc., is a wholesale franchiser. He recruits franchisees by visiting with them in their own independent establishments. What Downey looks for, he says, are entrepreneurs who "know consumers and care about customers." He insists on strict standards and procedures for his franchisees, but he offers them advantages as well. They don't have to worry about warehousing because they buy all their inventory from Downey (who deals with over 100 suppliers) and Downey provides daily deliveries to replenish the franchisee's stock as fast as it turns over. Downey also provides total backup: initial financial assistance, remodeling help, signs, advertising, training in counter selling, and profit management.

The only written agreement between Downey Automotive and the franchisee is the agreement "to take back inventory, shelving, lease—everything," says Downey. "And we do that so if a guy wants out, he can get out. But, more important, if he dies, it'll leave his family with some options."[2]

To become a franchisee you need a certain amount of capital, especially if the franchiser requires the franchisee to construct and equip a building to precise specifications. You also need to obtain territorial rights. If a Robo-Wash or a Century 21 Real Estate franchise is already operating in your neighborhood, you will not be able to open a new line (although you could purchase an existing operation). Of course, if you were first to operate a franchise in your community, you would not want another one to cut into your business! Franchisers seek to protect each franchisee.

Franchisers will usually help you select a location, supervise construction, handle promotion, and stage the opening. The franchiser will also train you in its standard procedures and help you to hire employees, to buy at discount rates, and to establish and administer your financial records. Many retail and some service franchises locate in shopping malls, where the mall developers are seeking well-known names. Banks and other lending institutions are often more amenable to making loans for such well-planned ventures.

Many franchisers also send out company representatives to visit franchisees and to ascertain whether they are maintaining quality standards. These people can provide managerial counseling as well.

When Frank L. Carney was in college, he opened a small carry-out pizza business with a friend in order to help pay his college expenses. When an employee left to open a similar business, Carney and his partner assisted with financing, management advice, and advertising. Later another former employee did the same thing. By the time Carney had completed his degree, he had helped several people launch their pizza businesses. Carney decided to develop

Advantages	Disadvantages
Established name brand/image: clientele are familiar with the quality and type of goods and services.	**Limited control:** can only offer those goods and/or services established by franchiser. Some entrepreneurial decisions require approval or are limited by the franchiser. May also have to implement standard advertising and accounting procedures.
Financial aid: potential loans from the franchiser and/or creditability with local lending institutions; may include getting more favorable credit terms.	
Established management methods: methods have been tested by trial and error and other systematic approaches, by the franchiser.	**Franchise fee(s):** one usually pays for initial or purchase rights and/or royalties, which are paid continually for the life of the franchise (may be an estimated percentage of sales, such as 5 percent of gross sales per month).
Management training: in advertising, purchasing, recordkeeping, and employee training and supervision; where available, helps to compensate for lack of entrepreneurial experience.	**Possibly undesirable identification—** or "guilt by association": if the company—its products and services—gain ill repute then your franchise can suffer as well, through no fault of your own.
Continuing help: in analysis and adjustment of managerial policy.	

FIGURE 4.1
There are advantages and disadvantages to operating a franchise, as shown on the T-Chart.

a franchise business he named Pizza Hut. Today of course this company is known throughout the world. Yet the assistance Carney originally provided is still part of the firm's overall management policy.[3]

Questions to Answer

In deciding whether to become a franchisee, you should ask yourself the following questions:

1. What can the franchise do for me that I could not do for myself in some other fashion?
2. Are the goods and services I could offer appropriate to my selected community?
3. Would the limitations imposed by the franchiser—on the types of goods and services offered, the management style, and so on—prevent me from running my company the way I want to?
4. Can I abide by the franchise contract? Will I want to?
5. What is the franchise's reputation in this community? If it's good, will I be able to maintain it (i.e., to live up to the franchiser's recommendations)?

6. Do I have the capital I need to purchase a franchise? Would my company be able to pay the continuing royalties (if any) without causing me and my dependents undue hardship?
7. Do I have the personality and attitude appropriate to working in a franchise relationship? That is, can I accept the limitations and controls of any one particular franchise?

You should take these issues into consideration before deciding to "go franchise." You can interview and observe selected franchisees and franchises in various locales on your own, apart from appointments made for you by the franchiser, in order to collect realistic data.

BUYING AN EXISTING BUSINESS

Because many firms go out of business, either for personal reasons or because of bankruptcy, there are numerous opportunities for you to buy a business that appeals to you and that is in your price range.

The factors to consider in buying an existing business include location, condition of the facilities, past performance and profits, legal obligations, and the extent and nature of goodwill. As with starting a new business, you should also assess the competition and the market area, projecting community, demographic, and economic trends.

Location and Condition of the Facility

A deteriorating neighborhood or the relocation of major thoroughfares and thus of customer traffic can mean that a location once considered good may no longer be satisfactory. Are the facilities and equipment outdated or just what you need to carry on business? Having good equipment in place saves you the time and money you would have to expend comparing prices and having new equipment intalled.

Past Performance and Profits

Conduct a marketing study to determine how satisfied customers have been with the existing business. Also have an accountant evaluate the current financial condition of the business. Preferably the business will have kept accurate records about depreciation on inventory, and so on. Long-term records can reveal past trends and thus help predict future ones. Financial statements, when available, are especially useful. However, many small business owners keep incomplete or perfunctory records (accountants say that they are often asked to prepare income-tax statements from no more than shoeboxes full of receipts and cancelled checks!), so there may be little data to base a comprehensive analysis on.

Legal Obligations

Have a competent legal adviser check for possible financial or legal problems with lease agreements or property titles, delinquent taxes or other unpaid bills, current liabilities, or pending litigation. Unscrupulous sellers may try to hide this type of information; other sellers may simply not know or have forgotten about their total commitments. In any event, you don't want the burden of having to assume unanticipated responsibilities.

Extent and Nature of Goodwill

A business with goodwill has an established and favorable clientele together with an outstanding reputation for integrity. The intangible asset of goodwill, which contributes to higher profits, should be evaluated differently than other assets.

Suppose that the seller has $70,000 invested in his business (which represents his "net assets") and an anticipated profit percentage (return on investment) of 10 percent, or $7000. If the business actually makes a profit of $10,000 a year, the difference of $3000 represents goodwill. This element increases profits 30 percent over the norm for the business. In this case, other factors being equal, a purchase price of $90,000 might be appropriate.

Closing the Purchase

The legal documents needed in closing the purchase include: the bill of sale, title insurance, contract agreements about making payments and guaranteeing protection to the seller, and certificates of assurance about taxes and other legal obligations. Both seller and buyer must understand all the terms of the purchase agreement and all the implications of signing.

The seller's realtor or attorney may have initiated the contact between seller and buyer, but the latter's own independent agent can furnish specific advice. Not all business purchases include the building in which the business operates. Where the firm operates in a leased facility, then the buyer is purchasing the business but not the building.

Why People Want to Sell

Many people want to sell their business for personal reasons, such as (1) they are tired of entrepreneurship—the long hours, the heavy drains on their energy (not to mention their money), the risks they did not anticipate and may not be equipped to handle; (2) they wish to relocate nearer friends or family; (3) they are ready to retire; (4) they have found other, more appealing, opportunities (e.g., starting another type of business, working for someone else, or going into politics).

Sellers might also use any of the above as excuses when their real reason for selling is that their businesses are failing. Yet even failure or potential bankruptcy is not necessarily a disadvantage. The current business problems may well be due to mismanagement. Maybe you can do better.

Another reason for selling is lack of capital: the entrepreneur has a low cash flow and no more money to invest in expansion, updating, advertising, or even the sales promotions necessary to match or beat the competition. When the entrepreneurial buyer enters business with enough capital, he or she can apply these funds to correcting whatever financial or management problems may have plagued the previous owner.

The Advantages and Disadvantages of Buying an Existing Company

Although there are many advantages to buying an existing company, the new owner may also be inheriting problems. The possible advantages are that the established firm has:

1. A proven track record of sales, services, profits, etc.;
2. An established clientele who are already familiar with the company's products and in the habit of shopping there or perusing its offerings;
3. A location with which the clientele is familiar;
4. Existing facilities—including equipment, materials, and supplies or stock—which are already obtained and in place;
5. Supplier and banking services that are familiar with both the existing company and its needs and practices;
6. A records system—appropriate to the type of business and in place; and
7. Employees who are also familiar with the operation.

Any or all of the above, however, may prove to be disadvantages as well, depending on the condition and creditability of the operating system. Some obvious problems would be a run-down facility, crowded or mismanaged space, and even the lack of buying customers. Observation of the company's daily operation at different times over several days can reveal such problems. It may cost a great deal more to buy an existing business because of the extras you are getting: the building, the inventory, and the goodwill (reputation and an established clientele). Many sellers expect to be paid for the intangible benefits as well as the tangible.

JOINING THE FAMILY BUSINESS

Being the boss's son or daughter doesn't necessarily guarantee success. Parents can serve as excellent role models and mentors, however, and the family-owned business can provide training in all aspects of business.

Yet parents, of either gender, can also be difficult to work for. Sometimes they fail to recognize that their children have grown to adulthood, no matter what the offspring's age or circumstances. Some parents seek to control and supervise their children in the workplace as in the home. Or they might try to satisfy their own dreams of fulfillment by living their children's lives for them. This type of parent-boss may vent more of their frustrations on their adult children than they would on other employees and might expect more of them than of others. Such behavior can impede the son's or daughter's smooth transition from worker to manager to ultimate owner. See the following two examples:

> Cindy Ross mastered the technical specifications for 45 industrial equipment machines and became adept at giving on-site demonstrations in her job as sales trainee in her father's company, where she worked on commission only. Although she performed well, she and her father had a difficult time working together. "When I brought Dad information from the field, he didn't take my ideas seriously," she claimed. Mr. Ross suggested that his daughter wasn't willing to listen to him either. "Kids don't always accept opinions from a father the way they would from a regular employer."
>
> After five years working and growing together, Cindy became a company vice-president and her husband, Doug, general manager. Mr. Ross, who had supposed he'd have to liquidate the company upon his retirement, was able to make other arrangements. Cindy and Doug negotiated a buy-out offer with her father and became co-owners.
>
> After establishing her own fashion retailing company in Dallas, Kathleen returned to Massachusetts to join her stepfather's firm, also as a sales trainee. In the first year and a half she had to work doubly hard to establish her credibility despite being the boss's daughter. Her stepfather conceded, "I may have expected more of Kathleen at first." Another problem arose from differences in their personalities. She wanted to plunge ahead and make innovative decisions, while he was slower, more conservative.[4]

Relatives or offspring who follow a parent into a professional firm often have at least one advantage in credibility. Their degrees have prepared them to function in the field(s) of choice, which is not always true of other business neophytes, who may have little background beyond ambition and the familial motivation to see the business succeed.

Yet this very sense of family, of seeking to provide continuity and succession, may be the biggest motivator of all when someone decides to join parents or relatives, buy into, or otherwise assume ownership of a family-owned business. If you have grown up in the family business—or have an inclination to return to it after having gained experience elsewhere—and if your goals and aptitudes mesh sufficiently with this ongoing enterprise, then here is where you may choose to set your sights. Applying effective entrepreneurial principles as you work through the company's labyrinth toward management may help you to assume ownership.

Perhaps you (or a parent) will recommend that you come or buy into the business as a junior or equal partner. Parents may want to retire or to assume a secondary role in the business. At any rate, you can avoid many of the problems associated with starting a new business by taking this route to company ownership.

Many new entrepreneurs get into business by buying an existing enterprise. They do not always look for successful businesses if their management ideas, plus a low purchase price, make buying a run-down business attractive.

SUMMARY

Among the options for going into business, besides starting your own independent company, are: contacting a franchiser and becoming a franchisee, buying an existing business, or joining a family-owned business with the ultimate goal of becoming the owner.

Franchise relationships have existed for many years. Chief among the earlier franchises were automotive dealerships and gasoline stations. Over the past few decades, however, many other franchises have emerged. Typical are the many retail establishments marketing brand-name products, fast-food places, motels and other restaurants, and personal and business services.

If you decide there is less risk in buying an already successful business, it is important to determine if those offered for sale have proven profitability. If not, you will want to look for compensating factors such as a low purchase price. Joining a family business has both advantages and disadvantages, but is a means of gaining valuable experience.

DISCUSSION QUESTIONS

1. Why is the failure rate for franchises lower than that for independently owned enterprises?
2. How do the advantages and disadvantages listed in Figure 4.1 compare in significance with those reported by the franchisees you interviewed? What comparisons can you make between your own and the interviewees' current or future business plans, needs, and personalities?
3. From the interviews you've conducted to date (and from the reports of your peers and colleagues), what differences do you perceive between starting a business from scratch and buying an existing enterprise? At this time, which route appears to suit your needs best? Why?
4. In buying an existing business, what other factors would you want to look at beyond those reported in the chapter and by your interviewees? How would you go about collecting the needed information?
5. What advantages and disadvantages do you perceive in joining a family-owned business, particularly as an employee? What privileges or problems do you think you would encounter by becoming junior partner rather than assuming full ownership? What recommendations would you make to someone whose family already has a successful business operation and who might want to join the company?

ACTIVITIES AND EXERCISES

1. Arrange to observe and interview a minimum of two franchisees. Contact one company involved mostly in product selling and another that offers services. Determine which of the advantages and disadvantages listed in Figure 4.1 were most important in the owner's decision of whether to "go franchise." Compare the two (or more) companies you visited.
2. Check the classified advertisements in local newspapers to see who is offering their businesses for sale. Use one or both of the following methods to obtain related data:
   a. In making an interview appointment, explain that this is a class assignment to determine why owners want to sell (record their answers). If possible, conduct telephone interviews with two or three different sellers in order to make comparisons among their situations.
   b. If you can, observe the selected companies informally. Visit each one to ascertain the condition of the building and facilities; also observe if the enterprise has many customers. Be ready to analyze your superficial findings and to evaluate the situation as a good or poor opportunity for buying an existing business.

3. Using personal knowledge or the "Yellow Pages," identify one or more family-owned businesses. (A clue is the company name, e.g., "Garcia *Brothers*," "Kisuke *and Sons*," etc.) Interview the owners to determine the relationship of the family members within the company's organizational structure. If a member of the family works in the company but does not yet have ownership status, try to determine the working relationship and when, if ever, the secondary (or minor) family member might expect to assume ownership. What conditions would be necessary to bring this to pass: additional exposure in the company, formal training, buying the principal out, or the principal's death or retirement?

CASE: WHY SOME PEOPLE BUY AND SELL

Some people buy a business only temporarily, to make a quick profit by getting a poor business back on its feet and reselling it. Other entrepreneurs purposely look for businesses with a poor performance and profitability record because they expect to get a bargain on the purchase price. The Whitmans' and Sanchezes' story illustrates both of these purposes:

When Mr. and Mrs. Whitman bought a local motel at a bankruptcy sale, they knew they had little capital to invest in bringing the dilapidated establishment back to par. What they did have was plenty of enthusiasm and elbow grease. Besides, their intention was not to make motel operation their lives' work but rather to turn it over quickly in a resale.

In 90 days they had accomplished a great deal, using no more than their time and energy, plus about $10,000 for paint, asphalt (to resurface the parking lots), and parts for repairing signs, etc. During this period they also had to meet mortgage payments and pay utilities and delinquent taxes. Nevertheless, the motel's exterior soon became appealing—to guests and potential buyers alike.

Mr. and Mrs. Sanchez arrived with a realtor (with whom the motel had been listed for sale). They were attracted by the location, by the outside appearance, and by the opportunity to apply their own ingenuity in creative marketing and management. The Whitmans readily opened their financial records, making clear the state the motel had been in for the previous five years (few guests, poor management, run-down condition, and unpaid local bills and taxes). With an "as-is" sale, the Sanchezes took over. They recognized that the motel's many internal needs would quickly use their resources. But their analysis was that the low purchase price would compensate for this anticipated exhaustion of their available investment funds. (Their capital of $100,000 came from selling two houses: their own residence and a rental property. With the motel's apartment, they would not need to buy or rent lodging for themselves.)

With their capital the Sanchezes bought and installed new heating, air conditioning, carpets, and color television sets; and they redecorated the guest rooms

Many businesses are family-owned. One attraction for women in business is that they can sometimes care for their children while at work, which is not usually possible if employed by others.

with new furnishings and accessories. Their greater capital resources made possible what the Whitmans' limited funds had not. Many guests arrived in response to the innovations and advertising and within nine months of buying the motel, the business was producing respectable profits.

The Sanchez couple might have used their funds to construct a new motel. But they chose to purchase an existing business, even though the financial records for the last five years (plus the obvious internal problems) clearly indicated a poor business. Had the motel been successful at the time of purchase, however, the buying price might have been three times what it was.

Coordinating Primary and Secondary Research Data

Prior to buying the motel, Mr. and Mrs. Sanchez remained in town a few days to get acquainted with the community and to conduct informal surveys, using both primary and secondary resources. Most business sellers in small towns and communities are aware of the many ways potential buyers can discover the truth about a business. Owners of other motels, chamber of commerce personnel, and other tradespeople willingly described to the Sanchez couple the motel's condition and its record of past poor performance, including the limited number of guests. Driving past all the other motels in town after 10 p.m., the Sanchezes counted the cars parked at each establishment for a week. This gave them an idea of customer traffic at each potential competitor's motel for each night of the week.

They coordinated this information with what they had found in the trade journals of the hospitality industry (hotels, motels, and restaurants). Thus they were not surprised to discover that all the motels did their biggest business during the work week. From these journals and by observing the practice of the competition, the Sanchez couple, although new to the motel business, discovered that special gimmicks and sales promotions were needed to attract guests on weekends.

Their research in secondary sources also produced a financial formula for purchasing an existing motel. The purchase price should ordinarily be no more than two and one-half to three times the annual gross income. In this case, however, the income had been steadily dropping, thus indicating a poor condition.

To overcome this price evaluation problem, Mrs. Sanchez called the chamber of commerce to get the room rates charged by local competitors. Multiplying that figure by the number of cars found in each motel over a week's period, she then extrapolated the annual income figure of each motel. Taking those motels most nearly competitive with the one they planned to purchase, the Sanchezes thus had a tentative earnings forecast (the most nearly competitive motels were those with a similar number of rooms to rent plus a similar location and comparable services, such as swimming pool, color cable television, and coffee shop).

Although the purchase price the Whitmans were asking was five times the previously reported income, the Sanchezes calculated that once they had brought revenues back to par, they would only be paying one and one-half times the income. The asking price was $150,000. Their second year's operation produced over $200,000 in revenues, proving that the Sanchez couple had been correct. (Meanwhile, the Whitmans made $100,000 on the sale since they had only paid $50,000.)

Discuss the following questions:

1. What motivation did the Whitmans have in buying an old run-down motel, when the establishment met virtually none of the criteria stated in the chapter?
2. What other options did the Whitmans have or that you would have considered if you had been in their situation?
3. What other steps would you have taken before deciding to buy the motel from the Whitmans?
4. How big a risk were either the Whitmans or the Sanchezes taking when they made their investment decisions?
5. What would you have done differently in either situation? Why? Make comparisons between this case and other types of enterprises in similar physical condition.

NOTES

1. Fran Weinstein, "Minding Your Business—What about Franchising?" *Working Woman,* January 1978, pp. 20–21.
2. Bradford W. Ketchum, Jr., "The Auto Man's Empire," *Inc.,* August 1982, pp. 77–84.
3. Speech given by Frank L. Carney, founder of Pizza Hut, Inc., at the Kansas Business Education Association conference, Wichita, Kansas, August 1976.
4. Andrea Fooner, "Dad & Daughter, Inc.," *Working Woman,* January 1983, pp. 79–82.

GENERAL CAREER INFORMATION
THE ARTS
BUSINESS
INTERNATIONAL
BUSINESS MAG.
JOB SEARCH INFO.
JOURNALISM-PUBLISHING
EDUCATION
SOCIAL SERVICE-PUBLIC INTEREST
HEALTH RELATED
FOURTH EDITION
Encyclopedia of CAREERS and Vocational Guidance
Vol. II Careers and Occupations

chapter 5

Deciding What Kind of Business to Open

Objectives

When you have completed this chapter and its suggested activities and used the checklists and tools in Appendices A and B, you should be able to:

1. Compare your own experiences, interests, hobbies, and aptitudes with the list of business classifications given in Chapter 3 to find what interests you most;

2. Identify any gaps in your technical and business background and explore possible means of filling those gaps;

3. Identify your personal strengths and weaknesses, and decide how to use the former in pursuit of entrepreneurship and how to compensate for the latter;

4. Use decision-making tools to develop short- and long-range plans for achieving your goals.

The task of choosing a business from the list of possibilities can boggle the mind. The decision you make (or the advice you give others) about what kind of company to open should be based on far more than whim. The investments and commitments you must make are too critical. The questions to ask yourself include:

1. What technical and business expertise are required to operate the business(es) of my choice? Do I have them, or can I get them?
2. What evidence is there that I would continue to enjoy owning this company despite long hours, hard work, and the possibility of numerous setbacks?
3. What products, services, and activities appeal to me most? Which could motivate in me the highest level of enthusiasm, even excitement?

ENTREPRENEURS—WHO ARE THEY?

It seems to take a special kind of person to succeed in business. Do you have what it takes? Or, perhaps equally important, can you acquire the training, the experience, and the qualities that separate those who succeed from those who fail?

Successful entrepreneurs are often independent, creative, adventurous, energetic, and willing to take risks. Leadership qualities are also essential, including the ability to persuade and motivate others, to sell (an idea, if not a product or service), to supervise, to communicate effectively, to relate well to others, and to make decisions and live by the consequences. Also important is the ability to think analytically and to take action as a result. A successful entrepreneur is a leader and a manager.[1]

Research has shown that any two or more of the following circumstances are typical of a leader-manager's background:

1. They have another entrepreneur in the family to act as a role model or a mentor;
2. They have had youthful experience as an entrepreneur, such as having a paper route, shoveling snow, or baby-sitting;
3. They are more interested in participating in sports and activities than in merely being an onlooker;
4. They are the oldest or only child in their family. Whether male or female, such children are more often thrown into adult company and roles than are their younger siblings. They may also have identified with their father, who in many families was the parent most involved in pursuing a career;
5. They have an independent, free spirit. They may find it difficult to take direction from others—parents, teachers, or employers—and thus may have a poor employment record, having changed jobs frequently or been fired. They tend to resist authority and to refuse to conform to established routines. (Somewhat surprisingly, however, entrepreneurs are not necessarily big risk-takers so much as they are "realistic gamblers"—i.e., they prefer having the odds in their favor before stepping out.)

6. They have a need to control their own lives and a desire to lead others. Leadership can take different forms. Some business owners prefer to motivate people (employees and customers alike) rather than to push products per se. Primarily, though, successful entrepreneurs like being in charge—of things, of people, and especially of themselves;
7. They have a need to work hard, often to the near exclusion of family and social activities—particularly in the early stages when the company is getting started. Some almost have to make a conscious effort to reserve time for others. Indeed, family and friends often call such people "workaholics." In fact, however, they may get more fun out of work than they do out of what other people call play.[2]

People who succeed frequently do work harder, or at least with more intelligence. The difference between a successful and a mediocre entrepreneur is often some small thing that makes a big impact—the winners are willing to go the extra mile!

Technical Skills and Vocational Education Programs

As a potential entrepreneur you can evaluate your training, hobbies, and work experiences to help identify your skills and the kind of business they equip you to run. Perhaps you have had technical training as a result of having enrolled in secondary or post-secondary school vocational education programs. Typically, students enroll in a comprehensive program beginning in the tenth or eleventh grade, or they get career exposure in high school to help determine the direction they will later take in a community college or business or trade school.

Although these vocational programs primarily focus on preparing students to work for others, the skills they teach can also be directed toward entrepreneurship. These programs are specifically named: business education (BE), marketing and distributive education (MDE), health occupations, trades and industry education (T & I), consumer home economics and related occupations, technical education, and vocational agriculture. Training in these fields often provides the technical expertise to operate numerous retail or service firms, and in some cases manufacturing enterprises, where specific skills are required to manage the selected products or services. If you have taken high school or post-secondary courses from the vocational disciplines of BE and MDE, you should also have received exposure to general or introductory business, accounting/bookkeeping, principles of management and marketing, data processing, and office systems.

Other Ways to Acquire Technical and Managerial Skills

Two-thirds of the owner-managers surveyed in a Canadian study had had no more than a high school education but they also had up to 18 years of experience in their lines of business.[3] Work experience in a related field seems to be a common denominator that many successful entrepreneurs mention. Lance Herndon's story is an example:

94   Chapter 5

Vocational training gives students specific skills that they will use in the business environment.

With vocational training and specific background, adults develop skills that they can use in a particular type of business.

Deciding What Kind of Business to Open

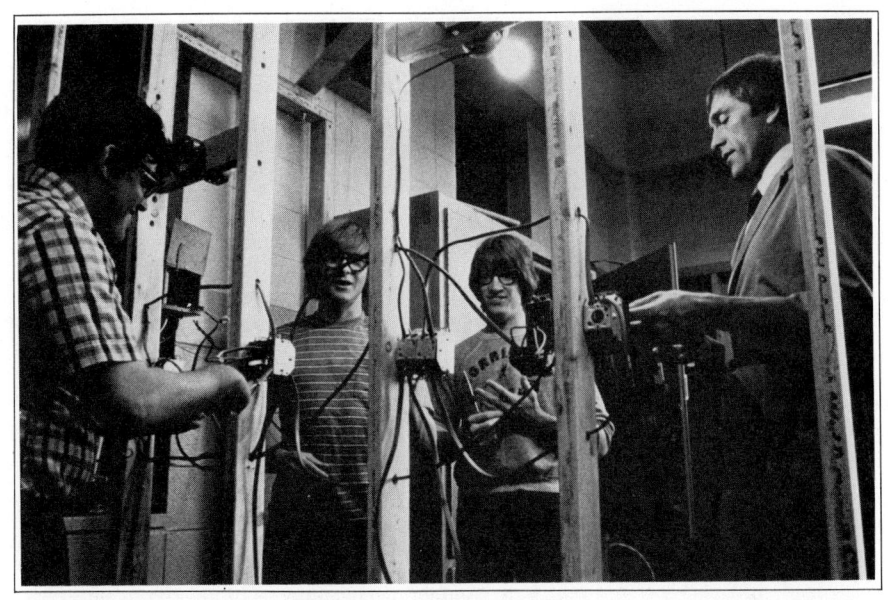

Electrical, electronic, and other industrial businesses require technical training and "hands-on" experience.

"I learned from the best," says 28-year-old Lance H. Herndon, speaking of the time he spent as a data processing consultant for two companies in New York. "I took notes for six years and then I realized I could compete with my employers." In 1980 Herndon took $3,000 from his personal savings and set up as a data processing consultant in Atlanta. For the 1982-83 fiscal year, Access, Inc. grossed $482,000 and is described by owner Herndon as "extremely profitable." Access, Inc. does application programming, installs and customizes software, and teaches corporate clients how to select and use microcomputers. "Because my background is technical, the hardest thing to learn was marketing and presentation. I had to become a professional marketer."[4]

If you dream of opening your own business sometime in the future, then you may find both the time and the opportunity to develop some of the traits and experiences you need by working for others, preferably in the type of enterprise you would like to open for yourself later. Although smaller companies cannot promise the rewards and steady upward movement through the ranks that large companies can, as an employee in a smaller company you have a greater chance of becoming a partner or of eventually owning the entire company. One survey revealed that almost a third of all small businesses were purchased by their present owners: "29 percent of the CEOs of small businesses polled said their business had been founded by someone else (other than a relative)."[5]

Another study of 1805 small businesses nationwide suggested that "small businesses are more likely to be breeding grounds for potential entrepreneurs than are larger companies." This survey also indicated that 70 percent of entrepreneurs started businesses in fields where they had job experience, while 50 percent had parents who owned their own businesses.[6]

"HE TELLS STUDENTS TO GO AND MAKE A BUSINESS HAPPEN"

Can entrepreneurs—those economic daredevils who risk everything on a new idea—actually be academically replicated? "Experiments" are under way at universities nationwide. So far, many seem to be working.

At Carnegie-Mellon University in Pittsburgh, for instance, Dr. Dwight Maylon Billy Baumann is hatching tycoons in the engineering building. He sends his students, programmed to wheel and deal, out into the economy. "We're doing a scientific experiment here," he says. "We want to see if we can raise entrepreneurs in captivity." When the student fledglings have learned to compose a bravura business plan, to figure cash flow, to keep a new company breathing, those with the peppiest proposals may receive aid for their new ventures.

Baumann's office is an incubator for new corporations: a computerized taxi service, a theatrical troupe, a newspaper chain, electronic bookkeeping for physicians, companies making new medical immunization serums, ultrasonic toy guns, microfiche atlases, diesel fuel from sunflower seeds. When he was a child on a North Dakota farm, Dwight Baumann's hero was Thomas Edison, crackerjack inventor, canny businessman, technological prestidigitator. Now Baumann wants to revitalize the kind of dynamic spirit that Edison personified.

After World War II, large corporations dominated the financial skyline, not the entrepreneur's made-it-myself business jerry-built from scrounged dollars, a wild idea, and lots of brass. Without those entrepreneurial powerhouses—the Carnegies, Fords, Eastmans, Bells, Westinghouses, Eli Whitneys, Edisons—would the American economy lose its fizz?

Now the indicators say that the entrepreneur, long dormant, is rallying. In 1981, 53,000 more business (than 1980) were incorporated, an 80 percent increase over 1975. In a recent report on the new entrepreneurial Zeitgeist, the *Harvard Business Review* noted that today "several hundred colleges and universities—versus only a handful a decade ago—offer courses on starting and operating small businesses."

According to Dr. Baumann, psychological studies reveal that, compared with the average person, the entrepreneur has no abnormal inclination to take risks. But entrepreneurs do like to feel that they have special information, a secret edge. Perhaps the universal trait is wanting no boss.

According to Jack Thorne, who sold his own successful Los Angeles electronics company, Scionics, Inc., entrepreneurs "want to do their own thing, their own way—they are very independent, don't want to fill out forms, and don't want to work for big companies."

Source: Richard Wolkomir, "He Tells Students to Go and Make a Business Happen," *Smithsonia*, January, 1983, pp. 111–193.

What technical skills, managerial talents, and related work experience do you need to put together a workable package? You may not have to have every skill, trait, talent, and experience cited above to make your enterprise succeed.

Taking in a partner is one solution. Perhaps you have the product or service expertise, but lack the managerial experience. You may be the kind of person who prefers working behind the scenes with machines, things, paper, or data. You may find it hard to make the public relations contacts you should to put your marketing scheme into play. The solution would be to seek out a partner who has the talents you lack. Should your sources of capital be limited as well, you can solve two problems at once by having a partner. The other person brings in half the needed funds, plus approximately half the needed skills. However, then the business must support more than one entrepreneur; i.e., produce at least twice the income.

You can also hire some of the talents you need, although employees will not provide you with start-up or operating capital. Some business owners tend to feel threatened by workers who have qualifications that they lack. They may try to negate the contributions of workers who have skills they do not or who can do what they cannot or prefer not to do. Understanding that you cannot be and do all things in your business can help you appreciate and keep the people you need to help you run it, whether they are partners or employees.

Another alternative is to pay for consulting services or for entrepreneurs to share their expertise with you, and particularly to recommend how to deal with problems you might expect to encounter. Your start-up costs (and/or the expenses of your first year of operation) might include the fees you would pay for obtaining specific assistance from, for example, an attorney, an accountant, or a professional consultant.

In addition, you need to overcome whatever fears and anxieties may hinder you from becoming a successful entrepreneur. Self-confidence will enhance whatever personal assets you already have. But to change yourself you must know yourself. How can you objectively determine what sort of person you are today and what you may become in the near future?

SELF-ASSESSMENT

The following characteristics of successful entrepreneurs seem to stand out: self-confidence, articulateness in both verbal and written communication, organizational ability, and analytical talents. Your self-confidence grows when you know you have a certain number and level of the traits and experiences needed to succeed. You need both self-confidence and eloquence to sell your ideas and your products or services.

Many people have been taught, by contrast, to be modest and humble. Leonard Baumgarten, a business consultant for the development of human potential, believes that a low self-concept is the single biggest reason that people fail to sell themselves. "People," he says, "refrain from tooting their own horns for fear of coming across as a bore or a braggart."[7]

Studies show in fact that a person must succeed at least 60 percent of the time in order to develop a positive self-concept. Well-being comes from liking yourself. A positive self-image comes from succeeding, however you personally define that term.

Positive Experiences

Too many people—perhaps because they have been conditioned by family and society to be modest—concentrate on their weaknesses and failures, not on their strengths and triumphs. Or they fail to learn from their mistakes. The first step in the process of self-assessment is to record and analyze your positive past experiences. The goal is to determine what actions merit repetition, so that you can continue to have successful experiences. (See Appendix A for Exercise no. 1.)

Bodily and Emotional Sensations

Practically everything we do produces bodily or emotional sensations. These are clues to the real self. If you are allergic to chocolate and you eat a huge piece of three-layer fudge cake, you can expect to break out in a rash or to get short of breath. These are bodily responses that remind you not to eat chocolate.

Less apparent are the emotional clues; it takes some practice to identify when and how these emotions occur and what triggers them. What happens when you are asked to talk before a formal group, for instance? People often fear speaking in public more than they fear heights, flying, or being attacked. What bodily and emotional sensations do you experience when you are afraid? Do your hands get clammy, does your breath come quickly? Does the blood rush to your face and make you feel as if you're blushing? Perhaps you develop knots in your stomach, or your legs feel like they are turning to rubber.

Anxiety or excitement may sometimes cause the same physical reactions as fear. Consider your first job interview. How did you react before and during the experience? Like public speaking, the interview may have made you very nervous, and you may have experienced similar emotions and bodily sensations. But if you were hired, you probably overcame these feelings of anxiety quickly once you got your bearings on the new job. Thus the sense of nervousness usually soon gives way to more pleasant feelings of excitement and renewed energy.

From a basis of self-confidence you can learn to use your nervousness. Professional performers often feel anxiety before they go onstage or step up to a podium to speak. Yet they have learned to channel the energy that accompanies these bodily-emotional sensations, which pump adrenalin into the body, to heighten their performance. Anxiety, then, can actually contribute to your ability to succeed.

Although you may have long wished to open your own business, anxiety about attempting the unknown may have held you back. Distinguishing the challenges that cause you undue discomfort from those that excite you and increase your self-confidence should help you decide whether you have the temperament to succeed in small business despite the inevitable setbacks and challenges. (See Appendix A, Exercise 2-A.)

Using Negative Experiences Positively

Young people are often embarrassed when they make mistakes, especially in front of their friends or authority figures. Yet humans are prone to error. We miscalculate, forget things, spill things, speak out when we should keep silent. Hindsight is invariably better than foresight. With maturity we come to realize that probably no day ever passes and few actions take place that will be entirely error-free. With experience we also become aware of the mistakes we have made before and develop some ideas about how to avoid mistakes in the future. What really counts is not the number of times you may have failed in the past but rather the end result—how these mistakes contribute to the future.

Learning anything new is invariably a struggle, of course. Remember how hard you worked to gain the skills for your favorite athletic games and leisure-time activities, even your occupational expertise—all of which you can now enjoy and benefit from. It takes time and effort to learn how to ski, swim, play racquetball, type, or drive a car—anything requiring the coordination of mind, eyes, and hands. Undoubtedly you made numerous mistakes before you got good enough at the activity to enjoy it. But the point is that you stuck with the effort, despite the discomfort of learning, until you mastered the skill.

When you can identify the things that give you pain, you can avoid some of them and thus minimize the chance of making excessive errors consistently. You can differentiate between those things that matter little and those that would contribute to entrepreneurial success and thus are worth the effort of learning or acquiring. (See Appendix A, Exercise 2-B.)

Work, Play, and Family as Clues to Self

You are unique. Developing this belief, if you do not already have it, can take time. By reviewing your youthful experiences from a mature and analytical vantage point, you can begin to develop the objectivity needed to perceive the positive traits that can work for you in the future.

What you have been—at work, at play, and at home with your family—contributes to what you are becoming. You may well be destined to become an entrepreneur, but of what type of business? With what legal structure? Your best chance of success lies in choosing the type of operation that can give you the most pleasure, that builds on the skills and aptitudes you already have while eliminating painful or otherwise disagreeable experiences. (See Appendix A, Exercises 3 and 4.)

Does your past include experience as a leader? Have you had charge of people, machines, or things, and did you enjoy that position? You may have volunteered for such a position, or others might have chosen you, or an authority figure (a parent, teacher, supervisor, or employer) may have assigned the role to you. Perhaps you were chosen as captain of a school ball team or elected to an office in a civic or church organization.

Leaders must be able to persuade and to motivate. Their job is easier if they have a clear authority. For example, business managers both supervise and control their subordinates; they set salaries and promote, transfer, or fire employees. It is usually much harder to control people in volunteer groups, however, because the leader has neither clear-cut controls nor authority. If you have led people to perform effectively in such a situation, you have exhibited excellent leadership skills. You have been able to get a job done by force of personality alone.

You may also have been given responsibility over machines or things in the absence of the usual caretakers. The people who assigned you the task believed that you were competent and responsible, or they would not have chosen you to take charge. (See Appendix A, Exercise 5.)

To summarize your analysis of life experiences, as recorded in Exercises 1-5, toward assessing who you are today, use Exercise 6. If you have doubts about your competence, abilities, or self-concept, now is the time to start changing. According to Dr. Baumgarten, "raising one's self-image can be learned."[8]

MAKING DECISIONS

To help you determine what sort of business you might want to launch, try the following techniques: (1) review the kinds of businesses in the different categories given in Chapter 3; (2) assess your skills, talents, training, work experience, hobbies, and likes and dislikes; and (3) brainstorm to produce ideas.

Webster's defines *brainstorming* as "the unrestrained offering of ideas or suggestions by all members of a group to seek solutions to problems" and a *brainstorm* as "a sudden inspiration, idea, or plan, to emerge from brainstorming." You can also ask for ideas from other people and do some research to identify enterprises that have proved successful.

By the end of this chapter, you should have made a tentative decision about what type of business you would like to operate. This decision will make the following chapters more meaningful. You can, of course, select several possible enterprises, perhaps similar operations from each business category.

For example, suppose your self-evaluation reveals that you prefer to work with machines. Your hobbies, training, and work experiences may suggest a particular class of machine, such as automotive or electronic. Then you might consider opening a retail operation in which you would sell the selected product(s) directly to consumers; or a repair service, either in combination with retail trade or as a separate entity; or else a small manufacturing plant to assemble or produce the product you have in mind.

Perhaps, instead, you discover that you enjoy having frequent contact with people, whether in selling products, persuading, or negotiating deals and compromises. You may want to start a service-oriented business where you will interact constantly with clients (or customers). If machines and/or things interest you little and you have no expertise with them, then you would want to steer clear of related products, services, or manufacturing, or consider seeking a partner who has the needed skills. The highly creative person may be attracted to some special kind of venture that cuts across several business categories, or may seek to develop an entirely new product or service.

The Classic Decision-Making Model versus the Results-Oriented Model

Two methods of solving problems and making decisions are presented. The first is the classic seven-step management model. In Appendix B you will find forms that can help you move smoothly through the problem-solving process. Although these tools are recommended in subsequent chapters for making other decisions, they can aid you here in solving the initial problem; namely, what business you would do best in.

Notice how these seven steps apply to the action you should have been taking since the description of various enterprises was introduced in Chapter 3:

1. Write the problem statement. If you are seriously interested in operating a business of your own, or in helping others do so, the response here is, "Choose a business."
2. State the hypothesis or premise. Determine what kinds of enterprises generally seem to appeal to you. (This is the step you should have taken after exploring the many possibilities described in Chapter 3. If your list up to this point is long, don't worry. The next two steps result in reducing the number.)
3. Gather information. Collect "data" not only via your self-evaluation but also by comparing the results with reviewing the numerous subcategories of business (Chapter 3).
4. Identify a series of alternatives. With the results from your self-assessment, return to Step No. 2 to reduce the list to no more than 10 or 12 enterprises.
5. List the advantages and disadvantages of each alternative. Using the T-Chart in Appendix B, list the advantages and disadvantages you perceive for each type of enterprise. These lists should also reflect the results of your self-assessment exercises. (A T-Chart is so named simply because of its format in the shape of a "T.")
6. Prioritize alternatives. Rank your alternatives in order of preference.
7. Select two to four potential enterprises. Choose the highest on your prioritized list.

Another system for making decisions and improving the likelihood of success is called "management by objectives and results" (MBO/R). The first step is to visualize a positive goal, a desired result, as opposed to stating "a problem." Which of the two approaches described below do you think has the greater chance of stimulating positive action?

Joan is overweight. She's aware of her "problem," of course; not only do her family and some friends remind her, but her full-length mirror and the limited choice of clothes open to her confirm this fact. Concentrating on the problem, she half-heartedly attacks one fad diet after another, resenting the fact that she must curtail eating all of her favorite foods when some of her taller and skinnier friends freely consume all types of edibles. She feels sorry for herself, and her self-image sinks to ever new lows. To compensate for her lack of self-esteem, for the resentment she feels toward others, and especially for the long dreary days when no "fun" foods are there to make life worth living, Joan gives up and binges.

Joan may well have followed the problem-solving steps described above. She may have gathered such data as calorie-counting books, information about and the prices for joining weight-control and exercise clinics, low-cal recipes, and charts for logging weight loss. She may have brainstormed for ideas and analyzed and prioritized the possible ways of losing weight. But approaching the whole task negatively can bring disaster before she's half-way to her goal. She resists all the way. Little wonder she fails, not once but time after time until she gives up the effort. Compare this with the MBO/R system:

Marcia and Bill, although also overweight, take another approach. They envision a series of positive achievements they can expect if they successfully complete their plan. They will be able to: (1) wear a smaller size and have more choice in clothes; (2) feel healthy, have energy and stamina; (3) present a good image to family and friends; and (4) feel better about themselves.

The next step for the couple is to determine the difference between where they are now and where they want to be. (This is a positive approach to "stating the problem.") As well as gathering and analyzing data and prioritizing alternatives, they must establish a series of checkpoints, or sub-objectives, along a time line from "Now" to "Results" (see Figure 5.1).

Marcia and Bill launched their results-oriented program by continually reinforcing a positive self-image: "I can do it, I'm in control of my life." Like Joan, both sometimes strayed from their plan. But unlike her, they had allowed for an occasional deviation. Their checkpoints were realistic. Sometimes, upon reaching one of these interim goals, they found they had to step up—even renew—their efforts. Simultaneously, however, the recognizable compensating factors (each five- to seven-pound loss meant one clothes size smaller, increased energy and endurance, compliments from their friends) clearly indicated they were moving closer to the ultimate goal ("Result"). Each small achievement was thus a source of pleasure.

The decision-making tools given in Appendix B provide an additional opportunity to apply the MBO/R principles. The primary difference between the classic management model and this one is in the attitudes they promote. And from changed attitudes, behavior modification can readily follow.

OBJECTIVE:	
Question:	What ideal benefits/situation could result?
Answer:	Record under Results column below.
Question:	How will I know when I have "arrived"?
Answer:	Record measurable indicators in the Benchmark columns below.
Question:	When should the stated benchmarks be reached (along the continuum from Now to Results)?
Answer:	Record specific time(s) for checking progress in the spaces above each stated benchmark.
Question:	Where am I now?
Answer:	Record in the first column at the left below.

Now	Benchmarks Time Line						Results
							Finalizing Activity Result

FIGURE 5.1 MBO/R Planning Tool for Facilitative Management. Adapted from the concept of facilitative management, courtesy of the Center for Constructive Change, Durham N. H.

SUMMARY

Knowing who and where you are, where you are going, and where you want to be is the first step in conducting a self-assessment. Analyzing your past experiences helps you delineate your aptitudes, interests, hobbies, training, work experiences, familial influences, and past leadership roles. You should be able to discover whether you are primarily oriented toward machines, people, things, data, or a combination thereof. This self-assessment can help you decide

Between the training period and the operation phases of opening your own business, there is a great deal of planning that takes place.

whether you want to become an entrepreneur and, if so, what direction you might pursue with most success.

Problem-solving skills can apply to all areas of your life, but particularly to the business world, where the decisions you make can mean the difference between failure, mediocrity, and flourishing success. Applying the self-assessment and problem-solving tools now can initiate you into a structured decision-making process appropriate to many subsequent issues, whether in business or elsewhere.

ACTIVITIES AND EXERCISES

1. Use the MBO/R decision-making tools (see Appendix B) to chart the progression of the following case from "Now" to "Results." Compare your completed chart with others to see if your plan for Paul is realistic. That is, can it be achieved? Are the time lines associated with each objective realistic?

MINICASE

Paul Wilenga has conducted a self-assessment to determine if he has the potential to succeed as an entrepreneur. The business he would like to open is a tax-form preparation service. He has the motivation and desire. Since early youth he has been inclined toward entrepreneurial activities: he operated a lemonade stand outside a factory when he was eight, had a paper route in junior high school, and provided a gardening and caretaker service in high school. Paul is an only child.

He took bookkeeping in high school and worked part-time for his uncle, a public accountant, during his two years of community college, where he also studied accounting. Another part-time job in college gave him experience as a waiter and cashier. Sometimes he also served as assistant manager. These two jobs gave Paul an insider's view of many of the problems associated with running a business of one's own.

In assessing his weaknesses, Paul discovered he has little patience with irate customers and with employees who fail to take responsibility. He has given himself one year (from "Now") to get ready to open his business. Between now and then, his objectives include: (1) interviewing entrepreneurs of small businesses, particularly of those similar to the one he wishes to open; (2) reading books and articles on entrepreneurship, (3) seeking part-time work in a firm that specializes in preparing tax forms for the public, and (4) conducting a market feasibility study in his local community to see if the service company he wants to operate has a chance of succeeding.

One year from now Paul wants to open his doors for business. Using the objectives shown above, plot his progress on a time line from "Now" to "Result." Compare your chart with that of others and discuss. Make modifications, if appropriate.

1. Conduct a self-assessment, using the exercises and forms in Appendix A. Then use the decision-making models described in this chapter and the materials in Appendix B to select several potential businesses that most appeal to you at this time. Compare your results with those of your classmates to reinforce your understanding of how to use these tools in coordination with the self-assessment.
2. Interview two entrepreneurs and ask how they prepared themselves to start their own companies. How does the enterprise they selected relate to their educational background, vocational training, hobbies, and prior work experience? You may also want to ask for advice about getting started. Take note of the responses and use the T-Chart to record the advantages and disadvantages. Also record your observations and your reactions to the operations. Compare your findings with others in your group who have also conducted such interviews.

3. Read one or more books about positive self-concept, assertiveness, persuasiveness, success in entrepreneurship, etc. Abstract the salient points and prepare a book report or an oral report. Some recommended books are:

   Phyllis Chesler and Emily Jane Goodman, *Women, Money and Power* (New York: Morrow, 1976; Bantam paperback edition, 1977).
   Wayne W. Dyer, *Pulling Your Own Strings* (New York: Avon Books, 1979).
   Joe Girard, *How to Sell Yourself* (New York: Warner Books, 1979).
   Thomas A. Harris, *I'm OK—You're OK* (New York: Avon Books, 1969).
   Napoleon Hill, *Think and Grow Rich* (Greenwich, Conn.: Fawcett, 1960).
   Dorothy Jongeward and Dru Scott, *Women as Winners* (Reading, Mass.: Addison-Wesley, 1976).
   Michael Korda, *Power! How to Get It, How to Use It* (New York: Random House, 1975).
   Jess Lair, *I Ain't Much, Baby—But I'm All I've Got* (New York: Doubleday, 1969).

4. Research the lives of one or more successful entrepreneurs, by reading autobiographies and biographies or by arranging interviews with local business leaders. Try to find how these people compensated for their weaknesses, and how many of them failed at previous ventures, under what circumstances, and how often.

END-OF-UNIT CASE APPLICATIONS

See Projects 1 and 2 in *Stanley Junction*, the comprehensive case supplement.

NOTES

1. These qualities were those most often stated by the 250-plus entrepreneurs the author interviewed in preparing to write this book.
2. Kenneth R. VanVoorhis, *Entrepreneurship and Small Business Management* (Boston: Allyn and Bacon, Inc., 1980) pp. 22–25. See also Margaret Hennig and Anne Jardin, *The Managerial Woman* (New York: Doubleday and Co., 1976).
3. Rajeswararao Chaganti and Radharao Chaganti, "A Profile of Profitable and Not-So-Profitable Small Businesses," *Journal of Small Business Management,* July 1983, pp. 43–51.
4. "Making It," *Black Enterprise,* September 1983, p. 27.
5. Charles Gould, "Large Company or Small?" *National Business Employment Weekly,* January 12, 1982, p. 13.

6. "Surveys: Small Firms Can Breed Other Small Firms," *Inc.*, April 1982, p. 33.
7. Olive Church, *How to Succeed: Not Pushy, Just Friendly* (Laramie, Wy.: Jelm Mountain Press, 1980, p. 3).
8. Ibid.
9. Adapted from the "Management by Results" concept proposed by the Center for Constructive Change, a management consulting firm in Durham, N.H.

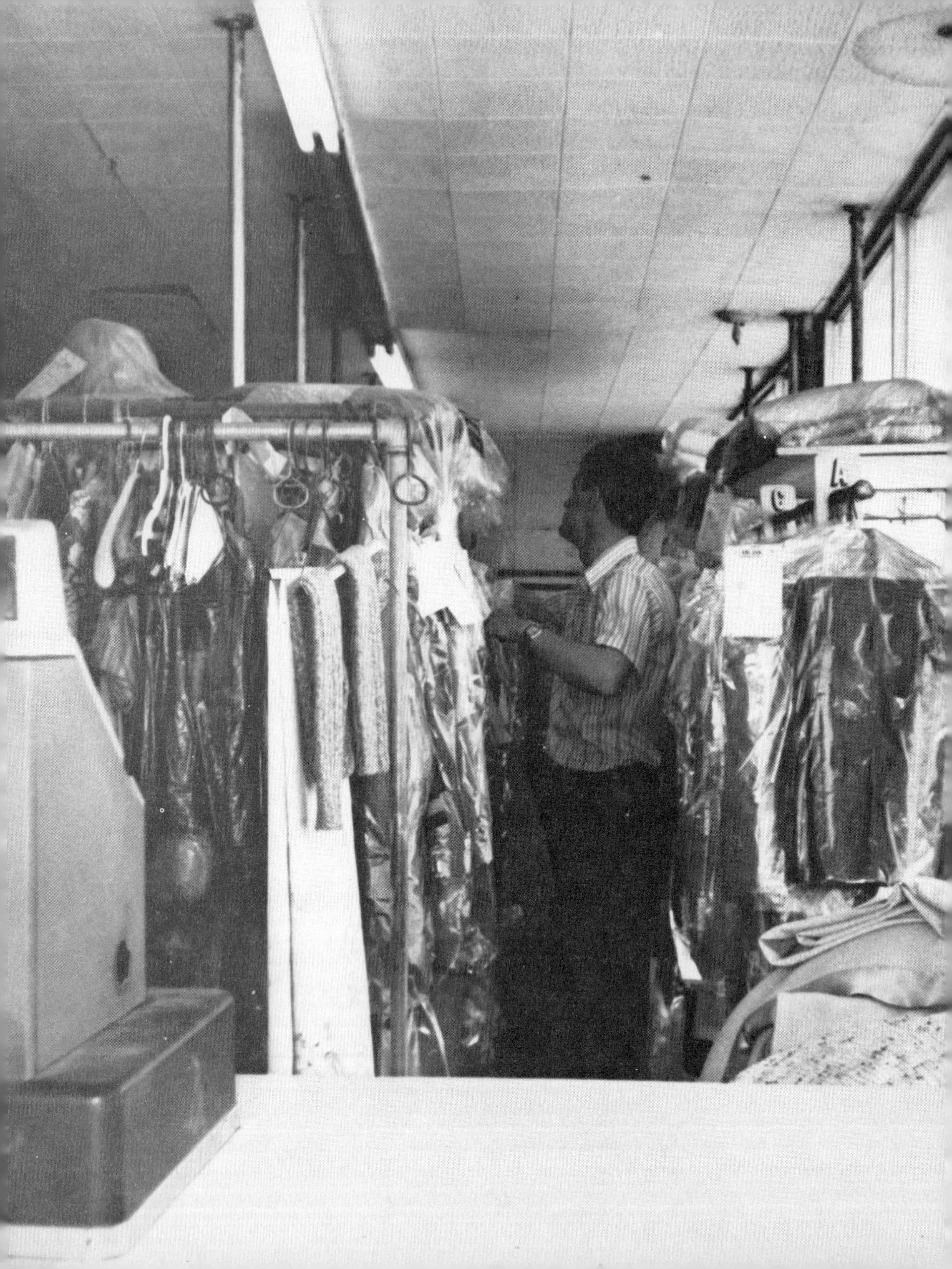

UNIT II

PLANNING THE SMALL BUSINESS

Management involves four steps, no matter what the activity or venture: planning, organizing, implementing, and controlling. Suppose you decide to have a party. The first step is to talk about and plan the event. Next, you organize to put the party into action; you send out invitations, order food and beverages, and arrange your house. Only after you have thoroughly planned and organized will you actually hold the party. The implementation occurs when you open the doors to receive guests and begin to put your plans and organization into action. At this point you also try to manage or control the affair, continually keeping an eye on everything that's happening, so as to make quick adjustments if needed.

Unit II opens with the preparation of a comprehensive business plan. This report can be used to attract financial backing, whether from bankers, investors, or family and friends. It is also, however, an important guideline for you as an entrepreneur, in planning where you want to go and how you're going to get there.

The unit then addresses other aspects of planning: how to conduct a market feasibility study; what criteria to use in selecting a location; how to plan and lay out the facilities; and how to purchase and place equipment, furniture, and tools. It will help you as well to select a legal structure for your business; to plan for staffing, if you anticipate hiring employees; and, finally, to establish pricing and credit policies.

PLEASE USE THESE
MACHINES
and the two on the opposite side.
FOR EXTRA DIRTY

chapter 6

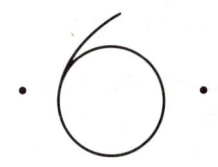

The Comprehensive Business Plan

Objectives

1. Explain the importance of a business plan for businesses of any size.

2. List the key sections (table of contents) of a comprehensive business plan.

3. Start developing a business plan for a hypothetical company of your choice.

PURPOSE AND STRUCTURE OF THE BUSINESS PLAN

The business plan provides a clear blueprint of where you are going and how you are going to get there. It can help you determine whether a company is likely to produce a reasonable income against expenditures and when it should pass the break-even point and become a going enterprise. The plan can form the basis for presentations to bankers from whom you may want to borrow money or to individuals and firms from whom you wish to entice investments (or "venture capital").

You can also use the plan to persuade suppliers to grant you credit and to convince prospective customers of the credibility of your company. Its formal development indicates that you know what you're talking about and that you mean business. Indeed, the comprehensive business plan is your key selling tool to the world until you can stand on your own financial feet, a script for what you hope and believe you can accomplish. It tells who, what, why, when—and how much! The toughest question you'll have to answer during the organizational start-up phase, whether it is asked by bankers, suppliers, customers, or even your own conscience, is: "What have you got to offer in the marketplace that is better than or different from what established firms are already offering?"

Eventually you should list your assets and needs; estimate your earnings and your start-up and continuing operational costs; and prepare formal financial papers based on these estimates. You should then have a pretty clear idea of the capital needed to get your company off and running.

The formal prospectus covers these topics, which constitute its table of contents:

1. Your résumé and background.
2. The company's purposes: what it is and what it will do.
3. An assessment of the competition and of how your company will match or beat it (see Chapter 7).
4. The company's legal structure (see Chapter 10) and its organization chart, if any.
5. Objectives and schedules: where you are going and how long it should take to get there, including short- and long-range goals and plans for growth and expansion.
6. Marketing strategy: pricing, quality, service, and distribution.
7. Location and facilities, including a list of the estimated costs of fixtures, furniture, and equipment (see Chapters 8 and 9).
8. The potential risks of the particular business, industry, or locale, and how you plan to cope with them (see Chapters 2 and 13).
9. Staffing and personnel management, when and if employees are hired (see Chapters 10 and 19).
10. Accounting and recordkeeping and mode of operation(s) (see Chapters 14 and 15).

11. Financial data:
    a. Statement of assets
    b. Earnings forecast
    c. Estimated expenses—fixed versus variable
    d. Credit and collection policies, if needed
    e. Finance (capital) requirements.

CREATING A BUSINESS PLAN

The Company's Purpose and Goals

The firm's products or services must be appropriate to the needs or wants of customers. (The marketing feasibility study should establish this for the selected community.) Customers must also be attracted to the goods or services offered. Retail customers, for example, have a wide range of needs, including, among others, type, style, size, color, price, and quality.

You should clearly state what the parameters of your enterprise will be. Corinne McGrady might have begun her business plan by giving the name of her company and then describing its purpose: "Leading producer of see-through cookbook stands. . . . The company plans to create, produce, and distribute these durable plastic stands at a price to attract consumers via retail stores and mail order."[1]

This one statement mentions both price and quality ("durable") and explains how the product will be marketed (via distribution to retail stores and/or by mail order). Note that McGrady also describes her business as a "leading producer." From the discussion of McGrady's company in Chapter 3, we know that competitors tried to "borrow" her design. This, along with the marketing research she conducted, justified McGrady's prediction that her company will be a leading manufacturer (especially as it may be the only producer!).

Consider this description of a retail firm: "The Hello Balloon Company, located in a shopping mall serving thousands of customers daily, will favorably compete with greeting cards and party favors to provide customers with a unique but inexpensive option. No other company sells individually decorated balloons in this city, but metro-marketing studies in like communities have proved that such businesses are readily accepted."

After this statement of purpose, another few specific goal-oriented sentences may follow. For example: "The company forecasts that it will be making a 12% net profit by the fourth quarter of operation, having obtained 15% of the market by that time. Revenues should also increase 10% annually for years two and three."

Although such forecasts logically demand expansion elsewhere in the business plan, this specificity mentioned initially should catch the attention of its intended readers. Money people (bankers, investors, suppliers, etc.) are impressed with descriptions and with specific but succinct facts and figures upon which they can base a decision.

Assessment of the Competition

The marketing survey should provide specifics about the competition, whether on the local, regional or national level (see Chapter 7). National statistics are appropriate to cite where the intended market is broad, as it often is for extraction, manufacturing, and distribution companies. Even for establishments that will focus their offerings locally, however, mention of research conducted elsewhere is sometimes appropriate. Note that in the purpose statement of the Hello Balloon Company the entrepreneur alludes to this factor: "metro-marketing studies in like communities have proved that such businesses are readily accepted." This portion of the business plan should not only focus on the scope of competition and perhaps name specific local companies, but it should reveal how your company's products or services will effectively compete. Will you be offering innovative features, better or new service and parts, entrepreneurial expertise, lower price, or better quality?

Consider, too, that the existing competition may be inadequate to meet consumer demand. Your marketing survey, for instance, may have determined that there are not enough drugstores in the community to serve the population (it takes approximately 4500 people to support one drugstore).

You can also use tables, charts or graphics to portray the significant advantages your company has over others in the field and/or community. Not only does the marketing survey contribute specific facts and figures for the development of this topic, but it can also give you more accurate data with which to forecast earnings.

Whether you plan to introduce new products or products similar to those already available in the market, your marketing survey can describe trends and growth patterns in associated industries. There you will want to elaborate on the sales and success that others have already obtained.

When Paula Nelson proposed starting Cortrex, a company that would produce and distribute audiocassettes about topics in business and finance, she explained that the cassette field "promises rapid growth" and that "the sales of cassettes have leaped from 5 million in 1966 to (approximately) 200 million ten years later." She cited such companies as Time-Life, whose tape division had an estimated sales volume of $2 million a year, and the Success Motivation Institute, with an annual sales volume estimated at $12 million.[2]

Nolan Bushnell invented the first videogame, "Pong," in 1972. Imagine the sales pitch he must have made, particularly when trying to describe the "existing competition." (Four years later he sold his company, Atari, to Warner Communications for $28 million, justifying his belief that the product would do well despite emerging competition!)[3]

You might also discuss how you intend to deal with potential competition. This discussion may also appear later, under the topic of "Coping with Potential Risks." Your decision on where to include the issue may depend on how extensive the current competition is and therefore on how important it is to delineate your strategy.

Legal Structure

If your enterprise is to be a sole proprietorship, then this section of the plan can be relatively short. You should outline your expertise, such as your education and training and your work experience. Your family background may be pertinent if it exposed you to the ownership and operation of a business.

With a partnership structure, you should describe both the capital and the skills that each partner will be bringing to the company. Although you need not attach the contract (the Articles of Partnership), its salient points should be mentioned. Describe the duties of each partner, how profits and losses will be shared, the restraints if any to be imposed on each partner, and how the partnership can be terminated (see Chapter 10).

If you are opening a franchise, describe the parent firm and its associated provisions—e.g., national advertising, ready customer acceptance of the brand-name product or service, and financial and/or management support—emphasizing how these will contribute to the success of the franchise. Have the contract with the franchiser at hand in case the potential investors wish to learn more (see Chapter 4).

You may attach the proposed articles of incorporation to the business plan. This section may give such pertinent data as the names and addresses of the officers, the duration of the corporation, the amount of capital stock to be issued, and the voting rights of the stockholders.

Organization chart. If you are going to be hiring employees, you need to construct an organization chart. When more than one person is involved in a business—whether as partners, corporate officers, or employees—a chart can clearly delineate duties, either by company function or department.

Figure 6.1 shows an organization chart for a business run by three partners with six employees. Figure 6.2 gives the chart of a corporation whose structure and nature entail several operations, with related functions.

Objectives and Schedules

To interest investors or stockholders, you should clearly indicate the company's potential for income, profits, and dividends. Venture capitalists, in particular, will be interested in these. Mention the type, prices, and quality of the products and cite realistic, quantitative objectives for each that contribute to and expand the central purpose and goals.

Automobile Sales and Service

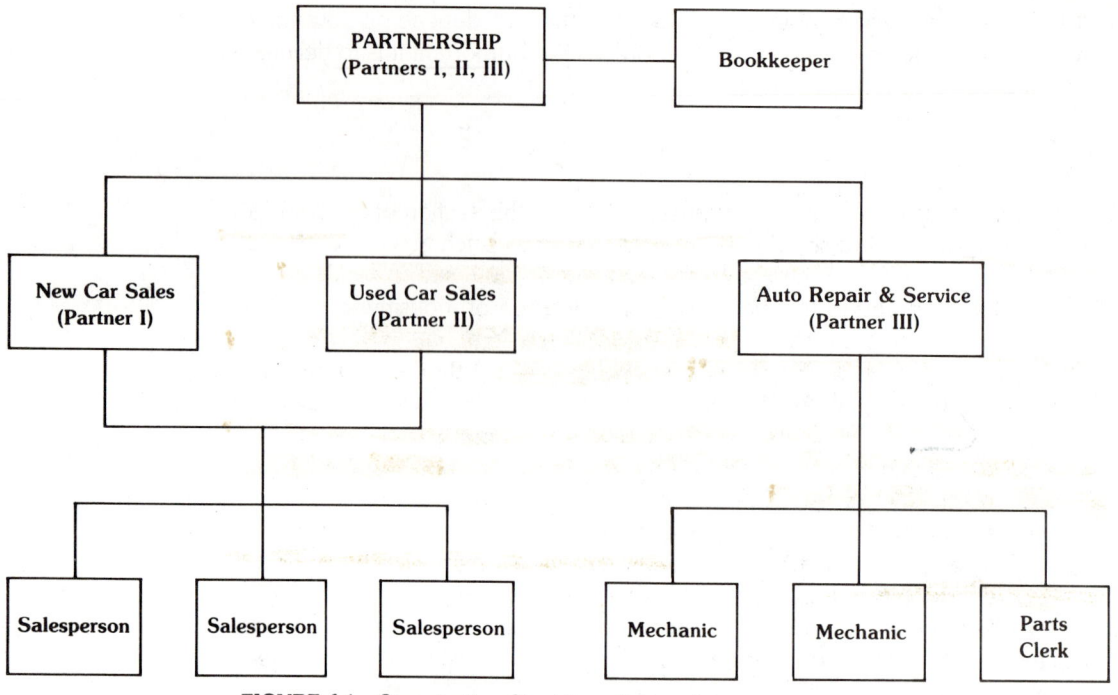

```
                    ┌─────────────────┐       ┌─────────────┐
                    │   PARTNERSHIP   │───────│  Bookkeeper │
                    │(Partners I,II,III)│     └─────────────┘
                    └────────┬────────┘
         ┌───────────────────┼───────────────────┐
┌────────┴────────┐ ┌────────┴────────┐ ┌────────┴────────┐
│ New Car Sales   │ │ Used Car Sales  │ │Auto Repair & Svc│
│  (Partner I)    │ │  (Partner II)   │ │  (Partner III)  │
└────────┬────────┘ └────────┬────────┘ └────────┬────────┘
         │          ┌────────┼────────┐    ┌─────┼──────┐
    ┌────┴────┐ ┌───┴────┐┌──┴─────┐    ┌──┴──┐┌─┴───┐┌─┴────┐
    │Salesper.│ │Salespr.││Salespr.│    │Mech.││Mech.││Parts │
    │         │ │        ││        │    │     ││     ││Clerk │
    └─────────┘ └────────┘└────────┘    └─────┘└─────┘└──────┘
```

FIGURE 6.1 Organization Chart for a Partnership

    Although most people would say that profit is their primary objective, your company may promise to benefit not only yourself as owner but also the customers and the business community—even perhaps society or the environment. For instance, you would perform a valuable service to a community that has no pharmacies by opening one. (Even if you are not a pharmacist, you could hire one or bring one in as a partner.)

    In this and similar situations, then, one of your stated objectives could be "To provide health care and aid to customers in a community now lacking adequate products and services." The owner of a light, clean manufacturing industry may stress that it will not harm the environment, or may propose creating an attractive industrial park. That industry could thus increase the community's ability to attract other companies while maintaining a healthful environment.

    A firm that would hire a number of workers at the outset, such as an extraction, manufacturing/processing, or distribution company, offers an objective of another type. The owner can promise an important community benefit: "The firm will need from 20 to 30 workers initially, thus providing jobs for local residents."

XYZ Manufacturing Company

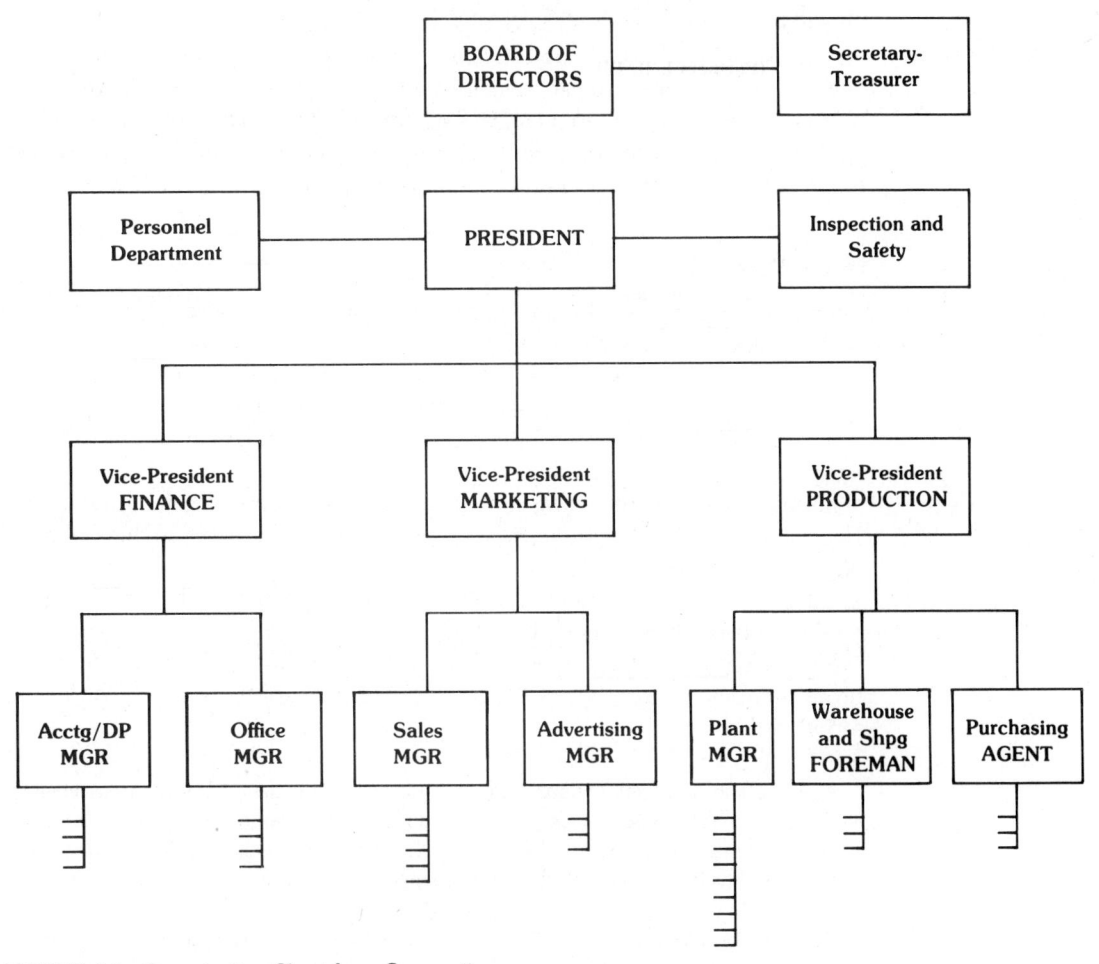

FIGURE 6.2 Organization Chart for a Corporation

You might address such topics as (1) the intended market—young people, senior citizens, business firms, do-it-yourselfers, householders, hobbyists, people interested in self-improvement, the general public, etc.; (2) sales forecasts and how the anticipated volume can be achieved to offset projected expenditures; and (3) long-range plans for growth and expansion (such as hiring more workers; changing the legal structure from a sole proprietorship or a partnership to a corporation; and raising additional capital by selling stock).

Draw up a schedule for those of your objectives that can be achieved by gradual steps. You can use the MBO/R chart in Appendix B. First state a clear-cut objective, then determine where you want to be and at what time. Assign checkpoints to measure your progress along the continuum from "Now" to "Results." Finally, assign a reasonable time in which to reach each checkpoint. Fill out one chart for each objective.

It would not be appropriate to include this series of MBO/R charts in a business plan designed to present to financial backers and others. They are an aid to help you forecast what results you should obtain by when. From this analysis you can draw succinct statements to accompany your discussion of objectives.

Marketing Strategy

Although you must do a great deal of planning before designing a marketing strategy, you should avoid lengthy detail in your business plan. The descriptive data you need to support this section can be derived from an analysis of the specific price/cost factors discussed in the financial section below.

It's important to indicate to prospective financial backers that you will have revenue coming in as quickly as possible.

In describing her marketing strategies for her educational/training tapes, Ms. Nelson wrote: "To bridge the normal, non-income-producing months of initial operation, Cortrex has begun negotiations with a cassette-producing firm to distribute a number of their tapes and allow Cortrex to realize substantial sales by the third month of operation."

Ms. Nelson then listed a number of subjects on which Cortrex planned to produce tapes. To emphasize the probable salability of these tapes, she further reported that:

> Cortrex is in final negotiations with an author who, it believes, brings great versatility to Cortrex. The author was previously director of personnel training for a leading financial institution. . . . Other authors have been tentatively selected for specific topics but will not be approached until financing for the company has been concluded.

The marketing strategy must also clearly indicate how you plan to tap the critical market. Thus Ms. Nelson continued:

> Cortrex will use both direct-mail campaigns and space advertising. For the business tapes, four-part direct-mail pieces will be sent to small and middle-sized companies. . . . It will arrange with other companies to distribute Cortrex's cassette programs when they become available. . . . These companies will afford Cortrex a highly trained, professional concept sales force to market its products.[4]

Production cost factors and schedules should also be described; e.g.:

> A recording studio in Los Angeles will be selected to produce the master tapes. We do not anticipate doing our own in-house tape duplication until the fourth month, at which time the volume will warrant the purchase of a cassette duplicator. . . . The price difference between in-house duplication and outside duplication is approximately 20 cents per tape, or 15 percent.[5]

Obviously, a small, local company will not need to provide data on national distribution or production techniques. However, both the costs of operation and the price(s) established must be clearly presented, along with the advertising and sales plan. Using a few facts and figures here helps establish that your planning and forecasting are realistically conceived.

Location and Facilities

If negotiations are in progress for one or more possible sites, attach pictures and/or layout(s) to the plan. Otherwise, describe what you estimate your needs will be in this area. The worksheet given as Figure 6.3 is designed to help you analyze the specific needs of a retail business; you can add to it items appropriate to service, extraction, manufacturing, or distribution firms, if you plan to open one of these. Later you will insert the estimated totals from Figure 6.3 into the overall financial plan (Figure 6.7).

Plan for Coping with Potential Risks

Chapters 2 and 13 discuss the risks you may encounter in business. Decide which of these risks you will probably face in your selected enterprise, noting as well the recommendations for coping with such contingencies.

Apple Computer, Inc., pioneered the manufacture of personal computers, but by the early 1980s, Tandy Corporation's Radio Shack TRS-80 was sharing the

Leave out or add items to suit your business. Use separate sheets to list exactly what you need for each of the items below.	If you plan to pay cash in full, enter the full amount below and in the last column.	If you are going to pay by installments, fill out the columns below. Enter in the last column your down payment plus at least one installment.			Estimate of the cash you need for furniture, fixtures, and equipment
		Price	Down payment	Amount of each installment	
Counters	$	$	$	$	$
Storage shelves, cabinets					
Display stands, shelves, tables					
Cash register					
Safe					
Window display fixtures					
Special lighting					
Outside sign					
Delivery equipment if needed					
TOTAL FURNITURE, FIXTURES, AND EQUIPMENT					$

Source: U.S. Small Business Administration.

FIGURE 6.3 Worksheet for Estimating Costs of Furniture, Fixtures, and Equipment. This worksheet can be submitted as an exhibit in the business plan (see Chapter 9 before completing this worksheet).

market lead with Apple (each had approximately 23 percent of the market). According to Apple's executive vice-president, A. C. Markkula, "We foresaw this (encroaching competition) when we wrote our business plan." Later, Apple projected a hefty $15 million expenditure (close to 5 percent of sales) for marketing and promotion to combat the competition. It further planned to maintain an innovative edge in research and development. In line with this decision, the R&D budget climbed from $3.6 million in 1979 to $27 million just two years later.[6]

Staffing and Personnel Management

Refer here to your organization chart, if you have one. You can also state the number of workers you will hire, the functions they will perform, and the qualifications they will need. It is not necessary to include complete job descriptions in the plan, although you can mention that they have been developed. Figure 6.4 gives a sample job description. Estimated salaries should also be entered in the financial worksheet, Figure 6.7.

Accounting and Recordkeeping System

Underlying the presentation of your marketing strategy and your financial data should be a description of the accounting system. Chapter 14 should give you some idea of what business and office functions are required in order to effectively manage information and make business decisions.

Financial Data

The heart of the prospectus is the financial papers you will include. Everything else is preamble, introduction, verbiage.

Earnings forecast. Data for the earnings forecast will come in part from the marketing survey (Chapter 7). You can also draw on interviews and observations of related enterprises in the selected community and elsewhere. (See Figure 6.5.)

The earnings forecast computes and subtracts the anticipated expenditures from the anticipated income to derive a gross profit. From that figure it then subtracts the operating or general and accounting (G&A) expenses to determine net profit before taxes. It may not be easy to make the initial projection of earnings. You must be realistic, however; prospective backers know that a new company isn't going to take off like a rocket in its first year of operation.

Sometimes they do, however. In 1978 the two-year-old Apple Computer company forecast $100 million in sales by the end of the following year. Not only did Apple reach its 1979 goal, but it went on to post a 43,154 percent gain over a five-year period (from $774,000 sales in 1977 to $334,783,000 in 1981)! Had cofounders Steve Jobs and Stephen Wozniak presented these figures in their initial forecast, who would have believed them?[7]

Title of Job Desk Clerk
Level of Job Level I
Department Front Desk

SUMMARY OF JOB: The person holding this job acts as a host/hostess to greet new arrivals, respond to their requests, and answer their questions. A general knowledge of office procedures would be helpful, since this job requires working with business forms and machines.

DUTIES OF JOB:

Most Frequent Duties: (Comprising at least 90 percent of work)

1. Greeting new arrivals and assigning rooms
2. Making reservations at other Ramada Inns for traveling customers
3. Receiving reservations from other Ramada Inns and the general public
4. Checking customers out by adding tab amounts to master folio and ringing up folio on cash register
5. Answering calls from outside the Inn and transferring those calls to the correct party
6. Answering questions about services, sightseeing, travel conditions, or other topics

Least Frequent Duties: (Comprising not more than 10 percent of work)

1. Open or route all incoming mail and post all outgoing mail
2. Sell postcards or souvenirs from the display cases
3. Make copies of correspondence or folios for office use

TOOLS AND EQUIPMENT USED:

Typewriter, reservation computer keyboard, cash register, telephone switchboard, file cabinet, reservations printer

FORMS AND REPORTS USED ON JOB:

Folios (both room customers and tabs from lounge and restaurant), telephone message forms, reservation computer printout

QUALIFICATIONS:

Education
Job holder must have knowledge of motel operations or be quick to learn. Also must have a high-school education or equivalent

Experience
Job holder needs no former experience in motel or office work but this knowledge would be helpful

SUPERVISED BY: General Manager or Senior Desk Clerk

RELATION TO OTHER JOBS: This is an entry-level position, which may lead to any other higher position in the organization, provided any knowledge/experience qualifcations are met.

FIGURE 6.4
Sample Job Description. If several employees are to be hired, it is appropriate to develop formal job descriptions and to include one as a sample in the business plan.

**FIGURE 6.5
Sample Earnings
Forecast.** An earnings forecast modeled after this style should be included in the financial papers of the business plan.

VICENTE FLOWER SHOP

Sales		$40,000
Costs of Goods and Services		
Wholesale purchase of inventory	$ 7,000	
Wages	15,000	
Operation, 2 delivery trucks	3,000	
Total Cost of Goods and Services		25,000
Gross Profit		$15,000
Operating Expenses		
Rent	$4,000	
Utilities	1,300	
Shop equipment	750	
Insurance	700	
Advertising	800	
Supplies	550	
Total Operating Expenses		8,100
Income before Taxes		$6,900
Income Taxes		2,300
Estimated Net Income or Profit		4,600

In her earnings forecast, Paula Nelson projected a gross profit (the difference between sales and cost of sales) of $102,161. Offsetting this was a total of $125,541 in G&A expenses—salaries and fees, rent, phone and utilities, postage, travel, office supplies, insurance, and contingencies. Thus she forecast a net loss of $23,380 for the first year of operation. This she described as "modest under the circumstances, but realistic when you consider the fact that I planned to keep operating expenses to a minimum." The next two years of Ms. Nelson's forecast "reflected a more cheerful attitude." It ran as follows:[8]

	Year 2	Year 3
Net sales	$370,000	$585,000
Cost of sales	144,000	222,000
Gross margins	226,000	363,000
Selling and G&A expense	178,000	282,000
Net profit before taxes	48,000	81,000
Income taxes	18,000	34,000
Net earnings	$ 30,000	$ 47,000

Tables 6.1 and 6.2 will help you understand the basis of Ms. Nelson's calculations.

The statement of assets. This statement describes your current financial capability. Here you list your savings and the funds available to you from other

TABLE 6.1 Reasons for Lower Earnings after Taxes

REASONS FOR LOWER EARNINGS	Construction	Manufacturing	Transportation	Wholesale	Retail	Agriculture	Financial Services	Nonprofessional Services	Professional Services	Number of Firms	Percentage of Firms
Sales volume	52%	71%	54%	54%	59%	22%	37%	45%	41%	477	53%
Labor costs	8	4	7	4	5	*	8	4	11	49	5
Cost of materials	7	14	11	11	10	16	8	17	11	100	11
Availability of materials	*	*	*	1	*	*	*	1	*	2	*
Higher prices for product or service	1	1	4	*	2	6	*	1	*	13	1
Unusual profit on inventories	14	2	7	7	5	13	16	4	5	67	7
Usual seasonal change	5	2	7	4	9	26	6	13	12	76	9
Other	9	4	7	16	6	15	20	8	20	86	10
No answer	4	2	3	3	4	2	5	7	*	34	4
Total	100%	100%	100%	100%	100%	100%	100%	100%	100%		100%
Number of firms[1] (October 1982)	108	119	28	96	293	51	62	91	56	904	

[1] Includes firms for which no industrial classification was ascertained.
* Less than 0.5%
Courtesy: National Federation of Independent Business (NFIB), *Quarterly Report*, October 1982

sources (i.e., a second mortgage on your house), plus equity capital—everything that indicates your net worth (assets equal liabilities plus capital).

Assets include both current and fixed assets. Current assets are those you do not anticipate holding for long, such as cash and other liquid items. Fixed assets are long-term holdings, such as real property, etc.

Liabilities are debts and notes payable that are likely to be long-term; e.g., a mortgage. The difference between the value of the assets and the value of the liabilities is the capital. (See Figure 6.6.)

Estimated expenses. The Small Business Administration has designed a worksheet (Figure 6.7) that can help you predict how much cash you'll need to get started and to keep operating until the company becomes profitable.

Credit and collection policies. If the company plans to operate on a cash basis only, then this data is not needed. Otherwise, you must allow for a negative cash flow in the beginning, and later for collections and bad debts. Also describe your system for accepting credit customers (see Chapter 11).

TABLE 6.2 Reasons for Higher Earnings after Taxes

INDUSTRY

REASONS FOR HIGHER EARNINGS	Construction	Manufacturing	Transportation	Wholesale	Retail	Agriculture	Financial Services	Nonprofessional Services	Professional Services	Number of Firms	Percent of Firms
Sales Volume	51%	62%	56%	56%	48%	20%	42%	55%	31%	161	50%
Labor Costs	2	7	*	3	5	*	3	2	*	12	4
Cost of Materials	4	*	*	3	3	*	3	*	*		2
Availability of Materials	*	*	*	3	*	*	3	*	*	2	1
Higher Prices for Product or Service	9	4	11	7	11	20	13	13	19	33	10
Unusual Profit on Inventories	*	*	*	3	*	*	*	2	*	2	1
Usual Seasonal Change	32	18	33	21	28	40	16	20	12	76	24
Other	*	9	*	4	3	20	17	8	32	22	7
No Answer	2	*	*	*	2	*	3	*	6	5	1
Total	100%	100%	100%	100%	100%	100%	100%	100%	100%		100%
Number of Firms[1] (October 1982)	53	45	9	29	92	5	31	40	16	320	

[1] Includes firms for which no industrial classification was ascertained.
* Less than 0.5%
Courtesy: National Federation of Independent Business (NFIB), *Quarterly Report*, October 1982.

Financial requirements. This is the bottom line, the difference between where you are now financially and where you need to be to get started and to realize the company's goals. Paula Nelson's introduction to this section read:

> As the financial forecasts show, Cortrex requires capital of $250,000 to realize its program. For this equity investment, the Company is prepared to issue 40 percent of its common stock to the investment group. The additional financing required to realize the expansion goals will be supplied from profits earned and bank credit which should be available to the Company after its first year of operation. The earnings forecast projects an efficient operation run with extreme frugality. Capital expenditures will be minimized at the outset in order to preserve the Company's capital.[9]

Note that this chapter's discussion of developing a business plan is introductory only. You will have the opportunity to continue the refining and updating of this plan as you complete Unit II on planning and Unit III on organizing.

```
┌─────────────────────────────────────────────────────────┐
│                   (name of person)                       │
│                   (current date)                         │
│   Assets                                                 │
│       Cash in bank                      $____            │
│       Real estate (appraised value)     ____             │
│       Furniture (current worth)         ____             │
│       Car (trade-in value)              ____             │
│       Accounts payable (owed you)       ____             │
│       Notes payable (same, long-term)   ____             │
│       Life insurance (cash value)       ____             │
│       Annuities (cash value)            ____             │
│       Other assets (cash value)         ____             │
│       Securities (stocks and bonds)     ____             │
│           Total Assets                  $ ____           │
│                                                          │
│   Liabilities                                            │
│       Bills payable                     $ ____           │
│       Unpaid mortgage                   ____             │
│       Notes and loans payable           ____             │
│       Other debts                       ____             │
│           Total Liabilities             $ ____           │
│       Total Assets (taken from above)         $ ____     │
│       Subtract total liabilities (from above) ____       │
│           Net worth                           $ ____     │
└─────────────────────────────────────────────────────────┘
```

FIGURE 6.6 Statement of Assets and Liabilities. This is another financial paper that bankers and other financiers look for in the business plan.

The Format of the Prospectus

Can you fit all this information into 12 to 15 pages? Your first draft may well be much longer. But to gain attention and a ready perusal, it must be not only clear and factual but also succinct. Edit out any flowery verbiage or merely "nice-to-know" discussions to leave the document "lean and clean."

Remember that the prospectus represents you: it's your selling tool. This means it should give an excellent impression of you and of the investment

**FIGURE 6.7
Financial Planning Worksheet.** This worksheet can be developed during Unit II and is refined with the completion of Unit III.

ESTIMATED MONTHLY EXPENSES			
Item	Your estimate of monthly expenses based on sales of $ _____ per year	Your estimate of how much cash you need to start your business (See column 3.)	What to put in column 2 (These figures are typical for one kind of business; you will have to decide how many months to allow for in your business.)
	Column 1	Column 2	Column 3
Salary of owner-manager	$	$	2 times column 1
All other salaries and wages			3 times column 1
Rent			3 times column 1
Advertising			3 times column 1
Delivery expense			3 times column 1
Supplies			3 times column 1
Telephone and telegraph.			3 times column 1
Other utilities			3 times column 1
Insurance			Payment required by insurance company
Taxes, including Social Security			4 times column 1
Interest			3 times column 1
Maintenance			3 times column 1
Legal and other professional fees			3 times column 1
Miscellaneous			3 times column 1
STARTING COSTS YOU ONLY HAVE TO PAY ONCE			Leave column 2 blank
Fixtures and equipment			Fill in Figure 6.3 and put the total here
Decorating and remodeling			Talk it over with a contractor
Installation of fixtures and equipment			Talk to suppliers
Starting inventory			Suppliers will probably help you estimate this
Deposits with public utilities			Find out from utilities companies
Legal and other professional fees			Lawyer, accountant, and so on
Licenses and permits			Find out from city offices what you have to have
Advertising and promotion for opening			Estimate what you'll use
Accounts receivable			What you need to buy more stock until credit customers pay
Cash			For unexpected expenses or losses, special purchases, etc.
Other			Make a separate list and enter total
TOTAL ESTIMATED CASH YOU NEED TO START WITH		$	Add up all the numbers in column 2

Source: U.S. Small Business Administration

opportunity you are offering. It should be professionally typed and photocopied. Begin with a title page, followed by a short summary (under one page) and a table of contents. Then comes the body of the report with financial pages at the end. Supporting documents can be supplied as appendices or mentioned (at the relevant point in the document) as "available upon request."

There should not be a single error, whether in spelling, grammar, punctuation, typing, or arithmetic calculations. Bind the report in an attractive cover, preferably black.

SELLING AND PERSUADING

Unless you have all the capital you need to open your business and to keep it going for the first few months, plus sufficient funds on which to live, you will need to sell your idea, the comprehensive business plan, to potential financial backers. The ability to sell yourself and your ideas continues to be important throughout the operation, of course. It is the foundation for marketing products and services, for publicizing your business, and for motivating employees to perform and customers to buy.

Why do so many people shrink from such public contacts as selling or from trying to persuade others? Many people claim they are not "sales-oriented," despite their desire to become entrepreneurs. Yet a key ability of the successful entrepreneur is a talent for selling, persuading, motivating, and negotiating.

At least two reasons lie behind this shyness. The first is fear of rejection—of one's self or of one's ideas, products, or services. The second is lack of experience. But, just as with any motor skill (coordinating mind with eyes and hands), practice makes perfect. With repetition comes experience, together with the confidence that one can cope (also see Chapter 5 and Appendix A).

All this "selling" often comes under other labels, to be sure, whether with the positive connotation of "persuasion" or the negative one of "manipulation." Selling is, in fact, both persuasion and motivation. We continually seek agreement and acceptance from others and, typically, try to incite them to some type of definitive action.

Most people will willingly share good news or bad with their friends, and even with an occasional stranger. When we are convinced of the goodness of something—up to and including the products or services we are offering and our own abilities and ideas—to tell others about it is no more than a form of sharing—"selling" with no bad connotations.

Your idea or plan must be positive and convincing, but even then it may be rejected. You may not have presented it clearly or enticingly enough. Whether you use a soft-sell or a hard-sell approach, the people you contact may need time to consider, to weigh alternatives.

Lack of experience also accounts for many anxieties. If you have never approached a banker for a loan or an investor for funds, you don't know what to expect, beyond what you have read or heard from associates. The same is true with selling or, for that matter, with any new experience.

To sell ideas, you need self-confidence. Having a complete written plan for presentation should help to alleviate some of the fears most neophyte entrepreneurs experience.

SUMMARY

Even if you don't need to seek large-scale financing, it's a smart idea to develop a business plan. It will serve not only as a prospectus for anyone you hope to interest in the venture but, equally important, it provides a clear blueprint for your own progress and self-analysis. In short, every business needs a plan! Once you have developed the plan, your reinforced belief in your potential enterprise and your ability to make it succeed should help you sell it to others.

ACTIVITIES AND EXERCISES

1. Arrange to visit one or more companies that appeal to you or are most familiar. Ask the entrepreneurs how much planning they did before starting the business. What were their plans for:

finance	location
marketing	equipment and supplies
competition	advertising and sales strategy
production	personnel
automation	records system

2. You will begin preparing your business plan now. By collecting data and making planning decisions throughout Unit II, you will be able to complete the first draft by the end of Chapter 11. The following guidelines apply to the draft when submitted in addition to the suggestions given in the chapter about format.

   Write the report, with underlined headings for each topic. Follow the guidelines given in the section on prospectus format above. Tables, charts, and graphics are appropriate for some topics and may be included in the body of the report if pertinent and brief. Otherwise, put these supporting documents in the appendices. Limit the final edited report to a maximum of 15 pages, exclusive of attachments.

   A proposed table of contents follows, with notations about where to obtain data.

   A. Introduction—brief overview
      1. Expertise and experience of the entrepreneur (résumé, prepare now)
      2. Goals (prepare now)
      3. Competition (see checklists in Chapter 7)
      4. Legal Structure and Staffing, with organization chart (see Chapter 10)
   B. Objectives and Schedules (prepare now and refine later)
   C. Marketing Strategy (see checklists in Chapter 7)
   D. Location and Facilities (see checklists in Chapters 8 and 9)
   E. Financial Data
      1. Balance Sheet—statement of personal assets and liabilities (prepare now)
      2. Earnings forecast (prepare and revise throughout Unit II)
      3. Estimated expenses (see worksheets and revise after Chapter 11)
      4. Credit and collection policies (see Chapter 11)
      5. Financial needs (finalize at the end of Chapter 11)

GETTING STARTED

Your building
  Have you found a good building for your store? ___
  Will you have enough room when your business gets bigger? ___
  Can you fix the building the way you want it without spending too much money? ___
  Can people get to it easily from parking spaces, bus stops, or their homes? ___
  Have you had a lawyer check the lease and zoning? ___

Equipment and supplies
  Do you know just what equipment and supplies you need and how much they will cost? (Worksheet 1 and the lists you made for it should show this.) ___
  Can you save some money by buying secondhand equipment? ___

Your merchandise
  Have you decided what things you will sell? ___
  Do you know how much or how many of each you will buy to open your store with? ___
  Have you found suppliers who will sell you what you need at a good price? ___
  Have you compared the prices and credit terms of different suppliers? ___

Your records
  Have you planned a system of records that will keep track of your income and expenses, what you owe other people, and what other people owe you? ___
  Have you worked out a way to keep track of your inventory so that you will always have enough on hand for your customers but not more than you can sell? ___
  Have you figured out how to keep your payroll records and take care of tax reports and payments? ___

Can you make decisions?
  ☐ I can make up my mind in a hurry if I have to. It usually turns out O.K., too.
  ☐ I can if I have plenty of time. If I have to make up my mind fast, I think later I should have decided the other way.
  ☐ I don't like to be the one who has to decide things.

Can people trust what you say?
  ☐ You bet they can. I don't say things I don't mean.
  ☐ I try to be on the level most of the time, but sometimes I just say what's easiest.
  ☐ Why bother if the other fellow doesn't know the difference?

Can you stick with it?
  ☐ If I make up my mind to do something, I don't let *anything* stop me.
  ☐ I usually finish what I start—if it goes well.
  ☐ If it doesn't go right away, I quit. Why beat your brains out?

How good is your health?
  ☐ I *never* run down!
  ☐ I have enough energy for most things I want to do.
  ☐ I run out of energy sooner than most of my friends seem to.

Now count the checks you made.
  How many checks are there beside the *first* answer to each question? ___
  How many checks are there beside the *second* answer to each question? ___
  How many checks are there beside the *third* answer to each question? ___

  If most of your checks are beside the first answers, you probably have what it takes to run a business. If not, you're likely to have more trouble than you can handle by yourself. Better find a partner who is strong on the points you're weak on. If many checks are beside the third answer, not even a good partner will be able to shore you up.

Source: U.S. Small Business Administration.

FIGURE 6.8 Checklist for Getting Started. Respond to this checklist periodically during the preparation and refinement of the business plan.

NOTE: Use the checklist entitled "Getting Started" (Figure 6.8) to help you develop and refine the business plan. Although you will submit the first draft at the close of Unit II, you will also update and revise it at the completion of Units III and IV.

NOTES

1. Mike McGrady, *Kitchen Sink Papers* (New York: Doubleday and Company, 1975).
2. Paula Nelson, *Joy of Money* (New York: Bantam Books, 1977), p. 81.
3. Alexander L. Taylor, III, "Striking It Rich," *Time,* February 15, 1982, pp. 36–41.
4. Nelson, *Joy,* pp. 82–83.
5. *Ibid.*
6. Robert A. Mamis, "Born to Grow," *Inc.,* May 1982, pp. 59–60.
7. *Ibid.*
8. Nelson, *Joy,* pp. 84–85.
9. Nelson, *Joy,* p. 85.

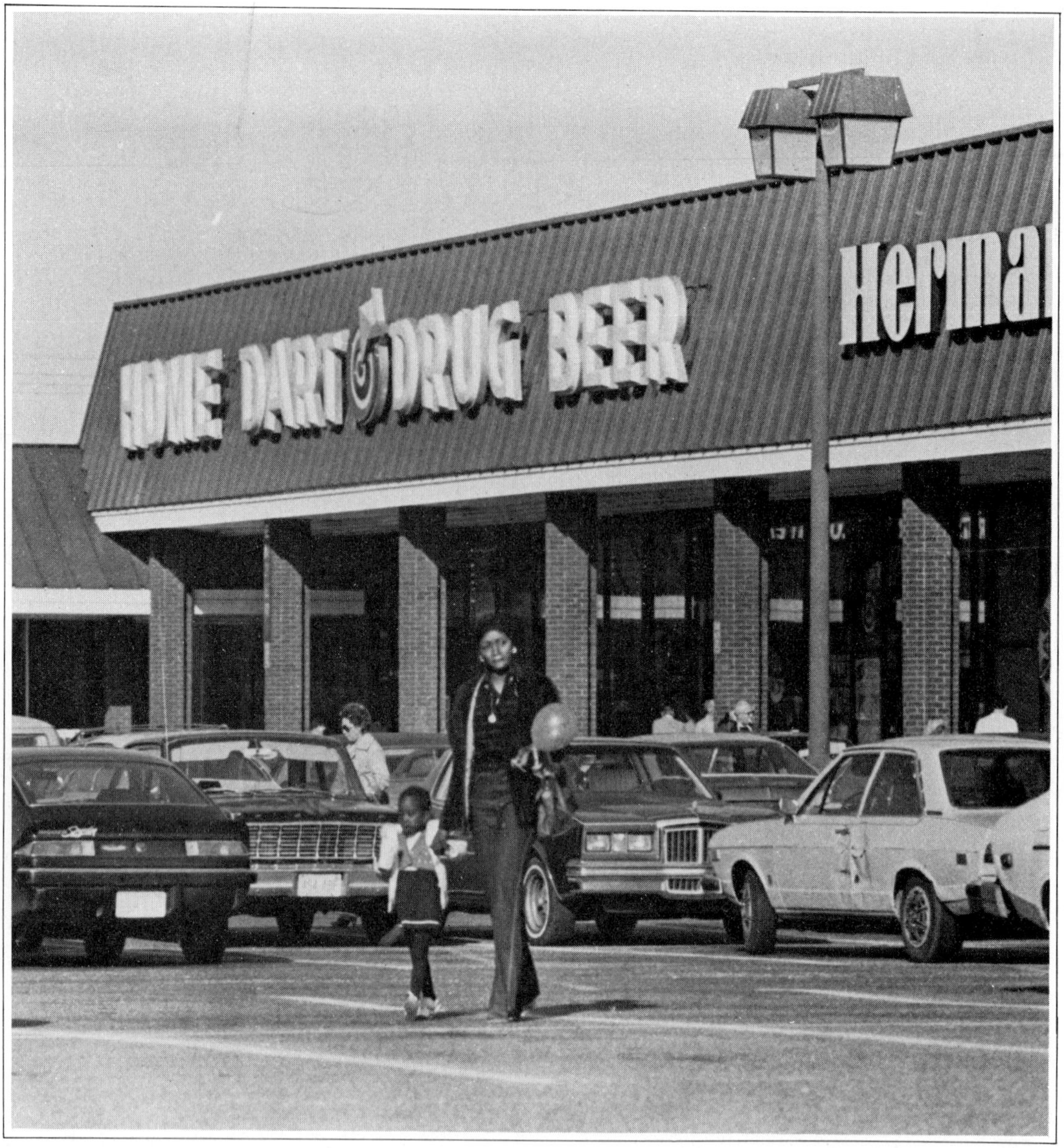
HOME DART DRUG BEER
Herma

chapter

7

Studying the Market

Objectives

1. Define market research and review the kinds of questions it can answer.

2. Describe how to use secondary resources to determine the demographic characteristics of a market area.

3. Use the data gathered to select a target population and a market area for the proposed company's products or services.

4. Identify what customers need and want in relation to your selected products or services.

5. Survey and evaluate the potential competition.

In planning your business, you need to determine whether there is a need for your product or service and whether you can generate sufficient sales from your share of the market to make your business succeed. To make these determinations, you must survey the market to identify what customers want and assess the competition to see what is already being provided.

If yours will be a new kind of venture, how can you discover if your idea has merit? And if you decide to buy an existing business, how can you find out if it has proven profitability or if you could solve any problems it may have?

MARKET RESEARCH

Market research is not a perfect science. Its object of study is people and their constantly changing likes and dislikes. And these can be affected by literally hundreds of influences, many of which cannot be determined specifically. Market research tries within these limits to learn about markets scientifically; that is, simply; "to find out how things are, not how you think they are or would like them to be; what people want to buy, not just what you want to sell them."[1]

Nevertheless, marketing research provides information that can be used to reduce the risk of making bad decisions. The need is for information that is reliable, valid, and actionable. "Reliability refers to consistency and stability over time, and a valid measure is one that provides an accurate representation of that which is being measured."[2]

A market study focuses and organizes market information. It ensures that such data is timely. It helps you reduce business risks and the potential of failure by providing the basic facts you need to make better decisions and establish plans for action.

In setting out to collect information, first list your own ideas and knowledge, based on your familiarity with a selected community and your projected business plans. Brainstorm with friends, family, or potential business colleagues to organize your ideas. Then plan a marketing study that uses both primary and secondary research sources.

Primary research is the data you collect directly, through interviews and by observing people, communities, and businesses. Secondary research involves the data that others have already gathered and reported, including the demographic, trade, business, and economic information published by various agencies and bureaus. Webster's defines *demography* as "the statistical science dealing with the distribution, density, vital statistics, etc., of populations."

Specific Questions

The following questions can help you to design your investigation of the potential market and to evaluate your ability to meet the competition. Ultimately, every answer relates to customers: who they are, whether there are enough of them, and what it will take to gain their patronage.

1. Who are your target customers? Should you try to appeal to an entire market (all the consumers within a given locale) or to one or more segments?
2. If you will concentrate on one segment, is it large enough to be profitable? Are there enough buying customers in this group to support your enterprise?
3. What are the demographic characteristics of these potential customers?
4. Can they buy? That is, are incomes in the community likely to remain stable? What is the condition of the local economy compared to that of the region, state, and nation?
5. Why do they buy? What needs and wants can your proposed business fill?
6. Will you be able to offer the goods or services your potential customers want at the best place, at the best time, and in the right amounts?
7. What is the competition like? Can you estimate the total market you might share with similar businesses? How can you make sure that your business differs from those that already exist?
8. What special appeals can you use to obtain customer patronage? Can you offer lower prices, better quality, wider selection, or more convenient hours than your competition?
9. What trade publications are available with information about your type of product or service?
10. What business or trade associations will you join in order to become and remain knowledgeable about your type of business, your market area, and your customers?

Networking

Interviewing owners of firms similar to yours is one means of gathering data informally. Potential competitors may not always be willing to advise you, but people in other communities can help you develop a realistic data base. Small-business owners with many years' experience in their lines of business often develop a feel for their customers—i.e., their markets.

If you have been an employee in a business similar to the one you wish to open you may already know a number of people who can advise or assist you in brainstorming. Using these contacts as resources is called "developing a human network." These people may help you now and also later, and you should be ready to return the favor, when and if they ask you.

> When Beverly R. moved to Kansas City from Canada, she knew no one. All she knew was that she wanted to go into business for herself. She wanted a partner to manage the financial end, about which she felt most nervous. Placing ads in the papers

produced no results. So she started attending career-oriented lectures, entrepreneurship seminars, and the like, "networking off each contact," to learn all she could about the city and to verify her own ideas.

The result was that she started Business Partner Search, a service company to help other budding entrepreneurs find partners for their ventures. Beverly also discovered she had a flair for training and soon added a series of seminars on various topics for other entrepreneurs—another arm of her company. She got her start via networking.

RESOURCES FOR SECONDARY RESEARCH

The Market Area

Secondary research information will seldom solve all of your information needs, but it is a useful starting point. Such data are not usually up-to-date, and often do not exactly fit your problem, but these sources can be very helpful in describing the general business environment, identifying needed information, and providing guidance concerning the collection of primary data.[3]

City, county, and state maps can help you identify market areas. Outside of metropolitan centers, towns of from 5000 to 30,000 inhabitants often serve as the center of a market area, drawing from smaller communities and the surrounding rural area.

Sedalia, Missouri, for instance, draws trade from 30 miles or more in all directions: from Tipton to the east, Sweet Springs to the north, Knob Noster to the west, and Versailles and Windsor to the south. Sedalia itself is a town of approximately 25,000 people. The surrounding communities and the rural trade, however, expand this market area to perhaps 50,000 people.

Geographic descriptions and census data. A "standard metropolitan statistical area" (SMSA) designates a county (or counties) containing a central city of at least 50,000 inhabitants, plus the contiguous counties that are socially and economically integrated with the central county.

There are 267 tracted SMSAs in the United States and Puerto Rico. Maps and census reports, based on population and housing data, are available on each.

Large cities and adjacent areas are divided into "census tracts" (subdivisions of SMSAs) for the purpose of showing comparable small-area statistics. The average tract has about 4000 to 5000 residents. Although the area covered in a census tract is usually small enough for a location analysis, you may want to examine even smaller units.[4] (See Figures 7.1 and 7.2.)

Within a census tract, block statistics are available for urban areas. The city-block data include the general characteristics of housing and the population demographics. By combining several block areas into trade areas, you can derive more information.

Proposed New Shopping Facility, Beaufort

Jean Ribaut Square will be the primary shopping facility for the city of Beaufort, for the military stationed at Parris Island, and for all of Beaufort County, which has over 67,000 residents including the 6000 permanent military personnel at Parris Island.

Population	County	67,345
	City	10,500
	Military	19,000*
Households		18,000
Per Household Income	County	$23,518
	City	$19,894
Disposable Personal Income		$502,956,000
Total Retail Sales		$341,188,000

*Figure includes 6000 permanent military personnel, 8500 dependents, and an average of 4500 recruits.
Sources: Editor & Publisher Market Guide for 1982; Beaufort Chamber of Commerce.

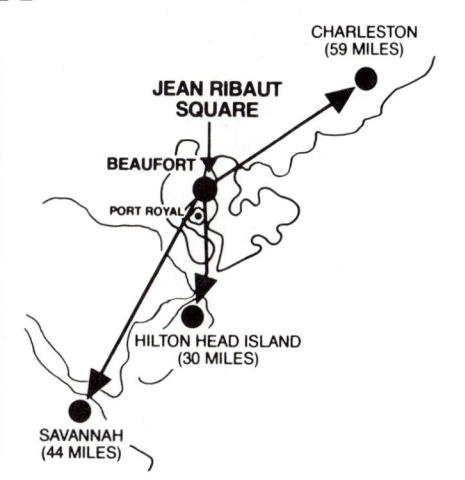

CHARLESTON (59 MILES)
JEAN RIBAUT SQUARE
BEAUFORT
PORT ROYAL
HILTON HEAD ISLAND (30 MILES)
SAVANNAH (44 MILES)

FIGURE 7.1 Trade Area Market Data. Before finalizing the choice of a business, future owners should make a thorough study of trade area market data. (*Courtesy of CBL & Associates, Inc.*)

Trade census. The Census of Business is taken every five years and published in years that end in 2 and 7 (1982 and 1987, for instance). It reports nationwide statistics on retail, wholesale, and service trade establishments. The data are compiled by county, by SMSA, by cities with population over 2500, and by "central business districts" (CBDs). A CBD is an area of very high land valuation with a dense concentration of retail stores, offices, theaters, hotels, and service firms. CBDs exist in most cities with populations of 100,000 and over.

The Census also publishes statistics for "major retail centers" (MRCs). An MRC has at least 10 retail establishments, one of which is a department store. It may include a planned shopping center as well as "string" or "strip" business districts and community developments. Both the MRC and the CBD are located inside the SMSA, but the MRC is outside of the CBD.[5]

Demographic Data

Demographic data include population totals, age groups, number of households, and cash income in various household groups. Such data tell investigators where and how people live and their gender, ethnic type, marital status, and age. Also reported are the number, type, and economic level of apartments, condominiums, and single-family housing units.

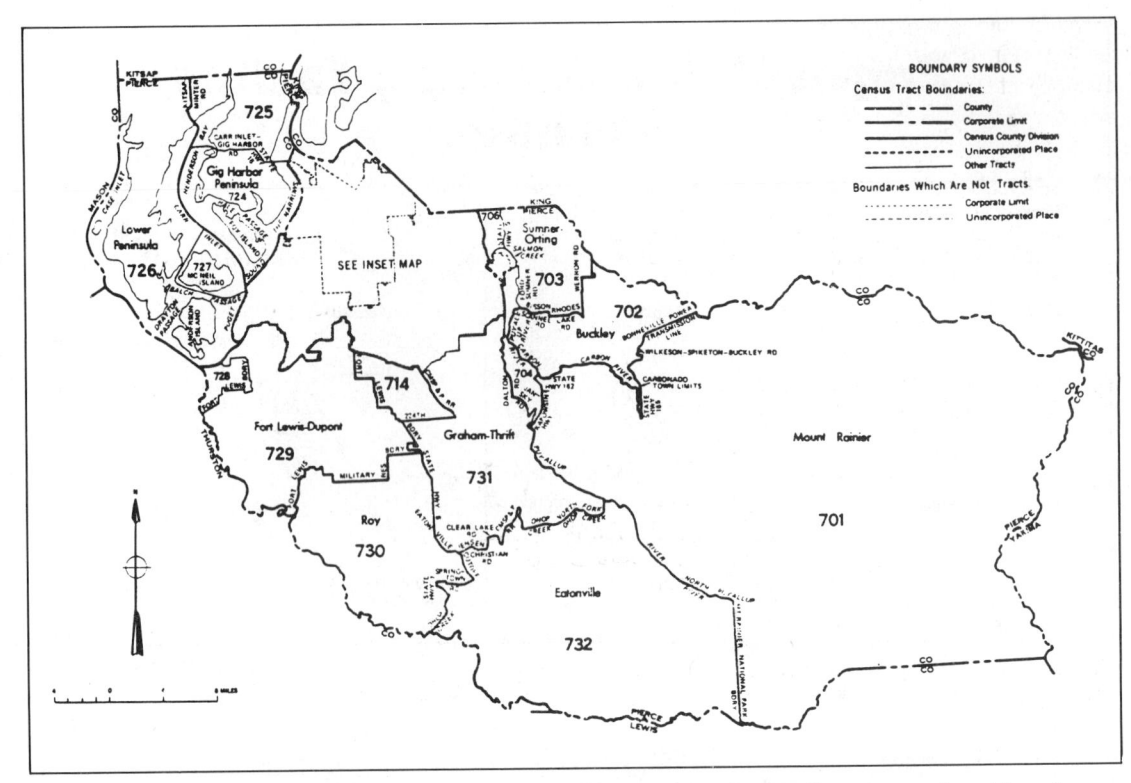

FIGURE 7.2 Census Tracts in the Tacoma, WA, SMSA. Characteristics that address demographics in various tracts and SMSAs include important data in the market study.

Education, occupation, and income have a strong interrelationship. Occupation is often determined by education, and better-educated people typically earn a higher income. This suggests that in communities with a high percentage of college graduates people would have higher-level jobs and higher incomes.

Higher-income people are more likely to purchase expensive items such as vehicles, home furnishings, and appliances. They can afford to purchase luxury items and are more likely to have developed a taste for art, books, travel, cultural activities, alcoholic beverages, fine clothing, and recreation.[6]

The highest incomes are earned by professional and technical workers and by managers and administrators. The cost of homes in a given tract is another index of income.

In coordinating demographic and geographic or tract data, the investigator identifies the types of people living in various neighborhoods by income, education, occupation, and other relevant factors. This information can help the entrepreneur to select a location or to identify specific products that are likely to suit potential customers.

"Groceries are groceries," said Howard B., a small grocery-market owner who lives in a Southern town. "Everybody has to eat. What difference does it make what the people are like?" In fact, knowing what your potential customers are like can make the difference between success and failure.

Suppose, for example, that Mr. B. stocks gourmet and specialty food items in his small grocery. But if his store is located in a predominantly lower-class neighborhood, where incomes are limited and where consumers are mostly "meat-and-potatoes" people, customers will shop elsewhere. To survive, the grocer must understand his market and cater to his customers' needs.

Rare and high-priced antiques often draw customers from the upper-income population segment. Secondhand goods, on the other hand, usually appeal to people with less income, including college students and young adults who are furnishing small apartments and first homes on limited funds. To combine both lines of products may diffuse a store's image and thus scare off both types of consumers. The entrepreneur who wavers between selling antiques or used goods should identify which type of consumer is more common within the selected market area and concentrate on serving that group.

Likewise, you could not expect heavy patronage and thus high profitability if you opened a maternity and baby-care store in a neighborhood consisting largely of apartments and condominiums occupied by people without children. A family shoe store caters to all ages but, depending on the quality and prices offered, the store may draw more customers from one income level than from another.

If you plan to open a cycle repair shop, then you must ask who will most likely patronize your establishment. Obviously, people have to own bicycles or mopeds before they will need repairs. Who are the most likely candidates? Children, teenagers, physical-fitness enthusiasts? If so, how many of each group live in the market area? (See Checklist no. 1, in Figure 7.3.)

Other Secondary Sources

From an analysis of small business in downtown redevelopment areas in New England, R. D. Norton concluded that "a healthy small business sector of owner-operated retail and service enterprises—rather than regional or national chains—are the touchstone of downtown vitality." He notes for example that Boston's Quincy Market is "a prime example of the small firm strategy, outdrawing Disneyland with a million patrons per month." During the time this report covered, the area was one of the most profitable retail clusters in the United States.[7]

Data regarding current demographic patterns and projected trends are available from many secondary sources and for many communities such as Norton's study in New England.

Besides using city, county, and state maps and census reports, and visiting chambers of commerce, you can obtain data from utility companies, railroads,

FIGURE 7.3
Checklist No. 1: Demographic and Economic Data by Comparative Locales. Find appropriate data to use with the checklist from secondary marketing-research sources.

Checklist No. 1
Demographic and Economic Data in Two Locales[1]

Item	Town/Community no. 1 (est'd no.)	Town/Community no. 2 (est'd no.)
A. Population: of town/city	_____	_____
of shopping area	_____	_____
B. No. of employed people:		
a. men	_____	_____
b. women	_____	_____
C. Age distribution:		
a. under school age 5	_____	_____
b. school age 6-19	_____	_____
c. teenagers	_____	_____
d. young adults ⎫ WORK	_____	_____
e. middle-aged ⎬ FORCE	_____	_____
f. senior citizens OVER 62	_____	_____
D. Marital status:		
a. single adults	_____	_____
b. married/mated adults	_____	_____
E. Types of residences:		
a. apartment or condo dwellers	_____	_____
b. house renters	_____	_____
c. house owners	_____	_____
F. Occupations:		
a. blue-collar	_____	_____
b. white-collar	_____	_____
OR		
a. office/clerical	_____	_____
b. sales	_____	_____
c. professional	_____	_____
d. managerial	_____	_____
e. technical	_____	_____
f. skilled	_____	_____
g. unskilled	_____	_____
h. farm laborers	_____	_____
G. Economic (income) level		
a. under $7000	_____	_____
b. $7000-$12,000	_____	_____
c. $12,000-$18,000	_____	_____
d. $18,000-$25,000	_____	_____
e. $25,000-$35,000	_____	_____
f. $35,000-$50,000	_____	_____
g. $50,000-$75,000	_____	_____
h. $75,000 and over	_____	_____

[1] This type of data can be found in such secondary sources as census reports, business-economic reports, and marketing studies, available from government and bureau/agency documents located in public libraries, marketing research firms, colleges and universities, and possibly local government offices.

city newspaper offices, and professional market-research firms. Numerous government bulletins, including those published by the Small Business Administration, can be found in public and university libraries. Librarians will help you locate the pertinent sources.

Small Business Institutes at approximately 500 universities each serve more than 8000 small businesses per year. College students, supervised by faculty members, are assigned to work on particular business problems at no charge. The Small Business Administration (SBA) is designed to draw on federal, state, local, university, and private consulting and management resources to assist small businesses. Small offices of the SBA agency are located in many locales.[8]

Applying Data

Using both primary and secondary sources, you can assemble data for analysis. Table 7.1 gives the number of inhabitants needed to support specific types of retail businesses.

Every 51 business establishments represent approximately 1000 households or about 3000 inhabitants. Thus a market area of 50,000 people can presumably support about 850 businesses, providing they supply goods or services needed or wanted by the buying customers.

Determining the market share. Suppose you want to open a general merchandise store. Table 7.1 tells you that it takes approximately 10,000 people to support this type of establishment. Your survey of the competition reveals that four similar stores are operating in your county, a market area of approximately 50,000 people. Your county thus has "room" for one more general merchandise store.

On this basis, you might expect to attract one-fifth of the total market. Your initial earnings forecast will be predicated on this market share. If county retail sales figures establish that the existing general merchandise stores currently share $1,000,000 in gross annual sales, your proportionate share could be $200,000.

This figure would then be your objective, and your marketing activities would be directed to achieving this goal. This estimate of potential sales would serve as the basis for establishing prices, budgets, and business policies (see Chapters 11 and 14). It would be unrealistic, however, to expect to capture a full one-fifth of the market in your first year. It takes time to make your products and services known and for customers to develop new shopping habits. Granted, they will be curious at first, producing an initial influx of potential customers to your business. To maintain their interest, however, you must continuously come up with attractive new advertising and selling plans (see also Chapter 18).

You can for example advertise and offer a wider range of products or services than the competition at lower prices or higher quality, as well as more attractive or serviceable facilities, better parking, and/or better trained and more courteous service.

TABLE 7.1 Number of Inhabitants Needed to Support Selected Types of Retail Businesses

TYPE OF MERCHANDISE	POPULATION NEEDED TO SUPPORT
Antiques, used goods	17,000
Appliances, household	12,500
Autos (new and used)	6,000
Auto parts, tires and batteries	8,800
Boats	61,500
Books and stationery	28,500
Cafés, restaurants, caterers	1,200
Candy, confectionary	31,400
Cocktail lounges	2,400
Dairy products	41,500
Drugstores	4,200
Family clothing	17,000
Farm equipment	15,000
Feed and grain	17,000
Flowers	13,500
Garden supplies	65,000
Gasoline	1,200
General merchandise	10,000
Gifts, novelties, and souvenirs	26,000
Groceries	1,600
Hardware	10,000
Hobbies, toys, and games	61,500
Jewelry	13,500
Liquor	6,400
Lumber and building supplies	8,000
Mail-order operations	45,000
Meat and seafood	18,000
Men's and boys' clothing	12,000
Optical goods	63,000
Radios, televisions, and stereos	20,000
Records and musical instruments	30,000
Shoes	9,300
Sporting goods	27,000
Trailers and recreation vehicles	45,000
Variety goods	10,000
Women's ready-to-wear	7,000
Women's accessories and specialty items	25,800

Source: Wendell O. Metcalf, "Starting and Managing a Small Business," Small Business Administration (Washington, D.C.: U.S. Government Printing Office, 1973).

When you are assessing the competition, be careful how you define the market. Define too narrowly and the result is omission of important competitors. Convention has identified the four basic components of the marketing mix as related to product, promotion, place, and price.[9]

The nature of the market is an important consideration. Some markets are essentially product markets. Others are more heavily influenced by place investments—most consumers will not really "walk a mile for a Camel." Some markets are promotion oriented, like cosmetics and music, while others are more price oriented: gasoline, for instance.[10]

Meeting Consumer Needs

It's difficult, if not impossible, to sell people what they don't want: remember the Edsel and the midiskirt. In both cases, many businesses suffered, from automobile and clothing manufacturers to retail auto distributors and clothes stores. They found themselves overstocked, their inventories collecting dust. Consumers were not buying.

If yours will be a "trendy" product or service, you might be ahead of your time. You may not be able to persuade enough customers to try what you have to offer. On the other hand, consumers may already be growing tired of the faddish idea or product. Such items come and go quickly: think of hulahoops, pet rocks, Rubic cubes, Pong and Space Invaders, decorated skateboards, and designer jeans. Of course, many of the manufacturers and retailers who got in on the action early made a killing.

Where is the market now? Where is it going—not only tomorrow, but two, three, even five or more years down the road? If a fad, fashion, or trend has already peaked, it may have nowhere to go but downhill. By the time you gear up to open your own business, it could be too late. If you don't recognize and plan for the short lives of many specialty items and services by diversifying your offerings, you could be heading for failure.

It may be obvious that "Nothing is easier than selling people what they want." The problem persists: "What do people want?" Regular perusal of the market data available in trade journals and through membership in related business organizations can help keep you aware of changing consumer needs, wants, and buying habits.

What Do Consumers Want?

To find out what the consumers want, you can interview people at random on busy street corners, in shopping malls, or block by block. You can administer questionnaires to civic or church groups or to a stratified random sample of the community's inhabitants. A "stratified sample" consists of questioning the same number of people in each socioeconomic, educational, occupational, income, ethnic, age, gender, and marital classification. You might ask the marketing students at a local college or university to conduct a study, or consult similar surveys they have already conducted. Another method is to select a certain percentage of the population segment you expect to serve; e.g., college students, senior citizens, parents of infants, etc. Improper sampling, in terms of both type and size, however, can invalidate results. Small businesses often use mail surveys, because they cost less than other methods. Yet, in instances where the

The customer is king. If people aren't interested in your product or service, you'll have few customers, if any.

study requires complex instructions, visual cues, or covers areas where the literacy rate is low, the mail survey may not be a suitable or cost-effective method.[11]

Furthermore, don't try to find out everything from a single survey. State the objective(s) of the study clearly and then design questions for the interviews or mailed surveys that reflect these objectives. The analysis of data obtained from any of these techniques should also include a meaningful interpretation. According to Boughton, "one often sees only percentages showing how many people felt this way or that way. A good analysis should interpret data and relate the information derived to the stated goals of the research."[12]

You could also draw on your own feelings as a consumer as an indication of customer needs, wants, and attitudes. Seek data pertinent to your intended kind of business. You can tailor the sample consumer survey given as Figure 7.4 to reflect your particular information needs.

The questionnaire asks consumers where they prefer to shop, at what times, and how (using cash or credit). You can use the information about credit, for example, to establish your own credit policies (see Chapter 11).

The questionnaire is useful for businesses that will deal directly with the public, such as retail stores, gas stations, word-processing services, etc. You can design a similar form to survey potential consumers of nonretail services as well, such as construction, agriculture, manufacturing, and wholesale distribution. (See Figure 7.4.)

FIGURE 7.4
Checklist No. 2: What Customers Want—Where, When, How.

Checklist No. 2

Product or service entrepreneur plans to offer: _____

	How Often (per month)	Estimated Amount Spent (per time)
A. On what do you spend money?		
1. _____	_____	$_____
2. _____	_____	_____
3. _____	_____	_____
4. _____	_____	_____
5. _____	_____	_____
6. _____	_____	_____
7. _____	_____	_____
8. _____	_____	_____
9. _____	_____	_____
10. _____	_____	_____

Check if "Yes"

B. 1. Where do you prefer to shop?
   a. downtown
   b. shopping center(s) (which?)
   c. out of town
  2. When do you prefer to shop?
   a. daytime
   b. lunch hour
   c. evening
   d. weekend
  3. If you buy on credit, what do you use?
   a. credit card
   b. installment plan
   c. layaway
   d. other_____
  4. What frustrates you as a consumer of (specify product or service)?
  If a product:
   a. lack of availability
   b. limited choice of type/size/color
   c. poor quality
   d. limited quantity
   e. high prices
  If a service:
   a. lack of availability
   b. discourteous personnel
   c. incompetent personnel

A New Idea

Suppose that you want to do something new and different and are open to ideas. Observing consumers' frustrations can suggest possibilities. Interviewing consumers about their wants can help you choose from among various options.

Be careful, however. If you gather data slowly, while simultaneously revealing to interviewees your new idea, someone else might start up first with *your* product or service.

What are your own frustrations? Do you dislike shopping, wrapping packages, cleaning, or preparing all the details for a party? Many others may feel the same way you do. Your consumer survey may reveal that there is enough market demand to support a shopping service, a gift-buying and mailing service, or a cleaning or catering service. Does your health prevent you from cleaning your drive and walks of snow, from cultivating your garden, or from conducting minor household maintenance chores and repairs? Again, you may not be alone. Nor are such ventures as these necessarily small operations. Major cleaning and catering services, employing many full- and part-time employees, have grown from such ideas.

"Mr. Glass," a household cleaning product sold by many supermarkets, was developed over four months of experimentation in the kitchen of its inventor. Frustrated that she couldn't clean as quickly and efficiently as she liked (when she despised cleaning in the first place), this soon-to-be entrepreneur tried numerous combinations of ingredients, using standard kitchen tools, until she had produced what she was looking for. A local manufacturer liked her idea, and voila! A new product, a new venture, was born.

SURVEYING THE COMPETITION

By using the Yellow Pages, contacting chambers of commerce and other reporting agencies, and taking a walking or driving tour you can begin to get an idea of the competition you might be facing.

You wouldn't have to survey an entire city, since in many cases a particular type of business is concentrated in only a few areas. Zoning laws often restrict heavy industry to one section of town, commercial businesses to another, and so forth. Customer shopping habits and other factors may also influence the distribution of businesses.

For instance, a central business district or business-strip area may primarily contain retail stores, with a smattering of business and personal services and a few restaurants intermingled. Downtown is usually the financial district, with banks and brokerage houses. Office buildings and related business services may be found here, too, as well as in outlying industrial parks.

Many communities have what is known as "auto row," a street lined with new and used car dealerships and associated parts and repair establishments. Warehouses and heavy industry are usually clustered together, convenient to such transportation arteries as railroads, waterways, and highways.

Shopping centers are generally found in suburbs or on the edge of town, and include mostly retail stores, with some service establishments. Motels, service stations, and some fast-food and other restaurants are usually located near heavily traveled streets and highways. Residential areas, particularly those adjacent to commercially zoned districts, may have personal-service establishments, repair shops, and some home-based operations, such as laundromats, beauty shops, a "corner grocery," and so on.

Location, as you will discover in the next chapter, can make or break a business. For now, it is important to realize that in surveying the competition, you don't have to study every section of a city or community.

Survey Procedures

Checklist no. 3 (Figure 7.5) will help you evaluate the competition. First count the number of businesses that are similar to your proposed business within the market area where you plan to locate. Then count the number of related firms. If yours will be a hardware store, for example, a department store with a hardware department would be a related firm, and auto distributorships or department stores with repair departments would be related to an auto repair shop.

Finally, count the complementary establishments. Such businesses support one another in motivating consumers to purchase related products: e.g., shoe stores and clothing stores, auto dealers and auto parts and repair shops, and appliance dealers and appliance repair services.

Checklist No. 3
Number of Competing and Complementary Businesses

Product or service entrepreneur plans to offer: _____

Number of	In Local Community	In Entire Town or City
Similar firms	_____	_____
Related firms	_____	_____
Complementary firms	_____	_____

Comments:

FIGURE 7.5
Checklist No. 3: Assessing the Competition by Number of Similar and Related Firms.

FIGURE 7.6
Checklist No. 4: Evaluating the Competition.

Checklist No. 4
Evaluating the Competition

General type of product or service entrepreneur plans to offer:
_____

	Company no. 1	Company no. 2	Company no. 3
A. Specific product or service:			
1. _____			
a. range of type, size, color	_____	_____	_____
b. quality	_____	_____	_____
c. quantity	_____	_____	_____
d. price	_____	_____	_____
2. _____			
a. range of type, size, color	_____	_____	_____
b. quality	_____	_____	_____
c. quantity	_____	_____	_____
d. price	_____	_____	_____
3. _____			
a. range of type, size, color	_____	_____	_____
b. quality	_____	_____	_____
c. quantity	_____	_____	_____
d. price	_____	_____	_____
4. _____			
a. range of type, size, color	_____	_____	_____
b. quality	_____	_____	_____
c. quantity	_____	_____	_____
d. price	_____	_____	_____
5. _____			
a. range of type, size, color	_____	_____	_____
b. quality	_____	_____	_____
c. quantity	_____	_____	_____
d. price	_____	_____	_____
B. Personnel:[1]			
1. courteous, respectful	_____	_____	_____
2. competent	_____	_____	_____
3. enough available:			
a. in daytime	_____	_____	_____
b. during lunch hour	_____	_____	_____
c. in evening	_____	_____	_____
d. on weekends	_____	_____	_____

[1]Rate by, for example, the following code:
   + outstanding   = good, satisfactory   − poor   0 nonexistent

Next you may wish to compare the findings of your survey of customer habits and frustrations with what the competition currently offers. Checklist no. 4 (Figure 7.6) can guide you in systematic observations of competing firms.

Visit these establishments (as though on a routine shopping trip) and take note of the quality, quantity, size and color ranges, and prices of the goods or services offered. Do you see any evidence of disorganization, unsafe surroundings, high prices, low selection, poor quality, or slow or discourteous service? If so, then despite the number of similar businesses currently operating in the market area, you could make your business a success by improving on the competition's poor service.

SUMMARY

To determine if your proposed company and its products or services have a chance to succeed, you need reliable data. To be successful, entrepreneurs must know their market. Market research is simply a logical, objective way of learning about potential customers and also about the competition.

DISCUSSION QUESTIONS

1. From your present familiarity with the product or service you plan to offer, which questions posed earlier can you already answer? Which ones can you guess at?
2. Define the market area of your own locale, whether a small town or a community within a metropolitan area. What different kinds of market studies might you initiate in these two areas?
3. How realistic is it to estimate the market share for each related establishment by dividing the number of existing competitors by the total county or metropolitan earnings reported? Why might one firm receive a disproportionate share of business?
4. Identify secondary sources one might use in gathering market data. Explain those with which you are already familiar. What kind of data do they supply, and in what form?
5. Why is it imperative to know what consumers need and want? Why are these factors sometimes difficult to determine?
6. Describe "stratified random sampling" techniques. How would you conduct a block survey?
7. How does the entrepreneur who has developed a new product or service identify what consumers need or want?
8. What's different and what's the same about conducting a market study for a new business and for an existing one?

ACTIVITIES AND EXERCISES

1. Determine the market share of a potential family-type restaurant in a market area of 50,000 inhabitants, given the following factors (also see Table 7.1): The market area has:

   - blue-collar workers employed by two major factories,
   - 10,000 students and 2000 professionals enrolled/employed in a local university,
   - senior citizens on limited incomes (10 percent of the population),
   - 31 churches and 17 schools (one junior high school and one senior high school).

   Existing competitive businesses include:

   - 10 fine dining establishments, serving cocktails,
   - 13 fast-food franchise establishments (serving hamburgers, pizza, tacos, chicken, and seafood),
   - two breakfast-type franchise establishments,
   - seven specialty cuisine establishments (Mexican, Italian, Chinese),
   - three bakeries/doughnut shops, with eating facilities,
   - two truckstops, with cafes,
   - three other family-type restaurants, not accounted for in the above categories.

2. Obtain demographic data for your county or SMSA/tract. Also contact the marketing department of a university or a professional market research firm to obtain the results of market studies conducted in your area. Record appropriate information from all sources on a chart such as Checklist no. 1 (Figure 7.3).

3. Conduct an informal survey by visiting the existing competition in the type of business that appeals to you. Devise a checklist for recording specific data about what the competition does or does not provide, such as the example given in Checklist no. 4 (Figure 7.6).

4. Using T-charts (Appendix B), chart the advantages and disadvantages of starting a business that is competitive with existing ones and of introducing a new product or service.

NOTES

1. J. Ford Laumer, Jr., James R. Harris, and Hugh J. Guffey, Jr., "Learning about Your Market," *Small Marketers' Aids* (Washington, D.C.: Small Business Administration, 1979), p. 3.
2. Paul D. Boughton, "Marketing Research and Small Business Pitfalls and Potential," *Journal of Small Business Management,* July 1983, pp. 36–42.

3. Ibid.
4. Louis H. Vorzimer, "Using Census Data to Select a Store Site," *Small Marketers' Aids* (Washington, D.C.: Small Business Administration, 1974), p. 2.
5. Ibid.
6. Laumer, Harris, and Guffey, "Your Market."
7. R. D. Norton, "Small Business and Downtown Redevelopment," *Economic Research on Small Business: The Environment for Entrepreneurship and Small Business* (Washington, D.C.: Small Business Administration, 1981).
8. Boughton, "Marketing Research."
9. James W. Culliton, *The Management of Marketing Costs.* (Boston: Harvard University Division of Research, Graduate School of Business Administration, 1948).
10. Victor J. Cook, Jr., "Marketing Strategy and Differential Advantage," *Journal of Marketing,* Spring 1983, pp. 68–75.
11. Boughton, "Marketing Research."
12. Ibid.

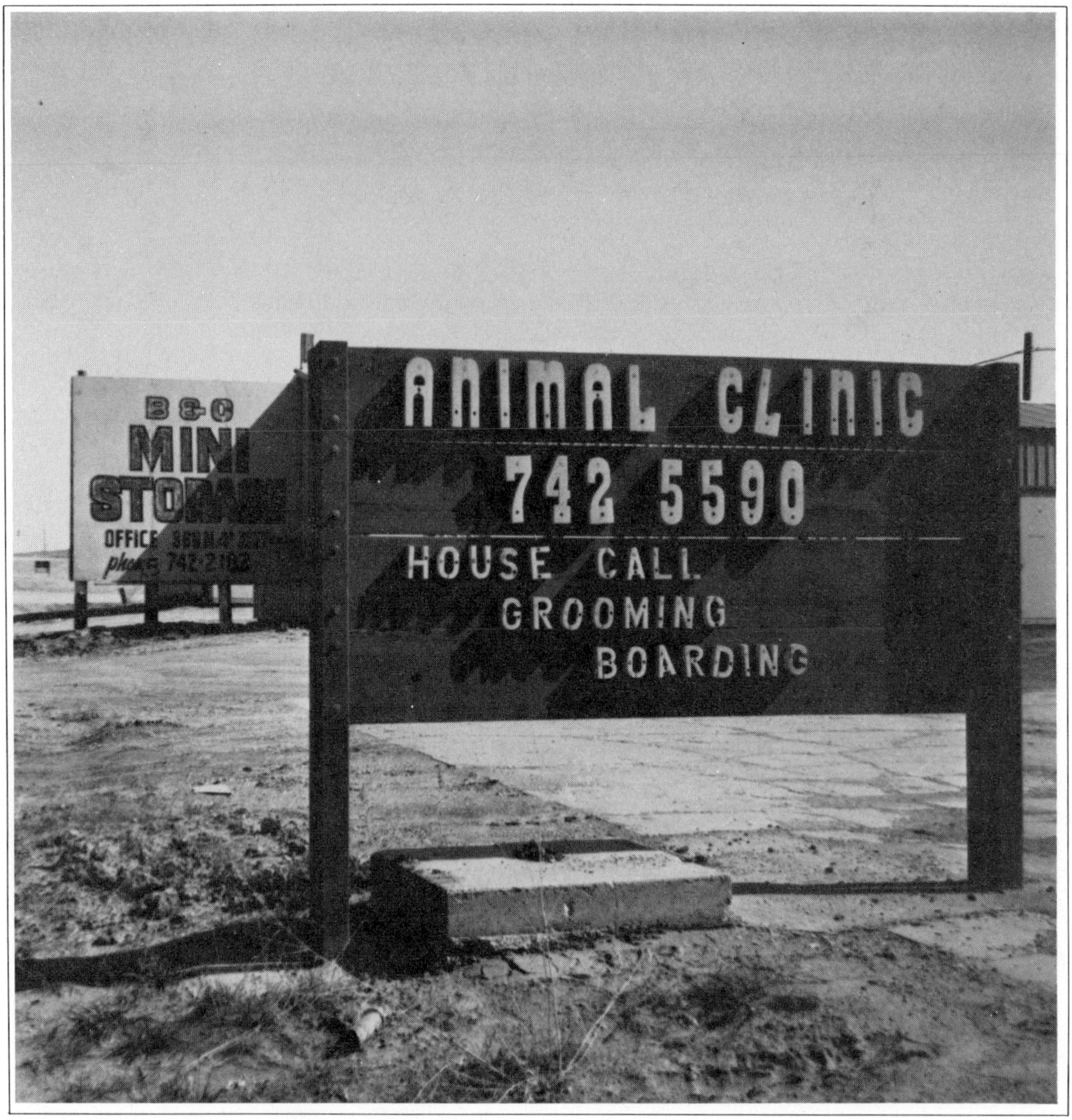
ANIMAL CLINIC
742 5590
HOUSE CALL
GROOMING
BOARDING

chapter 8

Selecting the Location

Objectives

1. Identify the factors to consider in deciding on a community within which to locate your business.

2. Determine the relative importance of neighborhood factors to consider in making a location decision for your type of business.

3. Debate the advantages and disadvantages of locating within a shopping center or mall.

4. Discuss the implications of leasing a facility.

5. Itemize the expenses that are related to and can help determine your choice of location.

Some experienced entrepreneurs and realtors claim that of the top possible criteria for business success, the first three are "location, location, and location!" The decision where to locate your business can make the difference between its success and failure.

Moreover, the first site you select may not be the best choice. As your business grows you may want to relocate or to open new branches. Whether starting up, moving, or expanding, then, you'll need some basic guidelines about how to choose a location.

There are three steps to choosing a location: choosing the state and city, choosing an area within the city, and choosing a particular site. Following is a checklist of factors pertinent to these decisions (some of which were also discussed in Chapter 7).

State and City

1. Size of the city's market or trade area,
2. Population characteristics and trends in the market area,
3. Total purchasing power and the distribution of this power,
4. Total market potential for your type of business,
5. Number, size, quality, and aggressiveness of the competition.

Location within the City

1. Attractiveness to customers,
2. Quality and quantity of competition,
3. Access routes, traffic patterns, and growth trends,
4. Zoning regulations,
5. Overall appearance.

Identifying a Site

1. Number and type of customers passing the site,
2. Ability of the site to intercept traffic en route from one place to another,
3. Complementary nature of neighboring establishments,
4. Type of goods sold and services offered,
5. Availability of parking,
6. Vulnerability of the site to unfriendly competition,
7. Cost of the site for start-up expenses including remodeling, and for continuing operations

SELECTING THE TOWN OR COMMUNITY

Metropolitan areas offer many different business sites. Your selection will depend on, among other factors, personal preference, community demographics, and proximity to markets and customers.

Personal Preference

People often choose to start their businesses near where they and their family or friends live—to start where they are rather than pulling up roots to move into unfamiliar surroundings. Their established credit gives them a better chance to get capital financing and credit and the developed reputation for integrity and dependability helps them create goodwill by attracting customers from among their acquaintances and others who have heard of them.

People who choose to relocate often select geographic regions on the basis of climate, population density, and the availability of cultural, sports, or recreational activities. They may also follow their preference in choosing an urban, suburban, small-town, or rural environment.

Sometimes people sell their homes or take second mortgages to finance new enterprises. When funds are scarce and people are willing to sacrifice to get the venture going, they sometimes choose to live on the business premises—in a small apartment above the store or in an adjacent mobile home, for example.

Sometimes people move not to seek a preferred lifestyle but rather out of economic necessity. They leave depressed areas for prosperous ones. They go where the action is.

> Hobbs, New Mexico, is a town created during the dust-bowl days of the late 1930s. People came there from the Plains states to seek work in the oil fields. Close on their heels were the merchants who quickly established thriving operations out of canvas tents along dirt streets. The merchants lived in the rear or in adjoining tents. Forty years later Hobbs was a bustling city of over 30,000 people.

Regional Growth Patterns

Some parts of the United States are growing, while others have been steadily declining. The Sun Belt area extending from Florida to California and most Western States are growth regions. Certain cities are also expanding rapidly. A city whose population continues to grow at a fairly steady rate offers opportunities for new businesses. (See Figure 8.1.)

One-industry towns, however, are subject to economic crises. Layoffs in the major or single industry will affect everyone, since purchasing power will plummet.

Community Demographics

Demographics, as noted in Chapter 7, involve population density and the socioeconomic, occupational, and educational levels of people living in a given area. It is also important to examine the condition of the neighborhood and its potential for growth or change.

Say you want to establish a teenage discotheque. If you open it in Sun City, Arizona, a retirement community with over 30,000 senior citizens, it may not stay open long. College or university towns, although sometimes small, nonetheless have many more young people than other towns of similar size. Here the

REGION I	REGION II	REGION III	REGION IV	REGION V
New England States	N.Y., N.J., Puerto Rico, & Virgin Islands	D.C., Del., Md., Pa., Va., & W.V.	Ala., Fla., Ga., Ky., Miss., N.C., S.C., & Tenn.	Ill., Ind., Ohio, Mich., Minn., & Wis.
Textiles High-tech mfg & services Mfg: leather shoes Extraction: lumber	Mfg: nondurable goods Transportation Finance Communications (out-migration from both N.Y. & N.J.)	Small business tops big business in: -dollars of sales -no. of employees -no. of firms -no. of new jobs (out-migration of -goods -services -skills -entrepreneurial techniques)	Finance Mfg Construction Services Profits are below national averages Small business accounts for up to 87% of employment (with 28% of small businesses employing fewer than 20 workers)	"Great Lakes Region has historically been the industrial heartland of America" 20.7% of U.S. 20.1%, Retail 29.8%, Mfg. 97% of firms have fewer than 100 employees Small business accounts for 45% of total employment opportunities Increasing: -services -government -finance Decreasing: -mfg. -trade -transportation -agriculture (out-migration since 1950s)

Source: Compiled from data found in Small Business Administration, *Economic Research on Small Business: The Environment for Entrepreneurship and Small Business* (Washington, D.C.: U.S. Government Printing Office), 1981. *(Continued on next page.)*

FIGURE 8.1 **Economic Profile of Small Business by Region.** Economic and business classifications to consider in making a regional location decision.

discotheque, together with other youth-oriented products and services, makes more sense.

Other choices may be less obvious. An elite boutique or a housecleaning service in a neighborhood of $300,000 homes might appear to have success potential. But the inhabitants may be used to shopping outside the neighbor-

REGION VI Ark., La., Ok., Tex., & N.M.	REGION VII Iowa, Neb., Mo., Kansas	REGION VIII Col., N.D., S.D., Mont., & Wyo.	REGION IX Ariz., Cal., Nev., Hawaii, Guam, & Pacific Isles	REGION X Alaska, Idaho, Oreg., Wash.
Small business employs 90% of workers Good environment for small business Problems: - transportation - lack of available capital Increasing: - services - trade (retail & wholesale) - finance (in-migration due to: - climate - economic growth trends - socioeconomic conditions favoring "personal liberty")	Rural influences, small communities, & predominance of small businesses (mutual dependency of agriculture & small business) Consistent & steady growth areas: - retailing - services - agribusinesses - mfg. (small) - finance Employment in companies primarily having less than 100 workers (with wages exceeding national averages) Growth area for economic & social prosperity	Retail & services represent over 50% of small businesses (particularly with 0-20 employees) Other fields: - construction - finance (insurance, real estate) - wholesaling - manufacturing - communications - utilities - extraction especially energy) - agriculture (ranching & farming) - tourism (skiing, etc.) Small businesses account for 99% of companies Problems: - lack of water - lack of capital (in-migration & growth in all fields)	Sharp contrasts in population & geography throughout the region; Cal. has the bulk of population, industry, & business High-tech region Nev., Ariz., & Hawaii: - tourism - recreation - hospitality Ariz., Nev.: - extraction (energy) - ranching (in-migration) Limits to growth: - lack of water - costs of energy - environmental controls	Sharp contrasts in geography & population Extraction: - timber, logging - oil - mining - agriculture Retail trade Services Wholesaling Manufacturing Retail & services far outnumber other types of businesses Boeing is the largest employer in the region; otherwise, small businesses abound

FIGURE 8.1 (Cont.)

hood or may have live-in or long-standing domestic help. If so, it might be difficult to break these consumer patterns—particularly if you ran the only luxury firm in the area rather than one of several boutiques or services in a shopping mall or area that caters to this economic class. Likewise, a firm specializing in lawn products and services would find few shoppers if it were located in an area of apartment and condominium complexes whose residents were not responsible for yard care.

Population characteristics differ from one town or city to another, as well as within cities. Variables include the nature of the local economy, such as the number and type of extraction and manufacturing industries, the prosperity of surrounding agricultural operations, and the number of blue-collar versus white-collar workers.

Midland and Odessa, Texas, are both supported primarily by the oil and petroleum industry. Located just 20 miles apart, both are equally surrounded by prosperous cotton farms and cattle ranches. Both are also of similar size. Yet one is essentially blue-collar, while the other is white-collar. Odessa is filled with thriving small industries serving the oil fields, together with oilfield brokers. Midland's high-rise towers contain many administrative offices (oil company executives and consultants, administrative support staffs, etc.). The two cities' shops and services differ widely, beyond those offering basic necessities.

Some communities have a special purpose. Like one-industry towns, there are also resort and tourist towns.

Solvang, California, Aspen, Colorado, Provincetown, Massachusetts, and Jackson, Wyoming, have more in common with one another although they are thousands of miles apart, than any has with a neighboring community. All are tourist spots and are therefore frequented by many sightseers and souvenir shoppers from all over the world. Restaurants abound with cosmopolitan and "home-cooked" cuisine to suit every socioeconomic level of consumer. Likewise, the popularity of leisure-time products and services attest to potential success for entrepreneurs serving customers.

Community Trends

Community demographics may also change. Are businesses drifting from downtown to suburbia? Is a neighborhood deteriorating, or is the clientele becoming older or poorer? Is the nature of the community shifting, bringing a change in the cultural, religious, or ethnic demand for certain foods, types of clothing, and products and services? If so, some established firms may be in for trouble, not to mention the similar firms that have not yet opened their doors.

On the other hand, if such enclaves are well entrenched, there is little point in trying to buck the tide. An auto repair shop or a new car agency would be hard pressed to find customers in Gap, Pennsylvania, for instance. The Amish people who have long lived there do not use mechanized vehicles. Bicycle sales and repair shops, though, are thriving!

Proximity to Customers and Markets

A retail business should be located conveniently near its prospective customers. Manufacturing, distribution, and wholesale businesses should be close to the source of supplies and raw materials and to transportation networks. Thus some business owners select locations for their nearness to warehouses and distributors, to railroads and rivers, and to airports and major highways.

Government Regulations

Cities and states that want to attract businesses to their communities may provide tax incentives. Other regions impose high taxes specifically to prohibit new business growth. Also imposed on businesses may be special levies or costly operating licenses.

Before deciding on any one location, check what city, county, and state requirements govern the locale. You can get this information from the secretary of state, county and city clerks, local chambers of commerce, and other business people.

LOCATION WITHIN THE SELECTED COMMUNITY

Once you have determined the town or community location, there are additional factors to evaluate, depending on the type of business you plan to open. A service firm or referral agency that operates over the telephone or by mail can locate almost anywhere. A desk within another enterprise, a home, or an answering service should suffice, unless you plan eventually to open an office and interact with customers personally.

Manufacturing and wholesaling firms tend to locate in industrial areas close to transportation and with space for loading docks. Retail establishments have different needs—with respect to customer traffic, parking competition, complementary businesses, and image. Repair shops often locate near related retail outlets. A car repair shop would locate near car agencies and auto parts stores, for example. Likewise, business services such as word-processing and accounting agencies do best when located near business customer firms.

Customer Traffic

Once you have accurately assessed the population characteristics of a neighborhood you must study the people's buying habits. What routes do they follow to and from work? Do they use public or private transportation? If there are many pedestrians, you will notice that when it's hot they walk on the shady side of the street, and that when it's cold they choose the sunnier side.

People usually do more shopping on the way home than on the way to work. You could open a drive-up, drive-through, or carry-out facility on the "going home" side of the street. Customers are more likely to patronize your establishment if it is on their regular route. They rarely go out of their way if they have a choice.

Pedestrian traffic count. You can begin by counting the number of pedestrians. First decide who to count, where, and when. Count only the type of people you expect to patronize your establishment. If you plan to open a men's clothing store, for instance, you will be interested in male pedestrians over the age of 16.

You may choose to make your count directly in front of one or more possible sites. You could also ask selected pedestrians about the reason for their trip, their destination, the stores they plan to visit, and their intended purchases. Shoppers on their way back to their cars or homes can tell you what goods they have bought and/or what services they have used.

Finally, be aware that the season, month, week, day, and hour all have an effect upon a traffic survey.

Automobile traffic count. Auto traffic can be divided into the work trip, the shopping trip, and the pleasure trip. Careful observation, together with a few interviews, can help you identify these categories.

Different types of retailers and service providers seek different locations, even though they may be serving the same type of customers. A dry cleaner would want to locate on the going-to-work side of the street, while a convenience store would choose the going-home side. People setting out on a shopping trip or to do errands frequently prefer shops on the right-hand side of a main street near other major thoroughfares.

People on pleasure or recreational trips patronize restaurants and fast-food establishments, motels, and service stations. You have a better chance of attracting this type of customer if your facility is located alongside a well-traveled highway and adjacent to a major entrance to a community.

Estimating company sales from observations of consumer traffic. You can make a reasonable estimate of sales volume if you have the following data (some of which you should have collected in your market survey):

1. Demographic characteristics of target customers (from pedestrian interviews),
2. Number of such individuals who pass the site during business hours (from traffic counts),
3. Proportion of passersby who will enter the establishment (from pedestrian interviews),
4. Proportion of those entering who will become purchasers or clients (from pedestrian interviews),
5. Amount of average transactions (from trade associations and trade publications).

One experienced retail owner is able to estimate not only who and how many people will make purchases but also how much the average purchase will be. Out of 1000 passersby each day, he estimates that 5 percent enter his store and each spends an average of $10. This produces an annual sales volume of $175,000.[1]

Customer Parking

Pedestrians can stop and shop with ease. But drivers can't become customers until they find a place to park the car. Shopping centers usually have plenty of

Selecting the Location   **159**

It's expensive for metropolitan businesses to provide customers with adjacent parking facilities, but in many cases this decision can mean the difference between having many customers or very few.

parking space. Yet some people dislike walking the long distances from outlying parking spaces to the mall itself, much less to the far-end locations within. A street or downtown area may be more to this type of shopper's liking, if there is a reasonable chance of finding a parking space.

Some people resist parking in metered spots or pay lots, and even where these exist, parking spaces may be at a premium. A business with its own private parking lot is the ideal—but attaining this ideal means purchasing additional high-rent-district land.

"Store Mix"

What is the "store mix" in your proposed location? Do the neighboring establishments provide related products and services and thus generate traffic for your firm? Or will they directly compete and thus draw business away?

For a small retail store or service establishment, particularly in its first year of operation, compatibility can be among the most important factors. Thus a clothing store next to a shoe store is a good combination, as is a used car agency near an auto parts or repair store.

Too many stores selling similar products will divide the trade among them. The competition could become fierce at all levels, from developing attractive displays and advertising campaigns to price wars.

Creating an Image

The site selected also affects the company's image and thus its total marketing package. The socioeconomic status of the community, the firm's compatibility with its neighbors, and the condition and appearance of the building all speak for you. What image do you wish to create: one expressing exclusivity and class or one communicating a reassuring ordinariness?

Location can project any image you desire, provided that the exterior and interior decor follow suit. Neophyte entrepreneurs might be tempted to use their limited capital to lease or buy a good building in a rundown neighborhood. Yet

Signs convey a message, create an image, and let people know who you are and what you do.

the money they spend on remodeling and decorating to achieve a desired image might be wasted if the neighborhood itself scares away customers.

Signs are such a powerful medium of communication that it is difficult to overestimate their influence. Signs help people find you; they attract the interest of people who are passing by your establishment; they present an image of your business.

Other media require the full attention of the person receiving the message. But people don't have to give their full attention to your sign in order to derive meaning from its presence. Subconsciously they are affected by the mood or atmosphere it creates. In brief, signs tell people who you are and what you are selling.

The sign is an investment in advertising and in image-creation. You have to balance factors such as size and design against the cost, including energy and maintenance costs. You can either buy or lease a sign, and you can either choose a standard design or have one custom-made. The most important thing is that the sign be both noticeable and readable.[2]

Manufacturing and Wholesaling Needs

When locating or relocating a small plant, you must consider the company's market and the availability of labor, transportation, raw materials, and buildings and/or building sites. Because of innovations in an industry, an old plant can become inefficient and a competitive disadvantage. Entrepreneurs should periodically explore whether a relocation is necessary for growth.

Manufacturing or wholesaling firms need more space than do retail and service establishments. Tractor-trailers have to be able to pull up to loading docks and to park in the rear. Wholesalers usually need a lot of storage space, and thus are typically located in low-rent districts or industrial areas. The discount houses and wholesalers that sell direct to consumers also need an attractive customer-receiving and ordering area, as well as customer parking facilities.

Whereas retailers want to locate near the center of the customer area to be served, processors need to be situated close to the source of raw materials. It makes more sense for a fruit and vegetable cannery to locate close to the orchards and farms that supply it because the produce is perishable. Likewise, putting lumber mills near forests avoids the expense of shipping heavy, bulky, uncut logs. The speed and efficiency of modern transportation systems have made these issues less critical than they were in years past. However, the cost of transportation continues to be important.

Zoning Regulations

Typical zoning classifications are single-family and multi-unit residential areas; business/commercial, light industry, and heavy manufacturing districts; and agriculture areas.

Zoning laws would not permit the building of a heavy industrial plant within either a residential district or a downtown business area. Light, clean industries often locate in industrial parks. Pleasantly landscaped and nonpolluting, these parks are often located in outlying regions, near highways but close to suburban residential communities.

Labor Supply

Wage rates differ from area to area, based on accessibility and established scales. The nature of the business and the level of skills needed may also influence the choice of location.

Manufacturing, milling, or warehousing firms that employ skilled or semiskilled labor might best locate near blue-collar communities. Motels and restaurants also depend on semiskilled workers to fill such relatively low-paying jobs as dishwashers, maids, janitors, groundskeepers, etc. However, it is generally more important for these operations to be located along highways, in downtown areas, or in tourist centers, than in respect to the source of labor.

A household-service agency that employs part-time homemakers would attract more applicants if located in a residential or suburban area than downtown. It might cost potential employees too much money, time, and energy to commute long distances. But an agency that supplies temporary help to downtown offices and benefits from this proximity would gain no great advantage by locating in suburbia.

Factors Often Overemphasized

When deciding on a location, many people overemphasize certain factors. One is the initial cost of the property. This, however, is a one-time charge, and if you are buying a small site (under 10 acres), an additional cost per acre may not be significant when amortized over the years you plan to remain at the site. A lower-priced property is not a bargain if the costs of operating on that site are much higher than they would be at a plant built on a more expensive property.

The cost of remodeling a facility is also sometimes overemphasized. The benefits to be derived from remodeling an appropriately located facility should be weighed against the cost of building a new facility.

Among the factors that have been increasing in importance, according to recent studies, are the availability of labor, market data, and financing arrangements. Among those that have been decreasing in importance are unionization, and access to raw materials.[3]

SHOPPING CENTERS AND MALLS

Customers appreciate a shopping center's convenience. They can drive in, park for free, and walk to their destination with relative ease and safety. There are generally four types of shopping centers:

1. **Neighborhood shopping centers.** The leading tenant is typically a supermarket or drugstore. Leasable space runs about 50,000 square feet. The center serves about 2500 to 40,000 people.
2. **Community shopping centers.** The leading tenant may be a variety or junior department store or a discount department store. The typical site covers 10 to 30 acres and serves 40,000 to 150,000 people.
3. **Regional shopping centers.** The leading tenant is one or more full-line department stores. The typical site covers 30 to 50 acres and serves 150,000 or more people. When there are several major department stores, the center can be called "super-regional." In these, smaller tenants offer a range of goods and services that approaches the appeal once found only downtown.
4. **Specialty theme shopping centers.** These centers do not necessarily have a major or "anchor" tenant. They offer highly specialized goods, including gourmet foods and custom-crafted, imported, and designer products. A greater number of the tenants may be independents (as opposed to franchises or chains). These centers often have an unusual architectural design and may be a tourist attraction.[4]

Shopping centers and malls are attractive locations to many entrepreneurs because of heavy consumer traffic and the benefits to be derived from group advertising. (*Courtesy of Blue Ridge Mall*, Kansas City, Mo.)

Shopping malls are roofed in and thus provide weather protection. Malls usually sponsor special events, such as visits from Santa Claus, art displays, and contests, to entice customers. They also have attractive common areas.

Highlighting the interior of Madison Square will be three major court areas. Two of these courts will feature fountains while the third will include a stage area for special events and promotions. The Garden, a food court with at least 15 eating places designed to accommodate more than 375 people at any one time, will be one of the most popular gathering places.

More than 25,000 square feet of skylighting will also be included in the two-level mall. Trees, some as high as 24 feet, will also be planted, with seating areas creating a park atmosphere.[5]

FIGURE 8.2
Mall Highlights, Chattanooga. Be aware of demographic data when selecting a town or community location.

Mall Highlights

Type Project	Enclosed, Two Level Air Conditioned Mall
Location	University Drive & Rideout Road
Acreage	118 Acres
Square Feet	1,092,989 Sq. Ft.
Total number of stores	100
Department Stores	Parisian (100,000)
	Castner-Knott (128,672)
	J.C. Penney (136,864)
	Pizitz (99,400)
	Sears (126,738)
	"F" — Junior Department Store (30,949)
Parking Spaces	4,869
Opening	Fall 1984

Source: CBL & Associates, Inc., One Northgate Park, Chattanooga, TN, Madison Square Mall, Huntsville, Alabama.

There are both advantages and disadvantages to locating within a shopping center or mall.

Advantages

Shopping area developers and owners look for successful retail and service establishments. First they sign on a prestige merchant as the lead tenant. Then they select other enterprises that will complement each other, so that the tenant mix offers a varied array of merchandise and services. This strategy bolsters the center's competitive strength and also supplies the market area's needs.[6]

Another advantage is that your market study has already been conducted for you. Center developers make this data available to potential tenants as noted in Figure 8.3. Developers of super-regional centers may also have improved roads

Trade Area Market Data

POPULATION:	
Huntsville (City)	146,597
Madison County	187,341
Trade Area*	516,413
HOUSEHOLDS:	
Huntsville (City)	50,292
Madison County	62,377
Trade Area*	176,152
PER HOUSEHOLD INCOME:	
Huntsville (City)	$22,897.00
Madison County	$21,584.00
Trade Area*	$20,200.00

*Includes 4 county area

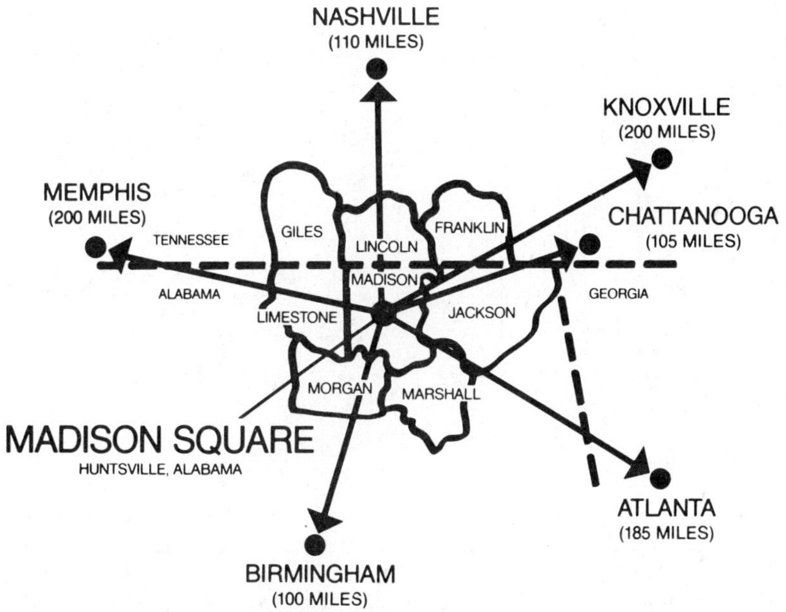
NASHVILLE
(110 MILES)
KNOXVILLE
(200 MILES)
MEMPHIS
(200 MILES)
CHATTANOOGA
(105 MILES)
TENNESSEE
GILES
LINCOLN
FRANKLIN
MADISON
ALABAMA
GEORGIA
LIMESTONE
JACKSON
MORGAN
MARSHALL
MADISON SQUARE
HUNTSVILLE, ALABAMA
ATLANTA
(185 MILES)
BIRMINGHAM
(100 MILES)

Source: CBL & Associates, Inc., Chattanooga, TN—describing the market trade area of Huntsville, Alabama.

FIGURE 8.3
Trade Area Market Data. Demographic data like that shown in Figure 8.3 are important in making location decisions.

and thus traffic patterns before starting construction of the center (see Figure 8.4).

Some developers help tenants plan their storefronts, exterior signs, and interior color schemes in order to ensure that store appearances will contribute to the center's overall image.[7]

Disadvantages

Leases are so tight you can't do anything

Tenants become part of a business team and thus have less independence when they locate in a mall. You must pay your share of the budget to support the team

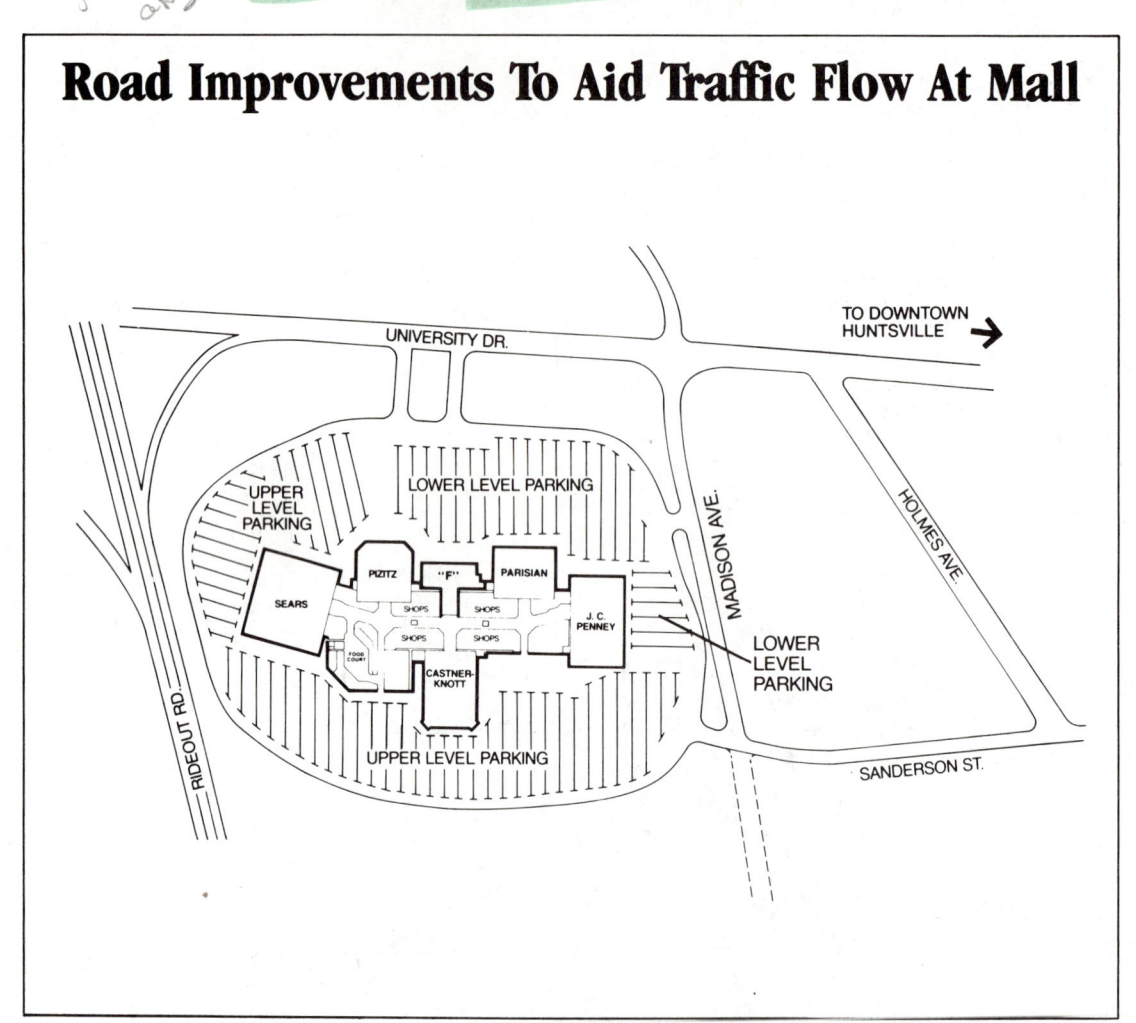

Road Improvements To Aid Traffic Flow At Mall

Source: CBL & Associates, Inc., Chattanooga, TN.

FIGURE 8.4 Road Improvements to Aid Traffic Flow at Mall. When locating in a mall, most important issues have already been addressed by the developers; when locating elsewhere, entrepreneurs have to be aware of traffic and road details.

effort. You must keep regular business hours, light your windows, and follow established procedures and regulations.

Generally, the mall owner furnishes the bare space. You do the "finishing out" at your own expense: you pay for light fixtures, counters, shelves, painting, and floor covering.

In shopping centers the rent is usually a minimum guaranteed amount per square foot of leased area or a percentage, usually between 5 and 7 percent of gross sales—whichever is more. In addition, you may have to pay dues to the center's merchant association, which maintains the common areas. Your company, then, will have to draw enough income to justify the added cost of locating in a center or mall.[8]

Getting In

To finance a center, a developer needs major leases from companies with strong credit ratings. The developer's own lenders favor tenant rosters that include the tripple-A ratings of national chains and franchises. A developer-owner may want about 60 percent of the tenants to be franchises and chain stores, but the other 40 percent are typically independent local businesspeople with good business records. This practice helps build customer rapport, since retail and service establishments with which local customers are already familiar will bring their clientele with them into the mall.[9]

Even small enterprises can locate in a shopping mall. The "Alley" is a popular place in Washington D.C.'s Crystal City Mall and on Waikiki (Honolulu), it's the International Market. The tiniest stores contain 80 square feet—and the kiosks even less. Craft businesses, specialty food stores, flea market goods, and small service firms are found in the Alley and the International Market, with short-term leases available.[10]

Many independent entrepreneurs report a high degree of satisfaction from tenancy in shopping malls. Malls provide numerous services and benefits, not the least of which are the mall promotions and special events that attract thousands of people.[11]

Factors to Consider

In considering whether to locate within a shopping center or to find your own site, you will want to ask yourself these questions:

1. Can I attract enough customers?
2. Does the center/mall offer the best sales volume potential for my kind of merchandise or service?
3. Can I benefit significantly from the center's access to a market? If so, can I attract the center's customers into my store?
4. Can I deal with the competition?
5. Can I cope with the regulations imposed on tenants?

Chapter 8

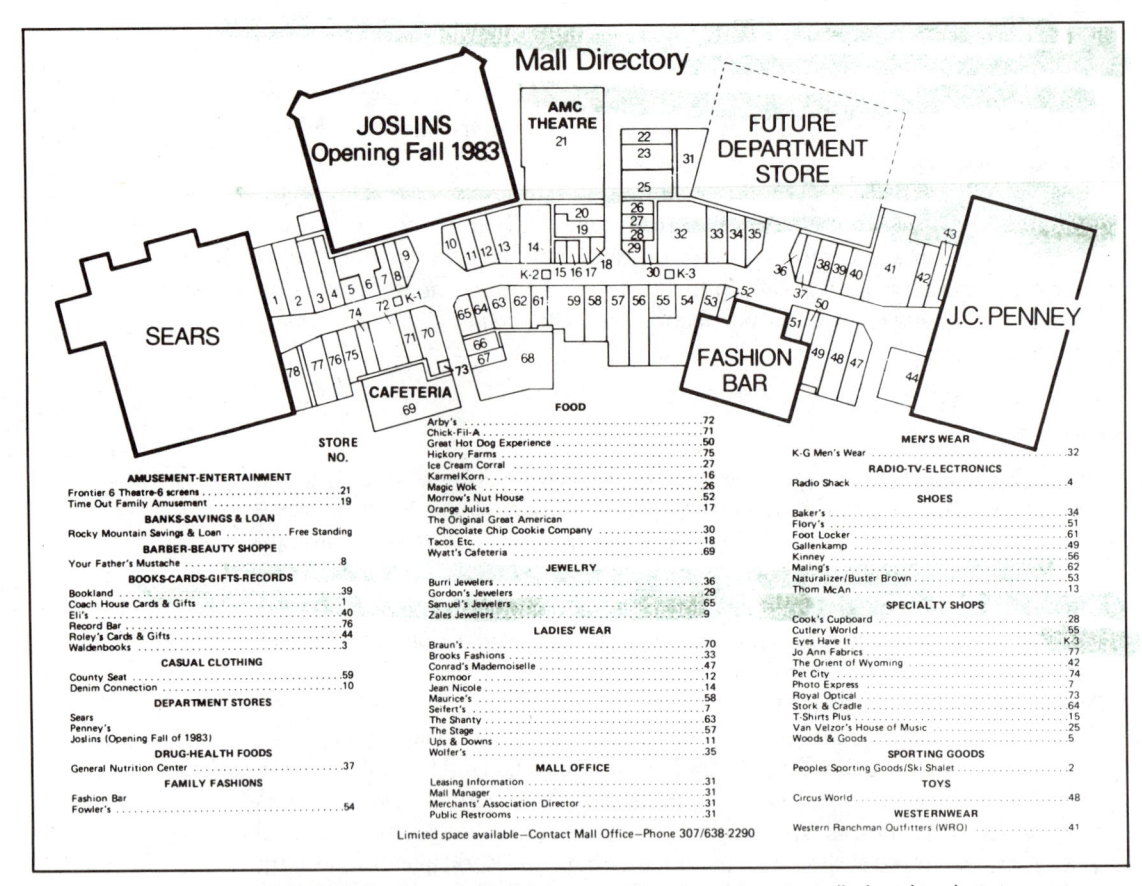

FIGURE 8.5 Frontier Mall Directory. The type of firms typically found in shopping centers and malls may help the potential entrepreneur in making a decision about the benefits of locating in such facilities.

LEASING A FACILITY

Many retailers rent rather than purchase or build their facility. This is particularly true in high-rent districts, whether located downtown or in shopping centers, where the owners are not interested in selling their properties.

Low rents can make a district very attractive. However, customer-oriented establishments such as retail and some service companies might find that the cost of the high-rent district may be offset by increased sales.

A lease is the legal document that binds the tenant to certain restrictions and limitations. You should seek legal advice before signing it. Typically, lease agreements, especially for retail establishments, involve a flat annual or monthly rate or a percentage-based rental fee. With the latter arrangement, the landlord usually receives a specific monthly minimum plus a percentage of sales. Both the leasee and the lesor should agree on the figures involved before signing the lease. (See Figure 8.6.)

SHOPPING CENTER
LANDLORD
TENANT

		Page
ARTICLE I—REFERENCE PROVISIONS, SHOPPING CENTER, LEASED PREMISES AND TERM		
Section 1.1	Reference Provisions	1
Section 1.2	Shopping Center, Leased Premises and Term	2
Section 1.3	Acceptance of Leased Premises	2
Section 1.4	Quiet Enjoyment	2
Section 1.5	Parties to Have No Liability If Shopping Center Not Constructed	2
ARTICLE II—RENT AND OTHER CHARGES		
Section 2.1	Minimum Annual Rent	2
Section 2.2	Percentage Rent	2
Section 2.3	Taxes	3
Section 2.4	Common Areas and Operating Costs	4
Section 2.5	Utilities Charges	5
ARTICLE III—CONSTRUCTION OF LEASED PREMISES		5
ARTICLE IV—USE OF LEASED PREMISES		
Section 4.1	Use of Leased Premises	5
Section 4.2	Joint Opening of Shopping Center	6
Section 4.3	Continuous Operation by Tenant	6
Section 4.4	Additional Covenants of Tenant	6
Section 4.5	Signs, Awnings and Canopies	7
Section 4.6	Retail Restriction Limit	8
ARTICLE V—INSURANCE REQUIRED OF TENANT		
Section 5.1	Insurance Required of Tenant	8
Section 5.2	Cost of Insurance	9
Section 5.3	Fire Insurance Rate and Requirements	9
Section 5.4	Waiver of Subrogation	9
ARTICLE VI—REPAIRS AND MAINTENANCE		
Section 6.1	Repairs by Landlord	10
Section 6.2	Repairs and Maintenance by Tenant	10
Section 6.3	Inspection	10
Section 6.4	Obstructions	10
ARTICLE VII—ADDITIONS AND ALTERATIONS		
Section 7.1	By Landlord	10
Section 7.2	By Tenant	10
ARTICLE VIII—DAMAGE, DESTRUCTION, OR CONDEMNATION OF THE LEASED PREMISES		
Section 8.1	Damage or Destruction	11
Section 8.2	Condemnation	11
ARTICLE IX—MERCHANTS ASSOCIATION		
Section 9.1	Obligation to Join	12
Section 9.2	Advertising	12
ARTICLE X—FINANCING		
Section 10.1	Financing	13
Section 10.2	Subordination	13
ARTICLE XI—DEFAULT BY TENANT		
Section 11.1	Default	13
Section 11.2	Landlord's Rights on Default	13
Section 11.3	Non-Waiver Provisions	14
Section 11.4	Inability to Perform	14
Section 11.5	Landlord's Expenses	14
ARTICLE XII—OTHER PROVISIONS		
Section 12.1	Definition and Liability of Landlord	14
Section 12.2	Relationship of the Parties	14
Section 12.3	Security Deposit	14
Section 12.4	Indemnity	15
Section 12.5	Damage to Property or Persons	15
Section 12.6	Assignment or Subletting	15
Section 12.7	Surrender of Premises and Holding Over	15
Section 12.8	Lien of Landlord for Rent and Other Sums	16
Section 12.9	Liens	16
Section 12.10	Interest	16
Section 12.11	Late Payments	16
Section 12.12	Consents	16
Section 12.13	Waiver of Right of Redemption	16
Section 12.14	Notices	16
Section 12.15	No Broker	16
Section 12.16	Short-Form Lease	16
Section 12.17	Entire and Binding Agreement	16
Section 12.18	Provisions Severable	16
Section 12.19	Captions	17
Section 12.20	Rule against Perpetuities	17
Section 12.21	Irrevocable Offer	17

EXHIBIT A—Shopping Center
EXHIBIT B—Construction of Leased Premises

(2/061581)

FIGURE 8.6
Sample Shopping-Center Lease. Be sure to have the lease for any type of facility checked by an attorney. Although a mall lease is often very comprehensive, this sample should give you some idea of what you can expect the lease agreement to cover.

Before renting a facility under either type of agreement, compare the rent with that paid by neighboring establishments of like condition, size, and purpose and estimate your probable volume of sales in order to ascertain that the rent asked is reasonable.

Don't as a neophyte sign a long-term lease—for, say, five or more years. Since you don't know how successful your business will be, or even if you will want to remain in the first site selected, don't commit yourself for more than one or two years if at all possible.

The lease may also specify the extent and nature of any remodeling and who pays for it; liabilities and responsibilities of each party; the permissible exterior treatment, including signs; limitations on the type of products or services offered or the activities performed; and so on.

Grade each factor: "A" for excellent, "B" for good, "C" for fair, and "D" for poor.

Factor	Grade
1. Centrally located to reach my market	_____
2. Raw materials available readily	_____
3. Quantity of available labor	_____
4. Transportation availability and rates	_____
5. Labor rates of pay/estimated productivity	_____
6. Adequacy of utilities (sewer, water, power, gas)	_____
7. Local business climate	_____
8. Provision for future expansion	_____
9. Taxation burden	_____
10. Topography of the site (slope and foundation)	_____
11. Quality of police and fire protection	_____
12. Housing availability for workers and management	_____
13. Environmental factors (schools, cultural, community atmosphere)	_____
14. Estimate of quality of this site in 10 years	_____
15. Estimate of this site in relation to my major competitor	_____

Source: Fred I. Weber, Jr., "Locating or Relocating Your Business," Small Business Administration, Management Aids No. 201 for Small Manufacturers, Washington, D.C.

FIGURE 8.7 Checklist No. 1: Checklist for Rating Sites.

COST AS A DETERMINANT OF LOCATION

There are many issues to be evaluated in deciding on a location, but the bottom line is invariably the capital you have available. Numerous costs are involved, besides rent or mortgage payments. The checklists in Figures 8.7 and 8.8 can be used to compare various locations on a cost-expense basis.

Utilities

Paying a low price for an old, uninsulated building may mean more expense than buying a modern, higher-priced but energy-efficient building. Heating, air-conditioning, and electricity expenses will all be lower. Manufacturing firms, which use a lot of power to operate their equipment and machinery, are particularly vulnerable to the escalating expenses of utilities. Customers must find the

	Location 1	Location 2	Location 3

Access to[1]
  Stock (inventory)
  Raw materials
  Customers
  Labor
  Service
  Parts			

Totals (points)			

Operating Costs[2]
  Heating
  Electricity
  Other utilities
  Rent (or depreciation)
  Wages
  Insurance
	$	$	$

Taxes[2]
  Property
  Income
  Sales
  Payroll
  Other			

Totals ($)	$	$	$

[1] Rate as "good" (10 points), "average" (5 points), or "poor" (1 point).
[2] Use estimated or exact dollar costs per month (multiply by 12 for annual cost).

FIGURE 8.8 Checklist No. 2: Comparative-Cost Analysis Chart. Use Checklists 1 and 2 in collecting realistic data on the business of your choice and specific sites included in the analyses.

establishment comfortable and reasonably attractive, and so must employees. It costs money to prepare a facility for efficient operation, a factor that should be taken into account in choosing a location.

Taxes and Insurance

Property, income, payroll, city, and state taxes are other variables in the location decision formula. Some of these rates may differ from site to site. The condition of the selected site and of the surrounding neighborhood usually determines insurance rates.

Wages and Salaries

As noted earlier, the location may affect the number and nature of the available labor supply and thus influence wage levels. If your employees are unionized, however, location may have little effect on wages.

Shipping and Transportation

Prospective owners of distribution and transportation firms should evaluate a location's closeness to sources of supply and to their market. The further away they are, the more it will cost to bring goods in or send them out.

SOURCES OF HELP

The following people and sources can provide advice and specific community data to help you decide on a location and site.

Government and Other Agencies

The field offices of the Small Business Administration and of the Department of Commerce as well as chambers of commerce and libraries can provide you with city and county maps, census figures, and information on city ordinances, tax rates, and labor laws.

Realtors, Bankers, Attorneys, and Accountants

Some banks have real estate departments where advice can be obtained. Realtors will tell you of buildings for sale or lease and can show you around the available facilities, allowing you to collect comparative data. Be aware, however, that realtors have a vested interest in selling properties, so that some of their more glowing remarks should be discounted.

Manufacturers and Wholesalers

Because of their expertise and familiarity with the community in which they are located, these people can be sources of information about local trends and patterns.

Shopping Malls, Office Complexes, and Industrial Parks

Space may be available, or may be about to become so, in any of these types of complexes. These sources, although they too have a vested interest, can supply data about the cost of utilities, typical wage and lease rates, the availability of vendors and shippers, labor supply, parking, and customer traffic and buying habits.

Utility and Transportation Companies

These sources can provide information about the availability and cost of utilities and transportation, the skill level and size of the labor supply, market potential, the stability of the community, and other population characteristics.

Business and Trade Associations

In any particular line or field, local or regional business organizations can also contribute helpful information.

SUMMARY

Whether moving or remaining in familiar surroundings, you have to consider numerous factors in selecting a neighborhood and a specific business site. Will you purchase or rent property? Should you locate your business in your home, in a shopping mall, an office complex, or an industrial park?

Location is very often the key to success. Entire books and many articles have been written on the subject, in relation to every type of business. Use the guidelines suggested here to gather all possible data before deciding on a location.

DISCUSSION QUESTIONS

1. From your experience or in your opinion, what factors differentiate those who relocate from those who remain in their present community? What would influence you to move?

2. What factors do you think should predominate in selecting a community and in choosing one neighborhood or site over another? Form two or more debate teams and try to convince each other of your opinions.
3. What is different and what is the same about selecting a location for a retail, service, manufacturing, or hospitality company?
4. If you can't afford either to construct or to remodel, how could you use the guidelines presented in this chapter to evaluate possible sites? Does the kind of business you have chosen to open influence how much weight you should put on each of these factors? Why or why not?
5. Would your type of business fit into a shopping center or mall? Discuss the advantages and disadvantages.
6. If the bottom line is cost, what guidelines are the most significant to consider? Why?

ACTIVITIES AND EXERCISES

1. Assume you are going to open the business you have chosen to operate in the area where you now live. Drive through or visit several neighborhoods. Which are the most attractive potential areas, on the basis of the guidelines presented in this chapter? Be ready to present your findings and conclusions to the group in a systematic manner. (Use the chapter checklists for recording information in addition to the decision-making aids in Appendix B, particularly the T-chart, to record the advantages and disadvantages of each site.)
2. Locate one or more buildings offered for rent or sale. Explain the class project to the owner or real estate agent and obtain their permission to tour the premises. Evaluate the place in relation to the guidelines given here and to the business you would like to operate. Note on your checklist what criteria are met by each site visited and decide what you would plan to modify and how, if you were to obtain the site. Report your findings and conclusions to the group. (Estimate operating expenses and record your figures on the worksheet in Figure 6.7 in Chapter 6.)
3. Talk with entrepreneurs located in shopping centers or malls. How do they evaluate the advantages and disadvantages of that location? Which factors weighed heaviest in their decision to locate there?
4. Visit an attorney or real estate agent to obtain a typical business facility lease form. Analyze the items and requirements. Would you prefer to rent or to purchase a facility? Why?

NOTES

1. James R. Lowry, "Using a Traffic Study to Select a Retail Site," *Small Marketers' Aid* (Washington, D.C.: Small Business Administration, 1979), p. 6.

2. Karen E. Claus, "Signs and Your Business," *Small Marketers' Aid*, (Washington, D.C.: SBA, 1979), pp 2–8.
3. Fred I. Weber, Jr., "Locating or Relocating a Business," *Small Marketers' Aid* (Washington, D.C.: SBA, 1979), p. 5.
4. J. Ross McKeever and Frank H. Spink, Jr., "Factors in Considering a Shopping Center Location," *Management Aid* no. 2.017 (Washington, D.C.: SBA, 1980).
5. Interview with John R. Martin, Jr., Director of Corporate Relations and Marketing, CBL and Associates, Inc., Chattanooga, TN, March 1983.
6. Interviews with John Griffin, Frontier Mall Property Manager and Robert J. Liedler, Blue Ridge Mall Manager, In Cheyenne, Wyoming, and Kansas City, Missouri, February and June 1983.
7. Ibid.
8. McKever and Spink, "Shopping Center."
9. Ibid.
10. Observations and interviews, Washington, D.C. (February 1983) and Honolulu (December 1983).
11. Based on observations and personal interviews, February–December 1983.

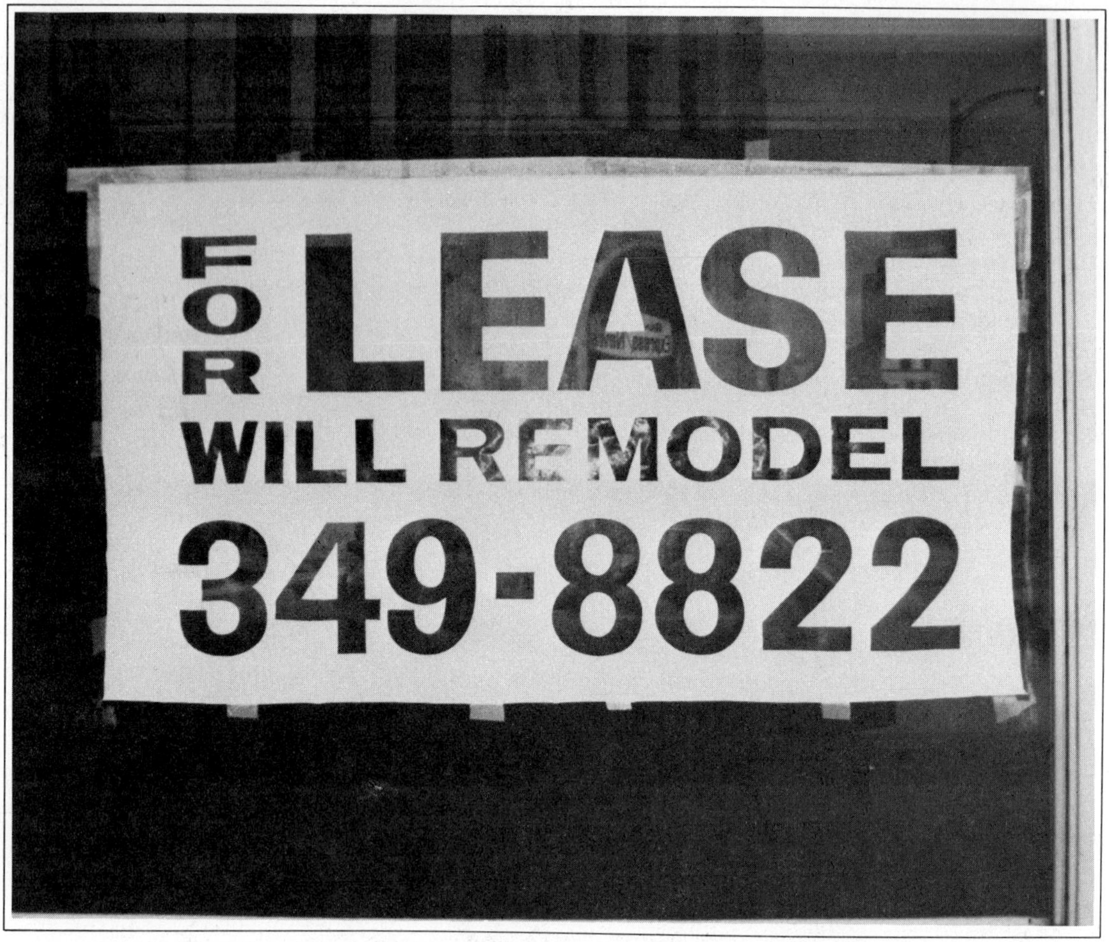
FOR LEASE
WILL REMODEL
349-8822

c·h·a·p·t·e·r ·9·

Facilities and Layout

Objectives

1. Identify and explain three criteria for judging the suitability of a facility for your business.

2. Explain important aspects of the structure of the building and the remodeling it might need.

3. Describe how to plan layouts and explain the layout needs of different kinds of businesses.

4. Evaluate one or more potential sites and select equipment and furniture.

5. Plan a layout for a specific type of business.

The building and layout of a business should be designed to facilitate its operations and to form a comfortable environment for customers and employees. The costs of remodeling the facilities and layout of your business are part of the capital you need to get started. Even if you find a building to purchase or rent that you can afford and that is suitable in size and design, you will want to plan your own arrangement of equipment, furniture, supplies, and tools.

CRITERIA FOR JUDGING A FACILITY

Although equipment and so on can be arranged after the business is operational, walls and built-ins cannot be altered so readily. Thus efficiency, comfort, and esthetics need to be considered from the beginning.

Efficient Function

Every owner wants to keep costs and expenses as low as possible. To do otherwise can be fatal: no profit, no business! The layout must facilitate the effective processing and flow of work and customers. To make a business facility not only efficient but also comfortable and attractive need not add excessive costs, if considered during the planning stage.

Comfort

Comfort involves things that contribute to people's physical well-being, including heating, air conditioning, lighting and noise control, safety, sanitation, well-designed work stations, adequate seating, and a lounging area.

Esthetics

Esthetic appeal involves the attractiveness of the decor, including the colors and fabrics chosen for ceiling, floor, and wall coverings as well as for furniture and equipment. All of these have to be some color, and it costs no more to choose colors that are pleasing to the eye and to the subconscious.

Comfort and esthetics contribute to the effective performance of employees and owner alike. They help raise morale and alleviate fatigue. These principles also apply anywhere customers will be received or served.

STRUCTURAL FEATURES

Whether constructing a new facility or remodeling an existing one, you should consider the following factors: energy efficiency, exterior, entrances and exits, accessibility to the handicapped, sanitation, security and safety, utilities placement and noise control, and psychological and physiological effects.

Energy Efficiency

High energy costs force people today to be interested in insulation, heating methods, and the tightness of doors, windows, chimneys, and any other openings through which heat or air conditioning might escape or cold and hot air find entrance. Compare the expense of gas, electricity, and hot-water heating in your selected community before deciding which type to install. Buildings that are already energy efficient may cost more. But remodeling old buildings to accommodate these needs can also be expensive.

The Exterior

The exterior should not only reflect the type of business conducted inside but should also attract customers esthetically. The facade should reflect your desired image and should attract attention, thus serving as an advertisement as well.

An important part of the building's external appearance is the sign. Will it be large, neon-lighted, and gaudy? Or small and discreet? Will it stand high above the neighboring stores or buildings and their signs? Will it stick out from the facade or be nailed flat to it? These decisions depend, in part, on the type of business you are opening as well as on the competition in the selected neighbor-

The price of leasing run-down facilities may be attractive to owners with limited capital, but remember the cliché, "You can't expect to put new wine in old bottles and get the desired results."

hood. The electricity expense of a flashing neon sign may preclude this choice no matter what your preference is. But where such a sign is very important in drawing in business (e.g., for a motel or restaurant along a highway), the costs may have to be borne.

Before putting up a sign, also check on community practices and regulations, including local zoning laws. Your lease, if you have one, may also impose restrictions on the type of sign that can be mounted on the property.

Entrances and Exits

To meet standards for the handicapped, doors should be wide, with at least one that is easy to open for people in wheelchairs or with limited strength. There must also be a rear or side exit, in case of fire or other calamity. Beyond these requirements, you will want your business's entrances and exits to be attractive, easily accessible to the nearest parking areas, and clearly visible.

Accessibility to the Handicapped

Public buildings are subject to government regulations that set certain standards to meet the needs of the handicapped. Although a small business need not comply with the following criteria, such accommodations will attract handicapped customers. Many of your competitors have already used these criteria:

1. Entrances and exits, as indicated above, are accessible; this includes installing electric eyes to open doors automatically and ramps to reach outside entrances with ease;
2. Ramps are constructed wherever there would ordinarily be steps;
3. Elevators are available to permit access to the second and higher floors;
4. Restroom cubicles have handrails and wide doors;
5. Sinks in restrooms are low enough to be reached from wheel chairs;
6. Buttons to control elevators, switches to open doors, etc., are in reach of people in wheelchairs;
7. Public telephones and other services are placed at appropriate heights for people in wheelchairs;
8. Loudspeakers or other audio devices are available to help hearing-impaired customers hear announcements, etc.;
9. Large-print signs and other visual devices are available to help seeing-impaired customers read notices, etc.;
10. Any other devices to make services convenient to physically handicapped customers and visitors.[1]

Sanitation

Wherever food and beverages are processed or served, sanitary procedures are vital, and periodic government inspections to assure the protection of the public's health are a fact of life. And in all types of business, employees and customers need clean restrooms—particularly in such establishments as food and beverage places and gasoline stations.

Trash cans should be ample, easily accessible (both inside and outside of buildings), and well-covered. All premises, whether open to the public or only to employees, should be kept clean and free of germ-producing substances (see also Chapter 20).

Ease of cleaning is one important factor to consider in selecting floor and wall coverings, furniture, and equipment and in locating restrooms, employee lounges, and trash-disposal areas.

Security and Safety

Try to limit temptations and opportunities for your customers to shoplift and for your employees to pilfer. Locate entrances and exits where you and your manager and trusted employees can keep them under observation. Install locks on built-in cabinets, counters, shelving, and storage areas, including employee lockers (see also Chapter 20).[2]

Almost any environment has potential for accidents and/or for health dangers. Counters may have sharp corners, electrical outlets may be overloaded, or extension cords may be laying about or strung across a room. Manufacturing equipment poses special problems, but careful planning can limit the number of hazards. Chemicals, including cleaning supplies, must be housed in safe facilities.

Utilities Placement and Noise Reduction

Effective planning of the type and location of heating, air conditioning, and lighting methods can reduce problems later. Noise control, too, is important. Heating and air conditioning outlets should be placed to provide maximum circulation but should not blow directly onto any one work station. Lighting can make the difference between fatigue and efficiency: it should be bright but not glaring, and a fixture should be located over or near every work station.

You can keep noise down by using acoustical floor and wall coverings. Where possible, group noisy equipment together, away from other work areas, and cover or isolate it with acoustical walls or room dividers.

Psychological Factors

The decor, including colors and fabrics, wall and floor coverings, drapes and furniture, can help raise or lower morale and thus productivity. Dark colors induce depression, too-bright colors overstimulate. Extensive use of nature colors such as greens and blues can soothe people to sleep. The best idea is to use unobtrusive colors, such as beige, pale lemon, and cream, accented with a few bright touches to stimulate positive emotions and productivity. Lighting can also contribute to or detract from the total effect, as noted above.[3] (See Figure 9.1.)

FIGURE 9.1
Checklist of Evaluation Factors—Existing Business vs. Remodeling.

| | Site no. 1 ||| Site no. 2 |||
Factors	Good	Adequate	Poor	Good	Adequate	Poor
Energy efficiency	___	___	___	___	___	___
Exterior	___	___	___	___	___	___
Sign(s)	___	___	___	___	___	___
Exits	___	___	___	___	___	___
Accessibility to the handicapped	___	___	___	___	___	___
Sanitation	___	___	___	___	___	___
Security	___	___	___	___	___	___
Safety	___	___	___	___	___	___
Utilities Placement	___	___	___	___	___	___
Overall Evaluation	___	___	___	___	___	___

THE LAYOUT

Before you decide on a site, be sure that it can accommodate your desired layout. We will examine the layout needs of several business categories, but first we will discuss their common requirements.

Modeling Layout

"Work flow" involves the movement of both products and information, while "traffic flow" is the movement of people, including customers, employees, delivery people, and visitors.

Time is money. And the time wasted in walking too far too often, or in dodging around fixtures or other people, or in waiting in long lines is both costly and frustrating. Employee frustration leads to decreased morale and productivity and to inefficient customer service. Frustrated customers are dissatisfied customers, and may not return.

Figure 9.2 shows the layout of a typical auto and engine repair shop. Customers enter the front door and approach the customer counter, where they order work or parts, pick up repaired objects, and pay bills. To deliver and to retrieve vehicles, they go to the side parking lot.

Is this the best arrangement? Can you perceive any problems? Chart the flow of both work and traffic and suggest possible improvements.

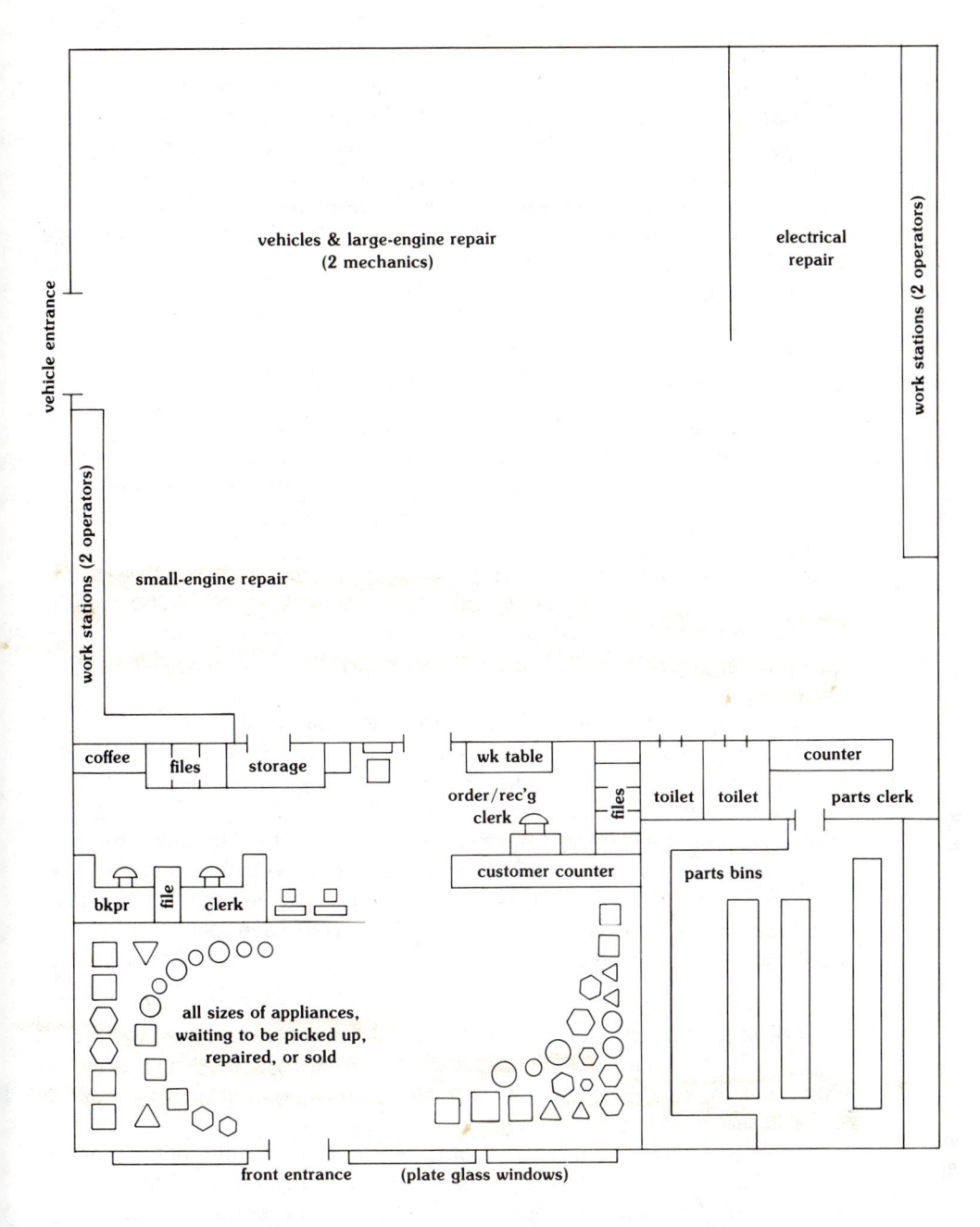

Repair shop employs 8 operators: 6 in the shop and 2 (1 of whom is owner) on the road to make service calls.
Office employs 4 workers: bookkeeper, assistant, order/receiving clerk, and parts clerk.

FIGURE 9.2 Layout of a Repair Shop.

You can experiment with layouts by using graph paper. You can draw proposed walls, storage areas, and built-in counters as well as equipment and furniture to scale. You can also cut out appropriately scaled models of movable elements and move them around, until you identify the best arrangement. You are trying to design the most efficient, safe, secure, comfortable, and esthetically appealing layout possible, within your given limitations.

You can construct such a model for each site you are considering. These graphic models, together with the cost-comparison charts in Chapter 8, can help you decide on a site, a facility, and a layout.

Layout for Retail Stores

Retailers deal with products and with customers, and they have to consider the needs of both in designing a layout. The relevant factors include: customer buying habits and service; image; product organization and displays; best utilization of space; appearance of spaciousness; security; and separation of activities.

Space value in merchandising. Each area of a store has a relative value; the front-right space has most, then the front center, the right middle, and the left. Rear portions of stores are generally the least trafficked, suggesting that these areas should be reserved for durable goods and for service and repair counters.

Since shoppers tend to move to the right and middle of the store, the most sellable and valuable merchandise should be placed there. This is also the appropriate place for convenience and impulse items. The latter can also be scattered throughout a store, using mid-aisle displays or other arrangements. As customers pass along the aisles to find specific goods on their shopping lists, they are often enticed to add some of these impulse items to their purchases.[4]

Seasonal goods are often placed directly in front of checkout stations. Such products include Christmas decorations and cards or lawn, patio, and garden equipment (in spring and early summer).

Organization, image, and security. An attractive and spacious-feeling layout helps create the image that "customers come first," that their needs and wants are considered. Heating and air conditioning, lighting, color, and fabrics are all used to enhance this image.

The store's layout should also unobtrusively facilitate security control. The law prohibits arresting shoplifters on the premises so that apprehending them can be very difficult—even when shopkeepers are certain they have evidence. Arranging the layout to make every section visible to yourself and your employees may prevent some potential shoplifters from taking unnecessary risks.

The alert shopkeeper displays small valuable items in locked glass showcases. Salesclerks can also be trained to greet customers almost immediately upon their entrance or to supervise browsers by hovering a short distance away, as if ready to assist when needed.

Retailers deal with products and customers. Layout guidelines include service and image; product organization and displays; and utilization of space, security, and efficiency.

Employee stealing is another problem, which will be discussed more extensively later (see also Chapter 20). For now we can note that an open but controlled physical environment can also serve to inhibit employee pilferage.

Layout of a Wholesale Business or a Factory

Efficiency, including speed and economy, is a primary consideration for the wholesale establishment or factory. Both types of business continuously process goods on mechanized or computerized assembly lines.

Wholesalers should place their most-ordered items in easily accessible areas. Organizing products, materials, and systems in the most efficient manner possible can save time and energy and produce a better utilization of wages spent.

Factories typically place raw materials close to the unloading docks and to where they will be used. If more than one delivery door is available, this principle is more readily applicable. Finished products should emerge from the inspection stations and the assembly line as near to storage facilities or loading docks as possible.

All operations should seek to minimize the movement from one station to the next. Time and energy are saved and efficiency raised.

Layout of a Service Company

Because service firms differ so much, few guidelines apply to all. Companies that have customer contact need to arrange their layout to accommodate those customers' needs and wants. Comfort and esthetics are very important in situations like these.

Any type of service business, however, should aim for an efficient layout that can speed and economize the efforts of owner and employees alike.

Comparing Hospitality, Retail, Manufacturing, and Service Businesses

Restaurants. Restaurants have to arrange tables, chairs, and service areas in a fashion that avoids crowding or inefficient service yet does not waste valuable space. Food preparation areas should, for sanitation reasons, be situated well apart from garbage disposal and dishwashing areas.

A respect for both comfort and esthetics in creating the layout and decor can reap sales benefits. The kitchen and the employee lounge, even though these are unseen by customers, should also be clean and safe to keep employee morale high and to protect customers' health.

Motels. Motels of the "ma-and-pa" variety offer perhaps the most potential for entrants into the hospitality industry. The owner/manager must determine where to house the laundry and service rooms (so that employees can function efficiently), the ice and vending machines (to serve guests), and the office, lobby, and, perhaps, living quarters (for the benefit of guests and staff alike). The smaller the establishment, the more likely it is that the owner will do most of the work, helped perhaps by part-time maids and groundskeepers. The motel staff should have quick and easy access to telephones, the front desk, tools, linens, and other products or services that guests typically require.

Shoe stores. Shoe stores should also be both attractive and comfortable. Carpeting, good chairs, and attractive displays can all enhance customer appeal. It is also important to minimize crowding and to make the customer-receiving and cashier station readily available. The behind-the-scenes space is used for inventory storage, employees' restroom, and office facilities.

Manufacturing and processing firms. Customers rarely enter manufacturing or processing plants. Thus the facility is designed primarily for efficiency and for the safety and comfort of the employees. The second goal contributes to the first, moreover, because employees who do not feel both safe and comfortable can suffer physically and psychologically. The result may be that morale and thus worker productivity plummet.

Barbershops. A barbershop is one of the easiest enterprises to illustrate and imagine. People come to get their hair cut and styled and to have a massage, a facial, or a manicure. Each chair should be placed close to a work station and a sink. At the front are space and chairs for waiting, with magazines and perhaps coffee or a soft-drink machine. The rear houses supplies and a restroom, out of sight of the work and service areas. The decor may vary from average to exotic, depending on the clientele sought.

Word-processing or data-processing services. Like the barbershop and the shoe store, the word- or data-processing company usually provides a single-purpose function. They produce fast and accurate paperwork, records, computations, and the like for customers. Workers need comfortable chairs, and the environment and atmosphere should be conducive to high productivity. A client waiting area is needed, although customers will usually be consulted with by telephone or when the operator(s) pick up and deliver materials.

Office Space

Every type of business needs facilities and equipment for keeping records and performing managerial analyses. At the very least, this entails a desk, file cabinet, telephone, calculator, and customer-receiving area.

Small firms often crowd the office into a small cluttered space in the rear. Yet recordkeeping and paper-processing are essential operations in any successful business. For maximum efficiency, esthetics and comfort should not be neglected here either, although the cost can be minimized. The layout, then, must also include space for office work. You can use the checklist in Figure 9.3 to evaluate possible business sites according to the criteria developed here.

SELECTING EQUIPMENT AND FURNITURE

Knowing what you need to adequately equip your establishment is important in making effective decisions. How should you set up the work stations and select equipment, furnishings, and tools?

A good idea is to visit entrepreneurs in businesses similar to the one that interests you and discover what arrangements and selections they have made. Then collect catalogs and survey the many alternatives of price range, function, and quality. These efforts should give you some idea of the costs involved in equipping and furnishing an establishment. Visiting with vendors is another alternative, but recognize that they have a vested interest in the products they offer. Enter the price data obtained from catalogs and vendors on the list of start-up costs (see worksheet No. 1, Fig. 6.3 in Chapter 6).

	Site no. 1	Site no. 2
	Good Adequate Poor	Good Adequate Poor
Efficient Function:		
Merchandise displays	___ ___ ___	___ ___ ___
Materials/stock storage	___ ___ ___	___ ___ ___
Traffic flow (aisles & space for customer & employee movement)	___ ___ ___	___ ___ ___
Work flow (adequate space & equipment for processing work)	___ ___ ___	___ ___ ___
Work stations (adequate space, per station, to process & complete work)	___ ___ ___	___ ___ ___
Customer receiving areas	___ ___ ___	___ ___ ___
Customer service areas	___ ___ ___	___ ___ ___
Comfort/Esthetics:		
Heating	___ ___ ___	___ ___ ___
Air conditioning	___ ___ ___	___ ___ ___
Lighting	___ ___ ___	___ ___ ___
Noise levels	___ ___ ___	___ ___ ___
Restrooms & lounge(s)	___ ___ ___	___ ___ ___
Colors & coverings:		
ceilings & walls	___ ___ ___	___ ___ ___
floors	___ ___ ___	___ ___ ___
equipment & furniture	___ ___ ___	___ ___ ___
Appropriate seating	___ ___ ___	___ ___ ___
Customer areas	___ ___ ___	___ ___ ___
Overall Evaluation	___ ___ ___	___ ___ ___

FIGURE 9.3 Layout and Associated Factors.

Ergonomics

Today, more than ever before, people are studying work ("ergonomics") and how it is performed and processed with respect to workers and work systems. The layout and facilities of a business should therefore be planned to accommodate the workers, i.e., anyone on duty, whether employees or owners/managers. Shelves, furniture, equipment, and supplies must be placed with thought for where and how work will be performed.[5]

If you or your employees will be standing all day, will you or they walk the aisles and then return to the cashier's stations? Should stools or chairs be available so that people can sit down when not occupied? These questions particularly involve work performed by waiters and waitresses, bellhops, porters, cashiers, tellers, gas station attendants, bartenders, salesclerks, cooks/chefs, beauticians, barbers, teachers/trainers, nurses, guides, guards, maids, janitors, and many others.

Conversely, what about those workers who must sit all day? The human anatomy was not designed to allow us to stay in one position for a long time. Stand-up workers need an occasional opportunity to sit down, and sit-down workers need chairs and tables/desks that are comfortable to work in or at. In both cases, the most frequently used supplies and tools should be housed within easy reach. Whether in a manufacturing or an office setting, machines should be placed at a convenient height so that the operators do not become fatigued with reaching and bending. Too short a reach over a long period can also tense the limbs and the back and neck muscles. Both morale and productivity drop sharply when worker needs are not perceived and planned for.[6]

People whose work requires them to sit for long periods of time must have chairs and work stations adjusted to suit their anatomy—to avoid back, shoulder, and arm fatigue.

Technical and Office Equipment and Tools

Presumably, you are not planning to open a business totally foreign to you. The experience you have gained by working for others and/or through education and training should suggest the technical equipment and tools needed for your planned company. Technical expertise is important for manufacturing and processing businesses but also in various service, repair, and retail establishments.

In your vocational training or on the job, were you aware of the machinery being used? Did you listen when the instructors or owners talked about the equipment they had chosen? Perhaps you may want to buy the same kind of equipment. It's possible, though, that the machinery and tools you have worked with in the past may now be obsolete.

There is a bewildering number of companies and models in the equipment industry. It's easy to end up buying a machine that is low-quality, inappropriate, and/or too expensive. Such mistakes can cost you both time and money, especially if they involve you later with frequent breakdowns, poor repair service, and the unavailability of parts. Downtime is lost time, and time is money.

Once you've tentatively chosen some equipment, it's wise to seek out a number of users and ask them if production has matched their expectations. Did they get good quality for their money? Would they buy something else if they had it to do over again? If so, what and why?

Service and parts will be easier to find for entrepreneurs located in metropolitan areas than for those operating in outlying districts. Yet there are significant differences among equipment companies, as in the cost of annual service contracts and the time it takes for a repair person to answer service request calls. Even if you are skilled enough to be able to repair your own equipment, you still have to get parts. Take the costs of continuing operations into account when evaluating each piece of equipment (see also Chapter 15).

Furniture

Practically everything that isn't built-in or that isn't operated mechanically or electronically is furniture. Industrial houses advertise heavy-duty furniture and specialized work stations for *every* need, including merchandise racks, shelving, service counters, couches, chairs, tables, desks, and file cabinets. They can supply furnishings for motels, restaurants, financial institutions, mortuaries, schools, clinics, and churches. Finally, they stock the special chairs and work stations needed by engineers and craftspeople, barbers and beauticians, and repair services and fix-it operators. Entrepreneurs with limited funds can also consider buying used furniture.

Leasing versus Purchasing

There are several reasons why some entrepreneurs prefer to lease rather than to buy equipment, tools, or furniture. Many owners hesitate to commit their capital resources to long-term payment for expensive equipment, especially when they fear they lack enough information to make wise decisions initially and when

Comfort and attractiveness applies to customers and employees alike. In this bookstore, browsers may rest awhile, which often leads to sales—when they otherwise might have tired before they looked over the possibilities.

models, performance, and prices are changing so rapidly. What appears the best on the market today may be obsolete tomorrow.

Leasing gives you the opportunity to get hands-on experience and to test how well various equipment suits your company's needs. Meanwhile, you can wait while new models—with increased capabilities and lower costs—emerge on the market. Many companies also offer a "lease with option to buy" alternative, whereby all or part of the lease payments are applied to the purchase price.

Furniture, too, can be leased. Some entrepreneurs whose investment capital is limited but who expect a high sales volume estimate that their income will cover a monthly lease expense. Smart business owners also look for tax breaks when they lease either equipment or furniture. For instance, the deduction allowed for leasing equipment is often greater than the depreciation that can be taken on furniture you have bought. But check current tax laws first before assuming that leasing is the better financial choice.

SUMMARY

Plan your facilities and layout and select your equipment and furniture to meet the criteria of efficient function, comfort, and esthetics. You have to think through what work will be performed, where, how, and by whom. The task of selecting equipment, machines, furniture, and tools from among numerous brands and models can overwhelm the new entrepreneur, and mistakes can have serious results.

The layout must accommodate the work flow and the procedures used—as well as the needs of customers, employees, and owners. The decor and design chosen for the facilities and the furnishings can affect people both physically and psychologically, thus contributing to or detracting from morale and productivity.

Since you must spend the money, why not buy things that will contribute to the success of the business? During the planning phase the wise entrepreneur thoroughly investigates all options before making final decisions.

DISCUSSION QUESTIONS

1. Evaluate the efficiency, esthetics, and comfort of businesses with which you are familiar. Draw comparisons, and discuss similarities and differences.
2. From your own experience or from related readings, discuss the importance of physiological and psychological factors when designing facilities and layout. How much attention would you give to the work stations of your employees? Why? What benefits would you expect to derive?
3. What do you think is the point of developing a comprehensive physical layout prior to or simultaneously with deciding on a location? How could you use the results of these investigations in the comprehensive business plan you will present to bankers or other financial backers and that you will also use as your planning guide?
4. Why is it recommended, at this point in the planning stage, that you make tentative decisions about the purchase and placement of equipment and furniture?
5. What legwork do you think is essential in planning your own business? Why should you visit businesses similar to the one you wish to open and look over equipment and furniture catalogs before contacting vendors?

ACTIVITIES AND EXERCISES

1. Find a vacant building in your community and apply the guidelines for remodeling. Use the checklist in Figure 9.1.
2. Evaluate an existing company similar to the one you envisage in terms of the efficient function, comfort, and esthetics of its layout. Use the checklist in Figure 9.3.
3. Look through catalogs and advertisements for equipment and furniture suited to the business/industry you have chosen. If you like the technical, office, or other equipment in a company similar to the one you plan to open, ask the owners for their sources—catalogs or other materials.
4. Plot the work flow and traffic flow of the vehicle and engine repair shop charted in Figure 9.2. Use a solid line for traffic and a dotted line for work. Ask yourself:

a. How would the employees pass from one station to another to complete their work, whether they are processing objects (i.e., parts, tools, etc.) or paper (records of orders, work completed, billing, etc.)?
b. How and where would customers move in the shop?

Based on your analysis, recommend possible improvements in line with this chapter's principles and guidelines. Incorporate your recommendations in a reconstructed layout, with new lines drawn for work and traffic flow.

5. Chart the layouts of two or more existing buildings, representing the feasibility of each proposed site. Use graph paper. Cut model furniture and equipment (including built-ins) to scale. Colored construction paper cut in blocks will suffice. Arrange and rearrange these until you are satisfied that you have found the design most appropriate to you and your business. Apply the principles discussed above. Show the layout to your colleagues and invite their suggestions. Modify it accordingly.
6. Estimate the costs of constructing versus remodeling and of purchasing appropriate equipment, furniture, tools, and working materials. Enter these figures on Worksheets 1 and 2 of your comprehensive business plan (Chapter 6).

NOTES

1. "Supervision of the Handicapped Employee," National Audio-Visual Center (Washington, D.C.: General Services Administration, 1977).
2. Bob Curits. *Food Service Security: Internal Control* (New York: Chain Store Age Books, 1975).
3. Olive Church and Anne Schatz. *Office Systems and Careers* (Boston: Allyn and Bacon, Inc., 1981), pp. 513–517.
4. Consumers tend to group retail products into three major categories, of convenience, shopping, and speciality. Definitions follow:

   Convenience or impulse items. Low unit price, frequency of purchase, low selling effort, habit buying, and sold in numerous stores. Examples are cigarettes, snacks, and such food products as milk and bread.

   Shopping items. Goods having these characteristics: high unit price, infrequency of purchase, more intensive selling effort; and consumers often spend time making comparisons of price and features before buying. Franchise products are typical. Examples include vehicles, furniture and appliances, and men's and women's higher-priced clothing.

   Specialty items. High unit price, infrequency of purchase, more intensive selling effort, few if any substitutes considered, and sold via brand name, often in franchise outlets. Examples are: jewelry, perfume, photographic equipment, etc.

5. "Forum: Small Business and the OA Maze," *Today's Office,* May 1983, pp. 48–62. (See also Stephen D. Channer, "White Paper Report: The Case for Furniture Befitting the Human Condition," *Modern Office Procedures,* June 1983, pp. 53–60; and "Facility Managers Emerge (at Last) As a Strong Professional Force," *Facilities Design and Management,* May 1982, p. 45.)
6. *Ibid.*

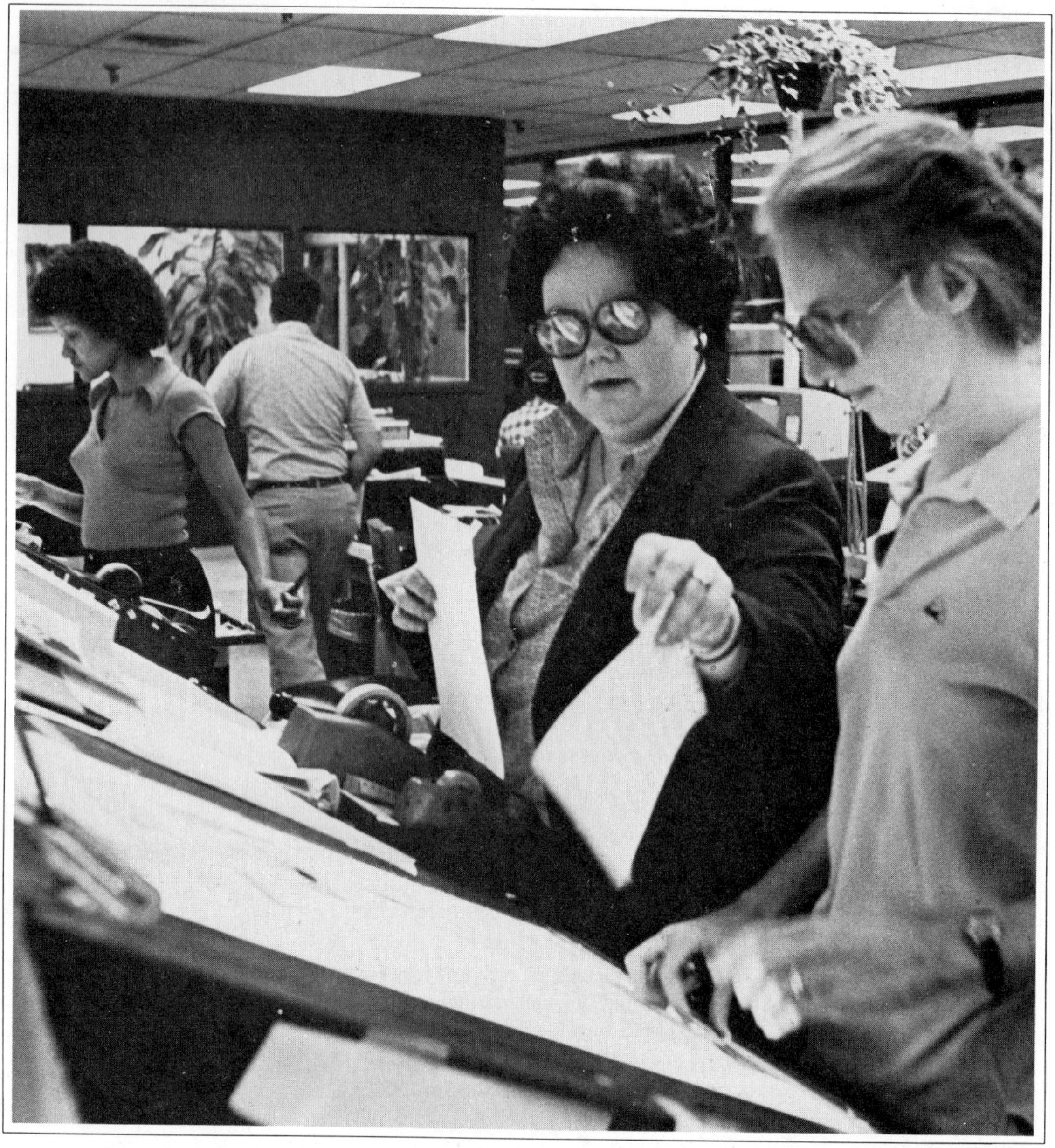

chapter 10

Legal Structures and Staffing

Objectives

1. Differentiate among the three legal forms of business: sole proprietorship, partnership, and corporation.

2. Explain the advantages and disadvantages of each legal organization and the legal procedures involved in organizing each.

3. Write a job description for one sales or service employee and prepare an organization chart.

4. Decide how much you will pay your employees and revise the earnings forecast in your business plan accordingly.

5. Hire and orient one employee in a simulated situation typical of a sales or service enterprise.

The issues of selecting a legal organization for your business and hiring employees are somewhat related. If you are the sole owner, for example, your staff will have to answer only to you. But with a partnership or corporate structure, you and your co-owners or corporate officers must decide on the lines of authority and responsibility, including how these decisions will affect your staff.

The organization chart that you create for inclusion in the business plan must also report the above decisions. Finally, what duties you expect your employees to perform impacts on the wages you are willing and able to pay and also on the earnings forecast (wage expense item) for the business plan.

LEGAL FORMS OF BUSINESS

Before opening your business, you must decide what form of legal organization best suits your needs and your inclinations.

You can organize a business as a sole proprietorship, a partnership, or a corporation. In deciding on the legal structure that best suits you and your type of business you should answer such questions as these:

1. Can I produce the needed funds to start my business and keep it operating for several months, or will I need loans or investors?
2. Do I have most or all of the expertise needed to assure the success of my company?
3. Does it matter whether I have complete control and flexibility in making business decisions?
4. How much liability am I capable of assuming?
5. Am I willing to share the profits from my business with others?
6. How much recordkeeping and report preparation am I willing and able to do?
7. Will one type of legal form allow me more tax benefits than another?
8. How private will I want to keep the financial aspects and internal operations of my company?
9. How will I ensure the continuity and survival of my business?

Sole Proprietorship

Legally, a sole proprietorship consists of one person, the owner. As the sole owner, you would receive all the profits, suffer all the losses, and assume all the legal responsibilities. The entrepreneur and the enterprise are one under the law. One legal implication is the concept of "unlimited liability." If for example the company experiences financial difficulties, not only the firm's assets but also your own personal assets as its owner are subject to liquidation.

In starting as a sole proprietor, the most typical legal requirement is to obtain whatever licenses are required in your city, county, and state, and for your type of business. This procedure includes getting a tax number assigned to your business. Then you may begin operations. Hence, this legal structure is the most widespread form of small-business organization. There is little formality and few legal restrictions involved in establishing a sole proprietorship. It requires little or no governmental approval to create, compared to a partnership or corporation.

As sole proprietor you don't have to share profits with anyone. There are no co-owners or partners to consult. You can respond quickly to business needs and thus you'll have more flexibility. (See Figure 10.1.)

FIGURE 10.1
Advantages and Disadvantages of a Sole Proprietorship

Advantages	Disadvantages
Easy start-up	One person rarely has all the skills and talents needed to run a business (e.g., management, selling, accounting, personnel, public relations, finance, etc.)
Control & flexibility in making decisions	
Minimum legal requirements	
Owner enjoys the profits	Limited personal assets often discourage potential lenders
Earnings may be retained within the business (to improve and expand, etc.)	If the business fails, the owner's personal assets are subject to claim by creditors (including house, vehicles, other properties)
Tax benefits: business losses are deductible from personal income (deductions against income on federal income-tax returns)	Limited life of the business
Privacy & confidentiality assured	Limited employee motivation: if the business is small, there are few opportunities for advancement or to buy stock
Compared with a partnership: Liability is limited to the owner's obligations	
No danger of loss as a result of a partner's death or withdrawal	
Compared with a corporation: No double tax when profits are distributed	
No capital-stock tax	
No corporate reports or inspections	
No restrictions on the nature of the business	
No penalties for retaining earnings in the business	

On the other hand, you are responsible in full for any business debts that may exceed your total investment. This liability extends to all of a proprietor's assets, including house and car. You would also be liable for such things as physical loss or personal injury. This risk, of course, can be lessened by obtaining proper insurance coverage.

Other disadvantages are that you would have less available capital, relative difficulty in obtaining long-term financing, and a relatively limited viewpoint and experience. Moreover, the enterprise may be crippled or require termination upon illness or death of the owner.

The Partnership

The Uniform Partnership Act, which has been adopted by many states, defines a partnership as "an association of two or more persons to carry on as co-owners of a business for profit." Although it is not specifically required by the act, for the protection of all partners it is best to draw up written Articles of Partnership. These articles outline the contribution each partner will bring to the business (whether financial, material, or managerial), and generally delineate the roles the partners will play in the business relationship.[1]

Each of the partners is an owner in the business and is subject to certain legal responsibilities, and each usually has unlimited liability, much the same as a sole proprietor. One partner can be held personally liable for the actions of the other partner(s). Suppose X and Y are partners in a retail store. X makes several bad purchases, which result in a financial loss. Assuming that X does not have enough money to pay for the loss, Y is legally responsible for paying the remaining debts.

It is often possible in a partnership to obtain more capital and a better range of skills than in a sole proprietorship. Partners are usually motivated to apply their best abilities because they share directly in the profits. Although less flexible than the sole proprietorship, the partnership is more flexible than a corporation. It also brings relative freedom from government control and special taxation.

A partnership, like the sole proprietorship, is also subject to unlimited liability for personal injuries. Appropriate insurance coverage, however, can provide protection against some foreseeable difficulties. The elimination of any partner automatically dissolves the partnership. The business can continue to operate if the remaining partner(s) exercises and/or seeks to create a new partnership. It can be difficult to buy out a partner unless specifically arranged for in the written agreement. (See Figure 10.2.)

Kinds of partners. An "ostensible partner" is active and is recognized as a partner. A "secret partner" may be active, but is not known or recognized. A "dormant partner" is both inactive and unrecognized. A "silent partner" is inactive but may be recognized as a partner.

Assuming they comply with the statutory formalities, "limited or special" partners risk only the money they invest in the business. As long as they do not

FIGURE 10.2 Advantages and Disadvantages of a Partnership.

Advantages	Disadvantages
Financing: with two or more partners, more capital is often availabile, and there is less need to borrow.	Divided profits: shared among the partners
Lenders may be more likely to make loans when needed	Divided authority: each general partner has a say in making business decisions
Responsibilities can be allocated by expertise and interest	
Tax benefits: business losses are deducted from the personal income of each partner (in taking deductions on federal income-tax returns)	Unlimited liability: each partner is liable for all debts incurred by the business
Employee motivation: perhaps more opportunity for advancement, if the partnership produces a larger business	Limited life: the partnership is automatically dissolved upon the death or withdrawl of a partner (unless the partnership agreement includes provisions for continuity, or where the legal form is a limited partnership)
Compared with a corporation: No state incorporation fees	
No capital-stock tax	
No double tax on dividends	
Income may be divided on several bases (other than amount of investment) such as talents or time devoted to the business	
The partners' salaries are not subject to payroll taxes	
No penalties accrue when earnings are retained in the business	

participate in the management of the enterprise or in the conduct of its business, limited partners are generally not subject to the same liabilities as general partners. In a limited partnership agreement, the general partner is usually the manager, the person with the most power and control—and liability. The general partner's role should be carefully defined in the written Articles of Partnership.[2]

The partnership agreement. Partnership agreements typically cover the following topics:

Name of the Business, Purpose, Domicile (location and address)

Duration of Agreement

Character of Partners (i.e., "general," "silent," etc.)

Contributions by Partners (at inception and/or later)

(continued)

Business Expenses (how they will be handled)
Authority (each partner's authority within the firm)
Separate Debts
Books, Records, and Method of Accounting
Division of Profits and Losses
Draws or Salaries
Rights of Continuing Partner
Death of a Partner (plan for dissolution or revision; insurance)

Rights of the Continuing Partner(s)
Employee Management
Release of Debts
Sale of Partnership Interest
Arbitration
Additions to or Alterations or Modifications of the Agreement
Settlement of Disputes
Required and Prohibited Acts
Absence and Disability

A partnership is distinguished from other forms of business organizations by its limited life, the unlimited liability of at least one partner, and the partners' co-ownership of the assets, mutual agency, share of management, and share in profits.[3]

The Corporation

The best-known definition of a corporation is that written by the Chief Justice Marshall of the U.S. Supreme Court in 1819: "an artificial being, invisible, intangible, and existing only in contemplation of law."[4] A corporation is a legal creation of the state government. Corporations that do business in more than one state must comply with the federal laws regarding interstate commerce and with the state laws, which may vary considerably.

To form a corporation you would ordinarily begin by taking subscriptions to capital stock and creating a tentative organization, unless yours will be a closely held corporation and will not issue stock to outsiders. You must obtain the approval of the secretary of state or another designated official of the state in which the corporation is to be formed. This approval comes in the form of a charter that states the powers and limitations of the particular corporation.

Corporations have a separate legal existence, and ownership is readily transferable. In the case of the illness, death, or other loss of a principal (officer or owner), the corporation continues to exist and to do business. The company thus has both stability and relative permanence.

You can acquire capital by issuing various stocks and long-term bonds. Securing long-term financing from lending institutions may be easier than with sole proprietorships or even partnerships because the company can take advantage of corporate assets and often of the personal assets of stockholders and principals or guarantors (personal guarantees are often required by lenders).

You can retain control because when you delegate authority it is to hired managers. The corporation can also draw on the expertise and skills of more than one individual.

However, business activities are limited by the charter and by various laws, although some states do permit very broad charters. You are subject to extensive government regulations and must provide some local, state, and federal reports. Also, to form a corporation you must pay state and attorneys' fees. Further, where managers do not share in profits, they have less incentive to function effectively. (See Figure 10.3.)

FIGURE 10.3
Advantages and Disadvantages of a Corporation.

Advantages	Disadvantages
Financing: funds may be obtained from several sources, including through sale of common or preferred stock, loans from the sale of bonds, exchanging assets, and retaining profits from the enterprise	Complex formation process: a charter must be prepared and obtained from the state(s) in which the corporation seeks to operate. Fees must be paid to an attorney for consultation and also usually to the state in obtaining the charter
Limited liability: as a separate entity, the corporation is obligated for debts incurred, not the owners personally or their assets; also includes liability for injuries, etc.	Charter restrictions: company can engage only in those activities specifically stated in the charter, unless an umbrella clause in the charter makes provision for diversification
Management expertise: responsibilities and authority divided, and employees hired, on basis of expertise	Geographic limitation to the state(s) in which the charter is granted, until and unless permission to operate elsewhere is sought and obtained (from every state in which the corporation seeks to function)
Easy transfer of ownership: by selling or transferring stock (with records kept of ownership in the corporate books)	
Continuous life for as long as allowed in the charter	Numerous regulations to comply with, plus many specific reports to be prepared and submitted for each state in which the corporation operates
Employee motivation: opportunities for advancement plus in some cases chance to purchase stock in the company	Double taxation: the corporation pays taxes on profits and stockholders pay taxes on their share of the profits
	Accounting and records: complete records must be kept, for reporting to government agencies, stockholders, etc.
	Little privacy: reports identifying sales, profits, and assets must be made available to all stockholders and others

Chapter 10

Steps toward incorporating. Guidance from an attorney will insure that (1) the articles of incorporation and the bylaws are tailored to the needs of your particular business enterprise, (2) you understand the various tax obligations involved, and (3) you will be in compliance with the state, local, and federal laws affecting the corporation in the location selected. This third point is especially important because the laws governing the procedure for obtaining a corporate charter vary widely among the states.

In any state, however, you will need to obtain a Certificate of Incorporation, to hold a meeting of officers and stockholders to establish the bylaws, and to ensure compliance with special laws and tax plans. To obtain the Certificate of Incorporation, you must:

1. List the name of the corporation. The law generally requires:
    a. that the name chosen not be so similar to the name of any other corporation authorized to do business in the state as to lead to confusion, and
    b. that the name chosen not be deceptive.
2. List the purposes for which the corporation is formed. Use language that is broad enough to permit territorial, market, or product expansion later but that is precise enough to clarify your general purpose and goals.
3. State the length of time the corporation will operate—for x number of years or "perpetually."
4. List the names and addresses of the incorporators. Some states require one or more incorporators to be a resident within that state.
5. Give the location of the corporation's registered office within the state of incorporation (you must establish an office or agent in other states as well, if you intend operating there).
6. State the maximum amount and the type of capital stock that the corporation wishes to issue. Set forth the proposed capital structure of the corporation, including the number and classification of shares and the rights, preferences, and limitations of each class of shares.
7. State the capital required at the time of incorporation. Some states require that a specified percentage of the par value of the capital stock be paid in cash and banked to the credit of the corporation before the Certificate of Incorporation is submitted to the designated state official for approval.
8. Provide for preemptive rights, if any, to be granted to the stockholders and for restrictions, if any, on the transfer of shares.
9. Provide for regulation of the internal affairs of the corporation.
10. List the names and addresses of persons who will serve as directors until the first meeting of stockholders or until their successors are elected and qualified.

The right to amend, alter, or repeal any provision contained in the Certificate of Incorporation is generally statutory, reserved to a majority or two-thirds of the stockholders. Still, it is customary to spell this out.

If the designated state official determines that the name of the proposed corporation is satisfactory, that the certificate contains the necessary information and has been properly executed, and that nothing in the certificate or in the corporation's proposed activities violates state law or public policy, the charter will likely be issued.[5]

Meeting of officers and stockholders. There must be a stockholders meeting to complete the incorporation process. This meeting is usually conducted by an attorney or someone familiar with corporate organizational procedure. The meeting will adopt the corporation's bylaws and elect a board of directors. The board of directors in turn elects the officers who actually manage the corporation's operations, i.e., the president, possibly a vice-president, a secretary, and a treasurer. In small corporations, members of the board of directors are frequently elected as officers of the corporation.

Corporation bylaws. The bylaws are often similar to the provisions contained in the charter and in state statues. They usually specify the:

1. Location of the principal office and of other corporation offices,
2. Time, place, and required notice of annual and special meetings of stockholders and the necessary quorum and voting privileges of the stockholders,
3. Number of directors, their compensation, their term of office, the method of electing them, and the method of creating or filling vacancies on the board of directors,
4. Time and place of the regular and special directors meetings, as well as the notice and quorum requirements,
5. Method of selecting officers, their titles, duties, terms of office, and salaries,
6. Issuance and form of stock certificates, their transfer and their control in the company books,
7. Dividends, when and by whom they may be declared,
8. The fiscal year, the corporate seal, the authority to sign checks, and the preparation of the annual statement, and
9. Procedure for amending the bylaws.

Readers who have participated actively in various school, civic, professional, trade, or religious organizations may find that creating a corporation is like organizing an association (with the added responsibility of assigning salaries and dealing with other financial matters). Indeed, active membership in such organizations provides good training for people interested in starting a corporation. Because it obeys legal requirements and has a board of directors (in those states where required), a corporation seems in some senses more "democratic" than a sole proprietorship.

Corporate directors and officers are certainly responsible to powers greater than themselves. They must report to the directors and the stockholders, and must file regular financial statements with the government. Some exposure to parliamentary procedure and to the process of developing bylaws is also useful, as these procedures are used in board of directors' and stockholders' meetings.

Subchapter S. Since 1958 certain corporations have enjoyed the legal status of operating in the corporate form and yet have paid no federal income tax. The Internal Revenue Code's Subchapter S permits a small-business corporation to have its income taxed to the shareholders as if the corporation were a partnership. Subchapter S provisions are designed to benefit small, closely held businesses that want to incorporate for legal reasons while remaining partnerships for tax purposes.

The Economic Recovery Tax Act (ERTA), passed by Congress in 1982, allows Sub S corporations to handle certain matters relating to income, deductions, and credits as if they were partnerships. The main thrust of the Act was to loosen the requirements for electing Subchapter S status, thus allowing more corporations to benefit from its use. It was this Act that also revised the tax treatment of a Sub S corporation, making it more closely related to a partnership than to a corporation.[6]

Notice some of these major differences between an ordinary corporation and a Subchapter S corporation:

1. Operating as a regular corporation subjects the earnings of the business to two levels of income taxation. First, the earnings of the corporation are taxed at corporate rates up to 46 percent. Second, the earnings that are distributed as dividends are taxed to the shareholders at rates up to 50 percent.
2. By law, a corporation can retain earnings beyond a stated amount only if it can show the earnings are needed for business purposes. The Sub S corporation eliminates the possibility of the IRS imposing the accumulated earnings tax. Since all income is passed through to the shareholder level on an annual basis, the corporation is not accumulating tax-free earnings.
3. By transferring ownership of the stock in a Subchapter S corporation to family members (i.e., children) in lower tax brackets, the overall tax assessment can be reduced and by transferring nonvoting common stock, which is permitted under ERTA, voting control is not diluted.
4. Since all income in the Sub S corporation flows through to the shareholders and is taxed currently, it makes little difference whether the income is treated as salary or dividends.
5. The losses from the Sub S corporation can offset earnings from other sources, since a shareholder can deduct corporate losses up to his or her investment in the stock.
6. Income that is tax exempt to the Sub S corporation would also be tax exempt to the shareholder.
7. A Sub S corporation carries with it the traditional legal benefits of operating as a corporation, such as limited liability.
8. The biggest disadvantage to the Subchapter S form of corporation is that certain fringe benefits that are provided tax free to employees are taxable to

owner and employees; including the exclusion of amounts paid to accident and health plans and the exclusion for meals and lodging furnished for the convenience of the employer.[7]

The rules for Subchapter S corporations may have limited use of companies seeking to retain earnings for growth. But closely held businesses with early-year losses, or those that are profitable and distribute their earnings as dividends, may find Subchapter S status worth looking into. Among the conditions of Subchapter S election eligibility are:

> That the corporation have 35 or fewer shareholders, all of whom are individuals or estates, that there be no nonresident alien shareholders, that there be only one class of outstanding stock, that all shareholders consent to the election, and that a specific portion of the corporation's receipts be derived from active business rather than enumerated passive investments. No limit is placed on the size of the corporation's income and assets.[8] (Table 10.1 gives data on firms that operate in the various forms we've discussed.)

The Relationship of Legal Structure to Hiring Employees

Many people prefer to go into business as sole proprietors because of the advantages listed earlier. However, as their plans mature and they discover that the type of business selected cannot be operated by one person alone, they

TABLE 10.1 Business Firms by Industry Division and Legal Form of Organization
(numbers in thousands)

INDUSTRY DIVISION	SOLE PROPRIETORSHIPS	PARTNERSHIPS	CORPORATIONS	TOTAL
All industries	11,345.6	1,153.4	2,241.9	14,740.9
Agriculture, Forestry, Fisheries	3,177.2	121.0	65.6	3,363.8
Mining	71.2	22.0	19.2	112.4
Construction	994.1	69.2	214.7	1,278.0
Manufacturing	224.1	28.0	231.1	483.2
Transportation, Communications, Utilities	385.3	16.8	85.2	487.3
Wholesale trade	307.2[1]	29.4[1]	237.6[1]	574.2[1]
Retail trade	1,862.4[1]	163.8[1]	432.8[1]	2,459.0[1]
Finance, Insurance, Real Estate	894.9	476.4	432.9	1,804.2
Services	3,302.5	226.6	516.4	4,045.5
Not Allocable	31.4	—	4.3	35.7

[1] Does not include unallocated returns.

Source: Department of the Treasury, Internal Revenue Service, 1977 Sole Proprietorship Returns, Table 1.1; 1977 Partnership Returns, Table 1; and 1977 Corporation Income Tax Returns, Table 1.

have to make other decisions. How many employees are needed, what duties will they be asked to perform, and can the business generate enough income to support their wages? Or will taking in partners serve to accommodate some of these needs?

When a prospective sole proprietor realizes that he or she cannot do everything or raise all the capital needed, it is often at this juncture that the partnership or corporate structure is considered. Simultaneously, an organization chart is constructed to reflect decisions about the business structure, the hiring of employees, and the interrelationship of duties that need to be performed and how authority and responsibilities are to be allocated.

Even with a partnership or a corporation, it still may be necessary to hire employees. How to find and staff your business is therefore a key issue and needs to be addressed during the organization phase.

HIRING EMPLOYEES

One often hears owner-managers say, "I just can't find any good people." The missing link, however, may be that they don't know exactly what they want when they advertise for and interview applicants.

Define What You Need

An effective way to begin your search for good employees is to develop a sound job description (see Figure 6.4 for an example). In two or three narrative paragraphs, describe the job precisely. Then list the specific duties involved. The value of the job description is that it forces you to be explicit about what the job requires and thereby can guide you in appraising the capabilities of prospective employees.

Suppose you are looking for a salesclerk. This job title means different things to different people, and there are various degrees of skill involved. So, what should the applicant be able to do? Perhaps your clerk only needs to tally sales receipts accurately. Or should he or she keep a customer list and occasionally promote your products to these people? Or even operate the store in your absence?

The skills level of the people you can expect to hire also depends on how much you are willing and able to pay and on what kind of training you can provide. The three basics of a good selling program are that your employees should be able to (1) identify the needs of customers, (2) know the product or service thoroughly, and (3) persuade customers that your products or services are better than the competition's.

Before advertising for applicants, you should also decide how much you are willing and able to pay the new hiree. Will you pay minimum wages, a weekly salary, commissions, or bonuses? What fringe benefits, if any, will you provide?

Define what employee skills you're looking for before advertising, whether it's a supervisor's or a laborer's job you want to fill.

Then, too, you need to establish personnel policies on such things as paid sick leave and vacations.

Know what you can offer so that you can discuss these factors intelligently with applicants. Don't wait for them to ask; explain the compensation package. They will be wondering about it anyway, and they may hesitate about accepting an offer if the compensation policies are not clearly stated.

Finding Personnel

You can look for employees through a variety of advertising means. Besides newspaper classified ads, you can use word-of-mouth advertising and can list your job specifications with public and private employment bureaus and with school and college placement offices. For entry-level jobs, you might even place a sign in the window of your establishment. And, of course, you can describe your needs to friends, customers, suppliers, present employees, and members of civic and merchant groups to which you belong. This is the word-of-mouth job applicant recruitment method, used by many small businesses in lieu of more formal methods.[9]

One good resource is secondary schools with strong vocational programs. Contact the teacher-coordinators of these vocational programs or the school administrators to find out about their graduates, particularly when you need to

Contact vocational teachers when you are looking for skilled workers; they supervise students not only in developing job skills but also in community jobs where training stations are coordinated with the schools.

fill entry-level, low-paid jobs. Unlike some others, these young people usually have a sense of responsibility, developed from the interrelationship of classwork and job experience. They recognize what businesspeople are looking for and what attitudes and work habits are expected.[10]

However, you cannot expect an immature or inexperienced high-school youth to assume extensive technical or managerial functions. If what you want is a high-ability, experienced worker, then you will have to pay more. If you are fortunate enough initially to find a highly capable person, of any age, who is willing to work for low wages, you can expect this person to soon become dissatisfied and to leave for a better job or to expect a promotion and a commensurate raise.

An alternative is to use temporary-help agencies or independent sales agents. You could also consider creating flexible working conditions and policies in order to attract experienced people who do not or cannot work normal hours or full time.

The temporary-help agency. Temp agencies will screen and send you the type of workers you need as you need them, such as during busy seasons and sales promotions. They process the paperwork, including the payroll and personnel records, withholding forms, etc. You pay the agency a flat hourly fee for every hour their worker is on your premises.

Through this practice you may also find someone to hire as a full-time employee. You can see a variety of people in action, find out what they can and cannot do, and observe their attitudes and behavior and their ability to provide courteous and sensitive customer service.

Many people work as temps, not only because they only want to work part-time but also because this practice gives them a chance to look employers over. Remember that hiring workers is a two-way street. You want the best people you can find for the money, and applicants want to find the best workplace available in return for the hours and services they are prepared to commit to it.

Temporary-help agencies advertise for, screen, and in some cases provide special training for the people they sign on. Workers are available in a variety of categories: salesclerks, office workers (secretaries, word processors, transcribers, clerk-typists, and data entry and processing people), medical technicians and aides, security guards, and skilled workers in other fields.[11]

Flextime and job-sharing. Some company owners use flextime schedules and job-sharing to attract able workers away from their homes. These people may have valuable work experience but for personal reasons (including their health, age, or parental duties) have temporarily removed themselves from the labor market.

Flextime allows people to work hours different from those normally observed in any industry. Some workers arrive early and leave early, while others arrive and leave late. Although the four-day week was touted more than two decades ago as a benefit to all, it has been little adopted as yet.

With job-sharing, two people together hold one job, each for part of the day or week. Job-sharing is another method of attracting and recruiting workers who are unwilling or unable to work a more normal schedule.

Interviewing and Hiring

Once you have attracted job applicants, the screening process begins. If your advertisements ask applicants to reply by mail, then you can expect to receive letters and résumés. If the ads tell them to phone, then someone must be ready to describe the position in more detail and to give the name and location of the company doing the hiring. If your ads give the company's address, then applicants will be arriving in person.

Once the applicants do arrive, ask them to fill out an application form. You may or may not wish to see people in person at this time. If you anticipate receiving a great many applications, you may want to assign someone else the responsibility of collecting and verifying the data given. You can then choose the applicants whose paperwork looks best and follow up with telephone calls or letters (if people apply from out of town) to set up interview appointments.

Chapter 10

Application forms and résumés. Having people fill out an application form accomplishes several things. Apart from collecting information on them, you can see how they respond to written instructions and how legible their handwriting is or how good their typing—important factors for jobs requiring employees to do a lot of writing or typing. You can verify the information supplied by contacting references and prior employers. Depending upon the nature of the job, some applicants will mail in or arrive with a typed résumé. This document can be used in lieu of an application blank, but be sure that all pertinent information is recorded.

The law forbids you to ask certain questions either on an application form or in an interview. You can buy standard application forms from an office supply store. These forms include appropriate questions about applicants' training and work history and military service. Applicants may leave some questions blank because they feel that the answer is none of your business.

Checking references. When young people with a limited work record apply, it is especially important to call their present and former teachers, counselors, and administrators. They can tell you about the applicants' attendance and promptness record and reputation for honesty and verify what classes they have taken and their grade-point average. This average indicates the applicants' perseverance and commitment if not their overall intelligence.

Written recommendations are not always completely valid. Applicants should have contacted the people they list in the reference section of their résumés or applications, but do not always do so. Reference providers are also often cautious about what they write about someone, because applicants have the right to see what people have written, unless they have specifically renounced this right. Reference writers do not want to be sued. For these reasons they may be franker and more accurate if contacted by phone.

Legal considerations. The law forbids discrimination, whether in screening and hiring or on the job, on the basis of race, sex, religion, age, or handicaps. Even if you decide that an applicant simply lacks the qualifications for your job, you must be careful about what you say and how you act during the interview. You don't want to be sued for discrimination because your attitude gave the applicant the idea that you wouldn't hire her or him under any conditions.

The 1938 Fair Labor Standards Act set the minimum working age at 16. Most states regulate the hiring of youths between the ages of 14 and 16. For hazardous occupations, the legal age may be higher. Check with your state to determine the criteria that affect you.

The 1964 Civil Rights Act, as amended by the 1972 Equal Employment Opportunity Act, forbids discrimination on the basis of race, color, religion, sex, or national origin. The Equal Employment Opportunity Commission was established as a result of these acts to receive and act upon complaints. States also have their own associated laws and regulations.

The 1973 Rehabilitation Act established guidelines for hiring handicapped people. Businesses that hold federal government contracts exceeding $2500 must take affirmative action to both hire and promote qualified handicapped workers.

Although you may want to collect personal information about applicants, to judge their stability and dependability, applicants may not have to answer questions about their race, sex, age, marital status, number of dependents, or status as renter or owner. Women particularly resent being asked if they use birth-control methods, which was a question once routinely posed during interviews—supposedly because employers wanted to determine if female applicants would be likely to remain with the firm for long.

Larger companies are more often required to follow specific affirmative action guidelines. However, smaller businesses can also be affected, if they employ a specific number of employees and hold government contracts and/or operate across state lines. Check with an attorney to determine what questions you may ask and which you should avoid.

Even if you are not required to comply with affirmative action guidelines, many applicants are familiar with them and may resent being asked personal questions that do not pertain specifically to work performance on the job for which they are applying. To avoid driving away good applicants, you may want to follow the criteria anyway.

The interview. First, you will want to make applicants feel comfortable. Have chairs available and provide a quiet place to talk together. You might open the dialogue by describing the position and your company. If you have developed a job description, use it as the basis for explaining the available position. Company literature can also be shared.

Remember, too, that you are being interviewed as much as you are interviewing. Even subconsciously, applicants are developing first impressions: Do they like what they see? Would they like to work for you, and in this type of business? Even though you may interview a dozen or more people for the positions, remember that eventually you will hire one of them, and that this person will be working for and with you for many days to come. Therefore, you will want to establish a positive climate at the outset, during the interview procedure.

Ask the applicant how her or his qualifications relate to the job description. Take the opportunity to test the applicant's verbal skills and ability to think and respond under pressure. Most jobs require these competencies, especially when they involve frequent customer contact as do sales or service companies.

To produce responses that indicate whether applicants do or do not have these abilities—particularly for customer-contact openings—you may ask questions like these:

- "Tell me about your most difficult work day and what made it trying. . . . How did you cope with the problems?"

- "How would you handle a complaining, difficult customer?... What if he was complaining to you about something that was not your fault?... What if these problems with a customer came at the end of a long, tiring day when both you and the customer were obviously exhausted?"
- "Why should I hire you over the other candidates for this job?"

Applicants are more likely to develop into the workers you need if, during the interview process and/or in their written application, they:

1. Exhibit a positive, wholesome attitude about themselves,
2. Exhibit an interest in the welfare of the company and of their potential supervisor and coworkers,
3. Refrain from criticizing or complaining about former companies and colleagues when, for example, they are asked why they left or to describe a really trying day at the former workplace,
4. Have a record of dependability, e.g., if their school and work references show regular attendance and participation in extracurricular activities and demonstrate an ability to follow through,
5. Demonstrate an interest in and an ability to increase company revenues, to help improve products or services, or to reduce expenses as evidenced in their responses to hypothetical situations and/or to questions about their former job(s).

SUMMARY

The legal form of business ownership you select depends on the type of company and its needs as well as on your personal inclinations. If yours will be a small company and you can acquire the start-up funds yourself, and have most of the expertise needed to manage its various functions, then you will probably opt for a sole proprietorship. If you do, you will be far from alone, since this is the most prevalent legal structure.

If you are willing to share both the control and the profits of your business, or if you lack either capital or expertise, then a partnership might be a good choice. A closely held corporation in which your family members or friends are the corporate executives and stockholders might also be desirable. Entrepreneurs rarely begin their careers by forming a corporation. But you may wish eventually to expand your business as a corporation.

If you will need one or more employees from the time you open your business, the people you hire may be critical to its successful operation. As a newcomer you may find it difficult to determine exactly what you want the employee(s) to do. A specific job description will help you in both recruitment and hiring. You must also decide what you are willing and able to pay your employee(s). Such decisions impact on the development of the earnings forecast in your business plan (see wage expense item and the total expenses anticipated).

Once you have screened applicants through an initial contact and/or by reviewing their application forms or résumés, you are ready to start interviewing. Recognize that you are being interviewed too and try to establish rapport. Be aware of what the law says you can and cannot ask during the interview.

DISCUSSION QUESTIONS

1. Which legal form of business is most common: the sole proprietorship, the partnership, or the corporation? Why?
2. Which of the advantages and disadvantages of partnerships seem most significant to the successful operation of the business? What potential does this arrangement have for the partners' mutual help or aggravation? From what you know about your own personality, would you like working with a partner(s)? Why or why not?
3. What would motivate you to select one legal structure over another for your business? Why? What would have to happen for you to contemplate changing your company's legal organization?
4. Describe the procedures you would use to incorporate your business. Compare the incorporation of a business with that of starting a civic or student organization, where it is essential to elect officers and prepare bylaws before you can get a charter from the headquarters of the organization you propose.
5. What relationship do you perceive between selecting the legal structure of your business, preparing the organization chart, and deciding whether you will hire employees?
6. How does the development of a job description relate to the organization chart and also to the wage expense item on the earnings forecast (financial section of the business plan)?

MINICASE

George and Larry operated a computer store and data-processing service as partners. The men, lifelong friends and highly compatible—despite their different personalities and areas of expertise—had few problems in allocating responsibilities or in sharing the profits from their enterprise. An oral "gentlemen's agreement," they believed, was sufficient, although George had contributed $20,000 and Larry only $5000. Larry, however, worked twice as many hours per week as George.

Both men were in their early forties and healthy. Although George had made out his will, with his wife his only heir, Larry had not. Then Larry suddenly died of a heart attack.

What do you suppose happened to the business? to Larry's widow? What difficulties do you think the survivors encountered? What could these partners have done to ensure the continuation of the business and to protect their heirs?

ACTIVITIES AND EXERCISES

1. If one or more of the companies you have already visited appeal to you, arrange to return for a more comprehensive interview. Otherwise, contact some new firms. Ask the owners:
   a. What legal form of business do you use? Why?
   b. Are you considering a change of legal form? If so, why?
   c. Do you use some form of job description for your staff?   And, if so, how do you use this form?
2. Proceeding either randomly or with a focus on the specific kind of companies that appeal to you, go through (a) the Yellow Pages, (b) one newspaper's advertisements or (c) one entire section (or block) of your community to discover how many are sole proprietorships, partnerships, or corporations. Company names should give you the clue: e.g., "The Legal Firm of Benjamin, Goodall, Jasinski, and Symington"—partnership; "Joe Marble's Repair Shop"—sole proprietorship; "American Warehouse, Inc."—corporation; and "Eldorado Import Motors, Ltd."—limited partnership. If you can't be sure, try phoning the companies and ask which legal form has been assumed and why.
3. Count the number of sole proprietorships, partnerships, and corporations in the *Stanley Junction* case supplement. From the background provided for each company, try to determine why the assigned form was used in each case. Recommend changes, if appropriate, and explain the advantages to be derived.
4. Arrange to visit with personnel managers in medium-size companies. Ask how they locate and recruit appropriate applicants to the positions they typically advertise. Ask what methods they use in the interview process and what procedures they use to comply with EEO and Affirmative Action guidelines. Report your findings to the class.
5. Write a job description for an employee you might need to hire in your business. Use the sample given in Chapter 6. Decide how much you will pay in wages and revise the wage item expense on the earnings forecast in your business plan accordingly.
6. Arrange to practice an interview scene with you as the business owner-employer and a classmate as the interviewee. Use the job description prepared in No. 5 above as background. You will expect the employee hired to be able to perform the duties listed and you anticipate hiring someone with the preferred qualifications.

NOTES

1. Antonio M. Olmi, "Selecting the Legal Structure for Your Firm," *Management Aide* no. 6.004, U.S. Small Business Administration (Washington, D.C.), April 1981, pp. 2–3.
2. Ibid.
3. Ibid.
4. Kay Fanning, William E. Jennings, and Otto Santos, Jr., *Law in Business* (Instructional Unit) (St. Paul: Minnesota Mining and Manufacturing Company, 1968).
5. Elizabeth Elliot and Wendy Susco, "Incorporating Yourself," *Working Woman*, June 1982, pp. 43–44.
6. Robert W. Merry, "Why Subchapter S Is More Alluring Than Ever," *Inc.*, January 1983, p. 94.
7. Ronald T. Mott and Richard C. Jones, "Should You Elect Sub S?" *Business*, April–June 1983, pp. 56–57.
8. "Incorporating a Small Business," *Management Aid* no. 223, U.S. Small Business Administration (Washington, D.C.), January 1976.
9. Olive Church, "A Business Community Resource Information System," paper presented at the National Delta Pi Epsilon Research Conference (University of Mississippi, November 1982). In this study, in which 32 Wyoming high school and community college teachers and counselors participated in interviewing 565 Wyoming business owners, it was learned that approximately 60 percent of companies use the informal word-of-mouth method for recruiting job applicants.
10. Ibid.
11. Olive Church, "Survey of Temporary-Help Agencies in Denver and the Rocky Mountain Region," independent study, (Laramie, Wy: University of Wyoming, 1980–81).

Travel Card
R TRAVEL CARD
WASHINGTON
BANKAMERICARD
VISA
NAL BANK

chapter 11

Establishing Price and Credit Policies

Objectives

1. Discuss the relationship of customer buying habits, prices, and quality.

2. Explain the systems of cost- and demand-oriented pricing and explain why pricing policies should be established during the planning phase

3. Describe the advantages and disadvantages of allowing customers to buy on credit and explain why credit policies should be developed during the planning phase

4. Delineate the various forms of credit

5. Establish pricing and credit policies for your products or services.

Will you be able to establish prices that seem fair to your customers, and still make a profit? The ability to forecast sales and earning potential with some accuracy is critical to making other decisions, such as how much merchandise, supplies, or raw materials to purchase, how many employees your company needs and can support, and how much financing will be required.

Chapter 7, you will recall, gave a simplified formula for determining your potential market share once you identify the competition. As noted in the market study, however, many other factors enter into this calculation, on which in turn you can base your earnings forecast. One of these factors is your pricing policy. And, of course, to set that policy you need to have some realistic idea about the costs of operating your business.

Also significant to the cash flow you can anticipate, particularly during those first crucial months of your business, is the amount of credit you receive, not only from banks, lending institutions, or venture capitalists but also from the vendors who will be supplying your needs. With a tight trade credit line, a retail or manufacturing business will be limited. In any case, you can expect at first to have more money going out than coming in. If you are operating in the red you will quickly exhaust your start-up funds. Thus the amount of credit or the type of trade discounts you can obtain from suppliers is important (also see Chapter 12).

Likewise, if your policy is to provide credit to your customers, your sales will not be generating cash-in-hand income until the buyers start paying their bills. Again, then, you will be taking in less money at first than you will need to spend.

PRICING POLICIES

The Relationship Between Price and Quality

Having conducted a market study and selected a location, you can zero in on the level of products or services that will attract the most customers in that area.

Suppose you want to sell shoes in a shopping mall in your locale. After meeting with the mall developer/manager and several franchisers, you find that there is room for your business in the mall and that you can become a franchisee. Your market study and an assessment of the mall's current store mix should allow you to decide the quality and type of shoes to offer. As a franchisee, you would be assisted by the franchiser in establishing pricing policies. If the shoes you will offer are of medium to low quality, then your prices will be lower than those of the mall's other shoe stores.

Similarly, when you deal with brand-name products, the manufacturers usually provide guidelines for pricing. A Cadillac will sell for more than a subcompact. Although the cost to you is certainly a factor in this difference, so is the quality of the product.

Independent businesses, especially those selling a wide range of products or offering a service, usually have fewer and less specific guidelines to follow. Here you can be guided by industry standards and your market study.

At shopping malls in the mid-1980s, a single chocolate-chip cookie sold for 55 cents in Casper, Wyoming; for 65 cents in Kansas City, Missouri; and for 85 cents in Washington, D.C. Obviously these stores do not compete with one another. The prices established in each might be reasonable, given the cost of living in each area.

But it is also true that the 85-cent cookie tasted better and had more chocolate chips than either of the others. If all three stores were located within ten miles of each other, chocolate-chip cookie buffs might willingly drive across town to buy the high-priced cookie. Of course, one reason the 85-cent cookie cost so much was that it had more chips, that it cost more to produce. However, to many people paying nearly a dollar for a single cookie would seem too great a luxury. Moreover, the total population of Casper is less than 90,000, while the Washington mall's market size is much greater.[1] One might conclude, then, that this location in the nation's capital city can better support the high-quality, high-priced cookie store than some other locales.

Location is even more important for larger luxury items. Everybody may occasionally treat themselves to an 85-cent cookie. But other high-quality, high-tag items will be bought only by well-to-do patrons or by the occasional middle-income consumer in special circumstances.

No Recession in the Luxury Market

"Spend now and enjoy it," is the attitude among the well-off, and that means big sales for prestige goods and services.

"There are more people with wealth today than ever, and they are no longer anxious to save millions of dollars for their children," explains Fred Hayman, owner of Giorgio's, a Beverly Hills clothing store.

For products and services as varied as crocodile-skin cowboy boots, custom-made baby clothes and luxury hotel suites, demand shows little sign of weakening. Business couldn't be better for thousands of companies which cater to the well-to-do. A survey of merchants by *U.S. News & World Report* bureaus found wide-spread evidence of free spending among the affluent, including:

—an Oklahoma City auto dealer who added Rolls-Royce to his line of imports was amazed when he quickly sold 26 luxury cars, ranging in price from $110,000 to $170,000.

—Atlanta, a gourmet shop in fashionable Lenox Square cannot stock enough caviar, even at $24 an ounce.

—Expensive linens, popular in Europe for years, are being snapped up at Frette, a Houston store where a set of pure-silk sheets sells for $1,500.

—Hammacher, Schlemmer of New York reports brisk sales of auto alarms with beepers that go off in the owner's pocket if anyone tampers with the car. Price: $400.

—Orders are running double what they were (last year) for Creme de la Creme, a Chicago-based catalog firm. Some three dozen porcelain carousel ponies—costing $975 each—have already been sold.

Excerpted, with permission, from the article, "There's No Recession in the Luxury Market," by Michael Doan; courtesy of *U.S. News & World Report*, November 23, 1981.

Customers will often pay more if they think they are getting higher quality products and better service.

Sometimes, though, a successful business can be located off the beaten track, provided that word of mouth and other advertising brings people to the door. In Cody, Wyoming, a small resort-type town near Yellowstone National Park, a furrier has for over 20 years successfully sold quality furs to customers from as far away as the East and West coasts and even Europe. Word-of-mouth advertising, among other marketing techniques such as the ability to offer lower prices, brings this furrier many new and repeat sales.

Today's sophisticated consumers are exposed to numerous consumers' guides and so on. Many will have made comparison shopping tours before they buy, particularly when purchasing expensive products or services.

Therefore, although business owners often charge "whatever the traffic will bear," many customer-oriented factors are also at issue. Entrepreneurs must take their customers' knowledge, habits, and needs into account when developing pricing strategies.

Cost-Oriented Pricing

Some entrepreneurs try to set prices that are high enough both to cover expenses and to assure a profit. In fact, Jackson, Hawes, and Hertel found that small retailers most commonly used "cost plus a reasonable percentage." The cost-oriented approach involves markup and/or markon.

"Markup" is the amount you add to what the merchandise cost you:

$$\text{Cost} + \text{Markup} = \text{Selling price}$$

If you buy a dozen greeting cards at $1 and sell them at $1.50, the figures plug into the formula like this:

$$\$1.00 + \$.50 = \$1.50$$

The markup here is 50 percent—i.e., you take half of what the item cost you ($\frac{1}{2} \times \$1.00 = \$.50$) and add those sums together to get the selling price ($1.50).

Another pricing formula is based on a percentage derived from the selling price, not the cost of the goods. Suppose you purchase an item for $1.20 and sell it for $1.60. The difference is called the *margin*, and here it is 40 cents, or 25 percent of the selling price. Thus the margin on this item is 25 percent.

If you need a margin of 25 percent to cover the cost of operation plus net profit, you will have to use a markup of 33 1/3 percent on the cost price (the 40-cent markup in our example is 33 1/3 percent of the cost, $1.20).

Why do merchants figure markup as a percentage of selling price rather than as a percentage of cost price? Theoretically, for every dollar taken in sales, the entrepreneur wants to know (1) how much is clear profit, (2) how much went to buy the product, and (3) how much went for operating expenses. (See Figure 11.1.)

Suppose a customer has paid one dollar for a small souvenir in your shop. That money might be distributed according to the pie chart in Figure 11.1. Of

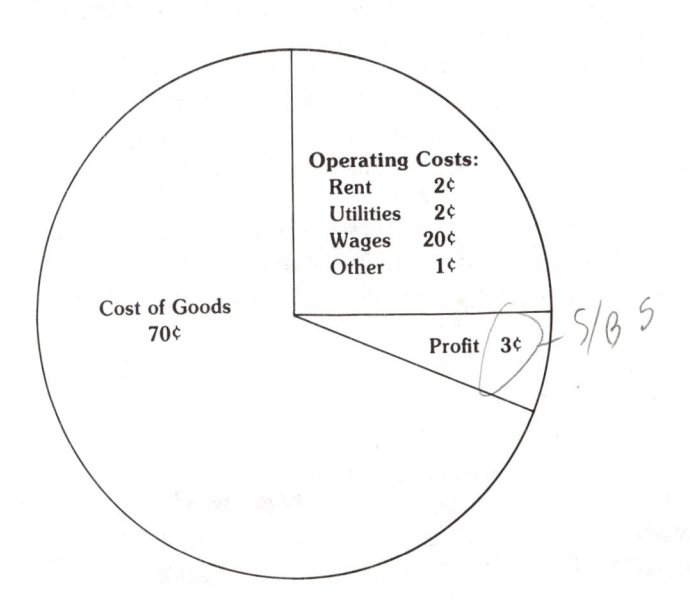

**FIGURE 11.1
Distribution of a Sales Dollar.**

Cost of Goods 70¢

Operating Costs:
Rent 2¢
Utilities 2¢
Wages 20¢
Other 1¢

Profit 3¢

course, entrepreneurs do not analyze each separate dollar. But multiplying this dollar by 10,000 can provide a realistic picture of a one-month business period. Here a markup of 30 percent on the cost price allows for a minimum profit.

Sales	$10,000	
Cost of goods	7,000	
Gross profit		$3,000

Operating and General Expenses

Rent	$ 200	
Utilities	200	
Wages	2,000	
Other	100	
Total operating expenses		$2,500

NET INCOME FROM OPERATIONS　　　　　　　　　　　$500

Markup Guidelines

There are many reasons for not pricing all products at exactly the same markup:

1. You might price some articles low to attract sales.
2. If you get a good buy on certain items, you can put a higher markup on them and still sell at competitive prices.
3. If the products are deteriorating or going out of style, you can mark them down to get them off the shelves.
4. If prices are falling and customers are buying elsewhere for lower prices, you will want to stay competitive by lowering your own prices.
5. You may sell high-turnover items at below markup.
6. You can increase sales volume by taking a lower markup.

Recognize, then, that the "average markup" should be a guideline, not a fixed rule. What you really want is to fix the markup at the point where you will earn the largest *overall* profit, although the amount of markup might be different for each article.

Demand-Oriented Pricing

Retail prices influence the quantities of products customers buy, which in turn affect total business revenue and profit. Thus, to be effective, pricing decisions must produce a successful operation. Prices must be low enough to meet the competition and attract customers but high enough to cover expenses and assure a profit. Customers react differently to prices. Some are conscious mostly of price while others seek convenience, quality, or knowledgeable and courteous assistance. The cost of merchandise should be at one end of the estimated price range and the ceiling above which customers seldom buy at the other.

Demand-oriented pricing is often superior to cost-oriented pricing. In the cost approach, a predetermined amount is added to the cost of merchandise, whereas the demand method attempts to identify what customers are willing to pay. (See Figure 11.2.)

---

1. Is the cost of this item very important to your target consumers?
2. Are prices based on estimates of the number of units that consumers will demand at various price levels?
3. Have you established a price range for the product?
4. Have you considered what price strategies would be compatible with your store's total retailing mix (including merchandise, location, promotion, and services)?
5. Do you have final pricing authority? Or do you have to assign prices according to a franchisor's or manufacturer's recommendations?)
6. What prices are your direct competitors charging?
7. Do you regularly review competitors' ads to check on their prices?
8. Should competitors' temporary price reductions ever be matched?
9. Have you established a profit objective for the first few months?
10. Have you estimated sales, operating expenses, and reductions (per season, if your business is seasonal)?
11. Given estimated sales, expenses, and reductions, have you planned initial markup?
12. Would it be appropriate to have different initial markup figures for various lines of merchandise or services?
13. Are additional markups called for because wholesale prices have increased or because an item's low price causes consumers to question its quality?
14. Will you consider the cost of merchandise before setting markdown prices?
15. Have you established procedures for recording the dollar amounts, percentages, and probable causes of markdowns?
16. If your state has an unfair-sales-practices act that requires minimum markups on certain merchandise, will your prices comply with this statute?
17. Are economic conditions in your trading area abnormal?
18. Do you display and promote your prices in a way compatible with consumerism (e.g., providing straightforward price information)?

FIGURE 11.2
Factors to Consider in Setting Retail Prices.

Source: Bruce J. Walker, "A Pricing Checklist for Small Retailers," *Management Aids* no. 4.013, U.S. Small Business Administration (Washington, D.C.), 1981.

FIGURE 11.3
Factors to Consider in Establishing Pricing Policies.

1. Is your tentative price compatible with established store policies?
2. Will you charge every purchaser the same price for all items?
3. Would prices ending in odd numbers, such as $1.98 and $44.95, be more appealing to your customers than rounded-off prices?
4. Will consumers buy more if you use multiple pricing, such as two items for $8.50?
5. Will you offer discount coupons in newspaper ads or through the mails?
6. Would periodic special sales, combining reduced prices and heavier advertising, be consistent with the store image you seek?
7. Would certain items sell better than others in a sale?
8. Should employees be given purchase discounts?
9. Should any customer group, such as students or senior citizens, be given purchase discounts?
10. Will you periodically review your pricing decisions?

Source: Bruce J. Walker, "A Pricing Checklist for Small Retailers," *Management Aids*, no. 4.013. U.S. Small Business Administration (Washington, D.C.), 1981.

Company Policies

Policy guidelines, preferably written and available to employees, are designed to provide direction in various situations. If developed carefully and used consistently, these written policies can help you make decisions and to treat customers and employees fairly. Figure 11.3 raises topics to consider in developing price guidelines.

Using Published Data

Trade publications, particularly those specialized for one particular industry or locale, provide data that can be helpful in making predictions. The National Federation of Independent Business, for instance, produces quarterly reports for each industry on numerous topics of importance to entrepreneurs.

Pricing for Manufacturing Products

Four elements make up the product sales price: direct costs, manufacturing overhead, nonmanufacturing overhead, and profit. Direct costs are the cost of the material and of the labor required to produce the product. These are the one-time costs of producing a new product.

Even nonproduction enterprises have some manufacturing overhead costs, such as janitor service, depreciation, and building repairs. Nonmanufacturing overhead includes selling and administrative expenses (including your salary).

TABLE 11.1 The Relationship between Price and Volume

	SELLING PRICE SET		
	At $5	At $4	At $4
Projected number of units sold	10,000	30,000	15,000
Projected sales	$50,000	$120,000	$60,000
Direct costs ($3 per unit)	$30,000	$ 90,000	$45,000
Contribution	$20,000	$ 30,000	$15,000

Source: Victor A. Lennon, "What Is the Best Selling Price?" *Management Aids* no. 1.002, Small Business Administration (Washington, D.C.: U.S. Government Printing Office, 1981).

Suppose you establish a price for a new product whose direct cost (materials and direct labor) is $3. If you charge $5 for the product, the difference of $2 is "contribution." For each unit sold, then, $2 will be available to help absorb both the manufacturing and nonmanufacturing overhead and to contribute toward profit. The amount of contribution will depend not only on the selling price you select but also on the number of units you expect to sell at the established price.

In Table 11.1, the $4 selling price, assuming you can sell 30,000 units, would be the best price for the product. However, if you can sell only 15,000 units at $4, the best price would be $5. That price would provide a $20,000 contribution, compared to the $15,000 contribution you could expect from 15,000 units sold at $4 each.[3]

In a manufacturing business, certain factors complicate the establishment of prices. You may be limited by the number of units that can be produced in a given time, by your capacity to employ sufficient workers, by the equipment available, or by your capability to obtain the raw materials needed. What the competition is doing can also be significant. Whether you ship to retailers, customers, or wholesalers also affects production, inventory, and operations. The direct-costing approach enables you to develop a pricing formula that recognizes these factors and to focus on any particular resource that is in short supply, such as labor, equipment, or materials.

The value of the materials used in manufacturing a product influences the contribution that accrues from each unit sold. When material costs are low, the contribution will be less, even though the same amount of direct labor and of machine use may be required to convert the raw materials into finished products.

In order to maximize profits, the manufacturer must realize the same dollar contribution per direct labor dollar, regardless of the cost of materials. If the material costs 15 cents and direct labor costs 10 cents, the selling price would be 50 cents, after you added a contribution of 25 cents. Basing the contribution on the labor hour assures a 25-cent contribution for each 10 cents of labor used to make a product, regardless of the value of the raw materials used.[4]

Return on Investment

In building profit into the pricing formula, "return on investment" is another approach often used. If the XYZ Manufacturing Company has invested $300,000 and seeks a 10-percent return, its profit before taxes should be $30,000. The formula to establish the unit selling price could then be:

Materials	$21.37	
Direct labor	1.80	
Contribution per unit	16.00*	
Price before profit		$39.17
Desired profit		−4.80 ($6 × .80*)
Selling price per unit		$43.97

*Calculated as follows: With a machine output of 1.25 units per hour, 80 percent of a machine hour is needed to produce one unit; the required contribution per machine hour is $20; therefore, $20 × .80 = $16.[5]

But what if $43.97 is not a competitive price? XYZ would then have two choices: (1) it could decide not to make the product if the machine time could be used to manufacture another product that would give the company its 10-percent profit, or (2) it could reduce the selling price, if the machines would otherwise be idle. Any price over $39.17 will generate some profit, which is better than no profit!

The direct-cost approach to pricing permits some flexibility. XYZ has to get $43.97 for the product in order to make the desired 10-per cent profit. Nevertheless, XYZ will *break even* at $39.17, meaning that any price over that figure will make some contribution to profit if not the total percentage desired. XYZ could even charge as low as $21.37, recovering the direct costs only. It will only take a few sales of the product at that figure, though, to produce a no-profit picture!

Break-Even Point for a Motel

When the Whitmans first bought their motel (see also Chapter 4), they knew that to survive while they repaired the dilapidated facility, advertised the enterprise as "under new management" to attract guests, and met the mortgage payments, they must reduce their break-even point to a bare minimum. Although the establishment had 40 rooms, they determined that by cutting corners they could break even if they rented an average of four rooms per night.

The four-room rental average allowed the Whitmans to meet their monthly mortgage payments and to pay the high cost of utilities, especially for the large neon signs they needed to attract potential guests. Any funds earned over this amount they used for capital investment, such as upgrading furniture and carpeting, asphalting the pavement, and repairing the swimming pool and restaurant.

To keep costs down the Whitmans did all their own laundry, room cleaning, and swimming-pool and courtyard maintenance, and simultaneously operated the restaurant single-handed. The Whitmans also reasoned that any income is better than none. Thus they often negotiated the price of any one rental, renting their rooms at discount rates and undercutting the competition in the process. Since they were in the beginning paying no wage expenses, even for laundry, renting rooms at a discount produced additional income.

They made little allowance for their own salaries or living expenses beyond the costs of groceries (their lodging and personal utility expenses were covered by living at the motel). As the average room rental began to climb, they could spend more money. With five rooms rented per night, they could afford one employee; with a six-room average, another; and so on.

Only after the Sanchezes bought the motel and used their start-up funds for additional capital investments (central heating and air conditioning, among numerous other improvements), did the motel actually show what could be called a real profit. With the addition of desk clerks and a night manager, plus salaries for the new owners, the break-even point became much higher; an average of 15 rooms had to be rented.

This situation demonstrates that new business owners cannot always start by basing estimates on the cost of operating a *successful* business. To merely survive until the business can pay its own way, you may have to take numerous shortcuts and undergo outrageous hardships, meanwhile keeping costs as low as possible in order to meet expenses. Until the company is fully operational, then, the standard formulas for establishing prices may not be applicable.

Pricing for Services

In order to assure profitability, service company entrepreneurs also need to understand the basic principles of costing and pricing. If you underestimate the costs per service performed, you can lose money, while if you overestimate, the high prices can turn patrons away. Checking your competitors' rates as well as those given in the trade literature can help to alleviate this dual problem. The cost of providing a service has three parts: (1) materials cost, (2) direct labor cost, and (3) overhead expenses.

"Materials costs" are the expenses for parts and supplies used on specific jobs. Develop a list of the prices suppliers charge for the needed parts and supplies to determine the materials cost. Shipping, storage, and related costs for these parts and supplies should be included.

"Direct labor costs" are those labor charges identified with a specific service job. Multiply the number of direct labor hours required by the cost per direct labor hour. To maintain accurate records you can use a time clock, worksheet, or daily time log for each job and each employee.

The hourly cost of direct labor can be priced two ways. You may use the hourly wage allocated to overhead, or you may add to the hourly direct labor cost the employer's contribution to Social Security, unemployment compensation, disability, holidays and vacations, and all other fringe benefits. The first addresses only the labor-related expenses while the latter includes all payroll expenses.

"Overhead expenses" are the indirect costs of the service, whether for materials, labor, or other items. This category includes machine lubricants and incidental supplies as well as wages, salaries, and other benefits for workers who do not perform direct services (e.g., clerical or janitorial workers). It also includes expenses for utilities, advertising, rent or mortgage, taxes, depreciation, insurance, and transportation. A common formula for allocating overhead cost to specific services is:

$$\text{Overhead rate} = \frac{\text{Total overhead cost}}{\text{Total direct labor cost}}$$

Where there is relatively little difference between the hourly wages paid to different employees, however, another formula can be used. Instead of dividing the total overhead cost by total direct labor cost, divide by the total direct and indirect labor hours. For this formula, overhead costs include primarily provision of the work space, the supervision, and the utilities that workers need to provide the service. Using this method, it is possible to determine the overhead cost per hour for *all* employees.[6]

In pricing various services, you will want to figure in a profit margin. Your price decisions may depend on: the competition's prices; the economic conditions of supply and demand; legal, political, and consumer pressures; productivity (of self and/or employees); and the volume of service jobs you can expect to attract.

Profit can be applied to all three costs independently, permitting you flexibility in allocating labor and overhead costs among jobs. For example, you might base your prices on a 10 percent profit on material, a 30 percent profit on direct labor, and a 30 percent profit on overhead:[7]

Cost Factor	Cost	Percent	Price	Profit
Materials cost	$20	10	$22	$2
Direct labor cost	10	30	13	3
Overhead cost	10	30	13	3
	$40		$48	$8

CREDIT AND COLLECTION POLICIES

The decision whether to operate your business on a cash basis or to allow credit purchases is usually based on these factors: the nature of the business, the competition's practices, the income level and potential to pay of the type of customers you seek to attract, and the availability of your own working capital. A store that sells durable goods is more likely to offer credit than, say, a souvenir shop. Transient workers, high school students, or residents of a nursing home are not usually good candidates for credit, particularly if you sell high-tag items where payments might be spread out over a long period. You will need more start-up capital if you allow credit buying. You will have to wait for your money, and funds tied up in accounts receivable cannot be used to pay current expenses.

There are both advantages and disadvantages to establishing a credit policy. A major advantage is that it increases people's ability to buy and may thus increase the number and frequency of sales, depending on the goods or services offered. A disadvantage is that you have to do more record keeping and more work, whether verifying credit ratings and making collections for slow payment or establishing accounts receivable and billing customers (see also Chapter 14). You must also allow for bad debts (uncollectible accounts).

Suppose you decide that the costs pertaining to the maintenance of accounts receivable are excessive and you issue a policy indicating that only cash sales will be accepted. This decision will obviously eliminate all costs of bad debts, late payments, resources needed to fund the receivables, credit approval costs, and other expenses. However, this cost reduction may be more than offset by the lost sales from customers who refuse to pay cash for goods and services.[8]

Will you accept checks or credit cards? Will you use indirect credit financing which can be a convenience to both customers and yourself? Will you be able to provide direct credit financing, if warranted, and how will you obtain trade credit, if needed? What policies will you establish if you are in a position to offer trade credit to others? Last, but hardly least, you'll want to establish both policies and procedures for handling collections.

Accepting Checks

Patrons often pay by check in such businesses as retail and food establishments, gasoline stations, and some service and hospitality firms. Companies usually require that the checks be written on local (or sometimes in-state) banks. Although not strictly a credit practice (since the passing of checks is usually considered a cash transaction), the acceptance of checks can sometimes involve collection activities.

Whatever policies you establish, it would be wise to verify standard community practices for your type of business, not only with the competition but also with such resources as the local credit bureau or Chamber of Commerce. You should post your establishment's check policies clearly—a popular spot is the cashier's station. It is important to make your established policies known not only to your employees but also to your customers. Following are recommendations:

1. Cash no payroll checks unless you are familiar with the company (even then you may want to avoid this practice unless you know your customers personally).
2. Accept no two-party checks.

3. Require proper identification, such as a driver's license or credit card. Record the ID or account number directly on the check so that if it's returned marked "Not Sufficient Funds," you can contact the credit bureau and/or the customer yourself. For the same reason, you should make sure that every check has the customer's address and telephone number recorded on its face. Verify, too, that each check is completely and properly filled out.
4. Allow customers to write personal checks for the purchase price only or with only a minimum overage, say $3, $5, or $10.

Accepting Credit Cards

Business owners who refuse to take standard national credit cards lose many sales, because customers have come to take this service for granted. Travelers especially would not purchase expensive merchandise, impulse items, and many services and products if they could not use credit cards. People do not like to carry much cash. Moreover, they are often more willing to buy now if they can pay later, when the credit-card bill arrives.

Since cards such as Visa and MasterCard are usually revolving accounts, people do not always pay all their charges each month. thus they can spread out the cost of such large seasonal expenditures as outfitting children for school, buying Christmas presents, and taking vacations. Credit-card companies also take responsibility for processing and collecting debts.

Against these advantages are some disadvantages. Credit-card companies charge from 3 to 7 percent (based on volume) for their services. They also charge rent on the stamping machine. Where net profit is already low, some entrepreneurs hesitate to add one more cost to their overhead. Another disadvantage is the work involved in processing credit cards. Customers may have to wait in line while you or your cashier fiddle with the machine, the card, and the record. Then you have to separate and bundle the receipts of the different credit companies and record the totals before transmitting each stack to the bank.

If you make few credit-card sales, then the advantages of accepting the cards may not be worth the time and expense. In short, each entrepreneur needs to establish an individual policy, based on the type of business, the competition's practices, and an assessment of the potential advantages and disadvantages.

Indirect and Financing Credit

You may not want to extend credit out of your own resources to finance purchases of such high-priced goods as cars, household appliances, furniture, sports equipment, and costly services. An alternative is to arrange with banks and other lending institutions for you to act as an intermediary. In some cases there is no charge to the entrepreneur, and in fact the loan company may pay you a finder's fee for bringing in clients.

Banks and finance firms can also assist a retailer by buying unpaid accounts or installment contracts. They may or may not buy these at face value. Banks typically buy contracts at face value "with recourse," meaning that in case of customer default the entrepreneur is liable. When loan companies purchase contracts "without recourse" (i.e., they accept responsibility for collections), the going rate may range from only 75 to 90 percent of face value.

The difference should be obvious: bad debts are a fact of credit life and it costs money, time, and effort to make collections. If you accept the responsibility of taking such action then you can expect a higher rate of return when you sell credit contracts to a lending institution.

Direct Financing

Several options are available if you want to finance customer credit yourself. Depending again on the type of business, your typical customers, your competitors' practices, and your own resources, you can establish installment buying or revolving accounts.

Installment accounts generally require a down payment (perhaps 20 percent or more), with regular payments extending over 12 to 36 months although for vehicles a duration of four years may be allowed. Interest rates are added. The Truth in Lending Act requires companies to disclose true financing charges to their customers.

You should also check state law to determine what security method can be used. Where "chattel mortgages" are the practice, legal title to the property purchased passes at the time of sale to the customer. With a "conditional sales contract," customers do not receive legal title until they make the final payment. The difference to the entrepreneur is significant. Under the latter system, you can repossess the item whenever a customer defaults on a payment. Conversely, with the chattel mortgage, although you retain a "seller's lien," you would have to take court action to obtain possession.

After making a credit check on applicants, you can establish a revolving account or line of credit for them. Usually a maximum credit allowance is specified, perhaps $500 to $1000, beyond which customers cannot charge purchases. Also, a percentage of the total debt must be paid each month, which supposedly motivates debtors to make regular payments against accounts. Finance charges are calculated on the unpaid balance and, again, the interest rate must be disclosed.

"Budget accounts" are short-term installment accounts for small purchases. Prices range from, say, $300 to $700. Payment should be completed in 90 days (or less). A low interest rate may be added, or none at all. Extensions may be negotiated, but in this case standard interest rates are added.

Trade Credit

As opposed to consumer credit, trade credit is established between manufacturers and wholesalers, between distributors and retailers, or, essentially, between any one company and another. As a manufacturer, you might decide to sell your goods to other companies (as opposed to selling them retail to consumers), and also to offer trade credit. If so, as with any other type of customer, you should keep accounts-receivable records on these transactions.

On the other hand, when you *seek* trade credit, you will establish accounts-payable records. You might for example order supplies and raw materials on credit from a vendor. (See Chapter 14 for how to establish and control records.)

A typical trade-credit term is "2/10, n/30": 2 percent discount if paid during the first 10 days following the invoice date or no discount if paid after 30 days (one month). If, however, you could be earning 5-percent interest or more if you left your money in a savings or "NOW" (interest-bearing checking) account, the 2-percent discount for paying within 10 days is no advantage.

In the recession of the early 1980s, some entrepreneurs— particularly those operating on slim profit margins—waited as long as 75 days to pay their bills, investing their funds in the interim. This practice reportedly often made the difference between profit and loss. Conversely, if you are on the receiving end, awaiting payment, this principle could work in reverse. Your cash flow could dry up.

Other credit terms are: "E.O.M."—the "end-of-month" bill covers all credit purchases made within the month and is due upon receipt; and "C.O.D." or "Collect on Delivery." As a new business owner, you may have to be satisfied with paying for your goods at the time they are delivered, at least until you have proved your ability to pay and are thus judged worthy of receiving credit. You would follow the same procedure, of course, in establishing credit for those who apply to your company.

Evaluating Credit Applicants

A business's evaluation of the potential credibility of credit applicants depends on four "C's": capital, character, capacity, and conditions. Corresponding to these are four questions:

1. Can the applicants pay as contracted?
2. Will they pay?
3. When will they pay?
4. If not, can the debt be collected?

In answering the second question, the creditor looks to the *character* or integrity of the applicants. Companies with integrity have sound business policies and follow ethical practices. Individuals with integrity are responsible people who pay their debts regularly and on time. A good index of reliability and dependability is the applicant's employment and residence status and stability, which you can verify by calling the character references listed on the application form.

Capital and *capacity* relate to collateral—to the cash and other assets against which loans and credit can be secured. Business applicants should have enough working capital to implement their business plans, not only in the start-up period but also to continue functioning over the length of the loan or credit period. To ascertain the business's capacity to pay, potential creditors want to examine its financial statement, balance sheet, and earnings forecast.

Conditions refers to the general economic climate. In times of recession or when major local industries are experiencing difficulties, loan companies and businesses offering credit are cautious about lending money or providing credit. Workers, no matter how stable in the past, may be facing layoffs. Companies that depend on local consumers may be in for trouble. Local competition and political factors will also influence an individual's or a company's ability to pay. A profitable business facing rezoning, rerouting of highways, and the like will not necessarily remain profitable—and may thus not be able to continue paying its bills or to make loan or credit payments in the future.

Credit Procedures

If you plan to offer credit to your customers, you will need to establish certain policies and procedures. First you will have to devise a method of identifying customers who can meet your criteria of using the four C's and their related questions. Potential credit customers can fill out an application form. Then you will want to verify some of the information reported and to check with the references provided about the character and capacity of the applicant. Check, too, with local credit bureaus and credit investigating agencies.

> One small clothing manufacturer has every sales order reviewed by a Dun & Bradstreet-trained credit manager who maintains a complete file of D&B credit reports on thousands of business customers. These reports, together with the dealer's financial statements and card, are the basis for decisions on credit sales.[9]

Credit limits should be established, next, for each consumer or business customer. Review the accounts periodically to see if debtors are making regular payments and the like, or whether an account is in arrears. (See Chapter 14 for how to prepare an "Aging of A/R and A/P.")

Some entrepreneurs bill debtors monthly, while others do not. For installment, revolving, and budget accounts, customers may be supplied with coupons or receipts at the time of arranging credit. They submit these with each monthly payment.

If these debtors pay in person, it presents another selling opportunity. Each time customers return to the store they may make new purchases they might not have considered otherwise. Personal interaction between entrepreneur or employees and customers also helps build rapport and goodwill. (See Chapter 14 for recordkeeping procedures).

Collections

"Intershoe, Inc., mounts a well-coordinated attack on what is today a nearly universal business problem: collecting overdue payments." Fifteen of the 120 people employed by this shoe manufacturer spend the majority of their work time "pestering retailers who have fallen behind in their payments." This company's accounts-receivable and collections staff service about 2500 customer accounts.[10]

Corinne McGrady, whose manufacturing company produces plastic see-through cookbook holders, assigned her husband the task of telephoning recalcitrant debtors. Although theirs was a small company with few employees, Corinne wanted customers to hear a different voice over the phone than hers.[11] Mike, like many credit collection people, grew accustomed to the many and varied excuses. The one that topped the list was: "I've already put the check in the mail."[12]

No matter how careful you are during the application and verification stage, you can't be 100 percent sure that every account will be a good one. You have to allow for bad debts when you prepare your business plan and during the organization phase. Your collections procedures should be in place when you need to use them.

The longer it takes to collect payment, the less likely you are to get anything at all. Two keys to extracting cash are (1) an efficient recordkeeping system that tells you who isn't paying and (2) polite, regular telephone calls to past-due debtors. Minimize the risk of a really bad debt by setting a maximum bill customers can run up and a maximum number of days they can run overdue before you cut off further shipments, sales, or service provisions. As owner, you have to decide whether to fight or accept a loss. To cover probable collection costs and losses, you may have to consider increasing prices.

A schedule of procedures is recommended, each step of which involves more pronounced action:

1. Periodically conduct an "Aging of Accounts Receivable" survey to determine the status of all accounts (see Chapter 14).
2. Contact overdue accounts with a courteous telephone call or letter. This notification might be a printed form stating, simply: "In case your check is already in the mail, we apologize for this reminder."
3. Recontact overdue accounts that are still pending, using a sterner tone and adding specifics such as "Please contact us immediately" or "Payment is expected within ten days of receipt."
4. Issue a "final warning."

If Step 4 produces no results, the contract or account can be turned over to a collection agency. Agencies can't do much that creditors themselves cannot do, however, aside from using the intimidating phrase, "collection agency." An agency normally charges clients 20 to 30 percent of the amount collected (see also Chapter 13).

Ultimately, creditors can take direct action and sue for their money—but suing usually involves more time and trouble than a debt is worth. Even in small-claims court, where companies may sue without an attorney for amounts under $1000 or so, garnishing a debtor's assets or wages requires half a dozen legal steps and could take months.

And if an attorney sues in district court—the only recourse if a debt is too large for small-claims court—a slow payer can use legal maneuvering to delay the case for a year or more. Often, filing suit is a worthwhile step for one reason: many delinquents settle as soon as they receive an official court notice.

In numerous lawsuits, however, bill collectors have had to defend themselves against claims that they harassed debtors unduly. Such suits were initially directed at professional bill collectors, but some individual entrepreneurs who use abusive tactics are now also being sued. To avoid lawsuits from debtors who claim you have used harassment, follow these guidelines:

1. Don't call debtors late at night or early in the morning; accurately identify yourself when you call; and limit the number of calls.
2. Don't mislead or deceive debtors by writing collection letters on a lawyer's or a credit agency's stationery or by using forms that appear to be sent from the government or a court.
3. Describe accurately the action you will take if the bills are not paid; avoid misrepresenting the legal status of your claim; and be cautious about what you say and do if you learn that debtors are themselves being represented by legal counsel.
4. Don't contact debtors' employers unless the debtors have given you permission to do so.
5. Protect debtors' privacy by sending written notifications in sealed envelopes (as opposed to postcards).
6. When turning accounts over to a collection agency or attorney, be sure that all documentation is complete and accurate.[13]

Although, as noted earlier, creditors who hold a conditional sales contract have the right to take repossession if the customer defaults on any payment, in reality it is not only more humane to give the customer a chance to pay but also sometimes a smart business decision. Problems do occur and people can forget to pay or temporarily be unable to do so. You don't want to risk losing an otherwise good customer because you took action arbitrarily and too quickly.

Nevertheless, where durable goods are at stake and where you hold a conditional sales contract, the final step can be to take physical repossession. There are many stories about the various and often devious means that vehicle, appliance, and furniture dealers use to repossess goods. Truly "bad debt" customers will use every ruse to hide an auto or themselves, for example, in order to avoid having the car repossessed or facing the bill collector.

If you are cautious in the beginning, when first considering customers for credit, you can avoid some of the hassles and the loss of both time and money involved in trying to make collections. Recognizing the problems that can occur should help you to establish both policies and procedures from the beginning.

The significance of credit in the phenomenal growth of U.S. commerce is well known. "Practically all of the goods and services which make up the well over one trillion dollar American Gross National Product move through the channels of distribution on credit. Credit, then, is a powerful force. And like any powerful force, it must be managed."[14]

SUMMARY

By thinking out your pricing, credit, and collection policies before opening your doors for business you can avoid many of the problems that face entrepreneurs who commence operations haphazardly, with little thought, planning, and organization behind them. Once you have assessed the costs of doing business, the competition, and the market, you can develop realistic policies and procedures.

The price structure you develop depends on the type of business you will open, although some factors operate similarly. You may be inclined to base prices on what the traffic will bear. Yet to do so you must have a thorough knowledge not only of what your competition offers but also of what customers are seeking—their needs and wants, their consumer awareness, and what they are willing to pay for what quality and what type of goods or services. Markup and margin formulas can help assure a profitability picture; they address the cost of providing goods and services and allow for both overhead expenses and the profit desired.

Establishing your credit policies also allows you to clearly envisage your start-up and continuing financial needs. Although cash flow can be a problem for a new business that offers credit to its customers, not offering credit—especially if you plan to meet or beat the competition's prices—can limit the business's sales and earning potential. This is particularly true if yours is the type of business from which customers expect to receive credit. The decision of whether to accept checks and national credit cards, although these are not strictly credit transactions, is relevant here because of the potential for uncollectibles. No matter what the specific procedures used, where any form of noncash is involved, entrepreneurs must consider how they will make collections.

DISCUSSION QUESTIONS

Use the data on prices and credit practices that you collected for Chapter 7's checklists as one basis for some of the discussion questions that follow.

1. Discuss the relationship among customer buying habits, prices, and quality.
2. Explain the systems of cost- and demand-oriented pricing and explain why pricing policies should be established during the organizational phase.
3. Consider the role of these factors: "whatever the traffic will bear," competitors' offerings in your locale, differences in quality, size, etc. Also, on what basis have your previous employer(s) made pricing and credit policy decisions?
4. From your own knowledge and from interviews, how are business owners helped to set pricing and credit policies by franchisers or by manufacturers' recommendations?

5. Discuss, from your own knowledge and observations, the prices that are charged by repair shops and other service establishments in your locale. Do you know or can you guess how they establish price and credit policies?
6. List the steps you would take to ascertain a credit applicant's willingness and ability to pay.
7. Delineate the various forms of credit.
8. What different action might an entrepreneur take in the collection process if the goods are held under a chattel mortgage or a conditional sales contract? What pitfalls can you foresee in making collections and what can you do to prevent lawsuits?
9. Describe the advantages and disadvantages of allowing customers to buy on credit and explain why credit policies should be developed during the planning phase.

COMPREHENSIVE PROJECT

The first two units of this book have covered a good many points about the planning involved in getting ready to start your own business. The next unit begins with a discussion about how to get the financing you'll need. The following chapters describe how to organize and set up your company.

At this time you should be prepared to refine and submit the first draft of your business plan. *Keep a copy to work with during the next unit.*

If you intend to open your own business in the near future, you should use real data in the updating of your plan. If not, then choose a business in Stanley Junction (a case supplement); namely, a day-care center, an energy service, or a laundromat.

Guidelines

1. Retrieve the business plan segments you have been developing since Chapter 6 and all checklists and worksheets prepared in the meantime. Reassess each topic, as proposed in the table of contents.
2. Decide on the legal structure of your business and prepare an organization chart.
3. Do you need to and can you afford to hire employees? Then review the job description(s) you wrote, if any, and determine the annual wage expense. Use this figure on your earnings forecast.
4. Use the marketing study (Chapter 7) and location and facilities checklists (Chapters 8 and 9) and adjust related figures on the two worksheets.
5. Use information provided in this chapter to establish a pricing structure for your products or services. If you will hire employees, allow for their wages and benefits in your formulas and calculations.

6. Establish other company policies. Include whether you will operate on a or credit basis. If you choose to offer credit, then outline how you will verify customer credibility and obtain collections.
7. Reevaluate your current assets in relation to your financial needs, as compiled from Steps 1-6 above. Identify the difference between what you have and what you need.
8. Prepare or revise the earnings forecast in line with the results of Steps 1-7 above.
9. Refine other sections of the comprehensive business plan as a result of completing Units I and II. Note the following possibilities:
   a. Estimate sales volume based on your assessment of the market population and of the competition.
   b. Determine the rent (or mortgage payments) of the site chosen. Calculate how much of your start-up and continuation funds these expenses will take.
   c. Estimate and record other costs associated with the site, whether one-time remodeling, equipment and furniture expenses, or ongoing expenses for utilities, etc. (See Figures 6.3 and 6.7.)

NOTES

1. Besides the 100,000 or so office workers employed in the 12-block area above the underground mall, there are also eight major hotels, lodging tourists and business travelers.
2. John A. Jackson, Douglas K. Hawes, and Frank M. Hertel, "Pricing and Advertising Practices in Small Retail Businesses," *American Journal of Small Business*, October 1979, pp. 22–23.
3. Victor A. Lennon, "What Is the Best Selling Price?" *Management Aid* no. 1.002 (Washington, D.C.: U.S. Small Business Administration, 1981).
4. Ibid.
5. Ibid.
6. James Salvate, "Profit Costing and Pricing for Services," *Management Aid* no. 1.020 (Washington, D.C.: U.S. Small Business Administration, 1981).
7. Ibid.
8. Fred A. Jacobs, Larry H. Beard, and Al L. Hartgraves, "Controlling Cash Flow in the Small Business," *Business,* January–March 1983, pp. 31–36.
9. H. N. Broom and Justin G. Longenecker. *Small Business Management* (Cincinnati: South-Western Publishing Company, 1979), p. 283.
10. Robert C. Wood, "Getting Cash from Slow Payers," *Inc.*, June 1982, p. 11.
11. Mike McGrady. *Kitchen Sink Papers.* (New York: Doubleday and Company, 1975).
12. Gordon Bizar, "The Check Is in the Mail, and Other Humbug," *Savvy,* September 1982, pp. 24–26.

13. Fred S. Steingold, "Bad Debts Can Cost You More Than You Think," *Inc.*, June 1982, pp. 101–2.
14. Cooke O'Neal, "Credit and Collections," *Management Aid* no. 1.007 (Washington, D.C.: U.S. Small Business Administration, 1981).

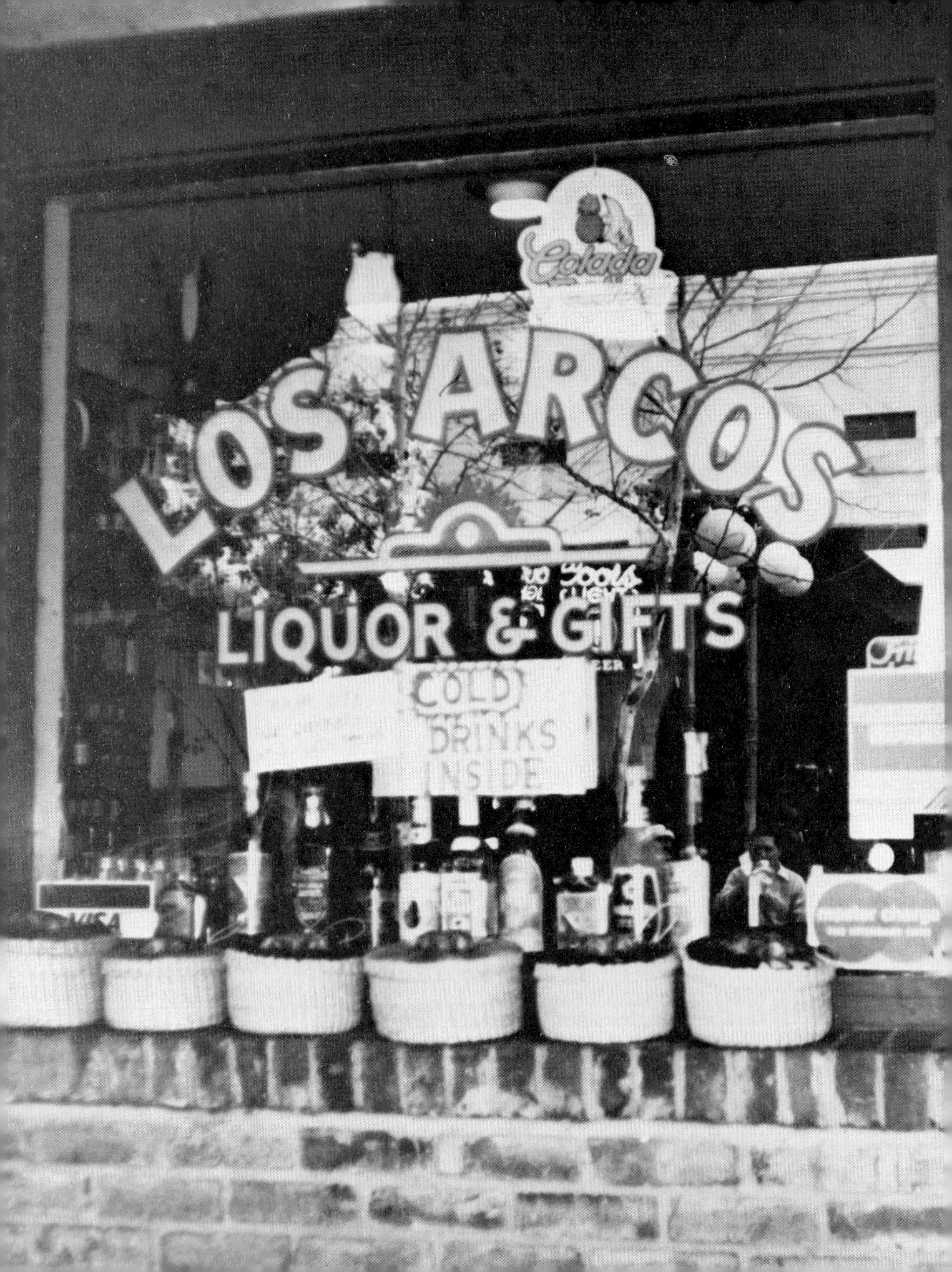
Colada
LOS ARCOS
LIQUOR & GIFTS
COLD DRINKS INSIDE
VISA

U·N·I·T III

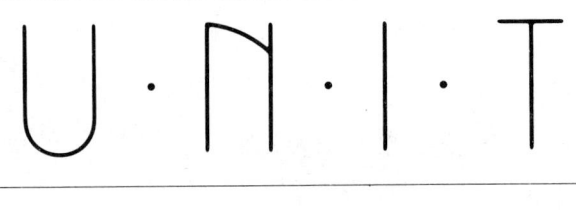

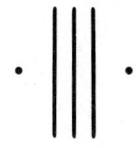

ORGANIZING FOR BUSINESS

Now that you have made certain basic decisions, if only tentatively, and developed the first draft of your comprehensive business plan, you are ready to organize your business.

Unit III commences by exploring various avenues for financing enterprises. Next we will discuss how to protect your business from risks associated with legalities and taxation.

In the organization phase you should also establish your records and office systems and decide whether to computerize operations. Such decisions depend on the nature and size of your business as well as on the extent to which you are willing and able to manage your business's financial systems.

Finally, there are two other significant organizational steps for you to take before launching your business: (1) the purchasing of inventory, materials, and supplies and, (2) the promoting of your business and its opening day. You must also arrange to continuously control the inventory and to manage an ongoing advertising program.

Periodically throughout this unit, you should look back over your business plan. As new and more complete information is added, this plan should ultimately reach fruition, representing concrete decisions and data.

Direct Sales TIRE WAREHOUSE
THANK YOU
PENNZOIL
AUTO SEAT COVERS

chapter 12

Financing the Enterprise

Objectives

1. Describe innovative means entrepreneurs use to finance business start-ups and continuing operations.

2. Identify sources of financing and describe similarities and differences in the characteristics of each.

3. Estimate capital requirements for one or more preferred businesses.

4. Prepare a cash budget to use in updating the business plan.

5. Sell your business plan in a simulated situation.

It isn't just the acquisition of money that assures business success. Management of the accumulated funds and the early production of a profit can make the difference between success and failure. Those who are in the business of loaning money—including banks and other financial institutions, government agencies, venture capital firms, and private individuals—are all interested in seeing your enterprise succeed, because your success is indirectly theirs.

Profitable businesses are good loan risks, because they produce the interest income or dividends that earn lenders and investors their profits. Thus everyone benefits from good financial management, while many suffer when failures occur. The challenge to you as an entrepreneur is to convince lenders that you are a good risk. The way to do that is to sell your idea effectively and to prove to them that you've done your homework and really know exactly what you're getting into.

THE CLIMATE FOR FUNDING

Capital-Gains Tax Rates

In 1969, Congress increased the maximum tax on long-term capital gains from 25 percent to 49 percent. (Capital gains are the profit made by investors on the sale of stocks, real estate, ventures, etc.) This action proved most detrimental to new business starts because fewer people and institutions were willing to invest money in potentially long-shot businesses. Venture capital investment dropped from $171 million in 1969 to a mere $10 million in 1975.[1]

In 1978, however, Congress rolled back the capital-gains tax rate to 28 percent. With the potential payoff increased, investors again began to take risks. By 1981, $1.3 billion in venture funds had accumulated, over 100 times the amount of six years earlier.[2] (See Figure 12.1.)

Innovations in Financing

> In 1979, after a fruitless search for start-up funds, David Sullivan went to Chicago's Esmark, Inc.'s venture capital division, and received $160,000 in cash and $300,000 in loan guarantees to finance his Indel Electrical Distributors company. In return, Esmark received 45 percent of Indel's stock, making the latter the first minority-owned firm to benefit from Esmark financing. (By 1982, Indel produced $1,563,000 in business revenues, up from $417,000 in 1980, its first full year of operation.)[3]

One reason for the success of many high-tech industries is that they are located in an area that has a well-developed business network and a positive attitude toward providing financial backing. In Santa Clara County, California, for example, an informal group of experienced executives, consultants, and development services had emerged by the mid-1970s to help new businesses get started. According to Adam Osborne of Osborne Computer, who amassed

$70 million in orders within his first two years of operations: "With a couple of local phone calls, a budding entrepreneur with the right ideas can round up $1 million in venture capital in a day. . . . Every single thing we need is within an hour's drive."[4]

Also located in Santa Clara County (popularly called "Silicon Valley"), Steven Jobs saw the commercial potential in Stephen Wozniak's easy-to-use small computer. The two friends decided to form a company to market the computer. They raised $1300 from the sale of Jobs' Volkswagen and Wozniak's scientific calculator and opened a makeshift production line in Jobs' garage.

Via networking, the company was mentioned to A. C. Markkula, a former marketing manager at Intel (a computer-chip manufacturer). When Markkula offered both his expertise and $250,000, Jobs and Wozniak made him an equal partner. Markkula helped arrange a credit line with the Bank of America and persuaded two venture capital firms to invest in Apple.[5]

George Gilder, a supply-side theorist, said "Entrepreneurs are fighting America's only serious war against poverty. The potentialities of invention and enter-

FIGURE 12.1 Estimated Venture Capital Fundings.

Year	New Private Capital Committed to Venture Capital Firms
1981	$1300
1980	900
1979	319
1978	570
Capital Gains Tax Decrease	
1977	39
1976	50
1975	10
1974	57
1973	56
1972	62
1971	97
Capital Gains Tax Increase	
1969	171

Total capital committed to the Organized Venture Capital Industry (September 1981 estimate)

Independent private venture-capital firms	$2.1 billion
Small Business Investment Companies	1.5 billion
Corporate subsidiaries	1.4 billion
Total	$5.0 billion

Source: Adapted from SBA, *The State of Small Business: A Report of the President*, March, 1982.

prise are greater than ever before in human history." Yet Gilder also suggests that few businesses begin with bank loans—small businesses especially.[6]

Some new entrepreneurs use networking to get in contact with funding sources while others use the more typical approaches of liquidating assets or using them as collateral to get capital.

> Suzy Bass found it difficult to get a bank loan when she wanted to start an ice cube delivery service. At first she could not even find anyone willing to lease her a truck, until through a friend she contacted a company that agreed to lease her the icemakers she needed. (Second-year revenues were $250,000 with 22% profits.)[7]
>
> Only three months after opening her shop, Sallye J. Orlando sought a loan of $35,000 to improve her cash flow. The bank turned her down. Following a friend's advice, she took three bankers to lunch and found one of them very supportive of women and small business. Her experience with that first bank, however, had led her to a Small Business Administration seminar, which led her to the local Chamber of Commerce. It was through Chamber activities that she met those three bankers. Her conclusion: "I've found it's very important to deal with accountants, attorneys, bankers—all those people you deal with on a consultant basis—who have the small business perspective." (Phone Marketing Services, Inc. earned $250,000 in revenues in its second year with $750,000 predicted for the third year.)[8]
>
> K. P. (Phil) Hwang emigrated from Korea in the early 1960s and worked as a busboy and waiter while attending Utah State University. In 1975 he used $9000 in family savings to found TeleVideo Systems, a company that makes computer screens and keyboards. By the early 1980s, Hwang had become a multimillionaire.[9]

A Denver broker, with 25,000 companies on file, runs a bartering service for small-business entrepreneurs who want to exchange products for services and vice versa. His small-company clients, particularly during their beginning days, sometimes find they can avoid seeking loans via this system. This broker, however, cautions his clients about income-tax reporting.[10]

The IRS is cracking down on services and/or products received through bartering, which may be considered income in some cases and should therefore be reported. However, where expenses exceed income, no income taxes at all may be due. Thus arranging to barter may make the difference between barely succeeding and going bankrupt. (See Figure 12.2 for typical funding sources.)

DETERMINING CAPITAL NEEDS

The funds you will need depend, in part, on the type of business you are opening. Like Jobs and Wozniak, you may seek outside help to promote your business or market your new product. If so, you'll have to pay specialists to provide this service, if not out of your own cash funds then by sharing the business on a partnership or other basis to help you raise the necessary capital.

Financing the Enterprise   **247**

STARTED BUSINESS, PREVIOUSLY NON-EXISTENT

Personal Resources - 60%
Lending Institutions - 23%
Friends, Relatives - 9%
Other - 4%
Investors - 3%
Government - 1%
Venture Capital Firms - 0%

PURCHASED EXISTING BUSINESS

39% - Personal Resources
37% - Lending Institutions
11% - Friends, Relatives
7% - Other
7% - Investors
2% - Government
0% - Venture Capital Firms

The most common source of financing a small business is one's personal resources. Financial institutions, friends, and relatives are also important.

The amounts obtained from different sources vary depending upon whether the owner starts a new business or purchases an existing business.

Source: Courtesy of the National Federation of Independent Business (NFIB)

FIGURE 12.2 Sources of Capital for Entrepreneurs.

Start-up Costs and Expenses

As discussed in Chapter 9, your company may require specific facilities, equipment, and furniture. Based on the capital resources you have available, you may decide to lease rather than buy some or all of these.

If yours is a retail establishment, then you must purchase stock; if a small factory, you will need raw materials in addition to equipment and supplies. Transportation, construction, and extraction companies will require vehicles, as will some service firms. Additionally, you must allot money to make mortgage payments on the land and building (if you plan to purchase), for promotional advertising, for prepaying supplies and insurance, and to carry accounts receivable, if any.

To obtain the stock or materials you need, you may at first have to pay up front. Buying from suppliers on credit is the best way to retain working capital, but this may not be possible until you have established your creditability. You will also want to secure your current and fixed assets by paying for insurance coverage. Another need is promotional advertising to attract customers.

Finally, you want to be sure that you have enough money to live on during those first typically tight months of business operation. If you don't anticipate this need, you may have to dip into your company's resources merely to stay alive.

Types of Capital

Working capital. This term describes a company's total current assets, or the excess of current assets over current liabilities. "Current assets" are those that are converted to cash within a year; while "current liabilities" are debts that are due and payable within the year. "Circulating capital" describes the conversion cycle of cash to stock to accounts receivable to cash, and so on.

Fixed asset capital. This category includes tangible and intangible fixed assets and fixed security investments. Assets are defined differently for different types of companies. A vehicle used for delivery is a fixed asset, but when offered for sale it becomes inventory or a current asset. Otherwise, tangible fixed assets usually include the company building, equipment, and land, as well as timber, mineral, and water rights, etc.

Intangible assets include copyrights or patents and goodwill. If you buy an existing business, part of the purchase price may be for the goodwill, and thus you would be starting with this intangible asset. Not many new businesses have either intangibles or fixed security investments, which can include pension or contingency funds and subsidiary stocks.

Estimating Capital Needs

Every chapter presented in the planning unit discussed some aspect of, and various methods to determine, what your capital needs might be in opening and operating the business of your choice. Here we can refine the process by estimating the money you will need for inventory, working capital, and accounts receivable (if any).

Inventory. Different businesses have different inventory needs. Retailers need to offer products in a range of sizes, styles, colors, and perhaps quality and price. Purchasing decisions are also influenced by the local competition and by the profit or sales volume desired.

You might strive for a sales-to-inventory ratio of, say, six to one. That is, if your estimated sales volume is $100,000, you would want an inventory worth at least $17,000. Suppliers can help you determine wholesale costs (see also Chapter 16).

Note, however, that when high interest rates are imposed for financing and credit, some business people reduce their inventories to a bare minimum. This strategy is made easier by the efficiency of telecommunications and transportations systems. If a consumer can't find the exact product she or he wants, the retailer will say, "We can have that item in stock for you by tomorrow." The store places a limited-number product order by an 800-line phone call, computer linkages, or facsimile transmission, and the customer's product is on the way that night by air freight, truck, railroad, or even bus or van.

Auto-parts firms and even small retail or larger department chain stores operate this way. In the latter, consumers can also select products from the chain's retail catalog. You should carefully survey local and industry practices to determine your inventory needs. You won't want to run short on available cash but at the same time you won't want to risk losing customers because you don't have needed items in stock.

Cash balance. The inexperienced entrepreneur must allow for unanticipated problems. To prepare a budget, estimate both your income and expenses. Then deduct noncash expenses (e.g., depreciation, which does not represent a cash payment). Suppose the amount remaining is $60,000 a year, or $5000 a month. You will need enough funds to cover two or three months' expenses, or at least a $15,000 cash balance.

Retailers or manufacturers must also consider turnover of inventory or raw materials. Suppose your stock or materials turn over about once per quarter, or every three months. With an estimated annual cash outlay of $60,000 for inventory, three months' worth of inventory would cost approximately $15,000. Both calculations, then, produce the $15,000 figure, or a $30,000 total.

Accounts receivable carrying funds. It is important to estimate this sum where credit is to be made available. Suppose approximately 25 percent of your sales will be made on credit. For a sales estimate of $100,000 per year, or of $8333 per month, about $2083 of sales a month will be on credit.

What sort of turnover in payments can you anticipate? As noted in Chapter 10, where NOW accounts and other savings accounts are paying relatively high interest rates, some business customers may take longer to pay their bills. For individual consumers, however, the average collection period ranges form 20 to 50 days, with a 35-day average. Using the figures above, you might need to add another $3000 or so to your cash reservoir to cover accounts receivable. Given this requirement, it should be obvious why some new entrepreneurs decide to operate, at least at first, without offering credit. The alternative, of course, is to have enough capital to underwrite this service. (Figure 12.3 is a worksheet for preparing your cash budget.)

FUNDING SOURCES

Typical sources of funding include: personal savings, personal assets that are liquidated or used to secure loans, loans from relatives and friends, and trade-credit or leasing arrangements.

If you have already lined up some funds (and prepared a comprehensive business plan that includes appropriate financial and forecast statements), you will probably have more success on approaching an established financial institution or venture capitalist. These financial people do want to invest in successful businesses. You can better convince them that you mean business if you have already made a real commitment to the enterprise as evidenced from your own financial investments.

Definitions

There are three kinds of loans; short-term, term, and equity capital. What kind you need depends on what you want it for and how you intend to repay it. People usually repay short-term loans by liquidating some current asset. Long-term loans, conversely, are normally repaid from earnings.

(For three months, ending March 31, 19 _____)

	January Budget	January Actual	February Budget	February Actual	March Budget	March Actual
Expected Cash Receipts:						
1. Cash sales						
2. Collections on accounts receivable						
3. Other income						
4. Total cash receipts						
Expected Cash Payments						
5. Raw materials						
6. Payroll						
7. Other factory expenses (including maintenance)						
8. Advertising						
9. Selling expense						
10. Administrative expense (including salary of owner-manager)						
11. New plant and equipment						
12. Other payments (taxes, including estimated income tax; repayment of loans; interest; etc.)						
13. Total cash payments						
14. **Expected Cash Balance** at beginning of the month						
15. Cash increase or decrease (item 4 minus item 13)						
16. Expected cash balance at end of month (item 14 plus item 15)						
17. Desired working cash balance						
18. Short-term loans needed (item 17 minus item 16, if item 17 is larger)						
19. Cash available for dividends, capital cash expenditures, and/or short investments (item 16 minus item 17, if item 16 is larger than item 17)						
Capital Cash:						
20. Cash available (item 19 after deducting dividends, etc.)						
21. Desired capital cash (item 11, new plant equipment)						
22. Long-term loans needed (item 21 less item 20, if item 20 is larger than item 20)						

Source: "The ABCs of Borrowing," *Management Aid* no. 1.001 U.S. Small Business Administration (Washington, D.C.), 1981.

FIGURE 12.3 Sample Cash Budget.

Short-term loans. Lenders often expect short-term loans to be repaid once their purposes have been served. Loans to cover accounts receivable should be repaid when the outstanding accounts are paid by your customers. Inventory loans may come due when the goods are sold. Banks grant such money either on an unsecured loan—on your general credit reputation—or on a secured loan against collateral.

Term loans. Term loans are paid back over a fairly long time. "Intermediate" loans last longer than one year but less than five, while "long-term" loans are for five years or more. Such loans are usually paid back in periodic installments from earnings.

Equity capital. Venture capitalists or other investors may buy a part interest in your business in return for providing you with equity capital. You do not repay this amount, as with a loan. Rather, you pay these people dividends from your profits.

Type of collateral. Not only your personal assets but also business equipment, accounts receivable, and warehouse receipts can serve as collateral.

The warehouse receipts show that the merchandise used as security has either been placed in a public warehouse or has been left on your premises under the control of a bonded employee (as in field warehousing). Such loans are generally made on staple or standard merchandise that can be readily marketed. The typical warehouse-receipt loan is for a percentage of the estimated value of the goods used as security.[11]

You can also secure loans by having endorsers, comakers, or guarantors. Although family members or friends may not be willing or able to loan you money, they can serve in these capacities. If the borrower fails to pay, however, the bank or other lender will expect the endorser to make the note good. The endorser may also be asked to pledge assets or securities.

A comaker creates an obligation jointly with the borrower. The bank can collect directly from either the maker or the comaker. A guarantor, on the other hand, guarantees the payment of a note by signing a guaranty commitment. If you organize your business as a corporation, the company officers may be asked to act as guarantors to assure continuity of effective management. Sometimes, too, a manufacturer, a franchiser, or a venture capitalist will act as guarantor.

Personal Resources

Preparing a personal financial statement often produces some surprising evidence: your net worth may be greater than you think. Since established financial institutions are not likely to make signature loans, you can expect to be asked to provide collateral and/or other personal guarantees. You should report your current assets in writing, not only to present to a bank but also in obtaining funding from other sources, such as relatives or friends.

Many businesspeople sell their homes to obtain funds. They either buy a less expensive place, rent an apartment, or even live temporarily in the business building itself. Instead of selling your house, you could also use the equity in your house and other current assets as collateral to secure a loan.

If your relatives or friends are willing to loan you money, they may also want "a piece of the action." You must decide if you want to share your business with partners, even ones whose contribution is silent or limited (see Chapter 10). Any resources you obtain in this manner should be supported with a written agreement that states the interest charges and your repayment schedule. You don't want to give relatives or friends an excuse to tell you how to run your enterprise, nor do you want to lose their friendship because of differences of opinion about the management of the business.

Partnerships and Corporations

You can acquire additional financing by organizing your business as a partnership or corporation, although you will thus be diluting your ownership. For manufacturing enterprises, this may be the only logical way to get a product on the market. Another approach is to offer stock for private sale, to relatives, friends, established customers, acquaintances, or even employees. Here again, however, you will be giving away part of your business.

"Going public" means offering stock to the public at large. Government regulations control such sales, which are supervised by the Securities and Exchange Commission. This agency, however, requires minimum financial-support data for offerings of less than $500,000.

Commercial Banks and Savings and Loan Institutions

With other data and action supporting your credibility, you may be ready to seek a loan from a bank or a savings and loan institution. S&Ls are appropriate if you are liquidating real property equity or arranging for refinancing. Another type of loan agency is the credit union. If you belong to one, you may be able to obtain from it a relatively small signature or secured loan.

Commercial banks can provide both short-term and long-term loans. For the former, you can expect to use as collateral the assets listed in your personal financial statement. In fact, you need not liquidate all of your assets if you can use some as collateral, including real estate, life insurance policies, and the like.

Permanent working capital and fixed assets should be supplied by your own investment or by long-term loans. Chattel mortgages and real estate mortgages can be used to support long-term loan requests.

For short- or intermediate-term borrowing, you want to be fairly certain your earnings will allow you to make regular payments. Fixed assets, when purchased with long-term debt, can be amortised by taking depreciation over a similar period as the loan. The depreciation time and the loan period should be designed to come out somewhat even.

You should select a bank carefully and then conduct most of your business with that firm. You will want to know the full range of services the bank provides to business people and how flexible it can be in assisting a business. Will it provide small signature loans, extend payment deadlines on loans in emergencies, allow you to act as intermediary for customers seeking financing, buy your credit or installment accounts? Your banker can be one among many in your financial and business network.

Equipment Loans and Leases

When interest rates are high, you want to avoid borrowing whenever possible. As Figure 12.4 demonstrates, when interest rates rise, so does the number of bankruptcies.

In such circumstances, you should explore every other possible option before committing yourself to making loan payments.

One of these options is to pay for equipment in installments (which is of course another form of debt). Equipment manufacturers are often amenable to such arrangements. Like you, they are in business to make sales—and you are a potential customer. You may be evaluated for this type of assistance as for any

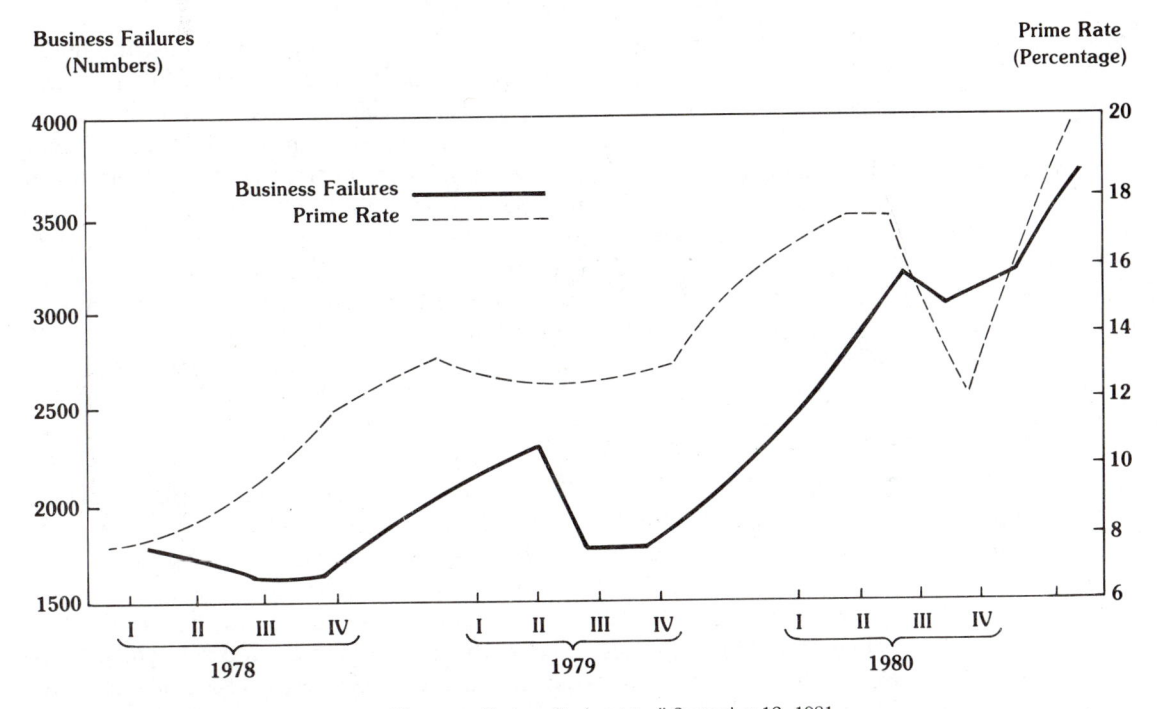

Source: National Small Business Association, "Report on Business Bankruptcies," September 12, 1981.

FIGURE 12.4 Business Failures and Prime Rate, 1978–80.

other form of credit or loan. The company will consider the four "C's"; namely, your character, capital, capacity, and conditions (see Chapter 11).

You can expect the credit to be extended in the form of a conditional sales contract or a chattel mortgage on the equipment. In either case, the seller holds a lien on the equipment, so you cannot simultaneously use it as collateral to secure another loan.

Another option is to lease equipment, which involves a smaller initial outlay of cash. This way you can also exchange older equipment when newer models emerge, as often happens with computer and other high-tech machinery. You should investigate this possibility, however, before signing a contract. With the rapid changes in electronic technology, in particular, some manufacturers may be reluctant to provide this option. Also investigate whether the lease payments—in whole or in part—can be applied to the purchase price, should you decide you want to buy later.

Trade Credit

You will want to explore carefully the type of credit available to you from vendors. The suppliers' decision about whether to establish a line of credit for you at the outset depends on the confidence they have in your ability to succeed and thus to make payments. One alternative is to use the C.O.D. method until you have established credibility.

Trade credit is the small retailer's most common source of short-term funds. Your accounts payable are the suppliers' accounts receivable. Thus they will expect you to pay after 30 days, or at least within 60 days. There may be a different arrangement about seasonal purchases, such as garden equipment, Christmas gifts, and so on. Like equipment manufacturers, vendors find their customers among small business owners. Thus they are willing wherever possible to make credit available to you. Usually trade credit, like bank loans, should be used primarily for working capital.

You will want to shop around, of course, to determine not only which vendors offer the best prices and quality, but also those with the best credit terms and conditions—and those whose national advertising will support your sales.

Government Assistance

The United States government enters the credit market directly through Treasury borrowing and indirectly through guaranteed lending sponsored by such agencies as the Federal National Mortgage Association and the Small Business Administration (SBA). The federal government accounts for or induces the lending of about one out of every four dollars raised in the borrowing market.

Federal aid to businesses and nonprofit entities is channeled through approximately 40 programs. Also, over the past two decades increased attention has been given to the specific needs of women and minorities who are trying to start, finance, and manage small businesses.

The small business administration. Congress established the SBA to help small companies that are experiencing difficulties in either financing or management. Loan assistance to small businesses grew most rapidly prior to 1974.

Nowadays the SBA concentrates much of its efforts on providing management training and assistance to would-be and existing entrepreneurs as well as conducting research on small business. Few direct-loan applications of late have been approved, although you can go after an SBA-guaranteed loan.[12] (Objectives in the SBA, like any government agency, depend on the attitude of any given administration, so don't despair. Government policies, like the weather, can change almost overnight.)

To evidence your eligibility in applying for an SBA-guaranteed loan, you must show that:

1. You have first sought a bank loan and been rejected,
2. You are of good character and have sufficient motivation and capability to operate your business successfully,
3. Your loan proposal is of sound value or sufficiently secured to assure repayments,
4. The financial prospects of your firm are good,
5. You possess a reasonable amount of your own capital to withstand possible losses, particularly in the early stages.

In short, the SBA wants to be sure it will get its money back!

Small business investment companies (SBICs). The Small Business Investment Act was designed to improve the national economy by stimulating (when necessary) the flow of private equity capital and long-term loan funds to small businesses. This policy is carried out to ensure the maximum participation of private financing sources. From this action emerged the SBICs, which are licensed and regulated by the SBA.

Under the aegis of this act, the SBA provides credit assistance to small businesses in the form of direct loans, loan guarantees, and certain other programs. Originally, the loan programs were designed to assure access to credit for those who possibly were discriminated against by the market. Over time, particularly in the case of direct loans, this objective was broadened to include the provision of subsidies to individual businesses that would otherwise fail.[13]

Similarly, SBIC loans now also seek to create jobs and promote regional economic development. Some SBICs provide free management advice in addition to the unofficial counsel that accompanies the original investment or loan.

Aid for women and minorities. Minority Enterprise Small Business Investment Companies (MESBICs) are solely devoted to making loans to, or equity investments in, companies owned and operated by members of minority groups. A MESBIC is privately owned and operated by members of minority groups and is regulated by the SBA.[14]

The Women's Business Enterprise program in the SBA and the Office of Women's Business Enterprise emphasize equal credit opportunity for women business owners, both present and potential. These programs seek "the systematic elimination of regulatory and procedural barriers which have unfairly precluded women from receiving equal treatment from Federal activities, including those affecting the opportunities for women in business." The Attorney General has the responsibility of periodically reviewing federal laws and regulations in order to identify and report any gender-based discrimination to the Cabinet Council on Human Resources. The Task Force on Legal Equity for Women, created by executive order, is then responsible for removing the inequities.[15]

To succeed in business, minorities and women need access to resources and to knowledge about business management and financing methods. To continue and expand its services to women and minority entrepreneurs, the Cabinet Council on Commerce and Trade reviews government assistance programs to determine how they can be made more efficient and effective.

Charged with assisting and advising minorities and women, Minority Business Development Centers (MBDCs) have been established throughout the United States in selected metropolitan areas with populations of more than 50,000. The

The U.S. Small Business Administration and other government agencies, such as the MESBICs, have programs designed to assist women in business.

WOMEN AND MINORITIES IN BUSINESS

In 1981 the first nationwide economic research project on small business was funded by the SBA's Office of Advocacy. It produced the following policy recommendations about women and minority entrepreneurs:

- Establish "special interest-group business service centers" to provide training and capital for minority- and women-owned businesses.
- Establish SBICs predominantly oriented to serving minorities and women.
- Expand existing loan and loan-guarantee programs.
- Develop guidelines for making the procurement opportunities program relevant to the needs of women and minority business owners. Disseminate these guidelines to ensure that the appropriate SBA staff is trained to carry out the expanded programs.
- Tie SBICs more directly to entities with paid staff, to overcome the need to pay staff out of earnings. (This would make possible lower interest rates for SBICs and MESBICs.)
- Develop more workshops for women to explain National Women's Business Enterprise Policy and the availability of assistance programs and seminars for women business owners.
- Engage in an extensive effort to recruit and appoint qualified women and minorities to positions in all levels of the SBA.
- Consider increased funding of direct SBA loans.
- Create insurance pools for lower-cost fire and theft insurance in high-risk commercial areas to stimulate the establishment of more women- and minority-owned businesses in inner-city areas.
- Monitor the percentage of loans granted to minority- and women-owned businesses in relation to total loanable funds and to the percentage of loans given to men versus existing minority- and women-owned businesses.
- Provide more prebusiness training for potential women and minority entrepreneurs.
- Continue and expand management assistance programs and workshops for women and minorities.
- Recruit more minorities and women for SBA's SCORE (Service Corps of Retired Executives), and ACE (Active Corps of Executives) programs to assist minority and women entrepreneurs.

Source: Adapted from *Economic Research on Small Business: The Environment for Entrepreneurship and Small Business*, Summary Analysis of the Regional Research Reports, 1981, pp. 26–28.

Note: For data unique to your locale, read the regional reports from the above source and others; statistics and program assistance can be found in these summaries.

MBDCs provide networking contacts for their clients, including referrals to business and financial consultants as well as to other agencies. Simultaneously, MBDC personnel review city, county, and state government contracts to assure that minority and women entrepreneurs have a chance to bid. MBDCs counsel their clients how to prepare and present proposals as bids for: construction, transportation, research and development, and other contracts.[16]

Small business innovation research (SBIR). Government agencies look for small companies that can tackle problems intensively. Traditionally, small businesses are far more productive in research and development (R&D). They produce two to three times as many innovations per employee as do large companies, and at a fraction of the cost. Between 1977 and 1982, for example, approximately 3500 firms that received National Science Foundation grants provided technological innovations in one area alone—embryonic biotechnology. A dozen government agencies have annual budgets of over $100 billion to identify and supply seed capital to small companies and individual inventors who meet agency R&D objectives. The research funds are awarded through various funding agreements, including grants and contracts. The 1987 target for small firms is $275 million. (Small firms seeking an R&D award should apply directly to the agency.)[17]

Venture Capitalists

While banks are creditors, venture capital firms are owners. They hold stock in a company, adding their investment capital to its equity. As noted earlier, banks

The SBA and MESBICs are also interested in helping minorities succeed in business enterprises.

are interested in the proposed debtor's character, capital, and capacity to pay, because they want the debt repaid (and to earn interest on it). Conversely, venture capitalists are more likely to concentrate on the product or service, on the market potential, and on the ability of the proposed company's management team to produce sizable profits. Since they hold equity ownership in the company, they look to returns on their investments.

You should pay careful attention to the degree to which you intend to retain ownership. According to a study that involved analyzing 197 prospectuses (business plans), representing unseasoned new equity issues, it was found that firms in which the entrepreneur retained higher ownership had higher values than those predicted by the standard measures of firm valuation. This study tested a model (developed by Leland and Pyle), which assumes that entrepreneurs know their firms' expected future cash flow, whereas potential investors do not. Therefore, the less willing you are to sell off your holdings, the more positive a signal this is to outside investors.[18]

Venture capitalists are seldom interested in investing less than $250,000. A venture capital firm usually receives over 1000 proposals a year. It chooses to investigate no more than 10 percent of these. The other 90 percent are usually rejected, because they don't match the technical, geographic, or market area policies of the venture capitalist firm—or, equally significant, because the proposals have been poorly prepared (see Chapter 6 for how to prepare a business plan).[19]

In its intensive investigation of every proposal component, the venture capital firm concentrates heavily on the expertise of the proposed company's management team. Each of the important areas—product design, marketing, production, finance, and control—should be under the direction of a well-trained, experienced and deeply committed member of the group. Responsibilities must be clearly delineated (with an organization chart and job descriptions).

If, after exhaustive investigation and analysis, the venture capital firm decides to invest in an applicant company, the two parties will negotiate a final financing agreement. This agreement will cover such important points as ownership, control, annual charges, and company objectives. Most venture firms prefer to own less than 50 percent of the new company, because they don't want to deprive entrepreneurs of their zeal and drive to manage their own companies.

Protective covenants in the contract, however, are likely to give the venture capitalists the power to take control if the company runs into financial, management, or marketing problems. The venture firm's investment can take several forms: direct stock ownership, straight loans with an option to convert to an equity position at a preestablished price, convertible subordinated debentures, or preferred stock.[20]

Types of venture capital firms. Traditional partnerships may be established by wealthy families who want to invest a part of their funds in small companies. Professionally managed pools consist of institutional money and operate like traditional partnerships.

Investment banking firms usually trade in more established securities, but on occasion they form investor syndicates. Insurance companies, which may make loans to smaller companies as a hedge against inflation, often require a portion of equity.

Manufacturing companies sometimes invest in smaller companies as a method of supplementing their R&D programs and keeping their own firms abreast of technological innovations. Small Business Investment Corporations (SBICs), as described earlier, are licensed by the SBA.

There are also many private investors and finders. The latter—either firms or individuals—are not usually sources of capital themselves. Instead, they are often familiar with the capital industry and may be able to help the small company locate resources.

Economic impact. Recently, venture capital has been needed in three major areas: (1) early stages of ventures, (2) the expansion of small-growth companies that do not yet have access to public or long-term, credit-oriented institutional funding, and (3) management/leverage buy-outs that revitalize major corporate divisions or absentee-owned private businesses. Figure 12.5 shows where venture capital funds were invested during the 1970s.[21]

The three key traits of venture capital investment are:

1. Equity participation, either through direct purchase of stock or through warrants, options and/or convertible securities;

FIGURE 12.5
Targets of Venture Capital Investment.

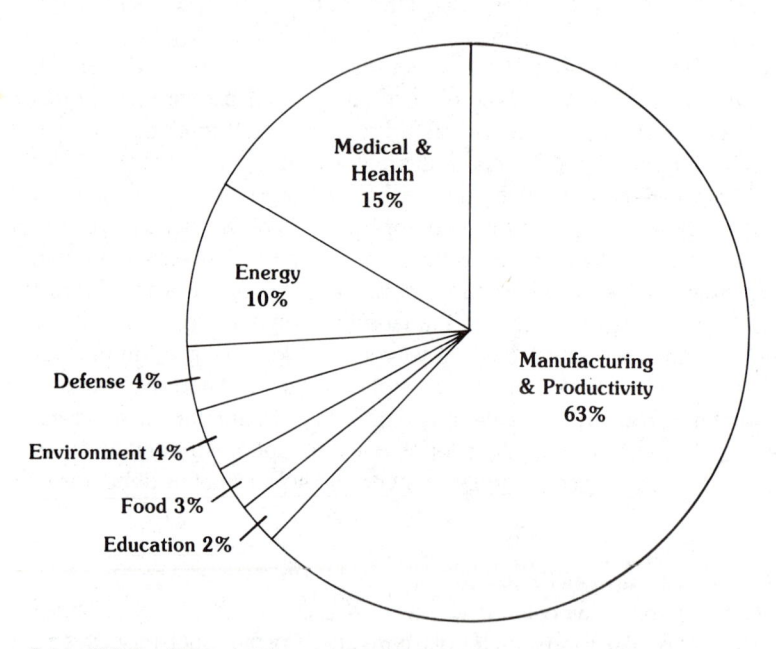

- Medical & Health 15%
- Energy 10%
- Defense 4%
- Environment 4%
- Food 3%
- Education 2%
- Manufacturing & Productivity 63%

Source: U.S. Small Business Administration, *The State of Small Business: A Report of the President* (Washington, D.C., March 1982), p. 147.

2. Long-term investment discipline that often anticipates a period of 5 to 10 years before the investment will provide a significant return;
3. Active, ongoing involvement in a company where value can be added to the investment.

SUMMARY

There are numerous methods of financing a business, if you can creatively combine your resources. Businesses typically start small— using everything from personal assets and those of relatives or friends to credit lines, leasing, short-term and long-term borrowing. But with effective management and marketing, many are also able to expand in a relatively short time. Entrepreneurs who run into difficulty can call on a wide range of assistance, from government agencies or their own network of business and financial consultants.

Some entrepreneurs organize their companies as partnerships and corporations in order to attract both an expert management team and venture capital. Other business owners wait until they are ready to expand before changing their legal structure (from sole proprietorships to other forms) or seeking venture financing. In summary, there are many directions to take and numerous options—that is, if you take the initiative in putting together a viable package and presenting it in a comprehensive business plan.

DISCUSSION QUESTIONS

1. Describe creative means entrepreneurs use to start up business and continue operations (besides examples given in the chapter, discuss businesses with which you are familiar).
2. Differentiate between (a) working capital and fixed asset capital and (b) debt capital and equity capital.
3. Discuss the various elements to consider when estimating capital needs. How would you go about determining these requirements for one or more specific businesses?
4. Explain the differences between short-term and long-term loans:
    a. From which sources are they sought?
    b. What would you use as security?
    c. How are they paid back—out of earnings or turnover in accounts receivable and inventory?
    d. Under what conditions should you (or should you not) consider borrowing?
5. How can you use your personal assets to finance your business? Discuss the differences between liquidating assets and using them as collateral.

6. What problems can you foresee in asking relatives or friends to help you finance your business? (What options are available in seeking these avenues to capitalize your requirements?)
7. What are the advantages and disadvantages of organizing your business as a partnership and as a corporation, in relation to obtaining financing? Will the type of business you decide to open make a difference in the type and amount of financing needed? If so, what impact will these needs have on the legal structure?
8. Compare direct loans with such subsidiary types of loans as trade credit and leasing.
9. List various sources of financing, including government agencies and venture capital firms, and describe the similarities and differences among them.
10. What financial benefits and services can you receive from government agencies?
11. How would you establish and use a network?
12. What is your opinion about having federal tax dollars allocated to the special needs of women and minorities? On what do you base your opinion? What special needs do you think these people have that the majority (namely, white males) does not have?

ACTIVITIES AND EXERCISES

The first three activities that follow are designed to help you develop a human-resource network. If you intend to open a business in a certain community within the next year or two, then you should conduct your interviews in the selected locale. These contacts can be very useful. If you are not actually planning to start your own business, then use the activities to collect current information that you can share with colleagues/classmates and that can add to your own working knowledge.

1. Visit with relatives or friends to discuss whether they would assist you financially in starting your business. Raise the possibility of not only obtaining direct loans but also of using their names as security or of sharing the business with them. Discuss both the opportunities and the potential problems this relationship might create.
2. Make appointments to talk with any or all of the following: banker, accountant, attorney, business consultant, venture capitalist, and successful entrepreneurs in a business like the one you hope to open. Use this chapter to develop a list of questions about how to estimate capital needs, refine the business plan, and obtain capital funding.
3. Visit a local office of the SBA or a MESBIC or MBDC to discover what services and financing they offer. You can also collect free publications for your file, get a schedule of upcoming business seminars, or ask for specific advice about the company you seek to open.

The next two activities can also help you understand the issues raised in this chapter.

4. Estimate the capital requirements of your business. To do this, follow these steps:
   a. Prepare (or update) your personal financial statement,
   b. Complete the cash budget given as Figure 12.3,
   c. Update your sales earnings forecast.
   d. Revise the section of your business plan that reflects your statement of capital needs.
5. Respond to Project 4 in the case supplement. This requires you to sell your business plan to one or more potential backers, using simulated situations.

NOTES

1. U.S. Small Business Administration. *The State of Small Business: A Report of the President* (Washington, D.C.: Government Printing Office, March 1982), p. 146.
2. Ibid.
3. "Making It," *Black Enterprise,* August 1983, pp. 27–29.
4. "Striking It Rich," *Time,* February 15, 1982, p. 38 (reported by Michael Moritz, San Francisco news bureau).
5. "The Seeds of Success: Apple Computer, Inc.," *Time,* February 15, 1982, pp. 40–41.
6. George Gilder. *Wealth and Poverty* (New York: Basic Books, 1979).
7. Geoffrey Leavenworth, "Business on a Shoestring," *New Woman,* July 1982, p. 78.
8. Mike Bulger, "The Right to Be Your Own Boss," *New Woman,* May 1982, p. 28.
9. "Striking It Rich," p. 39.
10. Interview, December 4, 1982 (interviewee asked to remain anonymous).
11. Leavenworth, "Business."
12. David E. Gumpert, "Tapping Into the SBA," *Working Woman,* November 1983, pp. 167–71.
13. "The ABCs of Borrowing," *Management Aid* no. 1.001 (Washington, D.C.: U.S. Small Business Administration, 1981).
14. "Effect of Federal Policy on Small Business," SBA's *State of Small Business,* p. 141.
15. Ibid.
16. Interview with a Boston MBDC director, Washington, D.C., January 26, 1983.
17. "Agencies Seek Inventive Firms," *NFIB Mandate* (San Mateo, CA: National Federation of Independent Business, December 1982), p. 5.
18. "Scanning Management Research Reports," *The Wharton Magazine,* Fall 1982, p. 9.
19. LaRue Tone Hosmer, "A Venture Capital Primer for Small Business," *Management Aid* no. 1.009 (Washington, D.C.: U.S. Small Business Administration, 1981).
20. SBA's *State of Small Business,* pp. 144–45.
21. Ibid.

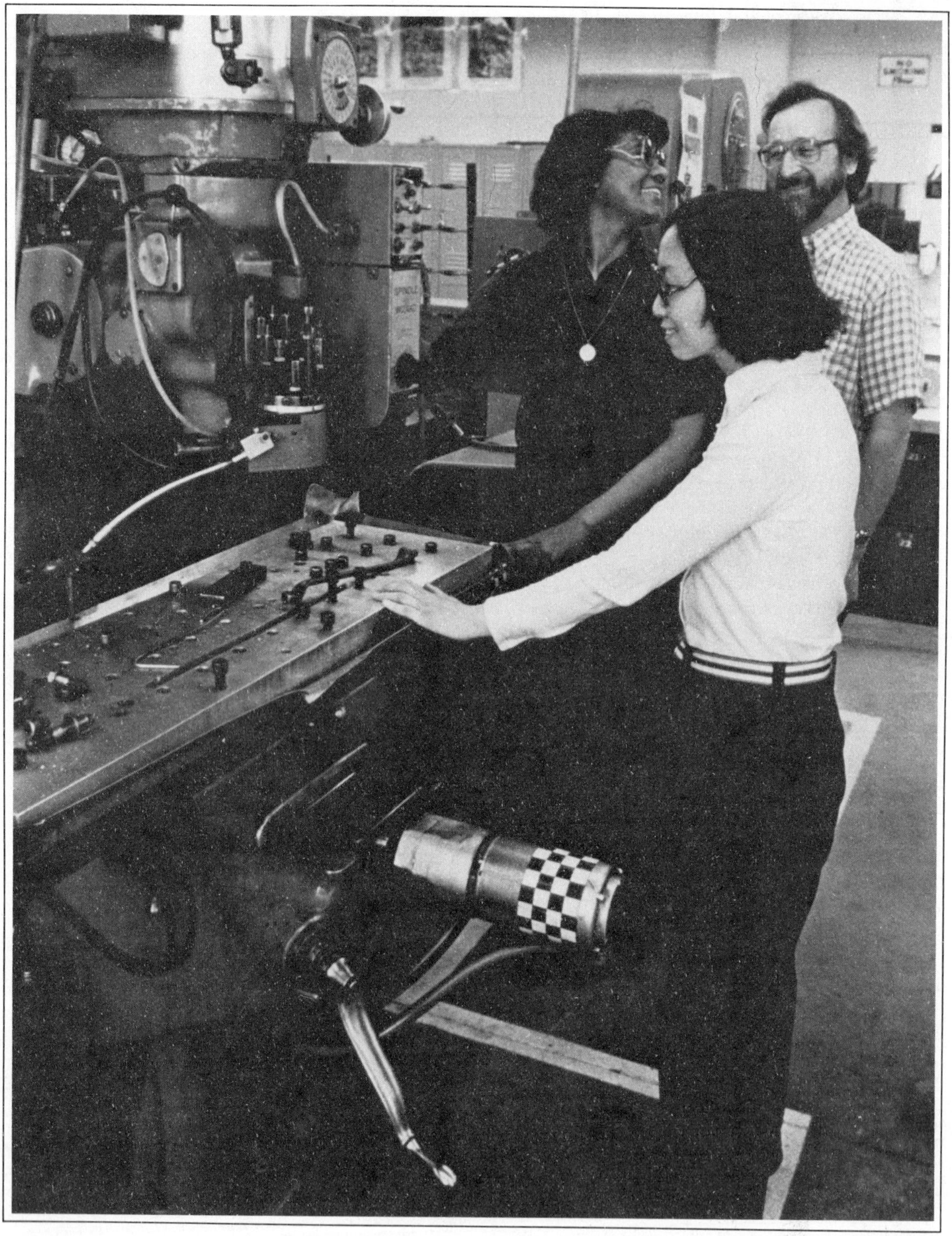

chapter 13

Legal, Tax, and Insurance Needs

Objectives

1. Discuss the purposes of legal requirements designed to protect the public, business owners, and employees.

2. Describe the elements in a contract, and give examples of possible situations between seller and consumer, principal and agent, employer and employees, and landlord and tenant.

3. Explain compliance procedures regarding tax laws that affect small business.

4. List potential risks in small business and the types of insurance best suited to provide protection.

There are many city, county, state, and federal laws and regulations that govern businesses and protect businesses from one another. Some laws are intended to protect the public's health, safety, and general welfare while still others are designed to protect workers. Certain regulations apply especially to hotels, restaurants, taverns, and gasoline stations, while others apply to most enterprises. They cover such areas as competition and trade practices, labor practices, licensing, business taxes, and the like.

Tax laws are also complex. In addition to the income taxes that individuals must pay to the federal government, there are special taxes and license fees that differ for various types of businesses. Theaters, bowling alleys, and other recreational businesses are subject to certain taxes. Luxury taxes must be paid on jewelry, gifts, and luggage. Also, retailing and service entrepreneurs must collect, report, and pay sales taxes.

Another source of expenditure is insurance, which can protect you in event of fire, theft, malpractice, liability, or other losses to building, inventory, or even life. Planning for these contingencies may help save a business that would otherwise go under when disaster strikes.

LEGAL CONSIDERATIONS

If you had lived in London 400 years ago and had opened a bakery, would you have had to deal with a mass of rules and regulations like those that exist today? The answer is, "Yes!" You could not have started the business at all without the permission of all the other bakers in town. The size of the loaf, exactly what ingredients you used, the price, and every other aspect of your business would have been subject to very specific regulations. Historical records indicate that even the businesses of ancient Babylonia, thousands of years ago, were bound by a multitude of laws.[1]

In many ways, entrepreneurs in the United States today have more freedom to open a new business or market a new product than those living in other times and other countries. Nevertheless, the regulations grow. More laws are passed and more reports seem to be required every year, and the regulations governing entrepreneurs, together with the reports they must file, grow steadily more complicated.

Most entrepreneurs will want to consult professional people regularly, including lawyers, accountants, and tax experts. Trying to stay up-to-date on your own can be exasperating, time-consuming, and ineffective. Remember, "Ignorance of the law is (usually) no excuse!"

The Goal of Legal Requirements

Regulations originate from various levels of government: from local (city, town, county), state, and federal governing bodies and from their various departments.

Trade associations, unions, and companies also make rules themselves. Many of these regulations emerge as law resulting from court decision.

Suppose you decide to open a restaurant. Before purchasing a building, you have to ascertain that zoning laws permit you to operate in the locale you prefer. The building and your remodeling are subject to dozens of inspections. Electric wiring must conform to safety requirements, and building and fire-department inspectors will keep checking the building to see that you conform to their codes. Once you've opened for business, the health-department inspectors will arrive to check on sanitary procedures. Other inspectors will check on your licensing, whether you're paying the minimum wage, or if you've employed underage youth.

In manufacturing and distribution, products pass through dozens of processes and hundreds of hands before they reach the retailer, much less the consumer. Regulations are imposed at each stage to protect the final consumer from, among other hazards, inferior food, drug, and cosmetic products and mislabeled, misrepresented, or otherwise falsely advertised products.

State laws about wages, working hours, workers' compensation, and safety are designed to protect workers. Also, however, laws governing patents, copyrights, unfair competition, price discrimination, and libelous acts are intended to protect people like you from the unfair, even unethical, practices both of big corporations and of other small business owners.

You will find it possible to conform with most legal requirements if you develop and maintain an accurate and regular recordkeeping system (see Chapter 14). Together with advice from a reputable attorney or accountant, when needed, such records should allow you to compile most reports without undue difficulty (certainly less than if, when asked for data, you tried to make it up out of your head!).

You can work through trade associations, unions, chambers of commerce, Better Business Bureaus, and with other entrepreneurs and legislators to seek changes in burdensome regulations that no longer serve any real purpose. Most existing laws are worthwhile, but others have outlived their usefulness. Legislators depend on their constituents, including businesspeople, to alert them to such situations. Groups can exert influence and speak with a common voice—another reason for developing a strong network.

Although it is impossible to cover in this chapter all the special federal, state, and local regulations governing every type of business, there are certain legal definitions and general laws that apply to the majority of businesses. The following discussion is not intended for legal reference, nor does it offer legal interpretations of statutes and regulations. It is no substitute for expert legal advice.

Negotiable Instruments

A "negotiable instrument" is a substitute for cash or goods and services, the use of which helps to expedite business transactions. An instrument is negotiable if it can be endorsed and transferred from one party to another.

"Bill of exchange" is an all-encompassing term for many different types of negotiable instruments. Basically, it is an order in writing that is addressed from one person to another and signed by the person transmitting it. The most common type is, of course, the check, which is drawn on a bank and is payable on demand.

The "bill of lading" usually represents goods in transit. It is a receipt for goods and provides documentary evidence of a person's title to the goods. A "note" is a written promise to pay another a certain sum of money at a specified time. The familiar I.O.U. is one kind of note.

Contracts

A contract is not a contract unless all of the required conditions are met; namely, it must be offered and accepted by competent parties for a legal purpose and with consideration. A contract may be oral or written; but if it is written, a contradictory verbal statement made by one party would make the contract invalid, especially if intent to deceive the other party is proved. (See Figure 13.1.)

"Consideration" refers to a monetary transaction or any reasonable exchange of goods, services, and the like. Both parties to the contract must be compensated or receive some benefit. Even an agreement not to do something may be defined as a consideration. If one party later claims to have been inadequately compensated, he or she would have to prove this claim in court.

Contracts can be unilateral or bilateral, but in neither case can a third party contract on your behalf unless previously granted authority to act as your agent. A unilateral contract offer would be, for example, a price posted on merchandise or listed on a menu, or jukeboxes, vending machines, laundromat equipment, or videogame machines placed on public display.

Suppose you have placed a videogame machine in a public place. When customers drop in their coins, they are accepting this unilateral offer, and as the machine's owner you are obligated to see that they either get the opportunity to play or have their money returned. Similarly, when you advertise a product at a specified price, in most cases you must sell the product at that price, even if it was the printer who made the mistake.

A bilateral contract is one that two parties enter mutually, both agreeing to and accepting all its terms. "Mutual agreement" has three elements: (1) there must be intent to contract; (2) there must be a definite and explicit offer, covering such details as price and payment method; and (3) the offer must be communicated to an accepting party.

People under 21 are not considered "competent parties," nor are people who have been committed to prison or to mental institutions, who have been declared mentally incompetent, or who are seriously intoxicated. The purpose for which the contract is drawn up must be legal. That is, if someone hijacked a truckload of furs and then offered them for sale, the sales contracts would not be legal and binding, because the goods offered had been stolen.

Legal, Tax, and Insurance Needs **269**

BUSINESS CONTRACTS

Conditions:

Oral

Offer and Acceptance
Competent Parties
Legal Purpose
Consideration

Written

FIGURE 13.1
Business Contracts. Whether oral or written, a business contract includes offer and acceptance, competent parties, legal purpose, and consideration.

Any deceptive or fraudulent action on the part of either party also invalidates a contract. For instance, if a seller claims a product is of higher quality than it really is and thus charges an inflated price for it, the buyer is not obligated to pay. Conversely, if a buyer pays with a forged check, then the seller is not obligated to supply the goods.

Chapter 13

Transfer of title. Under a conditional sales contract, as noted in Chapter 11, customers do not receive legal title to their purchase until they make the last payment. By contrast, a chattel mortgage gives the customer legal title to the property at the time of sale.

A cash sale, typified by the over-the-counter exchange of products for cash, transfers title at the time of sale.

The vendor, as cosigner, passes goods to retailers or consignees via transportation companies who serve as the intermediaries. Although title does not pass to intermediaries, it is expected that they will take reasonable precaution over goods in transit.

Contract remedies and precautions. Repossessing goods, passing an account on to a collection agency or attorney, or initiating court action are all typical remedies when customers who have received goods fail to pay for them. To protect yourself against such cases, you should check the credibility of the customer or credit applicant; you can also ask for collateral to secure the contract.

Another claim against property is the "mechanic's lien." Business people who do construction or major repair work or who deal with large volumes of materials and supplies can have a lien against the property if the customer defaults on payments for either labor or materials.

To recover losses resulting from breach of contract, you have these options: taking direct action, when you have the right and the ability to repossess goods or to garnish wages; turning accounts over to a collection agency; or seeking restitution through the courts. You can sue for small debts in small-claims court, where you can avoid the high cost of retaining legal counsel.

The statute of limitations protects debtors from being harassed for repayment years after the contract was entered into. Thus you should not wait too long before trying to recover funds or repossess goods. Check the laws in your state to determine the provisions and time requirements.

As a new entrepreneur, you may be entering into numerous contracts with many different people. Be sure to do so cautiously. For real estate and other major deals, see an attorney. For smaller deals, don't sign until you understand all facets of the contract. Read all the fine print and express to the other party your understanding of what you are entering into.

The Uniform Commercial Code (UCC)

To ensure that common law is uniformly applied throughout the United States, the Uniform Commercial Code (UCC) was adopted in 1962. The UCC clarifies and condenses all of the laws concerning contracts, sales, stock transfers, negotiable instruments, and many other topics dealing with business law.

Article 9 of the UCC is the model upon which the secured credit rules of most states are based. It is designed to assure that creditors will be able to enforce their rights to specified collateral as long as they observe certain legal formalities.

Many of the disputes under Article 9 arise when several creditors—a bank and two suppliers, for example—seek to claim the same piece of collateral to satisfy the credit obligations of a defaulting or bankrupt debtor. The law also provides some protection for debtors to assure that their rights are not abused when a repossession takes place.

The usual rule is that the first secured creditor to file or "perfect the interest" takes priority. (A bank, say, might thus lose to the supplier in a battle over inventory collateral.) This is because the supplier's interest is what the UCC calls a Purchase Money Security Interest (PMSI). (The PMSI is a security interest that finances the purchase of particular equipment or inventory.)[2]

Agency

An agency is a relationship wherein one party, the agent, represents another party, the principal, in dealing with a third party. For example, employees, including managers, act on behalf of business owners; a partner serves as agent for the partnership; and realtors represent buyers and sellers. General agents and special agents have different degrees of authority. A real estate agent, for instance, is authorized to act only in a specific transaction and therefore is a special agent.

In the agency relationship, both principals and agents have certain obligations. You, as the principal, would have to inform your agents of the details of the agency relationship, including both the scope of authority and its limitations. Principals are liable to third parties for the performance of contracts made by their agents, when these agents act within the scope of their authority. You would also be liable for negligent or fraudulent acts of your agents when they make decisions within the scope of their authority.

For these reasons you want to be careful when selecting people to represent you and also in specifying the scope of their authority. When you act as an agent (as in a partnership situation), you want to be equally certain that you understand what the agency relationship does and does not cover. As an agent, you are liable if you exceed the specified authority granted by your principal (or by the partnership). This becomes significant if you, inadvertently or not, cause damage or loss to a third party.

Antitrust Laws

The U.S. Congress has passed several laws to sustain the American free-enterprise system by promoting and protecting competition. The first one, the Sherman Antitrust Act of 1890, was designed to prevent conspiracies in the restraint of trade and to prevent monopoly (defined as the control of an industry by one firm).

The second law, passed in 1914, was the Clayton Act, designed to prevent unfair practices that would have an adverse effect on competition. The third significant piece of legislation affecting free enterprise, the 1936 Robinson-Patman Act (an amendment to the Clayton Act), was designed generally to prevent unfair price discrimination that would affect competition.

In 1914 the Federal Trade Commission (FTC) was established to enforce antitrust laws. The FTC, with the aid of the Justice Department, can take a business to court for using illegal practices. Courts do not act, however, until business people complain.

Antitrust laws prohibit entrepreneurs from:

1. Requiring a customer (wholesaler, retailer, or consumer) to buy certain products in order to purchase another (an arrangement known as a "tie-in" agreement). For example, a company that sells a copier cannot insist that purchasers buy their copying paper as well.
2. Initiating unfair pricing competition.
3. Using false or misleading information in advertising.
4. Using misleading or deceptive business practices.

Several businesses that agree to charge the same or similar prices for one kind of goods are practicing unfair competition. Likewise, antitrust laws prohibit a business from buying other companies in the same product line if such purchases will give that business control over 30 percent or more of the market.

No pricing violations exist if sellers are simply trying to meet or beat their competition. It is a violation, however, to sell the same product to one customer at a lower price than to another.

Real and Personal Property

In purchasing or leasing property, there are some basic facts to consider. Entire books have been written on real estate law, and new financing options regularly emerge. Before buying any real property, you are best advised to seek legal counsel.

Real property consists of land, buildings, and any attached installations. Personal property is movable and unfixed, e.g., equipment, machinery, furniture, tools, supplies, and inventory.

If you decide to lease a facility, you should have a written lease contract that delineates the rights and obligations of both tenant and landlord. A "tenancy at will" may be terminated at any time upon the request of either party, although some states require sufficient notice prior to termination. You will want to negotiate the best contract terms possible, including whether you are allowed to make renovations, whether you can remove your installations and take them with you, and whether you can sublease the property.

Also determine if, by state law or otherwise, the landlord must pay taxes and insurance and if he or she will repair structural damage to the facility or pay for it to be remodeled to your specifications.

Other Protections for Small Businesses

Will you need to protect your products, inventions, or creations from infringement by others? Then you will need to know about trademarks, patents, or copyrights. You also want to protect yourself from libel lawsuits.

Common law acknowledges a property right in the ownership of trademarks. A "trademark" is a symbol, figure, or word used to identify a product or service offered by a specific company. It may also be used as a company logo on business papers and in media advertising. Although states have different requirements, a trademark registration usually lasts for 20 years with an option to renew.

Company personnel must oversee the use of trademarks, especially as popular usage tends to put them into the public domain. For example, the word "aspirin" was once the name of a specific product. To preserve their product's uniqueness, manufacturers try to remind consumers that, for instance, "a Xerox" is not just any photocopy but one made on one of Xerox Company's machines.

A "patent" is the registered right of an inventor to make, use, and sell an invention. Patents are good for 17 years, although an improved product can be repatented for another 17 years. Not only machines and products but their original designs and redesigns can be patented. To obtain a patent, you pay a fee. You should also retain a competent patent attorney to represent your claim. If someone else has already patented your design or improvement, then you may not be able to obtain a patent yourself. You might have to pay royalties to an inventor whose design you have improved.

"Copyrights" protect the works of creators—such as designers, artists, authors, and composers—for the duration of their lives plus 50 years. Even photocopying of large sections of a work is prohibited without previous permission from the copyright holder. Those who use such material may have to pay royalties, or at least acknowledge the copyrighted source.

Holders of trademarks, patents, and copyrights can sue violators to obtain restitution or cessation of infringement. Such suits may, however, prove costly to the plaintiffs.

"Libel" is defined as printed defamation of one's reputation. You may not think that you are likely to be libeled or to libel others. If so, think again. You can even be held liable for what you write in collection letters (because, if you dictate your correspondence, someone else knows your comments, which can thus be construed as a published statement).

Protection for Consumers

There are numerous federal, state, and local laws to protect consumers. Gone are the days when entrepreneurs could proclaim, *"Caveat emptor"* (Latin for "Let the buyer beware"). Indeed, consumers today are protected in many ways (see Figure 13.2).

Many agencies and laws are designed to regulate and enforce business practices. Chief among these are the U.S. Food and Drug Administration (FDA), the Federal Trade Commission (FTC), and the Consumer Product Safety Commission (CPSC).

Also, Better Business Bureau (BBB) offices, found in most communities, often take action locally. Once a BBB receives a certain number of complaints about

**FIGURE 13.2
A Consumer's World.**
There are consumer protection laws designed to protect customers from unscrupulous business practices.

to buy...
or not
to buy...

BRAND
PRICE
GUARANTEE
QUALITY
RELIABLE DEALER

any one business, it warns the entrepreneur that it will pass along such complaints to other customers as well as to the media. BBBs can also report gross violations for police or court action.

The FDA requires foods, drugs, cosmetics, and the like to be appropriately labeled. Manufacturers must give not only an accurate list of ingredients but also note how dangerous these products could be in overdosages or if used by children. Food additives also must be reported.

False or misleading advertising. The FTC monitors advertising claims of product effectiveness, capabilities, and limitations. It also takes action against ads that are false and misleading. Some retailers, for instance, use the "bait and switch" technique. They advertise a product at an attractively low price to attract customers, only to tell them upon arrival that the item has been sold out or even that the advertisement was a misprint. Then they try to get the customer to buy a more expensive or higher-quality item.

Another practice is to "doctor" commercials to make a product seem to perform better than it can. Some examples:

> The makers of a soup commercial added marbles to the soup to float with the vegetables and make it look more appetizing. Coffee commercials sometimes showed a liquid that was hot wine instead of coffee. The wine looked darker and richer than real coffee. Children's toy commercials gave the toys animation that was not realistically possible for the children to duplicate.[3]

FEDERAL CONSUMER-PROTECTION LAWS

Besides the rules and regulations administered by the FDA, the FTC, and the CPSC, there are many other Federal laws that protect consumers. A few of these are briefly outlined below:

Fair Packaging & Labeling Act	Protects consumers against misleading packaging and labeling.
Consumer Product Warranty & FTC Improvement Act	Covers warranties: a warranty must be attached to a product, and it must state what the manufacturer will do if the product fails.
Fair Debt Collection Practices Law	Prevents collection agencies from harassing debtors in various ways.
Consumer Credit Protection Act ("Truth in Lending")	Requires disclosure by lenders of annual interest rate and total cost of loan.
Fair Credit Reporting Act	Permits consumers access to, and reason for, and source of credit rejection.
Hazardous Substances Labeling Act	Requires accurate labeling of hazardous household products. Extremely flammable, corrosive or toxic substances must have the word "Danger" on the label; those less dangerous must have "Warning" or "Caution" on the label.
Poison Prevention Packaging Act	Among other things, this law requires that medicines and household chemicals be put in child-proof containers to prevent accidental poisoning.

Additionally, there are many state and local regulations. Some concern the safety of automobiles, the construction of houses, food preparation, the treatment of medical problems, barbering and hairdressing, and food services.

Source: Adapted from Roy W. Poe, Herbert G. Hicks, and Olive D. Church, "Protection for Consumers," *Getting Involved with Business*. (New York: McGraw-Hill, 1981), pp. 455-56.

Advertising testimonials come under this heading, if they make questionable or false claims. For example, a professional football player probably should not be directed to claim in a television commercial, "I owe my Super Bowl win to Crunchy-Wunchy Bran Flakes!"

Door-to-door sales. The FTC also regulates door-to-door sales and mail-order merchandise operations. For instance, a buyer can cancel within three days any order for merchandise placed with a door-to-door salesperson, providing the value of the order is over a certain amount, say $25. The salesperson must tell customers both in person and in writing about their right to cancel an order.[4]

Mail-order merchandise. Consumers do not have to accept, pay for, or even return any merchandise received through the mail that they did not order if the items were addressed to them. (Customers are expected to return shipments that are misaddressed, though.)

Other unfair practices. Three other unfair practices of interest to the FTC are fictitious pricing, lowballing, and selling used goods as if they were new. "Fictitious pricing" is the practice of claiming to have marked down a sale item from a higher price that was never actually assigned to it. Lowballing takes place when repair shops do more work than required without their customers' permission, and then charge for the extra work. Sometimes repair shops also falsely claim to have done more work or to have taken more hours than they really did. Finally, even when something new has been added to a used article—such as a coat of paint—it is illegal to advertise or sell the item as new. All of these are considered unfair practices.

Protection for Workers

Over the centuries, Americans have passed many laws designed to protect employees. In the early industrial revolution, workers were grossly mistreated in some industries, until laws were passed to restrict such practices. Another major problem in our society has been the economic insecurity that results from unemployment, accidents, and sickness. The U.S. government has also sought to provide help for those who cannot help themselves.

Thus we find laws regulating many aspects of the work environment, including the work hours, minimum hourly wages, the type and number of breaks, working conditions and facilities, safety provisions, and the availability of Social Security and workers' compensation.

Workers' compensation laws protect employees who suffer accidents on the job or sicknesses related to or caused by the job. These laws are not standard throughout the United States; each state has its own plan. States also make provision for loss of employment not related to sickness or accidents through unemployment compensation laws. You should become familiar with the various laws affecting workers in your state. States, however, must follow federal guidelines on wages and hours.

Legal, Tax, and Insurance Needs   **277**

Certain labor laws protect workers' rights, including the right to have safe working conditions, breaks, and the like.

LABOR LAWS

1935—Social Security Act (Federal Insurance Contributions Act—FICA). FICA is designed to assure the worker continuity of income after retirement age. A certain proportion of each paycheck is regularly deducted for Social Security under FICA. As amended in 1965, OASDI (old age, survivors', and disability insurance) is a provision of the Social Security Act and is financed by a tax, in equal amounts on both the employer and the employee, on income earned in the calendar year up to a specified maximum. (The tax on this amount of income for the self-employed is higher.)

1935—National Labor Relations Act (Wagner Act) is administered by the National Labor Relations Board (NLRB), which provides that employees shall have "the right to self-organization, to form, join, or assist labor organizations, to bargain collectively through representatives of their own choosing, and to engage in concerted activities, for the purpose of collective bargaining or other mutual aid or protection."

1936—Walsh-Healy Act made provision for overtime pay and also required firms with government supply contracts in excess of $10,000 to pay "prevailing wage rates," no matter what the prevailing state minimum wage was.

1938—Fair Labor Standards Act provided for minimum hourly wages for employees of most firms engaged in interstate commerce (which rate, established by Congress, is changed periodically). Also apparent was the "time-and-a-half" overtime pay, designed to inhibit employers from requiring excessive work time beyond the "normal" 40-hour week.

1947—Taft-Hartley Act. Among other provisions, the intent of this law was to equalize the union-oriented Wagner Act.

1959—Landrum-Griffin Act, passed to protect the rights of workers from the autocratic use of union power. Additionally, the unfair labor practice provisions in the Taft-Hartley Act were strengthened.

1963—Equal Pay Act (amendment to the Fair Labor Standards Act). This law requires employers to "pay equal wages within an establishment to men and women doing equal work on jobs requiring equal skill, effort, and responsibility which are performed under similar working conditions." Different wages between "classified male-female jobs are permissible only if there are demonstrable differences in job content."

1964—Civil Rights Act, Title VII (see EEO Act of 1972)

1970—Occupational Safety and Health Act (OSHA). This act primarily regulates industrial safety and health, although many types of businesses find they must comply with safety and health standards.

1972—Equal Employment Opportunity Act (EEOA, amending Title VII of the 1964 Civil Rights Act) prohibited discrimination in any avenue of employment on the basis of race, color, sex, religion, and national origin. The Equal Employment Opportunity Commission (EEOC) seeks to enforce the provisions of the act via court initiated class action suits and other means.

1975—Age Discrimination Act. This law adds provisions to the EEO Act regarding discrimination against people not only because of age but also due to handicaps, health problems, and those with arrest records.

The list of laws continues to proliferate. To keep updated on new and amended laws, see an attorney and appropriate agencies, including those with the U.S. Department of Labor and the U.S. Small Business Administration.

Choosing an Attorney

Small business and the legal business are vital to each other. An *Inc.* magazine survey showed, for instance, that 94 percent of small companies regularly rely on outside legal counsel, while close to 88 percent of attorneys consider small-business clients important to their practices.[5]

Legal fees, however, can be costly. You want to make the best possible use of time spent consulting a lawyer by finding the one who best suits you and your type of business. Don't wait until you're in trouble and then call the first attorney in the Yellow Pages or the one nearest you. To find a lawyer:

1. Use your network of fellow entrepreneurs, customers, and other professionals, such as a banker or accountant.
2. Ask these acquaintances about the reputation and experience of law firms you are considering.
3. Meet with several lawyers *before* you need one to determine their availability, their interest in taking you as a client, and, especially, their expertise in dealing with companies of your type and size and with the problems you are likely to encounter.

Although price is certainly a consideration, as is location, neither of these criteria belong at the head of the list. If the fee appears relatively low, there may be a reason: the attorney may lack both expertise and experience. You may pay more in the long run for having made this initially "least painful" decision.

TAX CONSIDERATIONS

If you are a citizen of the United States you have become accustomed to the fact that taxes are a way of life. Even if you earn so little that you owe no income taxes to the federal government, you know that you must keep records and report your income and expenses.

Entrepreneurs actually serve as government agents, in one sense, by collecting Social Security and state and local sales taxes. Money that is withheld (from employee earnings) or collected (added to the sales price) should be retained, recorded on the books, and passed on to the appropriate agency when or before due. Simultaneously, entrepreneurs are also debtors, in that they owe taxes on their own earnings and personal property as well as matching funds for their employees' Social Security and related taxes.

If you are self-employed, your income will be subject to FICA/OASDI under the Social Security Act, even though you have no employer to withhold funds from your wages. Some states levy an unincorporated business income tax on net income derived within the state. As either a sole proprietor or a partner you must file federal and perhaps state personal income tax forms. Good records, as we will see in the next chapter, are the key to meeting tax obligations on time and without undue difficulty or trauma.

Federal Taxes

The two best-known federal taxes are income taxes and Social Security taxes. The federal government also collects unemployment taxes and excise taxes.

Income taxes. In addition to filing the standard personal income tax form, you will also have to attach Schedule C to report the expenses of operating your business. If you compare this form to your financial statement, you will see that they are similarly structured. (For now, you can compare Schedule C to your forecast of earnings statement in your business plan.) Income tax forms change every year, however, so you should obtain a new instruction booklet annually. These booklets will alert you to any changes and explain how to report your business expenses.

Individual proprietors and partners are required by law to file a Declaration of Estimated Tax form on or before April 15 of each year. In it you would estimate how much income and self-employment taxes you will owe the government that year, based on your sales forecast and estimated expenditures. You would pay this amount in quarterly portions, due by April 15, June 15, September 15, and January 15. You can adjust the original estimate either up or down at the time of making each payment.

The individual retirement account (IRA). Although tax provisions and allowances invariably change from year to year, in essence self-employed people are allowed to establish tax-sheltered plans, commonly known as "Keogh accounts." Formerly, entrepreneurs could not establish their own Keogh accounts unless they also set aside retirement funds for their employees. Now they can. Get your banker to explain how to extablish and contribute to an IRA or a Keogh account.

Investment tax credit and tax credit for creating jobs. Businesses that use a lot of machinery and equipment can receive an investment tax credit. There are other tax credits for companies that create new jobs and hire employees. Since small business is more labor-intensive than big business, the cost of labor as a percentage of total business costs is much greater and hurts small businesses. The credit for new jobs created can be applied directly against rising payroll taxes and thus aids small firms that employ workers.[6]

Keep track of changing tax regulations and provisions so that you can take advantage of potential benefits—whether retirement plans or deduction possibilities. In fact, tax laws often benefit small business entrepreneurs. For one thing, there are allowable deductions for the legitimate expenses of operating your business, but also the laws and regulations stimulate the keeping of good records.

Withholding and paying taxes. Your role as an agent in collecting taxes begins when you have employees fill out and sign a Form W-4, indicating the number of their dependents. This certificate gives you the authority to withhold a portion of their regular earnings each pay period, as determined by a tax withholding table. At the year's end, you also supply each employee with a copy of Form W-2, indicating the total amounts earned and withheld. This form also reports how much was withheld for Social Security (FICA).

In paying Social Security taxes, you are both an agent and a debtor. As an agent, you deduct the tax each employee owes. As a debtor, you match these deductions, paying to the government the same amount you withheld from each employee. Additionally, you must match the FICA funds withheld from employees' wages. These funds, as well as income taxes, must be deposited in a separate bank account—either in the Federal Reserve bank that serves your district or in a commercial bank authorized to accept tax deposits.

You use tax return Form 941 to report withholding and Social Security remittances to the government. To make deposits of funds retained, fill in Form 501, "Federal Tax Deposits, Withheld Income and FICA Taxes." Generally, the smaller the amount of your total tax liability, the less often you are required to make a deposit.[7]

Unemployment taxes. Your business is liable for federal unemployment taxes if you pay a certain level of wages, say $1500 or more, in any calendar quarter, and in certain other situations. Each deposit (made like those for income taxes and FICA) must be accompanied by a preinscribed "Federal Unemployment Tax Deposit" form (no. 508). An annual return must be filed, using Form 940, on or before January 31 following the close of the calendar year for which the tax is due.

Excise taxes. Federal excise taxes are imposed on the sale or use of some items, on certain transactions, and on certain occupations. Check with the nearest Internal Revenue Service (IRS) office to ascertain your tax liabilities. If liable, you must file quarterly returns, using Form 720. When you owe more than $100 per month in excise taxes, you must make monthly deposits of that tax, in the same manner as described above.

A supply of the forms listed here is available from the nearest IRS office. Meanwhile, you should apply for an employer identification number when you open your business or hire employees.[8]

State and Local Taxes

If your state imposes income taxes, then you will also have to withhold these funds from your employees' earnings, just as for federal income taxes. Determine practices in your state.

Each state has its own regulations about unemployment taxes. In some states, employees also contribute through payroll deductions.

Sales taxes. Many states, even cities, impose sales taxes. In this situation you act as an agent only, collecting taxes due and passing these funds on to the appropriate state and/or city agency. Each taxing jurisdiction will have an established collecting, reporting, and transmitting system for these monies. Check with the tax authorities for the requirements.

Local taxes. Your town, city, or county may impose a variety of local taxes including real estate taxes, personal property taxes, taxes on gross receipts of businesses, and unincorporated business taxes. A license to do business is also a tax, even though some entrepreneurs think of it otherwise. And some communities, mostly metropolitan areas, may also have their own income taxes.

RISKS AND INSURANCE

Entrepreneurs face risks every hour and every day they are in business. These risks include fire, natural disaster, internal and external crime (also see Chapter 19), and injuries to life and property.

Your ability to meet the challenge of these many possible risks depends, in part, on your management plan (see Chapters 17-21). If you have foreseen the problems and contingencies, you will know how to take appropriate action if and when they occur. The first task is to decide what insurance coverage is appropriate for your needs and how much you want and can afford.

Needs Assessment

To determine what insurance coverage you will need, consider the following questions:

1. What property requires protection? Include any real and personal property, such as land, and building, equipment, furniture, stock, supplies, delivery vans, and other vehicles.
2. Are any personal injuries likely to occur, for which you would be liable? If you employ no workers or if your type of operation does not bring customers or salespeople to the business, then your liability might be limited to general passersby, if any.
3. Would you suffer a loss of income if you or any other key employee were to become ill or incapacitated or to die? Provisions should be made to cover the interests of partners or family members in case of your death (or of that of a key employee).
4. Is your business located in a high-crime area? How much would you expect to lose annually through burglary, robbery, shoplifting, employee pilferage, and bad checks?
5. What is the right balance between your need for working capital and your need for adequate insurance coverage? You don't want to place your entire business in jeopardy to save the price of insurance premiums, but you also don't want to tie up scarce capital in unneeded policies.
6. What are the greatest risks facing your business? Is there some other way besides insurance coverage to protect yourself?

Coping with Risks

It's virtually impossible to cover every type of potential risk by insurance. Other ways to cope with risks are summarized in these four key words: "Eliminate, Minimize, Shift, or Absorb."[9]

Suppose you are experiencing problems with shoplifting, with bad-debt collections, or with employee injuries. To *eliminate* or *minimize* these problems, you could:

1. Install mirrors or otherwise step up surveillance practices to decrease the incidence of shoplifting,
2. Improve procedures for verifying credit references and making collections,
3. Draw on workers' compensation, provide safety training to employees, and remodel facilities to meet OSHA standards (see also Chapter 21).

Two other common problems are high interest rates and having too much working capital tied up in inventory. To *shift* the risk you might decide to reduce your inventory. This solution became a common practice during the early 1980s as manufacturers, wholesalers, and retailers alike reduced inventory volume in order to reduce their credit load with the financial institutions that were carrying them. The new risk they now encountered was that they could not always supply their customers with products on demand.

In *absorbing* risks, you would decide not to insure yourself against unlikely contingencies. If one of these contingencies then really came to pass, you would have to absorb the cost involved. To protect yourself, you might set aside funds to cover such unlikelihoods.

Types of Insurance

[handwritten: Depending on business. Shop around. Know your needs. Don't things you don't need.]

In general, the following types of insurance are available:

1. Fire and general property insurance—covering losses due to fire, vandalism, hail, and wind damage;
2. Consequential loss insurance—covering loss of earnings or extra expenses if the business is suspended due to fire or other catastrophe;
3. Burglary insurance—covering forcible entry and theft of merchandise and cash;
4. Fidelity bond—covering theft by employees;
5. Fraud insurance—covering counterfeit money, bad checks, and larceny;
6. Public liability insurance—covering injury to the public, such as a customer who falls while on your premises;
7. Workers' Compensation insurance—covering injury to employees at work;
8. Product liability insurance—covering injury to customers arising from the use of goods bought in the establishment;
9. Life insurance—covering the life of the owner or of key employees.[10]

Shop around for insurance. Visit independent insurance agents in your locale to compare the coverage, cost, and restrictions and limitations offered by various companies and policies. Simultaneously, use your human-resource network to find out what coverage other successful entrepreneurs in your line of business have adopted. Your insurance needs will depend on the neighborhood in which your firm will be located, the type of business you will operate, and whether you will hire employees.

Business Life Insurance

This coverage can include one or several of the following provisions:

1. A sole-proprietorship insurance plan to provide for the maintenance of the business upon the death of the sole proprietor.
2. A partnership insurance plan to retire a partner's interest at death.
3. A corporation insurance plan to retire a shareholder's interest at death.
4. Key-employee protection to reimburse you for loss and to provide a replacement in the event of a key employee's death.
5. A group plan for employees. A group annuity or pension plan may be a good idea if you have a lot of employees. If you have only a few employees, some form of individual retirement policy can be used. You and your employees can share the costs in any proportion desired and negotiated.
6. Reserve for emergencies. Most business life-insurance plans have cash value. This fund grows over the years, and can provide your business with a valuable reserve for emergencies. The policy's cash value can also be used as the basis for loans. Finally, in the event of your death, this policy provides your family with ready cash and aids in liquidating your interest in the business.[11]

Once you have established an insurance program for your business, you should review it periodically. Financial conditions change, tax laws vary, valuations of the interest of the owner are seldom constant. Any of these factors may affect the overall plan. Any change in legal structure also calls for a reassessment of insurance coverage. In conducting this annual review, you should work with an insurance agent you have come to trust.

SUMMARY

Business people must identify and observe those legal requirements that exist to protect their own and others' enterprises as well as employees and consumers. By seeking legal counsel, as well as advice from accountants, tax experts, and insurance agents in your human-resource network, you can protect yourself from disabling lawsuits and other potential difficulties.

It is no simple matter to stay fully informed about taxes and the related forms, procedures, and payments required under the law. Various taxes must be reported and paid periodically to federal, state, and local authorities, including special taxes and license fees unique to different types of businesses.

You can cope with potential risks by analyzing those that apply to your business. There are many kinds of insurance policies to protect entrepreneurs, but not all potential risks can be planned for or should be covered with insurance. Experienced entrepreneurs can minimize many risks by effective management.

DISCUSSION QUESTIONS

1. Discuss the purposes of legal requirements designed to protect public, business owners, and employees.
2. Describe the elements in a contract, and give examples of possible situations between seller and consumer, principal and agent, employer and employees, and landlord and tenant.
3. Describe antitrust laws designed to ensure that entrepreneurs can conduct their business without undue interference from others.
4. Describe laws that are designed to protect consumers.
5. Describe laws that have emerged to protect workers, including women, minorities, and the handicapped.
6. How must entrepreneurs comply with the various tax laws that affect them, including those that apply when they hire employees?
7. List potential risks affecting entrepreneurship. What types of insurance can best provide protection?
8. What risks can a successful manager cope with without recourse to insurance? How?

MINICASE

In the absence of Carl Gilchrist, a junkyard owner, two of his employees agreed to sell a used pickup-bed attachment to Mr. Reinhardt for $100. Mr. Reinhardt gave them a check for $100 but did not take the item with him since it needed a missing part. The employees verbally promised to locate the part and have the truck-bed attachment ready for Mr. Reinhardt the next day.

The next day, however, the customer was told by Mr. Gilchrist that the price his employees had quoted was wrong, and that the truck bed actually cost $250. Naturally, Mr. Reinhardt was very upset. However, he did write a check for the $150 difference, and took possession of the truck bed attachment. Later, it occurred to him to call his bank and cancel the second check for $150, leaving the junkyard dealer with the original $100 asked for by the two employees. But in the several hours that had passed before he made this decision, Mr. Gilchrist had already deposited both checks in the bank and they had cleared (both parties having the same bank).

Mr. Reinhardt took the case to small-claims court. He contended that he had taken in good faith the price quoted by Mr. Gilchrist's two employees. Reinhardt claimed they were agents of the junkyard owner and thus he should have been able to count on their verbal contract.

How would you resolve this case if you were the judge? Consider:

1. The nature of the contract.
2. The type of title that was passed, and at what point.
3. Whether an agency relationship did exist as claimed by the buyer.
4. What do you think the judge ruled in this case, and upon what basis?

ACTIVITIES AND EXERCISES

1. Select one or more of the following activities. In the process, collect samples of these items: a recently negotiated contract, an insurance policy, pertinent tax forms used to report sales, property, and state and federal income taxes.
    a. Interview an attorney or a paralegal aide in a law firm of your choice. Discuss the services that the firm provides for a small business and identify the issues about which entrepreneurs most often seek legal counsel. You may also want to ask about how the small-claims court functions.
    b. Visit a local Better Business Bureau to determine how the organization operates and what it does to protect consumers and small business owners.
    c. Make appointments with any of the following to discover how the agency protects employees:
    (i) Equal Employment Opportunity Commission,
    (ii) Local office of the U.S. Department of Labor,
    (iii) OSHA or MSHA (Mining Safety and Health Act) offices,
    (iv) Labor union officials,
    (v) Employment Security Commission, Job Service.
    d. Visit with entrepreneurs and discuss their procedures for reporting and paying business taxes. Identify what local taxes and licenses they must pay.
    e. Ask entrepreneurs about the scope of their insurance program and what other ways they seek to manage risk. Also find out how many insurance agencies they deal with and, if they use several, why.
    f. Arrange to interview some insurance agents to identify policy coverages, costs, and stipulations.

2. Meet as a group to share and discuss the results of your experiences and findings from a through f above.
    a. Debate the question: "Who is most protected—small businesses or big businesses, consumers or employees?"
    b. Review the sample copies of contracts, insurance policies typically taken out by owners in your locale, and tax reporting forms and procedures.
3. Using the earnings forecast from your business plan, assume that this represents actual revenue, costs, and expenses for your company's first year of operation. Transfer these figures to Schedule C of last year's federal income tax form. (Note: If you were already in business and had kept accurate records for the year, it would not be difficult to prepare this required form, which must be submitted annually.)

NOTES

1. William D. Hailes, Jr. and Raymond T. Hubbard. *Small Business Management* (Albany, NY: Delmar, 1965), p. 15.
2. Richard Stone, "The Law of Secured Credit: A Trap for the Unwary," *Inc.,* May 1982, pp. 155–56.
3. James F. Moreau. *Effective Small Business Management* (Chicago: Rand McNally, 1980), p. 195.
4. Roy W. Poe, Herbert G. Hicks, and Olive D. Church, "Protection for the Consumer," *Getting Involved with Business* (New York: McGraw-Hill, 1981), p. 453.
5. Bradford W. Ketchum, "You and Your Attorney," *Inc.,* June 1982, pp. 51–56.
6. "Tax Credit for Creating Jobs," *NFIB Mandate* (San Mateo, CA: National Federation of Independent Business), February 1983, p. 6.
7. Stephen P. Radics, Jr., "Steps in Meeting Your Tax Obligations," *Management Aid* no. 1.013 (Washington, D.C.: U.S. Small Business Administration, 1980).
8. Ibid.
9. Dan Steinhoff, "Risks and How to Deal with Them," *Small Business Management Fundamentals* (New York: McGraw-Hill, 1978), p. 236.
10. Clifford M. Baumbeck and Kenneth Lawyer, "Insurance and Risk Management," *How to Organize and Operate a Small Business* (Englewood Cliffs, NJ: Prentice-Hall, 1979), p. 288.
11. Institute of Life Insurance, "Business Life Insurance," *Management Aid,* (Washington, D.C.: U.S. Small Business Administration, 1980).

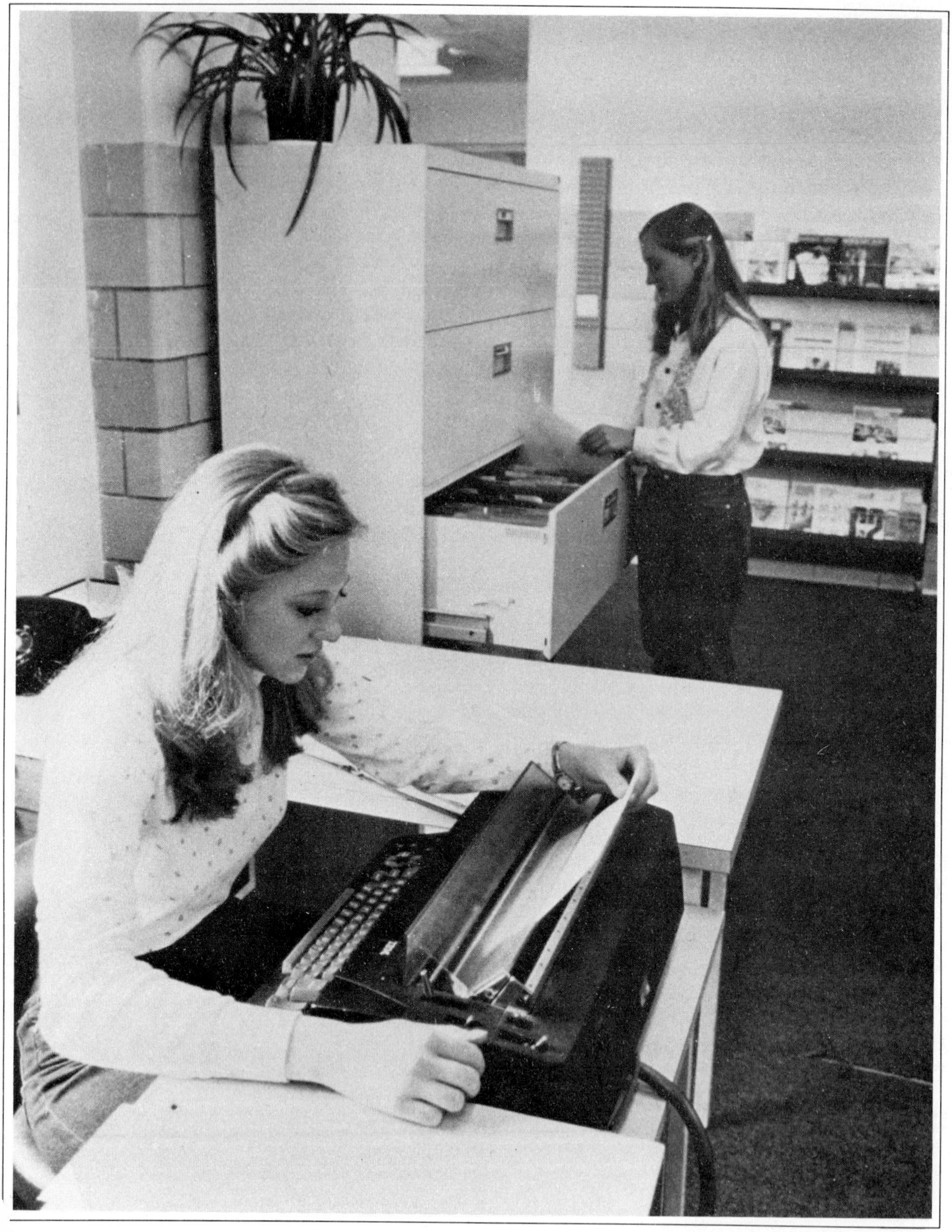

chapter 14

Establishing the Records and Office Systems

Objectives

1. Compare the cost of establishing an accounting or recordkeeping system with the benefits to be derived, including factors associated with both time and wage expense.

2. Describe a basic recordkeeping system and its purpose.

3. Demonstrate the use of pertinent records and controls, from the source document phase through balancing the books.

4. Evaluate the use of financial statements and their impact on effective management and control; give examples from your proposed business.

5. Describe and give examples of office functions and procedures, whether maintained by manual or mechanical modes.

A major problem during the first year of any business is merely staying alive! While a manager must necessarily focus on many areas simultaneously, seeking to earn enough money to cover basic expenses should be the first objective. It's a common practice during the first hectic weeks, particularly for inexperienced entrepreneurs, to keep scant records. They let receipts and canceled checks collect dust in a bottom drawer and keep minimal records of their sales and expenditures. Many small business owners commence operations on a cash basis, without even opening a bank account.

THE IMPORTANCE OF KEEPING RECORDS

An accurate set of books can provide you with a data base, a road map. Up-to-date and accurate records will tell you where you have been and where you are, so that you can make sound decisions about where to go next. A complete bookkeeping system will furnish you with the specific figures you need to prepare your tax forms. The system can also alert you to problems, serious or otherwise.

Sound data can help you find realistic answers to such questions as:

1. Did I make any profit last month? If so, how much?
2. Where is the money going?
3. Which customers warrant the most attention, good or bad? Who should be encouraged to buy more? Who should be encouraged to pay their overdue bills?
4. Which suppliers give the best discounts or provide the fastest services?
5. How effective was the last sales promotion?
6. How does this year (month, season, etc.) compare with the same previous period?
7. What percentage of revenue am I spending on each budget item? How can costs be reduced? Where should more money be spent?
8. What is the current ratio of assets to liabilities? Is this a safe margin? If I seem headed for trouble, what can I do about it?

Internal Controls

All recordkeeping systems should have built-in internal controls for maintaining accuracy, honesty, efficiency, and speed. Controls exist at various points in the bookkeeping cycle. Conducting a trial balance, a post-closing trial balance, and a bank reconciliation illustrate accuracy controls.[1]

To ensure honest accounting, you can divide the responsibility so that one person's work can be checked against another's. No one person, whether employee or partner, should have total responsibility for handling cash and also for keeping the records of cash expenditures.

Entrepreneurs use both single- and double-entry accounting methods. Because regular and systematic bookkeeping takes time, it's wise to see an accountant—at least during the establishment phase—and perhaps hire a bookkeeper.

The use of special journals (e.g., sales and expenses) allows businesses to achieve efficiency and speed. With more than one journal at least two people can be working on the books at once. Also, special journals increase efficiency because all data regarding one kind of business transaction is collected and journalized in one place.

Components of the Recordkeeping System

The four components of a recordkeeping system are people, records, equipment, and procedures. Business owners or their designees process and interpret information. These people make the system work. Where more than one person is involved, each person relies on the work of others; they must interact, and work must flow from one to another.

Source documents, papers, forms, journals, ledgers, and other records are used to retain data and to facilitate internal controls. A document's format can enhance efficiency, while prenumbered forms stimulate honesty and preprinted forms improve accuracy. Equipment for both manual and computerized systems helps increase efficiency and speed (see also Chapter 15).

Specific procedures guide data through the recordkeeping system. The choice of procedures depends on the type of information needed, the expertise and preference of the owner (and/or bookkeeper), and on the equipment used.

Double-entry bookkeeping is usually the preferred method for keeping business records and making use of journals and ledgers. Transactions are entered first in a journal, and then monthly totals of the transactions are posted to the appropriate ledger accounts. The ledger accounts include five categories: (1) income, (2) expense, (3) asset, (4) liability, and (5) net worth. Income and expense accounts are closed each year; asset, liability, and net-worth accounts are maintained on a permanent and continuing basis.

Single-entry bookkeeping, although not as complete as the double-entry method, may be used effectively in the small business, especially during its early years. The single-entry system can be relatively simple, recording the flow of income and expense through a daily summary of cash receipts, a monthly summary of receipts, and monthly disbursements journals (such as a checkbook). This system is entirely adequate for the tax purposes of a small business.[2]

Time and Cost Constraints

It takes a certain amount of time each day, each month, each quarter, and each year to keep adequate records. Many entrepreneurs lack a basic understanding of the rudimentary procedures for establishing and maintaining a records system. Ignorant of the benefits to be derived, they neglect to organize for this phase of their business and to set aside the time needed to perform the related tasks satisfactorily. Without having established a system or maintained it, they have no data base upon which to make managerial decisions.

A comprehensive accounting and financial program differs from a simple recordkeeping system. To implement the former, it should be understood at the outset, you need both training and experience. If you haven't got this background, you should use a competent certified public accounting (CPA) firm. To expect such expert service from a low-paid company bookkeeper or an ill-informed family member is unrealistic.

After the system is established, it also must be maintained. You, the business owner, will have to spend the time this takes or else you must pay someone else to do so. Meanwhile, having an accountant assist you with setting up the books can save you many headaches later.

ORGANIZATION PROCEDURES

A useful recordkeeping system includes having journals for cash receipts and disbursements. Every amount received or spent should be entered. A general ledger records assets, liabilities, capital, revenue, and expense accounts. You'll need a sales journal and, if you hire people, employee compensation records. If you offer credit to customers, you'll have to establish subsidiary ledgers of accounts receivable, and if you buy on credit, you'll need accounts payable. You'll also need inventory-control records, if you deal in products or merchandise.

Decide what forms you want to have printed and place the order. You can buy many standard business forms at office-supply stores, but for advertising reasons you may want to have your company's name and address printed on some "external papers," i.e., papers that will be seen by your customers. External papers include checks, sales slips or statements, stationery, envelopes, business cards, and purchase orders. Although you can use a rubber stamp, your company's name and logo will make a better impression if they are printed.

Other organizational steps include opening a bank account and retaining an accountant to help you establish the records system. Be ready to answer the accountant's questions, such as: What will be the company's source of income? What expenditures do you anticipate? Will you operate on a cash basis only, or will you seek to obtain credit and make credit available to your customers? Will you be stocking inventory regularly? Will you employ others? Do you want to use a double-entry or single-entry records system? Will you use the cash system or the accrual system of accounting? And how do you plan to handle depreciation?

The Business Bank Account

Open a separate checking account for your company. Business checking accounts often do not work like personal accounts. Some banks require a minimum balance but make no charge per check. Ask the bankers such questions as: What different plans are available for a company in my category? What are the advantages and disadvantages of each? How much assistance can I receive—i.e., free printed checks, night depository, automatic teller, safe deposit box, and so on?

Make it a habit to pay every business expenditure by company check. This practice provides you with a record of specific expenses on each checkstub and on the monthly bank statement. Also deposit all your receipts regularly, whether in cash or checks. Not only does this remove temptation from your employees (and save losses if you are robbed!), but it keeps the record of your deposits current. Never mingle personal funds with business funds.

The Bank reconciliation. Know where your bank balance stands. Balance your business account each month (many banks allow 10 days for making corrections). Check the bank statement and the canceled checks against the checkstubs. Note which checks are still outstanding and whether any deposits do not appear on the statement. Correct any errors that you or your staff have made, either in the checkbook or in the cash disbursements journal.

Keep all bank statements and canceled checks for a minimum of three years, which is the normal statute of limitations for federal income tax audits. Retaining them for five years may be smarter.

Source Documents

"Transaction" or "source" documents include canceled checks and deposit slips; sales slips, receipts, or cash register tapes; statements, invoices, or bills sent to credit customers; and supplier invoices or bills received for purchases made. Record at the time of processing all pertinent data about each of these papers, or at least about those for which the company is responsible. Preprinted forms can help to assemble this data. Be sure to record the purchaser's name, address, and telephone number; the specific items sold and their quantity and unit and total price; and any terms or conditions, including whether bought by cash or credit.

Source documents should be maintained in a regular fashion, using a readily accessible filing system. Prenumbered forms, which must be used in consecutive order, help to assure honesty as well as control. Even if you are the only person who works with the records, you may wonder what happened to check or sales slip no. 157, for instance, should you find it missing. Thus it is important to file voided documents. Otherwise you might wonder if an employee tore up the form and pocketed the money. By using prenumbered documents and retaining them systematically you can alleviate such worries.

Large companies—with numerous departments and many people responsible for processing papers—often use multiple copies of source documents. A small business, however, usually finds this practice unnecessary. The processing of source documents can work this simply:

1. The original copy of the sales slip goes to the customer and another is filed.
2. For monthly bills or statements sent to customers buying on credit, the original is submitted to the customer and the copy is filed.
3. For checks, the original is given or mailed to pay for the purchase, while the checkstub remains in the office. When the canceled checks are returned, together with the bank statement, these become the property of the owner and are filed.
4. In preparing purchase orders, submit the original to the supplier and retain the copy, preferably in an open book or pending file until the order has been completely filled (until no back orders are outstanding). Upon receipt of the goods ordered, together with the supplier's bill, check the accuracy of the bill. Then pay with a check, and the transaction is completed.

Journals and Ledgers

A journal is the basic recordkeeping book. All transactions are taken from source documents and recorded here. Because both the money coming in and the money going out need to be recorded, two journals are commonly used. One records cash receipts and the other cash disbursements, whether payments are made by cash, check, or other means.

Cash-receipts journal. Entries should be made in chronological order. Show the date of the transaction, the person or company from whom the money was received, the amount, and the nature of the transaction—cash sale, payment on account or loan, etc.

Cash-disbursements journal. Enter all payments in chronological order, separating those made in cash from those made by check. Some people like to keep small amounts of cash on hand. They may write a check to petty cash, and keep separate vouchers against expenditures in this fund (perhaps $50 to $100 in a locked box). If so, the recordkeeping system should reflect this practice.

In the disbursement journal you may want to enter payments for merchandise or for materials separately from other expenditures. If you employ a staff, you will need another separate section (or journal) to record payroll expenditures and deductions for income tax and Social Security, etc.

All transactions must be recorded completely, regularly, and in an organized manner. The benefits of the system are lost if the entrepreneur records data haphazardly, and only when the mood strikes. Too much important data can easily be lost otherwise.

Together, these two journals chart the daily money flow in and out of a business. Any office supply store offers a range of such books, with various numbers of columns.

Posting to ledgers. Next "post," or transfer, the data from the journal entries to various ledger accounts. An "account" is a single classification of information within the conventional accounting system. It summarizes all the transactions within a particular period that affect a specific asset or liability. The ledger page is arranged into two columns, with debits on the left and credits on the right.

Assets include cash and inventory on hand, while accounts payable and notes payable are liabilities. Assets are listed in the ledger first, in order from most to least liquid; and liabilities follow. Next come the equity accounts of the sole proprietor, partner, or stockholders, depending on the legal form of business (see Figure 14.1).

Balancing the books. Transactions should be entered daily into the cash-receipt and cash-disbursement journals, but posting to ledgers may be handled once a month. At the end of each month you should balance your books. Add up the debits and credits within each account. By subtracting one from the other, you can discover whether there is a credit or a debit balance.

Subsidiary accounts (A/R, A/P). The amount that customers owe you is "accounts receivable" (A/R). The amount that you owe suppliers or others is "accounts payable" (A/P). If you either extend credit to customers or buy on credit yourself, then you should establish subsidiary A/R and/or A/P ledgers. Typically, a ledger page is established for each account, including one A/R page (or section of pages) per credit customer. Charges are posted in the debit column and payments in the credit column. You also establish a separate A/P page for each supplier to whom your company owes money.

FIGURE 14.1
Chart of Accounts.

**Chart of Accounts,
ODC Word-Processing**

	Acct No.		Acct No.
Assets		**Liabilities**	
Cash	111	Accounts payable	211
Petty cash	112	Notes payable	221
Accounts receivable	121	Sales tax payable	231
Bad-debt allowance	012	Employees income tax payable	241
Furniture/Fixtures	131	FICA tax payable	251
Depreciation allowance	013	State income tax payable	271
Prepaid insurance	141		
Stationery/Supplies	151	**Capital**	
		Proprietor, capital	311
Income			
Income from services	411		
Expenses			
Rent	511		
Advertising	512		
Salaries	513		
Bonuses	514		
Office supplies	515		
Depreciation	516		
Insurance	517		
Employer's payroll taxes	518		
Bad debts	519		
Utilities	520		
Telephone	521		

Other Records and Decisions

Where inventory is an issue, then accurate records must be kept. You will want to keep enough merchandise or raw materials on hand to stock your shelves or to supply your production, but you do need to know their status at any given time so you will not run out or overstock. If you employ workers, then you will have to maintain payroll records. Records are also kept of insurance and depreciation.

Inventory. There are three types of inventory: raw materials, materials in process, and finished goods. Retailers deal with finished goods. Manufacturers must maintain all three types. Wood, steel, chemicals, semiconductors, reels of wire, bolts of fabric, sand, and gravel are all raw materials.

Materials in process, as the term implies, are incomplete products, such as partially upholstered or unpainted furniture. The balance sheet must account for everything, however, including direct labor and factory overhead.

For finished goods, the accounting system includes the total cost of units completed but not yet sold. The cost of inventory must also include the cost of transportation in addition to the invoice price.[3]

Payroll and personnel records. In either a sole proprietorship or a partnership, the money removed from the business by the principal(s) is not considered part of the payroll. For tax purposes, these people are self-employed. Stockholders in a corporation may receive a salary; they would thus be part of the payroll.

When you employ people who are not principals, then you have a "payroll" and must keep specific records. For no more than one or two employees, you can use the cash-disbursements journal. Otherwise, you should use a payroll journal. This record includes, for each employee, the name, total wages, deductions, and the net amount paid. To find withholdings tables and other regulations, obtain a current copy of the Employer's Tax Guide from the U.S. Internal Revenue Service.

Insurance. You will want to record what insurance policies you hold, when the premiums are due and in what amounts, and the type and extent of coverage each provides. It's a good practice to keep insurance policies in a safe-deposit box at the bank. You do not want to lose such valuable papers in case of fire.

Depreciation. Buildings, vehicles, equipment, machinery, and furniture all depreciate. A certain percentage of the value of these items can be charged off each year as an expense of doing business.

Suppose you purchase a truck for $10,000, and you deem it has a useful life of five years. This means you can write off $2000 each year for this five-year period. Your record notes this vehicle's worth each year as an asset. Thus the first year the truck is an asset worth $10,000, but the second it is worth only $8000. In your records, list each item, its original cost, the depreciation taken each year (on income tax forms), and the remaining value as an asset (shown on the balance sheet).

Cash versus accrual system. You can keep records according to either the cash or the accrual system. The first reports income and expenses at the time that the money is actually exchanged, the second when the obligation to pay is first made, as when the products are first sold or the services performed. Where inventories are involved, the business is legally required to use the accrual system. Although somewhat more complicated, this practice usually produces a more realistic picture of the actual operation.[4]

Suppose Carl, who operates an appliance repair firm, decides to use the accrual system. Each time he makes a service call he records the transaction as earned income. The resulting records tell Carl how profitable any given period has actually been. Yet Carl may make his service call in one month, pay for the parts he used the following month, and receive payment from the customer the third month. The cash system makes for easier recordkeeping, requiring no more than a checking account and a billing procedure. It would not however, give Carl a clear picture of his real earnings in any given time period.

If your business is not legally required to use the accrual system, then the decision is up to you. An accountant can advise you, and if you choose the accrual system, he or she will help you establish it.

Separating Family and Business Records

Family finances and business finances must be kept strictly apart. The entrepreneur who dips into the cash register and takes out $100 when the family needs groceries cannot know how the business is doing. The merchant who takes some of the inventory home for personal use without recording it is also confusing the records. The contractor or operator who uses company work crews for personal projects at home must absorb the cost somewhere.

No matter how small your business, even if you only run it part-time to supplement other family income sources, always keep your business accounts separate from your personal or family accounts. This includes establishing separate bank accounts.

THE USE AND INTERPRETATION OF FINANCIAL STATEMENTS

It is not enough merely to establish the books or even to maintain them. Developing analytic abilities and the habit of regularly interpreting the data available to you can make the difference between success, mediocrity, and failure. Yet the interpretation and effective use of data is often the forgotten step, particularly by new and busy owners. Financial-statement analysis is the process of forming judgments about the present and past financial health of a company, from evidence available in its balance sheets, income statements, tax returns, and other financial statements.[5]

The Balance Sheet

Compare the Chart of Accounts (Figure 14.1) with the Balance Sheet (Figure 14.2). Both are for a word-processing service company. Note how the ledger data, derived from the processing of source documents and the transaction entries in journals, is summarized on the balance sheet. Assets must equal liabilities plus capital.

Current assets are those that the owner does not anticipate holding for long. This category includes cash, finished goods in inventory, and accounts receiv-

Balance Sheet,
ODC Word-Processing
July 31, 19—

FIGURE 14.2
Balance Sheet.

Assets		
Cash on hand and in the bank	$25,000.00	
Petty cash	580.00	
Accounts receivable	2,547.57	
Furniture and fixtures (net)	55,300.00	
Prepaid insurance	250.00	
Stationery and supplies	2,380.75	
Total Assets		$86,058.32
Liabilities and Capital		
Notes payable	$14,500.00	
Accounts payable	4,750.44	
Total Liabilities		$19,250.44
Proprietor, capital	$40,000.00	
Proprietor, retained earnings	26,807.88	
Total Capital		$66,807.88
Total Liabilities and Capital		$86,058.32

able. Fixed assets are long-term assets, including plant and equipment. A third possible category is the intangible asset of goodwill.

Liabilities are debts owed by the business, including both accounts payable, which are usually short-term, and notes payable, which are usually long-term debts such as mortgage payments. The difference between the value of the assets and the value of the liabilities is the capital. This category includes funds invested by the owner plus accumulated profits, less withdrawals.

The Income Statement

This statement is also known as a profit and loss (P&L) statement. It shows how a business has performed over a certain period of time. An income statement should be prepared at least once a year, and more often for new firms. The income statement specifies sales, cost of sales, gross profit, expenses, and net income or loss from operations.

Comparative Financial Statements

Comparative financial statements can be developed for any period. You can compare this month against last month, this season against the same season last year, and so on. During the first year of operation the wise entrepreneur charts changes from month to month and item by item. Thereafter, owners commonly compare the results of one year or season against the last such period.

Horizontal comparisons. Also known as a horizontal analysis, this procedure compares the same items with one another at different times. Businesses that experience seasonal fluctuations are particularly interested in this type of analysis. Recreational facilities, for example, can discover whether it is more profitable to focus more on winter or summer sports. Retail establishments, too, experience seasonal changes. Their peak periods are before Christmas and in spring and late summer, when children are returning to school. Florists find the spring and early summer a busy period, featuring Mother's Day, spring proms, commencements, and weddings. (See Figures 14.3 and 14.4.)

Vertical comparisons. This type of comparative analysis takes the entrepreneur down the list to compare items within categories. Perhaps you want to know the percentage of cost of sales to sales. If your income is $97,569 and the cost of sales is $38,912, this percentage equals 40 percent (see Figure 14.4).

The same method can be used to determine the percentage of each expense item against the gross sales figure. These figures, however, can't tell you whether the amount you are spending in each category is realistic. Trade association and

FIGURE 14.3
Comparative Balance Sheet.

Comparative Balance Sheet
Wiseman Appliance Repair

Assets

	Dec. 31, 1983	Dec. 31, 1984	June 30, 1985 (6 mos)
Current Assets			
Cash on hand	$ 5,000	$ 4,000	$ 3,973.38
Accounts receivable (Net of bad-debts allowance)	8,112	11,946	11,832.06
Inventory	30,500	29,500	28,500.00
Add:			
Plant & equipment (cost, less accumulated depreciation)	11,410	8,393	5,654.00
Total Assets	$55,022	$53,839	$49,959.44

Liabilities and Equity

Short-term debt	—	—	$10,623.66
Long-term debt	$32,000	$31,000	29,986.72
Accounts payable	2,704	3,982	4,243.89
Total Liabilities	$34,704	$34,982	$44,854.27
C. Wiseman, Equity	20,318	18,857	12,729.34
Total Liabilities and Equity	$55,022	$53,839	$57,583.61

**Profit and Loss Statement,
Wiseman Appliance Repair**[1]

FIGURE 14.4
Profit and Loss Statement.

	Dec. 31, 1983	Dec. 31, 1984	June 30, 1985 (6 mos)
Sales	$97,569	$126,216	$73,783.70[2]
Cost of merchandise/services sold	38,912	29,860	18,445.90
Gross Profit	$58,657	$ 96,356	$55,337.80
Operating and general expenses			
Salaries (less jobs. credit)	$27,354	$ 15,287	$28,800
Travel	5,019	5,893	2,500
Advertising	2,493	793	—
Depreciation	3,017	2,739	1,366
Freight (not in above)	1,122	1,934	—
Insurance	2,060	1,432	716
Interest	2,410	3,402	1,701
Supplies (office)	466	487	243
Supplies (shop)	3,888	4,746	2,373
Rent	3,600	3,600	1,800
Utilities	2,254	3,973	1,896
Taxes	4,215	12,482	6,241
Legal fees	—	267	135
Other	3,482	3,689	1,845
Total Operating Expenses	$61,380	$ 60,724	49,616
Net Income (or Loss) from Operations	($ 2,723)	$ 35,596	$ 5,721.80

[1]Data taken from Wiseman's tax return, Schedule C.
[2]Gross sales (1983 and 1984 Sales) represents net sales.

government and other survey agency publications can give you data on industry averages for different types of businesses. This sort of analysis can help you identify areas where you should spend more or less.

Cash flow. Another statement most entrepreneurs want to see explains where they stand on a cash-flow basis. What revenue is coming in from what sources? And how much is going out, for what purposes? The cash-flow statement summarizes and classifies this monetary flow. It is often prepared month by month. (It is this type of financial paper, also, that treasurers of civic and other organizations periodically present to their membership.) (See Figure 14.5.)

Aging of accounts receivable and payable. You will want to know how you stand in relation to both accounts receivable and payable. Preparing an aging statement from the A/R and A/P ledgers allows you to assess the status of either at a glance. (See Figure 14.6.)

FIGURE 14.5
Cash Flow Statement.

**Cash-Flow Statement,
Wiseman Appliance Repair**

For the Month of June 19—

Cash Available, Beginning		$ 4,000
Cash Received:		
Cash sales	$16,000	
Payments on account	2,675	
Cash from other sources:		
Loans	600	
Owner's investment	1,000	
Total Cash Received		$20,275
Total Cash for Month		24,275
Cash Expenditures		
Cash purchases	$ 5,800	
Salaries	6,100	
Payments on account	1,000	
Loan payments	2,500	
Insurance	—	
Utilities	350	
Taxes	—	
Other operating expenses	950	
Owner withdrawals	1,600	
Total Expenditures		$18,300
Cash Available, Ending Balance		$ 5,975

Budgeting, Planning, and Forecasting

Many small business owners prepare budgets simply by assuming that future expenditures will parallel those of the past. But good managers are always making new and different decisions for the future.

Suppose you want to increase the insurance budget, but you do not anticipate any increase in sales. You will probably have to cut back on some other item in order to make the funds available.

In seeking to increase sales, you might decide to hire more salespeople. That course will increase the wage expenses. Perhaps you will buy new equipment to streamline operations and produce more units at less cost each. Then you must allot funds to pay for the equipment. If you think you can acquire more customers without new expenditures for equipment or workers, then how will you accommodate the needs of these customers? A service or repair installation may concentrate on improving methods. All such managerial decisions should be reflected in your budget for the next year or season.

Aging of Accounts Receivable and Payable, Wiseman Appliance Repair

For Year Ending June 30, 19—

FIGURE 14.6
Aging of Accounts Receivable and Payable.

ACCOUNTS RECEIVABLE

Age Interval	Balance	Estimated Uncollectible Accounts Percent	Amount
Not due	$ 9,372.83	2	$ 187
1-30 days past due	700.88	5	35
31-60 days past due	653.80	10	65
61-90 days past due	116.55	20	23
91-180 days past due	407.15	30	122
181-365 days past due	259.46	50	130
Over 365 days past due	571.39	80	457
	$12,082.06		$1,019

NOTE: Approximately $1,119.28 worth of accounts have been turned over to a collection agency for a 50-percent possible recovery for the firm.

ACCOUNTS PAYABLE

Age Interval	Balance
Not due	$2,202.14
1-30 days past due	1,577.85
31-60 days past due	610.41
61-90 days past due	51.94
	$4,442.34
Less credits	296.08
	$4,146.26

Local or national economic trends can affect your planning. Is a major new industry coming into the market area? Will there be many new workers arriving as a result, to construct the plant or as permanent employees? Will local industrial layoffs, the result of a national recession, change your current and future plans? Are you planning to expand or to introduce new products or services on the market? All these activities should appear on your budget. (See Figure 14.7.)

To estimate future income, prepare an earnings-projection statement. If your forecast suggests an increase in sales, many if not all expenditure items will

Monthly	July	Aug	Sept	Oct	Nov	Dec	Jan	Feb	Mar	Apr	May	June
SALES	$17,000	$16,000	$15,000	$14,000	$13,000	$12,000	$10,000	$10,000	$11,000	$13,000	$15,000	$16,000
[1]Cash Collectibles	14,675	15,675	16,675	15,675	14,675	13,675	12,675	11,675	9,675	9,675	10,675	12,675
LESS												
[2]Cash Purchases	4,125	4,125	3,875	3,600	3,375	3,100	2,750	2,500	2,700	3,000	3,500	3,800
[3]Salaries	3,625	4,100	4,100	4,100	4,100	4,100	3,625	3,625	3,625	3,625	4,100	4,100
[4]Mortgage (SBA)	1,700	1,700	1,700	1,700	1,700	1,700	1,700	1,700	1,700	1,700	1,700	1,700
[5]Insurance	750	—	—	—	—	—	750	—	—	—	—	—
[6]Utilities	250	250	250	250	250	350	450	450	450	350	250	250
[7]Taxes	4,000	—	—	4,000	—	—	—	—	—	4,000	—	—
[8]Operating Expenses	750	750	750	750	750	750	750	750	750	750	750	750
Cash Available	$ 1,725	$ 5,750	$ 6,000	$ 1,275	$ 4,600	$ 3,675	$ 2,300	$ 2,650	$ 450	($ 900)	$ 375	$ 2,075
Cash Total	$30,575 for year											

[2]Cash paid 30 days after order (i.e., 20 for shipping and 10 days for payment [max]) at rate of 25% of Sales for parts cost and on a 60-day sales moving average.
[3]Add ½ time person in August through December, and then again in May.
[6]Utilities includes added heat cost in cold months; otherwise estimated at $250 per month.
[7]Taxes paid on 4/15, 7/15, and 10/5, for a total of $12,000.
[8]All other general expenses (i.e., supplies, advertising, legal, etc. = $9,200, which does not include depreciation.

FIGURE 14.7 Pro-Forma Cash Budget.

Sales (average of $13,500 × 12 mos)	$162,000	
Cost of merchandise sold at 25% of sales	40,450	
Gross Profit on Sales		$121,550
Operating expenses		86,650
Net Income (before depreciation and interest expense on building to be purchased with SBA loan—and before income taxes)		$ 34,900

FIGURE 14.8 Yearly Earnings Projection.

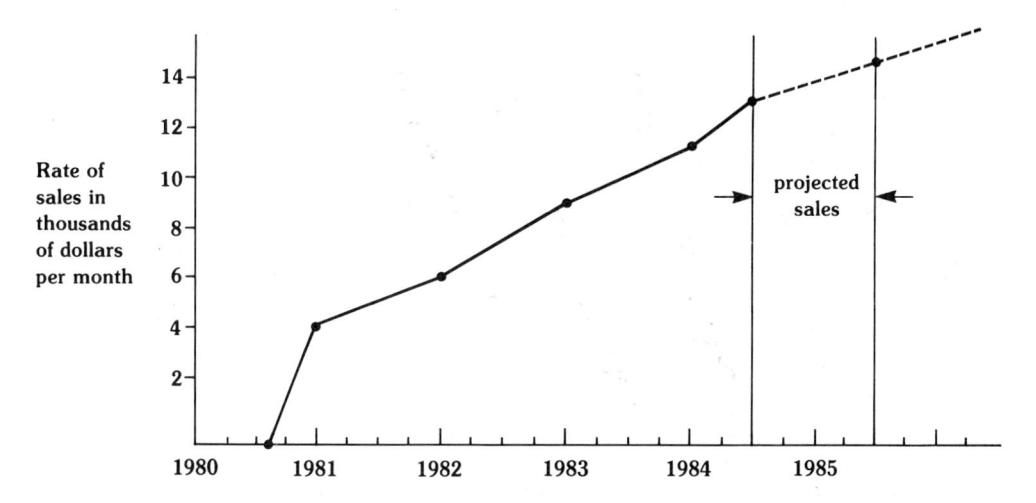

[Graph: Rate of sales in thousands of dollars per month, 1980–1985, showing growth from ~4 in 1981 to ~13 in mid-1985, with projected sales beyond.]

¹Sales projected on a growth curve graph using actuals for 1980–84, and six months of 1985. Sales on June 30, 1985, are projected to total $14,500.

FIGURE 14.9 Sales Projection.

increase as well. By identifying the percentage of each line item against past gross sales, you can make predictions about future expenses. (See Figures 14.8 and 14.9.)

As each period passes, compare the actual revenue and expenditures against the original projection. This "budget variance report" can tell you where you spent more or less than originally anticipated. This report can help you budget more realistically for the next period.

Interpreting Ratios

In some industries, maintaining a two-to-one ratio of assets to liabilities is recommended, i.e., two dollars of current assets to every dollar of current liabilities. Current assets include cash, receivables, and inventory. Current liabilities include accounts payable and short-term notes payable. A ratio lower than the 2:1 industry standard suggests potential weakness, while a higher ratio may imply a poor use of funds.

$$\text{Current Ratio} = \frac{\text{Current Assets}}{\text{Current Liabilities}}$$

The quick ratio—that is, the current ratio exclusive of inventory—is determined by dividing the total cash and receivables by current liabilities. A ratio of 1:1 is considered adequate for the quick ratio. This computation tells you how well your business would measure up if required to liquidate its current assets rather quickly in order to meet liability payments.

$$\text{Quick Ratio} = \frac{\text{Cash} + \text{Receivables}}{\text{Current Liabilities}}$$

The next ratio is a measure of how the company can meet its total obligations from equity. The lower the ratio, the higher the proportion of equity relative to debt and the better the firm's credit rating will be. The formula for determining the ratio of total debt to net worth is:

$$\frac{\text{Total Debt}}{\text{Net Worth}} \times 100 = \text{Total Debt Ratio}$$

Knowing Your Business

The first step in developing a cash-management attitude is to determine where the cash comes from and how it is used in one's own business. Cash, remember, is an asset of a firm, and like all resources, there is an optimum amount that should be held at any given time. A business receives cash from cash sales, from collections of accounts and notes receivable, from the sale of assets, and from creditors and owners. Debt and equity are external sources of cash, while the acquisition and sale of goods and services are the major internal sources of cash for the business. Cash is also most commonly used to reduce payables, to acquire fixed assets, to pay taxes and interest, and to return a profit to the owners.[6]

The cash operating cycle. The two critical dimensions of the cash operating cycle are breadth and depth. The breadth of the operating cycle refers to the average length of the cycle in time (number of days). The depth of the cycle is the average amount of cash flowing through the cycle at a given time (dollars invested). Both of these aspects of the cash operating cycle must be properly managed. They can be managed by controlling: (1) the level of cash invested in inventories and receivables, and (2) the length of time necessary to recover cash invested in inventories and receivables.[7] (Also see Chapter 16.)

SMALL BUSINESS NEEDS

What records will you need in your business? What office functions and related activities? Will you buy a computer? (see Chapter 15). To help you answer such questions, we will trace the typical operations of "XYZ Manufacturing Company" (see Figures 14.10 and 14.11), from ordering supplies and raw materials through production to the end result, the sales. We will note how recordkeeping, accounting, and office functions fit into this picture.

Processing Data

Written, verbal, mechanical, and computerized methods of handling or transmitting information are all forms of data processing. When clerks prepare receipts for cash received, they are processing data. When secretaries take telephone messages, they are processing data. Typing a letter, adding a column of figures, putting papers in a filing cabinet, and opening and reading mail are all forms of processing data. Recording, computing, communicating, transmitting, storing, and retrieving all involve data processing. The purpose of the office function is to manage information, and to do it quickly and accurately so that managers can make effective use of this data.

Traditionally, with the high cost of office machines and equipment, few small companies ever considered computerizing their office and business functions. Yet with wages and the other costs of running a business escalating, it often can be far too expensive to process data manually or even mechanically.

Manual operations. This method implies using a pen or pencil to handwrite letters, total columns, prepare reports, take dictation, write checks, or make ledger and journal entries. Wherever someone is required to write data, and then to rewrite it again (and again!), opportunities for making errors multiply. This is one reason why the name, address, and number of credit-card holders are embossed on their cards and are recorded by machine.

The pegboard method of preparing payroll also allows people to "write it once." An example is the payroll procedure: payroll data of individual earnings record, check, and company journal are hooked to the board, via pegs. Pegs align various forms on top of each other, so that each line of data only has to be written once.

Mechanical operations. This method involves the use of various machines, such as an electronic 10-key calculator, a cash register, or an electric or electronic typewriter. Most businesses have some or all of these machines. For businesses with duplicating needs, the photocopier is now the most common machine. Bookkeeping machines post simultaneously to a general ledger and to the customer's account. Rotary calculators were once popular but they are both expensive and bulky. In most companies they have been replaced by small, inexpensive electronic calculators and/or by microcomputers.

Xerographic copiers are more popular than the old-fashioned duplicating methods of carbon paper or mimeograph.

Systems and Subsystems

All the functions of any company, whether retail, service, manufacturing, extraction or distribution, are interactive and interdependent. Figures 14.10 and 14.11 illustrate this fact for a manufacturing company. The first figure depicts the flow of products, while the second traces the flow of information by means of business forms and of paper or paperless transmissions.[8]

Whether organized according to business functions or departments, every company is a system, and every operation a subsystem. And within each subsystem there are subsets, procedures, and methods. The accounting department (or function), for example, handles the following subsystems and procedures: accounts receivable (A/R), accounts payable (A/P), cash receipts and payments, sales, purchasing, personnel, payroll, taxes, and general recordkeeping for reporting, analyzing, and forecasting.

Business forms and procedures. Notice the number of papers (or paperless transmissions) in Figure 14.11 that must move from one department or function to another in order to activate the flow of goods (Figure 14.10). Each function's tasks are interdependent. Sales orders must be submitted in order to

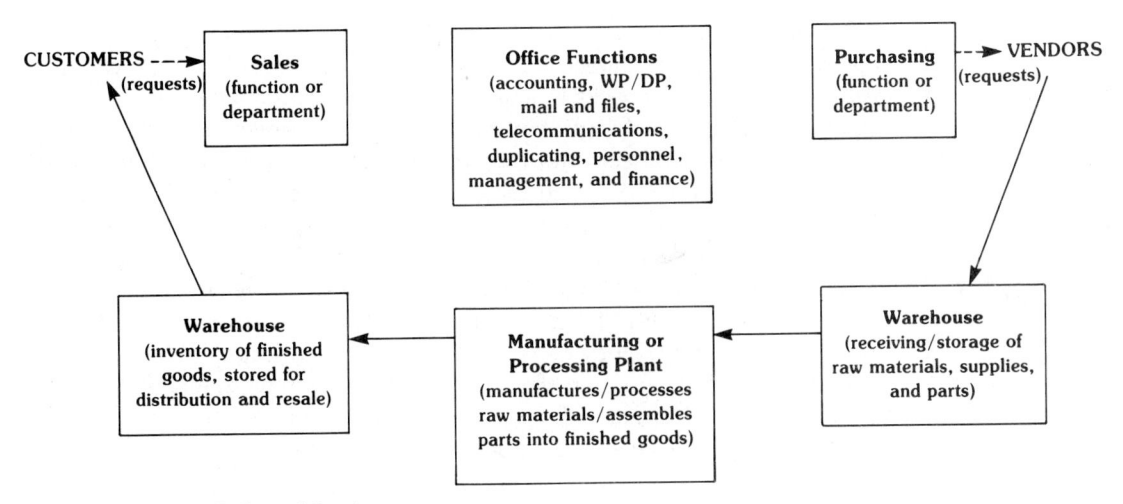

FIGURE 14.10 XYZ Flow of Goods.

move goods from the manufacturing plant through the warehouse to customers. But raw materials, small parts, and supplies must be ordered and received from vendors before they can be processed into finished goods. To replenish the inventory of raw materials, requisition orders go from manufacturing to warehousing and, if the materials are not in stock, on to the purchasing department, whose personnel prepare purchase orders and send them to vendors.

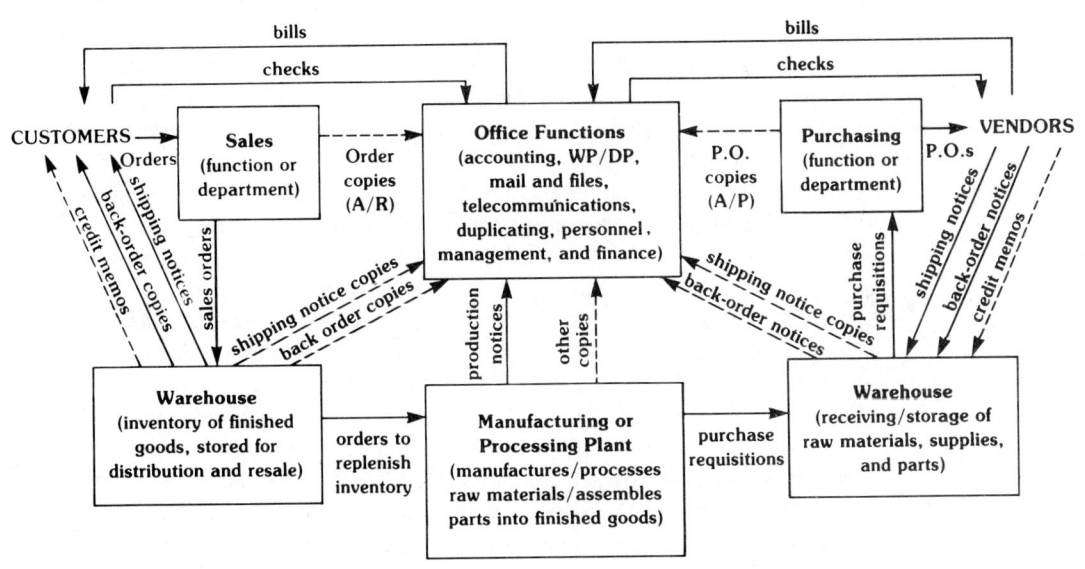

FIGURE 14.11 XYZ Flow of Information.

The vendors then prepare and transmit shipping orders (and transportation companies submit freight bills) to the company. The accounting clerk records to A/P and later writes checks in payment. From the customer orders, the office clerk records to A/R, while presenting the customers with invoices or statements (bills). The latter, in their turn, respond with checks in full or partial payment.

Where only a portion of a customer's order can be filled, the remainder must be back-ordered, a step that requires additional procedures. When the company receives partial orders from vendors, other steps are needed in the purchasing-receiving-paying subsystem(s). Some customers will overpay or underpay. Company personnel must then prepare a credit memo and adjust records in the general ledger, the customer's account, and on other documents.

Before customers are even allowed to purchase on credit, someone has to run a credit check and approve the practice. A subsystem is necessary for collecting on late or partial payments, and provisions must be made for uncollectible or bad debts.

For all of this data processing, the office staff receives form copies to activate their functions; namely, that require the staff to record, compute, communicate, transmit, store, or retrieve data. Whether small, medium, or large, every business has these functions to perform.

Business communications. Standardized business forms and reports are used because situations and procedures repeat themselves and because businesses need to keep records in order to keep track of what is happening, should happen, or fails to happen. People could simply place telephone calls or write notes, if hard-copy (paper) records were not needed for transmission and for retention. Even checks written out on scratch paper are legal tender, providing all needed data is included and a legitimate signature on an established bank account appears.

The need to retain (i.e., file) hard-copy data for legal and other purposes has generated formalized and accepted styles for memoranda and letters, together with the many standardized business forms common in most companies. Memos are used for internal communications, and letters for external contacts. Wherever data is used repeatedly, however, it is more practical to have as much information as possible already printed and standardized. This reduces both the time it takes to process data and the possibility of error. Hence printed forms.

Instead of communicating verbally or writing out information on scratch paper, or even in memos and letters, most businesses transmit data by means of forms, such as: purchase requisitions, purchase orders, invoices, statements, inventory forms (with or without preprinted stock numbers), shipping notices, back orders, sales orders, credit memoranda, production logs, scheduling reports, and checks. Internally they use employee performance rating forms, employee earnings records, personnel applications and related records, and insurance and tax forms. The need to systematically retain and readily access copies of forms and other documents requires a file system and equipment to process and store data.

Equipment to facilitate the office system includes typewriters, calculators, cash registers, file cabinets, desks, tables, and chairs, among other things.

SUMMARY

Keeping records is an important aspect of a business. Not to establish and maintain an effective system—one that reflects the nature of your business and works well for you—is foolhardy. Without such systems and procedures, you would find it difficult to determine when and to what extent your business is in trouble. You would have no idea, either, of when or why you are doing well.

You can establish and maintain your records system more effectively if you have some knowledge of what machines are available and how to manage both manual and mechanical operations. Recordkeeping and office functions accompany each phase of a company's operation, and their significance in the total management process cannot be ignored.

DISCUSSION QUESTIONS

1. Compare the cost of establishing an accounting or recordkeeping system with the benefits to be derived, including factors associated with both time and wage expense.

2. Describe the recordkeeping system and its purposes.
3. Explain the use of pertinent records and controls, from writing source documents through balancing the books.
4. How are various financial statements used in analyzing, forecasting, and making management decisions?
5. What are the advantages and disadvantages of having a cash budget?
6. How would one or more office functions be processed manually? How could the same functions be handled with machines?
7. What is meant by a "system"? By a "subsystem"? Trace the flow of goods through a small manufacturing plant; compare that with the flow of information.

ACTIVITIES AND EXERCISES

1. Choose from the following recommended personal contacts and be prepared to report your findings and experiences. Wherever possible, also collect literature and exhibits to share and keep in your files.
   a. Visit with entrepreneurs to ask about their recordkeeping methods and whether they use a single- or double-entry system. Do they prepare financial statements? If so, what kind, and what use do they make of them?
   b. Contact a certified public accountant (CPA) and ask what problems he or she typically encounters when dealing with owners of small businesses. What functions would be best handled by entrepreneurs themselves, and what services and assistance can the CPA best provide? Identify, if possible, typical fees for services of various types.
   c. Talk with agents in the Internal Revenue Service and/or your local tax office about the assistance, forms, and advice these personnel make available to owners of small businesses.
2. Prepare and submit a report on your findings from no. 1 (a.–c.) as an oral or written report or as a member of a panel.
3. From the following data, prepare a balance sheet as of December 31st: Cash on hand, $5,000; Accounts Receivable, $8,000; Inventory, $22,000; Equipment, $18,000; Accounts Payable, $3,500; Notes Payable, $1,500; Mortgage Payable, $29,250. Also determine the Owner's Equity. Apply the ratio formulas given in the chapter to analyze the financial health of this business.
4. From the following data, prepare a P&L statement as of December 31st: Sales, $95,000; Cost of Sales, $38,500; Wages, $15,330; Advertising, $3,500; Depreciation, $3,000; Insurance, $850; Utilities, $3,600; Rent, $4,800; Supplies, $4,500; Taxes, $5,300; and Other, $3,750. Determine the percentage of gross profit and net profit. Then calculate the percentage of wage and advertising expense items. What decisions would you make as a result of this analysis?

5. Revise the cash budget for your business plan.

   EXTRA PROJECT: If you are unfamiliar with accounting/bookkeeping procedures, you may want to practice, using samples of actual journals, ledgers, and source documents.[9]

   NOTE: Project 5 in the *Stanley Junction* case supplement deals with financial decisions. You will have opportunity to work with the P&L Statement and the advertising budget for one of two companies: service station and U-Haul rental, or a clothing store.

NOTES

1. Connie Kestella, "Accounting Systems: Seeing the Whole Picture," *Business Education World,* March–April 1982, pp. 3–4.
2. *AEA Business Manual* no. 71 (Los Angeles, CA: *Entrepreneur* Magazine, 1981), p. 56.
3. Larry H. Beard, Al L. Hartgraves, and Fred A. Jacobs, "Managing Inventories in a Small Business," *Business,* April–June 1983, pp. 45–49.
4. Bernard Kamoroff. *Small-Time Operator* (Laytonville, CA: Bell Springs Publishing, 1983) p. 40.
5. Ralph Heatherington, "Interpretation: the Forgotten Step of the Accounting Cycle," *Business Education World,* May–June 1981, pp. 25–26.
6. Fred A. Jacobs, Larry H. Beard, and Al L. Hartgraves, "Controlling Cash Flow in the Small Business," *Business,* January–March 1983, pp. 31–36.
7. Ibid.
8. Olive Church, "The Whole and Its Parts," *Office Practice Activities* (Portland, ME: J. Weston Walch, Publisher, 1978), p. 17.
9. See the working papers and illustrations for how to implement various recordkeeping tasks, available in such materials as Kamoroff's *Small-Time Operator* (includes all the ledgers and worksheets "the new entrepreneur will need for a year"); and David A. Weaver, David E. Gynn, and Virginia Rose. *Pro-Lawn Service Accounting Application* (New York: Gregg/McGraw-Hill Book Co., 1982).

(Courtesy of Victor Business Products)

chapter 15

Microcomputer Systems in the Small Business

Objectives

1. Demonstrate familiarity with terminology appropriate to using microcomputers in small business.

2. Describe business applications that can be performed by microcomputer and make comparisons with manual and mechanical means.

3. Explain some of the difficulties entrepreneurs often have in selecting hardware and software appropriate to the needs of their business.

4. Give examples of new entrepreneurial opportunities emerging as a result of technological and electronic innovations.

People from many market segments—businesspeople, at-home workers, educators, agriculturalists, and freelance writers, for instance—have accepted and are becoming familiar with microcomputers (otherwise known as "micros," "personal" or "desktop" computers). No one questions the legitimacy of computers anymore. Instead, people now ask: What is the best size and price for a microcomputer? Is there software available that can meet my specific needs? What hardware is compatible with that software? And, how can I learn what I need to know to use my microcomputer effectively?[1]

As the microcomputer industry has matured, new applications have been developed. Enhanced graphics and electronic mail, for example, can now assist financial planning and accounts receivable. Table 15.1 shows how people were using micros as of 1982.

Some industry experts have predicted that the price reductions for small business computers will end as vendors find they have to recover their production and marketing overhead. "The user's buying motivation changes from pure price on the lowest end to service, support, and software on the other." In fact, many specialists see software support as the growth area for the late 1980s.[2]

What Micros Are and What They Do

A small business computer typically consists of a microcomputer processor, a keyboard/display unit for data entry, a disk or diskette unit for file storage, and a

TABLE 15.1 Use of Microcomputer Applications in Business

FUNCTION	AVERAGE PERCENTAGE OF USE
Accounts receivable/billing	40%
Text-editing (word processing)	28
Mailing lists	23
Financial planning	18
Stock/investment analysis	9
Sales tracking	8
Payroll/personnel	7
Inventory	7
Data base	5
Graphics	5
Program development	4
Invoicing	4
General ledger	3
Scheduling/communications	2
Business records, other	2

Source: Lecture in Cheyenne, Wyoming, February 4, 1983; by Colorado State University Professor Ed Rademacher; Conference on "Microcomputers for Small Business Operations."

A COMPUTER

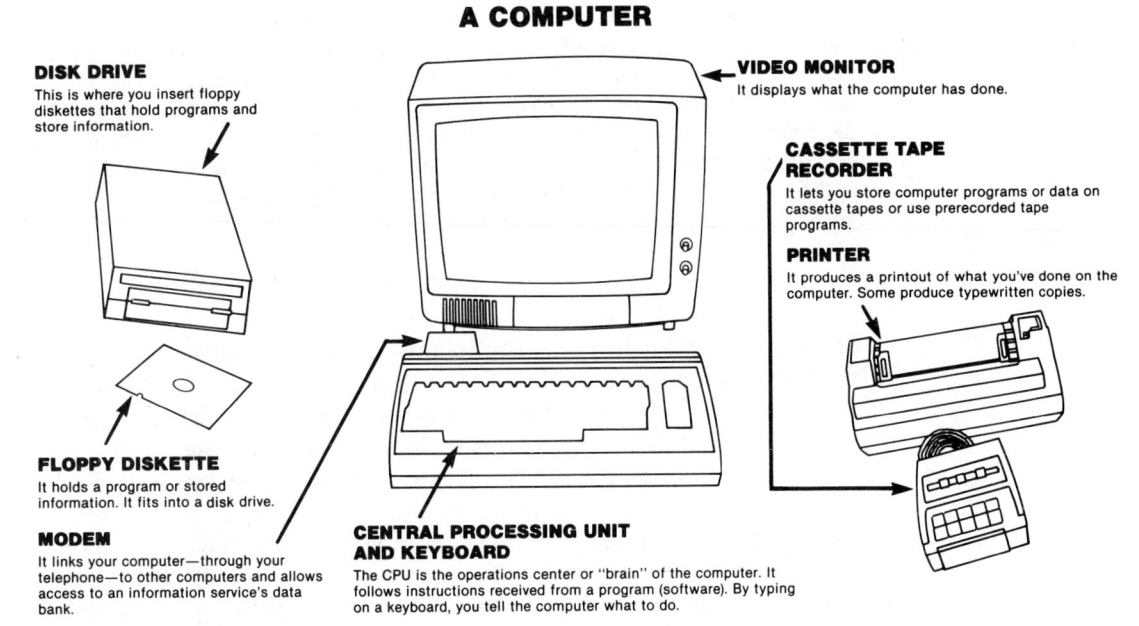

DISK DRIVE
This is where you insert floppy diskettes that hold programs and store information.

FLOPPY DISKETTE
It holds a program or stored information. It fits into a disk drive.

MODEM
It links your computer—through your telephone—to other computers and allows access to an information service's data bank.

VIDEO MONITOR
It displays what the computer has done.

CASSETTE TAPE RECORDER
It lets you store computer programs or data on cassette tapes or use prerecorded tape programs.

PRINTER
It produces a printout of what you've done on the computer. Some produce typewritten copies.

CENTRAL PROCESSING UNIT AND KEYBOARD
The CPU is the operations center or "brain" of the computer. It follows instructions received from a program (software). By typing on a keyboard, you tell the computer what to do.

FIGURE 15.1 Microcomponents and Descriptions.

serial printer for hard-copy (paper) output. Another common component is the modem, which uses telephone lines to link one computer system with others. Micros are programmable in BASIC or other computer languages, have a minimum of 4k of memory (RAM), and can cost from under $1000 to $5000 or more (see Figure 15.1). (For technical terms such as "RAM," see the glossary at the end of this chapter.)

Small business computers are designed primarily to process the business data of small companies. In addition to processing routine transactions, a computer can produce analyses that help managers decide how to improve customer service, reduce inventory, tighten cost control, and increase production. Appropriate software programs can summarize data and forecast anticipated results, based on a number of variables. Here is how one businesswoman uses a computer for her small operation:

> Maria Fernandez sells fruit and cream pies out of her kitchen. Her customers are mostly restaurants, which buy dozens of pies each week. Ms. Fernandez wants to forecast sales under several situations for the next few months.
>
> To begin, she enters some basic data about her pie-making business, such as a one-month income statement. In a typical month she sells 650 pies at an average price of $5 per pie. Next, she specifies on the computer the costs of doing business: buying flour, sugar, fruit, butter, etc.; utilities; employee wages; delivery costs; and the ads she places in several trade journals. The bottom line is her net profit of $1.90 per pie, or $1235 per month.

But in business, little is certain; prices fluctuate and business gets better or worse. What if a bad fruit harvest raises the price of Ms. Fernandez's raw materials by 60 percent? What if the number of pies she sells doubled, but her staff simultaneously demanded raises? What if advertising rates increased and the bottom dropped out of the pastry market? To answer such "what if?" questions, Ms. Fernandez merely changes the appropriate piece of data (or "variable")—the price of fruit, for instance, or the number of pies sold. In seconds, the software program she has chosen refigures all the costs and computes a new profit prediction.

Electronic spreadsheets. The software programs marketed in the early 1980s under the trade names of VisiCalc, SuperCalc, T-Maker II, and TARGET allow business owners to make fast and accurate decisions. VisiCalc is essentially an electronic "spreadsheet"—a financial analysis program designed for nontechnical users. It enables businesspeople to do in seconds what used to take hours or days. Ms. Fernandez's analysis of her pie business is one example.[3]

For instance, these spreadsheet programs provide a visible matrix of rows and columns on the computer screen that the user can fill in with labels, numbers, and computational directions like "sum this column." Not only are individual entries easily changed, but all computations throughout the sheet, like subtotals and totals, are instantly recalculated whenever a change is made.[4]

It used to take three people three days to close the books of one medium-sized company at the end of the fiscal year. Now it takes them six hours. Furthermore, the business owner can ask for, and get, many other reports that analyze and project the health of the company. The beauty of these canned programs is that they can work with dozens of variables and hundreds of assumptions. The output: a 10-year income and cash-flow statement for a proposed factory; a three-year profit-and-loss statement for a retail store selling hundreds of items; a cost-efficiency study of a 10-member law or medical firm. (See Figure 15.2.)

Word processing. Many microcomputers offer software packages for word processing (WP). "Text editors" are microprocessors dedicated exclusively to word processing. They are designed primarily to produce typewritten material for business correspondence and reports.

WP programs offer text editing, spelling verification, and the ability to move whole paragraphs and pages from one place to another. One of the biggest expenses involved in adding WP capabilities to a microcomputer is the cost of the printer. A good printer, one that produces typewriter-quality copy, is relatively expensive. Moreover, the price difference between a manually fed, "slow" printer (about 180 words per minute) and one that feeds paper automatically and prints faster (over 500 wpm) can run into the thousands. Where a great deal of quality typing is required, however, the automatic fast-speed printer can save the operator time and trouble, and so contributes to the efficiency of the system.[5]

Another option has been made available. Many electronic typewriters can now be interfaced with micros and word processors to provide quality typewritten output. With this purchasing decision, you will still have a typewriter for doing small jobs (e.g., typing envelopes, cards, labels, etc.). You'll have to manually feed the electronic typewriter, though, and you should not expect it to handle heavy work such as printing 10,000 original advertising letters every month.

Electronic mail is the name given to paperless messages that are transmitted electronically from one place to another over telephone lines. The sender can input memos, letters, reports, and simple messages at his or her station. The "mail" will wait at the receiving end until an operator is at hand to accept the message. Like an answering machine, the receiving computer stores communications and other documents until retrieved. When both sending and receiving operators are present, they can interact and "talk" to each other. Printers can be used to provide hard copy if desired.

Percent of EDP by Functions

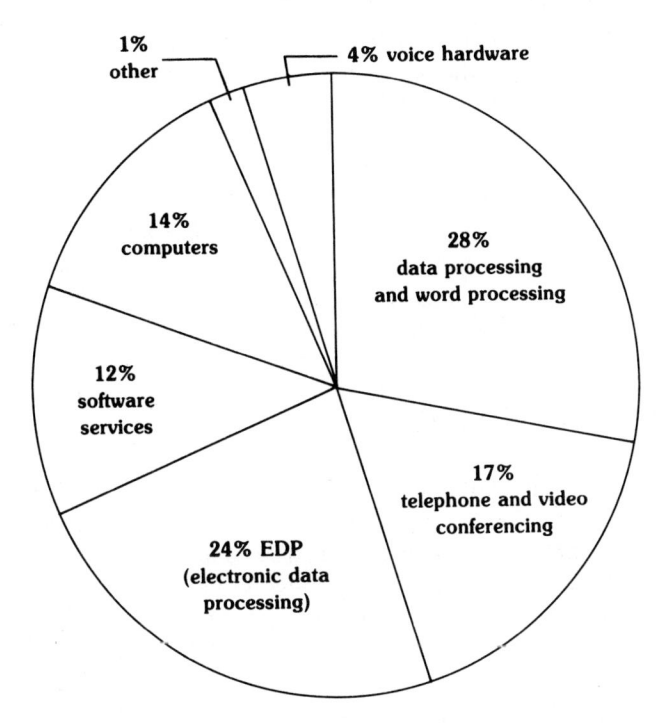

- 1% other
- 4% voice hardware
- 14% computers
- 28% data processing and word processing
- 12% software services
- 17% telephone and video conferencing
- 24% EDP (electronic data processing)

FIGURE 15.2
Application Allocations of EDP.

An estimated $1050 billion will have been spent between 1982 and 1986.

Source: A lecture presented to a conference on "Microcomputers for Small Business Operations," Cheyenne, Wyoming. Ed Radamacher, Colorado State University Professor of Computer Science.

Facsimile is the method whereby photocopiers are linked, also by modems and telephone lines, to transmit and receive hard copies. Unlike electronic mail, facsimile simply transmits pieces of hard data from one place to another.

Unnecessary applications. Commercials describe how some owners have put their daily appointment books or telephone listings on computer. This is "advertising overkill." A computer should only be used for things that it can do better, faster, and more accurately than you can.[6]

MAKING DECISIONS

Entrepreneurs who are interested in the technology must start somewhere in conducting feasibility studies and analyses. A microcomputer on one's desk is a constant invitation to experiment and to develop better ways of doing things. Indeed, micros offer several advantages over outside time-share computer service companies; they can provide fast application development, personal control, and quick turnaround time. They are easier to access, simpler to work with, and they usually are less expensive to purchase and to use.[7]

Ironically, the last thing you should look at when searching for a computer is—the computer! First, you need to know what your business does, what functions it uses, and how these are performed. The planning process must include defining detailed output and processing specifications. You must also know who will be using the equipment—yourself, your partner(s), and/or employees.[8]

A danger of microcomputer acquisition is that some owners may have unrealistic expectations about computers. It is easy to overlook the hidden-dollar cost of buying software and the substantial time costs involved in learning to use the machine and developing useful applications. Without a commitment to the necessary personal time investment, the hardware investment may sit idle on your desk.[9]

Your feasibility study then must consider your business needs, the users' needs, and how these can be met using existing software programs. With the many packaged programs now available on the market, we use the analogy of searching for the "right" book in a library full of hundreds of thousands of volumes housed there. You have to know what you want in order to identify it when you see it. After you make these decisions you can then zero in on the appropriate hardware. For the average business, though, it simply doesn't matter a great deal which computer is purchased, based on technical specifications. You simply want to buy hardware on which your chosen software will operate. Beyond that, other considerations are those of preference, price, and service.

Software and Hardware

Small business computer systems often fail because the owners moved in the wrong direction: they bought the hardware before the software. To ensure a successful system, you should identify the software that meets your business needs. Ask yourself:

1. How willing and able are the potential users to be trained as computer operators? ("Users" includes yourself as the business owner as well as any partners or employees who would be using the equipment and programs.)
2. What sort of records system should my type of business have? And, what accounting, finance, and office functions should the system perform? Do I want it to handle financial analysis, inventory control, payroll, billing?

If you are unsure, ask your accountant for help. If yours is a manufacturing company you may want computer-assisted design (CAD) or computer-assisted manufacturing (CAM) functions; if you're going to offer educational or counseling services, perhaps you'll want computer-aided instruction (CAI). The list of computer capabilities seems inexhaustible. But the point remains: know your business system before buying.

Once you have answered these questions, you can select the software to meet your exact needs. With literally hundreds of thousands of programs from which to choose, you may find no more than a few hundred that do what you want in the way you want it.

If a particular vendor doesn't sell a program which meets your needs, some other vendor will. How should you choose among competing claims? For one thing, you should choose a viable, ongoing concern that you think will still be in business a few years from now when you want to upgrade or integrate old software with newer offerings. Probably even more so than in hardware, "a penny saved on a computer program may cost you a dollar somewhere down the road."[10]

Once you have taken the above steps, you can select the hardware upon which the software works. Thus business needs and the user are more important than the equipment, and the software must suit the users as well as the company's systems. If you or your employees are unfamiliar with computers and high technology, you or they may resist changing from a manual or mechanized system to a computer system. In fact, your staff may be afraid of being displaced or even of appearing inadequate.

Four prime factors often determine the choice of microcomputer: (1) company reputation, (2) the availability of compatible software, (3) cost, and (4) distributor support. About 26 percent of the 860 business users interviewed by the Eastern Management Group in 1982 identified software availability as *the* primary criterion for selecting one microcomputer over another. Company name ranked second (25 percent); cost third (22 percent), and distributor support last (about 10 percent), with the remainder unsure.[11]

Unfortunately, too many business owners think they lack the time to become familiar with this vital technology. "I've seen too many company owners march through here hoping to make a final decision in less than an hour," says the sales manager of a computer store in downtown Detroit. "In almost every case, they end up either paying too much for the right equipment, or too little for the wrong equipment."[12]

Most experts recommend that before you buy you should form a clear picture of what you expect your computer to do for you. Consider, for example, your need for expandability. Will you want to add on components to your computer system? Do you want a system whose hardware and software can both be upgraded?[13]

You also want a manual you can use without too much difficulty. Instruction manuals are becoming increasingly easy to follow, just as software programs are using more simple English phrases. BASIC, the fundamental computer language, requires little data-processing knowledge to begin with.

Neophyte entrepreneurs and those new to computers should invest some time in exploring what is available to meet business needs. (See Figure 15.3.) To develop the computer literacy you need in order to make a sound buying decision, you can:

1. Read the literature, including both articles and advertisements.
2. See hardware and software in use by visiting computer stores, attending trade shows, or inviting vendors to your business.
3. Visit companies similar to yours and ask specific questions about the computers they use and how satisfied these owners are about the chosen system's performance.
4. Join or organize a group of people like yourself so that you can explore and learn together.

MINICASE

One businessman who set about systematically to buy a computer and gain computer literacy is Henry Lee, chief executive officer (CEO) of Lee Pharmaceuticals. He repeatedly visited six different computer stores and saw demonstrations of numerous software packages. He also read many articles and joined a microcomputer club. Once he bought his first microprocessor, he brought it home. He trained himself to operate it by using the instruction manual, frequently calling the store or the manufacturer for further guidance.

Mr. Lee also learned to use his micro as a word processor. Under the old system Lee would handwrite his documents—letters and reports as long as 15 pages and full of technical detail—have his secretary type a draft, correct the draft, and have the final version retyped. "Sometimes it took a week to get a long letter off." His word-processing (WP) program changed all that. "I could usually sit down first thing in the morning and have it done by noon, and it was a finished product!"

Next Mr. Lee bought several micros for the company and persuaded his staff to use them for word processing. He provided moral support by describing how many reporters and writers do all their own work on word processors. Now the technical writers freely exchange work, transferring a paragraph or a page from one person's disk to another's.

FIGURE 15.3
Checklist for Evaluating Hardware and Software.

1. Is the vendor a: manufacturer_____, distributor_____, or an original equipment dealer_____?
2. How long has the vendor been in the computer business? _____years.
3. Has the number of units sold increased over the past few years? Yes_____ No_____
4. How many distributorships does this micro have (approximately)? _____
5. What does the vendor provide? equipment_____ installation_____ training_____ service_____ repairs_____ support/advice_____
6. Does the vendor itemize the prices for hardware components, software packages, supplies, services, training costs, etc.? Yes_____ No_____
7. How much memory is available in the CPU? minimum K_____ maximum K_____
8. How many additional CRT stations can be added to the same system? _____
9. What are the additional costs, per station? $_____
10. If several additional stations operate simultaneously, can each process a different job? Yes_____ No_____
11. Can these stations be housed in different rooms? Yes_____ No_____
12. What is the maximum disk capability—i.e., how many characters can be stored? _____
13. What types of storage does the vendor offer for this micro?
14. How long does it take to copy (back up) one disk to another? _____min.
15. What types of printers are available? What is the cost and capability of each?

Type	Cost	Capability
	$	

16. Will the vendor maintain the operating system? Yes_____ No_____
17. Are software packages available for this micro? Yes_____ No_____. If yes, how many? _____. Of what variety/application, at what cost?

Software	Applications	Cost
		$

18. Will the vendor demonstrate live, installable software programs prior to purchase? Yes_____ No_____
19. Does the vendor document the software programs to assure your ability to understand and use them? Yes_____ No_____
20. Who takes responsibility for installation and at what cost? _____
21. Is service available locally? Yes_____ No_____. If No, how far will servicepeople have to travel? Miles_____
22. What is the average service response time (in hours or days)? _____

Gradually, Mr. Lee's staff also integrated the personal computers into such critical business functions as budgeting, market analysis, and planning. The new technology helped upgrade the quality of data and permitted more informed and timelier decisions. Mr. Lee and his managers also use software programs to handle taxes, complex financial calculations, personal scheduling, project planning, and personnel management.[14]

Many small businesses use microcomputers. (*Courtesy of IBM*)

Dealing with Vendors

Never buy a software package without insisting that the vendor demonstrate how the program runs through the computer and how it looks on the display terminal. Also be sure to use the software yourself and personally test each machine you evaluate. Vendors can make the operations look easy when in fact they may not be all that user-friendly.

Don't buy either hardware or software from companies with little or no reputation. You will need support for your system. Only established companies can provide a full range of support services, including quality installations, instructional assistance (both printed manuals and individual guidance over the telephone or in person), timely repair, service contracts, new programs, and updating.

Ask the vendor for a list of the small businesses that have bought its computers and software programs. If its products and support services are living up to claims, the vendor should not hesitate.

Note that "peripherals" are computer "accessories," such as printers. One type of printer can produce copies that look typewritten, while another does graphics. To link your computer to an information service by telephone, you will need a modem. Some peripherals need a special hookup to the computer. You may also need a system expansion unit. Ask the vendor about installation fees and any cables that may be needed to connect an accessory to the computer.

Four types of vendors. Small business computers are marketed by four distinct types of vendors. The most visible group consists of the old-line mainframe manufacturers such as Burroughs, IBM, and Sperry Rand. All of these companies offer broad product lines and worldwide marketing and support organizations.

The second vendor group consists of such established minicomputer makers as Digital Equipment Corp., Hewlett-Packard, Microdata, and Wang Labs. These companies typically offer a small business package consisting of a minicomputer and the associated peripherals, often accompanied by an operating system, compilers, and applications software.

Turnkey firms make up the third group of suppliers. These companies generally buy minicomputers and peripheral devices from manufacturers, package the configurations, develop software for specific business applications, and market the whole system to end users. The prime appeal of a full turnkey system is that the necessary software is provided by the vendor.

The fourth group consists of the microcomputer companies (such as Apple, Commodore, and Radio Shack). These companies initially designed their low-priced systems for home use. Now such products provide the level of performance, reliability, and software support demanded by business applications.

A significant development in small-computer marketing is the advent of computer stores, which allow prospective buyers to see and evaluate the available equipment before buying. Computer stores significantly reduce the overhead costs vendors incur in selling and supporting small business computers. As a prospective buyer you can either visit these stores or request a vendor to send a sales representative to your office. (See Table 15.2.)

Compatibility. Be sure that your computer can function successfully in your work environment. Computers of any kind cannot operate reliably under very hot and humid conditions. Also, programs may be affected by microwave ovens or by electric sparks or electric "noise," such as from generators. Ask vendors about any environmental specifications.

For the benefit of users, you will want to select chairs, tables, and desks that fit the human anatomy, particularly where anyone will be sitting in front of a

TABLE 15.2 Microcomputer Sales in Units

YEAR	$100–$800	UNDER $1000	AVERAGE $3000	AVERAGE $10,000
1982	315,000	2,250,000	820,000	160,000
1985*	1,440,000	9,300,000	2,235,000	480,000

* Estimated.

Source: Future Computing, Inc., *Kansas City Star*, February 27, 1983.

A forecast made by Dataquest is that by 1990, 25 percent of all American homes and 60 percent of all American businesses will own at least one of these small computers.

terminal for long hours at a time. You will also need storage facilities for filing software programs and computer supplies. All the following factors should be compatible:

1. The system with the people using it,
2. The equipment and furniture with the users,
3. Hardware and software with the environment in which they are used,
4. Each software package with every other software package that must be interactive, such as:
   a. perpetual inventory and purchasing systems,
   b. sales with general ledger,
   c. word processing with microforms (see the Glossary).

Users' Complaints

During the 1970s, computers were often ridiculed because the hardware was unreliable and the software faulty and inadequate. The mid-1980s, however, have brought some different complaints.

The reliability problems have been brought under control by improved technology and the availability of service contracts and troubleshooting hot lines. Users continue to complain, however, that software programs are not intelligible to the average person. Obsolete programs also need updating. Alert companies that seek to maintain their competitive position continually simplify and upgrade their existing programs while trying to create new ones at ever-lower cost.

Users will keep making some mistakes—forgetting to "end" a document or to remove the diskette before turning off the computer, for instance. In these cases one cannot fault the industry, except for not emphasizing these points in their training programs.

Other problems are associated with how the system is used in relation to the business's needs. Whether manual, mechanized, or computerized, a business system always must be current to serve needed business functions, and this includes the business's subsystems which are performed on computer.

Business Opportunities in the Computer Field

Programming. By 1983 there were more than 500 vendors of microcomputers in the U.S. market. About 500,000 people were also employed as programmers to write the incredibly detailed instructions that put a computer through the mathematical or technical acrobatics of a videogame or a tax accounting program. The fast-growing market for software has generated a multibillion-dollar business. There are hundreds of thousands of computer programs on the market. Software lists are updated weekly in a variety of computer trade magazines.

One of the most popular programs is VisiCalc, the "financial spreadsheet" used by Ms. Fernandez in the example described earlier. This flexible program permits entrepreneurs to work out a series of "what if" scenarios to test solutions for potential business problems. With over a hundred thousand copies sold in its first five years, VisiCalc has generated tens of millions of dollars' worth of business.

"Being a software programmer is like being an unknown rock 'n' roll singer or a writer starting out," says Jim Dishman, a young computer programmer in St. Petersburg, Florida. "What you need is to create that one big hit, that best-seller, and you've got it made for the rest of your life."[15]

However, such dreams may not be realistic. Fads come and go. For instance, a 13-year-old youngster who wrote a program to solve the Rubic Cube puzzle had phenomenal sales for one year, but when the Rubic Cube fad passed, so did interest in his computer program.

The software industry also needs people to market the programs. It demands new kinds of desks and tables to hold the equipment. Also needed are cases to carry portable models, cleaning agents to keep the equipment clean, and hosts of skilled programmers to keep it working.

Publishing. An estimated 150 special-interest, technology-related publications appeared on the market between 1981 and 1983 alone. The fastest-growing and most lucrative of these magazines concentrate on the computer industry and in particular on the booming personal-computer market, which alone grossed approximately $6 billion in 1982. Revenues for the 53 computer-related newspapers and magazines were $252 million that same year.[16]

> One successful publisher in the computer industry is CW Communications, Inc., of Framingham, Massachusetts, which publishes the weekly tabloid *Computerworld*, two other national biweeklies and 16 foreign computer publications. Revenues climbed from $11 million in 1977 to $60 million in 1982.
>
> In August, 1976, New Hampshire publisher Wayne Green set up a $30 canvas sign at an Atlantic City computer technology convention, hoping to attract subscribers for his fledgling magazine, *Microcomputer*. About a thousand computer buffs signed on, and the one-time radio announcer/psychologist had launched a new business.
>
> By the mid-1980s, he had seven monthly magazines, a 25-book annual output, plus a software division that had produced over 1000 different packages. 1982 revenues had climbed to $30 million, double that of 1981.
>
> "I tell people it's easy to make a lot of money," Green says. "The key to success is finding a niche. And from my viewpoint there is almost an infinite number of niches opening up in the microcomputing industry."[17]

Farm and ranch operations. An estimated 20 percent (about a half million) of the nation's farmers regularly bundle reams of their personal production history off to management firms and then wait for the computer-calculated plans that will help them decide what's most profitable for them to grow. By

1983 another 6 or 7 percent of farmers and ranchers were using microcomputers directly to keep records but also to get current information. Most microcomputers, for instance, are wired so that they can use a modem device to tap into bigger central computers filled with market prices and news. Many land-grant colleges offer market information services for individual users, with perhaps 1000 or so regional and crop packages available.

Seven northern states, for example, are connected by the Agriculture Network (AGNET). The terminals, located in all county extension agencies and in the homes of some farmers and ranchers, are linked to central computers at the University of Nebraska. The system includes several dozen prepackaged software programs that address the economics of farm/ranch management (feed mixes, crop production projects, etc.). AGNET also contains several consumer-oriented programs, from nutrition and weight-loss diets to budgeting, income tax preparation, and financial management. A databank offers up-to-date local agricultural information. Using AGNET requires minimal computer knowledge; one only needs the ability to keyboard (type) and to choose from a menu (a list of the program's functions).[18]

Some agriculturalists even hook their computers to switches that run the machinery for tending livestock or moving grain. Farmers print out cash-flow and balance sheets and keep records on equipment, finances, and so on. Because they can juggle variables—from the morning's quote on soybeans to the cost of diesel fuel—they can get fast answers to such questions as: Should I hold a crop off the market? How would two weeks of drought affect prices? What should I plant and when?

Computer and WP services. Small businesses that cannot afford to hire employees, and owners who don't want to bother using new systems and learning or upgrading their own skills continue to use outside service companies. Thus the computer and WP service businesses continue to offer opportunities for entrepreneurs who do have these skills to get into business.

The at-home worker. Whether you are considering a computer or WP service or are a free-lance writer or researcher, you may decide to locate your business at home. With a telephone modem, your home office can be linked to offices elsewhere and with numerous data banks and other information services.

Your home might also be organized so you can use facsimile (you need a copier with a modem) or electronic mail. You might have opened a business elsewhere but because of emergencies or new situations occurring at home (such as a new baby's arrival), you prefer to work part time at home. The above-mentioned telecommunication devices will make it possible for you to centralize your company's operation.

Self-employed freelance writers and researchers make extensive use of dedicated word processors (text editors) and of microcomputers with WP software packages. Journalists also use the technology, as do entrepreneurs in publishing and mass communications. The text-editing capabilities are an advantage, as is the ability to access numerous commercial, public, and government databanks.

Free-lance people and others who work at home can be equipped with electronic work stations—like this woman, who can care for her own child while operating the Telestaff home satellite transcription system used in conjunction with the Lanier EZ-1 work processor (*Courtesy of Lanier Business Products, Inc.*)

Differences between Accounting and Data Processing Terminology

The terminology used in accounting and recordkeeping does not always match that used in data processing (DP). For instance, in accounting one "records in a journal and posts to the ledger." DP often calls journals "transaction registers" and ledgers "listings," and permits an operator to record directly to the ledger.

Entrepreneurs who are new to both accounting and DP may find an instructional software package useful. Although professional software may say "transaction registers" and "listings," a good instructional software package should follow the traditional accounting cycle, furnish an audit trail, and operate on a double-entry basis. In fact, users should still be able to define a chart of accounts, record in the journal, and post to the ledger, although by electronic means. A good instructional program will help you, step by step, to adapt yourself to automated methods of accounting.[19]

SUMMARY

Many business people today are deciding to computerize their operations, particularly the office and business functions, because of two major factors:

1. Improved technology, with associated price reductions, is making it possible for owners of small businesses and consumers alike to have their own microcomputers.
2. Because of the escalating costs of operating a business and the risk of employee errors, it usually costs more to hire workers than to buy a computer system, particularly over the long run.

There is a great deal to learn if you desire to become computer literate. Without adequate preparation, exploration, and analyses, both experienced and neophyte entrepreneurs can make costly mistakes. If you have never been exposed to computers, it's still not too late to begin.

GLOSSARY OF DATA PROCESSING AND MICROCOMPUTER TERMS

Abbreviations

BASIC	Beginners' All-purpose Symbolic Instruction Code
CAD	Computer-Assisted Design
CAI	Computer-Aided Instruction
CAM	Computer-Assisted Manufacturing
COBOL	Common Business-Oriented Language
CP/M	Controlled Program/Monitor
CPU	Central Processing Unit
DP	Data Processing
EDP	Electronic Data Processing
EMail	Electronic Mail
IC	Integrated Circuits
MIS	Management Information System
RAM	Random-Access Memory
UNIX	An operating system
WP	Word Processing

Words and Phrases

Binary	Two-digit number system "understood" by computers.
Databanks	Information systems that can be accessed via computer networks.
Facsimile	Hard-copy transmission over telephone lines.
Hard copy	Paper.

Hardware	The physical computer and its related equipment and peripherals.
Microform	Hard copy photographed, reduced, and stored on film. One needs a microfilm or microfiche reader to read the material in this form and/or reproduction equipment to return it to hard copy.
Micropad	A paper pad used to enter data into the computer; what you write or print goes directly into the computer.
Operating system	The operating system should include all files, and the system has text-editing (WP) and utility (a back-up system and the capability to duplicate). Examples are CP/M and UNIX.
Software	Preprogrammed packages carrying detailed instructions that tell the computer how to perform some specific application.
User-friendly	Fast and easy to learn, remember, and operate.
Text editing	The electronic editing and rearrangement of copy in word processing.

Automated Office Systems

Conferencing	Telecommunications systems, ranging from basic telephone service to video conferencing, that facilitate human interaction.
Information transfer	Electronic message systems, whether message is transmitted by keyboarded characters, facsimile images, or voice.
Information retrieval	Computer-assisted recall of information stored as data, text, graphics, or audio or video input.
Personal processing	Interactive computer-assisted writing, editing, calculating, and drawing, including word processing, personal computing, and interactive graphics.
Activity management	Systems such as electronic tickler files and automated task-project management that track, screen, or expedite schedules, tasks, and information.[20]

DISCUSSION QUESTIONS

1. Discuss and share your knowledge of computer business applications. Base the discussion on your work experience, personal knowledge, courses, readings, etc.
2. How do you think the exposure that children today are having to computers will affect the business and consumer world? Give and discuss examples. Compare your own background to that of your parents and of other preceding generations.
3. What relationship is there between choosing hardware and software, and what are the potential dangers in making selections? How can you learn to avoid pitfalls, other than by costly trial and error?

4. Why is it important to evaluate the reputation, training, software, and service(s) of computer manufacturers?
5. Give examples of some entrepreneurial opportunities the computer industry has created.
6. Describe how microcomputers are being used in small businesses, on farms and ranches, and by at-home workers, freelance writers and others. What other uses of computers in business have you encountered?
7. Once upon a time each office function was clear-cut, each separated from every other by the specific procedures and equipment it used. For example, telephones were used for voice transmission; typewriters for producing paper documents; computers for calculating, summarizing, designing experiments, and analyzing; and duplicating equipment for reproducing paper copies. Now, with the merging of information systems (including telecommunications, facsimile, electronic mail, and word and data processing), many office functions are interdependent. From your own experience and readings, discuss recent innovations in office technology and describe how various equipment and systems work. Make applications to small businesses in various classifications.

ACTIVITIES AND EXERCISES

1. Arrange to visit one or more companies. Interview the owner and ask to observe operations. If microcomputers or other sophisticated office technology are in use, ask why and how decisions to purchase were made. Otherwise, discuss the potential benefits of such equipment and what would motivate the owner to purchase it.
2. Read and compare advertisements for office technology in a series of office and business journals. Discover what you can learn from advertisements and discuss your conclusions.
3. Visit a computer store or a vendors' trade show. Ask for demonstrations. Also ask about various companies' reputation for training and service. Using T-Charts (Appendix B), compare several microcomputers.
4. Find a directory that lists software programs—if possible, those that best suit the business you would like to open. On the basis of your current knowledge, evaluate several of the programs listed.
5. Locate one or more software packages and evaluate how well they provide the business applications they are designed for.
6. *Reporting:* If you have access to a word processor (WP) or a microcomputer with a WP program, write a report on any of the activities recommended above. Use word-processing procedures to write, edit, rearrange, revise, check spelling, and print a final copy. Report your experience to your group orally or in writing.
7. Select a sole proprietorship or partnership from the *Stanley Junction* case supplement that you believe could benefit from installing a microcomputer. Compose and submit a letter directed to the entrepreneur of this company

that explains why the firm might benefit. Be specific, describing company functions as they are now performed and the improvements and savings a computer could realize. Assume you have been hired by the company as a management consultant.

NOTES

1. Helena Smejda, "Small Business Systems: State of the Art," *Small Systems World*, January 1983, pp. 24–36.
2. Joel Makower, "Computers: The Executive Generation," *United*, June 1982, pp. 91–108.
3. *Chicago Tribune*, "Business," February 28, 1983, sect. 4, p. 6.
4. Robert E. Good, Robert R. Harmon, and Kenneth M. Jenkins, "Managing with Microcomputers," *Business*, January–March 1983, pp. 37–43.
5. This book (my fourteenth to be published), for instance, was written entirely on a dedicated word processor with an automatic-feed, fast-speed printer. Each chapter must have had nearly a hundred revisions. Each additional interview, piece of data, or updated statistic could be appropriately inserted—right up to the point of submission (both the hard-copy manuscript and the magnetic disks go to the publisher). While the printer turns out each new draft of finished copy without operator attention, I can continue composing and editing. The magnetic disks go from the publisher to the photocompositor who inserts them in another computer without recourse to additional keyboarding.
6. John M. Garris and E. Earl Burch, "Small Business and Computer Panic," *Journal of Small Business Management*, July 1983, pp. 19–24.
7. Good, "Managing with Micros."
8. Gerald M. Ward and Mark D. Lutchen, "Before the Micro Arrives, Plan for It," *Data Management*, August 1983, pp. 12–15.
9. Good, "Managing with Micros."
10. Garris, "Computer Panic."
11. Gregory S. Blunbell, "Microcomputer Market Soars on All Fronts," *Data Communications*, December 1982, p. 90.
12. Makower, "Computers."
13. Mark Stevens, "What to Look for in a Small Computer," *National Business Employment Weekly* (a publication of *The Wall Street Journal*), February 13, 1983, p. 17.
14. Bruce G. Posner, "Learning to Live with Micros," *Inc.*, July 1982, pp. 33–36.
15. Patricia Bellew, "Yearning for That One Smash Hit," *Kansas City Star*, February 27, 1983, p. 10G.
16. Arthur Howe, "Publishers Cash In on the Demand for Computer Know-How," *Kansas City Star*, February 27, 1983, p. 11G.
17. Ibid.
18. Roy W. Poe, Herbert G. Hicks, and Olive D. Church, "How Computers Serve Consumers," *Getting Involved with Business* (New York: McGraw-Hill, 1981), pp. 525–26.
19. Diane Kaylor, "Conversations with Steve Hamilton," *Business Education World*, January–February, 1983, p. 9.
20. Harvey L. Poppel, "Who Needs the Office of the Future?" *Harvard Business Review*, November–December 1982, p. 147.

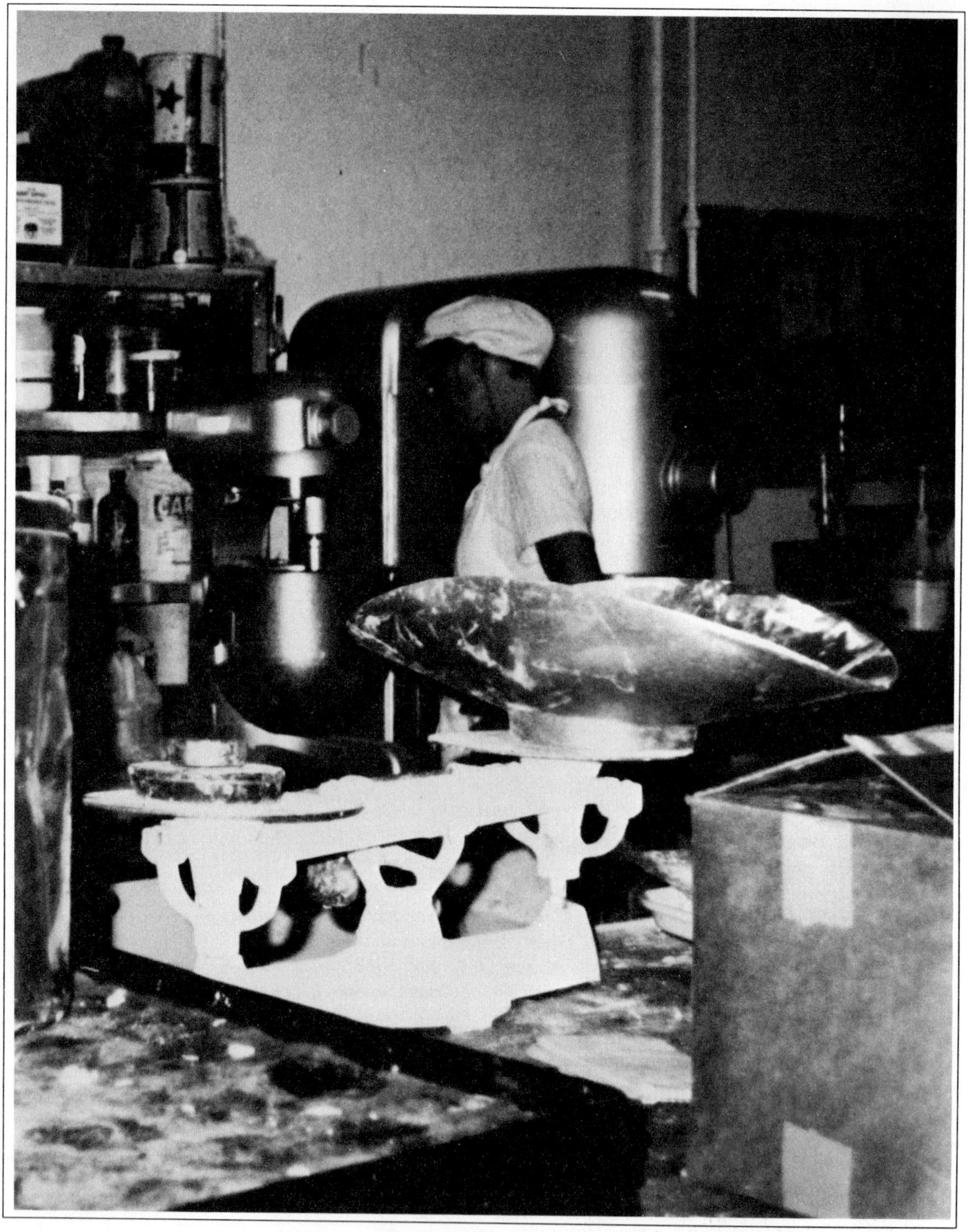

chapter 16

Purchasing and Promotion

Objectives

1. Describe channels of distribution for different types of goods or services, from the point of production and purchasing to consumption.

2. Give a rationale for making several purchasing decisions and give examples.

3. Illustrate methods of inventory control appropriate to one or more specific businesses.

4. Explain the interrelationship of developing an initial promotion program with that of conducting a marketing study and establishing pricing policies.

Before opening your doors for business you have at least two final tasks to complete. You must purchase stock or raw materials plus any supplies you will need for the next few weeks. And you must promote your business to your target customers. (See Figure 16.1.)

If you plan to hire employees, of course, you will also need to implement management techniques for their effective orientation and supervision (this topic is discussed in Chapter 19).

PURCHASING

Channels of Distribution

Both business people and consumers pay less for products bought directly from producers or extractors. When you buy milk and eggs from a local farmer, for instance, the channel of distribution is direct. Some people even buy wood and coal direct from woodcutters and coal mine sites, when they are conveniently located near such sources. In buying direct from extractors or producers you avoid the price markup that comes with transportation, packaging, warehousing, packing, wholesaling, and retailing of the product.

Depending on the type of business you have selected, you may find yourself anywhere along this distribution path as producer, broker, wholesaler, or retailer. You'll observe that if your business is a local bakery you will not only be a producer of sorts but you will also sell direct to consumers.

FIGURE 16.1
Grand Opening!

GRAND OPENING!
MONDAY

The closest you'll come to an authentic New York Deli is finally here! The Gateway Delicatessen and Restaurant will be open to serve you January 17. Enjoy Corned Beef, Whitefish, Tongue, Pastrami, and many more "Deli"cacies. We specialize in All Occasion Platters for your parties too! Give us a try!

OPEN FOR BREAKFAST, LUNCH AND DINNER
Monday-Friday 7am to 7pm
Saturday and Sunday 10am to 6pm

Your position along the channel of distribution will influence some of your purchasing decisions. As a retail or service entrepreneur, will you buy direct from manufacturers, from an agent or broker, or from wholesalers?

If the products you choose to offer are national brands, the manufacturers' national advertisements will support your start-up promotional activities. However, you cannot expect to receive direct assistance from the manufacturers in advertising your own specific enterprise simply because you plan to purchase and sell their products. (See Figure 16.2.)

The Relationship between Inventory and Sales

In order to "sell right," you must "buy right!" This involves choosing the suppliers that can provide both the best prices and the best services for your business and locale.

Some entrepreneurs offer the formula: quality plus quantity plus price equals success. That is, to maximize your profits, you have to order in quantities that allow the most efficient or cost-effective balance between the cost of possession (maintaining inventory) and the cost of acquisition (purchasing).

Inventory, to many owners of small firms, is one of the more visible and tangible requirements of doing business. "Inventory" literally refers to products offered for sale. (The materials needed to operate are called "supplies.") The inventory represents a large portion of the business investment. An overstocked inventory can tie up valuable funds: merchandise only contributes to profits when it is sold.

Raw materials, goods in process, and finished goods are all forms of inventory encountered in manufacturing organizations.

FIGURE 16.2
If you handle name-brand products, you can use such names in your own advertising to build credibility with consumers even before you open.

Manufacturing. One of the most important tasks in a small plant is the management of industrial purchasing—of securing the materials, supplies, and capital stock needed for the production operations. An effective industrial purchasing program can have a vital impact on profit.

The following purchasing guidelines can help you save money:

1. Use less costly material that still meets quality standards.
2. Improve quality or change specifications to save production time or steps.
3. Develop new sources of supply.
4. Order in large volume wherever discounts are available.
5. Negotiate with suppliers to reduce unit prices.
6. Consider whether it's cheaper to make or buy items.
7. Apply different purchasing techniques.

Wholesaling. The primary job of a warehouse is to receive, unpack, store, transfer, and repack goods for distribution. Money can be saved through efficient transportation, warehouse organization, and use of labor. To match their competition, some warehouse owners agree to take back unsold inventory. They may plan special quarterly or seasonal promotions. They purchase in large quantities from various manufacturers in order to provide competitive prices to their customers.

In turn, they make discounts available to retailers who make large purchases. These special prices, promotions, and services are advertised through brochures and newsletters and by sales representatives. Warehouses, too, must meet their competition in appealing to retail and service customers.

Retailing establishments. According to several shopping-center managers, the major problem facing small independent retailers today is remaining competitive with the many franchise and chain-store establishments.[1] The latter firms pay less for their stock because of the large-volume purchases made by their central headquarters.

One mall manager, whose experience in developing several very large shopping centers throughout the country makes him an expert, suggests that even small chains—those with no more than seven stores—experience difficulty in getting the competitive prices they need. Those independents who specialize in a narrow market, however, sometimes have a better chance of succeeding. They need less space and their competition is limited.

Retailers who specialize, who are located in small towns or in areas that shoppers seldom leave, or who sell luxury products may have less difficulty in meeting the competition. Nevertheless, all retailers must consistently seek the lowest possible prices from suppliers, in order to offer competitive prices to their customers.

Questions to Ask in Making Purchasing Decisions

The following questions can help you develop your buying plans:

1. Will you establish a merchandise budget for each season?
2. Will this budget take into consideration planned sales for the season?
3. Will it achieve a planned stock turnover?
4. Will you break this budget down by department or by merchandise classification?
5. Will you establish a formal plan for deciding what to buy and from whom?
6. Will you establish a system for reviewing new items coming onto the market?
7. Have you considered using a basic stock list or a model stock plan in your buying?
8. Will you use some sort of unit control system?
9. Will you keep track of the success of your buying decisions from one year to another and/or from one season to the next, so that you can make informed purchasing decisions?
10. Will you make most of your purchases from two or three principal suppliers?
11. Will you set up a system for evaluating the suppliers' performance?
12. Have you established a planned gross margin for your firm's operations and will you buy so as to achieve it?[2]

Advantages of purchasing from manufacturers. Today, with many manufacturers advertising and selling through mail-order catalogues, retailers can often circumvent several middle operations to obtain lower prices by buying direct. The advantages of purchasing directly from manufacturers include

Many retailers buy from manufacturers' and wholesalers' sales representatives who come to the store.

access to the latest fashions and trends, to potentially lower prices, and to assistance in the form of advertising and sales aids and financial and credit help.

Advantages of purchasing from wholesalers. You can usually depend on your wholesaler to keep you informed about primary market conditions that would affect the supply of a particular product. Foreknowledge of the possible scarcity or surplus of consumer goods or of anticipated major shifts in prices can be very useful when you are drawing up your buying plans.

The advantages of purchasing from wholesalers include:

1. Their ability to sell in smaller quantities than producers and purchase in even greater quantities for bigger discounts,
2. Lower transportation costs because of proximity (there are more wholesalers than there are original manufacturers),
3. Faster delivery on a wide variety of products because wholesalers buy from many manufacturers,
4. Potentially better terms and credit services than from producers,
5. Savings of time and trouble because one wholesaler can supply goods from many different manufacturers.

By pooling your orders with other independent retailers, you can cooperatively feature selected merchandise and secure price concessions or other favorable terms. Generally, the wholesaler passes some of the savings obtained from manufacturers on to you, the customer, to help you counter the price appeals offered by large retailers who buy directly from manufacturers in large quantities. In other cases, a wholesaler-distributor may sell selected items at cost in an effort to obtain a major part of your other business orders.

Processing Orders and Receiving Delivery

The order cycle begins when an order is placed. (See Figure 16.3.) The cycle has six stages:

1. Order preparation and transmittal,
2. Order receipt and entry,
3. Order processing,
4. Warehouse selection and packing,
5. Order transportation,
6. Delivery and unloading.

The first three phases of the cycle are expedited by good communication between customers and the customer service personnel employed by the manufacturers or wholesalers. Order-receivers may be equipped with computer terminals or may accept orders over 800-number telephone lines.

If you plan to open business as a manufacturer, wholesaler, or transportation carrier, you should organize to process all incoming orders efficiently. If you

FIGURE 16.3
Purchase Order.

PURCHASE ORDER		THIS NUMBER MUST APPEAR ON ALL INVOICES-PACKAGES, ETC.	8766
TO	American Rug Manufacturers	DATE	1-18-19--
ADDRESS	P.O. Box 3782	FOR	
SHIP TO	Battle Creek, MI 49016		

PLEASE NOTIFY US IMMEDIATELY IF YOU ARE UNABLE TO SHIP COMPLETE ORDER BY DATE SPECIFIED

	QUANTITY	PLEASE SUPPLY ITEMS LISTED BELOW		PRICE	
1	10	Stock # 96 S 4510 Hook Rugs (8'6" x 10'4")	49.00	490	00
2					
3					
4					
5					
6					
7					

DATE REQUIRED (2 weeks hence)   HOW SHIP common carrier   PLEASE SEND 3 COPIES OF YOUR INVOICE

TERMS E.O.M.   PURCHASING AGENT

Rediform 1H 134

become a retailer, you should deal with efficient companies. Delays in handling requests slow customer-companies' order cycle.

Today's improved methods all along the order cycle, including high-speed communications, can reduce inventory carrying costs. And consistency of delivery reduces the need for safety stock (to avoid running totally out of stock), and therefore also reduces inventory carrying costs. In return for speed you may have to pay or charge higher prices, though.

As a retailer you must, at the time of delivery, verify that you are receiving as many cartons (or pounds, etc.) as are indicated on the delivery receipt. Examine the outside of cartons for damage. If visible damage appears, note this fact on the delivery receipt and have the driver sign your copy. Immediately following delivery, open the cartons and inspect the contents to see if the merchandise is damaged.

Retain damaged goods at the point received and call the carrier to report the damage. Also confirm the call in writing, for your own protection. Then you can seek replacement from the supplier as well as compensation from the carrier who was responsible for the damage.

Buying the Minimum Needed

Assuming that goods are nearby and readily available on call, you may choose to purchase only what you need for short durations. With this method, you would display only sample items. As customer needs dictate, you would place calls to purchase specific items.

This practice becomes common during periods of inflation and high interest rates. With instant telecommunications available to place orders, followed by fast (same-day or overnight) delivery service—and depending on the type of products—customers are not as inconvenienced as they might once have been. Car parts, specialty items, and the like all fall into this category.

The advantages of the "buy and pay as you go plan" are that the purchasing system is simplified and the inventory investment is minimized. The disadvantages are that: (1) prices will be higher because a smaller quantity is purchased, (2) some sales may be lost or operations hampered because of the unavailability of goods or because of delays in delivery, and (3) shipping costs will be higher. That is, if you order fewer items each time, you will be purchasing more often and delivery charges will be assessed on every order.

Identifying and Evaluating Suppliers

Both new and experienced entrepreneurs should continually search for new suppliers. Just as consumers periodically go on comparison shopping tours, so should company owners. Peruse supplier catalogues, talk with sales representatives, and find out which suppliers companies similar to yours are using, and why.

In evaluating potential suppliers, you should ask yourself:
1. Who sells my line of products to retailers? Can I buy direct from manufacturers or through wholesalers and distributors?
2. What delivery service is available? Would I have to pay shipping charges?
3. What are the terms of buying? Can I get credit?
4. How quickly can the supplier deliver?

Keeping a good relationship with suppliers. To avoid misunderstandings, you should specify all the details of an order, preferably in writing and on a preprinted form. The form should define prices, terms, dates of shipment, and liability for shipping costs. When an agreement is in writing, any errors can usually be corrected without damaging your relationship with suppliers.

To maintain this rapport, you as a company customer should remember how you want your customers to treat you, and treat your suppliers accordingly:
1. Pay your bills when due or shortly thereafter.
2. Avoid canceling or changing orders at will.
3. Negotiate in a businesslike manner but don't demand special or unreasonable concessions on prices or services.
4. Treat suppliers' sales representatives with courtesy—they visit you not only to make sales for their company but also to assist you; they can provide a fund of information if encouraged.

Several suppliers or one? Although you want to establish a mutually beneficial and positive relationship with suppliers—and thus may prefer dealing with a single firm—there are advantages to diversification. The supply house you choose because it offers the best prices and service may some day experience difficulties. Strikes, catastrophes, or change of management and thus of company policies can all influence future dealings. Using two or more suppliers can insure you against such contingencies.

Conversely, dealing primarily with a major supplier assures you the best discounts for large-volume purchases. Other benefits include speedy deliveries (rush-order handling may be reserved for regular customers), advertising assistance, and the possible availability of extended credit terms.

Principles of Inventory Control

Successful inventory management must balance the *costs* of inventory with the *benefits*. Many new entrepreneurs fail to understand the true costs of carrying inventory. There are the direct costs of storage, insurance, taxes, etc., but inventory also ties up money that could be used elsewhere. Small reductions in this inventory investment can change the company's overall cash position. Obviously, money not tied up in inventory is available as working capital, but lost sales significantly reduce profit in the long run as well as the short run.

Inventory types. Differences exist between a merchandiser's inventory and a manufacturer's inventory. In a merchandising company, such as a retail store or a wholesale operation, inventory is purchased in a form ready to be sold without further processing or conversion. In contrast, a manufacturing company has three types of inventory—raw materials, work-in-process (WIP), and finished goods. "Raw materials inventories" can include unprocessed commodities such as iron ore or farm products, as well as technologically advanced subcomponents such as a computer for an airplane. The "WIP inventories" comprise all products that have been placed into the production process but have not yet been completed. The cost of the WIP inventory includes not only raw materials but also the labor and overhead incurred in converting raw materials into finished goods. "Finished goods inventories" contain all the finished products that have been through the manufacturing processes but have not been sold. For all practical purposes, the finished goods inventory of a manufacturer is identical in character to the merchandise inventory of a retailer in that it is ready to be sold.[3]

Ratios for computing inventories and inventory turnover:

$$\text{Raw materials inventory turnover} = \frac{\text{Cost of raw materials}}{\text{Average raw materials inventory}^*}$$

$$\text{Days in raw materials inventory} = \frac{\text{Number of days in a year}}{\text{Raw materials inventory turnover}}$$

$$\text{WIP inventory turnover} = \frac{\text{Cost of manufacturing}}{\text{Average WIP inventory}^*}$$

$$\text{Days in WIP inventory} = \frac{\text{Number of days in a year}}{\text{WIP inventory turnover}}$$

$$\text{Finished goods inventory turnover} = \frac{\text{Cost of goods sold}}{\text{Average finished goods inventory}^*}$$

$$\text{Days in finished goods inventory} = \frac{\text{Number of days in a year}}{\text{Finished goods inventory turnover}}$$

* Calculated by adding the beginning and ending balances and dividing the sum by 2.[4]

Economic Order Quantity. The EOQ formula is widely used to compute the minimum annual cost for ordering and stocking each article. The EOQ computation accounts for the cost of placing an order, the annual sales rate, the unit cost, and the cost of carrying the inventory.

EOQ-based inventory management uses a maximum/minimum system of inventory control. This system assumes the use of a standard order that represents the most economical quantity to purchase. Once this figure is established, it can be used almost automatically for deciding when is the proper time to reorder.

This method is adaptable to products and materials whose prices seldom fluctuate widely and that are used in substantial and regular quantities. See the formula for calculating EOQ, Figure 16.4.

FIGURE 16.4
Calculating Economic Order Quantity (EOQ).

Calculating Economic Order Quantity (EOQ)

EOQ = Economic Order (Quantity)
A = Cost Per Order (Dollars)
C = Carrying Costs (Percent)
U = Unit Cost (Dollars)
D = Units Used Annually

Formula: $EOQ = \dfrac{2AD}{UC}$

Estimated Cost Per Order		Estimated Carrying Cost Per Unit	
Order Preparation	$ 5	Interest Rate on Loan	12%
Order Folllow-up	10	Insurance Costs	3
Inspection Cost	20	Property Taxes	4
Office Expense	10	Storage Costs	1
Total	$45	Total	20%

Suppose that you wish to order something that costs $5 each and you anticipate selling 400 units annually. The above costs and percentages represent estimates for estimated costs per order and estimated percentages for carrying costs per unit. Apply the above formula to this illustration, as follows:

Formula Applied:

A = $45
C = 20%
U = $5
D = 400

$$EOQ = \dfrac{(2)(45 \times 400)}{(.20)(5)}$$

= 36,000 (.36 × 400)
= 144 units per order maximum

The increasing demand for more accurate, timely inventory systems has been matched by advances in computers and their associated software. "Material requirements planning" (MRP), a computer-based information processing system, can help to facilitate the ordering and scheduling of materials, components, subassemblies, and the like. Small businesses have been reluctant to take advantage of MRP because many were unable to purchase computers. Since microcomputers have become affordable, however, small manufacturers can now reap the benefits of MRP techniques.[5]

MRP provides information that can be used to develop and control an inventory accounting system. According to some studies, a number of companies have successfully used MRP II to realize 10 to 25 percent reductions in inventory control and 10 to 15 percent improvements in productivity.[6]

A stock control system. For the small nonmanufacturing firm, this need not be elaborate. The kind and amount of recordkeeping necessary for effective stock control depends largely on the type of merchandise handled and the size of the company. Many perishable items, such as milk and bread in a grocery store, are controlled visually—by merely looking at the quantity remaining. Such products are stamped with a "use before" date. The supplier's route people also have an interest in helping keep these stocks fresh.

An inventory control system may work by counting stocks or counting sales. First, decide what items you want to control. Prior work experience in a related industry, plus advice from people in your resource network and published guidelines, can help you decide this point. Then prepare a model stock list. On it you should record specific products and the amount of each to be ordered and maintained on hand.

Clothing and department store owners must keep a range of sizes, styles, and colors in stock for any given item. Make comparisons between this example and your type of business. For opening day you must have some idea of what will appeal to your customers and plan accordingly. Thereafter, you can use sales records to update the model stock list.

Stock control records help prevent memory lapses. Keep a stock record card for each item you sell, recording on it all details, such as style, color, and size. Use these records—whether processed manually or by computer—not only to maintain a count of what is on hand, but to tell you at what point you should reorder and in what quantities. (See Figure 16.5.)

Some model stock lists, such as those for women's clothing, include a special section entitled "maintained selection items." The objective is to flag those articles that are affected by fashion trends. Although you may proceed to order at the point designated by your records, you may order a different style. Thus reorder records are filed by classification, item, and price. Such notations will assure that you continue to offer current fashions.

Counting stock versus sales. To get the data you need for effective inventory control, you can count stock on a periodic basis or you can count it

FIGURE 16.5
Sample Stock Record Card.

Description	HOOK RUGS—8'6" x 10'4"			Stock No. 96 S 4510		
Supplier 1.	American Rug Manufacturers		Location Floor 3	Unit Quantity 1	Reorder Quantity 10	
2.					Reorder Point 25	

DATE	EXPLANATION	UNIT COST	RECEIVED	ISSUED	BALANCE	REORDERED Req. No.	Date
1-20	standard order	$49—	10	—	35	99	1/20
Feb	sold	—	—	12	23	—	—
3/5	rush order	49—	20	10	33	191	3/5
March	sold	—	—	13	20	—	—
4/10	standard order	49—	10	—	30	201	4/10
Ap-May	sold	—	—	4	26	—	—
June	sold	—	—	11	15	—	—
7/5	standard order	49—	20	—	35	527	7/5
Ju-Aug	sold	—	—	7	28	—	—
9/20	standard order	49—	10	—	38	621	9/20
Sept-Oct	sold	—	—	22	16	—	—

daily by counting sales. To count stock, you keep track of an article, such as shoes, by listing: (1) what is on hand, (2) what is on order, (3) what has been received, and (4) what has been sold. Periodically, such as once a month, you recount the stock to identify how well the product is selling. (See Figure 16.6.)

FIGURE 16.6
Inventory Tally Sheet.

Priced By _____ Extended By _____ Date _____ Page ____

Location								
CABINET	SHELF	STOCK NO.	DESCRIPTION	QTY.	UNIT COST		AMOUNT	
		8	In-Out Baskets	15	3	00	45	00
		10	Staplers	5	5	00	25	00
		11	Staples (per strip)	10		50	5	00
USE LOCAL		12	Scotch-Tape Dispensers	5	2	50	12	50
COMPANY		13	Paper Clips (per 50)	500		25	2	50
INFORMATION		16	Correction Material (strip)	20		25	5	00
		18	Ink pads	5	1	00	5	00
		19-a	Date Stamp	5	2	50	12	50
		19-b	"Paid" Stamp	3	2	50	7	50
		19-d	"Cancelled" Stamp	1	3	50	3	50

Subsequent purchasing decisions are based on sales. If sales are dropping on any particular item, then you may decide to close it out. At this point a special sale might be in order. If the product is moving as anticipated, then the reorder number on the stock control card or model stock list would stay the same. The formula for using the "rotated unit control" system is:

$$\text{Old Inventory} + \text{Purchases} - \text{New Inventory} = \text{Sales}$$

If products are disappearing but are not represented by sales, then something obviously is amiss. Check first for errors in counting either the stock or the sales; if you find none, then the problem may be shoplifting or employee pilferage.

"Perpetual inventory" is a means of maintaining control over stock by continually deducting sales from the inventory on hand. To use this method, you must record sales on an item-by-item basis. This is most easily done by computer. In fact, a computer system is of great help with all inventory tasks: keeping track of stock on hand, of raw materials, of goods in process, and of finished goods.

THE OPENING-DAY PROMOTION

Assume that one month from today you will open your doors for business. By this time you should have: established the image you seek to project; selected a sign that reflects that image; assessed what promotional activities the competition uses, particularly when starting up; developed a human-resource network to advise you; and identified the advertising media that can best attract customers to your establishment. (See Figure 16.7.)

You have to have something to say before you can advertise effectively. When you have established an image, a price range, and customer services, you are ready to tell prospective customers or clients why they should shop in your store or deal with you. Simultaneously, you want to prepare an advertising budget and work within this framework in developing your opening-day promotion.

Grand Opening Give-A-Way!
Over 25 Prizes -- Come In And Register!

THIS AD IS WORTH $5.00 OFF YOUR
PURCHASES OF $25.00 OR MORE!

FIGURE 16.7
Grand Opening.

Know Your Company and Your Customers

The first step in developing promotional objectives is to look, once more, at your business and its target patrons. Ask yourself again:

1. What business am I in?
2. What quality of merchandise or services am I offering?
3. What image do I want my establishment to project?
4. How does my business compare with that of the competition? How does it benefit customers more?
5. What services am I offering? How will these services enhance sales? How are they different from those offered by the competition?
6. What are the demographics of my target customers?
7. Why would these customers find my merchandise or services more attractive than those of the competition?

Knowing just who you want to attract and what you have that will attract them will allow you to organize a start-up promotion that will bring people to your door and cause them to buy. (See Figure 16.8.) Even during the opening days, you want to get the most for your advertising dollar.

The Image Projected

A company has an image whether or not the owner is aware of it. The image begins with promotional advertising and also with the signs you put up.

FIGURE 16.8
Use some special gimmicks for the opening day or week, such as reducing prices or giving away gifts or having a contest.

INTO FISH?

TROPICAL FISH ½ PRICE SALE!
Purchase One Fish At Regular Price, And Get It's Mate For ½ PRICE!!

The first image you want your enterprise to project will probably depend on the appearance of the exterior and the sign that you choose.

Signs. Signs represent you and your image, no matter where they appear. Signs are the most direct and continuing form of visual communication available. They give information about your store and build your image. They are a relatively inexpensive means of advertising, are easy to use, and are always at work for you. They appeal directly to people already in your vicinity—unlike advertisements, which may be seen by many people who never come to your trade area.

Less expensive and more permanent than advertising in other media, signs are also practical. When special items are displayed on a sign, sales of these items increase. Studies have shown that people do read and remember what appears on signs.[7]

To promote your business effectively, your signs must be noticeable and readable, and they must project the desired image. The sign's design, therefore, is important. Simple designs and materials suggest discount prices and no frills. Elegant and expensive sign materials suggest luxury goods and services.

Three basic design considerations are important: physical dimensions, graphic elements, and legibility. You must first decide on the size, placement, materials, and structure of the sign. Different businesses have different needs. A roadside firm designed to attract trade off busy thoroughfares needs a sign that is both large and high. The sign must also be durable enough to survive weather conditions—you don't want it to blow over or its colors to fade.

Graphic elements include the colors, lettering, shape, symbolism, harmony, and lighting of the sign. Finally, the message must be easy to read and understand.

In addition to exterior signs you might consider billboards. This type of permanent advertisement directs people off of thoroughfares to your business and is especially appropriate for motels, restaurants, gasoline stations, and fast-food establishments.

Window displays in service firms. Visualize and compare the two scenes which follow. An appliance repair shop that had large plate-glass windows on each side of the entrance fills the display area with broken appliances waiting to be repaired. Passers-by see a lot of dusty junk—not very appealing.

By contrast, an office services establishment creates a well-balanced display. On one side are authentic antique typewriters and other office artifacts; on the other side, a huge and colorful poster showing computerized equipment. Hanging above and between these contrasting scenes is a sign bearing the simple message: "With our up-to-date equipment and efficient, courteous staff, we can help you meet your business deadlines. Fast, Quality Service."

Financial, legal, or accounting companies often arrange an attractive office layout, complete with carpeting, wall hangings, plants, and neat desks that is visible through the street windows. Although this view is obviously more appealing than the window full of broken appliances, promotional opportunities are still being lost.

Discrete but enticing displays and signs can advertise services, special one-time offerings, the latest news, etc. A stock-market brokerage could feature current stock prices; a tailor could display "before and after" pictures of mended clothing.

Merchandising; window displays in retail stores. Owners of most retail stores and of many small service firms purchase or lease buildings that have plate-glass windows at the front. This area usually has space for developing attractive displays that can help bring passers-by inside.

Large department stores and many specialty shops make wise use of this window space, but some small retailers forget or ignore the benefits to be derived. Yet they may be paying a higher rent for a good location with much customer traffic—and window displays are an excellent way to divert that traffic into a store. A study conducted by a trade publication revealed that one store spent a sum equal to as much as 40 percent of its rent on decorating its windows.[8]

Merchandising; inside the establishment. What do you want to happen when people walk into your firm? If you are a retailer, you hope that they will buy some of your stock and leave as satisfied customers. You want repeat customers and money in the cash register. Service firms also want patrons to return. In either case, the interior of the establishment can contribute to or detract from the image desired.

Window displays provide information, advertise special sales and products or services, and help project a particular image.

Toss some products on shelves in a dimly lit store and customers will decide it's a junky, dirty place. Arrange things neatly and conveniently and your customers will return. The type of business selected should suggest the image you want to project. A floral design shop or gift boutique, for example, should look and smell good.

> Phyllis Brooks and Jelaine Norton operate a partnership that supplies hotels and restaurants with flower arrangements for conferences, weddings, and banquets. They also teach floral design, Christmas decorating, and silk-flower-making.
>
> To create their desired image they filled their establishment with fine furniture and unique antiques. They sought to develop a "backyard effect" with flower trellises, green carpeting that looked like grass, and potted trees and plants. The appealing combination of wood and flowers reflects the desired image and attracts customers like a magnet.

The Promotion Campaign

Begin with a sound selling idea such as a special sale, price discounts, a liberal credit plan, a contest, or a premium offer. You can find many suggestions for promotional campaigns in trade journals and newsletters and in books on advertising and marketing.

Assistance and advice from your network contacts. Alert the local Chamber of Commerce to your opening. Some communities designate certain people as "ambassadors" (or a similar title). These people, plus the mayor and other city officials, may come on the day the establishment opens to cut the ribbon and assist with other promotional events.

You can ask the ambassadors to greet people, serve refreshments, tell people about you and your business, and conduct tours of the facility. Their praise of you, the entrepreneur, your qualifications and your business's attractions provide valuable free advertising. Customers usually believe opinions they hear from outsiders.

Your resource network can also provide help; i.e., advertising agents (for a fee), shopping-mall managers, and radio, television, newspapers, and/or magazine reporters. Experienced business people in similar or related fields may sometimes give you advice.

Merchandising help from wholesalers. Some wholesalers offer free or inexpensive help with sales promotions. Wholesalers are also major sources of display material designed to stimulate "impulse buying" for both nationally advertised and private brands. They usually accompany this service with advice on how best to merchandise the displays.

In some instances, wholesalers will even help you build effective window, counter, and bin displays. You might invite a representative to assist you during the opening-day promotion.

A checklist for planning the campaign. Before putting your promotion campaign into action, ask yourself the following questions:

1. Am I familiar with the strengths and weaknesses of various promotional methods?
2. Have I considered how each type might be used for my firm?
3. Do I know which media (radio, television, newspapers, yellow pages, handbills, etc.) can most effectively reach my target group?
4. Do I know what I can and cannot say in my ads (see Chapter 13 for "truth in advertising" requirements)?
5. Can I use direct mail?
6. Are good mailing lists available; if so, should I use them?
7. Have I contacted people in my network for advice or technical assistance?
8. Can I get help from local newspapers, radio, or television?
9. Are cooperative advertising funds or other aids available from suppliers?
10. Have I studied the advertising of other successful firms, as well as of my competitors?
11. Have I decided how much I am willing to spend for my grand-opening promotional campaign? Is this figure in line with the first year's advertising budget?[9]

A GENTLE TAN

nordic sun

First Session Free

A TANNING SALON

FIGURE 16.9
Free or cut-rate appeals will bring new customers to your door that first week, but you want to ensure that they will return.

Developing Printed Advertisements

Advertisements for a "Grand Opening" should give the date, location, type, and name of the business. As a promotional "gimmick" you could offer extra-low prices, two-for-one specials, or coupons. The coupons serve the consumers who clip them from the paper as a reminder to visit the establishment on opening day. (See Figures 16.9 and 16.10.)

ENTIRE STOCK OF GOLD FILLED
Earrings, Pendants, and Bracelets

50% Off!

- Convenient Charge Accounts
- 90 Day No Interest Accounts
- Most Bank Cards Accepted

SAMUELS
JEWELERS

FIGURE 16.10
It's a good idea to list special terms in addition to reduced prices to avoid legal problems later.

Some ads also give the terms of sale. For instance, a coupon may state: "This coupon is not redeemable for cash and may not be applied to layaways." The ad may say that reduced prices will be in effect for the first week only. Refund and return policies may be highlighted, and credit conditions may be stated.

Some service businesses advertise that the first session or referral is free, give a discount for charter subscribers or patrons, or offer special treatment to contest winners. You may want to feature free deliveries or extra-fast service, such as one-hour dry-cleaning or a 24-hour turnaround on developing photos or repairing goods.

Also highlight in your ads any special events that will accompany the start-up campaign. There may be contests, games, free refreshments, or entertainment. A store selling children's clothing, toys, or pets might feature a clown or other performer.

Designing a good ad. Your advertisements can introduce people to your business itself, not only to what you have to offer. Develop an appealing, eye-catching logo that will remind people both of the opening promotional events and of a continuing business of repute.

Use a simple layout for your ad that will draw the readers' eyes directly through its features—art or graphic, message, price and conditions, etc.—directly to the bottom line: the name and location of the firm. The logo, illustration, and/or message must clearly indicate what type of business you're operating. You don't want to keep the nature of your company and its potential benefits a mystery!

Illustrations should show your product in use or someone benefiting from your service. The ad should convince readers that there are specific reasons why they should patronize your establishment and not others. Essentially, an ad should project one primary benefit, with perhaps two or three secondary points, all of which will entice people to spend their money. (See Figure 16.11.)

If you plan to sell brand-name products or services, highlight that fact. Check with the franchiser, wholesaler, or manufacturer to see if and how you can coordinate your ads with national advertising.

Although it's always good to highlight special bargains, you shouldn't be afraid to quote high prices—if, that is, your ad makes clear the benefits to be derived. In short, support your statements with valid, believable, and appealing claims.

Selecting the Media

Typical local advertising outlets include newspapers, radio, television, direct mail, handbills, and word of mouth. To take advantage of word of mouth, tell everyone you know about what you are doing. If you have been constructing or remodeling a facility, local business people, passers-by, and many other residents will already be curious. Using your network, including the contacts made by joining several business and civic clubs, you can pass the word around about what type of business will open and how it will benefit people.

FIGURE 16.11
This advertisement describes that all sales are final, there will be no refunds, and exchanges must be made within 30 days.

Newspapers. Newspapers offer the advantages of local coverage and precise timing. The results are often measurable, particularly when consumers clip out coupons and bring them in. Newspaper advertising rates are based on circulation and on the number of newspaper lines, columns, or inches used for the ad. If you have the choice, decide where in the newspaper you want your ad located and ask for your preference.

Radio. Radio goes everywhere—into people's homes, into offices, and into cars as people drive about town or travel on highways. Radio characteristically offers early, if not immediate, scheduling, comparatively low rates, and few, if any, production costs.

The station's audience—in addition to the length of your advertisement, how often it will be aired, and at what times—determine the advertising price range. Where you have a choice of airing time, think about your target audience. Teenagers will be in school during the day, so it makes less sense to advertise products that appeal to them in mid-morning than in the late afternoon or evening.

Direct mail and handbills. If you want to attract charge-account customers, then you should try to get access to a current and accurate mailing list of credit-card holders. Perhaps your services or products will be directed to senior citizens; if so, then you'll want a list of retirees. In direct-mail promotions, the mailing list should include the names and current addresses of the customers you most want to target.

Check with the Post Office for current regulations, bulk-mail rates, and advice about how to get the most from your postage dollar.

"Handbills" are one-page ads that are distributed at random on the street, placed on windowshields, and perhaps taken from door to door. Although you do not have to worry about the "line" or "column-inch" ad rate in this case, the same principles for ad design and layout apply. People are busy, and many resent having their car windows cluttered up or papers stuffed into their hands as they walk by. Thus the layout must immediately catch their attention and the message must be succinct but revealing. Given the time and expense of promoting your business in this way, you want the handbill to bring in at least a minimum percentage of those who receive it. (See Table 16.1.)

Developing the Advertising Budget

In preparing your advertising budget, first decide what percentage of your anticipated sales volume you will allocate to this expense. This percentage will vary according to the type and condition of the business, to local competition, and to the nature of products or services.

Trade journals offer comparative industrywide statistics. By multiplying your total anticipated sales by the standard percentage, you will get the total amount of advertising money you can budget for the year. (Also see Chapter 14.)

Some entrepreneurs develop monthly budgets. Suppose you anticipate that sales for the month will be 12 percent of the year's total income. Then you might also devote 12 percent of the year's advertising budget to that month. For the

TABLE 16.1 Typical Monthly Advertising Costs of Various Advertising Media

ADVERTISING MEDIUM	TOTAL ADULT AUDIENCE/1,000 EXPOSURES	MONTHLY COST	COST TO REACH EACH 1,000 ADULTS*
Newspaper (1½ page ad per week)	685,000	$1,008	$1.47
Radio (6 one-minute spots per week)	91,200	264	2.90
Television (6 one-minute spots per week)	1,176,000	1,580	1.34
Outdoor billboard, painted	900,000	500	.56
Junior posters	192,000	25	.13
Sign (8' × 6' double-face, acrylic plastic, internal illumination)	1,050,000	58	.06

* In a community of approximately 130,000 population.

Source: K. E. Claus and R. J. Claus, "Signage: Planning Environmental Visual Communication" (Palo Alto, Calif.: Institute of Signage Research, 1976), p. 31.

grand opening, however, your advertising expenses may be included in the start-up costs. At any rate, you may want to develop the annual budget at this time. (See Figure 16.12.)

If your business will experience seasonal fluctuations, your budget should account for that. A florist shop will experience more business during spring and early summer, for instance (because of Mother's Day, banquets, proms, weddings, etc.); while gift shops and related retailers will have hefty sales prior to Christmas. The busy period for firms that prepare tax forms is from the first of January through April 15. Although advertising generally precedes such seasonal shopping and service periods, it is not always necessary to maintain an advertising budget level commensurate with the total trade anticipated.

SUMMARY

Whatever kind of business you have, you will find that the fewer the number of middle operations, the lower the prices you will be able to obtain—simply because every establishment must add its own markup. But there are also

Account	Month		Year to Date	
	Budget	Actual	Budget	Actual
Media Newspapers Radio TV Literature Other				
Promotions Exhibits Displays Contests				
Advertising Expenses Salaries Supplies Stationery Travel Postage Subscriptions Entertainment Dues				
Totals				

FIGURE 16.12
Advertising Budget.

certain benefits and services that each middle operation provides as part of the total price package.

Purchasing decisions depend on numerous factors, including the type, size, and location of your business; what prices your competition is paying and charging; and your success in developing effective relationships with suppliers.

Buying in small quantities avoids tying up capital in inventory. However, buying in large quantities gets you lower prices. If you buy loyally and often from one supplier, in large quantity, you may earn special services, including marketing and financial help. On the other hand, if that wholesaler runs into some difficulty, you may be left without a supplier. If you are contemplating a manufacturing business, you will be especially interested in applying ratios and formulas to ordering, inventory turnover, and carrying costs. Every business that handles stock, however, must develop an inventory control system.

This chapter also covered the promotional activities you can use to advertise the grand opening of your business. Advertising begins with the image you create. The signs, window displays, and the merchandising techniques used inside your establishment can add to or detract from the appeal your business makes to passers-by.

You can use your human-resource network to obtain advice and assistance in promoting the opening of your business. You can spread the news through newspapers, radio, television, direct mail, and word-of-mouth advertising. The ads you design for any of these outlets also have a significant effect on your image.

With the grand opening, you are actually in business. From this point on you will have little time for leisurely planning and organizing. The business plan should have been revised repeatedly, until by now you feel confident that the plan will work. Of course you can expect to continually analyze your ongoing business operations so that you can make effective on-the-spot management decisions. And that's what the next unit is all about.

DISCUSSION QUESTIONS

1. Describe the channel of distribution by using examples of companies with which you are familiar. Also describe how consumers can buy directly from extraction, manufacturing, or producing businesses.
2. Where does the type(s) of business you are most interested in operating fit into this channel of distribution? Why?
3. Explain the relationship of extraction industries to producers, manufacturers to wholesalers, wholesalers to distributors (including transportation companies), and either of the latter to retailers and consumers who buy direct or ultimately from local stores. Think imaginatively and state your own opinions.

4. Describe how orders are processed, using each of the above steps in no. 3 in relation to the others. What is the effect of sophisticated communication transmissions and fast-speed deliveries on the processing of orders? Compare how yesteryear's system might have worked with what happens today.
5. Discuss how various service industries use channels of distribution and order processing and where they appear along this channel.
6. Why might you decide to use one supplier or several? To buy only as needed or in volume? To work cooperatively with other retailers?
7. Which kinds of inventory control are appropriate for which kinds of businesses: the counting method versus the sales method; the formula and ratio approach; the perpetual inventory method; manual versus computerized modes? Why is inventory control essential?
8. How is an initial promotion program related to the market study and pricing policies? Discuss this relationship in one or more specific businesses, your proposed business especially.
9. Why is it important to develop a positive image—one that effectively reflects the nature and quality of a business? Give examples of how to create this image in both merchandise and service firms.
10. What resources would you use from your network of contacts? How would you use these sources in planning your grand opening?
11. How important is it to develop an annual advertising budget? A monthly budget? What relationship does this budget have to the start-up costs of promoting the business?
12. If the usual expense for advertising in your line of business were 3 percent of sales, would you be justified in establishing a 5-percent advertising budget for the first year? What about budgeting 10 percent, or 20 percent? Why or why not?

ACTIVITIES AND EXERCISES

1. Arrange to interview owners of businesses like the one you wish to operate. Find out all you can about their purchasing policies.
    a. Use discussion questions 1-4 above to develop a structured interview format. Be ready to share your findings with your peers.
    b. Ask the owners how orders are processed and what forms and procedures are used.
    c. Ask how inventory is controlled.
2. Visit with new owners of businesses like yours to determine how they promoted their business prior to and during the opening days.
3. Observe several businesses of your choice to identify the image they project. Analyze the exterior signs, the window displays, merchandising strategies, and the advertisements they place in newspapers or on radio and television.

Does the advertised image accurately reflect the actual establishment and its merchandising?
4. Select a packaged product and describe the packaging and design of the product's container. Prepare drawings if desirable. Then explain how products of this nature would be purchased, controlled as part of an inventory management system, and promoted during a grand-opening campaign.
5. For the business you have selected:
   a. List several products or services and decide to whom advertisements should be targeted.
   b. Analyze the unique selling points of this product or service.
   c. Develop a promotion program for attracting the target customers to your business.
6. Design possible promotion activities for a selected service business. Write a 30- or 60-second commercial for radio and design an advertising layout for a newspaper, a direct-mail piece, or a handbill.
7. Prepare a one-year advertising budget for your business, using the form shown in the chapter. (You may revise this budget later.)
8. Select one of the vacant Stanley Junction facilities. Decide what type of business(es) would have the most likelihood of success in this location. Then decide upon and plan for:
   a. The channel(s) of distribution you will use in purchasing products, raw materials, or supplies.
   b. Whether to use one or several suppliers or to buy only as needed.
   c. How to process orders, and the procedures involved.
   d. The type of recordkeeping and control system you will establish for managing inventory.
   e. A promotion campaign—select from given ideas (from the chapter or as listed in nos. 5 and 6 above).
   f. Your human-resource network—from among the people who live and operate businesses in Stanley Junction—who you will ask for help in organizing your grand opening. What kind of assistance can they provide?
9. Participate in the case discussion from case supplement Project 6.

NOTES

1. Interviews conducted with mall managers in Casper and Cheyenne, Wyoming; Denver, Colorado; Kansas City and St. Louis, Missouri; Indianapolis, Indiana; Chattanooga, Tennessee; Washington, D.C.; and Honolulu, Hawaii; February–December 1983.
2. George Kress and R. Ted Will, "Marketing Checklist for Small Retailers," *Management Aid* no. 4.012 (Washington, D.C.: U.S. Small Business Administration, 1982).
3. Larry H. Beard, Al L. Hartgraves, and Fred A. Jacobs, "Managing Inventories in a Small Business," *Business*, April–June 1983, pp. 45–49.
4. Ibid.

5. Charles H. Davis, Feraidoon Raafat, and M. Hossein Safizadeh, "Production and Inventory Information Processing: Material Requirements Planning," *Journal of Small Business Management,* July 1983, p. 25.
6. Frederick J. Davenport, "Financial Management Through MRP," *Production and Inventory Management,* Second Quarter 1983, pp. 63–70. (See also Earnest Pennents and Ted Levy, "MRP on Microcomputers," *Production and Inventory Management Review,* May 1982, pp. 20–25.)
7. Karen E. Claus and R. J. Claus, "Signs and Your Business," *Small Marketers' Aids* (Washington, D.C.: Small Business Administration, 1977).
8. Ovid Riso, "Advertising Guidelines for Small Retail Firms," *Management Aid* no. 4.015, (Washington, D.C.: Small Business Administration) p. 2.
9. Kress and Will, "Marketing Checklist."

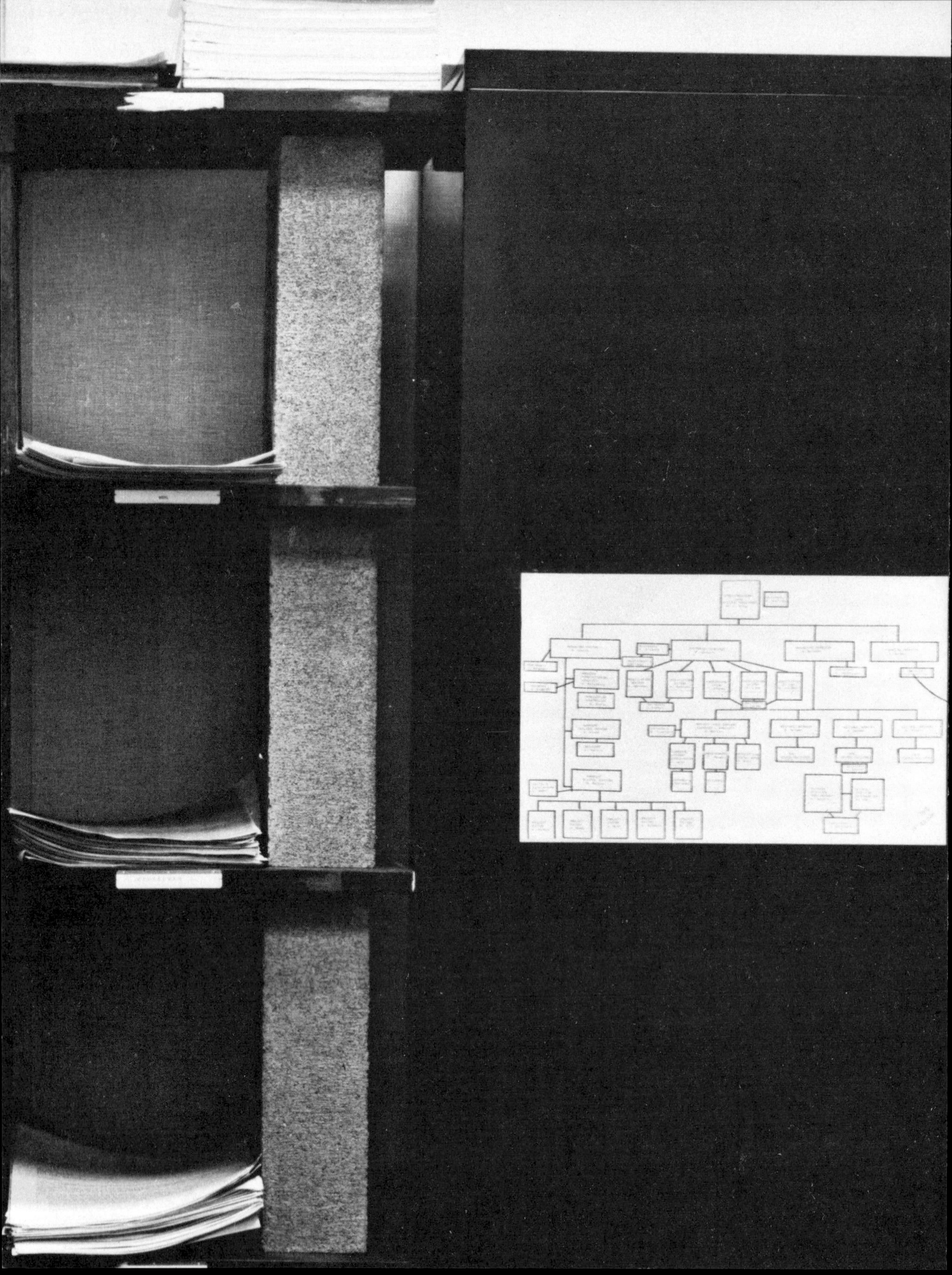

U·N·I·T

·IV·

MANAGING AND CONTROLLING THE SMALL BUSINESS

Inattention to any of a business's subsystems or parts can ultimately spell disaster for the whole enterprise. This unit commences by defining both the systems and the creative approaches to management and offering tools and methods for planning, organizing, implementing, and controlling new and emerging objectives. You will learn that you must continually analyze and make adjustments in your business. It is also important to establish good communications with your employees and to consider if and how you might want to involve them in the decision making process through participative management.

The interconnecting parts of a business that require facilitative management include marketing (along with purchasing and inventory), the physical environment, security, people and productivity, and financial analysis. This unit's chapters are devoted to these major subsystems.

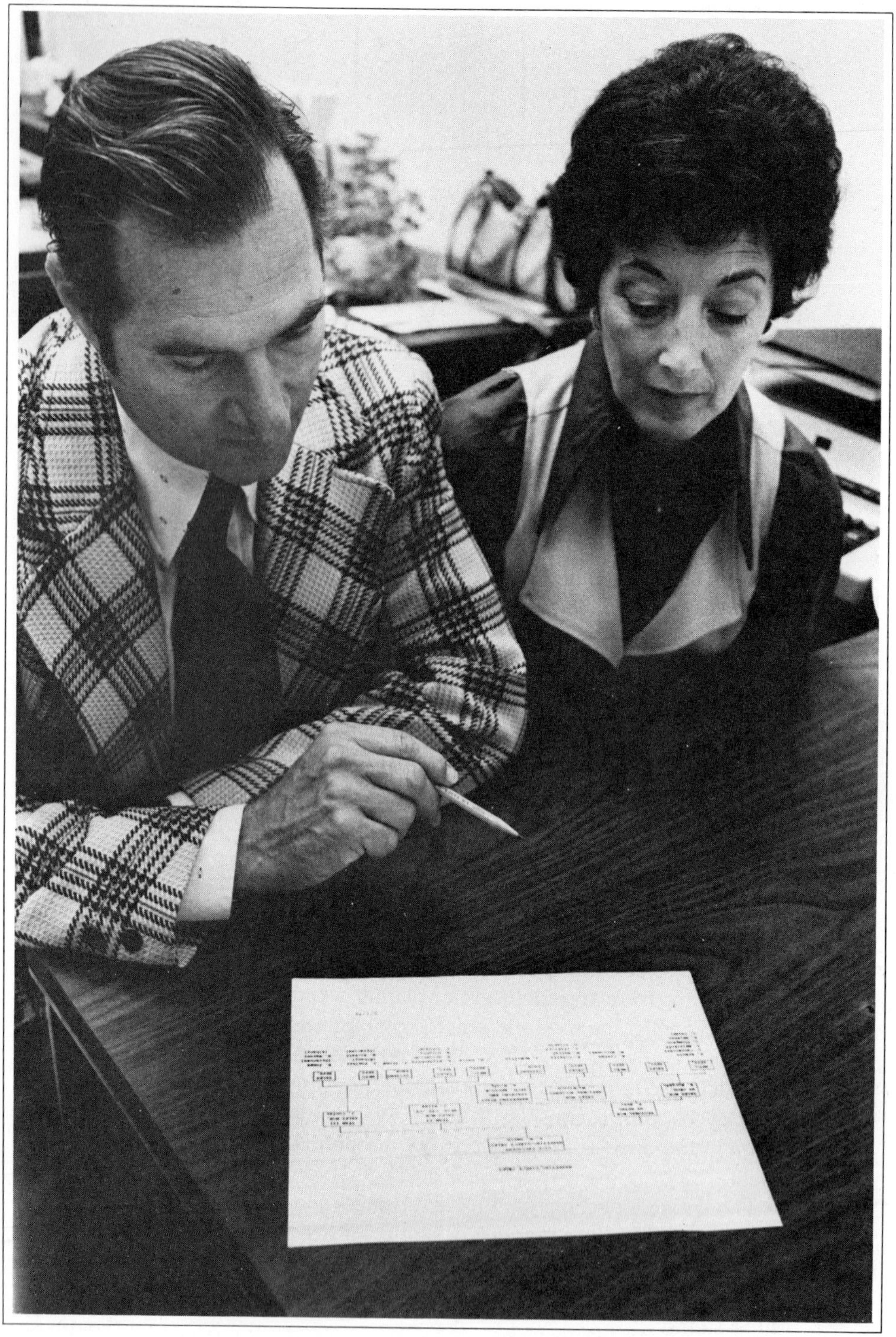

chapter 17

The Systems Approach to Management

Objectives

1. Develop objectives for your business, using the MBO/R management tool.

2. Assign responsibilities and a time for achieving objectives, using the management planning tool.

3. Describe why people fear change and give examples of how you can prepare employees to accept change.

4. Develop a job description (JD) for one of your employees and flowchart a single task within the JD, allowing for exceptions.

5. Compare a horizontal flowchart with a repair shop layout and make recommendations for improvements.

6. Apply time-and-motion principles in analyzing a personal, work, or school activity.

BUSINESS SYSTEMS AND SUBSYSTEMS

Webster defines system as "an assemblage of objects (principles, facts, parts) united by some form of regular interaction or interdependence; an organized whole; a regular method of order; as, to have a system in one's business." Thus a system is a whole that contains many parts or subsystems, which in turn have subsystems of their own. In any one business, the accounting system is divided into subsystems of accounts receivable, accounts payable, payroll, inventory control, and the like.

Although subsystems within any one business seem to act independently at times, all are connected. If any one subsystem fails, the entire system may become inoperable. To avoid such a disaster in your business system, you must continuously apply effective management principles to all its interrelated subsystems.

The processing of diner orders is a subsystem of restaurants. Because restaurants have a high turnover rate, it's often difficult to keep experienced waiters and waitresses. Employing the total number of people necessary to effectively manage a restaurant is also expensive. In responding to both of these problems, many restaurants have gone to a telephone system for taking orders. Using this method, the owner and key employees also have better control over the system.

You must also be aware of your business's place as a subsystem within the community's competitive system of relationships. Marketing, for instance, is not

Bob likes his telephone system for taking diner's orders. The method saves servers' time and also helps him maintain control.

only a subsystem within any given business but it also serves as a subsystem within the community's business system—making all competitors interactive. In this instance, we see how each company within a competitive system serves as a subsystem. The process of quantification, data collection, and system synthesis can be described, for instance, as a system of relationships, as follows:

1. All competitors who persist and survive have a unique advantage over all others. If they did not, then others would crowd them out.
2. The more similar competitors are to each other, the more severe their competition.
3. If competitors are different and coexist, then each must have a distinct advantage over the other.
4. If competitors are to coexist, each must have an advantage and each must match different environmental factors.
5. Since each and every pair of competitors acts as a constraint on each other, then the equilibrium point between them constitutes a segment boundary.
6. Any change in the environment changes environmental characteristics.
7. Competitors who can adapt best or fastest gain an advantage from environmental change.[1]

FACILITATIVE AND PARTICIPATIVE MANAGEMENT

Whatever simplified master planning forms you use, they should guide you in strategic planning and also in facilitating the management of your business. The use of forms can help you diagnose the status quo. Forms prescribe the major moves which you as the chief executive should plan for the next few months or years.[2]

You may or may not decide to permit your staff to participate in the decision-making process. "Facilitative" and nonfacilitative management is compared, as shown in Table 17.1. Other options to employee participation include using outsiders—consultants or business peers.

Logic and Creativity

Entrepreneurs manage their businesses from the basis of both right- and left-brain hemispheres, whether they realize where logic versus creativity, intuition, and attitudinal behavioral responses originate or not.

The left brain is logical, factual, systematic, and functions in consecutive order; the right is emotional, intuitive, subconscious, and functions in random order. The left-brain hemisphere deals with data or our collection of knowledge and is the "cognitive domain." The right brain, or the "affective domain," processes data on the basis of attitudes, values, and socio-psychological patterns gleaned from family and peer-group influences.

TABLE 17.1 The Effect of Facilitative Management on Business Operations

BUSINESS FUNCTION	WITHOUT FACILITATIVE MANAGEMENT	WITH FACILITATIVE MANAGEMENT
Managing	Owner controls and changes situations, problems, budgets, and strategies from day to day.	Owner manages progress toward full utilization of human, technical, financial, and material resources.
Decision-Making	Decisions are made from the top down; owners and managers direct and closely supervise subordinates to ensure proper implementation.	Employees monitor their own progress; owners and managers provide them with information for making appropriate decisions at the point of action.
Coordinating	Management uses administrative layers and frequent reports to coordinate functions that operate with different purposes and contradictory criteria.	Owner and managers construct missions that provide everyone with a common basis for making decisions and working together.
Recruiting Employees	Owner looks for the "right people for the jobs." If they perform well they are rewarded; if not, they are fired.	Owner recruits, hires, trains, and supervises employees based on targeted outcomes for each position; helps employees develop and test new approaches.
Performance	Management follows accepted patterns, systems, procedures and methods; strives to meet standards.	Management establishes essential results and outcomes; sets ambitious targets, monitors progress, and replaces unproductive systems.
Compensation	Owner rewards employees who meet annual profit goals, possibly jeopardizing the future health of the enterprise.	Owner rewards employees who meet benchmarks (indicators) of progress—financial and otherwise—that lead to long-term viability.

Source: Center for Constructive Change (Durham, New Hampshire).

The right brain, then, has the ability to select at random data stored in the left. Also emerging from the right side is the ability to look at old things in new ways and to creatively devise new methods of dealing with current or potential problems. Western civilization, particularly since the advent of systems analysis and the rapid growth of technology, has too often failed to acknowledge even the existence of feelings and intuition, much less their contributions to human behavior and business decisions.

Yet if we do not look at "wholes" in new ways, we cannot make sense of the many parts/subsystems that constitute any one system. Carl Jung, the Swiss psychoanalyst, drew attention to a transcendent dimension of consciousness usually ignored in the West; namely, the union of intellect with the intuitive, pattern-seeing mind. "I see through the eye, not with it," said eighteenth-century poet-engraver William Blake. "The enemy of whole vision is our reasoning power's divorce from imagination."[3]

It is easier to analyze the various components of your business's systems and subsystems when you are alone, when the pressures of business are far removed. This is the time to store precise-method data (i.e., "program the left brain"), available from using the recommended forms and procedures that follow. This is also the time to objectively analyze past performance and to creatively devise new methods.

During the hectic pace of a typical business day you are also more likely to be affected by numerous right-brain (affective domain) influences than you are when alone. It isn't always easy when under pressure to respond with logic and common sense. In the heat of emotion, for instance, you're more likely to act on impulse. And where do you think our impulses come from, if not from the feeling-intuitive right side of the brain?

Visualize the following scene, for instance:

> You have just arrived late at your place of business, having already suffered through a fight with your mate over breakfast, squabbling children on their way to school, and an early-morning traffic jam. As you walk in the door you hear the telephones ringing and one or more employees complaining. Nearby stands a supplier you had a confrontation with last week, frowning and shuffling his feet. Your pulse rate quickens and you feel your temper rise. Just then an obviously irate customer approaches. . . .

Just how "logical" and poised do you suppose you'll be? Wouldn't it be better to have already programmed your (left) brain with clues and information about how to handle a variety of situations?

The specific management tools and methods that follow can help you plan, organize, implement, and be ready to control your business. It's up to you to decide what specific objectives you'll address and where, when, and under what conditions each is appropriate to you and your business.

Management by Objectives/Results (MBO/R)

The MBO/R program leads you first to state your business objectives and then to project the results and when they should be realized. Although MBO is a comprehensive system of managing, when reduced to its essentials the MBO process involves the following steps: (1) setting objectives, (2) planning for action, (3) implementing plans and the MBO program, and (4) controlling organizational performance as well as appraising individual accomplishments.[4]

"Results" (in the MBO/R formula) are measurable by quantifiable criteria. The effectiveness of a marketing program, for example, can be measured in one way by identifying the number of new customers who come into the establishment or by noting the increased number of products sold on a broader market.

Figure 17.1 illustrates an MBO/R chart in use. Each chart has a single objective—in this case, to satisfy more of the store's existing customers (whose positive word-of-mouth remarks will in turn bring in more customers).

To use an MBO/R chart, follow these steps:

1. State a single objective, clearly and concisely.
2. List under "Now" the conditions in your enterprise that now exist in relation to the objectives.

OBJECTIVE: Create satisfied customers for the store

Now	Benchmarks				Results
	Month #1	Month #2	Month #3	Month #4	
1. Clerks are elsewhere (stocking inventory, visiting, etc.)	Training program	Buddy system (best clerks w/less ex'd)	Observe results	Clerks are available and courteous	1. Customers are greeted pleasantly by knowledgeable clerks
2. Display racks and counters are crowded	Rearrange	Observe and record data	Rearrange again if needed	Displays are well spaced and attractive	2. Customers have space to browse
3. Many products of one kind; not enough of others	Conduct marketing research with customers	Adjust stock orders	Observe and record data	Desired products are available	3. Customers find what they're looking for
4. Sometimes there are long lines of customers waiting at cashier stand	Observe and record data	Add 1-2 cashier stations or training program	Assess results and adjust	Clerks check out customer as needed	4. Customers are waited on when ready
5. Not all clerks know how to handle "exceptions"—i.e., making refunds or exchanges, getting back orders, processing layaways	Training program	Check results of training (observe and/or ask customers)	Fewer complaints occur	Complaints, backorders, and layaways are handled efficiently	5. Customer complaints are satisfied
					Ultimate Result More satisfied customers; increased sales and more new customers

FIGURE 17.1 MBO/R Planning Tool.

3. Devise a series of actions or benchmarks (including times to monitor progress) that will gradually change these conditions and show when the incremental changes should be met.
4. Under "Results," list the ideal outcome of each proposed action.

Once you have planned your campaign, organize your resources and start to implement it. Periodically measure progress against the benchmarks you devised and at the times designated. When the allotted completion time has arrived, evaluate the effectiveness of the project by assessing the bottom line. Do you now have more satisfied customers? (Or, have sales or productivity increased?) Was the net return achieved worth the cost of implementing the project?

If your anticipated results have not been achieved, you can reimplement any of the individual benchmark actions, abandon the plan, or redraft it and start anew. Of course, the efficient entrepreneur is simultaneously designing, implementing, and analyzing many such MBO/R-based projects (using both logic and creativity).

It takes most people awhile to fill out an MBO/R chart successfully. It is especially hard to devise good benchmarks on the way to the desired result. Also be sure that the time assigned to each interim task is realistic. Employee training, data collections, or visiting with customers will necessarily consume time over and above that needed to conduct routine business affairs each day.[5]

Communicating New Objectives

It also takes time to communicate new plans to subordinates. If they do not understand what is going to happen and why, their morale and thus their productivity may be affected, to the detriment of both the plan and the performance of their ordinary duties. Wherever people are involved, in fact, the potential for disruption and lowered morale exists. Even where no employees are affected, customers, vendors, or others may feel the impact of the change.

Brenda keeps track of progress toward meeting actions and time lines for each objective.

Facilitating Change

People fear change. They are comfortable with what they are doing and the methods they are using. They suspect that a new procedure will make them both feel and look inadequate.

There are five types of people with respect to change: innovators, early adopters, adopters, late adopters, and non-adopters. The "innovators" are people who set fashion or who, as a group, create new fads. "Early adopters" follow shortly thereafter to join the innovators, after discovering that innovation in some area or another has occurred. (People in both groups who can afford it have already purchased microcomputers.)

"Adopters" are the middle-of-the-roaders. They don't want to be first to change or to follow fashion, but they don't like being left behind either. "Late adopters" reject many fads and trends. They are conservative and traditional. They prefer the status quo, and any change makes them nervous. Only after the majority are doing something else will they change at all, and even then they often resist and complain.

"Non-adopters" don't change! Typical of this group are people who still use manual typewriters or wear crew cuts.

Change means learning, and learning is painful. Thus people have to see a need behind the change, an ultimate benefit it will bring—to themselves and/or to the business. People will accept change more easily if their peers accept it. Thus it is important to seek member involvement and interaction in instigating any change, however minor.

People also need time to practice the new ways and to unlearn the old ones. Take a person who types relatively well, using two fingers. The greater the speed (and accuracy) obtained using this method, the longer it will take before the person can type as well using the 10-finger or touch method.

There are four basic ways in which people change their minds:

1. Change by exception. The old belief system remains intact but allows for a small handful of exceptions.

2. Incremental change. Change occurs small step by small step; the person is basically unaware that change is taking place.

3. Pendulum change. One method or belief is completely relinquished for another—as when the fashion swings from long skirts to short ones, when people switch political parties, when a promiscuous person becomes a prude, or when smokers stop smoking.

4. Paradigm change. A "paradigm" is a pattern, and a paradigm change is one that brings a new perspective or insight to the data and allows it to come together in a new form. Paradigm change refines and integrates; it avoids the illusion of either-or.[6]

Peer Support

Few entrepreneurs are proficient in every aspect of their business. One source of advice to help you better facilitate the management of your business is business peers.

MINICASE

At AAA TV, Inc., a small television sales and service operation in North Miami, six appliance dealers from out of town converged to scrutinize the firm. Some dealers talked with a service technician, another group with front-office employees, while a third team poured over the company's books. This was a review of a business by a half-dozen of the owner's peers, who owned similar stores and knew what to look for.

All of the dealers were members of the Southeastern Critique Group, an informal organization of dealers from six states. The process spotlights a dealer's weaknesses and recommends better methods for managing the business.[7]

Most entrepreneurs would never expose their operations to a competitor. But, as one analyst remarks, "There are real emotional advantages (to everyone involved)—you can unload on each other." The owner of AAA TV, for example, received his colleagues' opinions on such questions as: "Should I concentrate on service or expand my sales effort? Should I add new product lines? How about employee morale? Where should the business be in ten years?" Nine out of ten participants in this network reported having improved their operations and/or their profits as a result of such critiques.[8]

Devil's advocate. Your employees can also be invited to advise you. Without an established system for gaining their productive input, however, your subordinates may volunteer no more than a "yes, sir" or "yes, ma'am." You can overcome this tendency by assigning someone (inside or outside of the company) the role of devil's advocate. It would be this person's role to provide an independent, objective analysis of a problem's nature and scope and to present fresh alternatives or modifications of an original proposal.[9]

Management Planning Tool

With the second management tool (Figure 17.2), you can plan out, organize, implement, and control business actions. You should design a different chart for each objective, identifying the target group—your customers, employees, vendors, or others—and devising a time line for each subset associated with the stated objective.

List, too, the resources needed, and forecast the hours required—from yourself, your subordinates, or others. Resources may include money, methods,

Objective: Improve security measures to reduce food and beverage pilferage

	Action Taken	Target Group	Time mo/wk	Resources Needed
Planning	Collect pilferage data	Businesspeople	8/1	Self (1-3 hours)
	Discuss legal implications (rights of employees and owner) Debate security measures and methods	Attorney, consultant, other business owners	8/2-3	Self (1-3 hours)
Organizing	"Quality control circle" discussions	Employees	9/1-2	Lawyer and/or consultant (2 hours)
	Devise new security, physical, records, and company procedures	Employees	9/3-4	Staff and selected employees (4-6 hours)
Implementing	New Systems Human: training and motivation, legal and other implications Physical: records, locks, interdepartmental procedures	Employees	10/2	Cost: $400-$500 (for consultants) Plus $400-$500, materials and new methods Also: lost time in discussion
Controlling	Assess morale	Employees	11/1-3	Self and employee time (assist in data collection and analyses)
	Collect and analyze pilferage data		11/4	Cost of program determined

Follow-up Branch back to "Planning" (using another system) or to "Quality control circles" if new pilferage data does not indicate decided improvement.

Finalizing Activity Analyze the results: increase in profit margin and employee morale; decrease in pilferage and losses.

FIGURE 17.2 Management Tool.

materials, machines, or such human resources as partners, employees, family members, attorneys, accountants, management consultants, or other business people.

During the planning stage, you may not be able to fill all the chart blocks in completely. Add this information as the plan progresses through the implementing and controlling stages. Here again you can invite your employees to participate.

PERT Chart

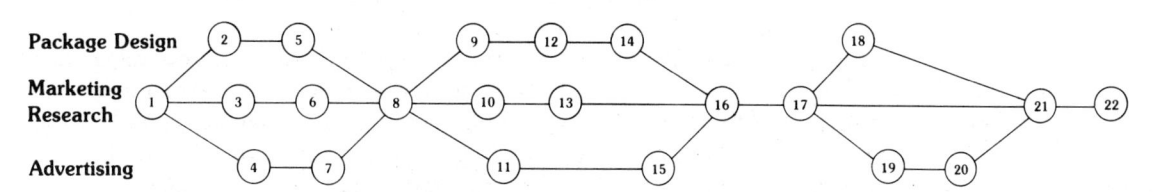

```
Package Design   (2)──(5)──────(9)──(12)──(14)──────(18)
                /                              \        \
Marketing   (1)──(3)──(6)──(8)──(10)──(13)──(16)──(17)──(21)──(22)
Research         \              /                   /
Advertising      (4)──(7)──────(11)──────(15)──(19)──(20)
```

1. Representatives from each subsystem meet to plan activities, resources, and needs, and to predict time lines

2. Commence gathering package-design data

3. Develop marketing research plan

4. Assess comparative promotion costs of various media

5. Submit several package designs

6. Identify the target group

7. Write initial advertising copy

8. Test the market re—two or more package designs

9. Create alternative package designs

10. Analyze marketing research data (reaction to the first 2-3 package designs)

11. Modify advertising copy as a result of #10

12. Verify cost comparison data to product alternative package designs

13. Modify marketing research plan: e.g., omit or add target groups (of different ages, interests, occupations, socioeconomic characteristics, etc.)

14. Coordinate with marketing research to select package design

15. Write new advertising copy to reach various target groups (see #13), using selected design (#14)

16. Test the selected package design on the target population.

17. Analyze marketing research data

18. Refine selected model design for package

19. Modify advertising campaign

20. Select media for product exposure

21. Coordinate implementation of advertising campaign

22. Analyze the results: increased sales; cost of production, advertising, and marketing research against net income

FIGURE 17.3   PERT Chart.

PERT Chart

To achieve even a relatively limited objective, you may have to pursue many steps simultaneously. The PERT—"Program Evaluation Review Technique"—chart (Figure 17.3) was developed by the Navy to coordinate the development and production of the Polaris weapons system. It allows you to visually trace a whole process.

Formal and comprehensive use of PERT for a complex project involves determining the "shortest critical path method" and identifying the longest (most pessimistic) and the shortest (most optimistic) times to achieve each subset.[10]

However, you can also use PERT informally as a simplistic visual depiction of what activities, from among three or four similar subgroups, must be conducted together and completed at given times.

Suppose you want to introduce a product in a new package. You will need to conduct three efforts simultaneously and interactively: (1) package design and development, (2) research on consumer response to the innovative design, and (3) writing the advertising copy and selecting the media that can best attract consumers. Mapped on a PERT chart, what results is a zigzag pattern of functions (subsets) performed in a staggered order.

In Figure 17.3, the top line traces those tasks that must be performed by the package design/development team. The middle line focuses on activities to be conducted by the marketing research group, and the bottom line on the tasks assigned to the advertising team. Steps 8, 16, 17, and 21 require coordination among the three teams. The product design people must have the first prototype ready for the marketing research group to test on the market (nos. 5 and 6) and the advertising people must be ready to write the copy (no. 7) prior to step 8—the first market test.

All three teams may not produce a "perfect" subsystem product on their first try. Thus the PERT chart allows for all three subsets to be modified and reimplemented.

Flowcharting

Flowcharts can trace many types of activities, including: work flow, traffic flow, an individual worker's activity (vertical flow), or a single task moving through the hands of several workers (horizontal flow).

Figure 17.4 gives the basic symbols that entrepreneurs in small businesses need to devise useful flowcharts.[11]

Vertical Flow and the Job Description

The easiest flow to describe and depict seems, at first glance, to be the duties of an individual worker. You may only have to list the duties in order of the preferred order of performance. The fewer different duties assigned, the more straightforward the chart—supposedly.

A receiving-order clerk may handle mail duties in addition to receiving callers and customer orders; but all tasks would be performed at the front desk or counter, making the worker consistently available to walk-in people and to the telephone. The task list (shown on the job description under the section, "Duties to Perform") might read in sequence like this:

1. Open the store/office and verify that the customer-receiving area and the lighting and heating are appropriate and operating properly, ready to receive visitors.
2. Open the mail; date-stamp and distribute it.

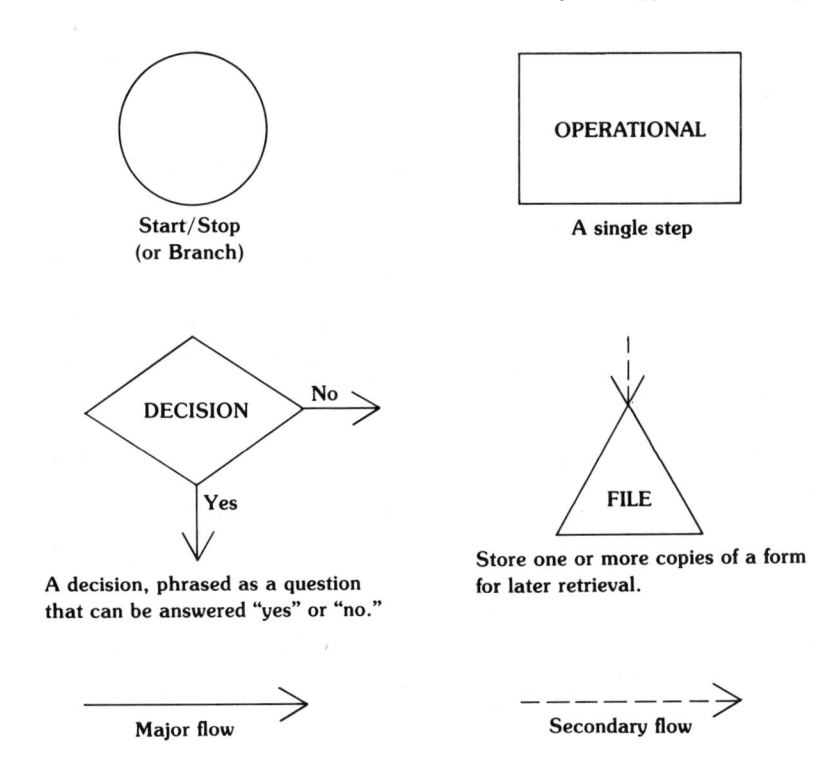

FIGURE 17.4
Basic Flowcharting Symbols.

Start/Stop (or Branch)

OPERATIONAL — A single step

DECISION — A decision, phrased as a question that can be answered "yes" or "no."

FILE — Store one or more copies of a form for later retrieval.

Major flow

Secondary flow

3. Greet visitors and make them comfortable; take orders as needed.
4. Answer the telephone and transmit calls as appropriate.
5. Impart information as requested by walk-ins or callers.
6. Make telephone calls as needed.
7. Keep the appointment calendar (for the owner or other employees).
8. Collect mail; seal and stamp it.
9. Close the office/store, verifying that lighting and heating are turned off or down, and the customer-receiving area is ready for closing.

Yet each of these tasks can require a separate chart of its own, once the subsets are clearly defined. A new employee, for example, would have difficulty if given this list with no further interpretation or training. Consider nos. 4-6 above. Without knowing where specific calls are to be routed, for what reasons, and under what conditions, a worker trying to "transmit calls as appropriate" could encounter many pitfalls. What if the owner doesn't want to talk to John Doe at all but absolutely must confer with Mary Moe before either the banker or the attorney arrives? The clerk must be made aware of such owner preferences in order to properly carry out the required task.

Nor can the receiving-order clerk "impart information as requested" without understanding a great deal about the company, its products and services, and what information it is and is not permissible to impart. Also needed are many bits of informal data. It might be all right for the clerk to tell a spouse that the boss is out on the golf course (or having a long lunch) with a client, but to reveal such news to a competitor might be inappropriate.

Thus the vertical charting of a clerk's sequence of duties might involve nine different charts. To keep the process as simple as possible at this point, only task no. 1 has been charted (Figure 17.5).

Although it is unlikely that you will want to prepare formal charts for every task performed by each employee and yourself, depicting at least several tasks by this means helps to "program the mind." It is often little things that spell the difference between effective performance and efficient, courteous service, on the one hand, and the disaster of failing at both, on the other.

Flowcharting for exceptions. If no exceptions occur, the task mapped in Figure 17.6 is fairly straightforward. But exceptions invariably do occur. As Murphy's Law says: "Nothing is as easy as it looks, everything takes longer than you think, and if anything can go wrong, it will."[12] All workers need to know how to deal with the many exceptions that occur every day in business, whether in working with customers or with machines, methods, materials, or money.

There is a story that circulated some years ago, when computers were beginning to gain wide acceptance. The moral was not only that machines make mistakes but that humans may not know how to deal with computer-related and other exceptions.

> Barry Parceau received his monthly electricity bill, which usually ranged from $35 to $40. This time, however, the computerized billing system had charged him $4035. When he stumbled into the electric company, shocked by this turn of events, the receiving clerk appeared puzzled. Smiling sweetly, she suggested, "Why don't you just pay the full amount, Mr. Parceau, and we'll credit you with the balance."

Apparently the clerk had only one alternative for adjusting to this type of exception. The decision symbol on the chart therefore represents those points where unanticipated options may occur. Note that every action that branches off the main track must loop back to pick up the next logical step in the flow process. No step can be left dangling. The sequence is complete only when all steps have been performed and the sequence closes with the Stop circle, indicating "the office is ready" to receive visitors and customers.

Developing job descriptions with MBO/R. Many job descriptions (JDs) merely list a worker's assigned tasks. The JD for the receiving-order clerk contains at least nine specific duties. One way to give employees a better idea of what you want them to accomplish in the job is to state an objective, using the MBO/R chart: e.g., "Increase counter sales by 15 percent."

This statement tells the clerk that he or she is responsible for more in the front office than merely processing repaired products and paperwork. Through participative management the employee contributes to developing the MBO/R chart, agreeing to the benchmarks, time lines for monitoring progress, and the desired

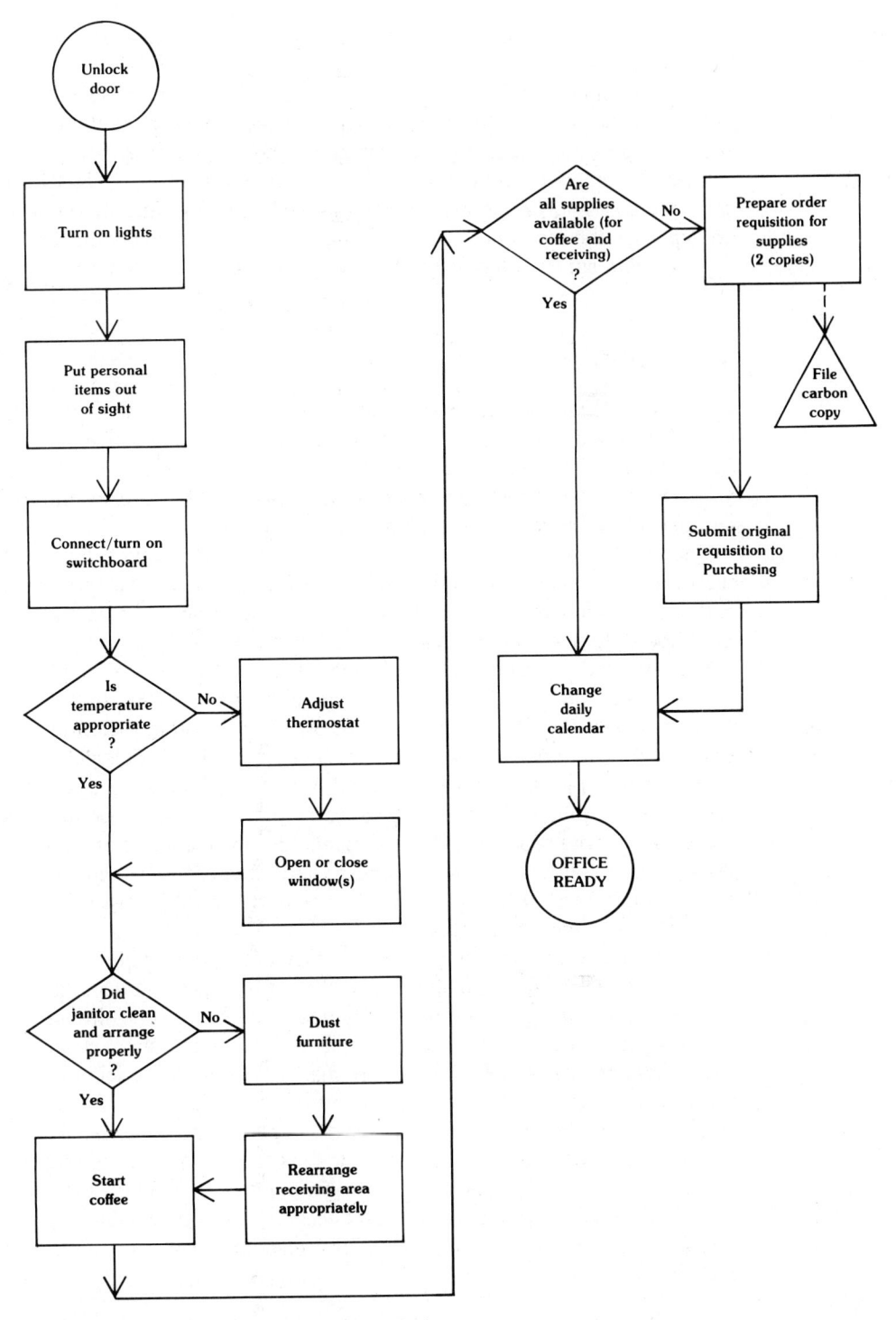

FIGURE 17.5 Vertical Flowchart of One Task.

result. Both in attitude and in behavior, this person can thus contribute to increased sales.

Another way of involving employees is to ask them to help define their own jobs. What are their major responsibilities? Then, for each duty assigned and accepted, you can effectively measure the worker's performance.

Inviting employees to help develop their own JDs and related MBO/R charts can have some surprising results, however. Often bosses and their workers do not agree on the major responsibilities involved. You may even find that no one is performing some of the functions that you consider important![13]

Horizontal Flow

This type of chart takes the vertical flowchart a step further, to account for the horizontal interaction when procedures involve more than one person. The chart (Figure 17.6) depicts the flow of a customer's repair order from the time the appliance leaves the latter's hands until the customer receives the repaired product plus a bill for services rendered.

Once vertical charts have been developed for each worker, the horizontal chart is easier to construct and to follow. At first glance, it may appear that the parts clerk has few steps to perform. But on the clerk's vertical chart this function would be only one among a variety of other duties.

The encircled "2" under the bookkeeper's list of steps stands for a branch, to another chart that leads the bookkeeper to additional activities. In this case, the no. 2 chart would include posting the customer's work order to accounts receivable and debiting the customer's charge account until the bill is paid.

The smaller the firm, the less likely it is that you'll need to develop either vertical or horizontal charts. As the repair company in the above example expands, hires more repair people, and inventories thousands upon thousands of parts for resale, however, the procedures and interactions become more complex, and the need for analytical supervision and control grows. Entrepreneurs who can systematically manage every part and function of their businesses can identify potential bottlenecks before or as they occur, and correct them quickly.

A horizontal flowchart can help you analyze current procedures, while seeking workers' input, and pinpoint where changes may be needed. It can diagram complex processes involving many people and things and show clearly how all these elements interact. Diagrams can chart the flow of a single element—of goods or information. But these factors must be coordinated. Otherwise, in the example given above, customers will likely experience the too-familiar frustration of waiting while some anxious clerk sorts through papers or tries to track down some other employee in order to get the data needed for the bill.

Such detailed coordination is less necessary in computerized operations, where all relevant data is input into the electronic files and is consistently available for retrieval.

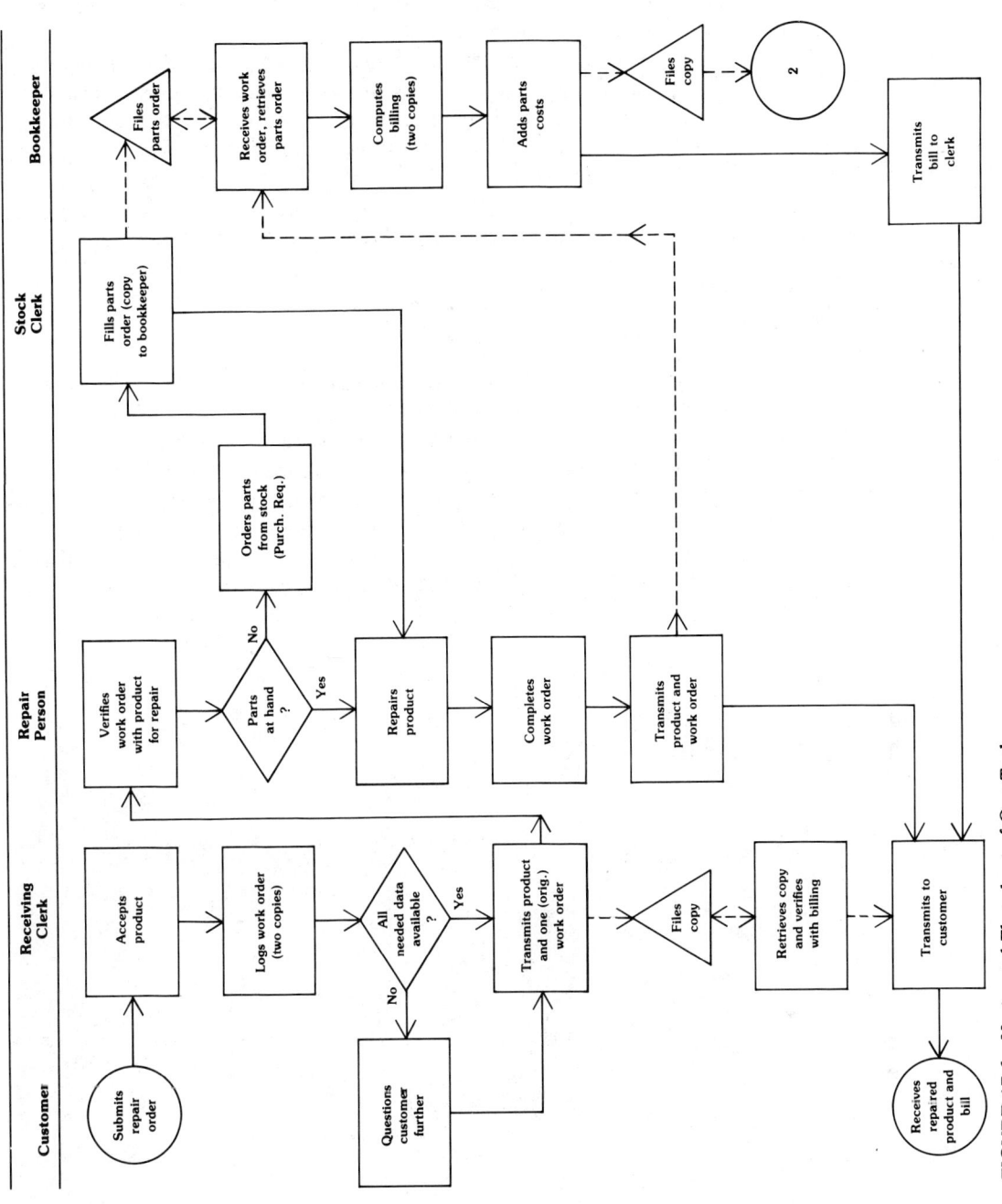

FIGURE 17.6 Horizontal Flowchart of One Task.

The horizontal flowchart combines both the work flow and the information flow. Thus the many activities involved in any given procedure—even complex ones—can be carefully coordinated.[14]

You can construct several horizontal flowcharts simply by watching your staff work. Systematically record on the chart the steps your employees follow. Then, at your leisure or theirs, you can analyze procedures and devise improvements.

A well-designed work environment will also promote the objective of efficiency, both behind the scenes and up front where customers are served. (See also Chapter 9 for how to analyze a physical layout. Compare the repair shop layout shown there with the horizontal flowchart in Figure 17.6 to identify additional recommendations.)

Time and Motion (T&M) Analyses

"Time is money," and wasted motion is wasted time. Watch the specific motions your workers make and the time it takes them to perform their tasks. Then experiment with new ways to do those tasks that might save energy, movement, and time. You can use a stopwatch to time the various methods. Those motions that take the least time and produce the least fatigue over a long period may be selected as the best method(s) for performing any one task. Another kind of T&M study clocks an employee's performance of the same activity at different times of the day. The sequencing of that person's tasks may be rearranged as a

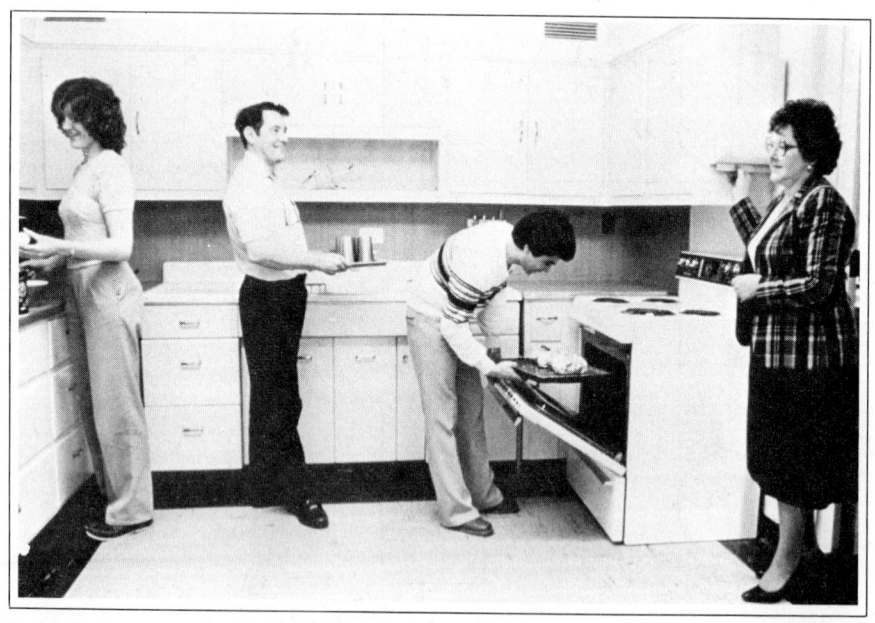

Dr. Gade, home economist, and her students chart kitchen-work flow, time motions, and analyze methods for making the work system more efficient.

result. Use your intuition and imagine how the company's operation appears to your customers or employees. You may hit on new and better ways of arranging and performing needed tasks.

Your employees will appreciate your helping them "work smarter, not harder." But only if you're sure to explain what you're doing and why.

Once faster, more efficient methods are developed, routine tasks can be performed quickly, without much thought. These repetitious (often menial) tasks then become "therbligs."

Therbligs

Frank and Lillian Gilbreth were early contributers to the scientific management school of thought. Among their activities were experiments conducted to improve work methods. In their micromotion studies, work was divided into its most fundamental or basic motions, known as "therbligs." The motions were studied separately and in relation to one another, and from these studied motions, when timed, methods of least waste and least motion were developed.[15]

Parents of a dozen children, these industrial psychologists also implemented T&M methods at home, determining the shortest path and quickest time for any one household task.

The Gilbreths invented the term "therblig," by inverting their last name. The word stands for those routine activities that can be performed in the same way (often at the same time). The same motions and sequence of steps are performed in the same manner each time until the person's brain and psychomotor subsystems function without conscious thought.[16]

Most people already employ many therbligs as they go about their everyday activities. For example, when you get up in the morning, you don't consciously decide what physical motions are needed to get from the bedroom to the bathroom, to open the medicine cabinet and take out the toothbrush and toothpaste, and to brush your teeth. Turning the many routine tasks at work into therbligs can help you and your employees accomplish tasks faster and more systematically, and thus free everybody's minds for more creative and demanding endeavors.

Time Savers

According to R. James Steffen, management consultant and author of two books on saving time, "Most people could be 20 to 30 percent more productive, and the exciting thing about it is that their increased productivity would be more satisfying to them."[17]

Most people don't know how to allocate their time and energy or how to get the most out of each moment because, for one thing, they find it difficult to separate those things over which they have control from those over which they have no control. Using the MBO/R method, you and your staff can apply these six steps:

1. Identify and write down your objectives, one per chart.
2. "Divide and conquer"—i.e., organize the objectives into subsets; as each one is "conquered," you and your employees will be so much closer to your overall goal.
3. Update your priorities regularly and rearrange the order of subsets as needed.
4. Implement subsets, on menial tasks at least, in the same way at the same time as often as possible, in order to routinize their performance (turning subsets into therbligs).
5. Write down anything you want to remember, when you think of it; use the same system for recording notes and put them in a regular place.
6. Have a convenient place for everything and keep everything in its place.

SUMMARY

If you'll arrange to conduct systematic analyses of your business and to devise creative management plans, you can circumvent numerous potential problems. Such organizational assessments can provide: (1) order and system; (2) division and specialization of labor; (3) direction and control; (4) an awareness of organizational needs; and (5) well-defined roles, relationships, communication channels, and responsibilities.[18]

Systematic methods of analysis, including the construction and use of the charts proposed in this chapter, can help you become objective and logical in the managerial tasks of supervision and adjustment so essential to business success. However, the ability to look at a system creatively and randomly is as necessary as the logical approach. Otherwise, new and different methods of doing things will seldom be discovered.

Explaining the reasons behind any given change and helping your employees adjust to change and overcome their fears can win you their valuable support. Using participative management, you can involve your employees in various decision-making processes. But also, their contributions will give you additional ideas and, as we shall discuss in more detail in Chapter 20, this involvement can serve as a motivator. When your employees are allowed to take some responsibility in facilitating the management and control of your business, they are more likely to contribute positively to achieving desired results.

Helping your employees make the best use of their time and energy can also save you money, while showing your workers that you care. For when you can help your employees and together manage tasks and responsibilities, they begin to perceive how they can contribute to the success of the company without feeling overworked or exploited.

DISCUSSION QUESTIONS

1. How do analytic and intuitive approaches operate together to produce effective, creative management—e.g., in systematic analyses, in attacking issues creatively, and in dealing with people?
2. Compare the MBO/R chart (Figure 17.1) with the management planning tool (Figure 17.2). Which instrument would you prefer to use? What advantages would there be in using them together? Note that the examples given reflect two different objectives. How would you use both tools for the same objective?
3. Compare the MBO/R chart with the PERT chart (Figure 17.3). How would these two tools contribute to accomplishing an objective if used together?
4. What are the relative advantages of participative management, inviting input from business colleagues, or appointing a devil's advocate as ways of assisting an owner-manager to assess conditions and make decisions?
5. Using the vertical flowchart (Figure 17.5), discuss other exceptions that might occur, other questions that might be asked (with a decision symbol), and the actions that would be needed to bring the loop back into line with normal procedures.
6. Compare JDs with the vertical and horizontal flowcharts to be sure you understand how these tools are used—singly and interactively.
7. Compare the shop/office layout (see the illustration in Chapter 9) with the horizontal flowchart. Discuss the work flow and the paper flow in relation to the layout.
8. Discuss how various types of analysis can reveal inefficient or wasteful uses of time and energy.
9. When workers are comfortable with any one method or machine, they typically resist change. Discuss methods you might use to gain their understanding and cooperation in changing a system or mode of operation (e.g., from manual to computer).
10. Discuss how you might save time and motions ("work smarter, not harder") in your own life now. When you have made personal applications of the principles of T&M and therbligs, you are more likely to feel natural about the process.

ACTIVITIES AND EXERCISES

1. Use the MBO/R chart and the management planning tool. Select a single objective to achieve in your personal or organization (civic, church, or school) life, and fill out these two forms in conjunction with each other. Have another team or person analyze the results. This peer evaluator takes the role of a business colleague or a devil's advocate.

2. Using the two charts prepared in no. 1, construct a PERT chart to reflect the times and simultaneous actions needed to complete the stated objective. Option: assemble several MBO/R and management planning tools that address objectives within a single major project. This method permits the coordination of several objectives into one comprehensive activity.
3. Select another task from the receiving-order clerk's partial JD. Then follow these steps:
   a. Write the statement in the form of a measurable objective—action that would make this person more responsible for improving company sales or services (revenue). Simultaneously, the "employee" should be able to feel good about himself or herself as a member of the participative management group.
   b. Construct a vertical flowchart of this one subset (task). Build in exceptions with decision symbols to complete the loop.
4. Apply some of the timesaving principles given above to your personal or work situation. Where can you save time and/or motions? Can you make activities that you currently dread into therbligs? Report the results and your reactions.
5. Participate in the *Stanley Junction* projects, "Brainstorming Socio-Economic Business Interaction" and "Time Management."

NOTES

1. Bruce D. Henderson, "The Anatomy of Competition," *Journal of Marketing*, Vol. 47, Spring 1983, pp. 7–11.
2. Rajeswararao Chaganti and Radharao Chaganti, "A Profile of Profitable and Not-So-Profitable Small Businesses," *Journal of Small Business Management*, July 1983, pp. 43–51. (See also Roger A. Golde, "Practical Planning for Small Business," *Harvard Business Review*, Reprint Series on Small Business, Part 1, pp. 11–109.)
3. Marilyn Ferguson. *The Aquarian Conspiracy: Personal and Social Transformation in the 1980s* (Los Angeles: J. P. Tarcher, 1980), pp. 46–47, 49.
4. Heinz Weihrich and Richard B. Babcock, "Relationships Between Organizational Phenomena and MBO Process," *Industrial Management*, July–August 1982, pp. 25–29. (See also Weihrich, "A New Approach to MBO—Updating a Time-Honored Technique," *Management World*, April 1977, pp. 6–12.)
5. "Management by Objectives/Results," procedures and chart adapted from methods used at the Center for Constructive Change, Durham, NH.
6. Ferguson. *Aquarian Conspiracy*, pp. 71–72.
7. Craig R. Waters, "Trial by Jury," *Inc.*, May 1982, pp. 81–86.
8. Ibid.
9. "The Devil's Advocate," *Small Business Report* (Monterey, CA: Small Business Monitoring and Research Company, October 1982), pp. 20–22.
10. Olive Church and Anne Schatz. *Office Systems and Careers* (Boston: Allyn and Bacon, Inc., 1981), pp. 290, 296.

11. Olive Church, "Employee Manual," *Secretarial Services Center* (Boston: Allyn and Bacon, 1979), p. 10.
12. Arthur Bloch. *Murphey's Law and Other Reasons Why Things Go Wrong* (Los Angeles: Price/Stern/Sloan Publishers, Inc., 1982), p. 11.
13. Raymond F. Pellissier, "Planning and Goal Setting for Small Business," *Management Aid* no. 2.010. (Washington, D.C.: U.S. Small Business Administration, 1981).
14. Hilda Turner, "Paper Management for the Entrepreneurship," *Business Education Forum* (Reston, VA: National Business Education Association), April 1979, pp. 23–25.
15. B. Lewis Keeling, Norman F. Kallaus, and John J. W. Neuner. *Administrative Office Management* (Cincinnati, OH: South-Western Publishing Co., 8th ed., 1983), p. 360.
16. Ibid.
17. "How to Stop Wasting Time—Experts' Advice," *U.S. News & World Report,* January 25, 1982.
18. Curtis E. Tate, Jr., "Organization Planning and Management Succession: Cases in Small Business Survival," *Economic Research on Small Business: The Environment for Entrepreneurship and Small Business.* (Washington, D.C.: U.S. Small Business Administration) pp. 103–104.

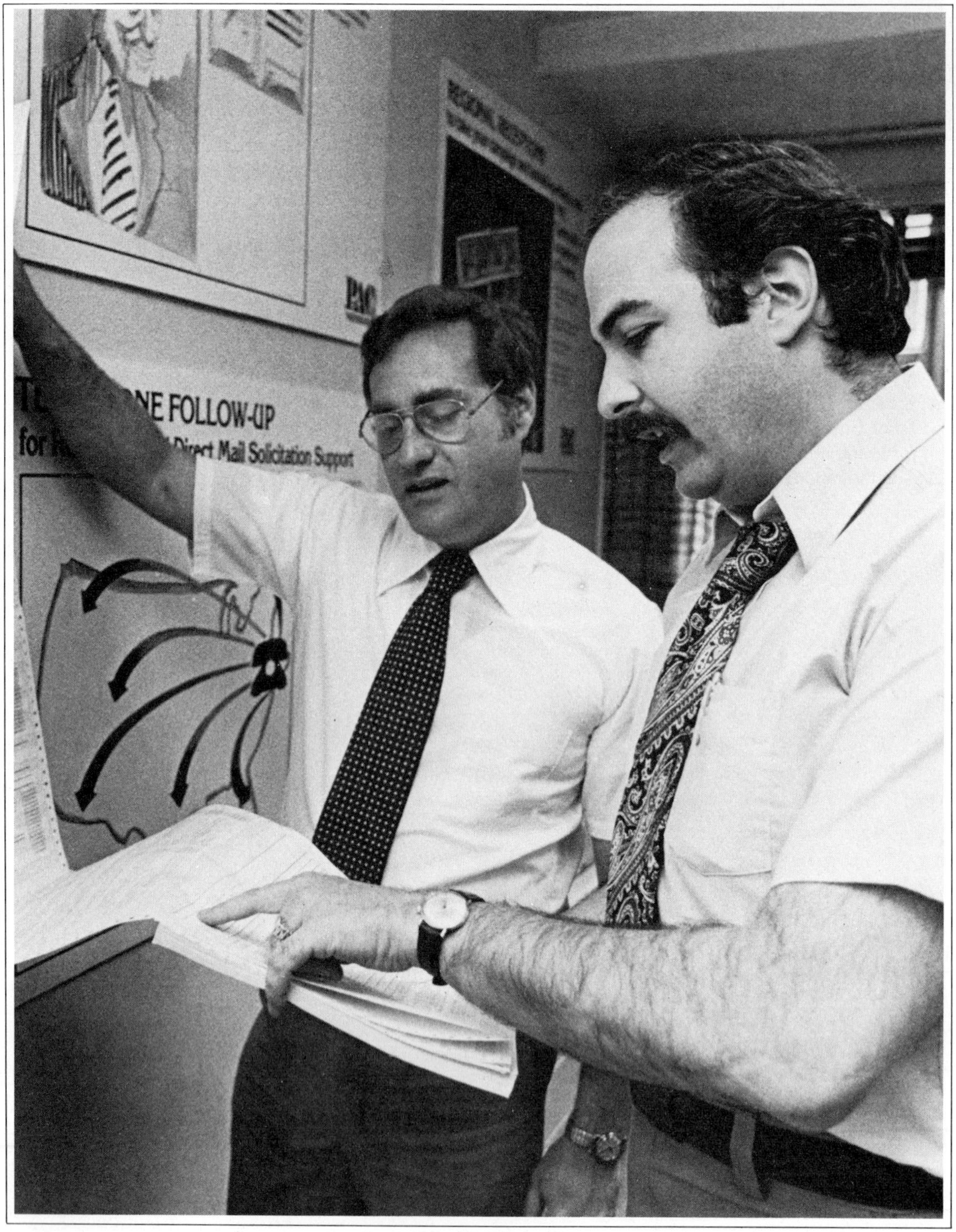
FOLLOW-UP
Direct Mail Solicitation Support

chapter 18

Market Research, Advertising, and Selling

Objectives

1. Use the MBO/R tool to implement and control a market research study for your business.
2. Develop a management plan for an advertising campaign in your business.
3. Describe Maslow's Hierarchy in relation to understanding customers' needs as a means of improving services and increasing sales.
4. Demonstrate effective sales techniques, from meeting the customer to eliciting action in closing a sale.

Assume that your business has been operational long enough to start turning a profit. Although it appears you can take a breather, now is not the time to grow complacent. Instead, you should continue to employ management techniques and tools to analyze your business and to adjust and create plans accordingly.

MARKET RESEARCH AND ADVERTISING

In Chapter 7 you learned how market research can provide important data about locations, demographics, and the competition, and can help you select products and services and establish policies. These same strategies can be used to improve your ongoing business practices.

Many owners, even of small firms, hire specialists to conduct their market research. Other entrepreneurs direct their own research, using both informal and formal techniques. Eventually, the methodology becomes second nature. Owners move about their stores, offices, and plants daily, visiting with repeat and new customers on a regular basis. Are customers satisfied? If not, what changes would they like to see? Do employees have suggestions? How would they: provide better customer service, improve advertising and sales, or change internal systems to achieve greater efficiency?

One retailer, who had set up several bargain tables, wanted to determine which product sold best. For one day, customers received a free sack of unshelled peanuts at the door and were told they could throw the shells on the floor. At the end of the day the entrepreneur simply followed the trial of debris to determine which parts of the store had experienced the most traffic.

Although this strategy may sound messy, even silly, it's a classic example of the creativity business owners use to informally test the effectiveness of their decisions. Entrepreneurs conduct informal polls and surveys, count pedestrian and vehicle traffic, and test products and services—all through random interviews and observation. They also use the services of market research.

Marketing Strategy

Marketing strategy is essentially the same as marketing management. Victor Cook, for example, views marketing strategy as an investment in the marketing mix variables in order to gain a specified strategic objective.[1]

Marketing management is concerned with target market selection and the design of the marketing program. Marketing management literature addresses issues at the level of the individual product or brand. Marketing strategy, on the other hand, addresses issues of gaining long-run advantage at the level of the firm or business unit. Marketing strategy, as the quest for long-run competitive advantage, sounds like it is synonymous with "business strategy." Indeed, marketing strategy is a major component of business strategy, although the latter also encompasses financial, product, technological, and human resource analysis.

Business strategy does rely heavily on marketing strategy, and many of the business strategy paradigms are based on "marketing" variables including market share, market growth, and target marketing decisions. But the specific formulation of these paradigms is the domain of marketing strategy.[2]

In a competitive market, as on a military field, a strategy can be defined with reference to the behavior of rivals. In marketing, the behavior is competitive deployment of marketing resources. Defining ambition is the first step in understanding strategy. Reference is often made to a firm's intention to "dominate" on media spending, to "match" its competitors' commitments, or to "flank" the superior product performance of a rival. "Dominate" is the most ambitious marketing strategy short of monopoly. At the other extreme is a retreat strategy. In the mid-range of ambition, a match strategy invests at a rate that matches or equals competitive resource deployments.[3]

Doing Your Own Market Research

There is no guarantee that today's effective marketing program will still be effective tomorrow. To keep a marketing plan strong you must continuously evaluate the program by comparing the results it is achieving against your objectives and schedule.

There are several reasons why the obtaining of reliable, valid information about the marketplace often proves to be a difficult task:

1. The marketing environment is dynamic. Conditions in the marketplace are in a constant state of change. Marketing variables such as customer needs, competition, government regulations, and economic events simply do not stand still. Marketing studies, on the other hand, are often static.
2. Failure to specify objectives. It is essential to determine why you want to do a marketing research study; that is, what data you want to gather and for what purpose. The specification of objectives establishes a foundation and a starting point for all that is to follow. These objectives should lead to the specifics of what you expect to accomplish.
3. Improper applications of methods and principles. The questions you ask determine the answers you get. For instance, many small business owners use mail surveys because of the low cost. Yet where the study requires complex instructions, visual cues, or includes areas where the literacy rate is low, the mail survey may prove ineffective.

In short, the type of research design depends on the type of market being studied. Industrial markets often dictate different approaches to market research than those used to research consumer and retail markets.[4]

Focus group interviews. Focus groups consist of unstructured, personal discussions, with a small group (eight to ten) of customers or subject matter experts. The purpose is to draw out opinions or feelings about a product, service, ad campaign, or other subject of interest. Group interviews can be moderated by the owner, someone in the business, or by an outside research firm or consultant. A word of caution: the focus group should be used for exploratory purposes only, and not as conclusive findings which represent a larger population.[5]

Keep your focus-group interviews (and other marketing surveys) simple. Some entrepreneurs have a tendency to throw everything into a study that they can think of. The idea seems to be, "as long as we're talking to them, let's find out a few more things." Avoid this tendency. Work on one problem (objective) at a time in the most straightforward way possible. You'll also want to follow up later. A few questions asked at different points in time can be more valuable than many questions asked only once. Such an approach will enable you to establish trends and to identify changes in variables.[6]

The following examples of data-collection methods can be used in different kinds of businesses on a routine but informal basis.

Hospitality establishments. Restaurateurs who change their menus often wander among their patrons to hear reactions. Other food-establishment owners regularly observe what food remains on patrons' plates. If a particular offering invariably goes half-eaten, the owners ask diners about that item.[7]

Many hospitality firms, in fact, leave customer evaluation sheets scattered about—in hotel and motel rooms, on restaurant tables, even in the restrooms of gasoline service stations. Although owners receive many criticisms of both services and facilities, some guests do make favorable and/or constructive comments.

Some evaluation sheets ask first-time guests how they were attracted to the establishment: through friends, business associates, or other word-of-mouth advertising; by roadside signs or the establishment's appearance; or through the Yellow Pages or newspapers, magazines, or radio ads. Guests may also be asked this question in person. Their responses give an informal measure of the effectiveness of various advertising outlets.

Motel owners count the cars parked in front of other motels and watch for the competition's advertisements in newspapers, on the radio, and so on. Simultaneously, whenever a motelier launches a new ad campaign, room sales can be tallied to see if more guests have been attracted.

Owners keep records of return customers and also of those who, after repeated visits, no longer return. The regulars are frequently invited to make comments and to offer suggestions. Those who stop coming back sometimes receive telephone calls or letters asking why they stopped patronizing the establishment.

All of this data influences subsequent managerial decisions. Attention is often directed to improving services and the attitude or performance of the staff who serve guests. There may be a need to upgrade physical facilites, buy new furniture, or otherwise remodel or rearrange the establishment.

Retail establishments. Chapter 16 discussed how newspaper coupons can remind customers of your offerings and attract them into the store. Coupons can also measure the effectiveness of advertising. The number of coupons turned in tells you how many people the ad brought into your store, and a comparison of the total sales on the advertised product with previous sales tells you how much the ad increased your intake. (See Figure 18.1.)

Advertisements for the same product(s) that appear in different media can be coded and compared against each other, if good records are kept. Suppose that specific lawn and garden tools are advertised by newspaper one week, and by radio the next. If nothing else varies—if prices aren't changed or displays rearranged for example—some comparisons can be made by counting the number of sales each week.

Following are topical questions around which you might build a market study. The data you gather might then become the basis for an improvement plan—one that should be both creative and realistic and whose effects should be monitored by follow-up studies. Ask yourself:

1. Which of the media reaches my target group most effectively?
2. What types of advertisements encourage the most purchases? (See Figure 18.2.)
3. Are my window displays attracting customers?
4. Are my store displays in the best possible location?
5. Which items are bought on impulse and should thus be placed in high-traffic areas?
6. Are my products displayed to maximize their appeal within the store? Which products have the most eye appeal?
7. Do my displays attract attention to other products nearby? That is, do I display related products together—e.g., shortcake and whipping cream near fresh strawberries?

FIGURE 18.1
Owners can conduct their own informal marketing research by keeping track of how many coupons are used on which products to test the effectiveness of specific advertising.

8. Have I established a schedule for changing various displays? Can I provide new and different displays without frustrating customers because they can't find what they want in the usual place?
9. Are the price tags easy to read?
10. Which of the special services I offer—such as credit purchases, deliveries, alterations, refunds, or free gift wrapping—appeals to customers most? To what extent do these services contribute to sales?
11. Do I contribute to charities, make donations, or provide free space or advertising to schools and civic organizations? If so, can I measure how much these contributions affect sales or create goodwill?
12. Do I participate in activities of the Chamber of Commerce, my merchants' association, the Better Business Bureau, or other civic organizations? Is there some way I can measure the benefits, if any, of my participation?[8]

Wholesalers often provide market information to aid retailers in attracting customers and satisfying their needs. Through their numerous contacts with local businesses and distant suppliers, wholesalers accumulate data on consumer demand, prices, supply conditions, and new developments in the market. Retailers have access to this information through the wholesalers' publications—bulletins and newsletters—and by talking with sales representatives.

Service establishments. Building a reputation for fast, reliable, and honest service is one of the best means of promoting service businesses. Of course you also will want to advertise in various media and develop an identifiable logo that can appear on the company's business cards, forms, and signs. Using the same symbol with every advertising method helps clients identify your business with its offerings and reputation.

Effective public relations are also important. Items 11 and 12 above suggest the kind of personal contacts that can establish your status with community organizations and institutions. People must not only learn about your company and what it has to offer but they must develop a feeling of confidence in your ability to satisfy their needs and wants. Positive and productive word-of-mouth advertising is critical to your success.

Manufacturing and broad-market establishments. Manufacturers sometimes develop a new consumer product, but few wholesalers or retailers are willing to invest their capital to stock a large volume of the items in their inventory. Manufacturers also sometimes discover that the seasonal products they want to sell pose such a capital risk to their customers that the products have little chance of reaching retail shelves during that season.

In such cases, manufacturers must make their products and terms of sale sufficiently attractive that their products can get on retail shelves and gain exposure to consumers. One means of promoting products until they achieve wide acceptance is consignment selling—shipping goods to dealers who pay the consignor only for the merchandise that sells.

Market Research, Advertising, and Selling 395

The dealer, or consignee, has the right to return, without obligation, the merchandise that does not sell. If you want to consider selling on consignment, check with an attorney for advice on the legal aspects involved and with an accountant for the recordkeeping procedures.

Many companies sell directly through catalogs, using an 800 telephone number. Companies also include their telephone numbers in newspaper or magazine ads. The personnel who take the phone orders can be trained to try to increase the intake by persuading the customer to buy related products or larger quantities of the product.

Telemarketing works for companies of all sizes, particularly if the market is broader than the local area. Sales representatives keep and refer to account

FIGURE 18.2
A Collage of Advertisements.

records, call accounts at preset times, and follow preset patterns in telephone selling. You can improve their productivity with effective training programs and thereafter measure the total amount of revenue booked.

Some telemarketing centers provide customer service by answering questions and dealing with problems. This kind of prompt, efficient service creates a competitive edge. It holds down returns, prevents the loss of accounts, and can result in additional sales.

Consumer complaints can also result in sales. Such situations offer opportunities to smooth ruffled feathers and to use personal selling techniques with the additional contacts.

Market research supports sales. One company offered product samples for people who called in. Those who did supplied valuable data about themselves and their product and service likes and dislikes.

Full-account management links sales and service into a "one-call" unit. Business customers can place orders, find out about stock availability, check on the status of a previous order, and get shipping and billing information. The turnaround time on orders in one company is 48 hours or better, and customers applaud the fast service.

Market Research Firms

Some market research firms specialize in one type of business. Researchers may gather demographic data and count pedestrian and vehicle traffic as part of a trade market survey. Others test products before they are introduced on the market or seek consumer reactions on various issues.

Suppose you want to offer a new food product in your bakery or restaurant. For a fee, people in the market research firm will prepare the food and then invite passersby or selected consumers to participate in a taste test. Disinterested researchers interview each consumer and record the reactions. The raw data goes to you, the client, but some companies will tally and analyze the results and make recommendations. As a result, you may decide to revise your recipe, test it further, or introduce the item as planned. You make the decision.

Business clients also submit potential television commercials and magazine ads to their market research firms. Focus groups are then invited to view the different commercials or ads and to give their preferences, stating a rationale if possible. To gain the participation of the general public—preferably of those people who are most likely to constitute the trade market—the market research firm gives away samples or pays a small fee (perhaps two or three dollars).

Researchers may stop passersby on street corners and in busy shopping malls. Ordinarily, only a minimum of questions are asked of consumers in this manner. After the people agree to participate in the survey, they are told of their rights and obligations. In return for their free gift or small payment they are asked to go to the research firm itself for lengthier involvement. Because these consumers deal with an intermediary and not you directly, you can expect to receive fairly honest responses.

Marketing research may be formal or informal. Before introducing a food product on the market or publishing a recipe, a firm may be hired to cook and taste-test the product or recipe.

It should be obvious that there are many benefits to be derived from using professional market research specialists. They can test and promote products and services, and they can learn what customers need and want—before you commit lots of money to development, production, and advertising. Of course these services cost money, too. In each case, you must decide if the costs are worth the potential benefits.

MATCHING THE CUSTOMERS' NEEDS WITH PRODUCTS AND SERVICES

The de-emphasis of personal selling by large-scale retailers leaves a gap in customer service that small retailers and service entrepreneurs can gain a competitive edge by filling.

Good selling essentially means matching customers' needs with the merchandise and products offered. Generally, the more skillfully this match is made, the better the selling job.

People who work at selling or servicing customers directly must: (1) be skilled at assessing the needs of the customer, (2) have a thorough knowledge of the goods and services offered, and (3) develop the ability to convince customers that their company can satisfy the customers' needs better than the competition.

A Hierarchy of Human Needs

Abraham Maslow devised a hierarchy of needs. The primary level is represented by basic needs for food, shelter, clothing, and sex. Next comes the security and safety level, suggested by such needs as job and financial security, health, religion, and protection from catastrophe. With these needs somewhat met, people usually need to give and receive love, interact with others on a social level, and be accepted. Next on the hierarchy comes self-esteem and needs having to do with respect, prestige, and other external rewards. Finally, Maslow hypothesizes that with most of the above needs met, people can become self-actualized. People at this level set their own goals and standards and develop their own internalized reward systems.[9]

You can generally expect that many of your customers will have needs somewhere in the mid-range of this hierarchy (from needs for security/safety through self-esteem). With this awareness, you can set about to match your sales pitch and services to accommodate customers at these levels. This suggests that you and your employees should treat people as worthy of your acceptance, attention, and respect.

If you offer basic-need level goods or services, such as in a grocery store or a hospitality establishment, you should understand that everybody needs to eat and sleep, and when they are tired or hungry they are likely to be irritable. Clothing, too, satisfies a basic need but perhaps—if your merchandise is of the high quality and price type—you may be appealing also to customers' need for prestige. Don't let yourself be fooled though. Although wealthy, some patrons dress down, drive old cars, or associate with those who are far beneath their own economic status.

The smart approach is to treat everybody who enters your establishment with equal respect and dignity, no matter your type of business or how you might judge your customers at first impression.

The Customer Is "Always the Customer"

Customers may not always be right, but they are "always the customers," which means they should be treated with respect and courtesy even when it's necessary to explain a misunderstanding. Customers are more likely to return when their needs or wants are satisfied by courteous, sensitive, empathetic, and patient people. Entrepreneurs and their staff who go that extra mile can keep a step ahead of the competition.

The ability to sell retail products begins with attractive displays and continues with the owner and sales clerks understanding both their products and the customers who are likely to buy. After that, it's a matter of using good sales techniques.

Courtesy. Courtesy is a constant. Some customers know exactly what they're searching for and merely seek advice or guidance. You or your employees can save these customers' time by helping them find items or by explaining the products or services. Other customers want time alone to examine your offerings, without having people with a vested interest (namely, you or your staff) make suggestions.

When you advertise your wares or services and open your enterprise for business, you are in effect inviting anybody and everybody to visit and look over what you offer. The same courtesies you extend at home are appropriate—within certain limits, of course—to your place of business.

Sensitivity. In business relations, personnel must often walk a narrow line between integrity and sensitivity. Suppose, for instance, a very obese man wants to try on a suit that is too tight for him. Although you want to make a sale, you'll also want the man to leave as a satisfied customer. Yet sensitivity to his feelings should not permit you or your staff to state aloud what he already knows—that, with his size, he simply won't look or feel good wearing that suit!

Other situations involve more subtle issues. Probably the best way to avoid offending is to take the burden of responsibility upon oneself. Compare the two possible responses given in each of the following examples. Which response is the most sensitive to the customer's needs?

The customer mumbles and cannot be understood. Responses: (1) "Speak up, you're not talking loudly enough." (2) "I didn't understand what you said; would you repeat that, please?"

The customer misunderstands what you said. Responses: (1) "You didn't listen to me!" (2) "Perhaps I didn't make myself clear."

The customer complains about a product, and it's not the fault of the store. Responses: (1) "Well, don't blame us, it's not our fault." (2) "Perhaps this particular item is faulty; I'll check with the manager (or the manufacturer). Would you like to exchange it for something else?"

A customer complains that another customer who arrived after her was served first. Responses: (1) "I might have taken you out of order; step right this way, please." (2) "I'm only human, you know. Why didn't you speak up?"

Notice that in none of the above examples is the company spokesperson unduly humble, subservient, or apologetic. Responses should be straightforward but courteous and sensitive.

Empathy and patience. Empathy goes beyond sympathy. It means putting yourself in the customer's shoes. Since we are all consumers as well as producers, we know what it feels like to be insulted or ignored in the marketplace. We don't appreciate having our self-respect stepped on, whatever problems the workers may have.

Where customers must wait in line or take their turns at getting noticed in a crowd, otherwise nice people can become disgruntled and ill-mannered. In such circumstances, entrepreneurs and their employees must exercise extreme care. It isn't easy to practice patience, and sometimes it is nearly impossible to feel empathy for rude or unkind customers.

That extra mile. In customer relations there should be no opportunity too small not to warrant giving superior service. To be successful, entrepreneurs and their employees alike should practice courtesy, sensitivity, empathy, and patience. Recognizing that customers have needs and desires, and making allowances for human error and fatigue by treating everyone equally and with respect, is a proven aid to success in business.

It is your willingness to go this extra mile that can bring customers again and again to your doors. Although your larger competitors may have the advantage in merchandise variety, pricing, and advertising, by establishing a well-developed personal selling policy you can make your company truly successful.

Making the Sale

Selling large-item consumer goods—such as vehicles, household appliances, furniture, and farm equipment—requires some special sales techniques. As a manufacturer or wholesaler, or as a door-to-door salesperson, you may be going out to find customers. Others, whether business customers or consumers, may be coming to you.

Yet getting a business customer to purchase a two-million dollar piece of equipment may be no more difficult than persuading a consumer to buy a $20,000 car or sign an installment contract on a set of encyclopedias, cookware, or a year's membership in a health spa.

In most sales-opportunity contacts you want to be able to stimulate action. Until the customer signs the sales contract or pays for the goods or services, you haven't achieved your sales objective. The steps in the sales process include:

1. Meeting the customer,
2. Talking the customer's language,
3. Getting the customer to perceive a need or want,
4. Demonstrating your knowledge and willingness to help,
5. Overcoming objections, and
6. Eliciting action.

Meeting customers. Getting acquainted is the first step. When you or your salespeople go door to door or into another's business establishment you must find a way to persuade people to give up their valuable time and pay attention to you. If appropriate, you may want to give samples or coupons.

When people come into your business, especially just to browse, you want them to buy something before they leave. After you have made a sale, you'll also want to entice buyers to make additional purchases.

How you and your employees dress is important and should reflect your company's desired image. Don't expect to make a sale if you are grubby. Your type of business and the customers you seek to attract should provide the clues about how to dress. If you're selling farm equipment, for example, then you may wish to wear work clothes like your clients.

Make customers feel comfortable. Persuade them that your taking their time will prove beneficial. Then, if the situation warrants, get to know them.

Realtors, for instance, should find out about their clients' lifestyles and demographics. It would waste both your time and theirs to show a $100,000 house to a couple who can afford only properties in the $60,000 range. If they have no children, it's unlikely that they'll be interested in a place with five bedrooms. Although you should avoid any appearance of prying too deeply, you should try also to discover what their hobbies and interests are. You can sense their attitude by listening carefully and reading their body language and facial expressions.

Talking the customers' language. If you and the customer are in the same industry, use your trade jargon. This demonstrates your respect for the customer as well as your own knowledge. If you propose to sell educational materials to teacher customers and you were once a teacher, then say so. This technique can establish rapport and indicates that you understand the customer's needs.

People like to talk. Listen carefully and respond, even if the conversation is not directly related to the products or services you provide. Your interest in the customer's needs can pay off later. People like to believe that others are interested and care about their problems.

Thus when women attempt to sell to homemakers they often discuss home management and explain how their products or services will help make the job easier. Business and professional women, however, usually do not want to spend much time visiting. They may already be "self-actualized," and although they appreciate being treated with respect, they're likely to prefer that you get right to the point.

When men approach male customers, they may discuss sports, the weather, or other topics of interest to the customer. Observations on the customer's environment might lead the conversation to the salesman's products or services.

Where one sex seeks to sell to another, or where the salesperson and the customer appear to have little in common, the burden of establishing rapport is on the seller. Getting to know your customers and their needs can help bridge the communication gap. You want your customers to listen to you, and these opening remarks and the climate you develop are critical to what happens next.

Getting the customer to perceive a need or want. As you launch your sales pitch, keep it simple. Use lay terminology, except when trade jargon is appropriate. Don't talk down to or over the heads of your customers. Relate to their needs. Are your offerings likely to save them money or time? To improve their health, their sex appeal, or their job opportunities? Show how your products or services can solve their problems and save them time and money.

Your products or services may also satisfy customers' psychological or social needs. Good health can increase their physical well-being, their energy level, and even their sex appeal. By improving their minds or their skills they can also increase their earning power and/or learn to appreciate the "good life."

Demonstrate your knowledge and willingness to help. You and your employees must know your company's products and services. Don't make claims that your offerings can't meet or that haven't been proved; i.e., by the manufacturer's research department or by consumer and federal agencies, etc. You will want to keep abreast of innovations in your area and of different or better sales techniques. To do this, you can subscribe to trade literature, attend or send your staff to seminars and trade conventions, and maintain active membership in related associations.

Know how your products operate and the various uses that can be made of them. You want your customers to realize that you and your staff know the products inside and out. Describe, illustrate, and demonstrate your products. Assure your prospects that buying this particular item and brand from you will be more beneficial than buying from your competition.

Your company may provide a service contract. Even if it doesn't, though, you'll want customers to be happy with your product. They need to know about guarantees and about where to go and how long they'll have to wait for repairs. Let them know where they can reach you or your service operators.

If your product's performance and your business's policies are better than those of your competitors, emphasize the fact. These selling points include special services, types of repairs available and the cost to customers under the guarantee, and the typical waiting time for repairs.

Handling objections. Sometimes customers only need to be assured that your product is better than the competition's. But they may also need more persuasion about why they should pay your price. At any rate, you can expect to hear objections and you should prepare yourself and your staff to handle them.

Turn every objection into a positive selling point. Above all, don't be tempted into arguing with the customer. You want to maintain attention, interest, and rapport. Customers typically raise objections on such issues as these:

1. They question the benefit of new products, because they are unfamiliar with them, with how they work, or with which of their needs or wants your product or service can satisfy.
2. They wonder how they will pay for it, and if it's worth the cost, even the "sacrifice."
3. They aren't sure (yet) that they really need it; despite the interest you have managed to generate, they wonder if they'll later regret a purchasing decision.
4. They wonder who else has bought the product. Business customers may wish to know if their competitors have already bought the equipment or furniture or supplies you're selling. Householders may be eager to keep up with—or outdo—the Joneses.
5. They are "sold," but they need input from other decision makers, whether a spouse or, for business customers, a partner, purchasing agent, executive, or employer.

Be ready for any of these objections. When customers object to the price, emphasize the quality of your product or service. Perhaps your product lasts longer and will thus save the customer money in the long run because it won't have to be replaced as often as other products. Maybe it has a record of top performance and will thus need repair less often.

When approval is needed from other decision makers, try to arrange a meeting with these people. You don't want them to hear your sales pitch secondhand.

Eliciting action. Sometimes it is difficult to tell when a customer is nearing the decision point. Suddenly he reaches for a pen and asks, "Where do I sign?" At other times the reaction to your sales talk is just the reverse. You think the customer is really interested and abruptly she turns around to leave or ushers you or your salesperson to the door.

After following all the steps described above as quickly, and smoothly, as possible, you want to get the customer into a purchasing frame of mind. When you believe this point has been reached, try to elicit action from the customer. However, instead of asking outright, "Do you want to buy?" you can slip into the decision-making sequence with a few subtle questions, such as:

"Would one or two items meet your needs better at this time?"

"Does the cash plan sound good, or would you prefer to buy on credit?"

"What other questions can I answer for you?"

Once the sale is made, don't linger too long. Any questions about delivery, installation, use, and service should already have been covered. With the sales contract in hand or the transaction completed, excuse yourself politely. Reserve for future contacts any other discussion you feel is pertinent.

Service and future sales contacts. Goodwill contacts can be made on various occasions: e.g., when you again meet with the customer to provide service or repairs or simply to see if you have satisfied customers. The referrals you receive in this manner can help build your clientele list. If you have sold consumable products or services, perhaps customers are ready to make repeat purchases. If not, you may try to sell them related products or accessories.

In any event, satisfied customers are a source of free advertising. From the good things they say about you, your business, and its products come other customers. Service counts. Don't neglect its benefits.

STAFFING FOR CUSTOMER CONTACT POSITIONS

Finding good sales and service people—those employees who will have routine and frequent contact with customers—is a problem for both large and small companies. As noted in Chapter 10, you need to know what you are looking for and how much you are able and willing to pay. Developing a concise but complete job description is the first step.

Besides recruiting your own employees, you can also contract with independent sales agents or hire part-time workers from temporary-help agencies. To attract older workers and people who are not available for full-time work, you may want to consider establishing flextime hours or job-sharing.

Independent Sales Agents

If yours is a manufacturing or processing plant, you may need outside sales representatives and find it difficult to afford them, at least at first. Selling for others is the business of independent sales agents. They make their money by representing several clients on a commission basis in their established territories.

Sales agents use various titles, including "manufacturer's agent," "manufacturer's representative," and "sales rep." The marketing functions that such agents perform vary from one industry to the next. In deciding whether to use an independent agent, consider the following list of advantages and disadvantages:

Advantages

1. They give you immediate entry into a territory.
2. They make regular calls on customers and prospects.
3. They provide quality salesmanship.
4. They cost you only a predetermined selling expense—a percent of sales as their commission.

Disadvantages:

1. Your control over their selling techniques is more limited than when you train and use your own employees.
2. On a large volume of sales, the selling expense may be greater than it would be with your own employees.
3. Their allegiance to your company and its products is not total because they serve other clients as well. They often need extra financial incentives to push your products.
4. If and when you cancel a contract, the agent may take many of your customers.[10]

Flextime and Job-Sharing

Some businesses must stay open long hours and hours other than the typical 9-to-5 office schedule, including restaurants, bars, motels, service stations, and recreational facilities. Retail stores, especially those located in shopping centers, are also usually open longer than the 40-hour work week. Your business may be one of these, or you may have other special requirements.

Age, health, and personal or family conditions often make it impossible for people who want work to fulfill the otherwise typical work-hour requirements. Establishing a policy of flextime or job-sharing gives you access to a broader employee market, from which you are likely to find many good qualified workers who have sales and personal-contact experience.

SUMMARY

The market-research effort should be constant and continuing, whether conducted by informal or formal means. Many strategies are available for assessing the effect of promotion and advertising efforts on sales. Successful entrepreneurs constantly establish or revise their objectives, using management tools to develop schedules and measure results.

An effective personalized selling program can counteract the competition from larger companies, many of which ignore the personal touch. Small business owners and their staff who are aware of customers' needs, wants, and motivations can keep customers coming back again and again. The many details associated with keeping customers happy, however, must be ingrained and practiced with every customer-contact opportunity—through study and application and for owner and employees alike.

Getting the type of employees who will care enough about your company, its products and customers, or who at least are trainable, isn't easy. Alternatives to doing your own employee recruitment include using independent sales agents or temporary-help agencies. However, you'll have a broader labor market from which to locate good customer-contact people if you are willing to offer such worker accommodations as flextime and job-sharing, and if you do not omit from your search the handicapped and the older or re-entry worker.

DISCUSSION QUESTIONS

1. Discuss informal market research strategies with which you are familiar, either from your own work experiences or from discussions with and observations of successful entrepreneurs.
2. What market research techniques can be used in business classifications not illustrated in this chapter: e.g., the extraction, construction, transportation, communications, and tourism industries? On what do you base your opinions?
3. What services are provided by market research firms?
4. What management tools would you use to evaluate the effectiveness of a market research project? Of an advertising program?
5. Describe Maslow's Hierarchy in relation to understanding customer's needs as a means of improving services and increasing sales.
6. How can a good, personalized selling program help build sales and customer rapport? Give examples of how small companies can compete with larger ones by designing an effective selling program.
7. This chapter commented, "The customer is always the customer." Compare this statement with the more familiar one, "The customer is always right." What differences do you perceive between the two viewpoints? How would each influence the way that entrepreneurs and their employees treat customers?
8. Have you as a customer ever been annoyed by service people who were discourteous, insensitive, unempathetic, or impatient? How could the business owner have trained these personnel to avoid such behavior?
9. How can an entrepreneur, through training and/or surveillance, keep employees from neglecting or insulting customers?
10. What are some advantages and disadvantages of using: sales agents, temporary-help agencies, flextime, and job-sharing?

ACTIVITIES AND EXERCISES

1. Use the MBO/R tool (see Chapter 17) to design and monitor a market research study for your business. Select a single objective. Describe a hypo-

thetical situation that you perceive could be happening in your business (record this situation under the Now column). State the result you want to achieve. In the benchmark columns between Now and Result, record a time line for monitoring progress and action steps, using quantifiable and measureable indicators.
2. Develop a management plan for an advertising campaign, using the tool(s) you prefer. For specific data use material from your business plan or from the Stanley Junction (case supplement) community.
3. Demonstrate effective sales techniques in a role-play situation. Base the demonstration on a specific product or service you expect to sell in your own business. Meet the customer and proceed through the required action steps, as described in the chapter, to demonstrate how you will close the sale.

NOTES

1. Victor J. Cook, Jr., "Marketing Strategy and Differential Advantage," *Journal of Marketing,* Spring 1983, pp. 68–75.
2. "From the Editor," *Journal of Marketing,* Spring 1983, p. 5.
3. Cook, "Marketing Strategy."
4. Paul D. Boughton, "Marketing Research and Small Business: Pitfalls and Potential," *Journal of Small Business Management,* July 1983, pp. 36–42.
5. Charles Keown, "Focus Group Research: Tool for the Retailer," *Journal of Small Business Management,* April 1983, pp. 59–65.
6. Boughton, "Marketing Research."
7. I confirmed this observation by an informal experiment conducted in several dozen restaurants of different types throughout the country. In each establishment I ordered either the house specialty or some unusual dish. After two or three bites, I pushed it aside and placed a second order. And then a third. Each time I carefully assured the waiter or waitress that there was no particular problem with either the service or the order—it was just that I didn't like it. The result? Nine times out of 10, either the owner or the manager arrived at my table to inquire—usually with a worried frown—what the matter was. Seventy-five to eighty percent of the time, the owners asked specifically about the rejected item and what I would have preferred and did I have any recommendations for improvement.
8. Based on George Kress and R. Ted Will, "Marketing Checklist for Small Retailers," *Management Aid* no. 4.012 (Washington, D.C.: U.S. Small Business Administration, 1981).
9. Abraham Maslow. *Motivation and Personality* (New York: Harper Bros., 1954).
10. Edwin E. Bobrow, "Is the Independent Sales Agent for You?" *Management Aid* no. 4.005 (Washington, D.C.: U.S. Small Business Administration, 1980).

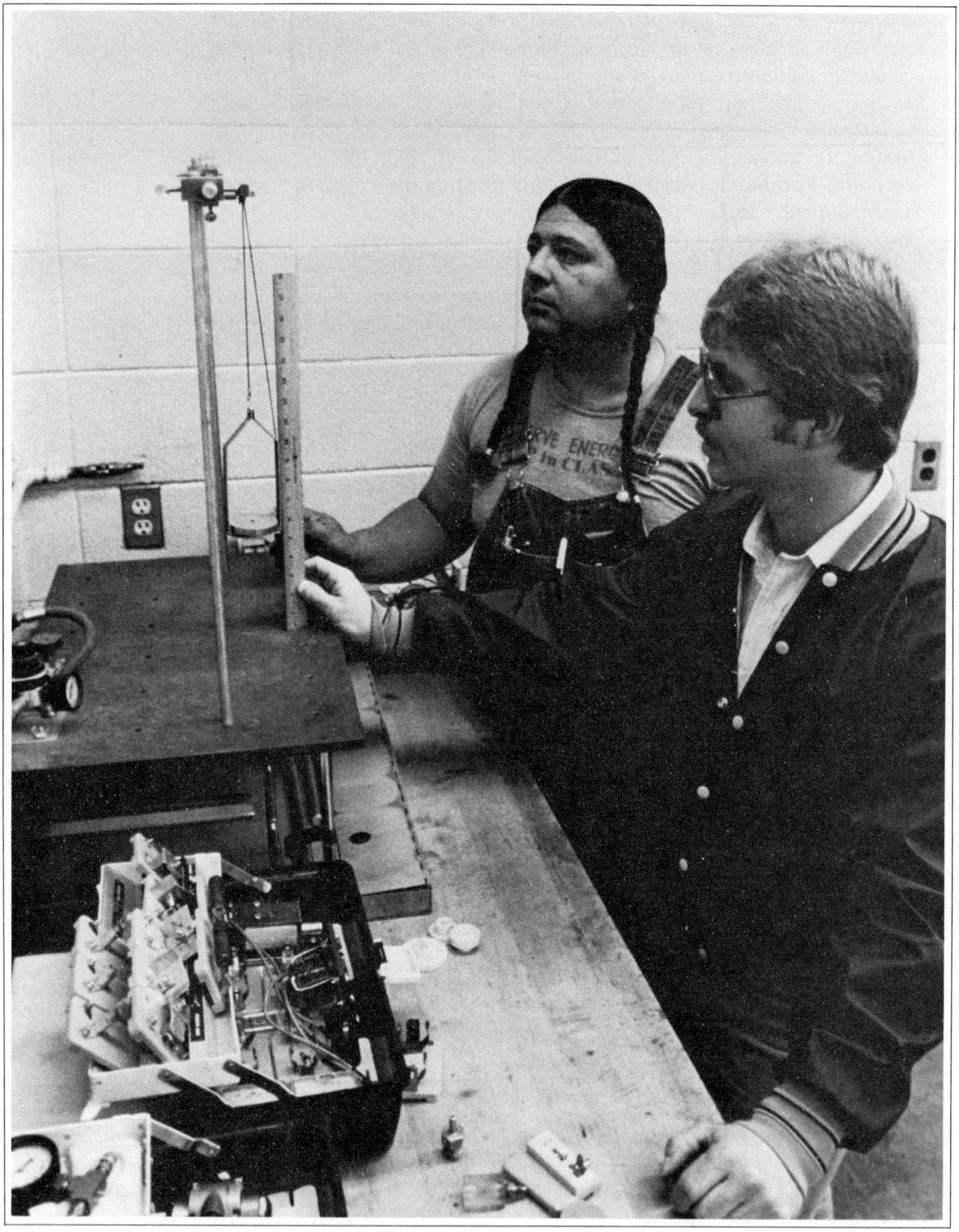

chapter 19

Training, Motivating, and Supervising Employees

Objectives

1. Establish objectives for an employee orientation and training program and describe methods of achieving the objectives.

2. Develop a table of contents for an employee handbook, based on your selected business and its operations.

3. Apply motivation theories in debate and simulated situations.

4. Design strategies for effectively supervising employees in two or more given situations as appropriate to your business.

5. Discuss the potential for unionizing and what you could do to avoid this possibility should it occur in your business.

Employees need orienting and training when they are hired, transferred, or promoted; when the job or equipment changes; and, generally, to improve their performance or attitude. As you add more employees, it is helpful if written policies and procedures are available, perhaps in the form of an employee handbook. Most disputes or questions can then be settled by referring to the handbook.

Every employee needs to be both motivated and supervised. The extent to which either are necessary will depend on the employee, the nature of your business, and your management style, among other factors.

Employee job satisfaction should be a management objective. Unless you are willing for your employees to join a union, you must make every effort to create a good management style, a positive climate of communication, and a pleasant working environment.

Once you have several employees, you should begin to consider what career opportunities your business can provide. You might then need to train your workers for such lateral moves. If employees are likely to transfer from one job or department to another or are promoted, they will be better able to contribute to your business if they are prepared.

ORIENTING NEW WORKERS

Once you have hired a staff (see Chapter 10 for procedures and recommendations), you have to orient them. Everything said, shown, or demonstrated to new hirees that first day and week at work combines to produce a dizzying kaleidoscope of sound and color, confusing and confounding to the senses.

At the basic-need level, new employees need to know where the eating and restroom facilities are located. Also describe, either verbally or in writing, the established policies governing coffee breaks, meal periods, telephone usage, smoking, and the like.

To meet their social needs, introduce new workers to any other employees and to repeat customers known personally by you and your staff. Have an established employee invite the new person to lunch, or issue the invitation yourself.

New workers should also start to develop a sense of participation, of proprietorship: "This is my work home. Together with a team, I'm responsible for the enterprise's success or failure." To plant the seeds of this attitude as early as possible, include as part of the orientation a tour of the plant, store, or office. Describe your processes, products, sales and service policies, and procedures. Use words like "our" and "we" rather than "my," "mine," and "I."

The Orientation Tour

See that new hirees understand how all departments and functions in your company are interactive and interdependent. If they will be selling to customers, see that they discover the interrelationship of the sales force with the stockroom and office staff, etc. If you're hiring office people in a manufacturing firm, include a tour of the plant; conversely, show factory workers the office and the customer showroom.

Make personal introductions wherever you go. And don't assume that the new employees will only want to meet people like themselves. People of all races and ages and of both genders can interact. If you have a single minority person on staff and you're hiring a second, for instance, don't make a point of trying to get these two people together. Also avoid making a special issue of having hired a minority member, a handicapped person, or a woman to fill a traditionally male position (or vice versa).

Orientation to the Actual Job

Don't provide too much information too quickly. Allow new hirees time to assimilate their new experiences. Trying to orient them in the middle of a busy work environment is also unrealistic.

After they have had time to become acclimated to the physical and social surroundings and to develop their initial impressions, the employees may be assigned to observe someone else, whether yourself or another employee. This approach can teach the new hirees what to watch for and emulate.

The new employees should see demonstrations and then get time to practice with the equipment, tools and materials, procedures and methods used to complete various functions. They should also understand in what sequence and by what criteria they are expected to perform. The new hiree needs to be exposed to every relevant detail—in not only the how but also the why of each procedure. Within a few days the new hiree may begin to "solo"—on selected functions at first, until finally all procedures and methods for performing the job have been successfully introduced and mastered.

Orientation to the Customer Service Role

The orientation and training for jobs that involve interaction with customers is difficult. Busy people do not appreciate having to stand around while the "big buddy" teaches the newcomer how to handle the cash register or fill out a form. Such orientation should ideally take place before or after hours, following observation and question-and-answer periods.

Many companies (e.g., banks, grocery and department stores, and small retail establishments) use the role-play plan during the orientation. Some large banks even have a completely outfitted teller simulation station in the designated training area. The supervisor or a senior teller acts as the customer to put the new hiree through a range of potential customer-teller contact situations. The trainee must also handle money, records, and computer transactions simultaneously with acting out the person-to-person contacts.

In grocery and department stores a similar simulation plan is used to train cashiers. Every possible situation is posed for the employee (by the owner or trainer playing the customer role), including problems that deal with potential or attempted theft and shoplifting, or honest misunderstandings on the part of the customer.

The hospitality industry, where customer service is so essential, is another field where employees (and thus the owner's business) can benefit from simulation and role-play training. Despite the relatively high turnover rate among employees in this business classification, the smart owner makes sure his or her employees know what to do and understand how to do their job well.

According to numerous surveys, one out of 10 workers is fired because of poor performance. The rest lose their jobs because of personality clashes, politics, organizational problems, mergers, and layoffs.[1]

TRAINING AND DEVELOPMENT

Between 1975 and 1982, employers spent from $30 to $40 billion annually to train and develop their own employees. In the same period the U.S. government spent a total of $53 billion through the Comprehensive Employment and Training Act (CETA) to help the hard-core jobless, including disadvantaged youths and welfare recipients. CETA focused on providing government-subsidized jobs and income support to employers who participated in the program.[2] (CETA was replaced by the Joint Partnership Act in 1982.)

Training and development is an integral function in most medium- to large-size organizations, but small businesses too have a need for constant personnel development. (See Figure 19.1).

Training for Customer-Contact Jobs

Sales training in small retail shops need not be formal, but it should be provided at regular intervals and on several topics, and not only to salespeople but also to service and repair workers, to telephone and receiving clerks, and to anyone else who ever comes into contact with customers. Even a complaint or a routine inquiry offers opportunities for making a sale.

Knowing products and services. Sales meetings can help train employees by covering such topics as:

1. New products—their features and benefits, how they work, how to demonstrate them, and how to interest customers in them.
2. New merchandising strategies—their objectives and rationale.
3. Changes in store policies—how they will affect workers and how to explain new procedures to customers.
4. Credit policies and procedures.
5. How to handle complaints and returns of merchandise.
6. How to turn a service, query, or complaint contact into a sale; or, at least, how to win and maintain satisfied customers.

Training, Motivating, and Supervising Employees

FIGURE 19.1
Selected Employee-Training Objectives.

- Orient and train new hires for the initial job.
- Improve selling techniques in response to customers' needs.
- Develop an individualized MBO plan.
- Improve performance by delineating steps involved in performing specific tasks.
- Point out the best way(s) to operate new equipment.
- Train employees to perceive why specific standards of quality must be obtained and how they can reach and maintain these goals.
- Reduce accidents and increase safety practices.
- Improve attitudes about work performance, safety, and security.
- Decrease tardiness and absenteeism.
- Improve communication and negotiation skills.
- Improve the handling of materials in order to reduce production bottlenecks.
- Train new workers in an expansion program.
- Learn to adapt to change, to control emotions, to manage time, and/or to manage stress.
- Train employees for newly developed or modified jobs.
- Train employees for promotion.

Developing employees' persuasion skills. Some people believe that it is virtually impossible to teach employees how to persuade customers to buy. "You either have the talent it takes, or you don't," they say. This skill is difficult to teach, but training can make a significant difference. Encourage your sales staff, particularly, to enroll in formal sales courses and seminars, and arrange frequent sessions of your own. Regular interaction with and among your staff, even for a half hour over coffee, can prove beneficial.

For instance, one salesperson might have developed a good method of handling objections while another may want to relate how she closed what appeared to be an impossible sale. Service operators and clerks may appreciate the opportunity of telling how they handled an irate caller.

Types of Training for All Workers

You can train your employees through on-the-job instruction, assigning a buddy or mentor to the learner, role playing, formal lecture and discussion sessions, apprenticeships or internships, individualized or correspondence studies, and off-site training and education programs.

On-the-job training. This method is often used to teach new hires their specific duties. The technique is also a successful way to introduce employees to new systems, products, and equipment.

The buddy or mentor system. You or another experienced employee can help guide a new worker through the job learning process. Often such relationships continue informally thereafter, as the learner develops respect for the buddy/mentor, and the latter enjoys continuing in the advisory role.

Formal lecture and discussion sessions. Formal training involves a specified meeting place and tools of instruction. You might set aside a room or area and equip it with a conference table and comfortable chairs, a chalkboard, learning manuals, writing materials, and so on. You yourself may serve as the instructor, or you can use a senior employee or hire a consultant to assume this role.

Vendors of new equipment may help train people. Franchisers or wholesaler's and manufacturers' representatives may participate, either on their own initiative or at your request.

Such a facility may also be used for company and sales meetings, for introducing new products, and for describing a market research or advertising program. This room or space can be reserved, too, for private conferences.

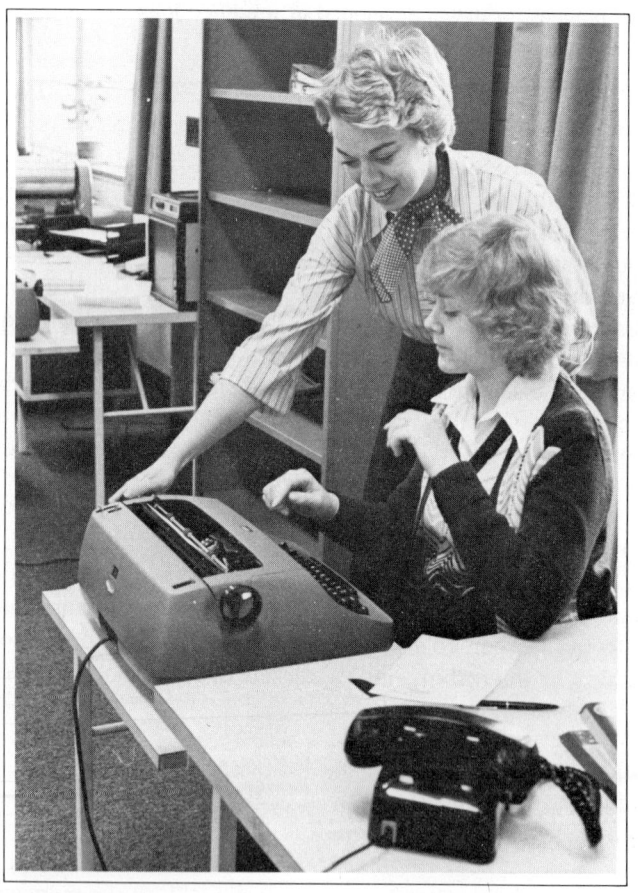

Assign a new hiree to an experienced worker who will act as a mentor during the orientation process.

Apprenticeships or internships. Carpentry, electricity, plumbing, and other trades require people to complete an apprenticeship before admitting them as fully practicing members. Such programs can last four years or longer. Apprentices receive both classroom instruction and on-the-job training.

Some high school or college work-experience programs also combine internship programs and government on-the-job training with formal instruction. Usually—but not always—you are required to pay minimum wages to such employees. In exchange for their relatively cheap labor you must agree to train the interns in an employable skill, evaluate their performance and productivity and report to the sponsoring school or agency coordinator.

Individualized or correspondence studies. You may assign employees the task of learning how to use new systems and types of equipment on their own. Many vendors supply instructional manuals with prescribed exercises in your particular industry or franchise operation.

Correspondence courses may also be available to people. You might or might not decide to underwrite the cost of this type of study, including tuition and work time spent studying. Having a training or study facility available can make this possible. Remember that employees who receive specific training that matches your needs become more competent. Motivated by the opportunities you are providing they may also become more productive and have a better attitude.

Off-site training. As you grow and expand, you may find the underwriting of off-site training a relatively inexpensive means of providing employees with further education, although you may not feel you are able to provide this benefit initially. Many community colleges and universities participate with companies in making courses available during the evenings and weekends.

You can offer to pay the tuition costs of employees who are interested in pursuing their education for the benefit of your business as well as for their own career advancement. Generally, though, this paid-tuition package covers only those classes or degree plans that specifically relate to the employee's current or projected job with your company. You may also wish to reimburse the employee only when he or she achieves a satisfactory record. You might pay full tuition for a grade of A, 75 percent for a B, and 50 percent for a C.

Another variation of this approach is to pay the full expenses of employees who take special training offered by a franchise or a manufacturer. Although there may be no tuition fees, you could expect to underwrite the cost of training materials, travel, lodging, meals, and incidentals. This type of training can benefit service and repair people, accounting people, sales personnel and those involved with new computer systems.

For any type of off-site training or educational program, however, you want to be sure that your employees will stay with you for a certain time thereafter. Their new skills and ideas make them eligible for other jobs, usually more advanced and at better salaries than you may be able to afford. Therefore, there should be a written agreement between you that details all your mutual obligations.

Some company training is conducted using computer-aided instruction for either independent or apprenticeship training.

Instructional Media

Education and training methods, materials, and media have grown quite sophisticated. A wide variety of multipurpose instructional media are available to schools and businesses. For instance, some of the same equipment and tools used for training purposes can also be used for conferences with advertisers, customers, suppliers, and others. A computer you use for accounting and financial management can simultaneously run training software for your employees.

Equipment you might wish to acquire, either now or later, includes:
- Projectors for motion pictures, filmstrips, slides, or transparency overlays.
- Computers and computer-aided instruction programs. Virtually thousands of software packages have been designed for educational institutions and for training in specific industries.
- Video cassettes or disks, which provide a variety of programs.
- Cassette players and training cassettes.
- Closed-circuit television, for developing and showing your own training programs and also for watching university-originated classes.

Special Training Topics

Many training programs that can help your employees improve their performance and attitudes on their current jobs are also appropriate for employees facing transfer or promotion.

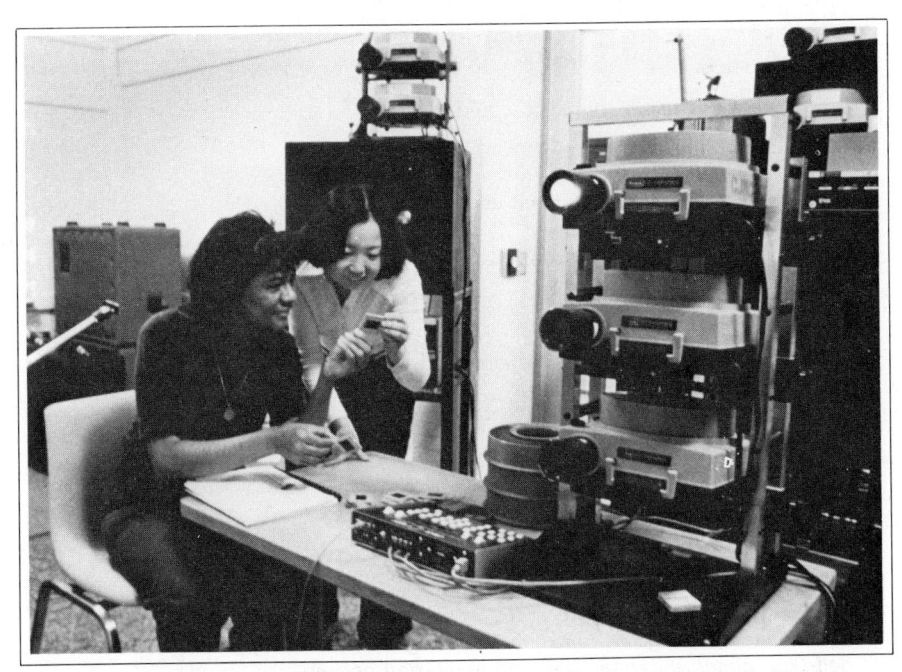

Many training materials are available for use with instructional media in company training sessions.

However, some ideas and skills are more abstract and thus more pertinent to advanced positions. These include the ability to communicate, to negotiate, to rethink existing systems, to analyze, to judge, to delegate, and to make decisions.

Higher-level employees have more demands on their time and more responsibilities. Thus they may have a particular need for training in how to manage time and stress.

Managing time. Training for the management of time is often difficult because so much that people do, and *how* they do things, is based on childhood and familial habits and on internalized value systems. Yet you as a business owner can establish policies and procedures that will help people make effective use of time, including arranging work stations to minimize time loss, motion, and fatigue. Having a plan and a schedule not only helps in managing time but also in managing stress. You can set the example and train your employees accordingly. See Figure 19.2 for a discussion of the wise use of time.

Managing stress. Stress is an unavoidable part of almost any job—certainly of any higher-level job. Studies show that stress can be as disruptive as any accident to an employee as well as to an organization. Consequently, the current era has appropriately been called the Age of Stress.[3]

FIGURE 19.2
Time Management

Time Wasters

What wastes time? A short list would include:

1. Telephone interruptions
2. Unexpected visitors
3. Unscheduled and unplanned events
4. Crisis situations
5. Lack of established objectives, priorities, or deadlines
6. Cluttered work spaces
7. Wasted physical motions
8. Disorganization, messes
9. Tasks that take longer than expected
10. Too "picky," too "petty"
11. Failure to delegate tasks
12. Wrong, delayed, or incomplete information
13. Indecision and procrastination
14. Inability to say "no"
15. Fatigue
16. Fear of what other people will say or think
17. A need to keep busy, despite lack of productivity

Efficiency: doing a job right
Effectiveness: doing the right job in the right way
Self-Discipline: understanding and mastering oneself

Do you count time? Or, do you make time count?
Have a plan . . . and work your plan. Work smarter . . . not harder.

Time Zones: "Sizzle to Fizzle"

People pass through up to five time zones, usually every day. These are:

1. "Sizzle" or peak times. You can concentrate easily and accomplish up to three times as much as during mediocre times. Hard tasks challenge you. You meet problems head on, more readily.
2. Near-peak times. You can still concentrate and get things done, but it may take a little longer.
3. Mediocre zone. Best time for menial, nonthinking work; you're easily irritable, don't appreciate challenges.
4. Slowing-down zone. Any task will take you three times or longer to complete than during your sizzle time.
5. "Fizzle" or near-zero zone. Time to take it easy, to relax your mind and body, let yourself recuperate. Watch television, rest, visit, prepare to sleep.

Knowing Yourself

Some people "sizzle" early, then wane. They may or may not ignite to the same level following a break or meal. Others climb slowly from mediocre through near-peak zones to hit their stride in midday. Once you recognize when your time zones regularly occur, you can adjust your work tasks accordingly, within the limits imposed by your business and its requirements. Early sizzlers will tackle their most difficult tasks first, and save the menial ones for later. Those who build to their peaks will choose just the reverse sequence of tasks.

(continued)

FIGURE 19.2
(continued)

Time Savers
1. Make notes and keep and use them.
2. Control the telephone. Be pleasant but set a pattern of giving and getting information quickly. Don't spend valuable time chit-chatting with telephone callers or walk-in visitors.
3. Have a place for everything and keep everything in its place. Organization includes the establishment of a good filing system.
4. Avoid indecision and procrastination. Get and analyze facts and make the easy decisions quickly, reserving time for the more complicated ones.
5. Have a plan and follow it. Draw up daily and weekly plans in writing, designed around company needs and your own time zones. Also establish long-range plans. Develop priorities and take matters in order. Train subordinates to recognize objectives and to meet them.
6. Organize work stations to eliminate unnecessary physical motions and to avoid unnecessary fatigue.
7. Delegate tasks to others.
8. Be realistic. Don't expect perfection in yourself or in others.
9. Be flexible. Be ready to *un*plan as well as to plan.

Some definitions of stress: Seyle defines it as "the nonspecific response to any demand. When some external force threatens the body, the common denominator of all adaptive reactions by the body means stress."[4] Schuler defines it as "a discrepancy of important needs and values. The more important or necessary the values and needs, the greater the stress."[5]

These definitions imply that the body can function well under reasonably stressful situations. "When it comes to instability, imbalance, and over-adaptation, the body has accumulated so-called stress; i.e., an overload of stress."[6]

When problems are seen as challenges, this "good stress" can actually help you and your employees perform at a higher level. Bad stress occurs when you feel you have little control over a situation. You lose concentration or even the ability to think clearly and you can get angry and express that anger badly. Too much bad stress can produce physical, emotional, and mental disorders. (See Figure 19.3, and the exercises in Appendix A).

In addition to providing training sessions on stress management, you can consider the following policies to help prevent bad stress in the workplace:
1. Physical fitness programs promoted and/or provided by the firm.
2. Job-sharing, task sharing, and flextime to accommodate employees's personal needs and commitments.
3. Communication channels to inform employees of issues and concerns that affect them, to alleviate their fear of the unknown, and to help them adjust to the changes you propose.
4. Training programs to address stressful situations.
5. Incentive programs and bonuses.
6. Career counseling and training for transfers and promotions.
7. Job descriptions that tell employees what is expected of them.
8. Written company policies and procedures, perhaps in the form of an employee handbook.

FIGURE 19.3
To avoid the potential of developing stress, whether among workers or the owner, the wise entrepreneur devises plans to alleviate the potential for developing undue and unmanageable stress.

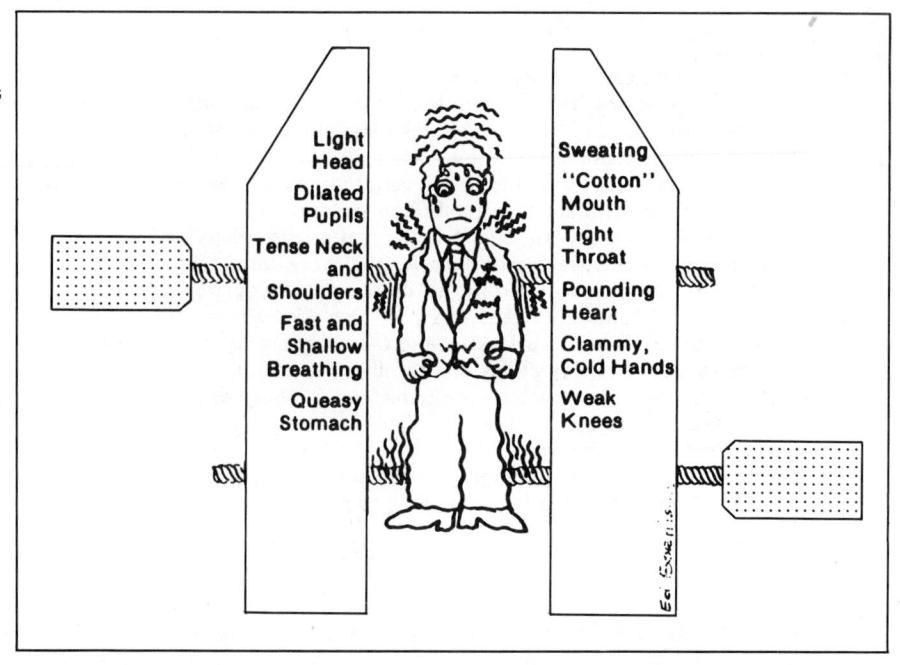

From *STRESSMAP: Finding Your Pressure Points* © 1982 by C. Michele Haney and Edmond W. Boenisch. Reproduced in *Small Business Management and Entrepreneurship* by permission of Impact Publishers, Inc., P.O. Box 1094 San Luis Obispo, CA 93406. Further reproduction prohibited.

Evaluating Training Programs

If you establish measurable objectives for each training program and segment, you should have some indicators against which to evaluate the results. Evaluation techniques can be informal or formal. You can ask employees what they thought about the program and what they learned. Approach them personally for their response or have them anonymously fill out written evaluation sheets.

You can also make comparisons of employees' performance prior to and following the training session. Note how much better they can operate a machine, implement personal selling techniques, describe products and services, and handle merchandise returns or customer complaints.

Written tests can help you evaluate the employees' grasp of new ideas. You can then develop the next training sesssion to "reteach" difficult but essential concepts. Since learners need opportunity and time to implement and practice their new knowledge, however, overall evaluation of the training program's value should be reserved until sometime later.

Finally, examine whether the training has achieved the intended objective. Have sales and sales revenues increased? Has the number of customer complaints decreased? Do the results match those projected on the MBO/R planning tool?

PERSONNEL MANAGEMENT

As your business grows and more employees are hired, a hierarchy of positions will emerge, requiring you to develop or expand the company's organization chart, the job descriptions for each employee, and the assignment of job titles. This specificity may permit the division and specialization of labor. Different and varying levels of skills are then required of people in each job title, with compensation designed to reflect these differences.

Attitudes of the Work Force

The values and attitudes of workers have changed over the last few decades and as an employer you must take these changes into account when you design personnel policies. For instance, many workers report dissatisfaction with their jobs on such issues as: lack of respect (i.e., failure of management to acknowledge the dignity of the individual and awareness of his or her strengths and needs); poor communication; lack of opportunity to provide input regarding those decisions which affect the job and the worker; too much or too little supervision; inadequate, improper, or unsafe working conditions; and lack of opportunity for promotions, raises, and career-development assistance.[7]

Since the mid-to-late 1960s there has also emerged evidence to suggest that many workers find more rewards and pleasure from leisure-time activities than from their work and also that the "work ethic is dead." Another tendency people exhibit is "mistrust of anyone in authority," and this includes one's boss.[8]

In an early 1980s study, it was found that there is an increasing mismatch between the realities of the workplace and the attitudes, abilities, and expectations of the work force. One mismatch exists, for example, between the reward system and incentives—in the United States, 73 percent of the 846 workers interviewed felt that there is no real relationship between their performance and their compensation.[9]

Further, the majority of jobholders in this study (56 percent of women and 48 percent of men) said they supported the work ethic, but three-quarters admitted they don't work as effectively as they could. In this study, the work ethic was defined as "I have an inner need to do the very best I can regardless of pay." Yankelovich reported on the cause for the higher percentage of women supporting the work ethic—based on the number who said they had chosen to work— that although some felt guilty (for going out of their homes to work), they also received self-expression from their efforts. Conversely, the men described a sense of entitlement.[10]

In times of recession when jobs become scarce, the above attitudes are often replaced by feelings of insecurity over potential labor-force cutbacks and individual job termination. With the return of prosperity, however, employees quickly regain their confidence, resuming anew their habits of expressing dissatisfactions, seeking change, and demanding additional benefits.

Organizing for Personnel Management

The objective of a good personnel-management program is to make effective use of employees' skills and talents—those they have when hired and those they can develop through training.

When your business has expanded to the point where you are employing workers in a hierarchy of jobs, you may want to hire a personnel manager, someone with expertise in all aspects of hiring, training, and evaluating the performance of employees. Until that time, though, all such tasks will fall to you, the entrepreneur.

For an effective personnel management program, you should implement policies and procedures that include the following, whether on a formal or informal basis and whether minimal or extensive:

1. Classify jobs and prepare wage and salary scales.
2. Recruit, interview, and hire.
3. Orient, train, and counsel employees.
4. Deal with supervisory, motivational, and discipline issues.
5. Develop safety standards and practices.
6. Manage benefit programs, including group insurance, health, and retirement plans; training opportunities; vacations; and sick leave.
7. Conduct periodic employee performance review appraisals; acknowledge strengths and needs and provide a system of recognition and rewards.
8. Assist employees in their efforts to develop and to qualify for more advanced jobs.

You may also have to negotiate with labor and service unions in the formulation of contracts, if and when your staff decides to join a union.

To help you develop the type of personnel policies that will promote satisfied workers who in turn will perform and produce for you, see Figure 19.4, which lists topics appropriate to cover in an employee handbook.

The Employee Handbook

Handbooks were once considered a frill that only large companies could afford. But no longer. Owners of small businesses now use handbooks to give employees information on policies, wages, and benefits.

Although face-to-face conversation is still the best way to exchange ideas and identify problems, having written policies gives employees something to check when in doubt. They may be unsure of what they are expected to do and of how they are expected to do it. And they need to know what benefits and opportunities exist for them in your company and how to take advantage of these. Figure 19.4 gives a table of contents for a typical employee handbook.

1. Welcome Message
2. History of the Company
3. This is Our Business
4. You and Your Future
5. What You Will Need to Know
   Working Hours
   Reporting to Work
   Rest Periods
   Absence from Work
   Reporting Absences
   Employment Record
   Pay Period
   Safety and Accident Prevention
   Use of Telephones
   How to Air Complaints
6. These Are Your Benefits
   Vacations
   Holidays
   Group Insurance
   Free Parking
   Training Program
   Savings Plan
   Christmas Bonus
   Suggestions and Awards
   Jury Duty
   Military Leave
   U.S. Old-Age Benefits
   Unemployment Compensation
   Equal Employment Opportunity
7. These Special Services Are For You
   Credit Union
   Education Plans
   Medical Dispensary
   Employee Purchases and Discounts
   Annual Outing
   Bowling League
8. Index

FIGURE 19.4 Suggested Table of Contents for an Employee Handbook.

Source: Adapted from Frank M. Cruger, "Points on Preparing an Employee Handbook," *Management Aid*, No. 197, U.S. Small Business Administration, Washington, D.C.

MOTIVATING EMPLOYEES

Satisfied employees are usually more productive and thus more likely to contribute to the success of your business. A major objective of motivating and supervising employees, then, is to help them reach as high a level of self-actualization, self-motivation, and satisfaction as possible within your business.

Management Style Theories

Douglas McGregor developed two management theories, which he labeled Theory X and Theory Y. The former is "job centered," the latter "people centered."[11]

Theory X. Generally, job-centered management focuses first on productivity and only secondly, if at all, on the needs of the workers. Some owner-managers, typified by the autocratic style, believe that workers: (1) hate to work, (2) need a club over their heads to make them work, (3) are by nature indolent, unambitious, and reluctant to take responsibility, and (4) prefer being told exactly what to do.

Theory Y. The people-centered theory, on the contrary, is based on the idea that most people can be motivated to achieve in order to attain self-respect and self-actualization. This theory assumes that workers: (1) do not dislike work but, rather, actively seek it, (2) do not need authoritative leadership but prefer participative decision making, (3) prefer establishing their own goals rather than having someone else establish them, and (4) do not shrink from responsibility but rather seek it.

Participative decision making (PDM). L. Coch and J.R.P. French, Jr. (1948) studied an in-house experiment conducted at the Harwood Manufacturing Company, in which management tested three schemes of employee involvement in decisions related to the production budget: (1) all employees affected were actively involved in budget decisions, (2) selected employee representatives participated in meetings with top management, and (3) the usual company procedure of simply informing employees of the final decision was followed. The results graphically revealed the relative desirability of the three schemes. Members of the third group experienced 17 percent resignations and significant deteriorations in productivity. The greatest improvement of productivity was made by members of the first group, who were fully consulted during the decision process. As in the second group, there were no resignations.[12]

A study reported in 1983 was the eleventh in a series of experiments designed to assess the effectiveness of participation and goal setting on employee performance. The series had as its impetus the early field studies by Coch and French (1948) and Meyer, Kay, and French (1965), as well as the theoretical work of Locke (1968).[13]

Of the 11 studies, 7 were conducted in the field. The population samples included typists, loggers, government workers, engineers and scientists. The tasks included logging trees, typing, brainstorming, and using basic arithmetic. In analyzing the results and their impact on participative decision making (PDM), the conclusions were the same: "The motivational effect of participation in itself does not affect performance. Participation affects performance only to the extent that it affects goal difficulty." However, these 11 studies provide strong support for PDM and goal setting; namely, that specific goals lead to higher performance than do generalized "do better" goals.[14]

Brownell's studies focused on participation in the budget process. However, the results achieved are applicable to the range of decisions facing owners/employers in the area of PDM: "Participation is most satisfying where individuals perceive that they have a valid contribution to make."[15]

Applying management theories. Not all employees can be involved in the full scope of managerial decision making. And few employees will precisely fit any one set of definitions. Generally, they will be motivated on some days and on some assignments more than they will on others. Some workers will actively seek participation in the decision-making process, others will respond well when invited to contribute, and still others will resist any such type of involvement.

Although as an entrepreneur you will soon develop your own management style, you should be ready to modify it to accommodate specific workers.

The mix of employee characteristics creates a specific work-group personality. When one employee is replaced with another, this group personality will change. A respected, productive worker can influence others to perform likewise, while a well-liked but mediocre worker will influence coworkers toward poorer performance. Observe who, among your employees, are likely to be leaders and who are the followers. Then you can work closely with the leader(s) to develop good communication and to inculcate the need for staff to comply with the company's objectives.

Employees who are denied the means of satisfying some of their psychological needs can become just as ineffective as if they were denied the means of satisfying such physiological needs as those for food, shelter, and clothing. Try therefore to create a working environment and working conditions that can provide a measure of both. Consider what your people need to perform their assigned duties. Remember that any system is only as effective as the people who operate within it.

SUPERVISING EMPLOYEES

The key to successful supervision of employees is good communications. People need to know what's going on and also how they stand within the organization.

Developing Effective Communications

The objectives of an effective communication program include: (1) improve morale by decreasing opportunities for employee dissatisfaction, (2) increase the potential for employee performance and productivity, and (3) reduce the potential for supervisory problems to emerge.

Follow these specific steps, in this order, for every employer-employee contact—e.g., to plan, make decisions, improve performance, analyze problems, settle disputes, etc. These communication guidelines should be used for one-to-one contacts but are also applicable to group situations:

1. Open the dialogue on a positive note.
2. Invite participation (in the communicative process and with the issue at hand) in a nonthreatening manner.
3. Seek and give feedback to ensure that each person—you as well as your staff—understands what the other one(s) is saying.
4. Elicit the employee's cooperation in planning the action that will follow.
5. Implement the plan or delegate its implementation to the employee(s) and establish a schedule for monitoring progress.
6. Praise the employee(s) wherever possible and build into the plan a means of recognition and/or reward.[16]

Two-way communication is used when policies or procedures are not yet established or when they are open to modification through employee participation. Two-way communication usually takes longer and is more cumbersome than when one person dictates the rules and subordinates are expected to follow. But such group or one-to-one communication can play an important role in developing your employees' sense of participation and involvement in those decisions that affect them.

A number of group decision-making studies have suggested that employers who discuss issues openly with their employees in a cooperative context will understand and incorporate other people's positions into the decisions they ultimately make. However, inviting subordinates into the decision-making process in order to gain consensus is not enough. People who are designated to participate in the management process must be able to express their opinions and differences openly. They must also avoid trying to win (whether they are employees, department heads, or the boss) but should rather seek to find and develop mutual goals. In short, it's not controversy that disrupts working relationships; it's the competitive, win-lose approach to controversy in participative management.[17]

Communication can also be "one-way," as typified by the employee handbook and by memorandums and reports designed to disseminate already established policies. In times of crisis, too, such as a fire, subordinates must respect their leader and obey commands without question.

Supervisory Problems and Issues

Effective orientation and training, in addition to positive communications, can ease the task of supervising employees, by giving them a solid understanding of their jobs. Nevertheless, problems will occasionally emerge. These must be dealt with as promptly as possible. You may find yourself needing to improve poor performance, correct absenteeism or tardiness, handle indiscretions, or help subordinates, especially those who regularly come into contact with customers, to control their emotions when under pressure.

Improving performance. When employees fail to perform at anticipated levels, the reason may be simply that they lack some necessary skills or understanding of the work. In such cases, the solution may be to provide both time and opportunity for training and practice of the skills.

In addressing the issue, though, be sure to use the specific involvement steps in communicating with the employee. Begin by explaining clearly why current performance is deficient and must be improved. Use the relevant job description to help the employee analyze his or her strengths and weaknesses. You may decide (together) to revise the job description to accommodate the employee's needs. Perhaps another worker is also performing below par with his or her particular assignment(s). A rearrangement of responsibilities could enable both to make better use of their talents, and make their work lives less stressful.[18]

Correcting absenteeism and tardiness. Employees who are often absent on Mondays and Fridays may be broadcasting a message that they are not receiving satisfaction from their work or that their jobs are stressful. They may not realize that their attendance is important to the success of your business or that they are forcing their co-workers to do their work for them during their absence.

Tardiness means getting to work late or returning late from breaks or meals. Some people are less aware of time than others. They invariably have excuses, of course, but the basic problem may be that they simply do not allow enough time for whatever they have to do, much less for emergencies. Tardiness also follows when a person assumes more responsibilities—whether at work or outside it—than he or she can handle.

Time-conscious people allow themselves enough time to conduct the normal routines of their day. But they also leave a margin for error, theirs or someone or something else's. They leave extra time in the morning; for example, in case the alarm clock fails to ring, the car's battery is dead, the snowed-up driveway needs shoveling, there's a big traffic jam on the way to work, or they simply are not moving too quickly that morning.

To help correct their tardiness or absenteeism, describe their importance to your company's successful operation and their place in the total picture (using the communication guidelines). Lead them to understand that their attendance or promptness record must improve. Then you can together zero in on the cause of the problem and devise a behavior modification plan the employee will agree to implement.

As suggested above, employees may fail to perform to standards because they lack the required skills. This kind of stress may lead to absenteeism or tardiness. In such cases, you can consider training in the needed competencies or redesigning the job description. The result should be a competent employee who arrives at work every day and on time.

Handling indiscretions or misbehavior. Absenteeism, tardiness, and poor work performance may also stem from drug or alcohol abuse, marital or family problems, or tension with colleagues at work. An employee may also practice dishonest, disruptive gossip, or other unethical or divisive behavior. In applying the specific communication steps be sure to: (1) emphasize the employee's value to the company, and (2) persuade the employee to acknowledge the indiscretion before (3) getting the employee to cooperate in designing a plan that will eliminate the misbehavior.

These employees should know that if their behavior does not change they will be fired. You may of course have to resort to using this ultimatum, if and when all else fails.

If the guidelines fail to produce improvements, however, it could mean the problem is very deep-seated. The employee may need counseling or other outside help.

Helping employees control emotions. Employees do get angry sometimes. Feeling frustrated or helpless, a woman may burst into tears and a man may start swearing or hit something or someone.[19]

Within the confines of an office, shop, or factory, nothing may be harmed but the person's own self-respect, unless of course a fellow employee is the recipient of this loss of control. Where customers are affected, however, your company may lose some business.

Crises often occur when several things happen at once or when equipment or systems break down and customers have to wait. It is especially at such times that employees *should* remain poised, yet these are the times they are most likely to lose control. Use the communication guidelines to work with employees who need to develop coping devices.

Specifically, though, make sure that: (1) the employee understands how appropriate business behavior is defined, under stress or otherwise, (2) you help the employee isolate his or her own "panic points," and (3) together, you devise alternative outlets.

You may also want to provide training under simulated conditions to allow the employee to practice maintaining control in the stressful situations that typically occur in your type of business.

Employee Development

If you are fortunate enough to get good workers, you will want to develop their potential in order to keep them and make them even more productive to your company. In establishing an employee development program, use the same communication guidelines. Specifically, you will want to:

1. Select an employee who appears able to take on increased responsibilities.
2. Describe the personal and professional benefits to the employee of accepting additional tasks—how the skills he or she will learn can lead to a higher salary or more responsible job.
3. Assign the employee one or more tasks that involve the use of new skills.

4. Grant the employee the authority needed to complete the new assignments. Instead of constantly supervising the employee's progress, allow him or her to exercise creativity—making it clear, however, that the employee may come to you with questions and requests for assistance.
5. Periodically evaluate the employee's progress and performance.
6. Identify, with the employee's input, what specific talents and strengths the new challenges have revealed.
7. If the employee has done well, continue to delegate the responsibilities—if possible, in place of some menial tasks formerly assigned. If no able employee is available to take over these tasks, assure the newly trained employee that he or she will be given more challenging responsibilities as often as possible.
8. Praise the employee for completing the tasks on time and with accuracy, and promise to note the achievement on the employee's personnel record.

Those employees who prove capable can take over for you in your absence. They can help develop creative marketing plans and contribute to the overall management of your company.

One of the most difficult managerial skills to learn is how to delegate work. New entrepreneurs often make one of two mistakes: either they delegate too few and only the most menial tasks; or they pass on all the tasks they themselves hate to do, but provide little if any instruction or supervision. The ideal path lies somewhere between these two extremes. The proper distribution of tasks can not only help motivate employees to take an interest in the business, perform well, and enjoy their job, but also relieves you of some tasks so you will have more time for doing your job; namely, overseeing the overall management of your business.

Remember, too, that as your business expands, you will want to have developed your employees' abilities so that they are ready to grow with you. A loyal, motivated, responsible employee can become your second or third in command. Such workers can assume new responsibilities as department or branch managers, production-line foremen or employee supervisors. Although some people may leave your employ to work elsewhere—even to start businesses of their own—many others may choose to remain—if, that is, you have provided them with opportunities to grow and advance. Meanwhile, having fostered a group of loyal, productive, responsible, and motivated employees, you will have less difficulty in the event other workers seek to unionize.

Unions

When you have 20 or more workers, your company may be open to unionization. If your employees initiate such a move, federal law requires that you must bargain with a union representative in good faith. In such a case you should retain a competent lawyer to help you negotiate with the union.

Workers think of unionizing when they become frustrated with their jobs. They may seek to increase their wages, to obtain job security, to improve working conditions, to increase fringe benefits, to correct what they consider unfair treatment, or to get recognition.

To avoid unionization, the smart entrepreneurs will establish fair and consistent policies, make these known to their employees and seek to effectively train, supervise and develop the skills of their workers.

SUMMARY

Personnel management concerns the effective use and development of the skills of a company's employees—whether salespeople in a store or on the road, clerks in an office, operators in a factory, technicians in a repair shop or laboratory, laborers on a farm, skilled craftspeople in a trade, or service and custodial workers in the hospitality industry. Personnel management starts with the recruiting and hiring of qualified people (see Chapter 10) and continues with orienting, training, supervising, and motivating their productive performance on the job. Wise entrepreneurs encourage their employees' growth and are available to assist as their subordinates encounter problems and stresses in the course of performing their duties.

Training is used to orient employees, to improve their performance, to modify their behaviors, or to prepare them for new responsibilities. Training can be offered formally or informally, one-on-one or in groups. Special training sessions can help correct poor performance, poor work attitudes, absenteeism, and tardiness.

Employees are more satisfied with their jobs when their working conditions are safe and appropriate and when they have access to their employer's attention. Motivated employees are usually more productive. When they have approachable employers—people who will listen to and respect them—employees are less likely to become frustrated. Satisfied workers, moreover, are less likely to seek unionization.

DISCUSSION QUESTIONS

1. How can an effective orientation and training program develop motivated and satisfied workers?
2. In what situations would training be appropriate in your particular type of business? What methods would you propose to use and under what conditions?
3. What types of problems emerge when employees manage time or stress poorly? How would you correct these problems?
4. How would you evaluate the effectiveness of a training program?

5. What is the difference between one-way and two-way communications? What circumstances would dictate using one or the other? Debate the potential benefits of taking time out from managing your business to communicate with your employees, using the recommended specific steps in the process.
6. How would you apply management theories X, Y, and PDM to specific situations that might arise in your type of business? Consider how you would modify your own style to meet the needs of the type of employees you would expect to hire.
7. Review suggestions for dealing with various supervisory problems. How would you implement these in dealing with various specific situations likely to occur in your type of business?
8. How does developing motivated, satisfied workers affect the potential for unionization?
9. Why is it difficult for many new entrepreneurs to delegate responsibilities? Discuss the benefits to the employer of taking time to develop employee skills, knowledge, and attitudes.

ACTIVITIES AND EXERCISES

1. Design an employee training program for your type of business. Develop benchmarks and a schedule for achieving your objectives. In responding, use the MBO/R management tool given in Chapter 17.
2. Draw up a table of contents for an employee handbook, based on your selected business and its proposed operations. Use the list shown in Figure 19.4 as a guide. Annotate the list—that is, indicate clearly what each topic will cover.
3. Organize a debate team to attack and to defend the following statements. Illustrate points by making specific references to the effect on company profits and employee satisfaction in the business of your choice.
    a. "Work groups whose managers spend a good deal of time doing nonsupervisory tasks are likely to have too many underproductive workers."
    b. "Close supervision reduces productivity. People seem to work better in a free atmosphere in which they carry out tasks in their own way."
    c. "Managers and supervisors who are 'work-oriented' as opposed to 'employee-oriented' get less work out of their people."
    d. "Managers who think of their people not as individuals but as hired hands are likely to have a negative effect on their workers. Loyalty to employers in these cases is obviously very slight."
    e. "Positive incentives are more desirable than negative incentives."
4. Identify classmates or colleagues who propose to open a business similar to yours. Then complete the following activities and present your findings in a panel discussion or by acting out simulated scenes.

a. Simulate orienting one employee for your enterprise. To do this, outline an informal script of potential situations. Be specific, using examples given in this chapter and/or derived from your own experience. Then form partnerships to play the roles of entrepreneur-orienter and new hiree. Decide exactly what tasks the new hiree should be trained for (see Chapter 17 on how to develop a job description).

Recommendations: to prepare you for dealing with specific situations, have the "new employee" act as if he or she is one of the following: (1) an inexperienced young worker who is totally unfamiliar with the world of work and its/your expectations, (2) a job re-entree, such as someone who has been unemployed for some time or a middle-aged or older worker who has been out of the job market for awhile and is trying to get re-acclimated to the work climate, or (3) a person in a wheelchair who you must introduce to using specific equipment.

b. Write a script involving one of the supervisory problems discussed in the chapter that is relevant to your planned venture. Represent the employer's communication (or training session) with one or more employees. Outline how you would apply the suggestions given here and your particular management style (X, Y, or PDM) to the situation.

Recommendations: practice role-playing the situation in your group. Change roles so that each member of your team can experience both the employer's role and that of the employee(s). Modify the script, based on how your role-playing turns out. As part of this revision, consider whether the "employer" would achieve better results with a different management style.

5. The related project in the case supplement provides another opportunity to simulate interaction between the employer and staff. The case activity may be used in lieu of No. 4 above.

NOTES

1. "Ways of Protecting Your Job," *U.S. News & World Report*, April 5, 1982, pp. 81–82. Also see Jeffery L. Sheler, "Why So Many Jobs for Youths Go Begging," *U.S. News & World Report*, November 23, 1981, pp. 77–78.
2. Jeffery L. Sheler, "Taking Shape: Smaller U.S. Role in Job Training," *U.S. News & World Report*, April 12, 1982, pp. 68–69.
3. J. M. Ivancevich and M. T. Matterson, "Optimizing Human Resources: A Case for Preventive Health and Stress Management," *Organizational Dynamics*, Autumn 1980, pp. 5–25.
4. H. Seyle. *The Stress of Life* (New York: McGraw-Hill Book Co., 1956). See also by the same author: "The Evolution of the Stress Concept," *American Scientist*, vol. 61, pp. 692–99.
5. R. S. Schuler, "Managing Stress Means Managing Time," *Personnel Journal*, December 1979, pp. 851–54.

6. Mu-Lan Hsu, "Monitoring Psychological Stress Means Preventive Management," *Industrial Management*, July-August 1982, pp. 7–11.
7. David W. Jamieson and James R. Warren, "Forces and Trends Affecting the Future: 1980–1990," source document and speech presented at the National Conference of the American Society for Training and Development (ASTD), Anaheim, California (April 28, 1980).
8. Merle Wood, "Directions in Business Education," speech presented at the national convention of National Business Education Association (NBEA), New Orleans (April 1981). Also see Richard Freeman, "The Work Force of the Future: An Overview," *Work in America: The Decade Ahead*, Kerr, Clark, and Rosow, editors (Van Nostrand Reinhold, May 1979); Lewis Lapham, "The Rage Against the Future: Further Reflections on the National Consensus of Anger," *Harper's*, November 1979; and Michael R. Schiavoni, "Employee Relations: Where Will It Be in 1985," *The Personnel Administrator* (March 1978).
9. Julia Kagan, "Survey: Work in the 1980s and 1990s" (conversation with Daniel Yankelovich), *Working Woman*, December 1983, pp. 16–23.
10. Ibid.
11. Douglas McGregor. *The Human Side of Enterprise* (New York: McGraw-Hill Book Co., 1960), pp. 33–57.
12. Peter Brownell, "The State of the Art: Participative Management," *The Wharton Magazine*, Fall 1982, pp. 38–43. See also by the same author, "Participation in the Budgeting Process—When It Works and When It Doesn't," *Journal of Accounting Literature*, Spring 1982; and "Participation in Budgeting, Locus of Control and Organizational Effectiveness," *The Accounting Review*, October 1981.
13. Gary P. Latham and Timothy P. Steele, "The Motivational Effects of Participation versus Goal Setting on Performance," *Academy of Management Journal*, vol. 26, no. 3 (1983), pp. 406–17.
14. Ibid.
15. Brownell, "Participative Management."
16. Olive Church and Anne Schatz. *Office Systems and Careers* (Boston: Allyn and Bacon, 1981), pp. 503–5.
17. "Using Controversy," *The Wharton Magazine*, Fall 1982, p. 13.
18. Robert F. Mager. *Analyzing Performance Problems* (Belmont, CA: Fearon Publishers, 1970), pp. 37–41.
19. Isabel Dienstback, "Women in Management," speech presented in Denver, Colorado (May 25, 1977). Also see Caroline Bird, "Differences and Similarities between Women and Men," *Born Female: The High Cost of Keeping Women Down* (New York: David McKay, 1970).

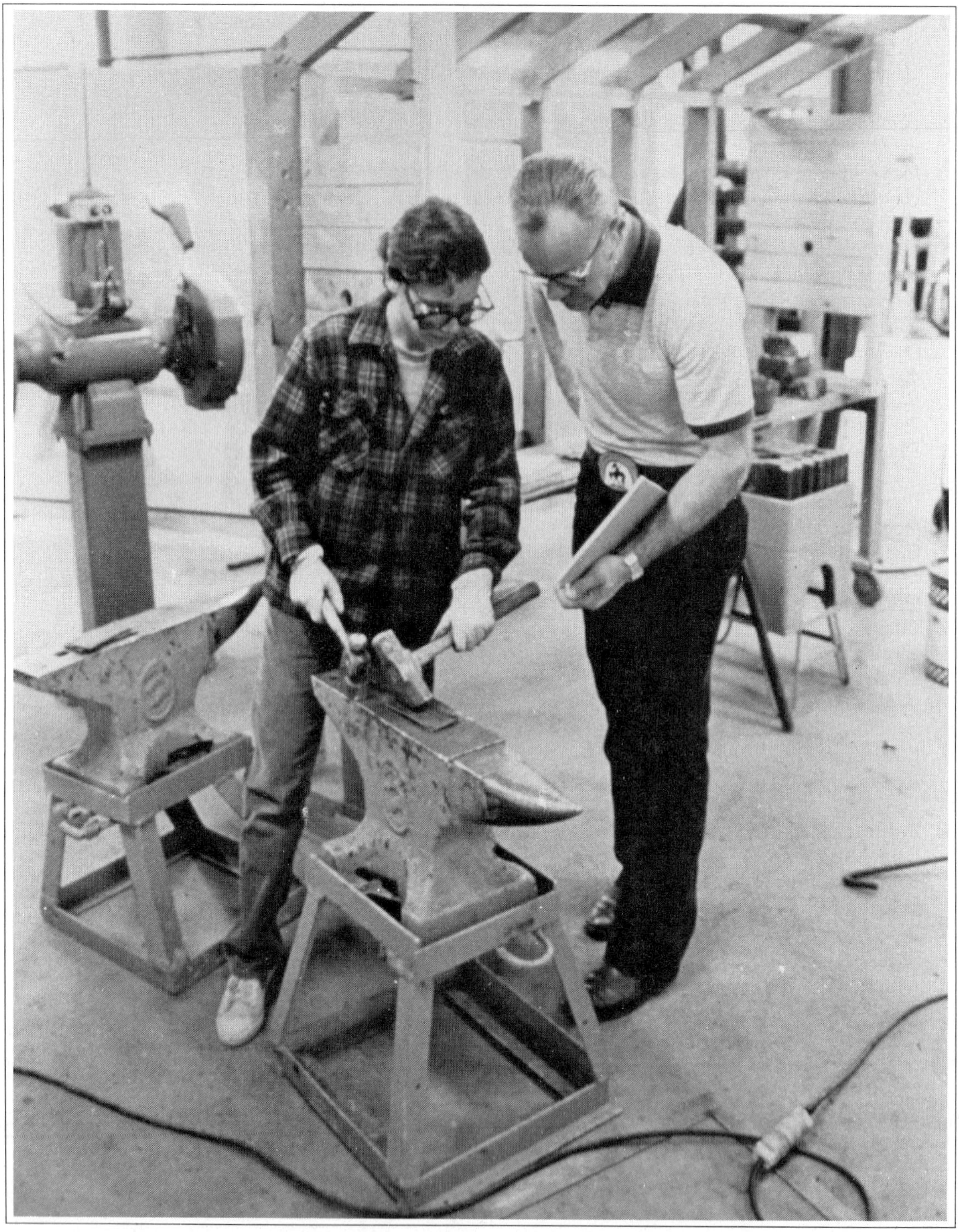

chapter 20

Managing the Physical Environment; Security and Safety

Objectives

1. Establish objectives for managing one or more physical environment factors in your business.

2. Design security measures for your business to reduce the potential of crime from both internal and external sources.

3. Develop an action plan for ensuring that the physical environment of your business is safe.

Employee morale and productivity are usually higher when the work environment is safe, healthful, and comfortable. The type, shape, and size of work station furniture and equipment can contribute to or detract from this objective.

Customers are more likely to return if they find your business premises not only esthetically appealing but also comfortable and safe. They appreciate, too, having their needs met quickly and accurately, although they may not know how you managed to create this efficiency.

You will also want to manage your business affairs so as to minimize the potential for crimes against you, your business, your employees, and your customers—whether the crime emerges from internal or external sources.

Federal, state, and local laws governing safety standards apply to many types and sizes of businesses. Your facilities must be able to pass routine inspection by fire and safety officials. Nor do you want complaints from employees, customers, or others to bring about special inspections.

THE READINESS AND MAINTENANCE OF THE PHYSICAL ENVIRONMENT

Utilities, Maintenance, and Repairs

To conserve on utilities, when your business is closed the air conditioning should be turned off or the heat turned down. Some owners install a master electrical switch that turns off every electrically operated machine at once.

Any premises will occasionally need minor repairs. You're lucky if you yourself have the necessary carpentry, mechanical, electrical, or plumbing skills—or can hire someone who does. Otherwise, you'll have to pay retail rates to service and repair operators every time something breaks down.

Cleanliness and Orderliness

Custodial tasks usually take place after the business closes for the day, although routine maintenance may also be required during operations. Cleaning equipment and supplies should be kept in closets near the place(s) of most use.

Printing establishments, repair shops, and manufacturing enterprises, where ink, oils, grease, chemicals, and the like are used, require special cleaning fluids. Carpentry and wood shops create sawdust. Where toxic chemicals or substances are used, exhaust fans, vacuum systems, and special cleaners are necessary. Various other products and processes require special precautions.

Restrooms and other common areas—whether designed for customers or only for employee traffic—should be kept clean and orderly. Floors should be swept and mopped; carpets, drapes, and furniture vacuumed or dusted; wastebaskets emptied; garbage taken out; and all surfaces—including counters, sinks, windows, walls, and door-frames—cleaned.

Managing the Physical Environment   **437**

The physical environment must be kept clean and orderly for the protection of customers and employees—but also in order to attract sales.

Workers should be made responsible for the orderliness of their own work places, repair areas, or customer-contact stations. They should clean up any messes they make themselves, rather than leave them for the janitor.

Hospitality establishments require continuous and special clean-up procedures. Most motels and hotels (and some restaurants) are open 24 hours a day, and management must decide what are the best times for maintenance. Late at night the facilities are relatively free of traffic, but sleeping guests or late diners do not appreciate being awakened or inconvenienced by cleaners. Motel maids usually start cleaning guest rooms in early or mid-morning hours, but to avoid waking late-sleeping guests they should be as quiet and unobtrusive as possible in the halls, outside, and in adjoining rooms.

Organizing Records, Materials, Tools, and Supplies

You should establish a procedure for reporting equipment breakdowns and another for ensuring that downtime is minimal. If outside service contracts have been made, the contractors should be called without delay. Where you or an employee are responsible for such repairs, time, opportunity, and tools should be available.

Workers should be responsible for the equipment, materials, tools and supplies they work with. At day's end these things should be returned to their proper locations, at the workers' stations or in common storage areas. Some materials may need to be placed under lock and key.

Both safety and security can be endangered if materials are left to lie about in disarray. Objects or materials that are hazardous to human health and safety should be controlled carefully. Confidential papers and records, valuable supplies, in-progress goods, and finished products should all be stored securely.

Your company's reputation may suffer if it looks disorganized or dirty to outsiders. Work or service stations visible to customers should not be any messier than is necessary to complete the job.

Protecting the Physical Environment against Loss

Although you will want to acquire insurance policies to cover your potential losses due to fire, theft, and other disasters, you should also seek to prevent such catastrophes from happening. Provide for regular maintenance of all equipment, and train your employees in safety procedures.

Nevertheless, not all contingencies can be anticipated and planned for. Thus you should design a recovery plan that will enable you to continue operating your business, no matter what disaster occurs or how much insurance you have purchased.

Accidents do happen. To expect employees to be immune is unrealistic, but the smart owner provides an environment and work systems that reduce the possibility of loss through human error or carelessness.

Recovering records and computer files. A study conducted by IBM indicates that from 1967 to 1978 there were 352 major disasters affecting data-processing records and systems. About half of these losses were due to fire; water and storm damage or theft accounted for the others. Such disasters have pushed many a company down the path toward financial ruin. According to another study, 75 percent of the companies with no contingency plans that lost data-processing operations in a fire never reopened their doors for business. Another 10 percent failed within the next two years.[1]

A contingency plan could simply involve housing computer programs, data files, and other documents in storage areas located away from the main establishment. Another approach is the use of "empty shells," or the joint lease of so-called empty facilities where computer equipment and files can be transferred and installed at very short notice. Analyzing employee functions, designating recovery teams, and training workers to handle recovery efforts are equally important in any recovery plan.

Meanwhile, insurance companies are now making policies available to cover the loss of records and other materials not only from specific disasters but also from internal theft, employee sabotage, and computer frauds.[2]

SECURITY

Theft, especially by employees, is a more serious problem than some small business owners realize. Dishonest employees account for two-thirds of the losses of some establishments. Shoplifting, burglary, and robbery are very high in others. However, there are many ways to discourage employee dishonesty, to protect your establishment and its contents, and to combat shoplifting.

Dishonest Employees

The U.S. Department of Commerce in 1975 estimated a total of $16 billion in business losses from reported employee thefts. Moreover, of businesses that failed in the mid-seventies, employee theft was listed as the major cause in 34 percent of the cases. Restaurants and beverage establishments particularly are subject to internal pilferage. Employee theft accounts for about 75 percent of a restaurant's inventory shortages.[3]

For instance, a restaurant with $500,000 in annual sales that finds a one percent shortage has not merely lost the $5,000 that a one percent shortage suggests. It has also lost all the profits on all the food that must be sold to pay for the loss. This means selling $170,000 worth of food without any profit at all in order to pay for the $5,000 shortage. Many restaurants are actually forced to operate without any profit at all from two to four months annually to pay for their losses.[4]

The dishwasher's pocketbook bulges as she takes food home for her children, her children's children, friends from the neighborhood, the church supper. . . . As owner, you finally have to fire the best pastry cook in town because you caught her red-handed carrying cartons of butter and bags of raisins out to her car—to say nothing of the bottle of Grand Marnier under her coat.[5]

Studies on work motivation show that how workers perceive their company is related to whether or not they will steal. People who are honest ordinarily, however, are often tempted to steal for various reasons: they see their peers do it; the amounts (particularly of small-item products) seem slight, insignificant to the total picture; they think they have a "right" because they work there, because they feel underpaid or unappreciated; or, in the case of food, "It will be left over anyway." All sorts of justification are used until behavior becomes habit and thus natural.[6]

Misplaced trust can tempt employees into pilferage, theft, or embezzlement. Many entrepreneurs feel close to their employees. They trust their people with keys, safe combinations, cash, and records, failing to realize that these opportunities for theft can tempt employees unduly. Management's indifference or ineptitude may allow employees to steal a little or a lot. Such a drain on a company may kill first the profit, and then the business itself.

Airlines examine everybody's luggage, even though only a tiny minority of passengers might ever want to hijack a plane or carry weapons aboard. Similarly, you should implement your anti-theft policies, procedures, and precautions without feeling guilty for "distrusting" your staff. In fact, honest employees will support your efforts. They realize that security measures will protect them and their possessions as well as the company and its assets. Meanwhile, by informing employees about the security system and precautions, you are influencing the employee's decision when he or she is faced with the choice—to steal or not to steal!

Methods by which employees steal. Sometimes profits go out the window—literally. One distributor caught employees lowering television sets and videogame machines from a third-story warehouse window to confederates below. A restaurant owner discovered that one of his long-term and supposedly loyal and trustworthy waitresses was throwing spoons out the window every night for her boyfriend to retrieve.

More often, however, employees carry off products, supplies, unfinished goods, and cash through doors, not windows. They also use shopping bags, purses, briefcases, and tool kits. They fill the pockets of their coats and sometimes even tuck things into their undergarments. Large items, however, may test their ingenuity. "Breaking out" is a term used when employees hide inside the business premises and leave with armloads of stolen goods—after closing hours. They may work in teams, in collusion with outsiders.

Many employees "lift" such small items as pens, stamps, paper, and paper clips. Some authorities question whether any employee, in fact, does not take something away at some time or another.

People juggle records to embezzle, establishing phony accounts and issuing checks to themselves. They alter computer programs to funnel money into bogus outlets, of which they are the recipients, often under fictitious names. They run up personal long-distance telephone bills or take cash from bank deposits, avoiding audit checks by taking full responsibility for all the related recordkeeping and activities. Or they pocket cash received and fail to record the transaction.

Cashiers in sales and service establishments have devised a number of techniques for stealing. "Put-downs," for instance, is a term used when a customer puts down at the cashier's station the exact amount due. The cashier may then pocket the money and simply not ring up the sales on the register. Another technique is to discard some sales slips—but this is possible only when the forms are not numbered and voided slips are not retained and verified.

Employees in retail establishments who are allowed to purchase damaged goods at discount prices sometimes exchange products so that they actually take home quality merchandise instead. Other dishonest employees simply switch price tags from one item to another.

Such crooked employees sometimes operate in collusion with others, either inside or outside of the company. They dump usable goods into the trash and arrange with the garbage collector to divide the proceeds. They sometimes keep what they steal, but often they steal goods for resale. Other employees give away products or services to their friends or fail to charge for all the items the friend buys. People who accept these favors are also dishonest. As a matter of fact, when they expect or invite their employed friends to participate in such actions, they promote stealing. Such people are often offended if they don't receive such preferential treatment.

Security Measures and Precautions

A variety of methods can be used to protect your establishment from internal theft. Some of these are directly related to the physical environment, while others deal with recordkeeping and other procedures. Note, however, that the best control method is one that inspires honesty in employees by making them aware of the relationship between theft and profits, and profits and their job security. No profits, no job!

Inventory and physical control. No one should take merchandise, supplies, tools, materials, or finished goods from their normal storage places without preparing a requisition or a removal record. Tight control should also be exercised over invoices and purchase orders. Unwatched or unchecked inventory invites embezzlement, fraud, and unbridled theft. Crooked salesclerks, office workers, and production and maintenance personnel dream about sloppily kept records and loose inventory controls.

You can conduct security checks or systems audits, change locks, and test alarms. Initiate these inspection and audit procedures at periodic but irregular intervals, so that they cannot be anticipated at any particular time.

When merchandise, materials, or finished goods are being received or shipped or when trash is being removed, you or a responsible employee should be present. Records should be kept and the person assigned should be held accountable for anything missing or out of order.

Entrances and exits can be secured with mirrors, security guards, closed-circuit television, and so on. These precautions can serve to deter both employees and customers from stealing. Inspecting lockers periodically, as well as bags and carry-out articles, is another means of deterring potentially dishonest employees.

Recordkeeping control. Important recordkeeping functions should be divided between at least two people:

1. Cashiering and account collections should be separated from bookkeeping.
2. The bookkeeper should not authorize purchases.
3. The cash-register tape should be checked against the amount of funds received by the cashier.
4. The entrepreneur should countersign all checks.
5. The bank deposits and the bank reconciliation should be handled by different people (unless, of course, the entrepreneur takes responsibility for both).
6. Expense records, such as long-distance telephone charges, postage and office supply purchases, invoices, and purchase orders, should be periodically checked.
7. An outside auditor should be used occasionally to check all records and systems.

Security control in manufacturing and distribution enterprises. The following guidelines can help reduce both the temptation and the ability of employees to steal from your company. Note that a number of these recommendations are also applicable to other types of businesses:

1. Every lunchbox, toolbox, bag, or package should be inspected by a supervisor or guard as employees leave the plant.
2. All padlocks, when not in use, must be snapped shut on hasps to prevent the switching of locks.
3. Keys to padlocks must be controlled. Never leave the key hanging on a nail near the lock where crooked workers can "borrow" it and have a duplicate made while they are away from work.
4. Do not allow trash to accumulate in, or be picked up from, an area near storage sites of valuable materials or finished goods.
5. If you have the slightest reason to suspect collusion between employees and trash collectors, inspect disposal locations and rubbish trucks at irregular intervals for the presence of salable items.
6. Supervise trash pickups.
7. Rotate security guards, if any, so that they won't become too friendly with any dishonest employees. Rotation also prevents monotony from reducing the alertness of guards.

8. Resist assigning two or more members of the same family to work in the same area.
9. Double-check incoming materials to ensure against collusive theft by drivers and the employees who handle receiving.
10. Let no truck approach the loading platform until it is ready to load or unload. At the loading platform, drivers should not be permitted to load their own trucks, especially by taking goods from stock.
11. Discourage drivers from taking goods or materials off the platform by:
    a. Putting heavy-gauge wire fencing up between bays, with a mesh too fine to provide a toehold.
    b. Mounting closed-circuit television cameras overhead so as to sweep the entire platform.
    c. Placing the receiving supervisor's desk or office where he or she can have an unobstructed view of the platform.
12. Number receiving reports and shipping orders in sequence to prevent duplicate or fraudulent payment of invoices and the padding or destruction of shipping orders.
13. Receiving reports must be filled out as soon as a shipment arrives. Delay in making out such reports can be an invitation to theft or, at best, result in recordkeeping errors.
14. Prosecute employees who are caught stealing.[7]

Computer Crimes

There are no accurate figures on either the number of computer crimes committed each year or the financial losses they cause—partly because the crimes are so difficult to detect and partly because even when they are detected many companies seem to be reluctant to reveal what happened (for fear of tempting others or worrying customers).

There are many different kinds of computer crime. In addition to tapping computer systems in order to steal funds, thieves also steal information: tax records, technological secrets, business accounts, mailing lists, marketing plans, and personnel records, to name a few. An irate employee may steal for revenge. Or a greedy one may hope to sell secrets to competitors.

Between 1978 and 1983, over 500 computer-security firms emerged. They offer a mixture of management advice and technological equipment to help entrepreneurs, corporations, and government agencies detect and prevent computer crime.[8]

Taking Action against Employees

When you suspect a theft, bring the police or a reliable firm of professional security consultants onto the scene. Where dishonest employees are bonded by insurance companies, you must uncover indisputable evidence of theft before you can file a claim with the insurance company to recover your losses. Professional undercover investigation is among the most effective ways to secure such evidence.

Although the reported financial losses from internal crime are high, only a fraction of incidents are ever reported. Too many entrepreneurs, particularly of small companies, simply fire the suspect on some other excuse than theft. In other cases, they accept an apology and restitution as an alternative to prosecution. But failing to take action helps perpetuate crimes. Dishonest employees who find it easy to steal will continue, whether they steal from you or from their next employer. Remember, too, that crooked employees may steal from other workers or from your customers.

Shoplifting

Petty thievery may not seem like major crime to the individual who casually pockets a ball-point pen, but overall, shoplifting costs each American over $150 per year. Nor is any store immune.[9]

Faced with the losses due to shoplifting, most entrepreneurs are forced to raise their prices. This common practice passes the cost of crimes along to the consumers. But in raising their prices, small store owners reduce their ability to compete.

Who are these crooks? They are of every socioeconomic class, any age, both genders, and all races. Nevertheless, we can categorize some typical offenders as juveniles, impulse shoplifters, kleptomaniacs, alcoholics, vagrants, drug addicts, and professionals. Amateurs are usually more nervous than professionals, so that an observant owner or employer often can detect their actions.

Children and young people actually account for about 50 percent of all shoplifters. At first they usually steal small items, things they want but that their allowances do not cover. They steal on a dare or as a prank. Frequently, they have been led to believe that retailers will excuse them because of their youth. If youngsters succeed in shoplifting they may go on to commit more serious crimes. They should be prosecuted through the proper legal channels and not "forgiven." The fact remains, overall this group costs retailers more money in lost goods and time than any other.

Many so-called respectable people shoplift on occasion and impulsively. Unattended or blind areas in a store make this type of shoplifter feel secure in succumbing to temptation. Kleptomaniacs have sometimes been glamorized in television shows because of the compulsion to steal, but their psychological problems don't change what they do. They steal from store owners, whether they need the items or not.

Drug addicts must support their expensive habit somehow, and shoplifting to acquire products for resale is one means. Together with alcoholics and vagrants, these criminals may seem clumsy or erratic, but beware. Because of their abnormal physical needs, they are often desperate. They may be armed. They can be violent.

Professional shoplifters are in the business of stealing. They steal to resell items. Thus their targets are high-demand, easily resold consumer goods such as television sets, videogames, stereos, and small appliances or small, expensive items, such as watches and jewelry.

Knowing their habits. Skilled professional shoplifters often work in pairs. One distracts clerks or causes a commotion while the other commits the crime. Juveniles also sometimes work in pairs or in gangs. In larger groups, these youngsters tend to feel secure, so beware: they, too, could be dangerous.

Shoplifters dislike crowds, preferring to work when store traffic is light or when clerks are tired and less alert. Early mornings and just before closing are typical hours. They hide merchandise in handbags, baby carriages, umbrellas, newspapers, magazines, bulky packages, knitting bags, and even in arm slings or under their clothes. Professionals may have had their clothes constructed with hidden pockets. Some use "booster boxes." Often gift-wrapped, to confuse clerks, a booster box has a hinged end, top, or side. The box is placed on a counter or on top of merchandise and the items are "boosted" into the box in just seconds.

Shoplifters also switch price tags on merchandise or write in lower prices. In dressing rooms they put on stolen garments and cover them with the clothes they wore when they arrived.

Guidelines for reducing shoplifting. To reduce theft from external as well as internal sources:

1. Teach your employees what problems to look for and why it is essential (to protect the company's profits) to reduce crime. You can invite police officers to assist in conducting the training. Employees must know, too, how to deal with shoplifters. Here are things you and your employees should watch for:
    a. Pairs or groups of shoppers.
    b. People who loiter near stockrooms or other restricted areas or who wander aimlessly through your store.
    c. Nervous people, people who arrive early or late, and people who distract clerks with seemingly aimless questions.
    d. Switched or altered price tags.
    e. Containers that may conceal items.
2. Limit the number of items customers can carry into dressing rooms. Count the items both before customers enter and after they return.
3. Mark prices on merchandise with a rubber stamp, marking machine, or other unchangeable device. Attach price tags firmly so that switching will be difficult, if not impossible. Some stores use metallic tags that are attached to an alarm system. When legitimate sales are made, clerks release the alarm before removing the tags. Many large stores use the Uniform Product Code, the magnetic strips that are read by a computerized system connected to the cash register. Prices are stored in the computer, and crooks cannot easily change the code.
4. When cashiers ring up legitimate sales, they should staple the cash-register slip or sales ticket to the outside of the sack (which also closes the bag so that additional items cannot be added).
5. Arrange the physical layout with deterrence in mind:
    a. Maintain adequate lighting in all areas,
    b. Keep displays low, so you and your clerks can see over them,

Posting signs, even humorous ones, can remind customers about the penalties for shoplifting.

    c. Lock small valuable items in display cases,
    d. Place convex mirrors to cover blind aisles and sections of the store,
    e. Guard or bar unauthorized exits in some fashion,
    f. Aim closed-circuit television cameras at vulnerable areas (someone will have to monitor the viewing screens).
    g. Post signs prominently warning would-be crooks that your store will prosecute offenders.[10]

Apprehension and prosecution. The laws in many states make it difficult to arrest shoplifters on the premises. However, some states permit store employees to detain a customer who has been observed concealing merchandise.

To ensure apprehension—and to avoid being sued for making a false accusation—you and your employees should be sure that you:

1. Actually see the person(s) take or conceal merchandise.
2. Can identify the merchandise as yours.
3. Are willing to testify that the merchandise was taken with intent to steal.
4. Can prove that the merchandise was not paid for.

If you are not able to meet all four criteria, you leave yourself open to countercharges of false arrest—even if all you do is prevent a person from conducting normal activities. In fact, even a light touch on the arm may be considered unnecessary and be used against you in court.

Generally, store personnel should not accuse customers of stealing. Nor should they try to apprehend suspected shoplifters themselves. Train your employees to alert you or the police. Avoid verbally accusing suspects. Instead, identify yourself and then say, "I believe you have some merchandise that you have forgotten to pay for. If you'll come with me, please, I believe we can solve the problem."

People often say they are first offenders. You can check the truth of this claim with your local merchants' association. Failing to prosecute when you know you're right encourages crooks to continue their operations. Also, news may get around that your store is an "easy hit."

Although each offender takes special handling, you may develop some guidelines for you and your employees to follow. Elderly people, for instance, may honestly forget to pay for merchandise because of senility, and you may want to accept their excuses. Juveniles, however, should be treated with a no-nonsense attitude. Besides protecting yourself, you can help to deter any future thefts. You should, however, contact the young offenders' parents as well as the police.

In most cases where the four criteria given above can be met, prosecution is in order. In fact, prosecution is essential if shoplifters are violent, if they lack proper identification and you suspect a prior record, if they appear to be under the influence of alcohol or drugs, if they have stolen valuable merchandise, or if they are professionals.

Burglaries and Robberies

Small stores and service establishments are prime targets for burglars and robbers. Burglary is any unlawful entry to commit a felony or a theft, even though no force is used to gain entrance. Robbery is stealing or taking anything of value by force or violence or by use of fear. Burglaries usually take place at night, while robberies often occur at opening or closing times or when customer traffic is light.

Almost 80 percent of all burglaries and 66 percent of robberies go unsolved. Lack of witnesses or evidence makes police prevention and detection difficult. And both crimes have been occurring with a steadily rising frequency. Some business owners have been robbed not just once, but repeatedly. In 65 percent of store holdups the robber uses a weapon, and the victims are often hurt.[11]

If your business is located in a high-crime area you will want to be especially cautious, but all entrepreneurs should take preventative measures. Some suggestions:

1. Install good physical deterrents:
   a. Suitable locks, such as dead-bolt and pin-tumbler cylinder locks with five or more pins. Give keys to as few people as possible, and keep a record of who gets them.
   b. Appropriate alarm systems, particularly the silent, central-station type. The burglar hears no alarms, but police officers or private detectives are alerted.

  c. Adequate indoor and outside lighting.
  d. Heavy window screens.
  e. Burglar-resistant windows.
  f. A secure store safe.

2. Keep only a small amount of cash in registers and transfer other funds to a safe until bank deposits can be made. Deposit these funds regularly but at different times and by taking different routes to the bank.
3. Opening and closing routines should be conducted by two people if at all possible. The system may vary, but the exchange should be systematic and consume the shortest amount of time possible. Some small establishments actually close their doors for the 5 to 10 minutes it takes to change the cashier or salesclerk shift.
4. Train employees to reduce risk. Emphasize the protection of lives as well as money. They should not try to be heroes but instead to stay calm and to keep the robber calm. Also, you and they should make mental notes of the robber's physical characteristics and mannerisms for reporting to the police.
5. If you run a drugstore or other emergency establishment, be cautious of night calls. Let someone know you are returning to the store, or inform the police. You might want to check on the telephone call before deciding to respond.

The Cost of Prevention

Obviously, many deterrent devices are costly. But the financial loss from both external and internal crimes is also high. Once you have been in operation for several months, make an analysis of your losses. Calculate the average monthly sum lost due to crime and multiply that figure by 12 or by 60 to give an annual or a five-year projection. Then determine the cost of preventative controls, including the one-time expense of installing permanent devices. When you compare the results, you may decide that installing special devices and systems is worth the expense. Meanwhile, it costs nothing but time to train your employees about what to look for and how to take appropriate action in various situations.

SAFETY

The Occupational Safety and Health Administration Act (OSHA), enacted in 1970, was designed "to assure as far as possible every working man and woman in the nation safe and healthful working conditions."[12] Under OSHA, you are required to provide employees with a workplace that is free of hazardous conditions, including exposure to toxic materials or other physically harmful agents.

Fire marshals and OSHA inspectors have found that the most frequent violations among small retail and service establishments involve hazardous piles of debris and poor lighting in storerooms, improperly marked or unmarked exits, and fire extinguishers not mounted or not easy to find when needed.

Safety and health inspectors may visit business premises at any time and without advance notice. When violations are found, companies may receive severe fines and other penalties, including a forced closure until the conditions cited are corrected.

OSHA activities. In October 1981, OSHA modified its inspection procedure, deleting from the official list of establishments those general industry firms with 10 employees or less. Additionally, under normal circumstances, OSHA no longer conducts general safety inspection at work sites where the number of workdays lost to injury each year is beneath the industry-wide average of 5.2 days per 100 workers (recalculated annually by the Bureau of Labor). However, OSHA continues to inspect small facilities if it receives a complaint. Current policies eliminate unneeded inspections, concentrate on protecting workers' safety and health where they are most threatened, and create a more favorable working relationship with small business. Further, OSHA now works with small business trade associations to consider better ways to assist small businesses, including the increased use of five-state consultation services.[13]

Mining Safety and Health Administration (MSHA)

MSHA is another agency that administers procedures and makes inspections. Under MSHA, every miner must receive a minimum of eight hours' annual training in safety and health procedures. MSHA has inspection and other regulatory authority over surface stone, clay, sand, gravel, and colloidal phosphate mining or milling operations and also over the surface construction activities of independent contractors.[14]

Although many people think of mining as a large-business industry, there are actually more small operations than big ones. Many entrepreneurs of small mining companies are unaware of the regulations that govern their operations. Yet it is in mining and manufacturing firms that many injuries and fatalities occur. Thus special precautions need to be taken to reduce if not eliminate the potential for industrial accidents. (See Figure 20.1.)

Computer-Related Health Hazards

Scientists have suggested that certain health hazards are associated with computer usage. Most studies have concentrated on the effects on operators of long exposure to video display terminals (VDTs, also called cathode-ray tubes or CRTs). The most frequent maladies brought on by VDT use are eye fatigue, muscle fatigue, backaches, and headaches. There appears to be no radiation

Number of Fatal Injuries in the U.S. Mining Industries
(in each quarter of 1980, 1981, and 1982)

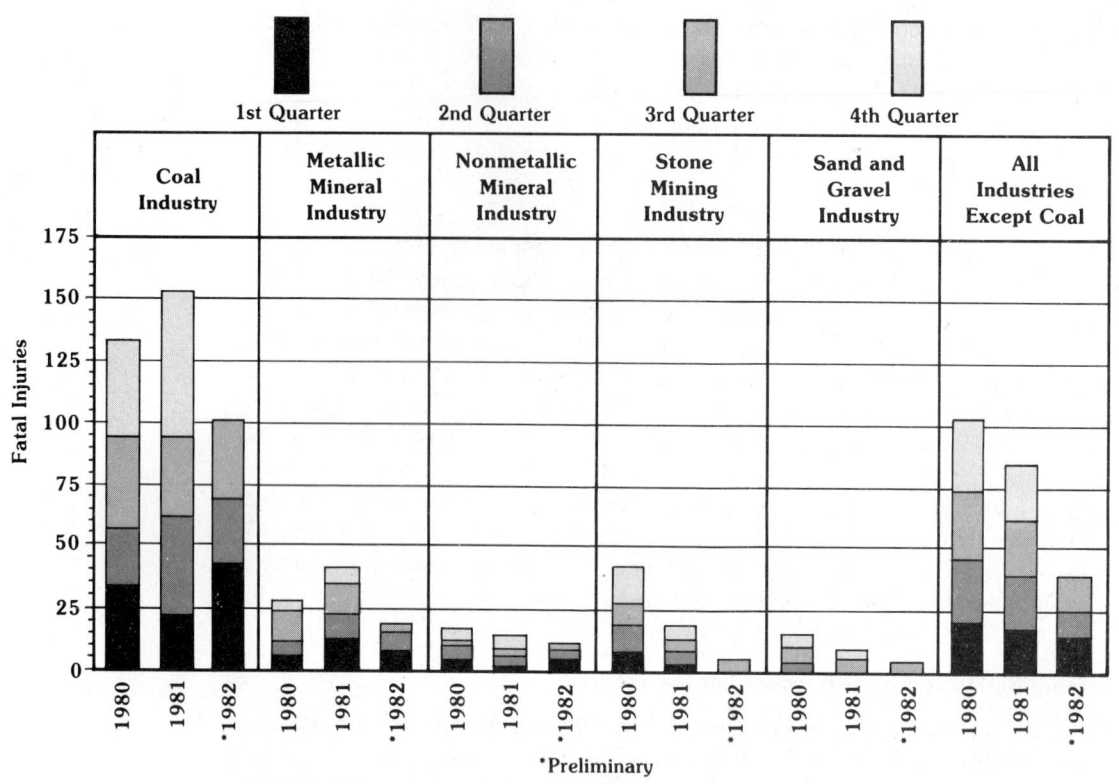

FIGURE 20.1 Fatal injuries in the U.S. Mining Industries MSHA

health hazard, but the evidence indicates that some users may develop skin rashes from using CRTs. According to Marvin Dainoff, a research psychologist with the National Institute for Occupational Safety and Health, "the problem of having the proper office environment has been neglected for a long time. The VDT has just added to the problem."[15]

To limit VDT-caused backache, muscle, and vision problems, you can use adjustable chairs that force people to sit up straight. Operators need to have a place for papers, and their furniture and chairs need to be positioned so that arms are parallel with the floor—not pointing either upward nor downward. Visors to remove the glare from terminal screens, regular work breaks, and adjusted room lighting can help reduce terminal-induced eyestrain.[16]

SUMMARY

Once upon a time retailers were called "storekeepers," and when they left their premises they trusted their employees to "mind the store." Like the word "housekeeping," the term clearly defines a basic management principle: any physical facility must be maintained. It also must be protected, which includes the safekeeping (or custodianship) of both the premises and their contents.

Facilities must be kept clean and orderly, to be sure, but owners also must by law provide employees with safe and healthful working conditions. Equipment and machinery must be kept operable, by means of preventative maintenance and with in-house or outside repair work.

Entrepreneurs must also seek to reduce the potential for both internal and external theft. Dishonest employees steal from their employers and from each other. They pilfer goods, embezzle funds, and commit computer crimes. Meanwhile, retailers particularly are plagued with shoplifting losses, and any type of establishment is subject to burglaries or robberies.

DISCUSSION QUESTIONS

1. How would you design a facility layout that provides for effective work and traffic flow and is simultaneously safe and secure?
2. What custodial duties would be involved in your type of business? To whom would these responsibilities be assigned? What authority will accompany the assignment of such tasks? How would you train an employee to perform these duties?
3. What kind of internal or employee crimes might you anticipate in your type of business? What physical deterrents could you use to prevent such crime? What policies and procedures could you use?
4. What types of external crimes might be most prevalent in your company and/or in the neighborhood you have selected to locate your business? Again, describe the preventative actions you could take.
5. How much would it cost to install preventative measures and procedures? How does this figure compare to the business losses due to theft?
6. How would you apprehend and prosecute the perpetrators of crimes against you and your business, whether the offenders are your own employees or outsiders?
7. How would you make sure that your employees have safe and healthful working conditions?
8. Debate the pros and cons of government inspections and regulations.
9. How would you train employees to follow safe procedures? Illustrate with examples from your type of business.
10. Describe your plan for an effective recovery system, should disaster destroy your facility, its contents, or its records.

Case Study

The following case describes seven crimes (or suspected crimes) that occurred in a single afternoon at a resort hotel. Decide how you would deal with each problem, if you were the security chief or the owner. Also, abstract salient points applicable to your type of business and be ready to draw comparisons.

Background. Ten plainclothes and two uniformed security guards are employed to protect the hotel and its grounds. The grounds include two tennis courts, a golf course, and a swimming pool as well as a parking lot and several cottages. The establishment includes two restaurants, snack bars at the golf course and swimming pool, a gift shop, a boutique, barber and beauty shops, a secretarial service, and a service station.

In the small security headquarters, employees rotate shifts to watch the closed-circuit television monitors, of which there are nine. The cameras cover certain exits and other blind spots. Also housed in this office are desks and equipment for keeping records and making reports.

Crimes (or possible crimes) during one afternoon:

1. In the security office, a guard sees (on a TV monitor) an unidentified pickup truck backing up to the exit nearest the room where liquors and wines are stored.
2. Another security clerk discovers by a phone call that a guest who has already checked out has no account at the bank on which he wrote a personal check.
3. A customer at the service station pulls away from the pumps without paying (the attendant has no idea whether the man is a guest at the hotel or merely a passerby).
4. An employee reports observing another employee removing packages of steaks from a big kitchen freezer, momentarily left unlocked. She believes the action was unauthorized.
5. A security guard reports seeing someone snooping around vehicles in the parking lot.
6. Another guard thinks he spotted a pickpocket in the lobby.
7. The boutique manager, robbed and beaten the night before and sent to the hospital, is ready to talk about the experience to the security guards and the police.

ACTIVITIES AND EXERCISES

1. Establish objectives for managing one or more physical environment factors in your business. Develop a separate MBO/R chart for each objective (see Chapter 17). Suggested topics include:
   a. Keeping the facility clean and orderly.
   b. Maintaining, servicing, and repairing equipment.
   c. Facilitating effective work and traffic flow.
   d. Ensuring workers' comfort and the reduction of fatigue.
   e. Securing records and planning for a recovery system in case of catastrophe.
2. Design security measures that can be implemented in your business to reduce the potential for crime from both internal and external sources. Use the MBO/R chart or management planning form.

3. Develop a plan for ascertaining whether the physical environment of your business is safe and healthful. Use the MBO/R chart or management planning form.
4. Participate in case discussions from the *Stanley Junction* case supplement.

NOTES

1. Steve Rosen, "Computers Create a New Market for Insurance Companies," *Kansas City Star,* February 27, 1983, p. 8G.
2. Judith Axler Turner, "Computer Crimes," *USAir,* January 1983, pp. 59–63.
3. Bob Curtis, *Food Service Security: Internal Control* (New York: Chain Store Age Books, 1975), p. 4.
4. Ibid., p. 6.
5. Kimberley Snow, "Why You Don't Want to Run a Restaurant," *Savvy,* July 1982, pp. 50–53.
6. Salvatore Didato, "Giving Employees a License to Steal," *The New York Times,* November 9, 1975, pp. 3–16. This article described industrial psychologist Laurence Zeitlin's concept of "controlled theft," which suggests that a company should determine how much it can tolerate in losses and then allow a controlled amount of theft, for the purpose of attempting to increase employee motivation and to keep labor turnover costs down.
7. Saul D. Astor, "Preventing Employee Pilferage," *Management Aid* no. 5.005, U.S. Small Business Administration (SBA) (Washington, D.C.), 1981.
8. Turner, "Computer Crimes."
9. Saul D. Astor, "Preventing Retail Theft," *Management Aid* no. 3.004, SBA (Washington, D.C.).
10. Ibid.
11. S. J. Curtis, "Preventing Burglary and Robbery Loss," *Management Aid* no. 3.007, SBA (Washington, D.C.).
12. *The State of Small Business: A Report of the President* (Washington, D.C.: U.S. Government Printing Office, March 1982), pp. 161–62.
13. Ibid.
14. *Mine Injuries and Worktime, January–September 1982* (Washington, D.C.: U.S. Department of Labor).
15. Steve Rosen, "New Technology May Bring Health Problems with Benefits," *Kansas City Star,* February 27, 1983, p. 8G.
16. Ellen Shea, "CRT Filters out the Glare," *Word Processing and Information Systems,* May 1982, p. 30.

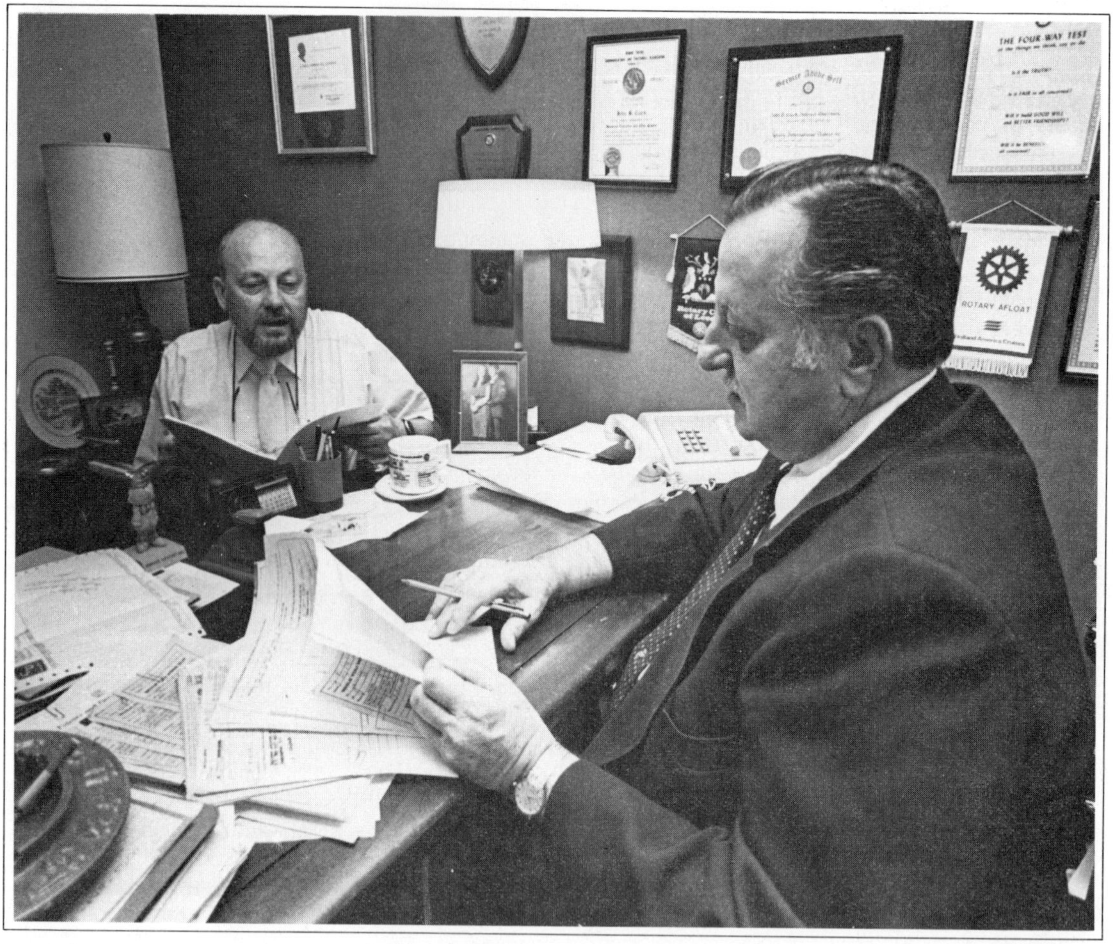
THE FOUR WAY TEST
ROTARY AFLOAT

chapter 21

Taking Stock; Managing Adjustments

Objectives

1. Establish criteria for evaluating the success of your business.

2. Identify management adjustment plans for weak areas that might occur in your business or aid you in getting out.

3. Design a plan for expanding a successful business.

Once you have been in business for a year or three or five you should be able to determine where you've been and where you are. To decide where you want to go next requires taking stock. In all likelihood, many of your decisions will have proven less than effective; you will have had good times and bad. One of the advantages of owning your own business, though, is that, compared to larger companies, you can decide how to adjust your management plan and can implement the changes quickly to redirect your enterprise toward increased profitability.

If your business has not been successful, you may decide to put it up for sale or you may even have to declare bankruptcy. Conversely, you may choose to bring in partners with additional capital and expertise or to incorporate and sell stock to raise needed funds.

If, instead of failing or faltering during those critical first months and years of operation your business proves successful, you may wish to expand by hiring new employees, making capital investments, opening new branches, or relocating in bigger facilities or in a better neighborhood. You might decide to add new services, products, equipment, or employees, or to go nationwide or international in your marketing program.

In any event, you will want to continue analyzing the competition and to devise new schemes to ensure your place in the market. You must not cease to conduct an effective personnel management and training program and to manage the physical environment. One of the excitements of operating a small business—at least to creative and adventurous spirits—is that no two days are ever quite alike. Ingenuity, energy, and a positive attitude are constantly required as you seek to turn problems into challenges and to make appropriate management adjustments.

MANAGEMENT EVALUATION AND FACILITATION

"Lousy" versus Effective Management

According to George L. Bernstein, a management consultant and executive partner in a major accounting firm, small business failures are often due to the type of management he calls "lousy." Such companies, he says, "can survive in good times because strong sales and profits tend to obscure their weaknesses. But in times of economic downswings, their deficiencies are exposed." He recommends that entrepreneurs establish a board composed of outsiders—experienced business people, retirees, even relatives—until they can afford professional advice.[1]

To survive, a company needs a strong competent owner(s) who has the ability to apply strategic and facilitative management to its operation. A business with great prospects but lousy management, according to Bernstein, "will either fail completely or become a marginal enterprise. Whereas a company whose prospects don't seem so bright may succeed marvelously because of the brilliance of its management."[2]

This kind of strong manager thinks strategically. That means thinking beyond the daily job and the weekly payroll and focusing on both short-term and long-term positioning in the marketplace. Strategic thinking addresses ways of gaining competitive advantages over others in the same industry. And it means constantly monitoring the marketplace, studying the external environment to keep aware of consumer's changing needs and wants. Facilitative management includes the ability to implement, direct, and control strategic plans, and to make good use of one's staff.

Evaluation Sessions

Using peer groups. Retailers in the boating, automotive, and jewelry industries use peer-review groups to help them evaluate their performance and make management changes. Numerous groups in other business classifications are also emerging. Many of these originated with contacts made at sales and trade conventions. The success of this type of informal association depends on several factors, among which are:

1. Locations that do not put members in direct competition with each other.
2. Similar type of businesses.
3. Similarity in size and volume of sales and revenue.
4. Different types of expertise and length of experience among the members.[3]

You can learn a great deal through such evaluations conducted by fellow entrepreneurs. But when your time comes, be ready to assume an objective attitude. You cannot benefit from the anlysis if your posture is defensive. It is, of course, up to you to decide what recommendations you will accept.

You may also want to ask the review team such questions as: Where should my business be in 10 years? Should I concentrate on service or expand the marketing program? What can I do about low employee morale?

Using participative management. When an important decision needs to be made in a Japanese organization, everyone concerned is involved in the process. A team of three people is assigned the responsibility of communicating with each person, and each time an important revision is considered, every one of the 60-plus people is again consulted. The team repeats this process until consensus is reached.[4]

This kind of participative decision making takes a long time, but once a consensus is reached, everyone involved will probably profit. According to Professor Ouchi, "Understanding and support may supersede the actual content of the decision, since five or six competing alternatives may be equally good or

Group sessions are meetings with key personnel for productive group thinking and to make strategic management plans

bad." What is significant is not only the decision but also how informed and committed people are.[5]

It's not the number of people who are involved, but the climate you promote by inviting staff opinions.

Yankelovich describes a scene where a company is facing foreign competition. Using the participative approach, management calls the staff together, where they hear, "Look, we have a problem. If we don't bring in new technology—we're not working in a vacuum—foreign competitors will get the job. If we bring in the new technology and become more competitive, a number of people—under ordinary circumstances—will lose their jobs. Let's work together on the problem." Yankelovich also believes in people. "Involve them," he says, "and they'll come up with job-sharing ideas, attrition plans, early-retirement plans—more positive results than if the owner(s) try to do it behind closed doors and people don't have any idea of what's going to happen to them."[6]

Managing for Profitability

To ensure business success, you must never lose sight of the ultimate objective: profitability. Year-end profit comes to entrepreneurs who strive for top-notch performance. You can achieve it by knowing your operation, by making timely, balanced judgments, and by controlling all your company's activities.

For the established concern, careful financial planning is a continuing necessity. A current shortage of funds is often the result of the unwise use of funds in the past. You should take care to (1) avoid an excessive investment in fixed assets, (2) maintain receivables and net working capital in proper proportion to sales, and (3) avoid excessive inventories.

According to some experts, "there is no financial difficulty of any firm, regardless of size, that cannot be traced to the violation of one or more of these three basic principles of financial management."[7]

To keep your business pointed toward profit, you must keep yourself well-informed. You must know its weak points before you can correct them. Some of the knowledge you need can be gathered from day-to-day observations. But records should be your principle source of information about profits, costs, and sales.

The income (or profit-and-loss) statement prepared regularly each month or each quarter is one of the most vital indicators of your business's worth and health. Be sure this statement contains all of the figures and facts needed for evaluation. It must cover every revenue, cost, and expense area. It should show the profit and loss for each of your products or services as well as for your entire operation.

You should not juggle records. The saying "garbage in, garbage out," used by the computer industry, applies to all records, whether maintained manually or processed by computer. If you put "garbage" into your records, the resulting reports also will contain "garbage." (See Figure 21.1.)

Break-even Analysis

All firms experience both direct and variable costs in doing business. Break-even analysis affords a method of finding out how much business your firm must do to just come out even during a given period. The method is straightforward in a routine operation.[8]

Break-even point analysis is performed in advance of an accounting year, although it utilizes information presented in earlier financial statements. It is more concerned with the future, however, than with evaluation of past performance.[9]

A break-even analysis can also help you assess the profitability potential of introducing a new product line. Contribution margin (CM) is the revenue that's left to cover fixed costs and profits after direct costs have been subtracted:

$$CM = \text{Revenue} - \text{Variable Costs (VC)}$$

When fixed costs (FC) are subtracted from the contribution margin, you get earnings (before interest and taxes). Then calculate the break-even level by dividing the fixed costs by CM. If CM is expressed on a per-unit basis, the break-

FIGURE 21.1
Evaluating for Profitability

Checklist for Evaluating Profitability

1. Choose an appropriate period for profit determination. Note that the accounting year need not coincide with the calendar year. A seasonal business, for instance, might close its fiscal year after the end of the season. Your selection depends upon the nature of your business, your personal preferences, or, possibly, tax considerations.

2. Determine your total revenues for the accounting period. Total Revenue = Net Sales + Nonoperating Income. Be sure to include gross sales, returns and rejects, discounts, and nonoperating income (such as interest on bank deposits, dividends from securities, rent on property leased to others, etc.).

3. Know your current ratio and your quick ratio.

4. Know your average collection period.

5. Compare your profit with your profit objectives.

6. Compare your profits (absolute and ratios) with profits made by similar firms in your line.

7. Prepare a sales report or analysis. Do you set up sales objectives by product, department, and accounting period? Are your objectives reasonable and are you meeting them according to the indicators and schedules established?

8. Do you have a buying and inventory system? Know what it costs you to order and carry inventory.

9. Keep records on the quality, service, price, and promptness of delivery of your sources of supply.

10. Keep ledgers for accounts receivable and accounts payable. Use journals for cash receipts and payments.

11. Prepare and use a budget.

12. Prepare an income (P&L) statement and a balance sheet. Use this data to decide on necessary management changes.

Adapted from: Narendra C. Bhandara, "Checklist for Profit Watching," *Management Aid* no. 1.018 (Washington, D.C.: U.S. Small Business Administration, 1981).

even volume will be expressed in units. If it's expressed as a percent of revenue, the break-even volume will be in dollars (see Figure 21.2).

The major problem with break-even analysis is that no one project really exists in isolation. Thus you must always consider not only the value of an individual project but also how it compares to other uses of funds, facilities, and labor.

FIGURE 21.2
Break-Even Analysis

Break-Even Analysis
Contribution on a Per-Unit Basis

$$\text{Contribution Margin (CM)} = \text{Revenue (Price)} - \text{Variable Cost (VC)}$$
$$= \$10 - \$7.50$$
$$= \$2.50$$

$$\text{Break-even volume} = \frac{\text{Fixed Costs (FC)}}{\text{CM}}$$

$$= \frac{\$250,000}{\$2.50}$$

$$= 100,000 \text{ units}$$

Contribution as a Percent of Revenues

$$\text{CM \%} = \frac{\text{Price} - \text{VC}}{\text{Price}}$$

$$= \frac{\$10 - \$7.50}{\$10}$$

$$= \frac{\$2.50}{\$10}$$

$$= 25\%$$

$$\text{BE} = \frac{\text{FC}}{\text{CM\%}}$$

$$= \frac{\$250,000}{25\%}$$

$$= \frac{\$250,000}{.25}$$

$$= \$1,000,000$$

Source: Peter G. Goulet, "Attacking Business Decision Problems with Breakeven Analysis," *Management Aid* no. 1.008 (Washington, D.C.: U.S. Small Business Administration).

Nor does break-even analysis permit proper examination of cash flow. It's generally accepted in basic financial theory that the appropriate way to make investments or capital decisions is to consider the value of a project's anticipated cash flow. If the discounted value of the cash flow exceeds the required investment outlay in cash, then the project is considered acceptable.

Break-even analysis does, however, have the following benefits and uses:

1. It's an inexpensive screening device. Discounted cash-flow techniques require a great deal of data, which is often expensive to get. Break-even analysis can tell you whether it's worthwhile to conduct more intensive (and costly) analysis.
2. It provides a means of designing product specifications. Each design has cost implications, which affect price and marketing feasibility. Break-even analysis permits comparison of possible designs before specifications are fixed.
3. It can substitute for unknown factors in economic projection formulas. Most formulas involve these variables: demand, costs, price, and miscellaneous factors. When most expenses can be determined, only two missing variables remain: profit (or cash flow) and demand. Demand is usually difficult to estimate. By deciding that profit must be at least zero (the break-even point), you can then find the demand you must have to make the project a reasonable undertaking.

Strategic Planning Techniques

A Dun & Bradstreet study of 11,452 business failures in 1975 reported that at least 34 percent occurred because of apparent liquidity or cash-related problems. Problems with cash flows are more common during recessions, when the demand for goods and services declines and fierce competition threatens a firm's market share. Cash-flow problems may also occur when times are good and there is rapid growth and expansion.[10]

A popular strategic planning technique used by manufacturers can also be applied to retailing. The Growth/Share Matrix Approach originated with the Boston Consulting Group. The multiple product unit retailer uses this technique to develop and manage an inventory of units, such as individual brands, merchandise groups, services, departments, or stores in a way that produces maximum cash flow over an extended period of time. The term strategic planning unit (SPU) is used generically to refer to these units. At any point in time, an inventory of SPUs can be plotted on a matrix that is defined by the market growth rate and market share dominance.[11]

To demonstrate the growth/share matrix approach, each category of merchandise is assumed to be an SPU. Four basic actions can be planned depending on the inventory location of the units:

1. "Stars" generally should be supported in order to hold or build their current position and thereby reap future cash flow. For example, underwear and hosiery represent such positions for discount stores in which allocations of money, space, and effort should remain high.
2. "Problem children" should be thoroughly audited and, if warranted, as the retailer you should either stop supporting these products by not stocking or by closing the department, or you can devise strategies that can develop such units into "stars" or "cash cows."

3. "Cash cows" should be maintained or harvested—depending on long-range market growth prospects—to provide cash support for developing or maintaining "stars" or for correcting "problem children."
4. "Dogs" generally should be withdrawn from the market as soon as reasonably possible if, in fact, it is possible.[12]

TIMELY DECISIONS AND GROWTH

A decision that does not result in action is a poor one. The pace of business demands timely as well as informed decision making. If you are to remain competitive, you must endeavor to control your destiny. To be effective, you also must be able to motivate key people to get the results planned for within the cost and time limits established.

In working to achieve results, entrepreneurs of small businesses have a major advantage over managers of big businesses. You can be fast and flexible, while many large firms must await committee action before making decisions and implementing actions. Equally important, you can personally supervise the changes you instigate and can focus on bottlenecks as they occur.

Winners and Losers

Based on the findings of a 1980 study, entrepreneurs would probably benefit by concentrating on building strength in cash management and innovativeness rather than attempting to excel in all possible management areas. Some of the strengths reported by the "winners" (more successful firms) in this study, such as cash management, can easily be acquired through training or by hiring trained personnel; innovativeness may be a lot harder to buy. Owner/managers who are creative and possess distinct know-how have the potential to do well.[13]

Product quality and manufacturing costs were the two most important items that separated the winners from the losers in this 1980 study. The most profitable as well as the intermediary groups of firms rated their product quality worse than that of their rivals. In contrast, the group of firms that had sustained losses rated their product quality as better. Profitable groups also paid higher wages and salaries than their leading competitors, and considered themselves managerially more competent.

Managerial competence might be the missing link that separates winners from losers. Another study of successful businesses found that their owners stress advertising, keep regular accounts, display better buying and selling skills, and have better customer relations.[14]

Business location is also deemed highly important in achieving success. Another significant factor is the ability to control costs.

Managing for Change

How will you handle change? Will you predict, control, cope, or adapt? Or will you plan for the management of change? Facilitative management helps entrepreneurs and their managers identify key areas where time spent will make the most difference, thus allowing for less and fewer meetings, paperwork, and housekeeping details.

Facilitative management focuses on profitability, quality, productivity, and effectiveness. Success in today's world belongs to the entrepreneur who can plan for and manage change, not to the one who merely reacts to today's problems and situations.

After some time in operation, you may wish to improve your facilities, to modernize existing systems, or to expand. If a building next door is available, your decision may involve no more than a remodeling expense. If you have been renting, however, a healthy profit picture may suggest that now is the time to consider constructing your own facility.

You may also be financially ready to consider opening branch offices or stores, buying another business, merging with another company, or expanding your market internationally. You may want to add new products to your line or

Whether out front or behind the scenes, crowded, cluttered, and unmanageable facilities may suggest that the time is ripe for relocating or expanding.

acquire additional customer accounts. Such decisions will depend not only on your financial position but also on the general state of the economy, both locally and nationally, and on current interest rates. (See Figure 21.3.)

Replacing and Updating Equipment

Equipment eventually deteriorates beyond repair. With frequent breakdowns, defective output increases, unit labor costs rise, and production schedules cannot be met. In deciding whether to replace a piece of equipment, weigh the costs of keeping old equipment against the cost of replacement.

First, determine cost of the new equipment and estimate its service life and salvage value. Then determine the market value of the old equipment and estimate its remaining service life and future salvage value.

Every piece of equipment generates an interest expense. Each asset you own ties up some of your capital. If you had to borrow this capital you would be paying for the use of the money. This "out-of-pocket" expense is one of the

FIGURE 21.3
Capital Expenditures

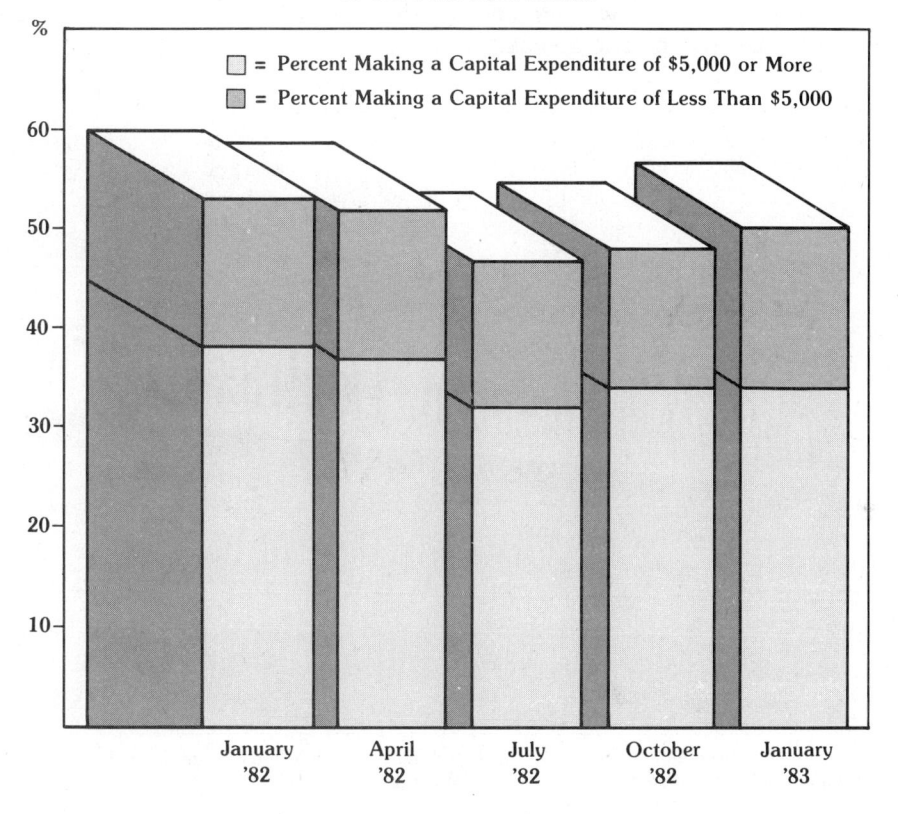

costs of owning equipment. The same is true when you use your own money. The amount involved is no longer available for other investments that could bring you a return. This is called "opportunity cost."

The third type of cost—the cost of operation—includes expenditures for labor, materials, supervision, maintenance, and power. These costs are affected by your choice of equipment. You may find it convenient to estimate them on an annual basis. You can get figures for each unit of equipment by estimating its next-year operating costs as well as the annual rate at which these costs are likely to increase as wage rates rise and the equipment deteriorates.

Once you have decided to purchase new equipment, you need to research the brands and models, to explore vendors' reputations, and to analyze the cost of operations. If total average annual costs are about the same, you will probably favor the equipment that requires a smaller investment or has the longer life. The same applies when you suspect that technological advances will soon make more efficient equipment available. You will probably prefer equipment that has greater output capacity, safety, and reliability. And finally, when you suspect that interest rates and the price of new equipment will increase significantly, you may be inclined to buy new equipment sooner rather than later.

In some manufacturing operations, numeric control (NC) is used to reduce the amount of human strength, manipulation, and accuracy required. The NC system uses tape punched with a numeric code to guide such equipment as mills and lathes through precise operations.

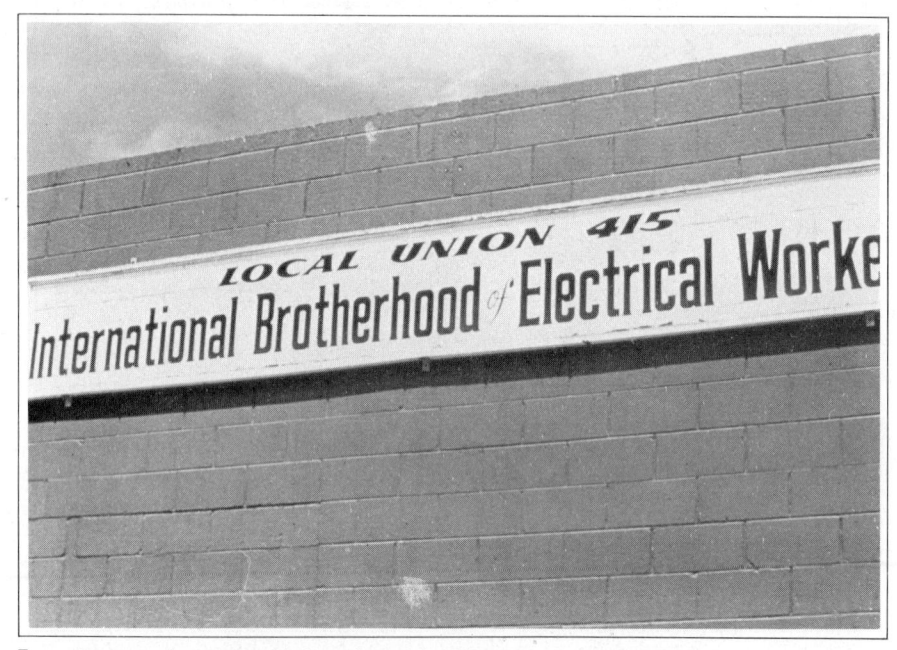

Expansion may also mean added employees (which may include negotiating union contracts if your employees are eligible and interested in joining a specific union).

Computer-aided manufacturing is used in many other operations. Next on the hierarchy of automatized functions is robotics, which eliminates even more human-initiated work. The cost of such sophisticated equipment and systems has decreased to the point where even small firms can automate many of their operations. (See Table 21.1.)

TABLE 21.1   Capital Expenditures

TABLE I

INDUSTRY[1]

TYPE OF PURCHASE	Construction	Manufacturing	Transportation	Wholesale	Retail	Agriculture	Financial Services	Nonprofessional Services	Professional Services	ALL FIRMS[1]—OCT 1982
Equipment, vehicles	39	52	52	42	28	50	38	34	48	38
Additional buildings	6	10	8	9	6	13	9	4	4	7
Improved buildings	8	17	20	20	16	18	11	14	15	15
Land	4	3	6	4	2	6	3	2	1	3
Number of firms	251	259	50	200	646	90	164	232	134	2026

[1] Includes firms for which no industrial classification was ascertained; columns do not add to 100% because more than one category could be checked by any individual firm.

TABLE II

SALES OF FIRM[1]

TYPE OF PURCHASE	Less than $50,000	$50,000–99,999	$100,000–199,999	$200,000–349,999	$350,000–799,999	$800,000–1,499,999	$1,500,000–2,999,999	$3,000,000 or more	Not Ascertained	ALL FIRMS—OCT 1982
Equipment, vehicles	21	33	37	34	39	40	53	57	32	38
Additional buildings	1	7	4	6	6	8	9	20	8	7
Improved buildings	9	13	12	12	14	17	22	29	11	15
Land	*	3	2	1	3	2	5	9	2	3
Number of firms	193	253	327	300	352	237	153	174	37	2026

[1] Quarter sales, at annual rates.

Source: Courtesy of the National Federation of Independent Business (NFIB), Research & Education Foundation, "Quarterly Economic Report for Small Business," October, 1982.

Technology and staff. In many industries, you need more than average performance from the work force, because that's what the competition is getting—particularly if you're competing on the international market. "So you need not technology instead of people, but the best technology *and* the most highly motivated people."[15]

Expansion may also mean adding new employees, which may include negotiating union contracts if your employees are eligible and interested in joining a specific union.

Expanding Internationally or Nationally

Similar principles that apply in any market feasibility study (see Chapter 7) are appropriate for a nationwide survey. However, the strategies are somewhat different, as are the resources you will need. In conducting a market analysis or in paying someone else to prepare it for you, you should collect factual, statistical, and map data on these topics, among others:

1. Appraising market opportunities.
2. Establishing marketing goals.
3. Developing sales promotions.
4. Allocating sales efforts and funds by territory.
5. Establishing sales quotas.
6. Controlling sales records and performance.
7. Designing sales compensation and incentive plans.
8. Planning the distribution facilities and methods.

International expansion. The U.S. government encourages small businesses to export. Sales to overseas customers help not only the exporters but also the U.S. economy. Each $1 billion in U.S. exports provides approximately 30,000 jobs. There are about 300,000 U.S. manufacturing firms, but only a small percentage sell their products abroad. Yet is is estimated that several thousand more firms could compete successfully in foreign markets if the effort were made.[16]

According to Yankelovich, the strongest force working on the workplace is international competition. "Our country depends very critically on growth, on expanding opportunity." Further, he predicts that "we'll become more competitive, more inventive, more entrepreneurial, more energetic, more aggressive, more efficient, and we'll have another wave of growth and productivity."[17]

The U.S. Department of Commerce's International Trade Administration (ITA) may be able to help you, if you are interested in:
· Entering the export field;
· Expanding your export sales;
· Locating an overseas agent or distributor;
· Licensing a product for manufacture abroad;

- Learning about opportunities for selling, exhibiting, and promoting your products abroad, including getting information on tariff and nontariff barriers, inspection, and shipping criteria;
- Keeping abreast of marketing, economic, governmental, and other developments overseas; and
- Exhibiting your products abroad and meeting foreign buyers. The list of federal departments and agencies that offer advice and publish materials includes: the Department of Agriculture, the National Oceanic and Atmospheric Administration (for fisheries or related businesses), the Department of State, the U.S. Export-Import Bank, the Overseas Private Investment Corporation, the Office of the U.S. Trade Representative (an agency of the Executive Office of the President), the Agency for International Development, and, of course, the Small Business Administration.[18]

Created by a 1982 law, export trading companies (ETCs) allow small and medium-size companies to band together to achieve economies of scale. ETCs are "one-stop-exporting shops," providing everything from financing, insurance, and transportation, to sales, marketing, and service. ETCs can arrange guaranteed loans from the Export/Import Bank and can obtain waivers of antitrust law enforcement, allowing companies with competing lines to export together.[19]

Nationwide expansion. When you seek to compete with major corporations, you want to be especially sure that your products or services are unique enough to attract and keep customers. You should also research how the competition markets their goods so you can emulate their best features and then offer something else besides. All of this takes money. You may be pouring funds down the drain if you are unable or unwilling to commit the resources necessary to make an impact on the marketplace.

MINICASE

Two textbook publishing companies have for many years dominated the secondary-level business education field. Only during the past few decades have other publishers attempted to break into this market to any extent. They attempted to market their business education products with the same sales techniques they used for their traditional publications. However, several of these companies experienced little or no success and have subsequently cancelled their business education line.

Why did these publishers who had already proved they knew how to market (other) textbooks fail in this specific line? As per their usual procedure, these companies listed their business textbooks in a general K-12 (kindergarten through twelfth grade) catalog, which they mailed to school principals, district curriculum directors, and state textbook-selection boards. Sales reps also visited these key personnel.

Publishers of the two dominant secondary-school business education materials on the other hand, develop catalogs specifically directed to business education products, and mail these catalogs directly to high school business education teachers. When their sales reps visit schools they go directly to the business teachers' classrooms. The latter not only get news about the latest textbook products but also hear gossip about their friends in the profession.[20]

These industry leaders also provide teachers with free teaching aids, exhibit their products at state, regional, and national business education conventions (where they also host cocktail parties), and support research and education in the field. Although major in size, both houses promote the personalized selling approach described in Chapter 18. Oh yes, they also mail literature to, and meet with, school principals and superintendents, curriculum directors, and state boards.

Not only were the new entries into the business education market up against very entrenched competitors, but those who failed must also have failed to analyze their rivals' methods and to benefit from their experience.

If breaking into the national market sounds difficult, it is! The revenues can be phenomenal, but only if you are willing and able to commit a great deal of money to the effort and if you direct those efforts appropriately. Remember Paula Nelson, Steve Jobs and Steve Wozniak? (Review Chapter 6 and descriptions of how these people started off thinking big.) It takes money to make money, yes; which is why so many entrepreneurs who decide to expand elect to form partnerships, to incorporate, to start a franchise, or to go after venture capital.

Buying Another Business

One method of acquiring new products or services is to buy all or part of another business. To become successful, many small companies with fine products may need the support of another company's money, equipment, facilities, personnel, or expertise in manufacturing, marketing, or management. If such companies are facing bankruptcy, their selling price may be low. However, such purchases are risky, and you need to be fairly certain your financial capabilities and managerial talents can bring such a company out of the doldrums before considering such a move.

You can find such companies by checking bankruptcy records, reading trade literature and the classified ads in newspapers, and contacting Small Business Investment Companies (SBICs) and investment bankers. These companies are continually examining existing and potential businesses. Contacts with these firms could lead to your acquiring a new product or an equity position in a business with desirable products. (Contact the nearest SBA office for a list of licensed SBICs in your area.)

Some entrepreneurs are able to take tired old, inefficient businesses and give them new life. No two buyouts are identical. But one thing they all share is the need to maximize the newly acquired company's cash flow. Among the most successful strategies are: (1) cutting costs unmercifully to bring them under control, (2) tightening financial controls, and (3) redeploying assets.

To create the kind of cash flow needed to service the debt, buyout owners reduce, and often eliminate, taxes by revaluing their assets upward. This can reduce taxes by increasing depreciation deductions. The balance sheet would then change, as described in this example:

1. First, assets are revaluated upward. The buyer takes the book value to the seller and restates it at a higher value. This "stepping up" can be achieved as a result of obtaining respected appraisals, which can include the reevaluation of property, plant, and equipment.
2. Purchasing patents or goodwill also increases the asset side of the balance sheet. A patent, recorded as an asset, can be depreciated over its estimated useful life.
3. On the liabilities side, the buyout financing may add a significant amount to the buyer's debt.

Thus taxes will be reduced through greater depreciation and interest-payment deductions. You should, of course, consult tax people early in the process of negotiating any asset-based deal.

GETTING OUT

Insolvency and Bankruptcy

If your company is plagued with nervous creditors, a tarnished reputation, defensive key employees, disgruntled workers, or assets and inventory worth a fraction of the value at which they are carried on the books—much less by outraged stockholders and by lawsuits and countersuits among principals and purveyors—then you may assume you are in for trouble! Because the bankruptcy laws change frequently, you should check with an attorney if you suspect your company is in any danger.

If you file under Chapter 7 of the National Bankruptcy Act, the assets of your company will be liquidated and the proceeds distributed to claimants. Under the provisions of Chapter 7, your business will be closed down for you—involuntarily—with no hope for you or your creditors to recover.

If you file under Chapter 11 of the Bankruptcy Code, however, your business will be protected against the full claims of creditors while you work out a plan of eventual repayment acceptable to them. A reorganization plan is then in order.

You may decide to sell your business—preferably to someone with the managerial and financial expertise to turn the business around. Or you may negotiate to retain a percentage of ownership and also some continuing role in the firm—with a title such as manager or vice-president.

If you suspect you are rapidly becoming insolvent, you can file for protection under Chapter 11. In fact, if you are forced by creditors into Chapter 7 liquidation, you can respond by filing under Chapter 11, which is automatically granted—a concept of business preservation dating back to the nineteenth century.

The bankruptcy act also establishes a system of priorities that gives preference to claimants in the following categories:

- Classes 1, 2, and 3: those entitled to priority status, such as the Internal Revenue Service and unpaid employees.
- Class 4: those creditors who have secured claims.
- Class 5: those who have unsecured claims up to $1,000.
- Class 6: all other claimants, to be satisfied out of future revenues.
- Class 7: holders of unsecured subordinated notes.
- Class 8: senior-preferred-stock owners.
- Class 9: junior-preferred-stock owners.
- Class 10: common stockholders.

Whatever you do, contact a competent lawyer with experience in dealing with bankruptcies. You might find you have other options.

Selling Your Business

Various offers and terms should be evaluated, whether you are a seller or a buyer. Among various considerations are the crucial tax consequences and estate ramifications that can, if you are not careful, eliminate all that you've achieved. Of course you will want to engage a competent attorney and a real estate agent to represent you in finalizing any transaction.

Even a losing or marginal company can be sold for a profit if your marketing approach is good and if you have prepared your business and its facility for sale. Terms are often more important than price. You may want to sell off your business but retain valuable assets, such as real estate.

With the help of your consultants, offer your company for sale in a manner that presents it in the best possible light. Then be ready to negotiate the best deal possible. Your plan should answer such questions as:

1. What is my business really worth?
2. Where are the buyers and how do I attract them?
3. What is a buyer looking for and thinking?
4. How do I separate the serious buyer from the merely curious?
5. How can I determine how much buyers are willing to pay?
6. Why it is important to know where the buyer gets the money to purchase my business?

7. Do I know the most common "deal killers" and how to overcome them?
8. How can I prevent losing in taxes what I gain from the sale?

You don't want to liquidate your business or file for bankruptcy if instead you can sell your business for a profit. Nor will you want to overprice the business and thus fail to attract qualified buyers, or underprice it and risk shortchanging yourself.

SUMMARY

To evaluate your business's success, you should develop procedures to compare your current position with your original objectives. As one analyst points out, however, "Entrepreneurs who develop the ideas, dream the dreams, and display the charisma that gives new businesses the initial burst of energy and innovation are not necessarily experts at follow-through."[21]

If your business has done well, you may decide to improve your facilities and equipment, to add branches or open new stores, to develop additional product lines, to expand your market to national or international proportions, or to buy other businesses.

If your business has not done well, it may be time to get out. You may then have to seek protection under the bankruptcy law or offer your business for sale.

FINAL ACTIVITY

Retrieve all financial papers, checklists, worksheets, and MBO/R forms and other management planning tools prepared throughout this program. Develop or revise objectives for each phase of your business. Adjust estimates. Complete the business plan and prepare it as a formal document to submit for final evaluation. See Chapter 6 for the guidelines about how to prepare an acceptable businesslike copy.

NOTES

1. Alan Gersten, "Lousy Management Cited for Failures," *Rocky Mountain News* (Denver, Colorado), May 11, 1983, p. 51.
2. Ibid.
3. Craig R. Waters, "Trial by Jury," *Inc.*, May 1982, pp. 81–87.
4. William Ouchi, "The Workings of a Japanese Corporation," *Modern Office Procedures*, January 1982, pp. 14–20.
5. Ibid.

6. Julia Kagan, "Survey: Work in the 1980s and 1990s," *Working Woman*, December 1983, pp. 16–23. This article reported on the findings of the Public Agenda Foundation survey; part of an international study that centered on job motivation and the work ethic, and the effect of technology on attitudes, among other topics. Daniel Yankelovich, president of the Foundation, discussed with the author some of his interpretations of the study's findings.
7. *AEA Business Manual* no. 71 (Los Angeles: Entrepreneur Magazine, 1982), p. 29.
8. Arthur H. Kuriloff and John M. Hemphill, Jr. *Starting and Managing the Small Business* (New York: McGraw-Hill Book Co., 1983), pp. 293–301.
9. H. N. Broom and Justin G. Longenecker. *Small Business Management* (Cincinnati, OH: South-Western Publishing Co., 1979), pp. 330–31.
10. Fred A. Jacobs, Larry H. Beard, and Al L. Hartgraves, "Controlling Cash Flow in the Small Business," *Business*, January–March 1983, pp. 31–36.
11. Glenn S. Omura and M. Bixby Cooper, "Three Strategic Planning Techniques for Retailers," *Business*, January–March 1983, pp. 2–9.
12. Ibid.
13. Rajeswararao Chaganti and Radharao Chaganti, "A Profile of Profitable and Not-So-Profitable Small Businesses," *Journal of Small Business Management*, July 1983, pp. 43–51.
14. Edward J. Chambers and Raymond L. Gold, "A Pilot Study of Successful and Unsuccessful Business Enterprises in Montana," study done for Montana State University, January 1961.
15. Kagan, "Survey."
16. "Market Overseas with U.S. Government Help," *Management Aid* no. 7.003, SBA.
17. Kagan, "Survey."
18. Kevin Farrel, "Exports," *Venture*, March 1983, pp. 62–66.
19. Ibid.
20. Nancy Ingram, "A Survey of Most- and Least-Used Professional Contacts and Resources Utilized by Business Education Teachers," master's thesis (Laramie, Wyoming: University of Wyoming, 1975).
21. Gersten, "Lousy Management."

appendix A

Self-Assessment Tools and Exercises

The exercises and tools in this appendix will help you evaluate whether you are most interested in people, machines, ideas, or things. Hobbies, leisure-time activities, work experiences, and familial influences are the focus.

Review of the results, as performed with Exercise 6, will identify your abilities in the areas of oral communications, risk-taking, organization, and analysis. Other attributes that may emerge include creativity and mathematical and mechanical skills. The first four, however, are perhaps the most important for entrepreneurial success.

1. *Oral communications.* Verbal articulateness, plus the ability to motivate and persuade others, are critical skills for entrepreneurs, who should enjoy talking and negotiating.
2. *Risk-taking.* A sense of adventure and excitement at taking small but potentially sound gambles is part of the picture. Notice the word *small*, however: the successful entrepreneur is likely to plan well and unlikely to make rash decisions.
3. *Organizational abilities.* The effective business owner is able to sort out and make sense of miscellaneous data and things, but also has the self-discipline to organize work and systems, to keep to a schedule, to set goals (and divide them into manageable subsets), and to follow through on self-assigned tasks.
4. *Analytical talents.* This includes the ability to perceive patterns and subsets in organized and random data, which may include dozens if not hundreds of seemingly isolated facts. Analytical thinking builds on organizational abilities. Also, from the talent for perceiving subsets grows the ability to think creatively, to come up with new ideas and methods of doing things.

5. *Creativity*. The creative person can pull out of assembled data/ideas those points that are most usable or important to other situations and needs. These data/ideas are then interrelated in new contexts to create new and different approaches and systems.

EXERCISE 1

Strengths and Successes

Divide the form into three age-life sections. If you are a teenager, use these classifications: (1) childhood—at home and school; (2) middle-school years—home, neighborhood, and school; (3) teenage years—home, neighborhood, and school. If you are an adult, use these phases: (1) childhood and elementary-school days, (2) teens and early adulthood, and (3) the years since adolescence.

1. Record at least three experiences for each age-life period in which you had an outstanding success. Identify one or more personal strengths (traits) that contributed to each success (column 1, exercise sheet 1-A).
2. State precisely why you consider each experience successful (column 2).
3. Check the categories in columns a–i that had an important role in making the experience successful. The subcategories are defined as:
   a. Leadership role: you were good at leading/motivating.
   b. Follower role: you were good at following (suggests you would be good at teamwork, would work well as a junior or equal partner).
   c. Self-approval: the experience was yours alone, and you were pleased with yourself. Nobody mentioned your triumph, and perhaps nobody knew about it but you; but no matter, you can work alone, without a boss or other person recognizing your success.
   d. Respected by others: your achievement was recognized and appreciated by one or more people. You may not have identified the action as an achievement until it was noticed and applauded by others (indicates your need for outside approval).
   e. Other people were involved: your feeling of success came from your involvement in a group effort (you may enjoy a partnership or corporate setting or being surrounded by people, as in customer and/or employee relations).
   f. Creative-original: the achievement was based on something you created or designed, with little or no contributions from others (a good attribute for a sole proprietor, particularly).
   g. Machines: the achievement involved the use of machines, and your technical/mechanical skills contributed to the success (indicative of the type of business you might be most interested in).
   h. Things, or data/information processing: the achievement involved the use of objects, paper, data, or information processing more than machines or people (also indicative of most compatible businesses).
   i. Ideas: the achievement involved your contribution or applying ideas, whether original or not.

Strengths and Successes

Patterns (check all appropriate)

Age-Life Period	Positive Experiences (Successful Ones)	What Made It Successful?	(a) Leader	(b) Follower	(c) Self-Approval	(d) Respect	(e) Others	(f) Original	(g) Machines	(h) Things	(i) Ideas	Other (list)
Childhood Home School												
Middle School (Grades 6-8) Home Community School (Or teens and early adulthood)												
Teenager Home Community School (Or time since leaving school)		Totals:										

Exercise 1. Strengths and Successes Exercise.

EXERCISE 2

Positive and Negative Experiences

This exercise invites you to identify both positive and negative life/work experiences and to record the emotional and bodily sensations associated with each. Obviously, you would do better in business situations that have positive associations than in those that arouse negative feelings.

In responding, use exercise sheets 2-A and 2-B.
1. Using sheet 2-A, record situations from the past few months that have aroused distinct bodily or emotional reactions (column 1).
2. Identify positive situations with a *P* and negative ones with an *N* (column 2).
3. Define the specific emotional/bodily sensations each caused (column 3), using such examples as these: *N*—sweaty palms, palpitating heart, shortness

of breath, inability to swallow, shaking legs, knots in the stomach (see Figure 19.3); *P*—feelings of excitement, peace, comfort, increased energy, lack of fatigue.
4. Using sheet 2-B, record related positive experiences. These are activities (or business enterprises) you might pursue to obtain similar positive or pleasurable feelings.
5. Analyze the negative experiences to determine the cause, for example: (a) fear of rejection—that people laughed at or shunned you, or that you might have; (b) lack of experience—you hadn't learned enough to be able to exhibit expertise; (c) other—define and describe.
6. Use Exercise 2-B to record what you would have needed for the negative experiences to have been positive: i.e., more expertise, additional practice or reading, etc. Avoid blaming either yourself or others. Concentrate, instead, on what *you* could have done differently in order to have succeeded. Finally, congratulate yourself on how well you did manage to cope, even if you weren't entirely successful.

Positive and Negative Experiences

Specific Personal Experiences: alone or with others (family, friends, school, new group), in last few months	P or N	Bodily/Emotional Sensations: racing heart, sweating, nervous; warm glow, peace/comfort, energetic, happy

Exercise 2-A. Positive and Negative Experiences—with Bodily/Emotional Sensations.

Positive and Negative Clues

Related Positive Activities: Record one or more activity related to each positive experience already stated. Use the bodily/emotional sensations as clues for finding other things you could do to bring the same responses.

Analyzing Negative Experiences: Record causes of negative experiences already stated. Then record what you could have done differently, to turn the negative experience into a positive one. Record the good things you did do to cope with the negative situation.

Summarize Experience	Cause: (a) fear of rejection or (b) lack of experience	Things I Could Have Done Differently	Good Things I Did Anyway to Cope

Exercise 2-B. Positive and Negative Clues Exercise.

EXERCISE 3

Work and Play as Clues to Self

This exercise focuses on your hobbies and favorite activities, both during and after your school years. Divide your life span into the same three stages used in Exercise 1. Identify your hobbies and pastimes, plus the chores you have done in your household (during youth and since).

In the columns to the right, record whether other people were involved or you enjoyed these activities in solitude and whether machines or things were used. Also, were these inside or outdoor activities? Did you need purchased materials or could you create your own? Finally, what bodily/emotional sensations did you experience when engaged in each? Total the checkmarks under each column.

Work and Play

Item and Age	Responses	Machines	Things	Inside	Outside	Others Involved	Alone	Mental/Quiet	Physical/Active	Purchased	Original	Bodily/ Emotional Sensations
Childhood Play Pastimes and Chores												
Middle School (Grades 6-8) Pastimes and Chores (For adults, use the teens and early adulthood)												
Teenager Pastimes and Chores (Adults, use the period since leaving school)	Totals:											

Exercise 3. Work and Play Exercise.

EXERCISE 4

Family Influences as Clues to Self

This exercise addresses the family setting. Since our parents and siblings strongly affect who we are and what we might become, these familial influences are important to analyze.

Interview family members, if necessary, in order to complete this form accurately. Use the column headings as a guideline. Also record your bodily/emotional sensations: how you feel/felt about the occupations pursued by family members.

Family Clues

Item	Response	Setting	People Involved	Things/ Machines Involved	Bodily/ Emotional Sensations
What type of job did/does your father have?					
What type of job did/does your mother have?					
What type of job did/do your sibling(s) have? (NOTE: If you have no siblings working, you may use other relatives or close friends. Also think of spouse and other influential people)					

Exercise 4. Family Clues Exercise.

EXERCISE 5

Classes, Jobs, and Leadership Roles: Likes and Dislikes

This exercise allows you to identify those classes and jobs that you like(d) best and least. Use L for like and D for dislike in the second column. Try to determine the causes for your feelings (column 3). Again, record your bodily/emotional sensations to make clear whether you liked or disliked each activity.

Record leadership roles for which you volunteered or were appointed or elected to, and managerial positions to which you were hired or promoted.

Classes, Jobs, and Leadership Roles: Likes and Dislikes

Item	Responses	L = Like D = Dislike	Causes: (a), (b), (c)*	Bodily/ Emotional Sensations
Classes: in any and all grade levels thus far experienced				
Jobs: part- or full-time that you liked/ disliked				
Leadership Roles: those you volunteered for, were chosen or elected for, or were assigned				

*(a) fear of rejection/failure; (b) lack of experience; (c) other—record

Exercise 5. Likes and Dislikes—Classes, Jobs, and Leadership Roles.

SUMMARY

Self-Assessment

In summarizing the self-assessment (Exercise 6), you should analyze the records from Exercises 1 through 5 to identify your patterns and thus develop self-awareness:

Knowing Yourself: Summary Analysis		
Item	Response	Cause, or Bodily/Emotional Sensation
Successful experiences (most imp.)		
Play, pastimes, hobbies most enjoyed		
Chores most enjoyed		
Classes most enjoyed		
Leadership roles most enjoyed		
Work that most appeals from that of family		
Patterns that show up most often: (inside or outside?) (things, ideas, or machines?) (alone or with people?) (active or quiet?) (physical or mental?)		
Things learned from mistakes or negative experiences		
Positive ways to cope		

Knowing Myself—Summary Analysis.

1. Compare the successes and positive experiences (Exercise 1 with 2-A and 2-B) to establish patterns. Record only the most significant ones on the summary sheet.

2. Compare the pattern categories in Exercises 1 and 3. Note similarities between your positive experiences (no. 1) and your favorite play, pastimes, and chores (no. 3). Record only the most salient experiences.
3. Return to the causes for each "Like" item in Exercise 5. Apply the checkmarked categories from Exercises 1 and 3. Record the factors that apply under the column "Causes" on no. 5.
4. Verify, from Exercise 4, the things that you liked most about family work pursuits with the column, "Things/Machines." Your clue to what you like is the response you made to each under "Bodily/Emotional Sensations." Circle the ones that stand out. Checkmark the things that also appeared on some of your other lists.
5. Use the summary analysis sheet to record some of the things that you now know about yourself (which you may or may not have suspected previously).

appendix B

Decision-Making Tools and Activities

A number of techniques used in solving problems and making decisions are used with specific tools. The T-Chart, so called because of its format, allows you to list advantages and disadvantages of any given alternative. This chart is sometimes used as the only analysis tool, particularly when you already know what issues to consider or what specific things you are looking for, such as during a business observation when you want to compare only two items. The T-Chart is shown as Step 3 with the figures contained in this appendix.

To keep the steps in order however, let's begin with Step 1. The example included in this appendix is the same as the MBO/R chart given in Chapters 5 and 17. This is the vertical format. You may choose whichever tool design you prefer. Expect to use this tool during Chapter 5, when you should make a decision about what business(es) you would prefer owning. You will use the technique and tool again in Chapters 17 through 21, on the management and control unit.

The brainstorming chart, shown as Step 2 in the following tools, is used less often. The idea is good, however, because when you (or you and your group) approach several different topics simultaneously, the subsequent ideas generated can be mixed and matched. Recording these ideas on a matrix like this allows you to use creativity in a logical fashion. For instance, an idea generated to serve one topic (issue or objective) may just as readily be suitable for another topic. Yet this matching may not have occurred to you until you see the ideas appear on paper. The key to having this happen is to use similar and related topics for the brainstorming session.

Phrase a question to find out the goal or results you want to achieve.

QUESTION: What would be the most perfect SSC week?
QUESTION: How would I know when the "Perfect Week" was happening?

WHAT IS HAPPENING NOW?

* Our branch office averages at least one person absent daily.

BRIDGING THE GAP FROM "HERE" TO "THERE" TECHNIQUES, STRATEGIES, METHODS	CHECKPOINTS
* Find out why people are absent. — Manager-employee conference to discuss cause & effect of absenteeism — Full-office meeting to discuss attendance — Employees would look for reasons why they are absent, try to eliminate causes (barriers to full attendance) — Full attendance employees would share their problems with absent workers by explaining about overload problems when a worker is gone. — Full attendance employees would be rewarded with recognition &/or a bonus.	After 2 weeks, absenteeism would drop to an average of 3 per week After 3 weeks, absenteeism would drop to an average of 1-2 per week After four weeks absenteeism would drop to 0-1 per week

ANSWERS: (Results)
1. My branch office would earn more profit than any of the others.
2. Nobody would be absent, so the others would not have a work overload.
3. Nobody would get mad at anyone, and everyone would get along just fine.
4. The Steno-WP jobs would be done more efficiently than ever before.
5. The clients would not return jobs to be done over.
6. The clients would be nice and not get irritable or mad.
7. I'd feel good about myself and the work I'd done.
8. We'd get some new clients, who had heard about our good services.
9. I'd get a bonus, and maybe a transfer or a promotion.
10. None of the machines would break down.

*Example topic: absenteeism

NOTE: A similar chart could be prepared for each of the RESULT topics.

Decision-Making Techniques, Step 1.

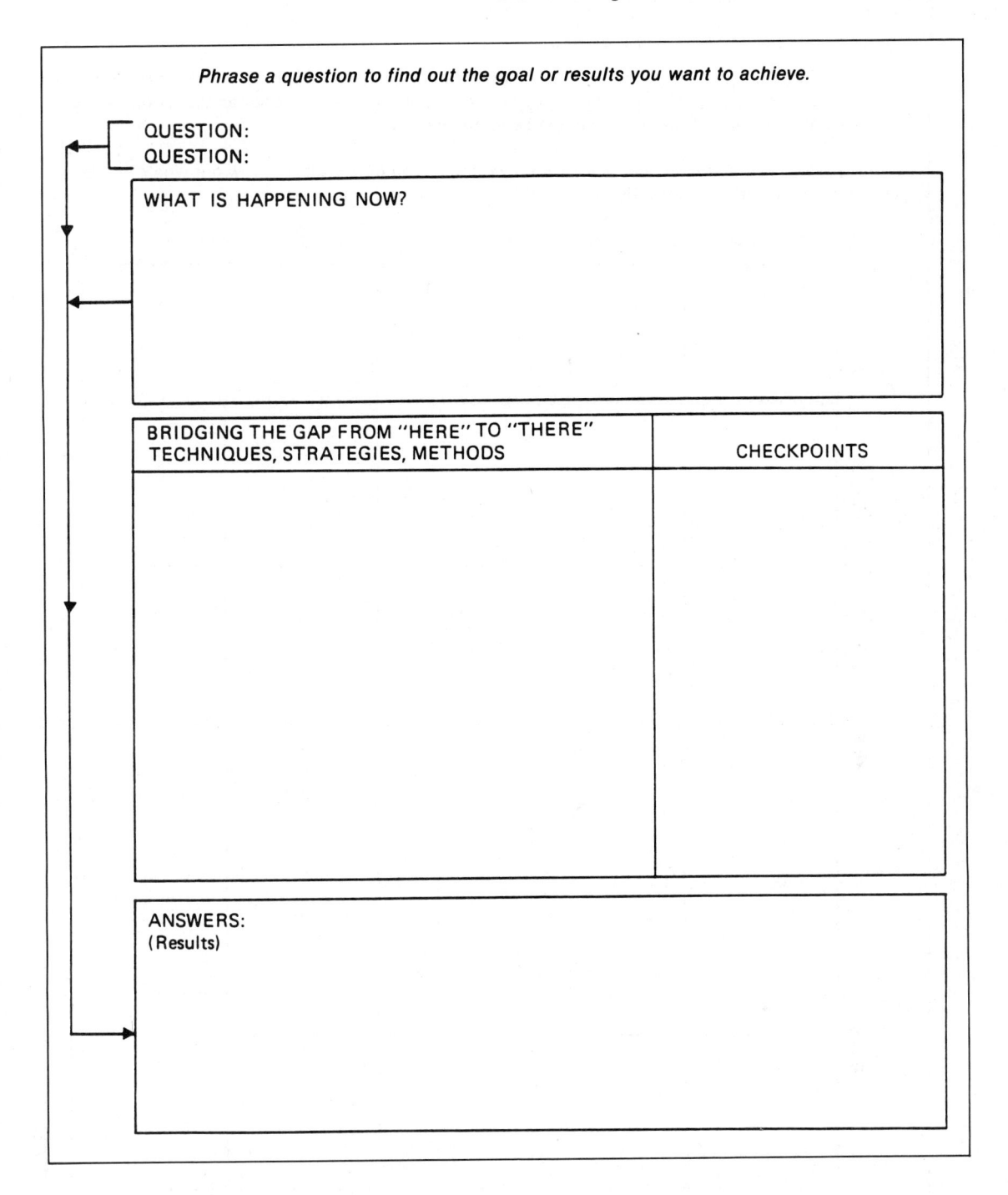

Phrase a question to find out the goal or results you want to achieve.

QUESTION:
QUESTION:

WHAT IS HAPPENING NOW?

BRIDGING THE GAP FROM "HERE" TO "THERE" TECHNIQUES, STRATEGIES, METHODS	CHECKPOINTS

ANSWERS:
(Results)

Decision-Making Techniques, Step 1.

"Brainstorming," or the generation of many different ideas, gives the person(s) faced with a decision many different avenues from which to choose. While a person can brainstorm alone, it is often useful to have other people generate ideas also.

You may want to tackle just one RESULT target, or you may want to throw out whatever ideas occur to you about many. Use the chart below to record responses.

*BRAINSTORMING CHART: One idea per square, under RESULTS, shown as topics

Topics:

Ideas:

*ALWAYS REMEMBER TO KEEP THE QUESTIONS FOREMOST!

Decision-Making Techniques, Step 2.

Decision-Making Tools and Activities

ANALYZING ALTERNATIVE SOLUTIONS — T-CHARTS: Listing what is good and what is bad about the most appealing ideas you generated during the brainstorming session. Try to be as objective and impersonal as possible.

T-CHART EXAMPLE

ADVANTAGES	DISADVANTAGES
STRATEGY IDEA: Manager-employee conference	**TARGET RESULT:** Attendance
— Employees would receive individual attention. — Employees might feel that "somebody cares." — Would give employee a chance to talk out problems. — Would help the Manager understand & know the employee better.	— The employee might be embarrassed. — The employee might be mad. — Too general an idea — Manager might act offensive or strict. — Conference would take too much time.

T-CHART

STRATEGY IDEA:	TARGET RESULT:
ADVANTAGES	DISADVANTAGES

Decision-Making Techniques, Step 3.

a·p·p·e·n·d·i·x

·C·

Checklist for Going into Business

BEFORE YOU START

How about YOU?

Are you the kind of person who can get a business started and make it go? Yes_____ No_____

Have you worked in a business like the one you want to start? Yes_____ No_____

Have you worked for someone else as a supervisor or manager? Yes_____ No_____

Have you had any business training in school? Yes_____ No_____

Have you saved any money or built any assets against which you can borrow money? Yes_____ No_____

How about the Money?

Do you know how much money it will take to get your business started? Yes_____ No_____

Have you determined how much of your own money you can put into the business? Yes_____ No_____

Do you know where you can borrow the rest of the money you need to start your business? Yes_____ No_____

Have you determined what net income per year you expect to get from the business? (Count your salary plus your profit on the money you put into the business.) Yes_____ No_____

Can you live on less than this so that you can use some of it to help your business grow? Yes_____ No_____

Have you talked to a banker about your plans? Yes_____ No_____

How about a Partner?

If you need a partner with money or expertise that you don't have, do you know someone who will fit—someone you can get along with? Yes_____ No_____

Do you know the good and bad points about going it alone, having a partner, and incorporating your business? Yes_____ No_____

Have you talked to a lawyer about the legal structure? Yes_____ No_____

How about Customers?

Do most businesses (of this nature) in your community seem to be doing well? Yes_____ No_____

Have you tried to find out whether companies like the one you want to open are doing well both in your community and in the rest of the country? Yes_____ No_____

Do you know what kind of people will want to buy what you plan to sell? Yes_____ No_____

Do people like that live in the area where you want to open your business? Yes_____ No_____

Do they need products/services like yours? Yes_____ No_____

If not, have you thought about opening a different kind of business or locating in another neighborhood? Yes_____ No_____

GETTING STARTED

The Building

Have you found a good building for your firm? Yes_____ No_____
Will you have enough space to expand, if needed? Yes_____ No_____
Can you remodel the building without spending too much money? Yes_____ No_____
Can people get to it easily from parking spaces, bus stops, or their homes? Yes_____ No_____
Have you had a lawyer check the lease and zoning? Yes_____ No_____

Equipment and Supplies

Do you know just what equipment, fixtures, furniture, and supplies you need and how much they will cost? Yes_____ No_____

Can you save some money by buying secondhand equipment? Yes_____ No_____

Can you save some money by leasing? Yes_____ No_____

Can you save some money by automating/computerizing? Yes_____ No_____

Merchandise or Raw Materials

Have you decided what products you will sell, manufacture, process, or distribute? Yes_____ No_____

Have you located alternative sources of raw materials? Yes_____ No_____

Do you know how much or how many of each (merchandise/raw materials) you will need to open your company with? Yes_____ No_____

Have you found suppliers who will sell you what you need at good prices? Yes_____ No_____

Records

Have you planned a system of recordkeeping that will keep track of your income and expenses, what you owe other people, and what others owe you? Yes_____ No_____

Have you worked out a system to keep track of your inventory (merchandise/raw materials) so that you will always have enough on hand for customers or production but not more than you need at any one time? Yes_____ No_____

Have you determined how best to keep payroll records and take care of tax reports and payments? Yes_____ No_____

Do you know what financial statements you should prepare, when, and by what mode of operation? Yes_____ No_____

Do you know an accountant who can help you? Yes_____ No_____

Your Company and the Law

Do you know what licenses and permits are needed? Yes_____ No_____

Do you know what business laws apply to your company? Yes_____ No_____

Do you know a lawyer you can go to for advice and for help with legal papers? Yes_____ No_____

Protecting Your Company

Have you made plans for protecting your enterprise against thefts of all kinds—shoplifting, robbery, burglary, employee stealing? Yes_____ No_____

Have you talked with an insurance agent about what kinds of insurance you need? Yes_____ No_____

Buying an Established Business

Have you listed likes and dislikes about buying an established business? Yes_____ No_____

Have you determined the real reason why the owner wants to sell the business? Yes_____ No_____

Have you compared the cost of buying the business with the cost of starting a new one? Yes_____ No_____

Are the building and facilities in good condition? Yes_____ No_____

Have you talked to neighboring businesspeople about the business and their opinion of its operations? Yes_____ No_____

Have you talked with the company's suppliers? Yes_____ No_____

Have you talked with a lawyer about it? Yes_____ No_____

MAKING IT GO

Advertising

Have you decided how you will advertise? (Newspapers, posters, handbills, radio-TV, direct mail?) Yes_____ No_____

Do you know where to get help with your ads? Yes_____ No_____

Have you observed what related firms do to get people to buy? Yes_____ No_____

Prices

Do you know how to figure what you should charge for products or services? Yes_____ No_____

Do you know what firms like yours charge? Yes_____ No_____

Buying

Do you have a plan for discovering what customers want? Yes_____ No_____

Will your plan for keeping inventory records tell you when it is time to order more and how much to order? Yes_____ No_____

Do you plan to buy most of your stock/materials from a few suppliers rather than a little from many, so that those you buy from will want to help you succeed? Yes_____ No_____

Selling

Have you decided whether to have salesclerks or self-service? Yes_____ No_____

Do you know how to persuade customers to buy? Yes_____ No_____

Have you thought about why you like to buy from some salespeople/sales representatives while you'd sooner avoid others? Yes_____ No_____

Employees

If you decide to hire workers, do you know how to recruit them? Yes_____ No_____

Have you written job descriptions, and do you know what qualifications you are looking for? Yes_____ No_____

Do you have comparative figures on the wages and salaries it will be necessary to pay employees in these job descriptions? Yes_____ No_____

Do you have a plan for training employees? Yes_____ No_____

Credit Policies

Have you decided whether to let customers buy on credit? Yes_____ No_____

Do you know the advantages and disadvantages of using a credit-card plan? Yes_____ No_____

Can you tell a deadbeat from a good credit customer? Do you have a plan for granting credit? Yes_____ No_____

Miscellaneous

Have you determined whether you could make more money working for someone else? Yes_____ No_____

Does your family support your plan to start a business? Yes_____ No_____

Do you know what resources to use for new ideas, products, services, and for help in various aspects of your business? Yes_____ No_____

Do you have a work plan (MBO/R) for your company, yourself, and your employees? Yes_____ No_____

Have you approached the nearest Small Business Administration office for help with developing your business plan? Yes_____ No_____

Source: Adapted from *Management Aid* no. 71 (Washington, D.C.: U.S. Small Business Administration), 1978.

appendix

D

References and Resources

BOOKS AND GOVERNMENT PUBLICATIONS

Entrepreneurship, General

Aronson, Charles N. *Free Enterprise* (New York: Arcade, 1979).
Bailey, Ronald W., ed. *Black Business Enterprise* (New York: Basic Books, Inc. 1971).
Baumbeck, Clifford M. and Lawyer, Kenneth. *How to Organize and Operate a Small Business* (Englewood Cliffs, NJ: Prentice-Hall, 1979).
Bird, Caroline. *Enterprising Women* (New York: Norton, 1976).
Broom, H. N. and Longenecker, Justin G. *Small Business Management* (Cincinnati, OH: South-Western Publishing Company, 1979).
Chamberlain, John. *The Enterprising Americans: A Business History of the United States* (New York: Harper & Row, 1974).
Economic Research on Small Business (Washington, D.C.: U.S. Government Printing Office).
Foster, Richard Dee. *Profits in Business* (St. Louis, MO: Milliken Publishing, 1980).
Handbook for Small Business (Washington, D.C.: U.S. Government Printing Office, 1980).
Huff, Ann S. and Doctors, Samuel I. *Minority Enterprise and the President's Council* (Cambridge, MA: Ballinger Publishers, 1973).
Kamoroff, Bernard. *Small-Time Operator* (Laytonville, CA: Bell Springs Publishing Co., 1983).
Kirzner, Israel M. *Perceptions, Opportunity & Profit: Studies in the Theory of Entrepreneurship* (Chicago: University of Chicago Press, 1979).

Kuriloff, Arthur H. and Hemphill, John M., Jr. *Starting and Managing the Small Business* (New York: McGraw-Hill, 1983).

Minority Business Enterprise—A Bibliography (Washington, D.C.: Office of Minority Business Enterprise, U.S. Department of Commerce, 1973).

Moreau, James F. *Effective Small Business Management* (Chicago: Rand McNally College Publishing Company, 1980).

Poe, Roy W., Hicks, Herbert G., and Church, Olive D. *Getting Involved in Business* (New York: McGraw-Hill, 1981).

Steinhoff, Dan. *Small Business Management Fundamentals* (New York: McGraw-Hill, 1978).

The Environment for Entrepreneurship and Small Business (Washington, D.C.: U.S. Government Printing Office).

The State of Small Business: A Report of the President (Washington, D.C.: U.S. Government Printing Office). Submitted to the Congress by the Small Business Administration, 1982.

Van Voorhis, Kenneth R. *Entrepreneurship and Small Business Management* (Boston: Allyn & Bacon, Inc., 1979).

Winston, Sandra. *Entrepreneurial Woman* (New York: Newsweek Books, 1979).

Entrepreneurial Traits and Successes

Characteristics of a Successful Business (New York: Competere Group, Inc.).

Characteristics of Successful Entrepreneurs (New York: Competere Group, Inc.).

Deeks, John. *The Small Firm Owner-Manager: Entrepreneurial Behavior and Management Practice* (New York: Praeger, 1976).

Dible, Donald. *Build a Better You—Starting Now* (New York: Hawthorne Books, Inc., 1979).

Types of Businesses and Business Opportunities

Beal, H. *How to Run a Restaurant* (Belfast, ME: Berne, Porter, 1978).

Becker, Benjamin Max. *The Family Owned Business* (Chicago: Commerce Clearing House, 1978).

Bermont, Hubert. *The Successful Consultant's Guide to Authoring, Publishing, and Lecturing* (Washington, D.C.: Bermont Books, 1979).

Brumbaugh, J. Frank. *Mail Order—Starting Up, Making it Pay* (Radnor, PA: Chilton Books, 1979).

Clark, L. W. *How to Make Money with Crafts* (Belfast, ME: Berne, Porter, 1978).

Dorland, Gilbert N. and Van Der Wal, John. *The Business Idea—From Birth to Profitable Company* (New York: Van Norstrand Reinhold Company, 1978).

Evers, Ona. *Sparetime Dollars from the Kitchen* (San Rafael, CA: Onaway Publishing, 1978).

Holmes, David. *The Millionaire Book of Twelve-Hundred Thirty-Six Unusual Successful Home Businesses* (Palo Alto, CA: National Finance, 1978).

Husack, Glen A. and Gibbons, Rudolph W. *A Do-it-yourself Feasibility Study: New Manufacturing Ventures* (Kitchener, Ontario, Canada: The Institute for Small Business, 1979).

Michaels, Richard. *The Over-50 Guide to Moneymaking Business Opportunities* (West Nyack, NY: Parker Publisher, 1978).

Seltz, David D. *A Treasury of Business Opportunities* (Rockville Center, NY: Farnsworth Publishing Co., Inc., 1979).
Smart, Albert. *Planning Guide for the Beginning Retailer* (New York: Lebhar-Friedman Books, 1980).
Stevens, Lawrence. *Guide to Buying, Selling, and Starting a Travel Agency* (Chicago: Chicago Review Press, 1979).
Temple, Mary. *How to Start a Secretarial and Business Service* (Atlanta, GA: Peachtree Park Press, 1979).
Vesper, Karl. *New Venture Strategies* (Englewood Cliffs, NJ: Prentice-Hall, Inc., 1980).
Watts, Gilbert S. *How to Make a Million Dollars from a Fruit and Vegetable Roadside Market* (Albuquerque, NM: American Classicale College Press, 1977).
Witt, Scott. *How to Make Big Profits in Service Businesses* (Englewood Cliffs, NJ: Prentice-Hall, Inc., 1977).

Franchising

Church, Nancy S. *Future Opportunities in Franchising* (New York: Pilot Books).
Finn, Richart P. *Your Fortune in Franchises* (Chicago: Contemporary Books, Inc., 1979).
Franchise Opportunities (Washington, D.C.: U.S. Government Printing Office).
Green, Michael L., ed. *Franchise Handbook* (Milwaukee, WI: DMR Publications, 1978).
Levy, Robert S. and Small, Anne. *A Woman's Guide to Her Own Franchised Business* (New York: Pilot Books).
Mendelson, Martin. *The Guide to Franchising* (New York: Pergamon Press, Inc., 1979).

Inventions, Innovations, and Technology

Braden, Patricia. *Technological Entrepreneurship* (Ann Arbor, MI: University of Michigan) Michigan Business Reports, No. 61, 1977.
Green, Orville M. and Durr, Frank L. *The Practical Inventor's Handbook* (New York: McGraw-Hill, 1979).
Nystrom, Harry. *Creativity and Innovation* (New York: Wiley-Interscience Publications, 1979).

Getting Started in Business; Financing

Clark, John J. and Pieter, T. Elgers. *The Lease/Buy Decision* (New York: The Free Press, 1980).
Dible, Donald. *Business Start-Up Basics* (New York: The Entrepreneur Press, 1978), distributed by Hawthorne Books, Inc.
Everything You Need to Know About Raising Money for a New Business (New York: Competere Group, Inc.)
Hayes, Rick Stephan. *Business Loans: A Guide to Money Sources and How to Approach Them Successfully* (Boston: CBI Publishing Company, Inc., 1977).
Hilton, Terri. *Small Business Ideas for Women and How to get Started.* (New York: Pilot Books, 1975).
Jessup, Claudia and Chipps, Genie. *The Woman's Guide to Starting A Business* (New York: Holt, Rinehart and Winston, 1976).
Leslie, Mary and Seltz, David. *New Businesses Women Can Start and Successfully Operate* (New York: Barnes and Noble, 1979).

Levy, Robert S. *Directory of State & Federal Funds for Business Development* (New York: Pilot Books, 1977).

Nelson, Paula. *Joy of Money* (Briarcliff Manor, NY: Stein and Day Publishers, 1975).

Preparing a Business Plan for Lenders or Investors (New York: Competere Group, Inc.).

Talking to Lenders or Investors (New York: Competere Group, Inc.).

Accounting and Office Systems; Legal and Tax Issues

Church, Olive D. and Schatz, Anne E. *Office Systems and Careers* (Boston: Allyn and Bacon, Inc., 1981).

Crumbley, Larry D. *Organizing, Operating, and Terminating Subchapter S Corporations: Taxation and Accounting* (Tucson, AZ: Lawyers and Judges Publishing Company, 1980).

Dible, Donald. *What Everybody Should Know about Patents, Trademarks, and Copyrights* (New York: Hawthorne Books, Inc., 1978).

Dyer, Mary L. *Practical Bookkeeping for the Small Business* (Chicago: Contemporary Books, Inc., 1976).

Harris, Clifford C. *The Break-Even Handbook* (Englewood Cliffs, NJ: Prentice-Hall, 1978).

Lane, Marc J. *Legal Handbook for Small Business* (New York: AMACOM, 1978).

Personal Payoff in the Closely Held Corporation, 4th ed. (Englewood Cliffs, NJ: Institute for Business Planning, Inc., 1980).

Ragan, Robert C. and Zwick, Jack. *Fundamentals of Recordkeeping and Finance for Small Business* (New York: The Entrepreneur Press, 1978).

Spiro, Herbert T. *Finance for the Non-Financial Manager* (New York: Wiley, 1977).

Tax Guide for Small Business (Washington, D.C.: Internal Revenue Service, yearly).

Sipple, Charles J. and Dahl, Fred. *Computer Power for the Small Business* (Englewood Cliffs, NJ: Prentice-Hall, Inc., 1979).

Still, Jack W. *A Guide to Managerial Accounting in Small Companies* (New York: Arno Press, 1979).

Walker, Ernest W. and Petty, J. William, II. *Financial Management of the Small Firm* (Englewood Cliffs, NJ: Prentice-Hall, 1978).

Marketing, Advertising, and Selling

Brannen, William H. *Successful Marketing for Your Small Business* (Englewood Cliffs, NJ: Prentice-Hall, Inc., 1978).

Breen, George Edward. *Do-it-yourself Marketing Research* (New York: McGraw-Hill, 1977).

Brownstone, David M. *Successful Selling Skills for Small Business* (New York: Wiley, 1978).

Feinman, Jeffrey. *Advertising for a Small Business* (St. Louis, MO: Corner Store Press, 1980).

Hisrich, R. D. and Peters, M. P. *Marketing a New Product: Its Planning, Development and Control* (Reading, MA: Addison-Wesley, 1978).

Lewis, H. G. *How to Make Your Advertising Twice as Effective at Half the Cost* (Chicago: Nelson Hall Publications, 1979).

Porter, Michael E. *Competitive Strategy* (New York: Harper Row, 1977).
Stanton, William J. and Buskirk, Richard, H. *Management of the Sales Force* (Hometown, IL: Richard D. Irwin, Inc., 1978).

Management, General and Personnel

Auditing & Managing Energy Use in Small Industrial & Commercial Facilities (Rye, NY: Reymond Associates, 1977).

Cross, Theodore L. *Black Capitalism, Strategy for Business in the Ghetto* (New York: Atheneum, 1971).

Curtis, Bob. *Food Service Security: Internal Control* (Garden City, NY: Doubleday and Company, 1975).

Dieker, Kenneth. *Management and Merchandising Aids for the Small Retailer* (Parsons, KS: Sun Graphics, 1978).

Friday, William. *Successful Management for One to Ten Employee Businesses* (San Francisco: Prudential Publishing Co., 1979).

Granick, David. *The European Executive* (Garden City, NY: Doubleday and Company, 1979).

Haney, C. Michele and Boenisch, Edmond, Jr. *Stressmap: Finding Your Pressure Points* (San Luis Obispo, CA: Impact Publishers, 1982).

Henning, Margaret and Jardim, Anne. *The Managerial Woman* (Garden City, NY: Doubleday and Company, 1976).

Mager, Robert F. *Goal Analysis* (Belmont, CA: Fearon Publishers/Lear Siegler, Inc.)

Telchin, Charles S. and Helfant, Seymore. *Planning Your Store for Maximum Sales and Profits* (New York: National Retail Merchants Association, 1975).

Expanding, Adjusting, or Getting Out

Export Marketing for Smaller Firms (Washington, D.C.: U.S. Government Printing Office, 1979).

Goldstein, Arnold S. *Strategies and Techniques for Saving the Financially Distressed Small Business* (New York: Pilot Books, 1976).

Hagendorf, Stanley. *Tax Guide for Buying and Selling A Business* (Englewood Cliffs, NJ: Prentice-Hall, Inc., 1978).

Henward, DeBanks M., III and Ginalski, WIlliam. *The Franchising Option: Expanding Your Business Through Franchising* (Phoenix, AZ: Franchise Groups Publishers, 1979).

Krauser, Peter M. *New Products and Diversification* (London: Business Book Limited, 1977).

Lewis, Mack O. *How to Franchise Your Business* (New York: Pilot Books, 1981).

Linneman, Robert F. *Shirt-Sleeve Approach to Long-Range Planning for the Smaller, Growing Corporation* (Englewood Cliffs, NJ: Prentice-Hall, 1980).

Stevens, Mark. *36 Small Business Mistakes and How to Avoid Them* (New York: Parker Publishing Company, 1978).

JOURNALS AND PERIODICALS

The Academy of Management Journal
  Academy of Management
  Post Office Drawer KZ
  Mississippi State, MS 29762

Advertising Age
  Crain Communications, Inc.
  740 Rush Street
  Chicago, IL 60611

American Journal of Small Business
  University of Baltimore
  1420 North Charles Street
  Baltimore, MD 21201

Balance Sheet
  South-Western Publishing Co.
  5101 Madison Road
  Cincinnati, OH 45227

Better Business
  Publication of the National Minority
    Business Council
  235 East 42nd Street
  New York, NY 10017

Black Enterprise
  Post Office Box 5500
  Bergenfield, NJ 07621

Business
  College of Business Administration
  Georgia State University
  Athens, GA 30601

Business Education Forum
  1914 Association Drive
  Reston, VA 22201

Business Education World
  Gregg/McGraw-Hill Book Company
  1221 Avenue of the Americas
  New York, NY 10020

The Business Owner
  Thomar Publications, Inc.
  383 South Broadway
  Hicksville, NY 11801

Business Week
  McGraw-Hill, Inc.
  1221 Avenue of the Americas
  New York, NY 10020

Chain Store Age
  Lebhar-Friedman, Inc.
  425 Park Avenue
  New York, NY 10022

Data Management
  Data Processing Management Association
  505 Busse Highway
  Park Ridge, IL 60068

Decision Sciences
  Institute for Decision Sciences
  College of Business Administration
  University of Florida
  Gainesville, FL 32611

Enterprising Women
  217 East 28th Street
  New York, NY 10016

Executive Female
  120 East 56th Street
  New York, NY 10022

Franchise Adviser
  2430 Pennsylvania, N.W.
  Washington, D.C. 20037

Harvard Business Review
  (Reprint series on small business)
  Boston, MA 02163

High Technology
  342 Madison Avenue
  Suite 1228
  New York, NY 10173

In Business
  Post Office Box 323
  St. Emmaus, PA 18049

Inc.
  38 Commercial Wharf
  Boston, MA 02110

Industrial Management
  25 Technology Park
  Atlanta, GA 30092

Journal of Marketing
  American Marketing Association
  250 South Wacker Drive
  Chicago, IL 60606

Journal of Purchasing and Materials Management
  496 Kinderkamack Road
  Post Office Box 418
  Oradell, NJ 07649

Journal of Small Business Management
  Bureau of Business Research
  West Virginia University
  Post Office Box 6025
  Morgantown, WV 26506

Kiplinger Washington Letter
 1729 H. Street, N.W.
 Washington, D.C. 20006
Management World
 Maryland Road
 Willow Grove, PA 19090
Modern Office Technology
 Penton/IPC, Inc.
 1111 Chester Avenue
 Cleveland, OH 44114
NFIB Mandate
 National Federation of Independent Business
 150 West 20th Avenue
 San Mateo, CA 94403
The Office
 Post Office Box 13205
 Philadelphia, PA 19101
Performance and Instruction
 1126-16th Street, N.W.
 Suite 315
 Washington, D.C. 20036
Personnel Administration
 30 Park Drive
 Berea, OH 44107
Personnel Management
 Personnel Publications, Ltd.
 One Hills Place
 London, W1R 1AG
Production and Inventory Management
 500 West Annandale Road
 Falls Church, VA 22046
Purchasing
 21 Columbus Avenue
 Boston, MA 02116
Quarterly Economic Report for Small Business
 National Federation of Independent Business (NFIB)
 150 West 20th Avenue
 San Mateo, CA 94403
Savvy
 111 Eighth Avenue
 New York, NY 10011
Time
 Rockefeller Center
 New York, NY 10020
Today's Office
 645 Stewart Avenue
 Garden City, New York 115230
Training
 731 Hennepin Avenue
 Minneapolis, MN 55403

Training and Development
 600 Maryland Avenue, S.W.
 Suite 305
 Washington, D.C. 20024
Travel Trade
 6 East 46th Street
 New York, NY 10017
Travel Weekly
 One Park Avenue
 New York, NY 10016
U.S. News & World Report
 U.S. News Building
 2300 N. Street, N.W.
 Washington, D.C. 20037
Venture
 35 West 45th Street
 New York, NY 10036
VocEd Journal
 2020 North 14th Street
 Arlington, VA 22201
Wall Street Journal
 Dow Jones & Co., Inc.
 22 Cortland Street
 New York, NY 10007
Washington Report
 Chamber of Commerce of the United States
 1615 H Street, N.W.
 Washington, D.C. 20062
The Wharton Magazine
 Centenary Hall
 University of Pennsylvania
 Philadelphia, PA 19104
Working Woman
 342 Madison Avenue
 New York, 10173
Your Business and the Law
 Research Institute of America, Inc.
 589 Fifth Avenue
 New York, NY 10017

U.S. SMALL BUSINESS ADMINISTRATION MONOGRAPHS

Copies of the following SBA Monographs are available free from: SBA, P.O. Box 15434, Forth Worth, TX, 76119. These monographs and bibliographies are published by the U.S. Government Printing Office, Washington, D.C.

"The ABCs of Borrowing," *Management Aid No. 1.001,* 1981.
Astor, Saul D., "Preventing Employee Pilferage," *Management Aid No. 5.005,* 1981.
Astor, Saul D., "Preventing Retail Theft," *Management Aid No. 3.004.*
Becker, Benjamin J. and Tillman, Fred, "Management Checklist for a Family Business," *Management Aid No. 3.002,* 1982.
Bobrow, Edwin E., "Is the Independent Sales Agent for You?" *Management Aid No. 4.005,* 1980.
Britt, Steuart Henderson, "Plan Your Advertising Budget," *Management Aid No. 4.018.*
"Business Plan for Small Construction Firms," *Management Aid No. 2.008.*
Claus, Karen E., "Signs and Your Business," *Small Marketers Aid,* 1977.
Cotton, John, "Keeping Records in Small Business," *Management Aid No. 1.017.*
Curtis, S. J., "Preventing Burglary and Robbery Loss," *Management Aid No. 3.007.*
Davis, Edward W., "Inventory Management," *Small Business Bibliography No. 75,* 1981.
DeBoer, Lloyd M., "Marketing Research Procedures," *Small Business Bibliography No. 9,* 1982.
DeBoer, Lloyd M., "National Directories for Use in Marketing," *Small Business Bibliography No. 13,* 1981.
Golen, Steven, "Effective Business Communication," *Small Business Bibliography No. 92.*
Gould, Douglas P., "Developing New Accounts," *Management Aid No. 4.010.*
Harling, Edwin L., "Stock Control for Small Stores," *Management Aid No. 3.005.*
Hedrick, Floyd D., "Purchasing for Owners of Small Plants," *Small Business Bibliography No. 85,* 1981.
Hosmer, LaRue Tone, "A Venture Capital Primer for Small Business," *Management Aid No. 1.009,* 1981.
"Incorporating a Small Business," *Management Aid No. 223,* 1976.
Institute of Life Insurance, "Business Life Insurance," *Management Aid,* 1980.
"Introduction to Patents," *Management Aid No. 6.005.*
Jacobson, Barbara, "Personnel Management," *Small Business Bibliography No. 72,* 1981.
Kramer, Edward C., "Can You Use a Minicomputer?" *Management Aid No. 2.015,* 1982.
Kress, George and Will, R. Ted, "Marketing Checklist for Small Retailers," *Management Aid No. 4.012.*
Laumer, J. Ford, Jr. and Harris, James R., "Learning about Your Market," *Small Marketers Aid,* 1979.
Lennon, Victor A., "What is the Best Selling Price?" *Management Aid No. 1.002,* 1981.
Litt, Danny S., "Cash Flow in a Small Plant," *Management Aid No. 1.006.*
Low, James P., "Association Services for Small Business," *Management Aid No. 7.002.*
Lowry, James R., "Using a Traffic Study to Select a Retail Site," *Small Marketers Aid,* 1979.

McKeever, J. Ross and Spink, Frank H., Jr., "Factors in Considering a Shopping Center Location," *Management Aid No. 2.017*, 1980.
Millican, Richard D., "National Mailing List Houses," *Small Business Bibliography No. 29*, 1977.
Muchnick, Paul, "Selling by Mail Order," *Small Business Bibliography No. 3*, 1977.
"New Product Development," *Small Business Bibliography No. 90*.
Olshan, Nathan H., "Recordkeeping Systems—Small Store and Trade Service," *Small Business Bibliography No. 15*, 1982.
Olmi, Antonio, M., "Selecting the Legal Structure for Your Firm" *Management Aid No. 6.004*, 1981.
O'Neal, Cooke, "Credit and Collections," *Management Aid No. 1.007*, 1981.
Pelissier, Raymond F., "Planning and Goal Setting for Small Business," *Management Aid No. 2.010*.
Pfeiffer, Paul L., "Retailing," *Small Business Bibliography No. 10*.
Radics, Stephen P., Jr., "Steps in Meeting Your Tax Obligations," *Management Aid No. 1.013*, 1980.
Riso, Ovid, "Advertising Guidelines for Small Retail Firms," *Management Aid No. 4.015*.
Salvate, James, "Profit Costing and Pricing for Services," *Management Aid No. 1.020*, 1981.
"Statistics and Maps for National Market Analysis," *Small Business Bibliography No. 12*.
Vorzimer, Louis H., "Using Census Data to Select a Store Site," *Small Marketers Aid*, 1974.
Vurpillat, Victor V., "Computers for Small Business," *Management Aid No. 2.019*, 1982.
Walker, Bruce, J., "A Pricing Checklist for Small Retailers," *Management Aid No. 4.013*, 1981.
Weber, Fred I., Jr., "Locating or Relocating a Business," *Small Marketers Aid*, 1979.

ASSOCIATIONS AND AGENCIES

Academy of Management
   Post Office Drawer KZ
   Mississippi State, MS 29762
Administrative Management Society (AMS)
   Willow Grove, PA 19090
The Advertising Council, Inc. (AC)
   825 Third Avenue
   New York, NY 10022
American Institute for Decision Sciences
   College of Business Administration
   University of Florida
   Gainesville, FL 32611
American Management Association (AMA)
   135 West 50th Street
   New York, NY 10020
American Communication Network (ACN)
   308 North Washington Street
   Knightstown, IN 46148

Appendix D

American Economic Foundation (AEF)
  51 East 42nd Street
  New York, NY 10017
American Enterprise Institute for Public Policy Research (AEI)
  1150-17th Street, N.W.
  Washington, D.C. 20036
American Production and Inventory Control Society, Inc.
  500 West Annandale Road
  Falls Church, VA 22046
American Society of Trainers and Developers (ASTD)
  Suite 305
  600 Maryland Avenue, S.W.
  Washington, D.C. 20024
American Vocational Association (AVA)
  2020 North 14th Street
  Arlington, VA 22201
Business and Professional Women's Foundation
  2012 Massachusetts Avenue, N.W.
  Washington, D.C. 20036
Chamber of Commerce of the United States (COCUSA)
  1615 H Street, N.W.
  Washington, D.C. 20062
Committee for Economic Development (CED)
  477 Madison Avenue
  New York, NY 10022
The Conference Board (CB)
  845 Third Avenue
  New York, NY 10022
Conference of American Small Business Organizations
  407 South Dearborn Street
  Chicago, IL 60605
Council for Better Business Bureaus, Inc. (CBBB)
  1150-17th Street, N.W.
  Washington, D.C. 20036
Distributive Education Clubs of America (DECA)
  1908 Association Drive
  Reston, VA 22091
The Entrepreneurship Institute
  90 East Wilson Bridge Road
  Suite 247
  Worthington, OH 43209
Future Business Leaders of America (FBLA)
  1914 Association Drive
  Reston, VA 22091

The Heritage Foundation (HF)
  513 C Street, N.E.
  Washington, D.C. 20002
Institute for Independent Business Women, Inc.
  4101 Nebraska Avenue, N.W.
  Washington, D.C. 20016
Institute of Industrial Engineers
  25 Technology Park
  Atlanta, GA 30092
International Council for Small Business (ICSB)
  929 North Sixth Street
  Milwaukee, WI 53203
International Entrepreneurs' Association (IEA)
  631 Wilshire Blvd.
  Santa Monica, CA 90401
Joint Council on Economic Education (JCEE)
  1212 Avenue of the Americas
  New York, NY 10036
Junior Achievement, Inc. (JA)
  550 Summer Street
  Stamford, CT 06901
National Association for Female Executives, Inc.
  120 East 56th Street
  New York, NY 10022
National Association of Manufacturers (NAM)
  1776 F Street
  Washington, D.C. 20006
National Family Business Council
  3916 Detroit Boulevard
  West Bloomfield, MI 48033
National Business Education Association (NBEA)
  1914 Association Drive
  Reston, VA 22091
National Federation of Independent Business (NFIB)
  150 West 20th Avenue
  San Mateo, CA 94403
The National Management Association (NMA)
  2210 Arbor Boulevard
  Dayton, OH 45439
National Minority Business Council
  235 East 42nd Street
  New York, NY 10017
The National Retail Merchants Association
  100 West 31st Street
  New York, NY 10001

National Small Business Association
  1604 K Street, N.W.
  Washington, D.C. 20006
Office Education Association(OEA)
  1120 Morse Road
  Columbus, OH 43229
World Association of Women Business Owners
  c/o *Enterprising Women Magazine*
  217 East 28th Street
  New York, NY 10016

Index

Absenteeism, 427
Accounting (see Records)
Accounting system, 120
Accounts (see Records)
Accoustics, 181
Active Corps of Executives (ACE), 257
Advertising,
   budgeting, 356
   designs, 353
   purpose, 17
   see also Image, Marketing and Promotion
Affective domain, 367
Agency, 271
AGNET, 328
Amway, 53
American Women's Economic Development Corporation, 23
Antitrust laws, 271
Apple Computer, 34, 53, 120, 245
Apprenticeship, 59, 415
Articles of Partnership, 46, 115, 199
Atari, 34, 114
Attorney, 279
Assets,
   current, 247
   statement of, 122

Bank account, 293
Bank reconciliation, 293
Bankruptcy, 471
Baumann, Dwight Maylon Billy, 96
Baumgarten, Leonard, 97
Better Business Bureau (BBB) 273
Bill of exchange, 268
Bill of lading, 268
Block areas, statistics, 134
Boycott, 18
Break-even point, 226, 459, 461
Budget account, 231
Budgeting, 302–5

Burglaries, 447
Burroughs, 35
Bushnell, Nolan, 114
Business,
   buying an existing, 80–82, 470
   categories, 50
   challenges of, 21, 42
   choosing a, 101–4
   continuity and survival, 43
   cycles, 20
   failures, 38, 39
   future of, 21
   opportunities for, 66, 144
   selling a, 81
   small, 13
   "string" or "strip," 135
Business plan, 111–27,
   financial data, 120–25
   format, 125
   guidelines for preparing, 237

Cabinet Council on Human Resources, 256
Capital, 244–51
Capital gains, 244
Carney, Frank L., 11
Cash,
   balance, 249
   flow, 301, 462
   operating cycle, 306
   see also Records
Catastrophe, 37
Census,
   of Business, 135
   data, 134
   tract, 134
Center for Family Business, 43
Central Business District (CBD), 135, 144
Change, facilitating, 372, 464
Channels of distribution, 336

Chattel mortgage, 231, 254
Checks, 229
Civil Rights Act, 210
Classification, (of businesses), 50–66, 326–28
Cleanliness, 436
Cognitive domain, 367
Collateral, 251
Collections, 234
Communication,
  classification, 50, 61
  correspondence, 310
  entrepreneurial skill, 475
  with employees, 425
  forms, 308
Community,
  demographics, 153
  trends, 156
Competition,
  assessing, 139
  defining, 16
  meeting, 34
  surveying, 144
Computers, 315–33
  crimes, 443
  glossary, 329–31
  robotics, 467
  vendors, 324
Conditional sales contract, 231, 235, 254, 270
Construction, 54, 58
Consumer Product Safety Commission (CPSC), 273
Consumer protection laws, 275
Contracts, 268–71,
  installment, 230
Convenience goods, 193
Copyrights, 273
Corporation, 200–205
  funding source, 252
Cost-oriented pricing, 220
Coupons, 353, 392
Credit,
  accepting checks, 229
  evaluating applications, 232
  trade, 231, 254
Credit bureau, 230
Credit cards, 230
Customers (consumers),
  company policies, 224
  determining needs of, 141, 397
  laws to protect, 273–76
  need for, 18
  proximity to, 156
Customer traffic,
  automobile count, 158
  pedestrian count, 157

Data bases, 50, 51, 328
Data Census, 134
Data processing,
  glossary, 329–31
  manual, mechanical, 307
Devil's advocate, 373
Demand-oriented pricing, 222
Demographics, 132, 135, 153
Depreciation, 297
Distribution,
  channels of, 235, 336
  classification, 50
  security control, 442
Double-entry bookkeeping, 292
Documents (see Records)
Douglas, Donald, 11, 53
Dun & Bradstreet,
  business failures, 39, 462
  data base, 51

Earnings forecast, 120
Economic Order Quantity (EOQ), 344
Economics, 13, 34
Edison, Thomas, 96
Electronic mail, 319
Electronic spreadsheets, 318
Employees,
  attitudes, 421
  dishonesty, 439–43
  orienting, 410
  supervising, 425
  training, 412
  see also Personnel Management and Staffing
Employment agencies, 207
Enterprise, 11
Entrances and exits, 180
Entrepreneur,
  advice to, 23
  characteristics of, 97
  circumstances predicting, 92
  definition, 92
  qualifications, 43, 475
  strengths, weaknesses 40, 476
  winners and losers, 463
Equal Employment Opportunity Act, 210
Equal Empolyment Opportunity Commission, 210
Equipment,
  leases and loans on, 253
  replacing, updating, 465
  selecting, 187–90
Ergonomics, 188
Evaluation,
  for profitability, 460
  training programs, 420
Expanding, 468

Index

Expenses, estimating, 123
Extraction classification, 50–55

Facilitative management, 363, 367, 456
Facilities, 119, 171–81, 178–88
Facsimile, 320
Fair Labor Standards Act, 210
Family,
    Center for Family Business, 43
    clues to entrepreneurship, 481
    female members, 43
    joining a business, 82, 83
    National Family Business Council, 43
    support from, 42
Federal aid and assistance, 254–58, 468
Federal Trade Commission (FTC), 272, 274
Fields, Debbie, 11, 13, 24, 53
Financial data, 120–25
Financial statements,
    balance sheet, 298
    income, 299
    personal assets, 251
    profit and loss (P&L), 301
    use of, 298
Fitzpatrick, Beatrice, 23
Flextime, 209, 405
Flowcharts, 376–82
Focus group interviews, 391
Food and Drug Administration (FDA), 273
Ford, Henry, 11
Forms and procedures, 308
Formulas, 303, 343–47, 459
Franchises, 76–80,
Free-enterprise system, 14
Furniture, 190
Funding sources, 249–56

Gilder, George, 245
Goodwill,
    intangible asset, 81
    need for, 18
Government regulations, 36
Gross National Product (GNP), 14
Growth/Share Matrix Approach, 462

Handicapped,
    facility accessibility, 180
Herndon, Lance H., 95
Hiring, *see* Staffing
Hobbies, in entrepreneurship, 11, 99, 144, 480
Home-based businesses, 67, 328
Hwang, K. P., 246

IBM, 35
Image, 160
    retail store, 184
    projected, 348
Impulse goods, 193
Independent sales agents, 404
Individual Retirement Account (IRA), 280
Industrial park, 144
Innovations, 15, 35
Insolvency, 471
Insurance,
    business life, 284
    costs and expenses, 172
    needs assessment, 282
    product liability, 37
    recordkeeping, 297
    types of, 283
Internal controls, 290
Internal Revenue Service (IRS),
    bartering requirements, 246
    data base, 50
    income taxes, 280
    investment tax credits, 280
    withholding taxes, 280
International Trade Administration (ITA), 468
Interviewing, 209 *see also* Staffing
Inventory,
    needs, 248
    physical control, 441
    relationship to sales, 337
    strategic planning unit, 462
    types of, 296, 337, 343
Investments,
    Individual Retirement Account (IRA), 280
    reason for entrepreneurship, 31
    return on, 226
    tax credits, 280

Job description, 121
    with MBO/R, 378
    and vertical flow, 376
Job sharing, 209, 405
Jobs, Steve, 11, 120, 245
Joint Partnership Training Act, 412
Jonovic, Don, 43
Journals,
    cash disbursements, 295
    cash receipts, 294
Jung, Carl, 368

Kitchens, Frank and Anne, 11, 53

Labor,
    protection laws, 277

Labor (*continued*):
  supply, 162
  see also Employees and Staffing
Laws,
  consumer protection, 231, 273–76
  small business protection, 270–73
  workers' protection, 276–78
Layout, 182–87
Leasing,
  a facility, 168–70
  equipment, furniture, 190
Ledgers, 295
Legal,
  forms of business, 196–205
  structure, 115
Liabilities, 247
Libel, 273
Loans, 249–58
Location, 151–73
  Central Business District (CBD), 135, 144
  importance of, 152
  leasing agreement, 169
  Major Retail Center (MRC), 135
  proximity to markets, 156
  site of, 152
  sources of help, 172

Mail order frauds, 68
Major Retail Center (MRC), 135
Management,
  of business plan, 117
  by objectives/results, 101, 102, 369–71
  facilitative, 367
  incompetence in, 44, 456
  skills, 92
  theories, 424
Maintenance, repairs, 436
Manufacturing and processing,
  advertising, 394
  classification, 50, 54
  location needs, 161
  pricing for products, 224
  purchasing, 337
  security, 442
  trade credit, 231
Market,
  defining the, 140
  determining the share, 139
  proximity to, 156
  trade area, 134
Market research, 132–47
  applying data, 139, 147
  firms, 396
  primary, 87, 133, 140–47, 157–60, 390–94
  secondary, 87, 134–39
Marketing strategy, 118, 390
Markup,
  example, 18
  guidelines, 222
Mary Kaye Cosmetics, 53
Maslow, Abraham, 398
Material Requirements Planning (MRP), 345
McDonald's, 34
McGregor, Douglas, 424
Media,
  advertising, 354, 393
  instructional, 416
Mentoring, 413
Merchandising,
  organization, 184, 350
  pricing, 218–24
  product definitions, 193
  window displays, 350
Mine Safety and Health Administration (MSHA), 55, 449
Minority Business Development Center (MBDC), 256
Minority Enterprise Small Business Investment Companies (MESBICs), 255
Motivation, 423

National Bankruptcy Act, 471
National Federation of Independent Business, 224
National Mortgage Association, 254
National Science Foundation, 258
Negotiable instruments, 267
Nelson, Paula, 114, 118, 122, 126
Network, networking, 3, 133, 246, 352
Norton, R. D., 137
NOW accounts, 232, 249
Numeric control (NC), 466

Objectives, 101–2, 115
Occupational Safety and Health Administration (OSHA), 37, 283, 449
Office functions, 307–10
Office of Advocacy (SBA), 37
Office of Women's Business Enterprise, 256
Office space, 187
On-the-job training, 413
Opportunities for entrepreneurs
  see Classifications
Organizational chart, 115
Osborne, Adam, 244

Parking, 158
Participative Decision Making (PDM), 424, 457
Participative management, 367

Partnership,
    articles of agreement, 199
    funding source, 252
    legal form, 123, 198
    reporting income taxes, 279
    types of partners, 198
Patents, 273
Peer groups, 457
Personnel management, 421–25,
    handbook, 422
Persuasion skills, 127, 413
PERT, 375
Pizza Hut, 11, 53
Planning,
    determine needs, 132
    forecasting, 302
    steps, 22
    strategic techniques, 462
    see also Business plan
Policies,
    credit collections, 228–36
    employee, 421–25
    pricing, 218–28
    written, 224
Pong, 114
Pricing, 218–28
Profit,
    how used, 20
    motive, 17
Psychological factors,
    of facility, 181
Promotion, 347–58
Purchasing, 335–47,
    relation to sales, 337
    opening campaign, 352
Purchase orders, 340

Radio Shack, 34, 119
Ratios, 305, 343
Records, recordkeeping, 290–98
    cash versus accrual, 297
    organization procedures, 292
    protection against loss, 437, 439, 442
    source documents, 293
    subsidiary accounts, 295
    time and cost constraints, 292
Rehabilitation Act, 211
Repairs, 436
Retail trade,
    advertising, 392
    burglaries and robberies, 447
    classification, 50
    description, 51
    pricing products, 218–24
    purchasing for, 338
    shoplifting, 444–47
    store organization, 184, 350
Revenue estimating, 120, 158
Revolving account, 231
Risks,
    coping with, 283
    definitions of, 32
    physical environment, 438
Robberies, 447
Robotics, 467

Safety, 448
Salaries, 172, 208
Sales,
    estimating, 120, 158
    related to inventory, 337
Sanders, Colonel, 11, 44, 53
Satisfactions, 30
Security, 439–48
    of facility, 181
    risks in business, 31, 37
Self-assessment, 97-100
Seller's lien, 231
Selling,
    and persuading, 127
    steps in, 400–404
    your business, 472
Service Corps of Retired Executives (SCORE), 257
Services,
    business, 63
    classification, 50
    financial, 62
    hospitality and recreation, 65
    personal, 64
    pricing for, 227
    professional, 62
    tourism, 66
Shaklee, 53
Shoplifting, 444–47
Shopping items (goods), 193
Signs, 179, 349
Silicon Valley, 245
Sims, Naomi, 11, 30, 24
Single-entry bookkeeping, 292
Small Business Administration (SBA),
    agency assistance, 139, 254
    data base, 51
    Office of Advocacy, 37
    recommendations, 37
    research, 43
Small Business Innovation Research (SBIR), 258
Small Business Institutes, 139

Small Business Investment Companies (SBICs), 255, 260, 470
SMSA, 134
Social Security (FICA/OASDI), 279
Sole proprietorship,
  definition, 196
  reporting income taxes, 279
Space value, 184
Speciality items (goods), 193
Staffing, 206–12
  applicants, 210
  defining needs, 206
  hiring, 206–12, 404
  interviewing, 209
  job description, 121
  legal factors, 210
  sources, 207–9
  wages, 208
Standard and Poors, 51
Standard Industrial Code (SIC), 51
Standard Metropolitan Statistical Area (SMSA), 134
Start-up costs, 247
Stock (see Inventory)
Stock control system, 345
Storekeepers, 450
Store Mix, 159
Strategic Planning Unit (SPU), 462
Stress management, 417
Subchapter S, 204
Suppliers, 342
Supply and demand, 16
Systems and subsystems, 308, 366

Task Force on Legal Equity for Women, 256
Taxes, 172, 281
Technology, risks in change, 34
Temporary-help agencies, 209
Texas Instruments, 35
Theory X and Theory Y, 424
Therbligs, 383
Time and motion, 382
Time management, 383, 417
Tract Census, 134

Trademarks, 273
Training and development, 412–20, 428
Truth in Lending Act, 231
Tourism, 66
Transfer of title, 270
Transportation,
  classification, 50, 60
Tylenol, 18

Uniform Commercial Code (UCC), 270
Unions, 429
Utilities, 181, 436
  costs and expenses, 171
  energy efficient facility, 179

Venture capital, 258
  investments, 244
  types of firms, 259
Vocational Education,
  disciplines defined, 93
  sources of employees, 207
  technical skills, 39, 93
Von Neumann-and-Morgenstern model, 32

Wages, 172, 208
Warner Communications, 114
Wholesale trade,
  activities, 338
  classification, 50
Window displays, 350
Word processing, 318, 328
Workers' Compensation, 37, 276
Workers,
  protection laws, 276
  see also Employees, Personnel Management and Staffing
Wozniak, Stephen, 11, 120

Zoning,
  definitions, 161
  laws, 144
  restrictions, 267